781.503   01816
Fea

Feather, Leonard.

The encyclopedia of jazz
in the sixties.

Date Due

DATE			
OCT. 18			

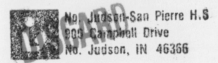

THE ENCYCLOPEDIA OF JAZZ IN

THE SIXTIES

by LEONARD FEATHER

THE

ENCYCLOPEDIA

OF

JAZZ

IN THE SIXTIES

Foreword by JOHN LEWIS

HORIZON PRESS · NEW YORK

Author's preface

The first edition of *The Encyclopedia of Jazz* was published in 1955. A second, substantially expanded edition appeared in 1960 and is still in print.

The Encyclopedia of Jazz in the '60s is what its title implies: an exhaustive examination of the many-faceted forms jazz has taken during this decade, through a survey of its principal personalities.

The task of compiling the biographies for this volume was one of unprecedented magnitude. The quantity of jazz produced, and the number of reasonably well known and musically important working jazz artists, have multiplied so rapidly that the main problem did not seem to be one of whom to add or retain, but more a matter of whom to leave out.

To those performers who went to the trouble of furnishing information—some to make their first appearances, others to bring earlier biographies up to date—my thanks are due, as well as to their wives, friends, agents, press agents, recording company representatives, and other associates whose time I took up in the gathering of what seemed like an endless trail of facts.

Ira Gitler, who was my associate during the preparation of the original edition, again worked in close and invaluable cooperation, not only in the writing and editing of biographies but in supervising the collection and coordination of material for the balance of the book. Mort Maizlish was an important assistant in the early stages, especially in the writing or collation of data concerning many of the avant garde musicians.

Others who, less officially but no less generously, contributed their time were, alphabetically, Joachim Berendt in Baden-Baden, Luke Breit in New York, Don DeMicheal of *Down Beat* in Chicago, Ralph J. Gleason in San Francisco, Miss Georgia Griggs in New York, Mrs. Randi Hultin in Oslo, Jean-Louis Ginibre in Paris, John Hammond and Dan Morgenstern in New York, Harry Nicolausson in Stockholm, Arrigo Polillo and his son Roberto in Milan, Eric Raeburn in New York, Miss Pauline Rivelli in New York, Grover Sales in San Francisco, Victor Schonfield in London, Frank Tenot in Paris, Elisabeth van der Mei and Eric Vogel in New York, Roman Waschko in Warsaw, Pete Welding in Chicago.

To the minority of artists who supplied information for which space could not be found, I can only repeat that the decisions entailed in assembling a representative cross-section of performers, in this decade of population explosion, provided the most frustrating moments of all during the long days and nights that went into the compilation of this book.

One important claim can be made, I believe, for *The Encyclopedia of Jazz in the '60s*. Every artist prominent in previous decades and still a conspicuously active figure on today's scene, along with every major new jazz personality of the present decade who had made his mark before these words went to press, can be found in these pages. For those who are not yet represented, may I add a reminder: this is not intended to be the last book in the *Encyclopedia of Jazz* series.

North Hollywood, Calif.

Contents

Illustrations

Foreword by John Lewis

Shortly before the 1960s it was evident that the decade ahead would be vitally important, perhaps crucial, in the development of modern music. The major trend that we associate with the jazz of the sixties began with the alto saxophonist and composer Ornette Coleman.

I first heard him one afternoon in 1959 in San Francisco and was greatly impressed both with his playing and with what he had to say about the future of music. I tried to see what I could do to help him, because he was one of the most interesting and original musicians I had heard in a long time.

Ornette today is the most important influence on young musicians. The opposition that he encountered at first, after he came to New York late in 1959, came mostly from his peers—the musicians of that day. But in the meantime a whole new generation of musicians has come along who are more interested in Ornette's music than his peers were back in those days. In 1965 Ornette went to Europe, and judging by all the reports that I heard and read, he enjoyed a success far beyond anything he had experienced in this country. He played at the Berlin Festival at the same time I was there with the Modern Jazz Quartet, and the response of the audience was remarkable. Jazz fans today are receptive to a greater variety of sounds than ever before, while the musicians themselves are naturally more concerned than they used to be with the utilization of all available forms, sounds and concepts. Because of what they have heard and read, listeners as well as musicians are more aware of the broad range of ideas around them.

My own history may give some idea of how a musician's background and experiences may shape his development. When I first came to New York, there were very few books on jazz, and certainly none remotely resembling Leonard Feather's *Encyclopedia of Jazz* series. Perhaps it was not a coincidence that the same man who introduced Leonard Feather to his publisher was the man who did the most for me when I arrived in town—John Hammond, who has dedicated his life to helping jazz and the people concerned with it. He lent me money, he found me jobs; I'll always be grateful to him, not only for what he did for me, but also for helping Benny Goodman, Count Basie and so many others.

I arrived in Manhattan shortly after coming out of the army, in November of 1945. The first job I ever played in New York was with a big band that the late Hot Lips Page had at the time. Joe Keyes was in the band, as were Walter Page and Joe Eldridge. I did that job three days after arriving, before I even had my union card. Then I played some jobs along 52nd Street that John Hammond helped arrange for me, with Shelly Manne, Allen Eager and others, on the offnights at the Three Deuces. I also played with Gene Ramey, the bassist, whom I'd known through Jay McShann's band during the couple of years McShann was living in Albuquerque, my home town. We had a couple of wonderful bands in Albuquerque. One was a Negro band from Oklahoma, although they called themselves the Bostonians. McShann played piano with them. Then we had a local band, Eddie Carson's Orchestra. There were lots of pleasant influences around Albuquerque.

Then through Kenny Clarke, whom I'd known in the army, I met Dizzy Gillespie. Kenny brought him some arrangements I had written; Dizzy liked them and asked me to arrange for the band. His pianist at that time was Thelonious Monk, but in 1946 I found myself out on the road playing with the band. I stayed with him until 1948 and during that time we went to Europe.

I regret now that I didn't know as much about music as I know today, because Dizzy needed some help, and I knew instinctively in what areas this help was needed, but I just didn't know how to go about doing it. I learned a lot of details of organization that I was able to apply later when I formed the Modern Jazz Quartet; and there was the question of the caliber of musicianship in Dizzy's band, but at that stage in the development of jazz there were not many musicians available who were capable of interpreting the things we were doing. Some of them were fine musicians, but they didn't suit the particular music we were making. Of course, that was at a time when there were many troubled musicians who had become drug addicts or had other personal problems. Fortunately this sort of thing has subsided considerably.

After five or six years as a sideman with Dizzy and others (Illinois Jacquet, Lester Young, Charlie Parker), I studied for three years at the Manhattan School of Music. I was lucky. This truly professional school had first-class teachers; they wanted people to come out of there to go to work, not only to teach. I had to stay on my toes to keep up. They had very small classes, too, so I was able to get more questions answered than would have been possible in a big university.

It was during the Manhattan School period that I decided I wanted to create some new concepts through a group of my own. I didn't want a band, but a quartet in which all four components could be heard clearly, and for which a very special kind of balance would be achieved, one that could be realized without microphones—a natural balance. This idea materialized in the Modern Jazz Quartet.

While the Quartet was being established, I maintained my interest in studying and listening to all forms of music, in looking at scores and analyzing them. My association with Gunther Schuller was and continues to be a very great stimulus. When we first met, he was a French horn player and composer who had developed an interest in jazz. Together we assembled two groups in which classical musicians were combined with such jazzmen as J. J. Johnson, Stan Getz, Lucky Thompson and Tony Scott, and under the name of the Modern Jazz Ensemble we recorded an album in 1955*, for which I wrote the music and some of the arrangements; Gunther did some of the arranging. I suppose some people would classify that album as "Third Stream"—a term that has been closely associated with Gunther; it could be applied to a venture in which he and I were involved a few years later, in the group known as Orchestra U.S.A.

Its purpose—I think perhaps it was a little too early and expensive to accomplish—was to show that it had become possible for American musicians to interpret almost any kind of music. This does not necessarily refer to the improvisational creative element, but the interpretive, and to the fact that there are in this decade creative improvisers who are also great interpreters. I am concerned with the introduction of jazz techniques to the artists who play in symphony orchestras, and believe that it should be incorporated into the training of young musicians who are to play in orchestras. Some of them are learning fast. Recently I became acquainted with a young violinist who can read music and make it sound like jazz—the first with whom I have had contact. There must be other such young musicians in America. The reverse has also occurred in the sixties. Young jazz musicians have learned to accommodate themselves to the requirements of symphony orchestras, as I saw in Orchestra U.S.A.

The increasing rapprochement between symphony and jazz musicians does not necessarily mean that jazz as an independent entity will cease to exist. Other musics that remind one of the manner in which jazz has developed—such as the folk music in the Balkan countries—still exist, yet they have produced such great composers as Bartok, Smetana and Dvorak. The folk music that inspired them has not disappeared, and I do not believe that jazz is in any danger of extinction, offering as it does a wonderful outlet for basic innovations, as we have seen in the case of Ornette Coleman. Moreover, we are currently paying much attention to some forms, such as rhythm and blues, that have been with us for a long time.

After traveling extensively between the United States and Europe, I have come to realize that European musicians may eventually well be superior to the Americans. In fact, the best jazz I heard last year was in Europe, played both by European musicians and

* This LP has been reissued under the title *Little David's Fugue* on Verve VSP 18.

expatriate Americans. With men like Ben Webster, Kenny Clarke, Jimmy Woode, Benny Bailey, Don Byas, the Continental scene is very stimulating.

Dizzy Gillespie once said in a magazine article that "jazz is too good for Americans." I would say rather that America is not yet sufficiently conscious of the possibilities of jazz as a contribution to its culture. Admittedly, the situation is changing, but very slowly. Though ours is still basically a North European-oriented country, many of the esthetic developments taking place here are native. There has to be a change in thought before the public at large is ready to accept what jazz can offer it. We don't seem to understand what our original cultural contributions are worth; there is still a tendency to imitate what is best in Europe. You can't do that; it proves nothing.

We should learn to think internationally. A watchful eye should be kept on the European scene, where the opportunities for development seem to be better: there are radio station house bands in all European countries, which give the musicians not only financial security, but also the opportunity to play different kinds of music. There is nothing remotely like that in the United States, except for the stage bands in high schools and colleges, which do not compare with European radio bands.

What we may need in America to help keep the music on a stable economic and musical level is either a new kind of night club or a new kind of concert hall, or something that is halfway between the two. One night not long ago we played a benefit at Lincoln Center in New York. They had taken out all the seats on the floor and put tables in. This made for a very nice atmosphere—not for a total, deep kind of concentration, since there was a little drinking, but, because the atmosphere was that of a concert hall, there was none of the kind of rowdiness that you encounter in a night club.

As far as the more recent avant garde manifestations are concerned, I feel that all these developments will ultimately make a contribution of value to the mainstream of music. The experiments vary greatly in their approach and some of them are not successful, but little details will turn out to have been valuable, as has been the case throughout the history of music. With the many kinds of creative thinking that are to be heard around us now—due to the shrinking of the world, the accelerated rate of communications —there will probably develop in due course a more international type of music that will use contributions from music of many countries; without doubt jazz will play a strong part in this. Certainly, the cooperation between musicians of very different backgrounds, some of whom have come to jazz from classical music and others who have moved in the opposite direction, plays a most important role in the jazz of the sixties.

Of course, along with the avant garde and the so-called Third Stream and various other developments of recent years, there are still the Duke Ellingtons and the other giants established in previous eras who continue to make a vital contribution, and their role is not neglected in this new book.

It is a great mistake to approach jazz as if it began in 1960, and as if Bird or anybody who preceded this period is now old-fashioned. I believe that although there are young students who undoubtedly have this attitude, they will grow out of it as they mature in experience. It is unfortunate that they can't do this immediately, instead of waiting and then having so much to catch up on later. This kind of thing happened to me too. When those Duke Ellington records came out in the early 1940s, I wasn't interested in anything else.

Representatives of the various forms I have mentioned, all the way from rhythm and blues artists to the avant garde musicians and many others in stages between those extremes, will be found in the pages of *The Encyclopedia of Jazz in the '60s*. This is the second of two currently available books of this kind, both of which Leonard Feather has gone to enormous trouble and effort to compile. His work benefits many people, not only those who are interested in jazz as fans, but also scholars, historians, musicologists and the players themselves. Works of this kind did not exist previously in any readily available form, and I for one am very grateful for this book, which contains information that you would probably never find elsewhere.

The Encyclopedia of Jazz in the '60s is a unique and valuable reference work. I believe it will find its way into all universities and music schools; I hope it will be translated into many languages and enjoy a substantial circulation in Europe and all over the world.

New York City

From the perspective of the late 1960s it is as difficult as ever to gaze into the future with any substantial measure of certainty; but it may be informative and helpful to look back and observe the changes that have taken place since this decade began. Certainly there have been more meaningful developments, proportionately more major new talents, and more variegations in the music since 1960 than in the entire 16-year period that separated that date from the bebop revolution.

A glance at the 1960 scene provides a reminder of the impermanence of much of the music, and of the cultism and sudden shifts of favoritism, winds of change that can work to an artist's advantage but more often hurt him and tend to confuse his place in history. According to a *Down Beat* critics' poll published a few months before the decade began, Tony Scott was the foremost jazz clarinetist, Barney Kessel the leading guitarist; in the "New Star" categories Benny Golson was the preëminent tenor saxophonist, ahead of John Coltrane; other winners were singers Ernestine Anderson and Jon Hendricks, clarinetist Bob Wilber, vibraharpist Buddy Montgomery, the harmonica player Toots Thielemans, Maynard Ferguson as leader of the best new big band, and the long-forgotten Mastersounds as the best new combo.

The personality cults and waves of affection that govern such awards clearly have little to do with the realities of the music. Actually the most significant current development of 1959-60 was the funky blues-gospel trend among small combos. Horace Silver's group had done much to initiate this phase and Cannonball Adderley's quintet, with the recording of *This Here* in 1960, did even more to perpetuate it. But during the next few years the groups led by Silver, Adderley and others, genuinely caught up for a while in this aspect of the small-group jazz sound, were to evolve into styles more challenging for the listener and far more demanding of the performers.

Ornette Coleman, as John Lewis has pointed out in his introduction to this book, was the new focal figure, whose arrival in New York late in 1959 triggered as great a controversy as had been generated in 1944 by the innovations of Dizzy Gillespie and Charlie Parker.

Cannonball Adderley said: "His followers believe that his is the shape of jazz to come. I feel that though Ornette may influence future jazz, so will George Russell's Lydian concept of tonal organization, Coltrane's sheets of sound, Miles' melodic lyricism, Gil Evans' clusters of sound in rhythm. Ornette Coleman is an innovator of the first water. But he is certainly no messiah." Along with Ralph Gleason, this writer and innumerable other skeptical critics and musicians, Adderley was later to adjust his evaluation upward.

There were many disquieting aspects to the jazz scene in 1960. Touring jazz concert packages, which had given so much exposure to major talents in the 1950s, had almost disappeared after a surfeit of such shows had driven the concept into the ground. Jazz festivals also were at a low ebb. One such event, held at the Hollywood Bowl, was a resounding financial disaster, and in Newport a riot erupted outside the Peabody Park festival grounds. Though this had nothing to do with the festival itself, the riot and the music were linked in headlines around the country; the damaging publicity resulted in George Wein's absence from Newport the following year. (A poorly handled festival staged by other producers in 1961 led to his return in '62 and to a steady improvement in the musical quality of the presentations.)

During the same year, the imminent racial revolt was reflected in a number of events involving musicians. Dave Brubeck canceled a lucrative Southern tour when he was asked to replace bassist Gene Wright with a white musician. Louis Armstrong was still refusing to play his home town because Louisiana enforced a rigid ban against public performances by mixed groups. More and more jazz composers identified with their heritage by writing suites dedicated to Africa and to freedom.

An auspicious news item of the year was John Coltrane's departure from the Miles Davis combo. Soon afterward he launched his own quartet, took up the soprano saxophone, and hired Elvin Jones.

Much of the big-band scene involved developments overseas. Duke Ellington went to Paris to start work on his background score for *Paris Blues*. Gerry Mulligan formed a 13-piece band and toured Europe under Norman Granz's auspices. Quincy Jones, after struggling for a year to keep his superlative orchestra working around the Continent, came home. In December Count Basie lost the services of his singer, Joe Williams, whose six years with the band had been invaluable in strengthening its popular appeal.

On the West Coast the annual "Dixieland at Disneyland" sessions were inaugurated in the fall. Shelly's Manne-Hole, which was to become one of the most successful night clubs launched by a modern jazz musician, opened its doors in November, a few days before President Kennedy's election.

Stan Getz, living in Copenhagen, was quoted as anxious to stay there living the quiet life: "I'm tired of tearing around making money." Another Copenhagen expatriate, Oscar Pettiford, died suddenly at the age of 37.

By 1961 Getz was back home, tearing around making fair money in the clubs with a quartet that included Scott La Faro, one of three young musicians who were to die tragically during that year (Lem Winchester, Booker Little). Guitarist Charlie Byrd, in a move that was to prove auspicious both for him and for Getz, went on a Latin-American tour for the State Department and heard some appealing melodies in Brazil.

Sonny Rollins returned to the jazz scene after his much-discussed two years in retirement. Another young tenor player, Eddie Harris of Chicago, whose sound was closer to Getz' than to Rollins' (or to that of the now influential Coltrane) earned sudden popular recognition with a recording of a movie-score lament, *Exodus*.

The Ornette Coleman controversy continued. Milt Jackson was quoted: "They're so afraid to say it's nothing. There's no such thing as free form. We're just getting around to knowing what Charlie Parker was playing. They threw Ornette on the public and said this is it. You can't do that."

The night club scene was increasingly erratic. Boston's Storyville, founded by George Wein, closed its doors permanently. But in New Orleans, the opening of Preservation Hall provided a long-needed showcase for veteran local musicians, and the establishment of the New Orleans Jazz Museum gave the city a belated opportunity to point with pride.

The interest shown by President and Mrs. Kennedy in all the arts had some slight effect on jazz. Benny Goodman appeared at the executive mansion in April. On November 19, 1962, a concert was given at the White House by the sextet of Paul Winter, a young alto saxophonist recently returned from a 22-week State Department-sponsored tour of South America. (During the next few years jazz was to be heard more frequently playing Pennsylvania Avenue gigs; the guests have included Dave Brubeck, Duke Ellington, Charlie Byrd, Louis Armstrong, Stan Getz and Gerry Mulligan.)

In the spring of 1962, under a cultural exchange program with the Soviet Union, Benny Goodman was sent to the USSR. It was the first time a modern jazz orchestra had ever toured the Soviet Union. Many objections were raised on the part of those who felt that others (Ellington, Armstrong, Davis) would have been more representative of contemporary jazz, and that Goodman had to put a band together for the occasion while many other leaders had permanently organized groups that were ready to go. The Goodman visit, with a band that included Zoot Sims, Joe Newman, Teddy Wilson, Victor Feldman and a generally strong line-up, was successful, but there were no more such ventures until Earl Hines took a small group on a Soviet tour in the summer of 1966.

The other well-remembered news event of 1962 was the emergence of bossa nova, details of which will be found under the biographies of Stan Getz, Charlie Byrd, Joao Gilberto, Antonio Carlos Jobim and others. The prodigious and totally unexpected commercial success of the Getz-Byrd *Jazz Samba* album led to the release of dozens more bossa nova records by artists who were simply attempting to jump on an economically handy bandwagon. The lyrical beauty of the Brazilian compositions, and of their treatment by the more sensitive of the American artists who adapted them, was lost in many of these bastardized performances. Bossa nova is essentially an intensely melodic, tonal music, a felicitous blend of North and South American idioms. Despite the crude attempts of many businessmen and musicians to vulgarize it, the music has persisted because its inherent validity has proved strong enough to outlast these onslaughts. Some observers have claimed that its survival beyond the initial vogue status may be due to the counterbalance it provided against the atonal complexities and intangible forms of some aspects of the avant garde, which, they say, alienated part of the jazz audience. (On the other hand, it is a matter of record that some musicians linked with the avant garde, among them Archie Shepp and Sonny Rollins, have themselves experimented with bossa nova.)

In terms of mass appeal, by far the most popular jazz artist of 1962 was Ray Charles, by now rapidly approaching the point at which he would aim most of his recordings at the commercial market while retaining most of his original following and his blues-rooted musical integrity. During the same year, Dizzy Gillespie enjoyed a significant success when he introduced *The New Continent,* an extended composition by his pianist, Lalo Schifrin, at the Monterey Jazz Festival. This was also the year when Herbie Mann, through his record of *Comin' Home Baby,* was established as an influential figure in Latin-oriented and other ethnic forms of jazz. Mann's success, though grounded in a musically valid form, earned him the contempt of many critics and led him to comment: "If you're in jazz and more than ten people like you, you're labeled commercial."

Much the same comment might have been made by Jimmy Smith, the organist whose albums reached a new peak of popularity in 1963. Smith by now had set a style for organ groups, usually featuring guitar, saxophone and drums, that was widely influential throughout the U.S. and overseas. His strong emphasis on the blues and on the use of tension and excitement as primary values did not connote that this was the only direction jazz was taking. On the contrary, during 1963 the diversification of jazz forms was clearly demonstrated by the Third Stream concerts of John Lewis' Orchestra U.S.A., composed of 29 classical and jazz musicians; by the growing interest in Ravi Shankar and other Indian musicians who began to bring the raga into the jazz orbit; by the development of a sturdy avant garde movement not only at home but also in England (Joe Harriott's *Abstract* album earned a five-star *Down Beat* rating); and by the important developments of that year in big-band jazz.

In 1963 Count Basie enjoyed successes without precedent in his 28 years as a bandleader. Four of his albums (two instrumental, one teamed with Ella Fitzgerald and one with Sinatra) became best sellers. Woody Herman's band of young musicians brought about a new resurgence of interest in the Herman orchestra and produced a series of buoyant, hard-swinging albums. For Duke Ellington it was, as always, an eventful year. He wrote the music for a production of *Timon of Athens* at Stratford, Ontario; organized a "second Ellington band" (supervised by Billy Strayhorn and conducted by Jimmy Jones) for his original production *My People,* seen at the Century of Negro Progress Exposition in Chicago; and undertook a tour of the Middle East for the State Department.

Theatricality was noted as a part of many jazz performances. Don Ellis, during a European tour, offered a series of "happenings," some of them of dubious meaning and certainly far less significant than the free-jazz music he was capable of creating. Sonny Rollins began to attract attention by appearing from backstage or from somewhere in the audience as he played his way onto the bandstand. Rollins was going through a stage of uncertainty about his musical direction, possibly caused by the emergence of John Coltrane as the principal tenor sax influence during Rollins' retirement.

Films and television continued to serve only as an occasional medium for the presentation of jazz. Dizzy Gillespie and Yusef Lateef played background music written by Mal Waldron for a film, *The Cool World.* Steve Allen financed a series of 26 half hour TV programs, *Jazz Scene USA,* that enjoyed a greater success abroad than at home. Critic Ralph Gleason was seen on many educational U.S. stations as host of a music-with-interviews series, *Jazz Casual.*

The night club scene grew bleaker. The Black

Hawk in San Francisco and Nick's, the long-established Greenwich Village home of Dixieland, closed down. During this period, however, the lower East Side of Manhattan began to replace the Village as an avant garde meeting place, not only for jazz musicians but for poets and painters.

There was an unusually great number of losses to jazz during 1963. Deaths included Pete Brown, Curtis Counce, Lizzie Miles, Glen Gray, Luis Russell and Dinah Washington.

As the mid-1960s approached, the international exportation of U.S. musicians increased continuously. In the year 1964 there was a climactic musical invasion of Japan, which for years had been growing as an outlet for American jazz artists. The visitors included Duke Ellington, on his first trip to the Orient; Philly Joe Jones, Shelly Manne and Roy Haynes heading a percussion package; Bob Crosby, Herbie Mann, Count Basie, Gerry Mulligan, Oscar Peterson, Harry James, George Lewis, and a "World Jazz Festival" comprising three shows (modern with Miles Davis, Dixieland with Red Nichols, swing with the Tommy Dorsey band), rotating for a week in five cities.

During 1964 jazz musicians became intensely active in appearances to help the civil rights struggle, playing benefits for the NAACP, CORE, SNCC and other groups. Duke Ellington's orchestra took part in *Freedom Spectacular,* a cross-country closed-circuit TV spectacular.

Important musical contributions during the year were those of Charles Mingus, whose group stirred the audience into a frenzy at Monterey; Earl Hines, whose first New York appearance in five years marked the beginning of a great upsurge in interest on the part of critics and musicians; Cecil Taylor, Jimmy Giuffre, Paul Bley and Rod Levitt, whose varied experiments were the subjects of frequent and heated debate. The Haitian-born Andrew Hill, a pianist and composer of exceptional talent, began to attract attention, as did another avant-gardist, the saxophonist and flutist Charles Lloyd, who left Cannonball Adderley's combo to form a combo of his own.

In 1964 jazz lost at least a dozen important figures, most notably Jack Teagarden, Don Redman, Meade Lux Lewis, Eric Dolphy, Joe Gordon and Joe Maini.

A development that reached the proportions of a full-scale trend during 1965 was the writing and performing of liturgical jazz. Though the association of jazz with divine worship had been attempted on various occasions during the previous decade, such events by now were frequent and often achieved their objective from both the musical and religious standpoint. Duke Ellington's concert of sacred music, for which the orchestra was augmented by a choir, solo voices and a tap dancer, was introduced in the fall at Grace Cathedral in San Francisco. Edgar Summerlin, long active in this field, presented his *Liturgy of the Holy Spirit* at the University of Bridgeport. Paul Horn's recording of a jazz mass composed and arranged by Lalo Schifrin, released under the title *Jazz Suite on the Mass Texts,* met with very little opposition and was praised as an inspired work, flawlessly conceived and performed.

Also in 1965, the Jazz Composers' Guild group, Archie Shepp and other avant gardists were presented at Newport; Ramsey Lewis' soul-piano reached a vast audience with his hit record of *The In Crowd;* Miles Davis and Mahalia Jackson were both sidelined by illness for most of the year; Maynard Ferguson and Lionel Hampton, abandoning their attempts to hold big bands permanently together, began to work either with small combos or occasionally with ad hoc larger groups. Louis Armstrong made his first tour of several Iron Curtain countries (excluding the USSR); a projected New Orleans Jazz Festival was called off because of the danger of racial discrimination, despite the passage of the 1964 Civil Rights law; the Harlem Cultural Council's Jazzmobile, bearing an impressive assortment of musicians who volunteered their services in a unique civic venture, started rolling in the streets of Harlem and the Bronx.

Birdland degenerated from jazz into rock 'n' roll, then quietly expired after a 15-year life as the world's best-known jazz club. Frank Sinatra sang with the Basie band at Newport; John Handy's quintet was the surprise success of Monterey. The year's deaths included Nat Cole, Denzil Best, Tadd Dameron, Carl Kress, Red Nichols, Clarence Williams and Spencer Williams.

By 1966 the situation in the South had stabilized itself to a point that enabled George Wein to stage jazz festivals in Austin, Texas, and Atlanta, Georgia. No segregation problems were encountered in housing, restaurants, onstage or at any other level. Even Mobile, Alabama, held an intercollegiate jazz festival, at which the winning combo was interracial.

Benny Carter, for some years a successful writer

of background music for television shows, completed the score for a Sammy Davis motion picture, *A Man Called Adam*. A Frank Sinatra film, *Assault on a Queen,* featured music by Duke Ellington. Also in 1966, Duke teamed with Ella Fitzgerald for a European tour arranged by Norman Granz, who described it as one of the most successful tours he had ever organized.

New big bands were started by Ray Charles and Buddy Rich. Buddy De Franco, after many years of erratic work, took over leadership of the Glenn Miller orchestra.

Friedrich Gulda organized an all-star orchestra composed of leading European and American expatriate musicians, fortified by a couple of Americans flown over specially, when he presented an International Competition for Modern Jazz in Vienna.

A 16-piece band from Indiana University completed a tour of the Near and Middle East for the State Department. It was one of many college bands that had begun to focus attention on the higher education centers as new media for the creation of first-class jazz, and for the regular presentation of concerts by leading jazz artists. Stanford University in California held a "Jazz Year" during 1965-6, involving concerts by name groups and a series of lectures by critics and musicians. The North Texas State Lab Band made a joint appearance with Stan Kenton and the Los Angeles Neophonic Orchestra, a large unit assembled in 1965 to present four concerts annually.

The losses to the jazz world included Dave Barbour, Papa Jack Laine, Johnny St. Cyr, Osie Johnson, Hank d'Amico, Fred Assunto, Avery (Kid) Howard, Bud Powell and Boyd Raeburn.

As the 1970s draw closer, the prediction of any firm future direction for jazz becomes increasingly difficult. The factionalism that has divided jazz for so many years seems today more bitter and unreasoning than ever. There is no meeting of the minds among the critics; the musicians themselves are no less sharply split. Some feel that the future of jazz may rest with its encouragement at the college level. Yet it is precisely here, and at the music schools such as Berklee, that young instrumentalists learn to go by the rule books, while in the professional world many jazzmen are founding their philosophy on the concept of throwing those books away. Freedom music, mainstream jazz, Third Stream adventures, big-band sounds in the traditions of Ellington,

Basie, Herman and Kenton, often appear to be incompatible forces whose adherents neither understand one another nor spend enough time listening to each other.

Many of the jazz musicians who have come to prominence during the past 10 to 20 years have been branded in scholarly critical essays as "popularizers." The use of the term is almost always implicitly derogatory. It has been left unclear whether the artists supposedly set out to popularize their music, or whether popularity was wished on them. In the sense that they try to communicate with their audiences, indulge in various forms of showmanship and are at times willing to make temporary compromises in order to sustain their reputations, some of the most catalytic and durably important figures in jazz might be classified as popularizers, from Duke Ellington and Louis Armstrong to Dizzy Gillespie and the numerous modern musicians (including several avant gardists) who affect unusual clothes, odd-shaped glasses or musical devices clearly designed to ensure that they will be talked about. The self-conscious attempt to become controversial is one of the most prevalent and obnoxious forms of would-be popularization.

On the other hand, should a George Shearing be relegated to the class of popularizer when history shows us that he was the first important European originator of a jazz style since Django Reinhardt? Should Herbie Hancock be similarly catalogued because he wrote the hit song *Watermelon Man,* even though he is in fact one of the most advanced of today's young jazz pianists?

If an unexpected change in popular tastes brought Cecil Taylor to the Ed Sullivan television show, the best-selling-record charts and an international tour as star of a series of festivals, no doubt he in turn would become, in the ears of some critics, a "popularizer," regardless of what modifications might or might not be found in his music.

Such a contingency is, of course, extremely improbable, for the avant garde jazz of the 1960s is far more esoteric and in most cases infinitely farther removed from mass acceptance than were Gillespie, Parker and the other avant gardists of the 1940s. The communication gap between musicians (or critics) and the jazz audience can be gauged by the results of the 1966 *Playboy* poll, in which Henry Mancini received almost 10,000 votes as leader of the mythical all-star jazz band (Ellington ran second with

3,748); Chet Atkins was voted second only to Charlie Byrd as a jazz guitarist; Al Hirt was runner-up to Miles Davis in the trumpet voting, and the leading avant garde musicians, with few exceptions, either trailed near the bottom or did not even receive enough support to be listed in the final tabulations.

The bitterness and hostility of some of the more inventive, adventurous artists, whose experiments appeal only to a minuscule in-group, can better be understood in the light of such figures. Yet it seems inevitable that those members of the new wave whose talent and patience are equal to the demands placed on them will survive and earn a lasting place in the history books.

In fact, if it is possible to make any over-all prediction for the jazz scene of the 1970s and 1980s, it is that the music will reach a significant third stage in its evolution as part of our esthetic life. In the first stage, to the extent that it was recognized at all, jazz was stigmatized as low-grade entertainment. In the second phase, with its acknowledgment by the intellectuals and the beginning of a rapport with the world of so-called classical music, it was accepted as a valid and serious part of our world of music. The third stage, one that seems to this writer to be close at hand, will find jazz in all its great diversity of forms established as a reflection and an incomparably vital part of the entire society in which we live.

—L.F.

For more than 20 years, artists from every area of jazz have been offering this writer their tape-recorded opinions of records played for them. Because they are given no prior information concerning the records, their reactions are never encumbered by the prejudices that are an unavoidable and natural consequence of such knowledge.

It is the aim of the Blindfold Test to elicit the honest subjective reaction of the listener. Secondarily, the musician blindfolded usually attempts to identify the artists on each record, though it is always made clear before the interview that the evelutions are far more important than the guesswork.

Since the Blindfold Tests of the 1960s had produced, at the time of going to press, a quarter of a million words of commentary by more than 150 subjects interviewed, the task of selecting the material most worthy of reproduction was an extremely complex one. For the most part, in choosing the following excerpts, Ira Gitler and I relied on comments involving music or musicians essentially associated with the 1960s.

The excerpts were selected on the basis of their general interest, without regard to the positive or negative nature of the comments. The ratings indicate outstanding records (five stars), very good (four stars), good (three stars), fair (two stars) and poor (one star.)

The excerpts are reproduced through the cooperation of Don DeMicheal, editor of *Down Beat,* and by permission of Maher Publications, a division of John Maher Printing Co.

The date after the artist's name before each comment indicates the year in which the interview was first published.

ORNETTE COLEMAN

Ornette Coleman. *Lonely Woman* (Atlantic). Coleman, alto.

Tyree Glenn (1960): Ha, ha, ha! I don't know—sounded like sump'n from India! You know, you hear these bands from India that play these flutes and different instruments—they've got so many moving parts it's hard to distinguish.

Ornette Coleman. *Congeniality* (Atlantic).

John Hammond (1960): . . . through all the sickness in his playing, there is a real, considerable talent here, and it's not just Charlie Parker talent either; the guy has got something of his own to say . . . but my prediction is that instead of this young musician getting better, he's going to become more and more of a bore.

Ornette Coleman. *Forerunner* (Atlantic).

Charlie Byrd (1960): . . . he's a very sweet and sincere guy, not a phony trying to capitalize on any freak kind of sound or idea . . . but I resent the fact that he is being touted as a great saxophonist . . . As for people making an analogy of Charlie Parker and Ornette Coleman, that's kind of ridiculous . . .

Ornette Coleman. *Ramblin'* (Atlantic).

Quincy Jones (1961): Whichever alto player it was, I wish he would play in tune. He's got good ideas, but it would help to get them across a little more, you know, if . . . unless that's considered to be a little bit more freedom—if you can take liberties with the intonation like that. If that's liberty, boy, they're making an ass out of Abraham Lincoln!

I think it would be a good idea for everybody to just leave Ornette alone and let him do what he wants to do for about five years and let him get himself together rather than subject him to all the controversial ends of it . . . he's searching and he should at least have the liberty to do it in peace.

Ornette Coleman. *Eventually* (Atlantic).

Rex Stewart: Wow! Protest! That reminds me of sitting in with Charlie Mingus . . . To me, music is much more than a lot of enthusiasm and a lot of notes. To me, there was a certain element, which I like to hear in music, that I'm afraid was missing.

Ornette Coleman, *Bird Food* (Atlantic).

Benny Golson (1961): Since none of us knows what the future holds, you might say this could be the music of the future . . . Some of the melodies he creates are very good . . . but the execution after the statement is on a lower level.

Ornette Coleman. *Focus on Sanity* (Atlantic).

André Previn (1961): Basing it on this record . . . the worst thing I can say about it is . . . that it is an unmitigated bore . . . If someone is bent on broadening that which has come before . . . developing upon precedents, then I'm for it, but turning your back on any tradition is anarchy.

[The following two entries are related, and should be read as one entry.]

Phil Woods (with Quincy Jones). *The Midnight Sun Will Never Set* (Mercury). Woods, alto.

Benny Carter (1961): Phil Woods does a wonderful job there, and this is the first record I'm going to give this rating—because of the wonderful alto solo —Five Stars.

Ornette Coleman. *Embraceable You* (Atlantic). Coleman, alto.

Benny Carter (1961): When people like Gunther Schuller and John Lewis, whose musicianship I respect, back and support this so openly and so fervently, I don't know what to think. I just can't figure it out. From the very first note it's miserably out of tune.

Afterthoughts by Carter: I should like to revise one rating. After hearing *Embraceable You* by the Ornette Coleman group, I'd like to raise the rating on Phil Woods' *Midnight Sun Never Sets* to 12!

Ornette Coleman. *Folk Tale* (Atlantic). Coleman, alto.

Sonny Rollins (1962): I'm in favor of Ornette and many of the things he has done . . . he does possess the basic elements that go to make up a jazz artist . . . a rhythmic drive . . . qualities you can find in everybody since Louis Armstrong—all the good guys . . . I can still see in his figures a certain quality that was exemplified by Bird.

Everybody says Ornette's playing sounds weird or so forth. But the basic jazz essentials, as I said . . . Ornette has—the drive and the rhythm. Rhythm is the most necessary part, the prerequisite for the jazz musician—the positive element. But, of course, harmony is the negative through which the positive must exert itself.

Ornette Coleman. *Enfant* (Atlantic). Coleman, tenor.

Frank Rosolino (1963): I like Sonny Rollins very much, generally, but they must have got him on a bad night here or something. Maybe he just got out of bed . . . The sound was awfully distorted too. Sonny Rollins generally sounds wonderful. I don't understand why they even released a record like that.

Ornette Coleman. *Beauty Is A Rare Thing* (Atlantic). Coleman, alto.

Jon Hendricks (1964): . . . for someone like Mr. John Lewis, who played with Bird, to call Ornette an extension of Bird, to me is charlatanism of the rankest order . . . And for people like Martin Williams and Nat Hentoff, who should know better, to propound this type of thing is either rank commercialism, which is a terrible thing to do to Ornette, or *complete* musical ignorance.

Ornette Coleman. *Enfant* (Atlantic). Coleman, tenor.

Joe Henderson (1966): In my estimation a very important date, along with some of Ornette's earlier dates. It was very important insofar as the direction of music; jazz, specifically the avant-garde . . . Ornette inspired me to move from the canal-like narrowmindedness of the '40s through the later '50s, to the later Grand Canyon-like harmonic awareness of the '60s . . . I think he might have had some bearing on Newk Rollins and the impeccable John Coltrane.

Ornette Coleman. *Snowflakes and Sunshine* (Blue Note). Coleman, violin and trumpet.

Dave Brubeck (1966): It has to be Ornette Coleman playing violin and well, it's wild. I wouldn't want to judge him as a violinist, because I don't think anyone could, and I don't think he wants to be. This is just a way he has of expressing himself with a violin, and I don't think I've ever heard anyone express themselves that way on the violin; but after all, that's what we're all doing, using music to say what we have locked up in us . . . When you play like this you lose a lot of the great qualities of music; you lose the quality of modulation, which is one of the most uplifting things in the world.

When I studied with Milhaud he said the reason he didn't like twelve-tone music is because you never have this great feeling of changing keys, rising and soaring into a new tonality; that's why he didn't particularly like twelve-tone music. This is not beautiful music at all, but it could serve Ornette and the musicians with him.

The trumpet player wasn't a good trumpet player, he didn't do things clean, I couldn't judge him . . . There's no way to judge this music. It'll have to be judged in the future . . . You *know* this can't satisfy many people, and you know it must satisfy Ornette and these fellows, or they wouldn't be doing it, so we'll keep listening. I think it's breaking the ice, it'll lead music somewhere; we don't know where yet.

THE AVANT GARDE

Archie Shepp. *The Girl From Ipanema* (Impulse). Shepp, tenor.

Herbie Mann (1966): The whole thing reminds me of like they were watching a movie and doing the sound track for it, and I wanted to see the movie too! I had no idea it was going to be *The Girl From Ipanema* (which it wasn't). It's a very interesting arrangement of the tune itself—it's a good arrangement . . . Archie Shepp's playing sounds to me like Eddie "Lockjaw" Davis with a sore throat. Really, he doesn't sound that far out to me.

Archie Shepp. *Naima* (Atlantic). Shepp, tenor.

Harold Land (1965): I recognized the tune that Trane wrote . . . And I wish he had been playing it, because it is a beautiful tune, and whoever this was didn't do justice to it. The great body of warmth in the tune was left out, in its entirety, to me. I just didn't receive any message; all I heard was a lot of calisthenics to no avail.

John Coltrane. *After The Rain* (Impulse). Coltrane, tenor.

Archie Shepp (1966): I think, aside from my own father, I respect John Coltrane as much as or more than any man in the world. John Coltrane is a tremendous man. He is the product of the same world which created and consequently murdered Bird, and Shadow Wilson, Billie Holiday, Ernie Henry . . . it attests to something: that he was able to overcome that and become the man that he is . . . he understands it's all about *growth!* It's certainly not just picking up a horn and playing it. You can't do that. A lot of youngsters think it's just pick up a horn and play it—but you don't. It's very hard work. It doesn't matter so much if a man learns to read music or not, or learns to notate. . . . I think the white man's made a great deal about his notation and about the fact that he introduced it to the world, but it's only a device really. It doesn't enable you to play music. . . . So, what would I give that? There are not enough stars for that man . . .

John put a group together that understood energy. Sonny Rollins' thing is his lyricism. Newk is lyrical. He can play ballads in the way that nobody can play them. But John's thing is his energy. And in order for a player today to really be worth his salt, he'd better listen to both of them, because they're coming out of the schools of Lester Young and Coleman Hawkins. Those are the two major schools of saxophone playing

right now. Like Ellington and Tatum are the major schools of piano playing.

John Coltrane. *Big Nick* (Impulse). Coltrane, soprano.

Cal Tjader (1965): I'm afraid I'm a little confused about whether it was John Coltrane on soprano or not. I don't think it was, although whoever it was was definitely influenced by the Coltrane style of playing . . . I really got a little bored, as I find myself doing on some of these things—it just gets to be too chaotic around the third or fourth chorus. The first chorus was very nice; going into the second was kind of interesting, but after that, I get bored. Frankly, I am sort of waiting till they take it out: the release from that tension.

John Coltrane. *Miles' Mode* (Impulse). Coltrane, tenor.

Stan Getz (1964): That's a good record . . . That Coltrane, he's a wonderful player.

The tune didn't move me too much. It's all built around one chord change and just goes on and on. Very monotonous. No matter how many substitutions they find for the chord, you still have that feeling of sameness.

John Coltrane. *Dahomey Dance* (Atlantic). Coltrane, tenor.

André Previn (1963): . . . from now on I'll take any saxophone player's word for it that he can play 6,000,000 notes per bar, have the fashionable unbearably ugly sound, play what they call superimposed changes, which in plain English means wrong, and make tracks that are never any shorter than 10 minutes.

There's no tune that I can detect, but, I'm sure, in keeping with the fashions today it's probably called *The Key to the Absolute* or *Let's See How Long We Can Play on G.* . . .

This is all purely personal, you understand, but the saxophonist, to me, is just this side of unbearable.

John Coltrane. *Lush Life* (Prestige). Coltrane, tenor.

Ben Webster (1962): I liked that . . . Seems to be hard for a real fast guy like Trane to slow down, but he did, and played some wonderful broad tones . . . really played it well. He played it like he should on a ballad—rather straight in places; yet he played his style too in spots.

John Coltrane. *Simple Like* (Roulette). Coltrane, tenor.

Sonny Rollins (1962): Great! That's one of my favorite saxophonists and favorite people—John Coltrane.

John Coltrane. *India* (Impulse). Coltrane, soprano.

Paul Horn (1964): I admire John Coltrane more than any other musician in the jazz field today. A lot of times, when a man is searching as hard as John is sometimes, you have to wade through a lot of things before you can get a certain meaty part of it. The ultimate in improvisation, while you want to be as free as possible, still has to be some framework to work within.

One of my favorite musicians—and I know one of Coltrane's too—is Ravi Shankar, the sitar player from India; and I think John hears a lot of those things in his mind when he plays and is maybe trying ultimately to get into the same bag. I'm not comparing him with a sitar player, because Coltrane is Coltrane, and Ravi Shankar is Ravi Shankar.

Though Indian music is free, there are still certain rules that are set up for the improvisation. You can maintain a great deal of freedom, but you can listen to a composition that goes on 20 minutes or longer, and it will add up to a totality.

John Coltrane. *Exotica* (Roulette). Coltrane, tenor.

Sonny Stitt (1963): It was interesting . . . but it was mysterious. The average human being who understands jazz, I don't believe, could interpret this, because it's quite heavy for the average layman. . . . I liked it, but it's difficult.

Cecil Taylor. *I Love Paris* (United Artists). Cecil Taylor, piano.

Ray Bryant (1960): You don't have to play this all the way through, you can take it off . . . That must have been Cecil Taylor. I don't have any comments. *No* stars.

Gil Evans. *Bulbs* (Impulse). Taylor, piano.

Don Ellis (1962): That is one of the best piano solos I have ever heard Cecil Taylor play . . . One of the things Cecil does is play patterns rather than actual notes, and I think this is good . . . In most of Cecil's work I find that most of his things should be limited. If you could extract a minute's work of Cecil Taylor's and round that out, I think you would have something tremendously moving, but Cecil loves to play, and he loves to extend himself, and it reaches the point where it loses any continuity.

Cecil Taylor. *Port of Call* (Candid).

Calvin Jackson (1962): You don't have a minus star, do you? Actually, this is even a little more neurotic than that one that sounded like the Motorola running backwards. It's sort of like gibberish, you know?

Gil Evans. *Pots* (Impulse). Taylor, piano, composer.

The Three Sounds—Andy Simpkins, Gene Harris, Bill Dowdy (1963):

Simpkins: I would guess Charlie Mingus. Whoever did the arranging did a wonderful job. This has a sense of direction, and it reminds me of life, because it's colored very good. It's really a very moody thing. Enjoyed it all very much, the harmonic concept too.

Harris: Even with all the syncopation going on, they were still all together. Might be George Russell.

Dowdy: I agree with Gene. . . . Dynamically it was very good too. Even if you didn't completely understand what was being played, you could feel the change in the mood.

Cecil Taylor. *Trance* (Fantasy).

Bill Evans (1964): I really got with that—it was interesting. I like it. In fact, I liked it a lot. I think that what they were going for they realized very well, and I would give it five stars except that I feel that with that wonderful beginning they could have realized a lot more with change of texture and dynamic exploration . . . For what it is, it's realized almost perfectly, but it just didn't explore enough areas of expression . . . all dramatic effect is achieved by change: by setting up one thing and then bringing in some sort of contrast. And that's the very thing that's lacking in this.

It's probably Cecil Taylor.

Cecil Taylor. *Lena* (Fantasy). Taylor, piano. Jimmy Lyons, alto.

Miles Davis (1964): Take it off! That's some sad ——, man. In the first place, I hear some Charlie Parker clichés. . . . They don't even fit. Is that what the critics are digging? If there ain't nothing to listen to, they might as well admit it. Just to take something like that and say it's great, because there ain't nothing to listen to, that's like going out and getting a prostitute.

Leonard Feather: This man said he was influenced by Duke Ellington.

Davis: I don't give a ——! It must be Cecil Taylor. Right? I don't care who he's inspired by. That —— ain't nothing. In the first place he don't have the—you know, the way you touch a piano. He doesn't have the touch that would make the sound of whatever he thinks of come off.

I can tell he's influenced by Duke, but to put the loud pedal on the piano and make a run is very old-fashioned to me. And when the alto player sits up there and plays without no tone . . . That's the reason I don't buy any records.

Art Farmer (1965): The piano player sounded like he'd been listening to Cecil Taylor . . . Sounded like it'd be good for TV—you know, where three or four guys are beating up the private eye? With the guns on the head and all that. I can figure out what they're doing if I set my mind to it . . . sounds like they're playing around in about two or three chords; it's not a very intricate thing harmonically.

There's lots of violence; it has a real frantic sound. It's not to my taste. Not that I don't like things that have life to them, but this didn't get to me.

Cecil Taylor. *Luyah! The Glorious Step* (Contemporary).

Ramsey Lewis (1966): The pianist is probably a very good piano player; however, he played a lot of little technical ideas, strung to each other, but one didn't necessarily lead to the other one. You wait for him to develop an idea, and give you a nice little climax, and it doesn't happen . . .

This is music for people who like their toast very dry. Good, say, for a class on jazz; it's more like laboratory or experimental-type music. If you took away the bass and drums the pianist wouldn't be swinging. Perhaps it would sound better that way—maybe as a background for a musical cartoon.

George Russell. *Waltz From Outer Space* (Decca). Russell, composer.

André Previn (1961): I found this fascinating. It's controlled and organized, and it really has something new to say within the realm of jazz . . . Contrary to the others you've played, here you don't have to have anything explained or pointed out. This is an attractive piece very well played and orchestrated.

George Russell. *Thoughts* (Riverside).

Kenny Dorham (1962): It sounds like something Sun Ra in Chicago would write, or Gil Melle or one of those guys—Ornette Coleman. Talk about freedom—they sure got a lot of freedom there. The way the composition is put together, harmonically and structurally. I don't hear any A-A-B-A; all I hear is A-B-C-D and so on down the line . . . it's a little Dukish in places, though I don't think it's Duke . . . I like tension, but I like rest too, and I can never rest when there's too much tension.

Calvin Jackson (1962): Well, for one thing, I wish the horns would tune up to each other, at least. This is very good descriptive music, I must say—but of what, I don't know. It doesn't swing, even though the tempi are consistent. I mean when they move to a fast tempo, they stay there for a while. Then they come back to a slower theme. . . . It sounds like a hurried imitation of Miles Davis with overtones of one of Ellington's small combos playing Hindemith!

George Russell. *Zigzag* (Riverside).

Mose Allison (1964): I don't know whether that was some of the junior members of the avant garde or whether that was some of the senior members of The Establishment burlesquing the junior members! I would say that, as jazz, it was completely inconsequential . . . Sort of a burlesque of *It's Time to Shine* . . .

Don Ellis. *Irony* (Pacific Jazz). Ellis, trumpet, in improvised performance.

André Previn (1963): . . . if this was improvised from beginning to end, then it's kind of a fascinating track. If this was supposed to have been written, then it's unsuccessful. Because there's no development of anything. . . . It's a series of very interesting sound effects.

You see, Edgar Varèse, in the '20s, actually did this an awful lot better. I don't think you can judge this as a jazz record, and I don't think it's meant to be judged as one. . . .

I got a little tired of it. I think it's a slight indulgence to let it go along this long. But, in contrast to some of the more pretentious things, it sounded naive and pleasant . . . I hope they were laughing, because if it's good-natured then they were successful, but if they were serious, then it's nothing.

Conte Candoli (1966): Well, the bird calls were genuine, weren't they? . . . I feel it has no validity as music. It's pointless—it really is. Maybe they could use it for a background as movie music or something like that, but it has no place in jazz, in music as I know it.

Was that an electric razor they started out with? It sounded like my electric shaver!

New York Art Quartet. *Short* (ESP). Roswell Rudd, trombone; John Tchicai, alto; Lewis Worrell, bass; Milford Graves, drums.

Charles Lloyd (1966): That's a way too. And I tend to like to hear someone working on that way of playing. They play the line together sort of well. I think those four people were really connected up together . . . The trombone player, he does some marvelous things with the instrument, and that opens up ways for people to look into the instrument. The trombone has had a rather limited kind of status.

The alto player had a kind of sliding intonation, but then he would play straight kind of phrases. He didn't really have a connection, it was like two different kind of things; sometimes it had an effect like Coleman's but never the kind of impact—Ornette's music is really marvelous, the energy flow is always running through it—with this music, the energy flow wasn't always there, and it left a lot to be desired.

Charles Lloyd. *Apex* (Columbia). Lloyd, composer, tenor; Ron Carter, bass; Tony Williams, drums.

Ray Brown (1966): I had a mixed reaction about

that chart. I liked the way it started off—the original line was fine, but they seemed to get a little away from the structure there for a while. This doesn't bother me, but it's something I've wondered about . . . I haven't played in any of these so-called outside groups, and I wonder if the idea is to play a composed line, a melody line, and then go outside. I'm just wondering, why not start outside and stay outside?

. . . the bass must have had his strings rather low, kind of soft; they got a kind of different sound, kind of a rubbery sound. The opening line was clear, but once in a while it got too rubbery—you couldn't make out the notes. I was trying to follow the line, but sometimes it got away from me.

Albert Ayler. *Bells* (ESP).

Shelly Manne: It's a shuck. It's easy to play that way, because you don't have to worry about swinging, don't have to create melody, don't have to adhere to any form, don't have to do anything except squawk on the horns; and anything goes. It seems a shame to me that musicians would practice that long, with this as the end result. It doesn't make any sense; there's no joy, no beauty, no nothing.

I realize maybe they are so angry that they don't see any joy or any beauty. If they don't, then I'm sorry for them. I hope some day they will be able to.

You can get the same results from sticking a microphone in the midst of all that humanity in Times Square on New Year's Eve—scream, rant, rave, blow horns, honk—the effect would be the same for me.

It may be another kind of music that I don't want to have anything to do with, but it's not jazz. Not in any way, shape or form.

THIRD STREAM

The Modern Jazz Quartet and The Beaux Arts String Quartet. *Sketch* (Atlantic). John Lewis, piano, composer.

André Previn (1961): I'm quite positive that is John's composition rather than Gunther Schuller's, because it is John's favorite century. Quite on purpose, I'm sure, it's harmonically archaic—the writing and the changes—which is something Gunther never does. I sometimes wish the two of them would hit an in-between groove. I would give this all stars possible for the playing, the execution, the blowing, the time, the recording, the whole thing—a marvelous record.

My only objection, and it seems funny after praising it so highly, is that I don't see anything terribly adventurous . . . I just don't see where they get off proposing that this is so adventurous that they have to give it a new name. *Third Stream Music.* It's just MJQ with a string quartet and that's it . . . nothing *outré* or *avant garde.*

Now when Gunther writes his pieces, they lose me, because I don't think he knows quite yet which side of the stereo speaker he's writing for . . . When I'm not working with my group or writing pop albums or jazz albums or movie scores, I write music meant for the concert hall . . . I've never been pulled in the direction of trying to combine the two . . . I would dearly love to do something the MJQ would deem worthy of playing, but to play both at the same time is an amalgam that doesn't come off yet . . . to write a kind of 1922 12-tone string quartet, and then have Percy Heath walk in four, isn't the answer.

I never mind being told that I sound like every pianist since James P. Johnson, but if somebody were to say that I'm imitating Gunther Schuller, I'd quit the business.

Modern Jazz Quartet and chamber group. *Exposure* (Atlantic). Lewis, composer; Gunther Schuller, conductor.

J. J. Johnson (1961): I heard this piece last year at Monterey. Schuller is very gifted and brilliant, likely to become one of the most important of American contemporary composers . . . Now assuming this was a Schuller arrangement—I'm almost sure that it was—it's a very crafty arrangement I think, a very crafty composition, with a lot of thought and skill employed in writing, notating, and voicing it.

Modern Jazz Quartet and Beaux Arts String Quartet. *Sketch* (Atlantic). Lewis, composer.

J. J. Johnson (1961): Great string playing, and the MJQ played in top form as they usually do . . . I'm sure this is John Lewis's composition. I know John's writing pretty well, and I don't think the composition is as crafty as the one you played for me before . . . The idea of bringing strings into the jazz context is a relatively new thing, and some strides in that direction have been made . . . The problem of bringing strings into the jazz idiom has got to do with inflections and the various intensities. Most of the really good string players have classical backgrounds, and this demands a specific kind of technique and interpretation. So that we've almost got to brainwash the string players.

Modern Jazz Quartet and Beaux Arts String Quartet. *Conversation* (Atlantic). Schuller, composer.

J. J. Johnson (1961): I'll bet money that's Schuller's arrangement. No question about that . . . One of the high points of the composition for me was that segment where the MJQ is wailing, and the strings come in with these little bits of things, little snatches of things, very effective . . . Actually, the concept is rather intellectual. Schuller is an intellect . . . "Third

Stream" music? Well. I'd have to take that up with Schuller. I'd like to find out just what he means by third stream. I'm not too clear on that. Because for sure, in all those compositions and on all of those performances, the classical portions were definitely classical, and the jazz portions were definitely jazz, and, for sure, it was a very compatible arrangement. One group and one idea did complement the other. It worked out very well.

I think that if and when a third stream comes about, it will be something different from what we heard today.

George Russell (1961): That's obviously a Gunther Schuller composition for the MJQ . . . and it is a piece of music with substance . . . I found it very interesting in terms of harmonic and instrumental color. I frankly reacted more to it at the times when the quartet was allowed to play without interruption. However, that may be because the other parts were not as accessible on first hearing as the free-swinging parts. It was the part I could pat my foot to that reached me; yet the other parts didn't strike me as particularly profound, in terms of say, Alban Berg.

There were parts when I thought the writing for strings was really ingenious, and that was during the non-jazz parts, but in the jazz I thought it was a little . . . well, maybe the composer intended, with this title, to have sort of conversation between the classical strings and the MJQ, but it sounded to me a little bit like an atonal David Rose or something.

John Lewis. *Abstraction* (Atlantic). Ornette Coleman, alto; Gunther Schuller, composer.
Calvin Jackson (1962): Well . . . it sounds like a Motorola running backwards. If this composition is supposed to be describing postnuclear panic, then it's very successful.

The raucous grindings of the strings, the strident sound of the alto sax are very neurotic . . . I feel it is nearer to electronic music than not.

I saw the electronic ballet that the New York ballet company put on here last summer. It was very interesting, because it had a visual thing to go with it, plus the staging. But just for bald listening, this sort of music has to be in the category of description.

I just hope the title is competent enough to describe the effort necessary in putting this down on paper.

Andrew Hill (1965): I liked the musical idea even though there were one or two things I didn't completely understand. But beautiful . . . This seemed to me to be about one-third premeditated and two-thirds solo work. I like a lot of things Ornette's done . . . calling it abstract doesn't mean anything because to me it didn't seem abstract, the way it worked out. To me it's just a beautiful piece of art . . .

Music For Brass. *Poem For Brass* (Columbia). J. J. Johnson, composer.
George Russell (1961): That's a wonderful piece of writing. It's J.J.'s piece for brass . . . I like especially the fugue at the end, and I think J.J. betrays in this piece his love for Hindemith . . . There were some parts of the piece that didn't strike me as keenly as the fugue thing at the end, but in general it was a very fine piece of music . . .

George Handy. *The Bloos* (Verve). Handy, composer.
Oliver Nelson (1964): . . . George Handy . . . He was one of the few people I felt really capable of extending everything . . .

For the composition (and I think that if anybody could have made Third Stream into anything, Handy could) it's strange, there was only one compromise, only one, where the band had to stop whatever it was doing, all that interesting music, and go into the blues, with this steady rock 4/4; I think that might have been just to get people to listen . . .

Duke Ellington. *Nonviolent Integration* (Reprise).
Louis Bellson (1964): . . . Of course anything that Duke does I like. He just seems to have a sixth sense about things turning out so good . . . But I liked especially the marriage between the strings and what he did with the band. He didn't confine the strings to just whole notes and half notes, which most guys do, but he gave them little pizzicato things and little staccato things in there, which works out beautifully . . .

Art Farmer (1965): . . . I wouldn't say that this was a combination of a symphony and a jazz orchestra; it was just some players from a symphony. But I think the idea can work if it's given enough time, and I don't think enough time was given to preparing this . . .

Duke Ellington. *La Scala, She Too Pretty to Be Blue* (Reprise). Ellington, composer; La Scala Orchestra with Ellington band.
Woody Herman (1964): In the past, things like this mostly got out of hand. Either there were jazz writers who didn't know how to write for strings or woodwinds, and it sounded weird. I remember one band . . . when this particular band had strings, there was an introduction and an ending of an old standard, it sounded like a bunch of cows mooing. Because the guy had all the strings like, down in the wrong register.

Guys like Artie Shaw, particularly when he used charts by Lennie Hayton, knew what they were doing; they were correct, and they were lovely. But this, this is even nicer, because it's jazz. This isn't the elegant arrangement of *Stardust*—this is jazz. The blues.

BOSSA NOVA

Cal Tjader. *Elizete* (Verve). Tjader, vibes; Clare Fischer, composer, arranger.

Lalo Schifrin (1962): I think this is a tune by Clare Fischer called *Elizete* . . . I think this is a very honest approach to bossa nova . . . He has the conception of vocal bossa nova, which American musicians got; their only source was Joao Gilberto's record. . . . the bossa nova has different faces. It has a face, not only vocal, which is a very mild melody, keeping the jazz changes and rhythmic pattern derivated from the synthesis of the old sambas, but they are also doing instrumental bossa nova.

The Brazilian musicians, they blow. They really blow on bossa nova, like American musicians blow on jazz. They take a tune, and they really go into that.

Charlie Byrd. *O Pato* (Riverside). Byrd, guitar.

Lalo Schifrin (1962): I don't have any idea who this guitar could be, but, of course, he doesn't have the same approach to bossa nova as the Brazilian guitarists do.

Now, I don't want to be a policeman—bossa nova is music, and music is something which is alive. I don't want to criticize in a way that says "if this is not bossa nova, this is not good," but as a point of view of music I think it is a bit monotonous . . . Even in the jazz flavor, it would be monotonous and dull.

Charlie Byrd. *O Barquinho* (Riverside).

Laurindo Almeida (1963): Was that meant to be bossa nova? I don't know who the guitarist was, but it sounds like one of those gauchos from the Brazil-Argentina border. Here again, they've been getting away without knowing, maybe, what the idea of this thing is supposed to be . . . I agree with Moraes, who said that bossa nova is a mood. It is a mood that comprehends a lot of things together. Inasmuch as it involves two styles from two different countries, both should be played here and there. First straight, the idea of the samba. Then straight with the improvisation, making the marriage. I didn't see this in that take.

Bola Sete. *Samba No Perroquet* (Fantasy). Sete, guitar.

Charlie Byrd (1963): It must be Bola Sete. It's a Brazilian, anyway; it has that kind of Brazilian time—and Brazilian sound. I liked it. I liked his ideas and phrasing; I don't like the sound. I don't like the recording sound first of all, but I also think the guitarist had something to do with it. Most of the Brazilians get kind of a dead sound that I don't care for.

Lalo Schifrin. *Desafinado* (Roulette). Schifrin, piano.

Mel Torme (1963): That's *Desafinado*, the bossa nova thing . . . I like the bossa nova trend; I think it's the first exciting thing in popular music and jazz since the progressive era began . . . The only thing that scares me is that something new like this comes out, and, immediately, everybody jumps onto the bandwagon, and they drive it into the ground . . . I like the piano player, but I think it's a reasonably undistinguished record, and I much prefer the Stan Getz version of this. For some reason, this song, and Stan Getz' version of it, did things for each other.

Stan Getz-Joao Gilberto. *Desafinado* (Verve). Getz, tenor; Gilberto, vocal.

Miles Davis (1964): . . . I'm not particularly crazy about just *anybody's* bossa nova. I like the samba. And I like Stan, because he has so much patience, the way he plays those melodies—other people can't get nothing out of a song, but he can. Which takes a lot of imagination . . . As for Gilberto, he could read a newspaper and sound good!

Stan Getz-Joao Gilberto. *So Danco Samba* (Verve).

Harold Land (1965): Well . . . just pleasant. I've heard several tracks on that that I think were a little more musical. They didn't really arrive at too much here. Bossa nova is effective on certain tunes, but this didn't say too much to me.

Bud Shank. *Samba de Orfeu* (Pacific Jazz). Shank, flute.

Sonny Stitt (1963): How do I feel about bossa nova? Latin American music is all right. I dig it, but I'm a jazzman! . . . That was a nice pleasant sound. I can see the Mardi Gras and all that kind of stuff going on, but, man, I'm a black American, and I play jazz. Now, I wouldn't mind playing with Africans—they've got good rhythm, good hand drummers. . . . But this is just an average . . . now, Machito, wow! . . . But this thing just doesn't have any message for me.

Zoot Sims. *O Barquinho* (Colpix). Sims, tenor; Jim Hall, guitar.

Oscar Castro-Neves (1963): I like very much this sound, this mixing of the instruments. In the feeling, this is more or less the feeling of how we play bossa nova in Rio . . . The rhythm is not quite right; it is too much like another Brazilian rhythm, baiao. It's hard to explain where they lose the samba beat to the other beat, but they go too much to the baiao.

Musically, though, it is very nice. As Lalo Schifrin said to me, many of the American musicians don't look for the real rhythm. They look for a new way of playing *their* ideas. It's a good thing in a way: perhaps not for bossa nova—from our point of view it would be better that they get the real rhythm, and also it would be better because it's our music; but I respect the idea.

Like you feel the 4/4, I feel the 2/4. It's in my blood. When you go out in the streets in carnival time in Rio and some players of samba are passing, most people stop what they are doing and go behind them, dancing and singing in the streets. It's our thing, we feel that.

Carlos Lyra. *Influencia Do Jazz* (publisher's demonstration record).

Herbie Mann (1963): That was Carlos Lyra, singing his tune *Influencia Do Jazz*. Funny thing— when the song was originally written, it was a put-down of how jazz has influenced the samba. Since then, I think Carlos has changed his feelings a little bit, because he came up here, and he's taking out papers.

Quincy Jones. *On the Street Where You Live* (Mercury).

Herbie Mann (1963): . . . when this date was made, it was just before I left for Brazil, and people were saying that was the closest thing to real bossa nova. Actually this tune, it's not really bossa nova, it's carnival rhythm, it's like the old-style samba.

Herbie Mann. *Desafinado* (Atlantic). Mann, flute.

Lalo Schifrin (1962): This is, of course, the popular *Desafinado*. With the wrong changes. I think that few people in this country record the *Desafinado* with the harmonic changes that the composer, Antonio Jobim, wanted . . . I know that among jazz musicians bossa nova is becoming a kind of fashion and I don't think it should be that way . . .

Now, if a jazz musician takes bossa nova as a point of departure to develop his own personality, it is all right. But trying to make jazz bossa nova because it is so fashionable, and because Stan Getz is selling so many records, I think is wrong for creative people.

Of course, this record is very honest, I give it for honesty three stars, but I don't think there is any creation at all.

Herbie Mann. *Bossa Velha* (Atlantic). Zezinho's School of Samba Orchestra. Recorded in Rio.

Shelly Manne (1963): I don't think that was recorded in the United States. I think it was definitely recorded in Brazil, they get a very authentic feeling and that rhythm section must be Brazilian. It reminds me very much of Brazilian street-carnival music.

Steve Allen. *Sweet Georgia Brown* (Dot).

Shelly Manne (1963): That's a combination bossa nova, Dixieland, swing and . . . everything else put in that will help sell a record. I have no idea who

that was, but that's a good example of how *un*authentic Brazilian rhythm sounds.

FUNK, SOUL, BLUES, GOSPEL

Les McCann. *Vakushna* (Pacific Jazz). McCann, piano.

Shelly Manne (1960): I think he used funky riffs just for the sake of being funky, so it sounded like a slightly affected attempt to create a feeling. But it was just the blues, and it's always nice to hear the blues, so even though it didn't impress me much, I'll give it two stars . . . The Gospel thing in jazz has become stylized, a fad . . .

Les McCann. *The Shout* (Pacific Jazz).

Maynard Ferguson (1960): My first thoughts are "humor and religion"—everybody's starting to get both of it . . . All the groups are doing things of a religious connotation, with a sense of humor . . . Is that Les McCann or one of those guys? . . . It's very entertaining, and I guess we're just judging a record and not the group, as I suppose they don't play like this all night . . .

Les McCann-Jazz Crusaders. *All Blues* (Pacific Jazz). Wayne Henderson, trombone; Joe Sample, piano; McCann, electric piano; Miles Davis, composer.

Miles Davis (1964): What's that supposed to be? That ain't nothin'. They don't know what to do with it —you either play it bluesy or you play on the scale. You don't just play flat notes. I didn't write it to play flat notes on—you know, like minor thirds. Either you play a whole chord against it, or else . . . but don't try to play it like you'd play, ah, *Walkin' the Dog*. You know what I mean?

The trombone player—trombone ain't supposed to sound like that. This is 1964, not 1924. Maybe if the piano player had played it by himself, something would have happened.

Rate it? How can I rate that?

The Three Sounds. *What Kind of Fool Am I?* (Mercury). Gene Harris, piano.

Horace Silver (1963): . . . I would say it was Les McCann funkin' it up as he can do so well. There's not much more I can say about it except that it's a pretty tune, played very well, funky and soulful, but there's not much solo space on it so I can't comment on it solowise.

Shorty Rogers. *Climbing to Heaven* (Capitol).

Mose Allison (1964): That sounds like Cecil B. De Mille in Mississippi! . . . It represents something, I guess; it's sort of like a symphonic version of the

Lolita song . . . Gospel, yes, sure it's synthetic, but it did capture some of that drive, some of the essence. Even if it was synthetic, it represents to me a certain basic rhythmical force that is underlying most of the music in this country today.

Kai Winding. *You've Lost That Lovin' Feelin'* (Verve).

Shelly Manne (1966) : . . . Sounds like some a&r man had a jazzman under contract and thought he'd try to make a hit. I don't think one good thing has come from rock and roll. Whatever good things you find in it were there long before, in rhythm and blues —the old records of Peetie Wheatstraw, the Devil's Son-in-Law; Roosevelt Sykes; Bessie Smith . . . all that influence was there many years ago. Rock and roll has taken all those things and blown them out of proportion into a grotesque, crude way of playing.

ELLINGTON-MINGUS-ROACH

One of the most provocative albums of the 1960s was a trio session featuring Duke Ellington in one of his less customary roles, as piano soloist, with the unusual rhythm section assistance of Charles Mingus and Max Roach. The music produced by this trio of giants elicited a variety of reactions. The album, issued in 1963, received a five-star review in *Down Beat*.

Very Special (United Artists). Ellington, piano, composer; Mingus, bass; Roach, drums.

Ramsey Lewis (1965): Duke Ellington on the piano, with Elvin Jones and Jimmy Garrison or somebody like this. If it is Ellington, the song didn't take on the form that, even when Ellington is improvising, he has a natural tendency to develop. Everybody was playing, but I don't think it went in a particular direction.

The bassist—this is the first time during this Blindfold Test that I've been inclined to say here is someone who is heavily influenced by Mingus. In connection with the Coltrane-type music, it reminds me that Mingus was playing this way several years ago, though I've never really connected him with this type music.

For the caliber of musicianship, I'd say three stars. Obviously these are three pros, and it's obvious, too, that this is not their best.

Junior Mance (1963): . . . I've never thought much of Duke as an outstanding piano player, but I rather enjoyed this . . . I liked the sound of the bass that Mingus got . . . and Max sounded very good . . .

In places it sounded a little muddled, like they had a lot going on at the same time . . . but it did swing.

Les Fleurs Africaines. Ellington, composer.

Horace Silver (1963): . . . I don't know the name of the composition, but it was very beautiful.

. . . What Charlie Mingus was doing in the background was very interesting—fascinating. I doubt if that bass part was written, but it complemented what was happening in the melody very nicely. It was a very pretty composition.

Caravan.

Miles Davis (1964): What am I supposed to say to that? That's ridiculous. You see the way they can —— up music? It's a mismatch. They don't complement each other. Max and Mingus can play together, by themselves. Mingus is a hell of a bass player, and Max is a hell of a drummer. But Duke can't play with them, and they can't play with Duke.

Now, how are you going to give a thing like that some stars? Record companies should be kicked in the ——. Somebody should take a picket sign and picket the record company.

MONK AT THE MICROPHONE

Not until the Blindfold Test had been appearing for almost 20 years did Thelonious Monk participate as a subject. The reason was clear: Monk is not the most voluble of personalities, and it seemed improbable that an interview could be obtained.

One day in 1966 Monk broke his long silence. Accompanied by his wife Nellie, he sat, stood or paced his way through eight records. When moments of silence engulfed him, Nellie succeeded in prodding him.

After the first minute of the first record, it became obvious that the only way to complete an interview and retain Monk's interest would be by concentrating mainly on other artists' versions of his own compositions. Accordingly, Records 2-6 were all Monk tunes. At this point, he seemed interested enough to listen to a couple of non-Monk works. He was given no information about any of the records played.

Monk's reaction to Record No. 7 may have a more than coincidental relationship to the opinions expressed openly by Oscar Peterson concerning Monk's own value as a pianist.

1. Andrew Hill. **Flight 19** (from **Point of Departure,** Blue Note).

(*After about two minutes, Monk rises from his seat, starts wandering around the room and looking out the window. When it becomes clear he is not listening, the record is taken off.*)

TM: The view here is great, and you have a crazy stereo system.

LF: Is that all you have to say about that record?

TM: About *any* record.

LF: I'll find a few things you'll want to say something about.

2. Art Pepper. **Rhythm-a-ning** (from **Gettin' Together,** Contemporary). Conte Candoli, trumpet; Pepper, alto saxophone; Wynton Kelly, piano; Paul Chambers, bass; Jimmie Cobb, drums.

TM: He added another note to the song. A note that's not supposed to be there. (*Sings.*) See what I mean?

LF: Did I hear you say the tempo was wrong?

TM: No, all tempos is right.

LF: How about the solos? Which of them did you like?

TM: It sounded like some slow solos speeded up, to me.

LF: How about the rhythm section?

TM: Well, I mean, the piece swings by itself. To keep up with the song, you have to swing.

LF: How many stars would you rate it?

TM: (*Indicating Mrs. Monk*): Ask her.

LF: It's your opinion I'm asking.

TM: You asked me for my opinion, I gave you my opinion.

LF: Okay, let's forget ratings.

3. Dizzy Gillespie. Medley: **I Can't Get Started, 'Round Midnight** (from **Something Old—Something New,** Philips). James Moody, alto saxophone.

TM: Dizzy. He had a crazy sound, but he got into that upper register, and the upper register took the tone away from him. That was the Freddy Webster sound too, you know, that sound of Dizzy's. (*Later*) That's my song! Well, if that's not Diz, it's someone who plays just like him. Miles did at one time too.

LF: You like the way they put the two tunes together?

TM: I didn't notice that. Play it again. (*Later*) Yes, that's the Freddy Webster sound. Maybe you don't remember Freddy Webster; you weren't on the scene at the time.

LF: I remember Freddy Webster. And the records he made with Sarah.

TM: Remember *I Could Make You Love Me*? The introduction? Play that for me.

LF: I don't think I can find it. You think Freddy influenced Diz?

TM: Every sound influenced Diz. He had that kind of mind, you know? And he influenced everything too.

LF: You like the alto player on here too?

TM: Everybody sounded good on there; I mean, the harmony and everything was crazy . . . play it again!

4. Bob Florence. **Straight, No Chaser** (from **Here and Now,** Liberty). John Audino, lead trumpet; Herbie Harper, trombone; Florence, arranger.

LF: You liked the arrangement?

TM: Did you make the arrangement? It was crazy.

LF: No.

TM: It was a bunch of musicians who were together, playing an arrangement. It sounded so good, it made me like the song better! Solos . . . the trombone player sounded good . . . that was a good lead trumpet player too . . . I've never heard that before. I don't know how to rate it, but I'd say it was top-notch.

5. Phineas Newborn. **Well, You Needn't** (from **The Great Jazz Piano of Phineas Newborn,** Contemporary). Newborn, piano.

TM: He hit the inside wrong—didn't have the right changes. It's supposed to be major ninths, and he's playing ninths (*walks to piano, demonstrates*). It starts with a D-Flat Major 9. . . . See what I mean? What throws me off, too, is the cat sounds like Bud Powell. Makes it hard for me to say anything about it. It's not Bud; it's somebody sounding like him.

LF: Outside of that, did you like the general feeling?

TM: I enjoy *all* piano players. All pianists have got five stars for me . . . but I was thinking about the wrong changes, so I didn't pay too much attention to the rest of it. Maybe you better play it again.

(*Later*) It's crazy to sound like Bud Powell, but seems like the piano player should be able to think of something else too. Why get stuck with that Bud Powell sound?

6. Bud Powell. **Ruby, My Dear** (from **Giants of Jazz,** Columbia).

TM: That's Bud Powell! . . . All I can say is, he has a remarkable memory. I don't know what to say about him—he is a remarkable person, musically.

LF: You think Bud is in his best form there?

TM: (*Laughs*) No comment about him, or the piano. . . . He's just tired, stopped playing, doesn't want to play no more. I don't know what's going through his mind. But you know how he's influenced all of the piano players.

LF: Of course. I was just questioning whether this is his best work.

Mrs. Monk: (*To Monk*) You don't think so.

TM: Of course not.

7. Oscar Peterson. **Easy Listenin' Blues** (from **With Respect to Nat,** Limelight). Peterson, piano; Herb Ellis, guitar; Ray Brown, bass.

TM: Which is the way to the toilet? (*Waits to end of record, leaves room, returns . . . laughs.*) Well, you see where I went. (*To Mrs. Monk*) Could you detect the piano player?

LF: How about the guitar player?

TM: Charlie Christian spoiled me for everybody else.

8. Denny Zeitlin. **Carole's Garden** (from **Carnival,** Columbia). Zeitlin, piano, composer; Jerry Granelli, drums.

LF: You liked that one?

TM: I like all music.

LF: Except the kind that makes you go to the toilet.

TM: No, but you need that kind too. . . . It reminded me of Bobby Timmons, and that's *got* to be good. Rhythm section has the right groove too. Drummer made me think of Art Blakey. Hey, play that again.

(*Later.*) Yeah! He sounds like a *piano* player! (*Hums theme.*) You can keep changing keys all the time doing that. Sounds like something that was studied and figured out. And he can play it; you know what's happening with this one. Yeah, he was on a Bobby Timmons kick. *He* knows what's happening.

MONK AT THE PIANO

Though only once involved in the Blindfold Test as a reactor, Monk has often been discussed by others whose comments about his records have provided an equally mixed range of opinions. Following are a few examples.

Remember (Riverside). Monk, solo piano.

    Gerry Mulligan (1960): Well, that record made me laugh all over the place—five chuckles, no stars! Well, I don't know if that was Monk . . . It sounded like something he was working on, and I think he picked a very unfortunate choice of songs to do it on, because when he got into the composition, it kept reminding me of MacDowell pieces. The things he did with the accents in the first chorus were the important parts for him . . . He wanted to do something with the first part of that tune . . . the changing durations and the shifting accents and making lines out of them.

    If you know it is Monk, there is a tremendously humorous approach to it . . . I think that's one of Irving Berlin's duller songs, is all. Monk did an orchestration on the first part—it's really funny.

Crepuscule With Nellie (Riverside). Monk, piano, composer.

    Benny Golson (1961): Count Basie at Town Hall . . . No, I'm only kidding; of course it was Thelonious Monk. There's been a lot of pro and con talk about Thelonious through the years, but from the beginning I was pro. I was fascinated, and I wondered how he arrived at these things. Eventually I found out, by studying and analyzing them.

    Now, he is not a virtuoso pianist, but there is real thought behind what he is composing. It's all very well laid out.

Darkness on the Delta (Columbia). Monk, solo piano.

    Bill Evans (1964): Sounded like *Concert by the Sea* there for a minute at the end! That is completely entertaining but it doesn't show Monk the composer. It does show a lot of humor and . . . there he is! There's nobody like that . . . Pianistically, I don't think Van Cliburn has anything to worry about, but if he (Monk) gets that stride going a little faster, I don't know . . . maybe Art Tatum will have to come back.

    Pianistically, he's beautiful. (A promoter I know uses that phrase; I guess he likes the way it rolls off his tongue.) But Thelonious *is* pianistically beautiful. He approaches the piano somehow from an angle, and it's the right angle. He does the thing completely and thoroughly . . . He hasn't been influenced through the traditional keyboard techniques because he hasn't worked through the keyboard composers and, therefore, has his own complete approach of musical thinking.

He is such a thinking musician, and I think this is something a lot of people forget about Monk. They somehow feel he's eccentric, but Monk knows exactly what he's doing. Precisely. Structurally, and musically, he's very aware of every note he plays . . .

Rhythm-a-ning (Riverside).

    Buddy De Franco (1963): I would venture to say it might be Monk, although I don't remember Monk doing that much playing—consistent playing—as far as the pattern.

    Tommy Gumina (1963): All I can say is, Monk writes some beautiful tunes. When it comes to being a piano player, I'll see you later . . .

Oska T (Columbia).

    Jack Wilson (1964): Unlike many piano players, I love Monk's playing very much. He was brought to my attention by Richard Abrams, a pianist in Chicago, and we used to analyze Monk's playing.

    We found that Monk's penchant for playing the piano is not in velocity, and not in dynamics, but in sound and overtones. He has a lot of other devices for producing the "sound"—I've noticed a lot of times, playing in clubs, where the audience is inattentive, you play something of a Monk nature and use that sonority, automatically their ears respond to it. No other piano player has done more to find out the notes that really produce sound than Monk. To completely toss him aside as a pianistic influence is an asinine view.

Sweet and Lovely (Columbia). Monk, solo piano.

    Hampton Hawes (1965): That piano player sounded honest as a little child. I think the left hand during the first part was a little hard. It could be Monk. Also it could be Mingus playing piano—sometimes he plays piano like that.

    I liked the record, the honesty of it and the good feeling it had. However, I think it could have been a little better; so I'll give it three. I'd rather hear wrong notes being played by a person with good feeling than another person playing perfect, like a typewriter, and sound cold.

Light Blue (Columbia).

    Charles Lloyd (1966): I thought Monk sounded particularly good on his solo. . . . His is the sort of music that spans time . . . it's something that's happening, and it always feels good to me. I can always readily identify with it, and it always has a freshness about it because of the way he constructs his phrases and the kind of twists it has.

    I sometimes would like to hear him in a context with some more adventuresome musicians . . .

The dual dilemma of deciding which artists are and which are not jazz musicians, and which jazz musicians are important enough to be included in an encyclopedia, has presented even more problems in connection with the present volume than were involved in the compilation of earlier books in this series.

If the broadest possible interpretation were put upon the term, one could define as a jazz musician any "folk-rock" or rock-'n'-roll artist; any classical instrumentalist who has ever happened to take part in a performance of a Third Stream work, regardless of whether he can improvise in the jazz idiom; any folk music personality who uses the same ethnic material as some of the early blues singers; and any performer in any country in the world who has ever played a solo on a recording and earned praise from reputable fellow-musicians and critics.

Clearly such a procedure would be impossible unless a book were planned that could run to thousands of pages. Thus, some arbitrary qualifications had to be set in order to limit the number of musicians included.

The musicians whose names will be found in the following pages have all earned a substantial reputation in this country or in a few other countries where the quality and quantity of the best jazz is close to U.S. standards. With very few exceptions, participation in at least one LP recording was considered as a qualifying factor. Significant new contribution to jazz during the 1960s was also taken into consideration.

Some of the folk-blues artists, who are more essentially a part of folk music than of jazz as the word is generally understood today, are referred to in the chapter by Pete Welding, immediately following the biographical section.

In the original *Encyclopedia of Jazz,* and to a lesser extent in the *New Encyclopedia of Jazz* which has replaced it, certain musicians were included whose role, in today's light, seems to have been less substantial than was originally assumed. This applies chiefly to performers who happened to be sidemen at one time or another in important name bands, but who were not vital contributors as soloists. These musicians have been eliminated in order to make room for the more extensive examination of the key figures of today (John Coltrane, Ornette Coleman, Charles Mingus et al) than space would otherwise have allowed.

The discographies, too, are selective, since the number of recordings by jazz artists released during the past few years has been unprecedented. Wherever it was possible, the records listed were selected by the artist himself, sometimes with an indication of his personal preferences among them.

Nancy Wilson *(Capitol Records)*

Gerry Mulligan *(Fred Seligo)*

Quincy Jones *(Mercury Records)*

Harry Carney *(Roberto Polillo)*

Gene Wright

Milt Jackson

Dizzy Gillespie *(Charles Frizzell)*

Tommy Vig

Ted Curson *(Roberto Polillo)*

Klaus Doldinger *(Philips)*

37

Teddy Buckner and his Orchestra
(Premiere Artists Agency)

Charlie Rouse and Thelonious Monk
(Columbia Records)

Double Six of Paris *(Jean-Pierre Leloir)*

George Shearing (*Capitol Records*)

Marion Williams (*Roberto Polillo*)

Al Cohn and Zoot Sims (*Don Schlitten*)

Neal Hefti

Benny Golson

Cecil Taylor (*Bernard Gidel*)

Roland Kirk *(Mercury Records)*

Stan Getz and Astrud Gilberto *(MGM/Verve Records)*

Lalo Schifrin and Dizzy Gillespie *(Jerry Stoll)*

Grachan Moncur III *(Francis Wolff)*

Curtis Fuller *(Francis Wolff)*

Peggy Lee *(Capitol Records)*

Rod Levitt

Bobby Hackett

Gil Evans (*Chuck Stewart*)

Astrud Gilberto and Gene Cherico *(Popsie)*

Laurindo Almeida *(Capitol Records)*

Anita O'Day *(Virginia Wicks)*

45

Barry Harris (*Don Schlitten*)

Paul Bley

Ella Fitzgerald and Duke Ellington

Benny Goodman

Mose Allison

John Coltrane
(*Impulse Records*)

Yusef Lateef *(Impulse Records)*

Jackie McLean *(Francis Wolff-Blue Note Records)*

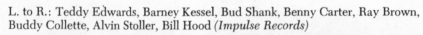

L. to R.: Teddy Edwards, Barney Kessel, Bud Shank, Benny Carter, Ray Brown, Buddy Collette, Alvin Stoller, Bill Hood *(Impulse Records)*

Abbreviations

ABC   American Broadcasting Co.
ABC-Par.   ABC-Paramount Records
acc.   accompanied, accompanying, accompanist
addr.   address
AFM   American Federation of Musicians
app.   appeared, appearing, appearance
a & r   artists and repertoire
arr.   arranged, arranger, arrangement
ASCAP   American Society of Composers, Authors and Publishers
Atl.   Atlantic
Aud. Fid.   Audio-Fidelity
b.   born
BBC   British Broadcasting Corporation
Beth.   Bethlehem
BN   Blue Note
bro.   brother
Bruns.   Brunswick
ca.   about
Cad.   Cadence
Cam.   Camden
Cap.   Capitol
CBS   Columbia Broadcasting System
cl., clar.   clarinet
Col.   Columbia
coll.   college
Comm.   Commodore
comp.   composed, composer, composition
cons.   conservatory
cont.   continued
Contemp.   Contemporary
Cor.   Coral
d.   died
Deb.   Debut
Dec.   Decca
Del.   Delmark
Des.   Design
Dix. Jub.   Dixieland Jubilee
educ.   educated, education
Elek.   Elektra
Empir.   Empirical
Fant.   Fantasy
fav., favs.   favorite, favorites
feat.   featured, featuring
Folk.   Folkways
GNP   Gene Norman Presents
Gold. Cr.   Golden Crest
gp.   group
Harm.   Harmony
Imp.   Imperial
incl.   including, included
JATP   Jazz at the Philharmonic
Jazzl.   Jazzland
JF   jazz festival
Jub.   Jubilee

KC   Kansas City
LA   Los Angeles
Lib.   Liberty
Lime.   Limelight
Lond.   London
LP   long-playing record
MCA   Music Corporation of America
Merc.   Mercury
MJF   Monterey Jazz Festival
MJQ   Modern Jazz Quartet
Mod.   Modern
mos.   months
mus. dir.   musical director
NARAS   National Academy of Recording Arts and Sciences
NBC   National Broadcasting Company
NJF   Newport Jazz Festival
NO   New Orleans
orch.   orchestra
Pac. Jazz.   Pacific Jazz
pl.   played, plays, playing
Pres.   Prestige
quart.   quartet
quint.   quintet
RCA   Radio Corporation of America; RCA Victor
r & b   rhythm and blues
rec.   recorded, recordings
Reg.   Regent
repl.   replaced, replacing
ret.   returned, returning
River.   Riverside
Roul.   Roulette
r & r   rock and roll
Sav.   Savoy
sch.   school
SF   San Francisco
SFJ   San Francisco Jazz
South.   Southland
Spec.   Specialty
st.   started
stud.   studied, studying
symph.   symphony
tpt.   trumpet
trom.   trombone
UA   United Artists
U., Univ.   University
Vang.   Vanguard
VSP   Verve Special Project
vln.   violin
WB, War. Bros.   Warner Brothers
w.   with
West.   Westminster
Wor. Pac.   World Pacific
yr., yrs.   year, years

* For detailed biographical information prior to 1960 on the artists whose names are followed by an asterisk, see *The New Encyclopedia of Jazz*, Horizon Press, 1960.

ABDUL-MALIK, AHMED,* *bass, oud;* b. Brooklyn, N.Y., 1/30/27. This scholarly musician, of Sudanese descent, has been increasingly active in recent years as an organizer and performer in programs at public schools and colleges, where he has introduced singers and combos in presentations of American, Middle and Far Eastern, Caribbean, African and Haitian music. He has been music adviser for the Fulton Art Fair in Brooklyn, N.Y. Abdul-Malik, who also plays tuba, violin, cello, piano and kanoon, was studying at New York College of Music in 1965, planning to earn a doctorate in music. Toured South America 1960, visited Africa, 1961. LPs: RCA, River., Pres., Status.

Addr: 749 Lafayette Ave., Brooklyn, N.Y.

ABNEY, JOHN DONALD (DON),* *piano;* b. Baltimore, Md., 3/10/23. Best known as an accompanist for several leading singers, Abney became a staff musician at NBC in NYC 1960, also did free-lance TV and radio work at CBS. For several months in 1961 he rejoined Ella Fitzgerald, whom he had accompanied in the mid-1950s. Settling in Los Angeles in '62, he worked mainly with Stanley Wilson and Benny Carter in TV orchs. at MCA Studios. Pianist with L.A. Neophonic Orch. 1966.

LP: *Nobody But Lou Rawls* with Benny Carter (Cap.).

Addr: 7024 Loyal Trail, Hollywood 28, Calif.

ACHILLES, ROBERT WILLIAM (BOB), *clarinet, saxophones;* b. Evansville, Ind., 9/30/37. Stud. pno. in Ind. 1944-7; clar. in Cheyenne, '47, later took up tenor sax at high school in Denver. Grad. from U. of Ill. '60 with BS in music ed. Moved to LA, gave lessons, stud. for three years with Lyle "Spud" Murphy. Worked mainly w. commercial groups, lounge acts, etc. until Oct. '63, when he joined Harry James band on bar. sax and clar. Has been feat. as a most effective clarinetist, one of the few to use this instrument extensively in a big jazz band of the '60s. Achilles is an accredited music and history teacher and has done substitute teaching between the band's engagements.

Fav. own solo: *Green Onions* w. James (Dot); also feat. w. James on *Harlem Nocturne* (MGM). Favs: Goodman, Shaw; Carney.

Addr: 3208 Glenhurst Dr., Las Vegas, Nevada.

ADAMS, PARK (PEPPER),* *baritone sax;* b. Highland Park, Ill., 10/8/30. When he was 12, Adams met Harry Carney; three years later he bought his first baritone saxophone and attempted to achieve a sound comparable with Carney's. Except for Army service in 1951-3 he was prominent in many local Detroit groups for about 10 years, playing w. Tommy Flanagan, Lucky Thompson and Kenny Burrell. After moving to New York in 1956 he was heard with Maynard Ferguson, Benny Goodman and frequently with Donald Byrd, an old friend from Detroit. He and Byrd continued to record together in the early 1960s, usually in a quintet under Byrd's name. Though he went on the road with the Lionel Hampton orchestra in 1962-3, Adams usually remained close to New York, gigging in various small combo contexts and w. Thad Jones-Mel Lewis band. Don DeMicheal of DB once described some of Adams' recorded solos as "flaming excursions into a sort of acid-dripping, jagged melodicism . . . he apparently is incapable of turning in a lacklustre performance." Some of his best work is to be heard on the two volumes of *Donald Byrd at the Half-Note Cafe,* also on *The Catwalk* and *Royal Flush,* on both of which he is also co-featured with Byrd (all Blue Note).

Addr: c/o Radio Registry, 850 7th Ave., New York 19, N.Y.

ADDERLEY, JULIAN EDWIN (CANNONBALL),* *alto sax;* b. Tampa, Fla., 9/15/28. By the mid-1960s Cannonball Adderley's quintet was firmly established as one of the most popular small combos in jazz, and as a group with a firm allegiance to the traditions of the bop era combined with a keen ear for newer developments. Adderley's pianists have included Bobby Timmons, Barry Harris and Victor Feldman; from April 1961 his pianist was Joe Zawinul. In 1961 the Adderley quintet became a sextet with the addition of Yusef Lateef. Charles Lloyd replaced Lateef in 1963, remaining until July 1965, when the group returned to quintet size.

Of his own style, Adderley has said, "I'm aware that jazz is changing, and I have listened to and absorbed many influences. I feel that Ornette Coleman was a most important force. However, what I play today is a logical development of my own style." Adderley was married June 1962 to actress Olga James. His combo played a tremendously successful tour of Japan in 1963, toured the European continent during the same year, and visited England in 1964.

Adderley was active intermittently as a producer of albums by other artists, including a Bud Powell LP cut in Paris and released on Columbia, and a Wes Montgomery set on Riverside. His own group recorded for Riverside and from 1964 for Capitol. Also LPs w. Nancy Wilson (Cap.), Ray Brown (Verve, VSP), *JATP in Europe* (Verve).

Addr: 112-19 34th Ave., Corona, L.I., N.Y.

ADDERLEY, NATHANIEL (NAT),* cornet; b. Tampa, Fla., 11/25/31. After leaving Woody Herman in 1959 Adderley rejoined the combo of his brother (see above). He also recorded with various groups of his own on Riverside and Atlantic. He enjoyed a growing reputation as a composer; several of his works were recorded (with lyrics) by leading jazz and popular singers. Among the best known are *Work Song, Sermonette, Jive Samba* and *Old Country*.

His style remained for the most part unchanged, though he was slightly influenced by the avant garde. He has expressed an admiration for the work of Freddie Hubbard.

Addr: 50 Beveridge St., Teaneck, N.J.

ADLER, HENRY, drums, teacher; b. New York, 6/28/15. First job with Wingy Manone at Knickerbocker Hotel NYC. Later was sideman with Joe Marsala, Larry Clinton, Red Norvo, Charlie Barnet, Vic Schoen, Georgie Auld, Jose Morand. Played at first Randall's Island Jazz Concert sponsored by Martin Block in 1938. Favs: B. Rich, L. Bellson, S. Payne.

Adler is chiefly important to jazz as an outstanding teacher. He has coached such musicians as Buddy Rich, Louis Bellson, Sonny Payne, Jack Sperling, Tiny Kahn, Don Lamond, Sonny Igoe and many others. Now a music publisher, he is the co-author with Buddy Rich of a drum method; with Humberto Morales of a book on Latin-American instruments; and with Don Lamond of *Design for The Drum Set.*

Addr: 136 W. 46th St., New York, N.Y. 10036.

AKIYOSHI, TOSHIKO,* piano, composer; b. Dairen, Manchuria, 12/12/29. After living for five years in the U.S., Miss Akiyoshi returned to Japan in 1961 and lived there with her husband, Charles Mariano. Returning to the U.S., she worked with Charles Mingus in 1962. From 1963-5 she again spent most of her time in Japan, but visited Cont. Europe in April-May 1964. Composed music for Tokyo International The-

atre '63; music for Swedish movie *The Platform* '64. Demonstrated unique two-hand 5/4 beat piano solo style in appearance at Newport Festival 1964. Toured Japan with J. J. Johnson sextet in World Jazz Festival, summer '64. Piano teacher on faculty of Summer Jazz Clinic August '65 in Reno, Nev., and Salt Lake City, Utah. Sidelines: writing monthly articles for *Japan Swing Journal;* dog raising.

Miss Akiyoshi, originally a Bud Powell-derived modern pianist, developed immeasurably during the early 1960s as instrumentalist, arranger and teacher. She showed a deep and sensitive understanding of new harmonic and modal approaches in jazz, and seemed to show the influence of Bill Evans in her piano style.

LPs: *Toshiko-Mariano Quartet* (Candid); album with big band in Tokyo (VJ); *Toshiko's Lullaby* (adaptations of children's songs from various countries) for Jap. Col.

Addr: 510 Grand Ave., Palisades Pk., N.J.

ALBAM, EMMANUEL (MANNY),* composer; b. Samana, Dominican Republic, 6/24/22. Active New York arranger since early 1940s. Still active in many phases of music, Albam teaches at Eastman School of Music, wrote music for TV and motion picture, composed jazz ballet. Visited England, recording with Tubby Hayes, Ronnie Ross. Own LPs: Victor, Impulse, Decca. Others with C. Fuller (Impulse) and J. Morello (RCA).

Addr: 349 South Boulevard, Nyack, N.Y.

ALBANY, JOSEPH (JOE),* piano; b. Atlantic City, N.J., 1/24/24. One of the first pianists associated with the bop movement of the '40s, Albany was considered an important influence in Los Angeles. He moved to San Francisco in 1959, wrote some songs which were recorded by Anita O'Day. Returning to Los Angeles, he gigged for a while; early in 1963 moved to New York, where he worked briefly with Charles Mingus and with various other groups including that of saxophonist Jay Cameron. Ret. again to Calif. '64. He is still represented on records by only one LP, taped in 1957 and released on Riverside.

ALEXANDER, ROLAND E., tenor sax, soprano sax, piano; b. Boston, Mass., 9/25/35. From a musical family, Alexander received a Bachelor of Music Degree from Boston Conservatory and went to New York in 1958. Has worked with J. Coltrane, M. Gee, Philly Joe Jones, M. Waldron, R. Haynes, M. Roach, Blue Mitchell and in 1965 with S. Rollins. Lists Johnny Griffin, Charlie Parker, Coltrane, Rollins, Ornette Coleman, Joe Henderson as influences. LPs w. Coltrane (Trans.), C. Persip (Beth.), Mitchell (UA). Own LP: *Pleasure Bent* (Pres.).

Addr: 220 Montgomery St., Brooklyn, N.Y.

ALEXANDRIA, LOREZ (Dolorez Alexandria Nelson), singer; b. Chicago, Ill., 8/14/29. Her mother, sister, aunts, uncles and cousins all sing and at one time were members of a versatile a capella choral group under her direction. Studied dramatics, later private singing lessons. Sang locally w. Jimmy Hill, King Fleming bands; while w. Fleming, comp. *My Very First Love.* Solo club work around Chicago, Midwest, East; began rec. for King, 1957. Seven months w. Ramsey Lewis at Cloister, Chi., 1958.

Moved to Los Angeles Feb. '61 and has since worked Calif. clubs, Steve Allen TV, etc. Married agent Dave Nelson. Four LPs on King, four on Argo and two more recently on Impulse, which she considers her best.

After a transition from gospel and spiritual music to a Sarah Vaughan-influenced modern style, Miss Alexandria developed into an exceptional performer with "the happy combination of a distinctive voice, great feeling, and the vocal equipment to handle a wide variety of material" (John A. Tynan, *Down Beat*). Favs: C. McRae, D. Washington.

Addr: 1675 S. Arlington, Los Angeles 18, Calif.

ALI, HASAAN IBN: see HASAAN

ALI, RASHIED, *drums;* b. Philadelphia, Pa., 7/1/35. Stud. at Granoff School and privately. Worked w. saxophonist Len Bailey and various local groups incl. rock 'n' roll bands. Forced to give up playing professionally, he drove a cab for almost two years, then resumed playing, with Arnold Joyner and others. After moving to New York in 1963 he began to acquire a reputation among the avant garde. He worked w. Bill Dixon, pl. concerts at Judson Hall and elsewhere; also w. Paul Bley, Archie Shepp, Marion Brown, Sun Ra and occasionally rock 'n' roll gigs. Joined the John Coltrane combo Nov. 1965, working at first as part of a two-drum instrumentation, the other drummer being Elvin Jones. A driving, impressive drummer in the freedom style associated with Elvin Jones, inspired by Max Roach, Philly Joe Jones and many others. LPs w. A. Shepp, (Impulse), Marion Brown (ESP).

Addr: 67 E. 2nd St., New York 3, N.Y.

ALLAN, JAN BERTIL, *trumpet, piano;* b. Falun, Sweden, 11/7/34. Studied piano at six, trumpet at 17. Played trumpet and piano in concert group with Lars Gullin, Georg Riedel, 1954. From 1955-60 pl. w. various bands at Nalen in Stockholm including Carl-Henrik Norin from '55-8. Co-leader with Rolf Billberg of a Tristano-inspired group '60-61. Since '63, leader of own combo touring Sweden. Has also been physicist, studying at U. of Stockholm. Favs: F. Navarro, C. Brown, M. Davis.

LPs on Swedish labels with Georg Riedel, Lars Gullin, Harry Arnold, Nils Lindberg, Rune Gustafson, and under his own name.

Addr: Orrvägen 57, Näsby Park, Sweden.

ALLEN, BYRON, *alto saxophone, composer;* b. Omaha, Nebr., 1940. Began playing in 1948. Influenced at first by Bartok and Ravel, he later heard Thelonious Monk

and used his knowledge of the classical composers, applying it to a new musical concept. First heard of in New York jazz circles when he recorded an album with a trio, Allen played an avant garde style described by Robert Ostermann as "total improvisation." Allen says, "I project what I'm experiencing at the moment . . . I'm trying to lay down something solid for the youngsters. I know there's lots of ugliness in the world, but I'm not giving that to anybody." Allen denies that he is playing jazz: "My mother didn't bring a jazzman into the world; she brought a human being. That's what I'm playing—human music." Own LP: ESP.

ALLEN, MARSHALL, *alto sax, clarinet, flute, oboe;* b. Louisville, Ky., 5/25/24. Mother was a singer. Started on clarinet at 10. Pl. w. Army band. Pl. w. Art Simmons in Paris '49-50, during which time also studied at Cons. of Music there. From '50s has been part of Sun Ra's Solar Arkestra in Chicago and NYC; also pl. w. Olatunji. App. in movies: *Individual* w. music by Bill Dixon; *Cry of Jazz.* Favs.: Hodges, Byas, Hawkins, but plays in more avant garde style. LPs w. Sun Ra (Saturn, ESP), Paul Bley (ESP).

Addr: 62 East 7th St., New York, N.Y.

ALLEN, HENRY JR. (RED),* *trumpet, singer;* b. Algiers, La., 1/7/08. Believed by some to be the trumpet link between Louis Armstrong and the swing generation, Allen during the 1960s enjoyed a growing reputation among critics and musicians. Nevertheless, he obtained little work commensurate with his talents. The Manchester Sports Guild brought him to England for a tour in 1964. He was seen on the NBC-TV special *Chicago And All That Jazz.* LPs: *Feelin' Good* (Columbia); *Red Allen Plays King Oliver* (Verve); *Mr. Allen* (Prestige), the latter displaying him effectively with rhythm section accompaniment.

Addr: 1351 Prospect Ave., New York, N.Y.

ALLEN, STEPHEN VALENTINE PATRICK WILLIAM (STEVE),* *songwriter, piano, vibes, leader;* b. New York City, 12/26/21. From the summer of 1962 until the fall of '64 the comedian-author-musician had his own TV series using in his staff band such jazz-oriented musicians as Donn Trenner, Frank Rosolino, Herb Ellis, Conte Candoli and Bob Enevoldsen. In 1963 Allen wrote the music and lyrics for a Broadway show, *Sophie.* Though the show was short-lived, his score was widely praised. He wrote lyrics for Ray Brown's jazz instrumental *Gravy Waltz.* The tune soon became a jazz standard and won a Grammy award as the best jazz song of 1964. An earlier song, *This Could Be The Start of Something,* also became a pop and jazz standard.

Though intensely busy in numerous other fields, Allen never lost contact with jazz. He even worked an engagement as a nominal sideman in a combo led by Terry Gibbs at Shelly's Manne Hole in Hollywood. He also feat. Gibbs as part of his own night club act, playing vibes duets with him.

Of Allen's many LPs, those closest to jazz were

Allen Plays the Piano Greats (imitations of other soloists) and *Bossa Nova Jazz*, both on Dot.

Addr: 15720 Ventura Blvd., Encino, Calif.

ALLISON, MOSE JOHN JR.,* *piano, singer, composer;* b. Tippo, Miss., 11/11/27. First heard in New York in 1951, again in the late '50s, Allison worked as a sideman with Stan Getz, Gerry Mulligan, and the Al Cohn-Zoot Sims Quintet. In the 1960s he was heard mostly as leader of his own trio, frequently playing night clubs in New York and Calif. Influenced by such singers as Muddy Waters, Sonny Boy Williamson and Percy Mayfield, he drew his vocal and instrumental ideas from a wide variety of sources, but as Nat Hentoff observed, "Allison has fused country blues and the modern piano tradition from Nat Cole to Thelonious Monk into a wry and unmistakably personal style." Own LPs: Pres., Col, Atl.

Addr: 34 Dogwood Dr., Smithtown, N.Y.

ALMEIDA, LAURINDO,* *guitar, composer;* b. Sao Paolo, Brazil, 9/2/17. In 1962 the rapid spread of popularity enjoyed by the bossa nova movement brought unprecedented prominence to the Brazilian-born Almeida. Though he was not (and never claimed to be) a founder of the movement, he was in a sense a precursor of the concept of combining native Brazilian music and American jazz. A series of World Pacific recordings he had made in 1953-4 in collaboration with Bud Shank was reissued and Almeida embarked on a number of new album projects featuring a popularized form of bossa nova. Though they enjoyed great commercial success, Almeida's most musically rewarding amalgamation with the jazz world during this period was achieved when he teamed up with the Modern Jazz Quartet, first at the MJF in 1963 and then on an extended European tour with the Quartet from Feb. to June 1964.

Almeida was also active as arranger and conductor for other artists, writing the LP *Softly, The Brazilian Sound* for Joanie Sommers (Warner Bros.). His compositions included both classical and popular works: in the former category was the award-winning *Discantus for Three Guitars*, while his popular items include *Choro for People in Love, Sahra's Samba* and *Twilight in Rio*.

The accidental success of the bossa nova movement had the side effect of drawing attention to Almeida's exceptional gifts as a guitarist in the fields of classical music, Brazilian popular music and as an all-around virtuoso.

LPs: Capitol; also *Brazilliance* Vols. 1, 2, 3 (World-Pac.)

Addr: 4104 Witzel Dr., Sherman Oaks, Calif.

ALPERT, HERB, *trumpet, leader;* b. Los Angeles, Calif., 3/31/35. Studied classical music with the first trumpet of the San Francisco Symphony. Later developed as a jazz musician but was known principally for his work in various studio groups in Hollywood. At one time, under the name of Dore Alpert, he was signed with RCA. In 1962, in partnership with Jerry Moss, Alpert began recording with a small instrumentation inspired by the Mariachi style of Mexican music. His first release, *The Lonely Bull*, sold over a million copies. During the next few years Alpert's group, known as The Tijuana Brass but actually composed of Hollywood studio musicians, enjoyed a phenomenal commercial success. The idea was widely imitated, even by jazzmen (an album entitled *Tijuana Jazz* was recorded by Clark Terry and Gary McFarland). The actual jazz content of the group's work, however, is virtually nil.

Favs: M. Davis, D. Gillespie, Clifford Brown. LPs: A&M.

Addr: c/o Braverman-Mirisch, Inc., 9255 Sunset Blvd., Los Angeles, Calif.

ALPERT, HERMAN (TRIGGER),* *bass, arranger;* b. Indianapolis, Ind., 9/3/16. Best known for work with Glenn Miller in '40s. Studio work with Garry Moore. Left CBS after 15 years in '65. Most active in TV and radio commercial jingles. Appearances with Eydie Gorme, Caterina Valente.

Addr: Cedar Gate Rd., Darien, Conn.

AMBROSETTI, FRANCO, *trumpet;* b. Lugano, Switzerland, 12/10/41. Son of saxophonist Flavio Ambrosetti. Studied piano 1952; self-taught on trumpet from 1959. Concert, festival, TV and radio appearances with father's group; often at Africana Club, Zurich, with own group. LPs w. Giorgio Azzolini. Favs: M. Davis, Gillespie, Hubbard, C. Brown.

Addr: Freigut Str., Zurich, Switz.

AMMONS, EUGENE (GENE or JUG),* *tenor sax;* b. Chicago, Ill., 4/14/25. Son of boogie-woogie piano pioneer Albert Ammons, he played in the Billy Eckstine and Woody Herman bands in the '40s. Popular during the 1950s, first in a two-tenor combo with Sonny Stitt, later on his own. In 1960-61 Ammons continued to play in night clubs, mostly in Chicago. Late in '61 he played at McKie's Lounge and was joined toward the end of a long run there by Stitt and James Moody. Don DeMicheal observed: "Ammons seems especially vigorous when he's teamed with Stitt. The musical exchanges between the two most often took the form of a good-natured blowtorch duel."

Ammons' career later was brought to a halt as a result of narcotics problems. In 1964-6 he was serving a long jail sentence. LPs: *Jug, Gene Ammons Bossa Nova, Velvet Soul, Sock, Angel Eyes* (all Pres.); *Dig Him!* with Sonny Stitt (Argo); *Boss Tenors* with Stitt (Verve).

AMRAM, DAVID WERNER III,* *composer, French horn;* b. Philadelphia, Pa., 11/17/30. Amram's career, largely devoted to jazz in the mid-1950s, by 1960 had taken a new direction and had established him as a major figure in the writing of dramatic and concert music. Writing of his music for the film *The Young Savages*, Jack Diether wrote: "Amram is very close to a perfect modern musician of the theater." Paul Hume of the Washington *Post* praised Amram's *Dirge*

And Variations as "frankly tonal, conceived with great skill for the instruments in mind, and holding a large degree of attractiveness of various kinds."

Credits: Mus. Dir., Lincoln Center Repertory Theater 1963-5, incl. jazz-oriented score for Arthur Miller play *After The Fall,* played by Amram-Barrow Quartet. This combo played one night a week at the Five Spot, NYC, 1963-5. Amram's opera, *The Final Ingredient,* was premiered April 1965 on ABC-TV.

Film writing-conducting credits: *The Young Savages, Splendor In The Grass,* 1960; *The Manchurian Candidate, 7 Days in May,* 1963. LPs: Amram-Barrow Quartet (Dec.); *Young Savages* score (Col.).

Addr: 461 Sixth Ave., New York, N.Y.

AMY, CURTIS EDWARD, *tenor sax;* also *soprano, alto saxes, clarinet, flute;* b. Houston, Tex., 10/11/29. Mother pl. piano. Clarinet in fourth grade; entered music prof. through high school band director. In service, '46-47; Kentucky State College '48-52, graduated with B.S. in music ed. Directed big band during last two years of college. Led own combo in midwest clubs for a few months, then spent two years ('52-4) as high school band director in Jackson, Tenn. Settled in LA 1955. Freelanced with various groups, rec. w. Dizzy Gillespie, Perri Lee; began recording as leader for Pac. Jazz 1960. Frequent gigs with own combos around LA and SF in 1960s, also concert and club dates with Gerald Wilson band.

Originally inspired by Gene Ammons and Sonny Stitt, Amy in the 1960s developed into an impassioned, technically adroit musician whose soprano work showed the strong influence of John Coltrane. He is an able composer of small combo lines such as *Native Land, Groovin' Blue, One More Hamhock Please.*

LPs on Pac. Jazz w. own groups and with Paul Bryant, Frank Butler, Gerald Wilson; own LP on Palomar 1965. Also feat. w. Onzy Matthews (Cap.); Lou Rawls (Cap.); Roy Ayers (UA).

Addr: 2111 Spaulding Ave., LA, Cal. 90016.

ANDERSON, WILLIAM ALONZO (CAT),* *trumpet, composer;* b. Greenville, S.C., 9/12/16. Anderson acquired an international reputation as the high note trumpet specialist with the Duke Ellington orchestra, in which he played from 1944-7 and again from '50-59. During the '60s he rejoined Ellington and took part in the band's tours in the U.S. and overseas. In addition to playing on numerous LPs with the Ellington orchestra, he was heard in several sessions featuring splinter groups from the band, among them *Inspired Abandon* with Lawrence Brown and *Everybody Loves Johnny Hodges* (both Impulse).

ANDERSON, ERNESTINE IRENE,* *singer;* b. Houston, Tex., 11/11/28. Vocalist with Lionel Hampton's band 1952-3. Popular in Sweden and the U.S. after an album she recorded in Stockholm, *Hot Cargo,* achieved commercial success in both countries. During the 1960s Miss Anderson, though still a singer of exceptional taste and gifted with a strong jazz feeling, was less successful in maintaining her career at a satisfactory level in the U.S. In 1965, after playing night club engagements in England, she decided to take up residence there. LPs: Several on Merc. and more recently on Sue.

ANDRUS, CHARLES E. JR. (CHUCK),* *bass;* b. Holyoke, Mass., 11/17/28. Well known for his freelance work in New York, Andrus joined the Woody Herman Orchestra in 1961 and remained for four years. He then resumed freelance work in New York. Toured Europe with Herman in '64. Feat. solo. w. Herman: *Satin Doll* (Philips). LPs w. Herman (Philips, Col.).

Addr: 134-39 Blossom Ave., Flushing N.Y. 11355.

ARCHEY, JAMES H. (JIMMY),* *trombone;* b. Norfolk, Va., 10/12/02. Has played with name bands since 1926. Became regular trombonist for Earl Hines combo, '55, and left Hines 12/62. LPs w. Hines (River.).

Addr: 785 Bayview Ave., Amityville, N.Y.

ARMSTRONG, LILIAN HARDIN (LIL),* *piano, composer;* b. Memphis, Tenn., 1903. Played with King Oliver, 1920; married to Louis Armstrong '24-32. Later worked with Red Allen, Zutty Singleton, toured Europe, played club outside Chicago from late 1950s. She has continued to be active in nightclub and recording work, mainly in Chicago, also visited Canada several times. Appeared on NBC-TV show *Chicago and All That Jazz* '61. LPs: *Chicago, The Living Legends* (River.); *Chicago and All That Jazz* (Verve); *Satchmo and Me,* documentary account of her background (River.).

Addr: 421 E. 44th St., Chicago, Ill.

ARMSTRONG, DANIEL LOUIS (SATCHMO or POPS),* *trumpet, singer, leader;* b. New Orleans, 7/4/00. Learned cornet in Waifs' Home while in mid-teens; later befriended by King Oliver, whose band he joined in '22 in Chicago. With Fletcher Henderson, '24-5; began recording as leader of own combos Nov. '25. Came to prominence in late '20s in Chicago and Harlem cabarets; fronted big band regularly from '29 and became an international star in early '30s, visiting England in '32 and touring Continent extensively in '33-4.

Armstrong appeared with Bing Crosby in *Pennies from Heaven,* his first film role as musician and actor, in 1936. In the late '30s he broadened his audience through recording of pop-style songs such as *Ol' Man Mose* and *Brother Bill.* Throughout the 1930s and most of the '40s he appeared always as nominal leader of a big band, usually under the musical direction of Luis Russell (later Joe Garland). The band, particularly the sound of its reed section, was patterned along the lines of Guy Lombardo's orchestra, Armstrong's favorite then and now. Two rare occasions when he was accorded the freedom of a small band context in those days were the *Esquire* concert at the Met. Opera House in Jan. '44, with a group of fellow-poll winners, and a Carnegie Hall concert, in association with the author, in Feb. '47, when in addition to his big band he was heard with the Edmond Hall Sextet.

Later in '47, after making a film called *New Orleans,* Armstrong abandoned big bands forever and was heard as leader of an informal sextet with clarinet, trombone, piano, bass and drums. He has fronted a group of this type ever since.

After World War II the international demand for Armstrong was incessant. He played a jazz festival at Nice in '48, toured Europe in '49 and '52, and made his first visit to Japan in '54. He spent six months in Europe in 1959, during which time he took part in four motion pictures, one in Denmark and three in West Germany. After the tour he became seriously ill in Spoleto, Italy, but recovered rapidly and was soon at work again.

During the 1960s Armstrong became more than ever a symbol of the basic beauty, simplicity and international appeal of traditional American jazz. In 1960 he undertook two tours of Africa. During the first, sponsored by a soft drink company, he visited Nigeria and Ghana; later he visited other parts of Africa under the auspices of the U.S. State Department.

Other foreign tours: 1961—Europe, Mexico and an extensive 19-country tour of Africa. 1962—Europe. 1963—Australia, New Zealand, Hong Kong, Korea, Japan, Hawaii. 1964—Australia, New Zealand, Singapore, India, Japan, Formosa, Okinawa. 1965—Czechoslovakia, East and West Germany, Romania, Yugoslavia, Hungary, England, France, Holland, Sweden, Denmark. During this tour he played before an audience of 93,000 in the Budapest Football Stadium.

After several years of comparative quiescence as a recording artist, Armstrong came to the forefront in 1964 with the release of *Hello Dolly,* a song by Jerry Herman from the Broadway show of the same name. The record, featuring Armstrong's regular sextet augmented by a banjo, became a phenomenal best seller both as a single and in an album (Kapp 3364). Armstrong found himself in the unprecedented position of outselling rock 'n' roll singers one third his age who normally dominated the best-seller charts.

The success of the song *Hello Dolly,* according to its composer, was due almost entirely to Armstrong's singing of this simple melody, which seemed perfectly tailored to his gruff, warm, globally imitated style. During the next two years there was an increasing tendency to concentrate more and more on his voice and less on his horn, though at important concerts and festivals he revealed the same brilliance and purity of tone, and the same gently syncopated manner of phrasing, that had marked his work since the first classic Hot Five records of the late 1920s. In 1966 he rec. another Herman song, *Mame.*

One of Armstrong's best-remembered appearances of the 1960s was his participation in *The Real Ambassadors* at the Monterey Jazz Festival, singing songs by Dave and Iola Brubeck (see Brubeck, Dave). He also appeared at Newport, Cincinnati and at festivals overseas. His TV appearances included the Ed Sullivan show (incl. one program taped in Berlin), *Hollywood Palace, I've Got A Secret,* BBC shows etc. His motion pictures in the '60s incl. *Paris Blues,* 1960 (for which he was joined by Duke Ellington, who wrote and recorded the score); *Where the Boys Meet the Girls,* 1965; *A Man Called Adam,* 1966.

Record catalogues list about 50 Armstrong albums currently available. Those released in the '60s (some are reissues) include *Satchmo—Autobiography* (Decca 78963, 74330, 74331); *Best of Louis Armstrong* (Audio-Fid. 6432); *Golden Favorites* (Dec. 74137); *Great Reunion,* with Duke Ellington (Roul. 52103, 52074); *Hello Dolly!* (Kapp 3364); *Hello Louis* (Metro 510); *I Love Jazz* (Dec. 74227); *Louis in the '30s and '40s* (RCA 2971); *I've Got the World on a String* (Verve 64035); *King Louis* (Dec. 74245); *Louis Under the Stars* (Verve 64012); *Louis Meets Oscar Peterson* (Verve 68322); *Louis Plays King Oliver* (Audio-Fid. 5930); *Rare Batch of Satch* (RCA 2322); *Louis with Dukes of Dixieland* (Audio-Fid. 5924).

Addr: c/o Associated Booking Corp., 445 Park Avenue, New York, N.Y. 10022.

ARNOLD, HORACEE (pron. Hor-as) E., *drums;* b. Louisville, Ky., 9/25/37. Older brother started him listening to jazz. Always wanted to play drums but did not until he was stationed in Calif. w. the Coast Guard and attending Los Angeles City College in 1957. Studied art and piano but was encouraged on drums by Maurice Miller, drummer w. Harold Land who admired his painting. Ret. to Louisville '58 and practiced daily. Pl. there w. Roland Kirk, and in Indianapolis w. Kirk, Dave Baker '59. Again in Louisville met Max Roach who was startled by Arnold's facial resemblance to him. Recommended to Lenox, Mass. School of Jazz by Roach but scholarship didn't come through. Came to NYC and rehearsed w. Hasaan and Henry Grimes. Pl. in trio w. Cecil McBee and Kirk Lightsey in Louisville. Back to NYC '60, pl. w. Mingus, Kirk; then four months w. dancer Carmen de Lavallade in Asia. Worked w. Barry Harris '62; Bud Powell '64; Hugh Masekela and Miriam Makeba '65; Tal Farlow and Don Friedman '66. Stud. comp. w. Heine Stadler '66. Orig. inf.: Roach; favs.: Haynes, Tony Williams, Clifford Jarvis. LPs w. Bobby Brown (Col.), Masekela (Merc.), Odetta (Five Star Prod.).

Addr: 735 E. 182nd St., Bronx 57, N.Y.

ARVANITAS, GEORGES, *piano, organ;* b. Marseille, France, 6/13/31. Played in Marseille, then to Paris in '54. Free-lanced in Paris clubs w. Bill Coleman, Don Byas, Sonny Stitt, Donald Byrd, others, and w. own combo at Club St. Germain '59-'62. Came to U.S. in '64 for jobs w. Ted Curson in NYC and touring w. Yusef Lateef. Returned to France '65; played in U.S. again '66. Also an active studio pianist in Paris, accompanying many singers and pop groups. In numerous European film soundtracks. Own LP: *Soul Jazz* (Fr. Col.) Others: w. Sonny Criss, Byas, Art Taylor, Doug Watkins, Toots Thielemans, Guy Lafitte, Louis Hayes. Available in U.S.: w. Curson (Atl.), Lateef (Impulse).

Addr: 638 West End Ave., New York 24, N.Y.

ASHBY, DOROTHY JEANNE,* *harp, piano, singer;* b. Detroit, Mich., 8/6/32. Daughter of Wiley Thompson, a jazz guitarist. Studied at Cass Tech. High. While continuing her studies at Wayne State U., she pl. piano for a choir, harp in the orchestra, and stud. vocal techniques. Sang folk songs on local radio and pl. many concerts in '50s. During the '60s she served as hostess of a jazz discussion show on WJR. Despite occasional excursions for concert and TV appearances, Miss Ashby has spent most of her time in Detroit and earned insufficient recognition for her remarkable virtuosity. She arrives closer to a true jazz feeling on the harp than any other performer, as was illustrated in a 1965 LP, *The Fantastic Harp of Dorothy Ashby* (Atl.). Kenny Dorham, reviewing it in DB, wrote: "Miss Ashby is taking care of business, which is quite a job with this traditionally clumsy instrument."

ASHBY, HAROLD KENNETH, *tenor sax;* b. Kansas City, Mo., 3/27/25. Pl. clarinet in school band. After two yrs. in Navy, took up saxophone and made prof. debut 1946 w. Tommy Douglas. After working w. many blues artists in Chicago in the early '50s he moved to New York, working there off and on w. Mercer Ellington and also subbing on several occasions in Duke Ellington's band, as well as taking part in numerous sessions w. Ellington sidemen. Worked briefly w. Basie '61; pl. in Ellington's *My People* orch. '63, led group at Minton's '64. Ashby is a warm-sounding mainstream soloist in a style reminiscent of Ben Webster.

Own LP: *Born to Swing* (EMI). *Colors in Rhythm* w. Mercer Ellington (Coral), *My People* (Contact), *Inspired Abandon* w. Lawrence Brown (Impulse), *The Soul of Ben Webster* (Verve).

Addr: 555 West 174th St., New York City, New York 10033.

ASHBY, IRVING C.,* *guitar;* b. Somerville, Mass., 12/29/20. Featured in '40s with Lionel Hampton; King Cole Trio; Oscar Peterson Trio '52. In 1963 he wrote and played background music for State Dept. documentary film at the USC School of Cinema. Completed modern guitar method for 1967 publication. In 1965 he completed 2½ years of landscape design study and has been free-lancing, designing landscaping for apartment buildings. He has also continued to play engagements around Los Angeles as a guitarist.

Addr: Rt. 1, Box 146, Perris, Calif.

ASMUSSEN, SVEND,* *violin;* b. Copenhagen, Denmark, 2/28/16. A professional musician from 1933, Asmussen has long been regarded, by those who have heard him in person, as one of the most gifted violinists in jazz. Unfortunately, his public performances

have been heavily larded with comedy, since he has been established throughout Scandinavia as a vaudeville star. In the early 1960s he appeared in night clubs with singer Alice Babs and guitarist Ulrik Neumann, the act being known as The Three Danes. In the summer of 1962 John Lewis, who had admired him for many years, went to Stockholm to record with him. The result was *European Encounter: John Lewis and Svend Asmussen* (Atl.). Asmussen can also be heard in a series of duets with Neumann on a Warner Bros. LP.

ASSUNTO, FRANK JOSEPH,* *trumpet, leader;* b. New Orleans, La., 1/29/32. Still leading the Dukes of Dixieland, Assunto for a time was based in Las Vegas but traveled extensively, playing clubs and concerts. In July of 1964 the Dukes took part in the First World JF on a tour of Japan. The group played the best part of 1965 in Chicago.

Many LPs w. Dukes of Dixieland, best of which incl. *Breaking It Up On Broadway*, 1960 (Col.); *Struttin' At The World's Fair*, 1964 (Col.); and *Live at Bourbon St.*, 1965 (Decca).

ASSUNTO, FRED J.,* *trombone;* b. New Orleans, 12/3/29; died Las Vegas, Nev., 4/21/66. Toured with Dukes of Dixieland (see Frank Assunto, above) but was sidelined by illness during much of 1965-6 and was replaced at various times by Dave Remington, Cutty Cutshall, Warren Smith, Jim Beebe and Bill Johnson. LPs: See Assunto, Frank.

ASSUNTO, JACOB (PAPA JAC),* *trombone, banjo;* b. Lake Charles, La., 11/1/05. Father of the Assunto brothers (see above), he continued to tour with them during the 1960s.

LPs: See Assunto, Frank.

ATKINS, CHESTER (CHET), *guitar;* b. Nashville, Tenn., 6/20/24. Self-taught. Started prof. as staff musician with KNOX, Nash. Tenn. Later achieved prominence as recording artist. As A&R man produced many hits by Al Hirt and other artists for RCA. Own LPs for RCA.

Toured South Africa 1963; Europe, 1964 and Japan, 1965. Has made guest appearances with Atlanta Pops, Nashville Symphony and Boston Pops.

Though he has won a *Playboy* Jazz Poll as no. one jazz guitarist, Atkins basically is not a jazz musician. His style is that of country music.

Favs: Johnny Smith, Django Reinhardt, Les Paul; also names Merle Travis and Jerry Reed as major influences.

AULD, GEORGIE (John Altwerger),* *tenor, alto, soprano saxes;* b. Toronto, Ontario, Canada, 5/19/19. Best known for his superlative solos on the Benny Goodman small combo records, 1940-41, Auld later led his own big band. During the 1950s he led various combos, lived in Calif. for some time, and returned to New York in 1958. In the 1960s he was rarely active in jazz, working various jobs mostly in Las Vegas. In 1966 he was briefly reunited with Goodman, playing in the latter's orchestra for a Las Vegas engagement. LPs: *Georgie Auld Quintet Plays the Winners; Here's To The Losers* (both Philips).

Addr: 445 Desert Inn Rd., Las Vegas, Nev.

AUTREY, HERMAN,* *trumpet;* b. Evergreen, Ala., 12/4/04. Best known as soloist with Fats Waller on most of his recordings between 1934 and '41. Later played with Stuff Smith, free-lanced in Calif., Canada and New York. Led quartet at Embers 1960; trio at Nevele '61; gigs w. Conrad Janis, Sol Yaged. In '65-6, member of traditionalist group organized by Red Richards known as the Saints and Sinners. LP with this group for Dobell (English label); w. Waller on many reissue LPs (RCA).

Addr: 760 Tinton Ave., Bronx 56, N.Y.

AYERS, ROY E. JR., *vibes;* b. Los Angeles, Cal., 9/10/40. Mother taught piano. Harmony at Jefferson High; further music studies at LA City Coll. Gigs around LA w. Gerald Wilson, Jack Wilson; Las Vegas Jazz Festival, '62; co-leader w. Hamp Hawes in quartet, '63; own quartet, 65-6.

Own LP, *West Coast Vibes,* prod. by L. Feather for United Artists. Also LPs w. G. Wilson, J. Wilson, L. Vinegar. Favs: Milt Jackson, Bobby Hutcherson, Cal Tjader, Vic Feldman. Comp. *Ricardo's Dilemma, Sound and Sense.*

Ayers is a vibraharpist with considerable technical finesse, a style clearly influenced by Jackson and an excellent rhythmic feeling.

Addr: 3927 West Adams Blvd., Los Angeles, Cal.

AYLER, ALBERT, *tenor sax, soprano sax, composer;* b. Cleveland, Ohio, 1936. Began playing at age of seven. First important gig was w. Cecil Taylor in NYC. Toured Europe with brother, trumpeter Don Ayler, and recorded in Denmark. Returned to NYC, recorded for ESP-Disk with Gary Peacock, Sunny Murray. Member Jazz Composers' Guild. Concert at NYC Town Hall May '65 w. Don Ayler, Murray, Lewis Worrell and Charles Tyler was recorded by ESP.

Ayler plays with a loud, sweeping tone. By turns he is romantic and sentimental, then screams and wails, then builds his solos to high emotional peaks similar to those used in the most recent work of Coltrane and Mingus. The tunes which he uses as starting points are often less related to jazz than to Scottish, Mexican or American folk music, especially with a martial air.

His first three recordings burst upon American music with a force comparable with that of Charlie Parker in the '40s, and provoked a mixture of admiration and hostility among both musicians and critics. Like Parker, he was accused of not knowing how to play his instrument, of childish lack of control, of not playing jazz, of destroying jazz and of trying to dupe his listeners. Reviewing *Spiritual Unity* for *Down Beat,* trumpeter Kenny Dorham stated that Ayler was "putting the listener on," playing "satirical comedy," playing without a mouthpiece, a baby, a "frustrated person," that "he doesn't know or care anything about

conventional music" and that "at this point it's not worth the paper it takes to review it."

Critic-composer Donald Heckman found the total effect of Ayler's sound very pleasing. In the *American Record Guide,* reviewing the LP *Bells,* he wrote, "Ayler's tenor saxophone is big, almost gargling in tone quality, with a heavily pulsating vibrato. The music has a frenetic, near-anarchic sound, but the fury is quenched by a curious second section that explores, in almost rudimentary fashion, the intervals of the major triad. The effect varies, reminding one variously of a Mexican mariachi band, of the title, and sometimes of a junior high school band rehearsal."

A number of experts, believing that Ayler represents an important breakthrough in the search for total human expression, have voiced the hope that he will continue in the direction he has found.

Own LPs: *My Name is Albert Ayler* (Fant.); *Spiritual Unity, Bells* (ESP).

AYLER, DONALD (DON), *trumpet, composer;* b. Cleveland, O., 10/5/42. Father plays tenor and violin; brother, Albert Ayler, is a modern saxophonist (see above). Studied at Miller Academy of Music in Cleveland from age 10 to 15; later at Cleveland Inst. of Music. Played occasional jobs with father. Worked independently in Europe during '63, especially in Sweden. Member of Albert Ayler Quintet since '64. Guest of John Coltrane at a Philharmonic Hall concert in NYC, April '66. Considered one of the most promising of the young avant garde trumpet players, he names Booker Little, Don Cherry, Miles Davis, John Coltrane, Eric Dolphy as influences and favs.

LPs with Albert Ayler (ESP, Impulse).

Addr: 29-78 Ripley Road, Cleveland, Ohio.

BABASIN, HARRY,* *bass, cello;* b. Dallas, Texas, 3/19/21. This underrated bassist and pioneer jazz cellist received an M.A. degree in composition at San Fernando Valley State College in 1961. Directed studio band there in 1960-61. Joined Phil Moody duo, 1963. LP w. Moody (Electrovox).

Addr: 12486 Wingo St., Pacoima, Calif.

BACCUS, EDDIE, *organ;* b. Lawndale, N.C., 1936. Stud. at School for Blind Children in Raleigh, N.C. Piano at 10. Family moved to Dayton; he continued his studies at School for the Blind in Columbus, Ohio where Art Tatum had been a student. Left school after his junior year to join Roland Kirk's group as pianist. Started organ lessons playing an extensive engagement with Kirk in Cleveland. Later formed own trio and made record debut 1962. Baccus is one of the more original organists, less given to melodramatics and funky clichés than most of his contemporaries. Own LP: *Feel Real* (Smash).

BACSIK, ELEK, *guitar;* b. Budapest, Hungary, 5/22/26. Cousin was Django Reinhardt. Studied classical and gypsy violin, then jazz guitar. Toured Switzerland, Spain, Portugal and Italy, then settled in Paris '59. Played regularly at Mars Club w. Art Taylor, Kenny Clarke, other U.S. musicians. Own LP: Phil. Other w. Dizzy Gillespie (Phil.).

BAILEY, ERNEST HAROLD (BENNY),* *trumpet;* b. Cleveland, Ohio, 8/13/25. Prof. since 1941. Starting in 1948, he made many trips to Europe w. D. Gillespie, L. Hampton, Q. Jones. Member of Swedish radio band '57-9; free-lanced in Sweden and around Continent during next few years, but was back in U.S. briefly in 1960 and rec. own LP for Candid. Feat. and lead trumpeter in Friedrich Gulda band as heard on *From Vienna With Jazz!* (Col.) Quincy Jones has observed: "Benny has phenomenal technique, great control, and his own sound and phrasing. He is a completely authoritative trumpet player who never resorts to clichés and is never at a loss for original ideas." Co-feat. on *Concerto for Benjamin and Jonathan* in *International Jazz Workshop* (Emarcy).

BAILEY, WILLIAM C. (BUSTER),* *clarinet;* b. Memphis, Tenn., 7/19/02. Member of Saints & Sinners Orch. 1961-5. LPs w. Jackie Gleason '62-3. TV: *Chicago and All That Jazz.* Newport Jazz Festival 1960-61 with Red Allen. Many freelance record dates w. Ronnie Gilbert, Odetta, Juanita Hall, Jimmy Rushing.

On July 4, 1965 the pioneer clarinetist, still playing in the fluent, academic yet swinging style that had identified him in the swing and pre-swing eras, joined the Louis Armstrong sextet. It was the first time he had worked with Armstrong since 1924-5, when they were members of Fletcher Henderson's band, both having left King Oliver's orchestra in Chicago to join Henderson.

Addr: 341 Washington Ave., Brooklyn, N.Y. 11205.

BAILEY, COLIN, *drums;* b. Swindon, England, 7/9/34. Drums at four. Piano and theory 1946-9. Prof. debut as accompanist to vaudeville pianist Winifred Atwell. Australia and U.S. with Australian Jazz Quartet, 1960-61. Settling in U.S., worked in SF w. Vince Guaraldi trio to Dec. '62. During next three years worked w. Vic Feldman, Geo. Shearing, Jim Hall, Clare Fischer combos. Japan w. Benny Goodman March '64; various other jobs w. Goodman quartet and band. Subbed for Tony Williams in Miles Davis quintet. Staff job w. Terry Gibbs combo on Regis Philbin TV series, winter 1964-5. Joined G. Shearing July '66.

Bailey has written two drum tuition books. His ambition is to play tympani and percussion in symphony orch. Influenced by Joe Morello, Philly Joe Jones and Shelly Manne, Bailey is held in high esteem by musicians who have worked with him.

LPs w. Guaraldi (Fant.), Fischer, Joe Pass (World-Pac.), Feldman (Ava, VJ), Goodman, (Cap.).

Addr: 8531 Lubao Ave., Canoga Park, Calif.

BAILEY, SAMUEL DAVID (DAVE),* *drums;* b. Portsmouth, Va., 2/22/26. Worked in '50s with Hodges, Mingus, and frequently from '59 with Gerry Mulligan. In recent years he has been free-lancing in New York, working principally with Mulligan, Billy Taylor and the Clark Terry-Bob Brookmeyer quintet. Participant in pioneer U.S. bossa nova record, a Curtis Fuller album entitled *South American Cooking* (Epic) recorded after his return from Brazil. He talked about and demonstrated the basics of bossa nova percussion long before it became nationally popular. A veteran AAF officer (1942-6), he now teaches flying at Westchester County Airport.

Bailey has made many tours overseas with Mulligan, Chris Connor and others. He is one of the most tasteful and adept of modern drummers.

LPs with Terry-Brookmeyer (Mainstream); B. Taylor (Cap.); Mulligan (Verve); Roger Kellaway (Pres.), etc.

Addr: 1158 E. 223rd St., Bronx, N.Y. 10466.

BAILEY, DONALD ORLANDO (DONALD DUCK),* *drums;* b. Phila., Pa., 3/26/34. After eight years on tour with organist Jimmy Smith, Bailey settled in Calif. and free-lanced at LA clubs w. Ray Crawford, Wm. Green, Bobby Bryant, Vic Feldman, H. Land et al. Visited Paris w. Smith, August 1962.

LPs: Many w. Smith (Blue Note, Verve); others w. Geo. Braith, Jack Wilson, Hamp Hawes.

Addr: 2476 Logan St., Pomona, Calif.

BAILEY, PEARL,* *singer;* b. Newport News, Va., 3/29/18. Featured in Broadway shows, movies and TV specials, Miss Bailey's reputation mainly is that of a leading show business personality. Nevertheless, there is a strong jazz element in much of her work. She has been married since Nov. 1952 to drummer Louis Bellson, who has frequently appeared and recorded with her.

In Oct. 1965 Miss Bailey taped a one-hour television special; with Ethel Waters as guest. LPs: *St. Louis Blues; Pearl Bailey + Louis Bellson = Happy Sounds; Pearl Bailey Sings Harold Arlen; Pearl Bailey Sings Jimmy Van Huesen; C'est la Vie,* etc. (all Roul.)

Addr: 8433 Melvin Ave., Northridge, Calif.

BAKER, CHESNEY H. (CHET),* *trumpet, fluegelhorn, singer;* b. Yale, Okla., 12/23/29. His best-known association was with Gerry Mulligan in the original Mulligan Quartet 1952-3. After working with small groups during the rest of the 1950s and visiting Scandinavia in 1957, he went to Italy in '59, but ran into the narcotics problems that had interfered with his career in the U.S., and was in jail in Italy during part of 1960 and '61. In 1962 he was arrested in Germany, but the charges were dropped and he was sent to Switzerland. Later he appeared in London. After spending some time in a sanatorium in Germany he arrived back in the U.S. 3/3/64 and during the next two years played night clubs, usually leading a quartet. At his best, he still showed some of the light, pure sound and lyrical quality that marked his best work in the early '50s. LPs: World Pacific, Prestige, Colpix, Limelight. Also feat. on *Michelle* with Bud Shank (World Pacific).

BAKER, DAVID NATHANIEL JR. (DAVE),* *cello; also trombone, bass trombone;* b. Indianapolis, Ind., 12/21/31. In 1961 the former Kenton and Maynard Ferguson trombonist toured Europe with the Quincy Jones Orch. He performed regularly with George Russell's experimental groups and received DB New Star Award for trombone in '62. In August '62 he switched to cello as the result of an illness. Does extensive private teaching; also composing and writing. Pub. book on Lydian chromatic concept; also article in DB '65. LPs: w. Russell (River., Dec.), w. John Lewis (Atl.).
Addr: 1237 Burdsal Pkwy., Indianapolis, Ind.

BAKER, HAROLD J. (SHORTY),* *trumpet;* b. St. Louis, Mo., 5/26/14. With Erskine Tate, Fate Marable, Don Redman in '30s; Teddy Wilson, Andy Kirk, Mary Lou Williams in 40s; also w. Duke Ellington in '30s, '40s and '50s for varying periods of time. Since leaving Ellington in Sept. '59 has free-lanced in NYC w. Own quartet and as sideman incl. Metropole. Inactive during part of '66 due to illness. LPs: one side of *Mainstream Jazz* w. own group (Cam.); *Shorty and Doc* w. Doc Cheatham (Pres.); w. Bud Freeman (Pres.).
Addr: Hotel Alvin, 223 W. 52nd St., New York 19, N.Y.

BALTAZAR, GABRIEL RUIZ JR. (GABE), *alto sax; also clarinet, flute, piano;* b. Hilo, Hawaii, 11/1/29. Father and brothers all musicians. Studied in high school in Honolulu; at Interlochen, Mich. Music Camp; at Baltimore Peabody Conservatory. W. Paul Togawa '57-'58, H. Rumsey '60. First alto sax in Stan Kenton band '60-'64. W. Onzy Mathews '63-'64, R. Peña '64, T. Gibbs '65, Gil Fuller at Monterey JF '65, Don Ellis '65. While w. Kenton appeared in Mexico and Britain, at Newport JF '63. A strong, hard-blowing altoist in the Charlie Parker tradition. Fav: Parker. Attends Cal. State College; plans to teach music, remain active in jazz. LPs: w. Kenton (Cap.), Togawa (Mode), Fuller (Pac. Jazz); Joe Castro (Clover).
Addr: 1684 Lucile Ave., Los Angeles 26, Cal.

BARBER, DONALD CHRISTOPHER (CHRIS), *trombone, leader;* b. London, England, 4/17/30. Made seven tours of U.S. 1959-63. The mass popularity of the band declined after that period, but it continues to make frequent European tours E. and W. of the Iron Curtain, and festival apps. in Eng. Barber is also active in auto racing as owner-driver.
Addr: c/o 18 Carlisle St., London, W.1., England.

BARBIERI, LEANDRO (GATO), *tenor sax;* b. Rosario, Argentina, 11/28/33. Pl. in Europe w. Jim Hall, Lalo Schifrin, Ted Curson. From '66 w. Don Cherry Quintet. LP with Cherry (Blue Note).
Addr: via F. Crispi 90, Rome, Italy.

BARBOUR, DAVID MICHAEL (DAVE),* *guitar, songwriter;* b. New York City, 5/28/12; d. Malibu, Calif.,

12/11/65. Best known for his professional partnership with Peggy Lee, to whom he was married 1943-52, Barbour was the co-composer with her of *Manana, It's A Good Day* and other hits. For the last 13 years of his life he was in almost total retirement. His only jazz LP during that period was *BBB & Co.,* with Benny Carter combo (Status). A few examples Barbour's excellent guitar work from the swing era can be heard on records with Teddy Wilson, Mildred Bailey and Red Norvo.

BARCELONA, DANIEL (DANNY),* *drums;* b. Honolulu, 7/23/29. A member of the Louis Armstrong band since 1958, Barcelona continued to tour with Armstrong in the 1960s and was heard on his albums, the most successful being *Hello Dolly!* (Kapp).
Addr: 115 S. Edgemont, Los Angeles 4, Calif.

BAREFIELD, EDWARD EMANUEL (EDDIE),* *clarinet, saxes, arranger;* b. Scandia, Iowa, 12/12/09. An intermittent associate of Cab Calloway since 1934, Barefield continued to serve off and on in 1957-60 as mus. dir. for Calloway, in Cotton Club revue that toured U.S. and South America. Cond. & arr. *Jazz Train* revue in Europe, 1960; free-lanced in NYC, '61-2; With Paul Lavalle at Freedomland and World's Fair, '63 and '65 respectively; also pit band work in B'way shows and jazz work w. Wilbur De Paris at Broken Drum, NYC, '64.
LPs: *Swing Goes Dixie* w. Roy Eldridge (Verve), own LP on alto (Cosmopolitan).
Addr: 861 Macy Place, Bronx 55, N.Y.

BARKER, DANIEL (DANNY),* *guitar, banjo;* b. New Orleans, La., 1/13/09. Known in N.Y. from 1930 for his work with James P. Johnson, Cab Calloway, Benny Carter and other leading bands, Barker free-lanced around N.Y. in the early '60s, playing several TV shows and festivals. Returning to New Orleans in 1965, he went to work as Assistant to the Curator of the N.O. Jazz Museum. Has written several articles on early musicians, pub. in *Evergreen Review* and *Jazz Review.* Lectured at Dillard, Tulane and other universities, discussing and demonstrating various traditional styles.
Addr: 1514 Sere St., New Orleans, La.

BARKSDALE, EVERETT,* *guitar;* b. Detroit, Mich., 4/28/10. The former Art Tatum guitarist has been a staff musician in recent years at ABC network in NYC, also playing and contracting many LPs for Dec., Merc., RCA, etc. TV, LPs with Lena Horne, Sammy Davis, Al Hirt, many others.
Addr: 19 Edgemont Pl., Teaneck, N.J. 07666.

BARNES, GEORGE,* *guitar;* b. Chicago Heights, Ill., 7/17/21. Swing guitarist from mid-'30s, active in radio, TV and recording. Formed duo w. guitarist Carl Kress in '63. Toured U.S., played White House Staff party '64, Japan '65, until Kress' death June '65. Teacher at Famous Guitarists School; wrote two books on guitar. Own LPs: (w. Kress) UA, Carney, MMO, Merc. Others: w. Louis Armstrong (Dec.), Bud Freeman (UA), Kai Winding (Carney), Sy Oliver, Gary McFarland, Bobby Hackett, Al Caiola, Mitch Miller.

Addr: c/o General Delivery, New York 1, N.Y.

BARNES, PAUL D. (POLO), *clarinet, soprano sax; also alto, tenor, baritone saxes;* b. New Orleans, 11/22/01. Stud. St. Paul Lutheran Coll. Took up alto sax 1919 and soon had his own first group, the original Diamond Jazz Band, later known as the Young Tuxedo Band. Joined Kid Rena in '22; Maple Leaf Orch. '23; Original Tuxedo Band '23. In 1926, while with Papa Celestin, he composed and recorded *My Josephine,* which earned great popularity and established his reputation.

Pl. w. Chick Webb '27; with King Oliver at the Savoy in NYC '27 and was with him again in '31 and '34-5. He toured and recorded with Jelly Roll Morton in 1928-9, had his own band in New Orleans from '32-3, and worked with Chester Zardis, '35; Kid Howard '37-9, and again in '41. U.S. Navy '42-5. Celestin's Tuxedo Band '46-51. To Calif., out of music '52-7. Back in New Orleans '59, where he joined Paul Barbarin's band the following year. From '61-4 he was in Calif. as member of Young Men From New Orleans on riverboat at Disneyland. In '64, back in NO, he played with many groups at Preservation Hall, Dixieland Jazz Hall, etc.

In addition to early sides with Morton (RCA) Barnes recorded with his own quartet in 1960 with the Icon label, also with Charlie Love's Ragtime Band and Kid Thomas' Eureka Brass Band. Barnes is one of the best surviving soloists in a tradition inspired by Sidney Bechet.

Addr: 2316 London Ave., New Orleans, La., 70119.

BARNET, CHARLES DALY (CHARLIE),* *saxophones, leader;* b. New York City, 10/26/13. Barnet, whose most successful band was the one he led between 1939 and '45, limited his activities to a few occasional gigs with a pickup group in the early 1960s. By 1965 he had gone into complete retirement. Some of his early work can be heard in *Dance Bands of the '30s and '40s* (RCA); later LPs are on Everest.

BARNUM, H. B., *singer, arranger, leader;* b. Houston, Texas, 7/15/36. Billed as the "Barnum Wonder Boy," he sang in churches where his father, a revivalist minister, was preaching. By the age of four, had won singing contest, played first movie role, and made piano debut, playing classics and jazz.

Barnum, who plays almost every commonly used instrument, writes songs and has had acting experience, was active in Hollywood in the 1960s, arranging for pop, jazz and r & b artists. Though his many talents include jazz work, he is not mainly affiliated with this field. LP: Capitol.

Addr: 6223 Selma Ave., Hollywood 28, Cal.

BARRETT, EMMA (SWEET EMMA THE BELL GAL), *piano, singer;* b. New Orleans ca. 1905. Self taught. W. Papa Celestin 1923; also pl. w. John Robichaux, Sidney Desvignes, Armand J. Piron. Long inactive, she began a comeback in '47. Since 1961 has been successful leader of her own band. Her trademark is a pair of bright red garters to which are attached brass bells which she jingles while keeping rhythm with her feet. Plays often in "The Quarter" in N.O.; concerts for NO Jazz Club. Disneyland 1965. Orrin Keepnews called Sweet Emma's group "far and away the best-organized jazz band now playing regularly in New Orleans." LP in Living Legends series on Riv.; other recs. on Southland, Jazzology, GHB, etc.

Addr: 3312 Short St., New Orleans, La. 70125.

BARRON, WILLIAM JR. (BILL), *tenor sax, composer;* b. Philadelphia, Pa., March 1927. Piano at 7 for two years. Stud. tenor sax at 13 in music dep't. at Mastbaum High where a classmate was Johnny Coles. Toured w. Carolina Cottonpickers. Pl. in Army special band unit w. Randy Weston, Ernie Henry. Discharged in '46, he stud. comp. and theory at Ornstein School of Music in Phila. Worked w. various groups in Philly '48-'58 incl. Red Garland, Jimmy Golden, Jimmy Heath. To NYC '58, pl. w. Cecil Taylor, w. Philly Joe Jones '61, then most often as co-leader w. Ted Curson through first half of '60s incl. European tours. App. w. Taylor at NJF '65. Early infl. was Dexter Gordon. Although Barron's work of the early '60s resembled John Coltrane's, Curson has said that he "was playing like this in Philadelphia a number of years ago when John Coltrane was still playing alto." Own LPs: Savoy; as co-leader w. Curson (Audio Fid.); w. Curson (Old Town, Atl.), Philly Joe Jones (Atl.).

Addr: c/o Ankar, Orvas Odds Vag 10, Stockholm K, Sweden.

BARRON, KENNETH (KENNY), *piano;* b. Philadelphia, Pa., 6/9/43. Stud. in Phila. w. sister of Ray Bryant. First job was in '57 w. Mel Melvin's band, of which his brother, saxophonist Bill Barron, was a member. Worked w. Philly Joe Jones, '59; in Detroit w. Yusef Lateef, '60; moved to NYC, Sept. '61, to work w. B. Barron and Ted Curson.

Joined James Moody sextet at Five Spot, Nov. '61; Roy Haynes Quartet, 1962. In November '62, recommended by Moody, he repl. Lalo Schifrin in the Dizzy Gillespie quintet and was heard in international tours and on LPs w. Gillespie. Very fluent modern soloist infl. by T. Flanagan, Wynton Kelly.

LPs w. Bill Barron (Savoy), James Moody (Cadet), Barron-Curson (Audio-Fid.), Dave Burns (Vang.), Gillespie (Verve, Philips).

Addr: 846 Prospect Place, Brooklyn, N.Y.

BASCOMB, WILBUR ODELL (DUD),* *trumpet;* b. Birmingham, Ala., 5/16/16. In 1960 Bascomb rec. new version of *Tuxedo Junction,* which he had originally popularized as soloist with Erskine Hawkins' band in 1939. Gigs w. own combo and big band, 1961-3; off-B'way show, *Cindy,* w. Sammy Quartet, 1964; mainly clubs and theaters w. Sam "The Man" Taylor from 1963, incl. annual concert and club tours of Japan.

LP: Savoy.

Addr: 434 West 163rd St., New York City.

BASIE, WILLIAM (COUNT),* *leader, piano, organ, composer;* b. Red Bank, N.J. 8/21/04. The departure from the Basie band of singer Joe Williams, in 1960, removed its most powerful commercial asset. Much of Basie's popularity during the previous six years had been attributed to the performances of Williams.

Nevertheless, Basie's career, with vocalists of relatively minor importance replacing Williams, continued on an upward trend in terms of popular success. The band toured the British Isles and the European continent in '61, '62, '63 and '65, and enjoyed a triumphal tour of Japan in May-June '63. Basie made motion picture appearances in *Sex and the Single Girl, Made in Paris* and *Cinderfella* as well as TV guest shots with Fred Astaire, Andy Williams, Tony Bennett, Edie Adams, Garry Moore, Frank Sinatra, Sammy Davis, Ed Sullivan and the Bell Telephone Hour.

The band's instrumental albums of original material enjoyed limited success, but when Basie recorded an LP entitled *Hits of the '50s and '60s,* with arrangements by Quincy Jones based on popular songs of the day, it was an immediate success and appeared on the best seller charts. It was followed by similar albums such as *More Hits of the '50s and '60s, Back with Basie, Pop Goes the Basie* and *Basie Picks the Winners,* with arrangements by Bill Byers. In '65-'66 the band, which had been recording mainly for Frank Sinatra's Reprise label, made a series of albums and personal appearances with Sinatra, all highly acclaimed by a wide audience, and mutually stimulating to Sinatra and Basie. Basie was also heard on records and in concerts with Tony Bennett, and in an album with Sammy Davis, Jr.

The tendency of the band to lean toward commercial songs of the day, and to emphasize arrangements more and improvisation less, did not set too well with many jazz experts. Some—notably John Hammond, who had discovered the band and was its most fervent supporter in early years—found a sharp deterioration in the musical interest of the band; Whitney Balliett dismissed Basie's music as "civil service swing." Other critics, particularly overseas, retained their belief that Basie's was one of the two or three remaining big jazz bands of any consequence.

During the '60-'66 period, it is true, the orchestra sustained the loss of several of the important soloists who had given it much of its character during the previous decade, notably trumpeters Joe Newman and Thad Jones, saxophonists Frank Wess and Frank Foster. In 1965 Sonny Payne, the flashy drummer heard with Basie since '55, was replaced by Rufus (Speedy) Jones. Payne ret. in '66. Despite the many personnel changes, Basie continued to maintain a nucleus of first-class soloists in the mainstream-modern style.

The personality of the band varied according to the arrangers employed. In addition to Jones and Byers, important contributors included Benny Carter, writer of two albums of originals, *The Legend* and *Kansas City Suite* (Roulette); Neal Hefti, whose association

with Basie was less frequent in the '60s (he wrote the score for *Sex and the Single Girl*); Thad Jones, Ernie Wilkins, Frank Wess and Frank Foster.

The Basie orchestra continued to win numerous awards both at home and abroad as no. one big band. The orchestra appeared at jazz festivals in Chicago, Detroit and other cities, also in '65 with Sinatra at Newport.

LPs: Some of the best are *Live Concert Recorded in Sweden,* featuring Louis Bellson on drums (Roulette); *Chairman of the Board* (Roulette); *Li'l Ol' Groovemaker . . . Basie* (Verve), *On My Way and Shoutin'* (Verve). Combo LP w. Kansas City Seven, rec. 1962 (Impulse).

In '61 Roulette released *The Count Basie Story,* a two-LP album comprising new versions in stereo of 23 jazz compositions associated with the Basie band of the '30s and '40s. The album included a history of Basie and the band in a booklet by this writer.

Addr: 174-27 Adelaide Lane, St. Albans, N.Y.

BAUDUC, RAYMOND (RAY),* *drums;* b. New Orleans, La., 6/18/09. Well known as member of Bob Crosby band 1935-42. Later w. Jimmy Dorsey, Jack Teagarden, and in late '50s in combo w. Nappy Lamare. In 1960 he played at Ben Pollack's Pick-a-Rib in Hollywood and Stardust in Las Vegas. Roaring 20s restaurant, Beverly Hills, Cal., '61-4; Robert E. Lee Riverboat, Newport Beach, Cal., '64-5.

Bauduc, still highly regarded as one of the best drummers in Dixieland circles, was reunited with Crosby for an LP on Dot in 1960.

Addr: 1228 N. Poinsettia Drive, Hollywood 46, Calif.

BAUER, WILLIAM HENRY (BILLY),* *guitar;* b. New York City, 11/14/15. Active with Herman and Goodman bands during 1940s and with Lennie Tristano and Lee Konitz mid-'50s. Led own groups in Long Island club 1961-'63. Staff guitarist for Ice Capades since '63. Has also appeared with Goodman and Ella Fitzgerald. Owns a music publishing company.

Addr: 121 Greenway, Albertson, N.Y.

BAVAN, YOLANDE (Yolande Mari Wolffe), *singer;* b. Ceylon, 6/1/40. Mother a concert pianist. Studied piano in Ceylon 1943, later cello. Own weekly radio show, *Swingtime,* in Ceylon 1955. Sang with Graeme Bell in Australia 1954-5, Toshiko Akiyoshi '55; variety shows in Ceylon '55-6. From 1956-9 she was in London singing with several groups including Joe Harriott, Vic Ash, Humphrey Lyttelton. Soloed at Blue Note in Paris, 1959. In 1962 she replaced Annie Ross in the Lambert, Hendricks & Ross Trio and toured with the group until 1964.

Miss Bavan has divided her career between singing and acting. She took part in several stage and TV plays in London, appeared with the New York Shakespeare Company in '64 and considers herself mainly an actress who happened to be sidetracked into singing. She earned great popularity touring with Lambert and Hendricks and can be heard on several of their albums on RCA.

Favs: Billie Holiday, who influenced her and personally helped her in Paris; L. Horne, C. McRae, S. Vaughan; also Horace Silver, D. Ellington.

Addr: 2, Winborne Mansions, Glenloch Rd., London, N.W. 5, England.

BAZLEY, ANTHONY (TONY), *drums;* b. New Orleans, La., 9/10/36. Studied with local teachers; voted best high school drummer in state of La. in band festival. Iceland, Greenland, Newfoundland, Japan w. Air Force show, '56-7. Studied at Los Angeles Cons.; spent five months w. Eric Dolphy in 1958, also poetry-and-jazz recital w. Buddy Collette, Langston Hughes. Other LA combo work w. Teddy Edwards, Ch. Lloyd, Dexter Gordon, Harold Land, 1959-61; Wm. Green at Marty's, '61-4; Curtis Amy, Roy Ayers, '64-6. Fav: Philly Joe Jones. Infl. Max Roach. Bazley, a skilled drummer whose first love was painting, says his ambition is to have his oils and water colors shown at Pasadena Art Museum.

LPs: w. L. Vinnegar (Contemp.), H. Geller, (Jubilee), *Montgomeryland,* 1960 (Wor. Pac.); Curtis Amy (Pac. Jazz), Roy Ayers (UA).

BELLSON, LOUIS (Louis Balassoni),* *drums, composer;* b. Rock Falls, Ill., 7/26/24. Worked with Benny Goodman, Tommy Dorsey in '40s; Harry James 1950-51, then two years with Duke Ellington. Subsequently toured with his own bands and combos, sometimes co-featured with his wife, singer Pearl Bailey.

In 1962 Bellson joined the Count Basie band briefly, touring Sweden. He then resumed his own career as a bandleader, fronting various groups of local musicians in New York, Chicago and Hollywood. He composed a jazz ballet and introduced it at the Las Vegas JF in July 1962.

Bellson took part in the World JF in July '64, as a featured soloist in the Tommy Dorsey orchestra. He returned to Japan six months later as part of an all-star percussion show featuring him with Buddy Rich, Charlie Persip and Philly Joe Jones.

In July 1965 Bellson rejoined the Duke Ellington orchestra after an absence of more than 12 years. He toured with Ellington for the rest of the year, rejoined his wife for concert work, then joined the Harry James band in April '66. Shortly before this, he took part in a presentation of his ballet on CBS Radio in Vancouver, B.C.

Bellson remains one of the most technically astonishing drummers in jazz. He plays with enthusiasm, a consistently driving beat, and an unusually tasteful solo style. His simultaneous manipulation of two bass drums at an incredible speed is one of the most popular features of his work. Though often used for spectacular effect, it is musically valid and never employed as a technical gimmick.

Own LPs and LPs with Pearl Bailey (Roul.); *Duke*

at Tanglewood (RCA) and other recent Ellington albums; *Basie in Sweden* (Roul.).

Addr: 8433 Melvin Ave., Northridge, Calif.

BENNETT, LOU (Louis Benoit), *organ, composer;* b. Philadelphia, Pa., 5/18/26. Stud. piano w. mother, aunt. After Army service, gigged in Baltimore w. own King Cole style trio. Worked as shoemaker for several years. Bought organ, '56; became full-time mus., on road w. trio '57, playing the so-called "organ circuit" clubs in East and Midwest. To Paris, 1960; since then, except for brief return to play NJF '64, has stayed in Europe, pl. all leading festivals and working in several films. Tour of East Europe countries fall '66 incl. Prague JF. Favs: Wild Bill Davis, Jackie Davis, Jimmy Smith. LPs for French RCA, Philips, Bel-Air and commercial '45s for French market. One track w. K. Clarke on *Americans In Europe,* Vol. I (Impulse).

Addr: 2 Rue Darwin, Paris 18, France.

BENNETT, MAX,* *bass;* b. Des Moines, Iowa, 5/24/28. In addition to many Hollywood studio jobs Bennett visited London and Monte Carlo in July 1961 with Peggy Lee, as her accompanist and conductor. Weekly gigs with Jimmy Rowles Trio at Carriage House, Burbank, from 1963. Concerts or club dates with Shorty Rogers, Pete Jolly. LPs w. J. Rowles, P. Lee, V. Feldman, Q. Jones.

Addr: 12208 La Maida, No. Hollywood, Calif.

BENNETT, TONY (Anthony Dominick Benedetto), *singer;* b. Queens, New York, 8/3/26. Though he is very popular with most jazz audiences and has appeared in concerts with Count Basie, Duke Ellington, and Woody Herman, Bennett is a first-class pop singer and not a jazz artist (see *Encyclopedia of Popular Music,* St. Martins Press).

BENSON, GEORGE, *guitar, singer;* b. Pittsburgh, Pa., 3/22/43. Stepfather, a guitarist, taught him ukulele and played Charlie Christian records for him. At age eight started playing ukulele in street for money; then pl. w. stepfather in after-hours club; also danced and sang there. In '54 began studying guitar. In same year recorded four sides for Label "X" as singer. While in high school got a guitar that stepfather made for him. Pl. w. cousin's rock and roll group, then formed own r&r group at age 17. On hearing Wes Montgomery and some Charlie Parker records, Benson became interested in jazz. With Jack McDuff '62 to winter '65; own group in Pitts. for three mos., then back to McDuff. Formed own group in July '65. Early infs.: Christian, Hank Garland; favs.: Montgomery, Grant Green, Kenny Burrell. A well-rounded, facile, inventive guitarist, and convincing jazz singer, Benson could well be one of the genuine new stars of the '60s. Own LP: Columbia; LPs w. McDuff (Pres.).

BERGHOFER, CHARLES CURTIS (CHUCK), *bass;* b. Denver, Colo., 6/19/37. Tuba and trumpet in high school. Started playing bass at 18, moved to LA 1945; studied with Bob Stone, Ralph Pena. Played with Skinnay Ennis, Bobby Troup, Pete Jolly. With Shelly

Manne in early '60s. LPs w. Manne (Contemp.); as sideman with Herb Ellis and other west coast groups.

Addr: 11323 Martha St., No. Hollywood, Calif.

BERNHART, MILT,* trombone; b. Valparaiso, Ind., 5/25/26. Active mainly as studio musician with Billy May, Pete Rugolo, Frank De Vol. Played in first Stan Kenton Neophonic concert 1965.

Addr: 1438 Pepper St., Burbank, Calif.

BERNSTEIN, ARTHUR (ARTIE),* bass; b. Brooklyn, N.Y., 2/4/09. A former lawyer who became a bassist during the 1930s, Bernstein pl. w. Red Nichols, the Dorsey Bros. and Benny Goodman. From the mid-1940s he worked in Los Angeles as a staff musician. He died of cancer in Los Angeles 1/4/64.

BERRY, WILLIAM R. (BILL), trumpet, fluegelhorn; b. Benton Harbor, Mich., 9/14/30. Father pl. bass, mother pl. organ. Started on piano in South Bend 1935, joined territory band 1948. Pl. w. Herb Pomeroy 1955-57; Woody Herman '57-60; M. Ferguson '61; Duke Ellington '62, and with Ellington's second-string orchestra for the *My People* show in '63. Has also done NBC and ABC staff work, pl. and recorded w. Gary McFarland, Thad Jones, Rod Levitt, sound-track trumpet part for Frank Sinatra Jr. role in film *A Man Called Adam* 1966. W. Thad Jones-Mel Lewis band '66.

Infl. by Gillespie and Ellington, Berry says his best work on records is heard on *Little David Danced* and *Montage* in the Ellington *My People* LP (Contact). Other LPs with Ellington, (Col., Reprise); Coleman Hawkins (Impulse); Ferguson (Roul.); J. Hodges-B. Strayhorn (Verve).

Addr: 420 E. 72nd St., New York City, N.Y.

BERRY, EMMETT,* trumpet; b. Macon, Ga., 7/23/16. With Fletcher and Horace Henderson bands in '30s; many bands in '40s incl. Teddy Wilson, Raymond Scott, Eddie Heywood, Count Basie; Jimmy Rushing, Johnny Hodges, Cootie Williams in '50s. Toured France and No. Africa w. Sammy Price '56, Europe w. Buck Clayton '59. In '60s pl. in band backing Nat Cole; then free-lanced in NYC w. Buddy Tate, Jimmy Jones et al. LP: *Jazz Reunion* w. Coleman Hawkins (Candid); Buddy Tate (Pres.).

Addr: 785 West End Ave., New York 25, N.Y.

BERT, EDDIE,* trombone; b. Yonkers, N.Y., 5/16/22. The former sideman with Kenton, Goodman and many name bands of the 40s and 50s worked mainly with Elliot Lawrence from 1955-65, playing Broadway shows, TV, etc. Concerts w. Chubby Jackson 1962-3, Gil Melle '62, C. Mingus '62, T. Monk '63-4. Featured guest soloist and conductor of Caracas Jazz Club at 8th International Jazz Festival, Venezuela Sept. '64. LPs w. Monk (Col.), Mingus (Merc.), UA, Fant.

Addr: 2 Park Lane, Mount Vernon, N.Y. 10552.

BEST, DENZIL DE COSTA,* drums, composer; b. New York City, 4/27/17. Prominent in the mid 1940s as

a member of combos led by Coleman Hawkins, Ben Webster, Chubby Jackson and others, Best achieved national prominence as a member of the George Shearing Quintet 1949-52. Also heard with Artie Shaw '54, Erroll Garner '56-7. In later years illness prevented him from performing at optimum level; he suffered from calcium deposits in his wrists. In May of 1965 Best fell down a flight of steps in a Manhattan subway, fractured his skull and died the following day, 5/24/65.

Though he was a tasteful and skillful drummer during his peak years, Best was better known as a composer of several melodies that became standards in modern jazz. Among them were *Wee, Move, Dee Dee's Dance* and *Bemsha Swing*.

BIGARD, LEON ALBANY (BARNEY),* clarinet; b. New Orleans, 3/3/06. The great soloist of the 1928-1942 Duke Ellington band by 1960 was regrettably in virtual retirement. In 1962 he played a record date with a group assembled by the author (*B.B.B. & Co.,* Prestige-Swingville). TV show w. Benny Carter; occasional concerts w. Earl Hines, Muggsy Spanier. Club dates w. Ben Pollack.

Addr: 3837 Gibraltar Ave., Los Angeles, Calif.

BIG BLACK (Danny Ray), conga; b. Georgia, 1934. Educated in the Carolinas, Big Black, who received his name from an older brother while a teen-ager, became interested in drums in childhood. While in high school he heard conga drums on a Cuban radio program. On leaving school he went to Florida and the Bahamas, traveling between the two places for the next five years. First prof. engagement w. Lord Flea's Calypso Band in the Bahamas; then w. Calypso Eddy Trio for three years. In Miami pl. w. Jack Costanzo, Moe Koffman; Contemporary Jazz Orch. at Rancher Motel Lounge. Then formed group w. Jamaican trumpeter Billy Cook in Nassau and began to explore jazz rhythms. To NYC in the '60s, he has worked most frequently w. Randy Weston's group; also pl. w. Ray Bryant, Johhny Barracuda, Junior Cook and Eric Dolphy. Was feat. performer at Caribbean Pavilion, NY World's Fair '65. App. w. Dizzy Gillespie at NJF and MJF '65.

Big Black is a powerful drummer, one who knows well how to blend his conga rhythms with the ensemble and soloists of a jazz group. LPs w. Weston (Bakton), Ray Bryant (Sue), Hugh Masekela (RCA); *Night of the Cookers* (BN).

Addr: Box 1458, Nassau, Bahamas.

BILK, ACKER, clarinet; b. Pensford, Somerset, England, 1/28/29. Formed his own New Orleans-styled Paramount Jazz Band '58, which soon became the most successful of the bands to enjoy mass popularity during the "trad boom," which lasted until ca. '63. Royal Command Performance and U.S. tour '62, also toured Far East, and extensively in E. and W. Europe. Solo and band LPs on Kapp.

Addr: 101 Wardour St., London W.1., England.

BISHOP, WALTER JR.,* *piano;* b. New York City, 10/
4/27. Feat. w. Art Blakey in late '40s; subsequently
w. Ch. Parker, K. Winding, many other small combos
during '50s. Gigged mainly w. Curtis Fuller in 1960.
Own trio with G. T. Hogan, Jimmy Garrison '61. Replaced Vic Feldman with Cannonball Adderley briefly.
Washington JF '62 w. Tubby Hayes. Opened new
Five Spot Cafe with Les Spann, Sam Jones, '63, also
worked the Golden Circle in Stockholm. In 1964,
toured w. Terry Gibbs quartet, later to Europe w. Geo.
Wein Fest. Trio and quartet work at Wells' and other
clubs in '65. The late Frank Haynes was member of
quartet, replaced after Haynes' death by Harold Vick.

Own LP: *Speak Low* (Jazztime). LPs w. C. Fuller
(Warwick, Epic); Ernie Wilkins (Everest); Jackie
McLean, Dizzy Reece (Blue Note); G. Ammons
(Pres.); K. Dorham (World Pacific). Others with
James Moody, Tubby Hayes, Roland Kirk et al.

Addr: 133 W. 113 St., New York 26, N.Y.

BIVONA, GUS,* *clarinet;* b. New London, Conn., 11/
25/17. The swing era soloist, heard off and on with
Steve Allen from 1958, incl. several TV shows, worked
in staff orch. at MGM studios during 1960s in addition
to leading own combos at clubs in LA and San Fernando Valley. Also active as deputy sheriff w. Malibu
Mounted Posse.

LPs: *Bivona Deals in Millions* (Warner Bros.); six
albums w. Glen Gray (Cap.), many others w. P. Rugolo et al.

Addr: 23058 Bryce St., Woodland Hills, Calif.

BLACKBURN, LOU, *trombone;* b. Rankin, Pa., 11/12/22.
Piano at Ind. High Sch., Birmingham, Ala. Two years
at Roosevelt U., Chicago. Spent eight years in U.S.
Army. Organized first group during service tenure in
Japan. Transferred to Europe, spent two years with
7th Army Symphony, 1955-6, w. Don Ellis, David
Amram, Fred Dutton. Discharged as M/Sgt. 1956.
Joined Charlie Ventura in Phila., 1956; house band at
Club Harlem, Atlantic City, N.J., '56-7; then joined
Lionel Hampton band. Toured Europe, N. Africa w.
Hampton '58. After leaving Hampton, played w. Cat
Anderson 1960. Spent eight months w. Duke Ellington,
1961. Settled in Los Angeles and became active in film
work (*Manchurian Candidate, Paris Blues, Sex and
the Single Girl*) and recording.

Influenced by Trummy Young and J. J. Johnson,
Blackburn is a consistently inventive trombonist with
a forcefully rhythmic style. He has written a number
of compositions incl. several for his own LPs on Im-
perial. Favs: F. Rosolino, C. Fuller, A. Mangelsdorff,
Aake Persson. Other LPs w. Hampton, Ellington; *Brass
Bag* w. Tricky Lofton (Pac. Jazz), *First Time* w.
Basie-Ellington (Col.), Onzy Matthews, Ch. Mingus.

Addr: 2322 W. 74th St., Los Angeles, Calif.

BLAKE, JAMES HUBERT (EUBIE),* *composer, pianist;*
b. Baltimore, Md., 2/7/1883. The pioneer vaudeville
and ragtime composer remained intermittently active
in the early 1960s, occasionally appearing in benefits

with his singing partner, Noble Sissle, with whom he
was first associated in 1915.

LP: *Wizard-of Ragtime* (20th Cent. Fox).

Addr: 284 A Stuyvesant Ave., Brooklyn, N.Y.

BLAKE, RAN, *piano;* also *organ;* b. Springfield, Mass.,
4/20/35. Studied piano in Hartford, but largely self-
taught. Began long association w. singer Jeanne Lee
'57. Highly successful tour of Europe '63, but received
little recognition in U.S. Duo was one of first to experiment with total vocal-piano improvisation. To
NYC, appeared w. Edythe Dimond, Barbara Belgrave
and at Columbia U. and Town Hall '64. Favs: G.
Russell, T. Monk, Mildred Falls, Ray Charles, M.
Roach. Infl: Heard more gospel music and Bartok
than jazz as child. Own LPs: RCA (w. Lee), ESP.

Addr: 281 N. Main St., Suffield, Conn.

BLAKEY, ART (Abdullah Ibn Buhaina),* *drums,
leader;* b. Pittsburgh, Pa., 10/11/19. Worked with
Fletcher Henderson 1939; B. Eckstine '44-7; Buddy
De Franco Quartet '51-3. Started working as leader
at Birdland in '54. His group evolved into the Jazz
Messengers, who came to prominence in '55 and toured
U.S. and Europe during the next five years.

Despite changes in personnel, Blakey continued to
dominate the particular area of jazz of which he had
become a symbol, i.e. hard bop, with a tremendous
kinetic force for which the leader's inventive and
stimulating work was largely responsible. Of the several groups he has fronted during the '60s, perhaps the
most impressive, and certainly the best organized, was
the sextet featuring Freddie Hubbard (or Lee Morgan),
Curtis Fuller and Wayne Shorter, from 1962-5. Shorter's arrangements gave the group a somewhat more
modern cast, though the basically dynamic quality of
the group was retained. After the breakup of the sextet
early in 1965, Blakey returned to quintet format. Toward the end of the year he started an entirely new
group incl. Chuck Mangione and Keith Jarrett.

LPs: Blue Note, UA, River., Impulse, Pacific Jazz,
Colpix, Epic, Limelight.

BLATNÝ, DR. PAVEL, *composer, piano;* b. Brno, Czechoslovakia, 9/14/31. Stud. with father, a composer and
music teacher. Has written 20 compositions for symphony orchestra, over 30 chamber works, 200 themes
for films, TV and radio, 40 Third Stream compositions and some 25 jazz works. He considers his most
successful recorded work to be *Passacaglia* as recorded
by Karel Krautgartner Orch. Film: *Concert for Jazz
Orchestra,* Prague 1965. Influenced by Stravinksy,
Webern, as well as Gunther Schuller, George Russell,
Ornette Coleman and Cecil Taylor, Blatný is one of
the most impressive of the experimental European
composers. One of his works, using quarter tones and
featuring a trumpet specially built for the purpose,
was introduced in the U.S. in 1965 by Don Ellis.

Addr: 19-21 Starobrněnská, Brno, Czechoslovakia.

BLESSING, LYNN, *vibes, drums;* b. Cicero, Ind., 12/
4/38. Started on drums in Indiana at age 10; played

with Freddie Hubbard, Larry Ridley in high school 1954-7. Formed his own group in Los Angeles 1960-61. This combo won the competition as best new group in the LA JF 1960. Also worked with Ray Crawford, Joe Loco, Don Randi, Fred Katz; regularly with Paul Horn 1965-6. Favs: Bobby Hutcherson, Gary Burton and Roy Ayers. Ambition: "To extend the use of the vibraphone into the field of classical music." Blessing's sound and style have been a valuable component of the Horn Quintet.

LPs: *Jazz Suite on the Mass Text; Here's That Rainy Day; Cycle,* all with Horn (RCA).

Addr: 3372½ Desconso Dr., Los Angeles, Calif.

BLEY, CARLA (née Carla Borg), *composer, piano;* b. Oakland, Cal., 5/11/38. Father a piano teacher and church organist; Carla sang in revival meetings as a child. Married to pianist Paul Bley in 1957 and began composing almost immediately, but did not devote full time to music until 1964. In Jan. '64 worked w. Charles Moffett and Pharoah Saunders at NYC Porpoise Club. With Mike Mantler was co-leader of Jazz Composers Orchestra from Dec. '64, for which she also composed and played. Went to Holland Jan. '65 for record date, radio and TV work. Back in U.S., in concerts w. Jazz Composers Orch. at N.Y. Contemporary Center, N.Y. Museum of Modern Art, Newport JF, N.Y. Judson Hall. Returned to Europe Nov. '65 for concerts, film work, radio and TV appearances in Germany and Italy. In Europe formed quintet w. Mantler and Steve Lacy.

Although she had not been recorded sufficiently as a soloist, by 1965 Carla Bley had gained prominence as a composer. Many of her works reflect the influence of her contemporaries in that they allow nearly complete freedom from rhythmic and time restrictions for soloists. Own LP w. Mantler *Jazz Realities* (Fontana). Compositions recorded by Paul Bley (GNP, Savoy, ESP, Fontana), Don Ellis (Pac. Jazz), Art Farmer (Atl.), Jimmy Giuffre (Verve), Jazz Composers Orch. (Fontana), Steve Kuhn (Contact), Steve Lacy (RCA), George Russell (Decca, River.), Attila Zoller (Merc.).

Addr: c/o ALRAC Music, P.O.B. 130, Cooper Sta., New York, N.Y.

BLEY, PAUL,* *piano, composer;* b. Montreal, Que., Canada, 11/10/32. Bley began to gain prominence among musicians of the growing avant garde in NY, the West Coast and Montreal during the '50s, playing with Charles Mingus, Ornette Coleman, Don Cherry. In 1959 he broke up his own LA group, which included Bobby Hutcherson and Scott La Faro, to return to NYC. There he worked with Mingus, Jimmy Giuffre, Don Ellis, Sonny Rollins and Gary Peacock. In '64 he again began appearing with his own groups, which included Steve Swallow, Pete LaRoca and Giuseppi Logan. Member Jazz Composers' Guild '64-'65; appeared in October Revolution '64 and subsequent N.Y. Judson Hall concerts. '65 led a quintet which, in Bley's words, found a "successful solution of total integration of compositions and solos." Toured Europe '60 and '65, Japan (w. Rollins) '63.

Although Bley is a "free" pianist in the conventional sense of harmony and group playing, his music is concerned less with the exploration of new forms than with the use of all forms to convey emotions with a characteristic easy flow. Of spontaneity, Bley told Don Heckman, "I like to rely on nothing but pure music, rather than bring something prepared into a situation." Bley has found a great deal of empathy with most of the important new bassists, including Mingus, La Faro, Charlie Haden, Swallow, Peacock, Dave Izenzon and Eddie Gomez.

Own LPs: Debut, Wing, GNP, Sav., ESP. Others: w. Mingus (Candid, Lime.), w. Giuffre (Verve, Col.), w. Rollins (RCA), w. George Russell (Dec.), w. Ellis (Pac. Jazz).

Addr: 639½ Hudson St., New York 14, N.Y.

BOBO, WILLIE (William Correa), *bongos, congas, timbales;* b. New York, N.Y., 2/28/34. Father a folk guitarist. Self-taught on drums. Began career in music as bandboy for Machito. Played w. Tito Puente '54-'58, Cal Tjader '58-'61, Herbie Mann '61-'63; also freelanced as soloist during that time. Given the nickname "Bobo" by Mary Lou Williams. Monterey JF '59 w. Tjader, Newport JF '63 w. Mann. Fav: Jimmy La Vaca. Ambition is to bridge gap between r&b and Latin music. Own LPs: *Bobo's Beat, Let's Go Bobo* (Roul.); *Spanish Grease* (Verve). Others: w. Tjader, Mann, Puente, Miles Davis, C. Adderley, L. McCann, Terry Gibbs.

Addr: 99-05A 195th St., Hollis, N.Y.

BOHANON, GEORGE ROLAND JR., *trombone;* b. Detroit, Mich., 8/7/37. First traveling job w. Premiers, then joined Chico Hamilton Quintet. Leads own groups around Wayne U. and for Detroit Jazz Society. Infl: Parker, J. J. Johnson. Considers own approach to trombone to be derived more from piano and sax than from conventional trombonists. LPs: two on Workshop Jazz, two w. Hamilton (Impulse).

Addr: 16168 Lawton, Detroit 21, Mich.

BOLAND, FRANCOIS (FRANCY), *composer, leader, piano;* b. Namur, Belgium, 11/6/29. Studied from age eight. Pl. w. Bob Shots at Paris JF '49; Germany with Al Goyens '50. Arrangements for jazz sessions in Paris with Bobby Jaspar, Bernard Peiffer et al, '51-4. Pianist-arranger with Aimé Barelli band '54-5. Toured with Chet Baker in Germany, France, Italy, '55-6; also briefly in U.S. '57-8. Has written arrangements for Count Basie, Benny Goodman, Kurt Edelhagen, Werner Müller, also a series of record sessions and concerts with big band and combos in collaboration with Kenny Clarke. Fav: Art Tatum. LPs: Blue Note, Atl., Col.

Addr: Neue Kantstrasse, Berlin 19, West Germany.

BOND, JAMES E. JR. (JIMMY),* *bass, tuba;* b. Philadelphia, Pa., 1/27/33. After traveling for a year with George Shearing, Bond settled in Los Angeles in 1959 and for two years worked mainly with the Paul Horn Quintet; also on road with Lena Horne. During the next few years he worked primarily with the Hollywood studios, playing the King Family TV show, many commercial sessions for Ralph Carmichael, Jerry Fielding, Benny Carter; movies for Lionel Newman. Favs: Ray Brown, Red Mitchell, Paul Chambers. His jazz work has included early albums with The Jazz Crusaders, also LPs with Curtis Amy, Gerald Wilson and Red Mitchell's cello LP on World Pacific. Appeared and recorded with Gil Fuller Orchestra 1965. LP w. G. Mulligan (Limelight).

Addr: P.O. Box 8551, Los Angeles 8, Calif.

BONFÁ, LUIZ FLORIANO, *composer, singer, guitar;* b. Rio de Janeiro, Brazil, 10/17/22. Father a guitarist. Bonfá began study of guitar at 12, first professional job 1946. Very popular radio and live performer in Brazil before first U.S. exposure '58. Wrote music for Brazilian film *Black Orpheus,* incl. widely performed *Morning of the Carnival (Manha de Carnival)* and *Samba de Orfeu.* Enjoyed much popularity after the impact of bossa nova in U.S. incl. engagements w. Stan Getz and w. wife Maria Toledo. Toured Germany, Italy '62. Bonfá is an accomplished classical musician. His goal is to do more film work and composing. Own LPs: Cap., Epic, Verve, Atl., Brazilian Odeon. Others: w. Getz (Verve).

Addr: 12 W. 72nd St., New York 23, N.Y.

BOOKER, WALTER M. JR., *bass;* b. Prairie View, Texas, 12/17/33. Father, a pharmacologist, plays piano and clarinet. Family moved to Wash., D.C., when Booker was nine and at that time he began studying clarinet w. father. Degree from Morehouse Coll. in psychology '56. Pl. alto sax and clar. in school concert band. Army '56-8 during which time he took up bass. After discharge stud. w. Joseph Willens in Wash. Pl. w. JFK quintet '60-3; Shirley Horn '64. To NYC Oct. '64 to pl. w. Donald Byrd. W. Sonny Rollins, Ray Bryant '65, Art Farmer '66. Orig. inf.: Percy Heath, Israel Crosby. A talented bassist who is an articulate soloist. LPs w. JFK (River.), Rollins (Imp.), Bryant (Cadet), Farmer (Atl.), Andrew Hill (BN).

Addr: 176 W. 87th St., New York 24, N.Y.

BOSTIC, EARL,* *alto sax, composer;* b. Tulsa, Okla., 4/25/13. Inactive in music for three years following a heart attack, Bostic resumed on a part-time basis in 1959, but remained generally close to his home in Los Angeles. In 1965 he decided to go on the road again, moving his residence to Detroit. He was leading a combo when he was fatally stricken with another heart attack in Rochester, N.Y., where he died 10/28/65.

Bostic's death took from the music world a remarkable performer whose florid, extrovert style had enormous appeal for rhythm-and-blues audiences. He was one of the biggest-selling jazz recording artists of the early 1950s. In his two final albums he showed evidence of an interest in a rapprochement with modern jazz, using such sidemen as Richard "Groove"

Holmes, Joe Pass, Shelly Manne and Al McKibbon, and arrangements by Buddy Collette.

LPs: Many on King. The two mentioned above were among his best: *A New Sound* and *Jazz as I Feel It.*

BOWMAN, DAVID W. (DAVE),* *piano;* b. Buffalo, N.Y. 9/8/14. Prominent in Dixieland circles, Bowman worked with Bobby Hackett, Jack Teagarden, Muggsy Spanier and Bud Freeman. After moving to Florida and free lancing there in the late 1950s he worked with hotel bands, also with Phil Napoleon's Dixieland band in 1964. He was killed in an automobile accident 12/28/64 in Miami, Fla.

BRADFORD, CLEA ANNAH ETHELL, *singer;* b. Charleston, Mo., 6/2/36. Stud. w. grandfather, a voice teacher. Debut at Faust Club, E. St. Louis. Heard in various Playboy clubs 1955-6. LP for Prestige, 1962; a more representative LP on Mainstream, '65. Miss Bradford, inspired less by other singers than by instrumentalists, chiefly James Moody and Miles Davis, is an artist with great potential, with an ear as musical as Sarah Vaughan's and a fluency not unlike Ella Fitzgerald's. Toured USSR w. Earl Hines July '66.

Addr: 5040 Ridge St., St. Louis, Mo.

BRADFORD, PERRY,* *leader, singer, piano;* b. Montgomery, Ala., 2/14/1893; raised in Atlanta, Ga. A pioneer producer and artist on early recordings, Bradford was the first man to arrange a session for a Negro singer, Mamie Smith, in 1920. He became a successful publisher, entrepreneur and recording consultant in the 1920s. Bradford later fell on hard times during the depression years. In 1965 his autobiography, *Born With The Blues,* was published by Oak Publications. Dan Morgenstern described it in DB as a repetitious and discursive diatribe in which the embittered Bradford blamed those who had failed to give him due recognition. The book, he said, lacked continuous narrative and contained little to help the novice or enlighten the serious student of U.S. entertainment history.

BRAFF, REUBEN (RUBY),* *trumpet;* b. Boston, Mass., 3/16/27. Self-taught, Braff worked locally with many small groups in Boston, and at several Newport festivals, starting with the first event in 1954. His style, sometimes compared with Buck Clayton's, was widely acclaimed by critics, but because he played in an idiom associated with an earlier era and came to prominence during the years of cool jazz and bop, he failed to gain the economic security and popular success he deserved.

During the 1960s Braff played many school and college concerts and festivals in the U.S. He appeared at the Newport, Ohio, Pittsburgh and other jazz festivals, sometimes playing with his friend and admirer, pianist-producer George Wein. He toured Europe with a jazz package in 1965. Later that year he visited England and worked as a soloist.

Braff has been poorly represented on record in recent years. Most of his LPs were on 10-inch records or have been deleted. One of the better and more recent items is *The Ruby Braff-Marshall Brown Sextet* (United Artists).

Addr: 5444 Arlington Ave., Riverdale 71, N.Y.

BRAITH, GEORGE (George Braithwaite), *soprano sax, tenor sax, stritch;* b. Bronx, N.Y., 6/27/39. Father a Pentecostal minister, mother and 5 sisters all musicians. Led own groups from age of 10, studied w. Garvin Bushell. Toured Netherlands w. own combo '57. Infl: Parker, Coltrane, Rollins; also Tatum, Berg, Bartok, Ellington. Always interested in possibilities of playing two horns simultaneously, has written book on subject. Plays custom-built saxes with expanded ranges. Own LPs: on Blue Note, incl. own fav. *Soul Stream;* also Prestige.

Addr: 725 Home St., Bronx 56, N.Y.

BRAND, ADOLF JOHANNES (DOLLAR), *pianist, composer;* b. Capetown, South Africa, 10/9/34. Studied privately from age seven, then studied on his own. First professional job with a vocal group, the Streamline Brothers; first band job subbing for regular pianist with the Tuxedo Slickers. After playing with Willy Max in Capetown, 1959, he was leader of his own group, the Jazz Epistles, in South Africa 1960-1, then moved to Europe, where he led his own trio from 1962.

Brand played at the Café Africana in Zurich in 1962-64; at the Antibes, Juan-Les-Pins and Palermo festivals in 1963; at the Blue Note in Germany 1964 and the Montmartre in Copenhagen 1964-5. His appearance at the Antibes Festival came as a direct result of his having made a record date under the sponsorship of Duke Ellington, who discovered him at the Zurich club.

Encouraged by Ellington, Brand came to the U.S. in 1965 and made a strong impression at the Newport Jazz Festival. By 1966 he had shown evidence of great potential stature in the jazz avant garde. W. Elvin Jones quartet '66. He names a South African alto player, Kippi Moeketsi, as a main influence on his playing; Ellington and Monk as his preferred pianists.

Brand's music is heterodox, angry and passionate, a reflection of the turbulent apartheid background in which he was raised. His mother and father are members of the Basuto and Bushman tribes respectively. He has absorbed in his playing, as he says, "all the different concepts of South African music—the carnival music every year in Cape Town, the traditional color music, the Malayan strains, the rural lament." Brand points out that he strives for freedom, and that prescribed shapes can cause trouble, "yet I wonder if you can ever tear yourself away from form. There is no such thing as free form."

The intensity and originality of Brand, both as pianist and composer, are unlike anything else in contemporary jazz. Among his compositions, his own preferences are *Ubu Suku, The Stride* and *Ode To Duke.*

LPs: One with Jazz Epistles for a South African album; *Duke Ellington Presents The Dollar Brand Trio* (Reprise); *Anatomy Of A South African Village* (Jazz Art).

Addr: c/o Tempo Music Inc., 52 W. 58th St., New York 19, N.Y.

BRANDT, HELMUT,* *baritone sax, composer;* also *tenor, clarinet;* b. Berlin, Germany, 1/1/31. In addition to working as a regular member of the RIAS Berlin Radio Dance Band, which he joined in 1959, Brandt has made several TV appearances with the Jazz Workshop, and has written many big band jazz works for RIAS and other German big bands.

Addr: Meraner Str. 49, Berlin 62, Germany.

BRANSCOMBE, ALAN, *alto sax, piano, vibraphone;* b. Wallasey, Cheshire, England, 6/4/36. Pl. in British army '54-6, then alto w. Tony Kinsey, Vic Ash (including U.S. '59), Stanley Black (including tour of Japan). Pl. piano and vibraphone w. Johnny Dankworth '60-5, inc. many Eur. concerts. LPs. w. Dankworth (Brit. Fontana), Harold McNair (Brit. Island), Stan Tracey (Brit. HMV).

Addr: 24 Fawcett St., London S.W.10., England.

BRAUD, WELLMAN,* *bass;* b. St. James, La., 1/25/1891. Braud, who came to prominence as bassist with the early Ellington band 1926-35, has remained occasionally active during the 60s, chiefly in concert tours, club dates and Capitol recordings with Barbara Dane and Kenny Whitson.

Addr: 4454 W. 116th S., Hawthorne, Calif.

BREEDEN, HAROLD LEON, *educator, arranger, saxophone;* b. Guthrie, Okla., 10/3/21. Entire family musical. Clarinet at 7 in Wichita Falls, Tex. Played with country and western bands in Okla. and Tex., and for a year with Ray McKinley, '52.

As an educator, Breeden came to prominence for his work at No. Tex. State College, where he carried on the formal-credit jazz and dance band course tradition established there by Eugene Hall. Student bands under his direction were first-place winners in several college jazz festivals at Notre Dame and U. of Kansas. He has also been prominent as director every summer of the jazz clinics held by the National Stage Band Camps. Favs: J. Hodges, B. Carter, Benny Goodman.

Addr: 1114 West Congress, Denton, Tex.

BRIGHT, RONNELL,* *piano, composer;* b. Chicago, Ill., 7/3/30. Accompanist for several vocalists, esp. Sarah Vaughan, during '50s, Lena Horne '61. Own tunes recorded by Vaughan, Gloria Lynne, J. Hartman, H. Silver, C. Tjader, Blue Mitchell. Single pianist-singer in N.Y. '63. Joined Nancy Wilson as pianist, mus. dir., conductor and arranger Jan. '64. A capable pianist, Bright has also recorded with a variety of artists. Own LPs: Reg., Vang., French Polydor. Others: w. Wilson (Cap.), Vaughan (Merc.), Coleman Hawkins (Pres.), Buddy Tate (Pres.), Rolf Kuhn (Vang.), Frank Foster (Sav.).

Addr: 4495 Don Tomaso Dr. Apt. 7, Baldwin Hills, Calif.

BRIGNOLA, NICHOLAS THOMAS (NICK),* *baritone sax;* b. Troy, N.Y., 7/17/36. Stud. and worked around upstate N.Y. during '50s, and on West Coast w. Tjader, Mastersounds. With Woody Herman '63, Sal Salvador '63-64. From '64 in Albany, Troy, Schenectady w. own group. Has own jazz show on Troy radio. Lectures and performs in area colleges. Experimenting with upper ranges of baritone sax. LPs: w. Herman (Phil.), Salvador (Aud. Fid.).

Addr: 11 Meadowview Dr., Troy, N.Y.

BROOKMEYER, ROBERT (BOB),* *valve trombone, piano, composer;* b. Kansas City, Kansas, 12/19/29. In August 1961 Brookmeyer formed a combo w. Clark Terry. During the next five years the two worked together intermittently, using various rhythm sections in New York, Los Angeles and on a visit to England in 1964. Brookmeyer also continued his association with Mulligan for some time, visiting Europe with him in 1962 and '63 and Japan in July '64. After leaving Mulligan April '65 he joined Merv Griffin TV show as staff musician. Married 9/1/64 to composer-lyricist Margo Guryan.

The music of the Brookmeyer-Terry team is personal, confidently swinging and often laced with touches of humor. Brookmeyer's intensely individual solo style has also been framed with great success in a series of other contexts. His most successful album as leader and composer is *Gloomy Sunday and Other Bright Moments* (Verve). Other LPs: *7 X Wilder* w. Jim Hall (Verve); *Brookmeyer and Friends* w. Stan Getz (Col.); *Trombone Jazz Samba Bossa Nova* (Verve); *Portrait of the Artist* (Atl.).

BROWN, GARNETT JR., *trombone, composer;* b. Memphis, Tenn., 1/31/36. Studied piano. A&R man for rhythm & blues record company before playing with Chico Hamilton, 1962. Toured Europe; Sweden, w. George Russell, 1964. Substitute teacher in NYC city schools. Favs: J. Cleveland, J. J. Johnson, F. Rosolino, S. Hampton, B. Woodman, B. Harris. LP w. Russell (River.), Roland Kirk (Lime.).

Addr: 1419 University Ave., Bronx 52, N.Y.

BROWN, JAMES, *singer, songwriter;* also *arranger, piano, organ, bass, guitar, drums;* b. Augusta, Ga., 1934. Raised in Augusta and Macon, Ga., Brown sang gospel songs and danced in the streets as a child to help his family pay the rent. Received encouragement from former champion Beau Jack to become a professional boxer; a leg injury ended sports aspirations which incl. prof. baseball, and he entered music full-time by forming his own group called the Famous Flames.

An audition record cut in '55 led to a recording contract with King. Since then, he has been one of the biggest attractions and record sellers in show business, touring the U.S. in one-nighters and theater engagements such as the Apollo, NYC, and Howard, Wash., D.C. with large company incl. big band.

It has been written of Brown: "The sound is what makes James Brown and the sound is not easily sus-ceptible of description. Soul music is a derivation of gospel singing, and of blues, a throbbing beat and a personal expression. With James Brown it is primitive and sometimes savage and it screams, but one of his first and best-selling records, *Please, Please, Please,* has the flavor of supplication and prayer."

LPs: King, Smash.

Addr: c/o Ben Bart, Universal Attractions, 200 W. 57th St., New York, N.Y.

BROWN, JEWEL HAZEL, *singer;* b. Houston, Tex., 8/30/37. Started piano lessons at age seven. Entered music professionally through her brother, Theodore K. Brown, a musician. Vocalist with Earl Grant 1957-8. Joined Louis Armstrong June 21, 1961 and has toured all over the world with him to South America, Western and Eastern Europe, Japan, New Zealand, etc. An admirable performer with an extrovert style and keen sense of phrasing, she has impressed audiences everywhere, but unfortunately by 1966 was still not represented on records. Favs: E. Fitzgerald, S. Vaughan, D. Washington, Ray Charles.

Addr: 2502 Eagle, Houston, Texas.

BROWN, LAWRENCE,* *trombone;* b. Lawrence, Kans., 7/3/05. A member of Duke Ellington's orchestra from 1932-51, Brown rejoined the band in June 1960. Originally known for his legato, highly melodic improvisations, on returning to the band he diversified his style by also playing plunger-mute solos of the type once associated with Tricky Sam Nanton. In addition to many LPs with Ellington, Brown can be heard on his own album, *Inspired Abandon* (Impulse), and in various sessions with Johnny Hodges (Verve, Impulse).

Addr: 100 Hirliman Rd., Teaneck, N.J.

BROWN, LESTER RAYMOND (LES),* *leader, clarinet;* b. Reinerton, Pa., 3/14/12. Formed his band 1938 and was popular through the swing era. Doris Day was his vocalist for several years in the early '40s. For almost two decades Brown has been associated w. Bob Hope, accompanying him on his Christmas tours to various parts of the world. In late '62 Brown announced his retirement from active leading, stating that on future bookings the band would be led by his baritone saxophonist-band manager Butch Stone. The arrangement was short-lived; Brown soon resumed appearing, on a limited basis, playing gigs with the band mostly in and around Southern California. TV series incl. *Hollywood Palace* 1965, Dean Martin Show '66.

Addr: c/o Kramer, 1614 N. Argyle, Hollywood 28, Calif.

BROWN, MARION JR., *alto sax;* b. Atlanta, Ga., 9/8/35. Mother sang in church, gospel groups. Studied sax, clarinet and oboe in high school and college. Played w. an Atlanta teen-age group, in an army band and w. Johnny Hodges in Atlanta '57. To NYC; first job w. Archie Shepp. W. Jazz Composers Guild Orch. Judson

Hall NYC '64, own group Newark Sept. '65. In USIA cultural film w. Bill Dixon June '65. Has written articles for *Kulchur, Change, The Negro Reference Book.* Acted in orig. production of LeRoi Jones' *The Dutchman.* Favs. and influences: B. Carter, C. Parker, O. Coleman, J. Coltrane. LPs: w. Shepp (Imp.), Coltrane (Imp.).

Addr: 224 E. 21st St. #12, New York 10, N.Y.

BROWN, MARSHALL RICHARD,* *leader, composer, educator, valve trombone;* b. Framingham, Mass., 12/21/20. Achieved note as educator, songwriter during '50s, especially after organizing and leading the Newport Youth Band in 1959. Organized own publishing firm for youth band compositions. During '60s played and toured w. Ruby Braff, Pee Wee Russell, Bobby Hackett, Wild Bill Davidson. Own LP: co-led w. Braff *Ruby Braff-Marshall Brown Sextet* (UA). Others: w. Russell (Col., Impulse), Hackett (Epic), Newport JF All-Stars (Impulse).

Addr: 247 W. 72nd St., New York 23, N.Y.

BROWN, OSCAR JR., *singer, songwriter;* b. Chicago, Ill., 10/10/26. His father, several uncles and cousins were all lawyers and he was expected to devote himself to this profession, but from an early age he showed a natural talent for songwriting. While at high school he had a regular acting role on a network radio soap opera. After graduating in 1943, he divided the next nine years between attendance at five different colleges and activity in a variety of side ventures. He wrote a daily news review, worked as an advertising copy man, ran for the Illinois State Legislature on the Progressive party ticket in 1948, and worked in public relations for the Musicians' Union. Occasionally he worked with his father in his law practice and real estate office.

After Army service, 1954-6, Brown continued to dabble in real estate, but gradually moved into professional songwriting. His first recorded composition was *Brown Baby,* sung by Mahalia Jackson. Brown also collaborated with Max Roach on the *Freedom Now Suite,* recorded in 1960 in an album entitled *We Insist!* (Candid).

In 1960 Brown signed as a Columbia recording artist, usually singing his own works. A long-projected play on which he had worked for several years, *Kicks and Company,* was presented in Chicago in 1961. Though the play failed, Brown's tunes were salvaged and he used them in his night club act and on records.

Though he has written both lyrics and music to dozens of compositions, Brown is particularly well known for having set lyrics to a number of instrumental jazz works, among them Nat Adderley's *Work Song,* Bobby Timmons' *Dat Dere,* Miles Davis' *All Blues,* Les McCann's *So Help Me* and Clark Terry's *One Foot In The Gutter.*

As Brown has observed, "My songs started when I was a kid flipping rides on the wagons that peddled down our alley, hiding and seeking and learning there is more than one world. Most of my worlds are Negro.

Being Negro is not always pleasant, but it is vigorous exercise for the soul. It can enrich an artist. The melodies I make up grow out of tunes, rhythms, chants, calls and cries that have always sung to me. My lyrics are verses about feelings I've felt and scenes I've dug. My aim is to deliver messages that swing and entertainment that is meaningful."

Brown's philosophy is brilliantly expressed in his writing and performances, which combine, as Billy James once wrote, "tenderness and turmoil, hostility and heart, clarity and confusion."

In 1962 Brown appeared as master of ceremonies of a series of 26 TV shows, *Jazz Scene USA,* which were still being screened throughout the world in 1966.

Own LPs: Columbia, Fontana.

Addr: 5056 Woodlawn Ave., Chicago, Ill.

BROWN, JAMES OSTEND (PETE),* *alto, tenor saxes;* b. Baltimore, Md., 11/9/06. A founder member of the John Kirby Sextet in 1938, Brown was prominent on a series of records in the late '30s and early '40s. He was Cecil Payne's teacher, and is credited by Paul Desmond as having been a strong influence on the latter's musical thinking.

After several years in and out of the hospital, Brown died 9/20/63 of a kidney ailment. His last public appearance was made at the Village Gate late in 1962, when he played with Dizzy Gillespie at a benefit.

Pete Brown's contribution to jazz has been vastly underestimated. His staccato, often humorous sound and superb sense of swing were unique; he was one of the great alto players of jazz history, a man whose talent far exceeded that of artists who were more fortunate in gaining publicity and economic security.

Unfortunately there is very little evidence of Brown's talent on available LPs. He can be heard in one track (*Allen's Alley*) on *The Bebop Era* (RCA) and took part in several sessions produced by this writer, for RCA, Decca and other companies, some of which, it is hoped, will be reissued in due course.

BROWN, RAYMOND MATTHEWS (RAY),* *bass;* b. Pittsburgh, Pa., 10/13/26. This greatly admired bassist is best known for his association with Oscar Peterson, which began on a regular basis in 1951. He continued to tour with Peterson in the 1960s, including annual visits to Europe, also a tour of Japan in 1964. In January, 1966 he left the Peterson trio and settled in Hollywood, Calif., where he divided his time between many studio assignments, composing and music publishing. His most successful composition, *Gravy Waltz,* was popularized through the TV show of Steve Allen, who wrote the lyrics for it.

Brown has continued to enjoy an almost unparalleled reputation among fellow musicians, as is indicated by the fact that he has won the All-Star's All-Stars Poll in *Playboy* every year since it was inaugurated in 1958. Own LPs on Verve. LPs w. Peterson (Verve, Merc., Limelight) and Milt Jackson (Verve).

Addr: 17814 Wexford, Detroit, Michigan.

BRUBECK, DAVID W. (DAVE),* *piano, composer;* b. Concord, Calif., 12/6/20. Studied under Darius Milhaud and others. Formed quartet in 1951 and began to rise to national prominence in '55. Made first Newport JF appearance and first overseas tour in '58.

During the 1960s Brubeck devoted more of his time to extended compositions. His *Points on Jazz,* commissioned by the American Ballet Theatre, was performed on the Ballet's 1960-61 tour. Excerpts from *The Real Ambassadors,* a musical play written in collaboration with his lyricist wife, Iola, were recorded in 1961 (Col.) and introduced at the Monterey JF in '62. The cast included Louis Armstrong, Carmen McRae, Lambert Hendricks & Bavan and Brubeck's quartet. In 1962 he recorded *Brandenburg Gate,* a fuller, orchestral version of a tune from his album *Jazz Impressions of Eurasia.* The following year he introduced *Elementals,* a major work for quartet and symphony orchestra. Brubeck also wrote the entire score for the CBS-TV show *Mr. Broadway,* 1964-5 season. Music from his albums *Time Out* and *Time Further Out* was used by various ballet companies.

The Brubeck quartet continued to enjoy unique popularity during the 1960s. Brubeck won first place in the piano division of the *Playboy* poll every year from 1961-6 and his quartet has placed first or second annually in the *Down Beat* readers' poll for more than a decade. The quartet played at the White House in April, 1964 at the request of Lady Bird Johnson. King Hussein of Jordan was guest of honor at the performance. Brubeck was the subject of a documentary television show, *Twentieth Century.* He has played with many major symphony orchestras, performing his own works. In Germany he played at the Berlin JF and performed *Elementals* with the Berlin Philharmonic in 1964. He has lectured on various musical topics in panels and symposiums at many universities.

Brubeck's compositions have been published in a series of 11 piano books and one organ book.

The quartet has made the following foreign tours: In 1960, Australia, New Zealand, Europe. In 1961: England in January and again in July (to take part in his first film, *All Night Long*); England and Continent Nov.-Dec. In 1962: Australia, New Zealand, Mar.-Apr.; England, Nov. In 1964, during a single two-month period (April-June), the group performed in the U.S., Mexico, Japan, Hong Kong and England. Another European tour was undertaken in Sept.-Oct. The quartet visited Australia again in Mar. '65.

In 1961 Brubeck received an Honorary Doctorate Degree from the Univ. of Pacific in recognition of his musical and humanitarian contributions.

More and more during the 1960s Brubeck's pioneering concepts of improvisation in polyphony and polytonality, and later in polyrhythms, were utilized in many areas of jazz. As a pianist, though his jazz style was not unanimously accepted by the critics, he became an important influence, particularly at the college-student level. Many of the young pianists of the '60s were as deeply indebted (perhaps unconsciously) to Brubeck as he in turn was to Tatum, Ellington and Waller.

LPs: *The Riddle* with Bill Smith, clarinet (8248); *Jazz Impressions of New York* (9075); *Bernstein Plays Brubeck Plays Bernstein* with Leonard Bernstein and the New York Philharmonic Orch. (8257); *Jazz Impressions of Japan* (9012); *The Dave Brubeck Quartet at Carnegie Hall* (826); *Tonight Only!* with Carmen McRae (8409); *Brubeck & Rushing* with Jimmy Rushing (8353); *Brandenburg Gate: Revisited* (8763); *Bossa Nova U.S.A.* (8798); *Countdown Time in Outer Space* (8575); *Time Changes* (8927); *Angel Eyes* (9148). All the above are on Col. *Near-Myth/ Brubeck-Smith* with Bill Smith (Fantasy).

Addr: 221 Millstone Rd., Wilton, Conn. 06897.

BRYANT, PAUL C., *organ;* b. Long Branch, N.J., 9/22/33. Started on piano in 1937 under Prof. John A. Gray, Gray's Cons. of Mus., L.A. A child prodigy, he appeared on CBS radio show in 1942. Appeared as actor in some 16 movies between 1938 and '48, incl. *Green Pastures, Tales of Manhattan, Star Spangled Rhythm, Cabin in the Sky, Stormy Weather, Saratoga Trunk, Knickerbocker Holiday, Jackie Robinson Story.* Radio shows w. Abbott & Costello. Turned to full-time music in late 1950s, appearing at Lighthouse, many other West Coast clubs, Steve Allen's *Jazz Scene USA* TV series.

LPs: Pac. Jazz, Fantasy. LPs w. Johnny Griffin (River.), Howard Roberts (Cap.).

Addr: 633 Miller Avenue, N. Las Vegas, Nev.

BRYANT, RAPHAEL (RAY),* *piano, composer;* b. Philadelphia, Pa., 12/24/31. From 1960 Bryant toured with his own trio, scoring a commercial success with his own composition, *Little Susie* (named for his daughter). He has enjoyed great popularity in Toronto, appearing there several times annually. Several of his compositions, notably *Cubano Chant,* have been popularized by other leading jazz groups. Own LPs: Col., Cadet; w. Sonny Rollins (Imp.).

Addr: 392 Central Park West, New York 25, N.Y.

BRYANT, WILLIAM STEVEN (WILLIE),* *leader;* b. New Orleans, 8/30/08. Though not a jazz musician, Bryant was a singer and leader of his own big band from 1933-9. His sidemen included Benny Carter, Teddy Wilson and Ben Webster. He was later active as a stage, screen and TV actor and disc jockey. After a few years of work in Los Angeles, mainly in TV, he died there of a heart attack 2/9/64.

BUCKNER, JOHN EDWARD (TEDDY),* *trumpet;* b. Sherman, Texas, 7/16/09. From the late 1950s through 1966 the former name-band trumpeter led his own group, which remained stable in personnel and spent most of the period from 1962-6 at the Huddle, a large restaurant in W. Covina, east of Los Angeles. In addition, the group was seen in the *Stars of Jazz* TV series, in *Jazz Scene U.S.A.* produced by Steve Allen, and in the award-winning CBS-TV documentary, *The*

Legend of Jimmy Blue Eyes. Buckner's sextet made several LPs for the Dixieland Jubilee label. His group's repertoire, and his own sound and style, remained firmly rooted in the Louis Armstrong tradition.

Addr: c/o Premiere Artists Agency, 1046 Carol Dr., Hollywood 69, Calif.

BUDIMIR, DENNIS MATTHEW,* *guitar;* b. Los Angeles, Cal., 6/20/38. Free-lanced in LA from '55, esp. w. Harry James, Chico Hamilton. W. Bud Shank, Peggy Lee '60-'61. In Armed Forces '61-'63. Returned to LA '63 to do studio work; also acc. Julie London, Bobby Troup, incl. tour of Japan '63. From '64 casual gigs w. Shank, Emil Richards. LPs: w. Shank, Gil Fuller-Dizzy Gillespie, Gerald Wilson-Les McCann (all on Pac. Jazz).

Addr: 2415 Hitchcock Dr., Alhambra, Calif.

BUDWIG, MONTY,* *bass;* b. Pender, Neb., 12/26/29. With several top LA combos during '50s, incl. Z. Sims, B. Kessel, R. Norvo, W. Herman, S. Manne. Joined B. Goodman quartet, playing several NYC concerts and tour of Japan '64. W. Terry Gibbs on staff of Regis Philbin TV show '65; Manne '66. Europe w. JATP. LPs: w. Manne (Cap.), w. Manne and Bill Evans (Verve), w. Victor Feldman (VeeJay).

Addr: 4112 Knobhill Dr., Sherman Oaks, Calif.

BUNCH, JOHN L. JR.,* *piano;* b. Tipton, Ind., 12/1/21. With W. Herman, B. Goodman, M. Ferguson bands and own quartet from mid-'50s. W. Goodman off and on during '60s, incl. Soviet tour '62, Las Vegas and NYC '61, US and Mexican tours '63. W. Buddy Rich at Birdland '60, Al Cohn and Zoot Sims at Half Note '61, '62, Gene Krupa quartet '61-64, Wild Bill Davison at Aspen, Colo. '65. With own duo at Luigi's NYC, '65. App. on Today TV show w. Don Goldie and w. Cohn-Sims, Telephone Hour w. Goodman '62. LPs: w. R. Kuhn (Pano.), B. Clayton (River.), J. Morello (RCA), Rich (Merc., MGM), S. Salvador (Dec.), Goodman (RCA, Col.), Krupa (MGM, Verve), G. Roland (Bruns.), C. Leggio (Jazz Unl.).

Addr: 350 W. 55th St., New York 19, N.Y.

BUNKER, LAWRENCE BENJAMIN (LARRY),* *drums, vibes;* b. Long Beach, Calif., 11/4/28. Top West Coast jazz and studio drummer from early '50s. Continuously active in movie and TV work, recording and performing. '62 w. Bud Shank, incl. concert at Palace of Fine Arts, Mexico City. Led own quartet '63, and worked w. Clare Fischer, Ralph Peña. Considers own most important job w. Bill Evans Trio on drums '64-'65, incl. European tour. To Australia '64 w. Judy Garland. Monterey JF w. Dizzy Gillespie. Toured Japan w. Stan Getz '65. Movie scores w. H. Mancini, N. Hefti, J. Mandel, Nelson Riddle. Bunker is a sensitive accompanist who can play a variety of assignments. LPs: w. Evans (Verve), w. Pete Jolly (Ava), w. Jim Hall (Pac. Jazz).

Addr: 2157 Sunset Crest Dr., Los Angeles 46, Calif.

BURCH, JOHN, *piano, composer;* b. London, England, 1/6/32. Became professional mus. in '59, and pl. w.

Bobby Wellins in France, and w. Allan Ganley. '62-4 w. Don Rendell, who rec. his comps. *Manumission* and *The Haunt.* Led own octet inc. Graham Bond, Dick Heckstall-Smith, Ginger Baker '64. Currently w. Tommy Whittle, but mainly songwriting at present. Has had several r&b songs rec. by Georgie Fame. LP w. Don Rendell (Jazzland).

Addr: 59a Chepstow Rd., London W.2., England.

BURNETT, JOE, *trumpet, fluegelhorn;* b. Dallas, Tex., 11/24/27. Began playing trumpet in high school. With W. Herman '53-54, M. Ferguson '56-'58, S. Kenton '58, C. Barnet '60. Married to singer Irene Kral. Did solo work for film *The Wild Seed.* Toured Japan w. Julie London '64. Favs: D. Gillespie, A. Farmer. Infl: Miles Davis. LPs: w. Kenton (Cap.); own fav. work on Dick Grove's *Little Bird Suite* (Pac. Jazz). Burnett has an exceptionally warm, rich sound and makes admirable use of the styles of his influences.

Addr: 727 N. East Ave., Oak Park, Ill.

BURNS, RALPH,* *composer, piano;* b. Newton, Mass., 6/29/22. Came to prominence as pianist and arranger with the Woody Herman band in 1944; later worked with small combos and as accompanist to singers. Though he won several awards as the number one jazz arranger in the early 1950s, Burns has been almost entirely absent from the jazz scene in the 1960s, much of his time having been occupied with the writing of orchestrations for Broadway shows. A prominent jazz composer, best known for *Summer Sequence, Bijou* and *Early Autumn,* he returned briefly to jazz in 1965, writing a few vocal arrangements for Herman.

Addr: 853 Seventh Ave., New York, N.Y. 10019.

BURRELL, KENNETH EARL (KENNY),* *guitar, composer;* b. Detroit, Mich., 7/31/31. BM from Wayne U. '55. Played with Dizzy Gillespie, Benny Goodman and many small combos in '50s. In early '60s he led his own group at Branker's Melody Room and free-lanced on innumerable record sessions.

Burrell, who is equally facile whether playing electric or Spanish guitar, is mainly self-taught, except for some classical guitar study in 1952-3. His versatility was well represented in a widely acclaimed album released in 1965, *Guitar Forms.* Five of the tracks were arranged by Gil Evans, with whom Burrell had frequently worked as a sideman. This LP is on Verve, as are others on which he played with Astrud Gilberto, Stan Getz, Jimmy Smith, Lalo Schifrin and Kai Winding.

Own LPs: *On View at the Five Spot Cafe, Blue Lights, Midnight Blue* (Blue Note); *A Night at the Vanguard* (Cadet); *All Night Long, Soul Call* (Pres.).

Addr: 550 Riverside Dr., New York 27, N.Y.

BURTON, GARY, *vibes;* b. Anderson, Ind., 1/23/43. Started playing at age six. Stud. only piano, comp. in high school, college; self-taught on vibes. Prof. debut in Nashville, Tenn., 1960. To South America w. own group, 1962; worked w. Geo. Shearing, '63, incl. Japanese tour; w. Stan Getz 1964-6, incl. appearance at

White House and two films: *The Hanged Man, Get Yourself a College Girl.* In '64 Shearing recorded an album, *Out of The Woods,* comprising works composed & arr. by Burton.

Though he names Bill Evans, Harry Partch and Stan Getz as influences, Burton has no favorite vibraharpist and has been sharply critical of a number of his colleagues. Though still immature, he is a performer and writer of unusual promise. Some of his vibes work involves a three- and four-mallet technique that is harmonically extraordinary and without precedent on this instrument in jazz.

LPs for RCA; also as sideman w. Shearing, Getz, Q. Jones, Joe Morello, B. Brookmeyer, Hank Garland. Own fav. LP: *Something's Coming* (RCA).

Addr: 36 W. 73rd St. Apt. 4B, New York, N.Y.

BUSHKIN, JOE,* *piano, songwriter;* b. New York City, 11/17/16. A sideman with many Dixieland groups from 1935, also w. Tommy Dorsey and Benny Goodman in the '40s and w. Louis Armstrong in '53, Bushkin occasionally led his own quartet in the '50s and '60s but spent much of his time in voluntary retirement, living in Hawaii. His best known composition is *Oh! Look at Me Now.* In 1965 he returned to U.S. for brief visits, pl. El Matador club in SF and rec. an LP for Decca. Also heard in own *Concert At Town Hall* (Reprise).

Early work reissued on *Chairmen of the Board* and *Eddie Condon: A Legend* (both Mainstream).

Addr: P.O. Box 687, Kamuela, Hawaii.

BUTLER, FRANK,* *drums;* b. Kansas City, Mo., 2/18/28. Worked w. Dave Brubeck in 1950; briefly w. Duke Ellington '54. Free-lancing in LA, was only intermittently active in 1960s, emerging from time to time for jobs w. Ben Webster, Harold Land and other combos. Played second drums w. John Coltrane (opposite Elvin Jones) for an engagement in late '65. LPs w. Vic Feldman (Ava), Phineas Newborn (Contemp.).

BUTTERFIELD, DON,* *tuba;* b. Centralia, Wash., 4/1/23. One of the first tuba players to be associated with modern jazz, he played with Teddy Charles and Charles Mingus in the 1950s. He played in the Dizzy Gillespie orchestra at the Antibes Festival on the French Riviera, July 1962; night clubs and Town Hall concert w. Mingus, '62; Newport JF '63 w. Dakota Staton; first jazz concert at Philharmonic Hall, Lincoln Center, with Oliver Nelson, Aug. '63. Films: *The Strange One, The Luck of Ginger Coffee, Act One.*

In addition to his jazz activities Butterfield has remained the principal tuba player in the Radio City Music Hall Orch. He is also a publisher, specializing in works on tuba, trombone, baritone sax, etc. Contributed articles to DB '62.

LPs w. Cannonball Adderley (River., Cap.); Nat Adderley (Atl.); Donald Byrd (BN); Maynard Ferguson (Main.); Dizzy Gillespie, Wes Montgomery, Oscar Peterson, Jimmy Smith, Cal Tjader (Verve);

Ahmad Jamal (Cadet); Charlie Mariano (Imp.); Charles Mingus (Limelight, Imp.); Oliver Nelson (UA, Pres.); Lalo Schifrin (Roul.).

Addr: Nydam Lane, Wyckoff, N.J.

BUTTERFIELD, PAUL, *singer, harmonica;* b. Chicago, 1941. As a teenager he developed a strong interest in traditional blues styles, partly through association with local Negro blues musicians such as Muddy Waters. He worked at the Blue Flame and The 1015 clubs on the South Side with an interracial group, and later at Big John's on Wells Street. In 1965-6 Butterfield's blues band rose to national prominence, appearing on major television shows. Pete Welding has called him "a vigorous, full-throated singer and feelingful, sensitive harp [harmonica] player . . . in marked contrast to the other white blues performer of his generation, Butterfield is committed wholeheartedly to the modern urban blues style long associated with his home town . . . so individual and fully assimilated is his approach that, listening to him sing and play, the question of his aping Negro style or specific Negro artists never arises. Butterfield is simply his own man."

LP: *The Paul Butterfield Blues Band* (Elektra).

BYARD, JOHN A. JR. (JAKI),* *piano, composer;* also *saxophones, trumpet, bass, trombone, guitar, drums;* b. Worcester, Mass., 6/15/22. Byard, as diverse in his styles and experience as in his instrumental ability, was a leader in Boston jazz from the early 1940s. In the '60s he began to come into his own as a composer of wide talents, synthesizing musics ranging from James P. Johnson and Earl Hines through Erroll Garner and Bud Powell to the contemporary avant-garde.

After three years with Maynard Ferguson, Byard left him in '62, moved to New York and joined Charles Mingus. In Byard's words, "Mingus had to get a piano player that could play 'old-fashioned' for his Town Hall Concert. There ain't too many cats who can go that way, play stride." Byard played a valuable role as arranger and pianist with Mingus at the '64 Monterey JF.

Aside from his work with Mingus, Byard has played with Eric Dolphy ("Eric was one of my favorite musicians"), Booker Ervin, Don Ellis, Ken McIntyre, Charlie Mariano, Sam Rivers, Roland Kirk, and has led several of his own bands in Boston and NYC. As a composer he has been able to incorporate "stride" into a modern setting and has written strictly modern compositions such as *Here to Hear* and *Twelve.* He has also been active in Boston educational TV. Byard's piano style is often tinged heavily with the blues, showing the importance of "roots" to a musician who can handle them without being repetitious or imitative.

Says Byard of his own music, "If you can relate to an audience, you can try to get the *feeling* of those people you dig. . . . I can't play one way all night and I wouldn't want to. . . . I don't play older styles 'tongue-in-cheek.' People say this about me and it's not true."

Own LPs: *Live!* (Vol. 142), *Hi-Fly, Out Front!* (Pres.). Also with Ferguson (Roul.), Dolphy (Pres.), Ellis (Candid, Pres.), Ervin (Pres.), Rivers (BN), Kirk (Merc.), and Mingus (UA, Impulse, Mingus).

Addr: 192-54 Hollis Ave. Hollis, N.Y.

BYAS, CARLOS WESLEY (DON),* *tenor sax;* b. Muskogee, Okla., 10/21/12. Prominent during the 1930s with the bands of Don Redman, Lucky Millinder, Eddie Mallory and Andy Kirk, Byas also played with Count Basie in 1941 and with the early Dizzy Gillespie combo in '44 at the Onyx Club on 52nd St.

After touring Europe in 1946 with Redman, he remained on the Continent, subbing in Duke Ellington's band in 1950, living in France for several years and then moving to Holland. Critic Joachim-Ernst Berendt has called him "the first to relate the classic tenor saxophone style of Coleman Hawkins to modern jazz." App. at Berlin JF '65. Though most of Byas' European recordings are unavailable in the U.S., he can be heard in good form in a 1963 concert recording made in Koblenz, Germany, which takes up one side of *Americans in Europe,* Volume 2 (Impulse); also *JATP in Europe* (Verve).

BYERS, WILLIAM MITCHELL (BILLY),* *trombone, composer;* b. Los Angeles, Calif., 5/1/27. Byers had a varied career as performer, arranger and conductor in LA, Paris and NYC during the '50s. After 1959 as a protege of Quincy Jones he played, arranged and toured w. Jones, and followed him as arr. for Count Basie. Wrote several albums for Basie and arrs. for Duke Ellington, J. J. Johnson and Q. Jones. Orchestrated several films, incl. Jones' soundtrack for *The Pawnbroker.* Arr. some of Andy Williams' TV shows. Own LP: *Impressions of Duke Ellington* (Merc.).

Addr: 244 W. 48th St., New York, N.Y.

BYRD, CHARLES L. (CHARLIE),* *guitar, composer;* b. Suffolk, Va., 9/16/25. Using his own Showboat Club in Washington, D.C. as home base, Byrd also undertook many other engagements during the 1960s. In 1961 he took his combo on a State Department-sponsored South American tour. A direct outcome of this trip was his discovery of the potential inherent in establishing the Brazilian samba rhythm in conjunction with jazz improvisation. On Feb. 13, 1962, an album entitled *Jazz Samba* was recorded at a church in Washington, D.C. by Byrd as co-featured soloist with Stan Getz, who was the leader on the date. Getz was impressed by the tunes Byrd suggested for the session, which included works by Antonio Carlos Jobim and others. The combination of Getz's subtly graceful improvisation and Byrd's harmonic and rhythmic ingenuity was not only an artistic success, but also a commercial hit of such magnitude that the entire bossa nova craze in the U.S. may be said to have sprung directly from this album.

Byrd toured Europe with Les McCann and Zoot Sims. He was featured on the TV shows of Edie

Adams, Steve Allen, et al, won several *Down Beat* and *Playboy* polls, and recorded extensively in the classical, jazz and bossa nova fields. In 1965 he gave a recital in the East Room of the White House for Mrs. Lyndon Johnson.

Because of his firm roots in jazz, his thorough classical training and his sensitive absorption of the sounds he heard in Latin America, Byrd developed into possibly the most versatile guitarist ever to play jazz.

Among his many LPs are a couple of early items on Savoy; several on River., incl. *Jazz At The Showboat* and *Byrd at the Village Vanguard,* two classical solo albums for Washington Records. In 1955-60 he recorded for Col. such albums as *Brazilian Byrd* and *Herb Ellis-Charles Byrd.*

Addr: 6435 Barnaby S., N.W., Washington, D.C. 20015.

BYRD, DONALD,* *trumpet;* b. Detroit, Mich., 12/9/32. First heard in New York in 1955 and well known for his work with the Jazz Messengers and many other small groups, Byrd by 1960 enjoyed the respect of jazz fans both domestically and in Europe, where he had appeared extensively.

In the 1960s he continued to progress on many levels. In the U.S. he worked from time to time in small combos, usually leading a quintet in partnership with Pepper Adams. Much of his time, however, was devoted to studying and teaching. He served as instructor at Music & Art High School, NYC, and at several of the jazz clinics conducted by the National Stage Band Camps.

Byrd acquired two educational degrees, a B.M. and Mus. Ed., and in 1966 was working on his Doctor of Education degree. He received a certificate of attendance for studying with Madame Nadia Boulanger in Paris, where he took up residence in 1963.

His continental appearances included jazz festivals at Juan-les-Pins, France; Recklinghausen, Germany; Stockholm, Sweden; and Molde, Norway. In 1965-6 he worked as arranger for the Norwegian Radio Orchestra.

Concurrently with all these activities Byrd continued his private studies of the classics, of Spanish music and many other music forms. As Nat Hentoff observed, "He is a man of many parts and many interests, and they coalesce with singular impact on his music." Of his trumpet playing, *Down Beat* editor Don DeMicheal remarked, "The sparkle and facility that Byrd has shown of late, added to his lyrical conception, marks him as possibly the best of the Diz-Miles-Brownie disciples." Byrd's mastery of the horn was eloquently explained in an article he wrote for *Down Beat* 1/19/61, entitled *Donald Byrd Talks To Young Trumpeters.* In it, he observed, "The complete mastering of the muscular aspects of brass playing produces ease of playing. The brass player who lacks this kind of mastery usually has a tense, nervous quality in his playing that is conveyed to the audience. And speaking specifically of jazz playing, tension makes it impossible for a player to swing."

Byrd's compositions, which have varied from the purest earthy blues to complex modern lines, include *Cecile, Pure D. Funk, The Cat Walk, Shangri-La, Elijah, Noah,* and *Bossa.*

Byrd's many LPs as leader included two excellent quintet sets recorded at the Half Note Cafe, as well as a series of studio sessions, most of them also with a quintet featuring Pepper Adams. Later he experimented with a new style involving a vocal group on several albums, among them *A New Perspective* and *I'm Tryin' to Get Home.* All the above were on Blue Note; later LPs, from 1965, appeared on Verve.

Addr: c/o Elgy Music Co., 202 Riverside Drive, New York 25, N.Y.

BYRD, GENE (JOE), bass; also *guitar, flute;* b. Chuckatuck, Va., 5/21/33. Brother is Charlie Byrd. Studied at Baltimore Peabody Conservatory, then free-lanced around Baltimore. Joined Charlie Byrd in '64. For tours and appearances see Byrd, Charlie. Favs: Scott La Faro, Keter Betts. LPs: w. Charlie Byrd (River., Col.).

Addr: P.O. Box 19123, Washington 36, D.C.

CACERES, ERNEST (ERNIE), * clarinet, baritone sax; b. Rockport, Tex., 11/22/11. Soloist with swing bands since 1937, inc. Jack Teagarden, Glenn Miller, Benny Goodman and Woody Herman. Since 1960 worked with Billy Butterfield in Newport, Va., area and played numerous concerts with own small combo and big band. Active composer in "progressive dixieland" style.

Addr: c/o Mrs. Lupe Duran, 1610 Laredo St., Corpus Christi, Tex.

CAIN, JACQUELINE RUTH (JACKIE), * singer; b. Milwaukee, Wisc., 5/22/28. Met Roy Kral after moving to Chicago in 1946; worked with Charlie Ventura. For further details see Kral, Roy.

Addr: 4715 Independence Ave., New York City, N.Y. 10471.

CAIOLA, ALEXANDER EMIL (AL), guitar; b. Jersey City, N.J., 9/7/20. First professional job w. CBS staff NYC as sideman. With H. Winterhalter '55, P. Faith '56, A. Kostelanetz '57. Leader and soloist for UA records from 1958. Performed own TV show and acc. Caterina Valente in Rome '62. Ambition is to display versatility of entire guitar family of instruments. Favs: Django Reinhardt, Charlie Christian, Joe Pass. Own LPs: UA. Others: w. Winterhalter (RCA), Faith (Col.), Kostelanetz (Col.).

Addr: 595 Seminole St., Oradell, N.J.

CALDWELL, ALBERT (HAPPY), * tenor sax; b. Chicago, Ill., 7/25/03. Active in traditional jazz from early '20s; played w. Armstrong, Condon, Waller, Hender-

son, own groups, From '60 free-lanced around NYC area w. Louis Metcalf, Jimmy Rushing, others. Led own quintet, playing club dates and at numerous Masonic affairs.

Addr: 207 W. 131st St., New York 27, N.Y.

CALHOUN, EDDIE, bass; b. Clarksdale, Miss., 11/13/21. Says he learned music "in the streets of Chicago." First professional job w. Prince Cooper after Army service. Pl. w. Dick Davis '47-9; Ahmad Jamal '49-52; Horace Henderson '52-4; Johnny Griffin '54; free-lanced w. Roy Eldridge, Billie Holiday, Miles Davis '54-5. Joined Erroll Garner '55 and has since app. w. him in clubs, concerts, TV and festivals throughout U.S., Canada and Europe. Names Wilbur Ware and Red Callender as main influences. Has rec. w. Jamal, Sonny Thompson. LPs: see Garner.

Addr: 6323 Ingleside, Chicago, Ill.

CALLENDER, GEORGE (RED), * tuba, bass; b. Richmond, Va., 3/6/18. Pioneer LA jazz and studio musician; w. Armstrong, L. Young, E. Garner in early '40s. Influenced many modern bassists. Wrote pop hit *Primrose Lane.* On NBC-TV staff, incl. regular Danny Kaye show from '64. Became Hollywood's most requested tuba artist, both for pop and jazz work. With Stan Kenton's LA Neophonic Orch. '65. Monterey JF '62-'64; with C. Mingus at Monterey '64. Own LPs: MGM, Crown. Others: *Mingus At Monterey.*

Addr: 4565 Don Milagro Dr., Los Angeles 8, Calif.

CALVERT, LEON, trumpet; b. England, 1927. Pl. w. Johnny Dankworth '50, later w. Tito Burns, Ken Moule, Dankworth big band, Tony Crombie, Bill Russo's London Jazz Orchestra. LPs w. Moule, Dankworth, Crombie.

CAMERON, JAY, * baritone sax; b. New York, N.Y., 9/14/28. Veteran of several bands both in U.S. and Europe, incl. R. Stewart, W. Herman, M. Ferguson. W. Slide Hampton 1960 thru '62, Paul Winter '63, own quartet w. J. Owens, D. Gojkovic. Toured France w. Hampton '62. Active in Union politics from 1964. Opened music store in Pennsylvania '66. LPs w. Hampton (Atl., Epic); own fav.: Winter's *Jazz on Campus* (Col.).

CANDIDO (Candido Camero), * bongo, conga drums; b. Regal, Havana, Cuba, 4/22/21. Popular Cuban drummer; toured in U.S. from '52 w. Kenton, Gillespie and own groups. 1960 in JATP w. Gillespie, S. Getz. Carnegie Hall concert w. Tony Bennett '62. App. on Mike Wallace TV show '62. Toured '64 w. all-Mexican revue. Took own Latin jazz combo to Virgin Islands, Puerto Rico '65. Candido is one of the most accomplished and widely recorded Latin jazz drummers. Own LPs: Roul., ABC-Par. Others: w. G. Green (Verve), W. Kelly (Verve), W. Montgomery (Verve), S. Rollins (RCA), L. Schifrin (Verve), S. Getz (Verve), D. Byrd (Verve), Willis Jackson (Verve), Joe Williams (RCA).

Addr: c/o Alamac Hotel, Broadway & 71st St., New York 23, N.Y.

CANDOLI, SECONDO (CONTE),* *trumpet;* b. Misha-waka, Ind., 7/12/27. In 1960, ending a six-year association with Howard Rumsey combo at the Lighthouse, Hermosa Beach, Calif., Candoli free-lanced extensively in Hollywood. He was heard with Terry Gibbs' big band off and on 1960-62, and with Woody Herman at Monterey JF in '60. Toured for four months in '61 with Gerry Mulligan's band, including European trip and Verve LPs.

From 1961-6 he was a regular member almost continuously of the Shelly Manne quintet. In addition, he played with TV staff orchestras: Don Trenner's band on Steve Allen Show June '63 to November '64, and the Elliot Lawrence band on Les Crane Show September-October '65. Frequent TV and recordings with Benny Carter.

Candoli has remained a first-class modern soloist, inspired by Gillespie and Davis, and particularly effective in muted ballad moods.

Own LP for Crown, 1961; LP with brother Pete for MGM, '63; Many sessions with Shelly Manne (Cont., Cap.), Steve Allen (Dot).

Addr: 2151 Sunset Crest Dr., Hollywood 46, Calif.

CANDOLI, WALTER JOSEPH (PETE),* *trumpet, composer;* b. Mishawaka, Ind., 6/28/23. With many name bands 1940-53 incl. Goodman, T. Dorsey, Barnet, Herman, Kenton. Own band '54-5. Mainly Hollywood studio work since mid-'50s; occasional rec. sessions w. brother Conte and appearances w. wife, singer Betty Hutton. Own LPs; Somerset, Kapp. LPs w. Conte (Dot, Warner Bros., Merc.)..

Addr: 30 S. Lacendo, Laguna Beach, Calif.

CARISI, JOHN E. (JOHNNY),* *composer, trumpet;* b. Hasbrouck Heights, N.J., 2/23/22. Pl. w. Glenn Miller's US Air Force Band; later w. Claude Thornhill, Charlie Barnet. Carisi sat in at Minton's in the early '40s but did not become widely known until his comp. *Israel* was pl. by the Miles Davis nonet in late '40s. Since then he has continued to write for various jazz and pop combos, and chamber groups. In '60 he took part, acc. a dance company, in a State Dept. tour of S.E. Asia and the Middle East. He did underscoring for *Breaking Point* and Jerry Lewis show on TV '62; chamber piece for NY Saxophone Quartet's Town Hall concert '65; music for Ypsilanti (Mich.) Greek Theater prod. of Aristophanes comedy '66. Three of his comps. are incl. in the Gil Evans album *Into the Hot* (Imp.). Other LP: *A Greek in Dixieland* for Gus Vali (UA).

Addr: 785 West End Ave., New York 25, N.Y.

CARLSON, FRANK L.,* *drums, percussion;* b. New York, N.Y., 5/5/14. Was a drummer w. original Woody Herman band; also rec. w. Glenn Miller, Benny Goodman. Has first-class radio engineer's license. Active at MGM studios, does cartoons, movies and TV shows. Regular on *Dr. Kildare*, etc. Member Neophonic Orch. '65. Was commercial radio engineer.

LPs: w. Stan Kenton, *Kenton Plays Wagner* (Cap.).

Addr: 203 N. Swall Dr., Beverly Hills, Calif.

CARMICHAEL, HOAGLAND HOWARD (HOAGY),* *songwriter, vocalist, piano;* b. Bloomington, Ind., 11/11/1899. Associated with jazz and popular music from '20s, the composer of *Stardust, Rocking Chair, Lazy River* and *Georgia on My Mind* remained active in TV and songwriting during the '60s. Wrote and hosted for Bell Telephone Hour; host for *Project 20* TV ragtime documentary. Wrote and appeared in numerous TV dramas. Two songs for film *Hatari* '61. Visited Japan '61 and '64. Published autobiography *Sometimes I Wonder* '65.

Addr: 9126 Sunset Blvd., Los Angeles 69, Calif.

CARNEY, HARRY HOWELL,* *baritone sax, bass clarinet, clarinet, composer;* b. Boston, Mass., 4/1/10. Joined Duke Ellington band at the age of 16 and has remained with him ever since. His four decades of contributions to the Ellington annals have made Carney the longest-lasting sideman in any orchestra in jazz history. More important, they have established him as the first and greatest performer on baritone saxophone, creator of a rich, deep sound that has never been duplicated. He is as important in his role as anchor man of the reed section as he is in a solo capacity. His occasional bass clarinet solos were the first ever to make extensive use of this instrument in jazz. As a writer, Carney is best known as co-composer with Duke Ellington of *Rockin' in Rhythm* in 1930.

LPs: See Ellington, Duke, and Ellington, Mercer.

Addr: 450 West 147th St., New York 31, N.Y.

CARR, BRUNO,* *drums;* b. Bronx, N.Y., 2/9/28. Cousin of Connie Kay of MJQ. Self-taught. Prof. boxer for seven years; Army, 1951-3. Bouncer in NYC club '53-55. Pl. w. Ray Charles (incl. European tour) '60-2; Sarah Vaughan, Betty Carter, '63; Lou Donaldson, Shirley Scott, '64, also w. Herman Foster, Abbey Lincoln, Bill Davis, Jean DuShon. Toured with Herbie Mann Septet '65-6. Favs: Sid Catlett, Jo Jones, Philly Joe Jones. LPs w. Ray Charles (ABC-Par.), Joan Shaw (Sue).

Addr: 2050 Valentine Ave., Bronx, N.Y.

CARR, IAN,* *trumpet, fluegelhorn;* b. Dumfries, Scotland, 4/21/33. Degree in Eng. Lit. at Durham Univ. Many unusual jobs before deciding on jazz career in '60. Pl. and rec. w. Emcee Five '60-2, then moved to London and pl. briefly w. Harold McNair before joining Don Rendell, with whom he has remained. Also founder-member of New Jazz Orch '63, leader and arr. of Animals Big Band from '65, and pl. w. Joe Harriott from '65. Wrote prizewinning film score for '63 Paris Biennale, pl. by himself, Jeff Clyne, Laurie Morgan. LPs w. Rendell (Brit. Col.), New Jazz Orch. (Brit. Decca), Michael Garrick (Brit. Argo).

Addr: 34 England's Lane, London N.W.3, England.

CARROLL, JOE (BEBOP),* *singer;* b. Philadelphia, Pa., 11/25/19. Featured with Dizzy Gillespie, 1949-53; later free lanced. Recorded an album, *Joe Carroll—*

Man With A Happy Sound, in 1962 for the since defunct Charlie Parker label. In 1964-5 he toured as vocalist with the Woody Herman orchestra and recorded *Wa Wa Blues* with Herman (Philips).

CARTER, BENNETT LESTER (BENNY),* *composer, alto saxophone;* b. New York City, 8/8/07. Though best known in the 1930s and '40s as one of the two or three foremost alto sax soloists in jazz, and as an occasional performer on trumpet, clarinet and other instruments, Carter by 1960 was so busy writing and arranging music that he rarely had time to play. Among his assignments were the Alfred Hitchcock show and many scores in 1963-5 for the Chrysler Theater TV series. He also acted as musical director for Peggy Lee in clubs and on records, 1961-2. Arr. & cond. albums for Sarah Vaughan, Pearl Bailey, Lou Rawls, Keely Smith et al. Two albums of original instrumentals for Count Basie band. Visited Australia with own quartet, 1960; Europe with JATP late '60. Collaborated with the author on 1962 Prestige record date (*B.B.B. & Co.*) and led combo that supplied background music for TV series *Feather On Jazz*, 1965. Own LPs on Impulse, VJ; *JATP in Europe* (Verve).
Addr: 2325 Kimridge Road, Beverly Hills, Calif.

CARTER, BETTY (Lillie Mae Jones),* *singer;* b. Flint, Mich., 5/16/30. This entirely jazz-oriented singer continued her career as a solo artist in leading nightclubs and theatres in the U.S. She appeared in a jazz concert tour of Japan with Sonny Rollins for a month in 1963 and worked at Annie Ross' club in London in 1964. LPs: *'Round Midnight* (Atco), *Inside Betty Carter* (UA), *Ray Charles and Betty Carter* (ABC-Par.).
Addr: 881 So. 15th St., Newark, N.J.

CARTER, RONALD LEVIN (RON),* *bass, cello;* also *violin, clarinet, trombone, tuba.* b. Ferndale, Mich., 5/4/37. Studied music at Detroit Cass Tech HS; Eastman School of Music at Rochester, N.Y., from which he obtained a B.M. '59; Manhattan School of Music, earning an M.M. '61. W. Eastman Philharmonia Orch. under Howard Hanson before first jazz gig w. Chico Hamilton. Much free-lance work with modern groups, including E. Dolphy, J. Adderley, Jaki Byard, R. Weston, B. Timmons. Earned greater recognition after joining Miles Davis in 1963. In Europe '63, '64 and Japan '64 w. Davis as part of Davis' radical and exciting rhythm section w. Herbie Hancock and Tony Williams. W. Friedrich Gulda in Europe '65. Won DB New Star Award for bass '65. On faculty of several summer jazz clinics.
As an accompanist, Carter's sense of time supports the most demanding artists. Byard describes his "time, tone and technique" as "brilliant." He also recorded as a cellist, and has expressed interest in expanding the use of the cello within its own framework. Of his cello, Pete Welding said, "Carter at times appears to be playing duets with himself . . . He has complete command of the instrument." Carter's solos and rhythm

work have had a profound effect on the new generation of bassists in the '60s.
Own LP: *Where?* (Pres.). Others: w. Davis, *Seven Steps to Heaven, In Europe, My Funny Valentine, E.S.P.* (Col.); Dolphy, *Out There, Far Cry* (Pres.); Don Ellis (Pres.); Jaki Byard (Pres.); Charles Lloyd (Col.); Mal Waldron (Pres.).
Addr: 156-20 Riverside Dr. West, #16D, New York 32, N.Y.

CARY, RICHARD DURANT (DICK),* *piano, trumpet, mellophone, alto horn, composer;* b. Hartford, Conn., 7/10/16. With many of best Dixieland and traditional groups during '40s and '50s, incl. Armstrong, Goodman, Condon, Hackett as soloist and arranger. Moved to LA in '59, free-lancing w. Red Nichols, Bob Crosby, Ben Pollack, Matty Matlock, Barnum and Bailey Circus, Disneyland. Toured Australia, New Zealand and Japan w. Condon '64. At Monterey JF '64 w. Pee Wee Russell. Greatly expanded writing activities, composing and arranging numerous charts for large bands and small groups. Private teacher of brass and piano. LPs: w. Condon (Epic), Hackett, Jimmy and Marian McPartland, Matlock.
Addr: 9828 Wornom Ave., Sunland, Calif.

CASTRO, JOSEPH (JOE),* *piano, composer;* b. Miami, Ariz., 8/15/27. For several months in 1960, Castro, Teddy Edwards, Leroy Vinnegar and Billy Higgins formed an excellent quartet that played at clubs in Hollywood. From '61 to Feb. '63 Castro served as musical director and arranger for singer Tony Martin. Since then he has divided his time between Honolulu and Hollywood. He has also accompanied several singers, among them June Christy, off and on since 1960 (including visit to Australia in '63), and Anita O'Day. In 1965 he formed a record company, Clover, producing sessions in Hawaii and the U.S.
LPs with Teddy Edwards (Contemp., Pac. Jazz), *Anita O'Day Sings Rodgers and Hart* (Verve), *Cool School* with June Christy (Cap.) and various sessions on Clover.
Addr: P.O. Box 8822, Honolulu, Hawaii.

CATLETT, GEORGE JAMES (BUDDY),* *bass;* also *saxophones, clarinet;* b. Long Beach, Calif., 5/13/33. Played w. Cal Tjader, Quincy Jones during late '50s. Joined Chico Hamilton in '61; w. Eddie Davis and Johnny Griffin '62, Count Basie Sept. '62 until Aug. '64, Maynard Ferguson for the remainder of '64, Coleman Hawkins early '65, Louis Armstrong from May '65. Toured Europe and Japan w. Basie '63, Europe w. Armstrong '65. LPs: w. Basie (Repr., Verve), Jones (Impulse), Curtis Fuller (Impulse), Davis-Griffin (Jazzl.).
Addr: 466 Berriman St., Brooklyn, N.Y.

CAVALLI, PIERRE, *guitar;* b. Zurich, Switzerland, 7/12/28. Parents amateur musicians. Studied violin from age of five. Settled in Paris '53 and free-lanced there w. Michel Legrand, Michel Magne, Quincy Jones, others, and wrote commercial arrangements and film scores. Went to Germany, appeared and recorded w. small jazz groups. With Friedrich Gulda in concerts in Vienna, Munich. TV appearances in Germany, Switzerland, Belgium. At Antibes, other European JFs. Only U.S. appearance was at Las Vegas Sands Hotel. Favs: Christian, Kessel, Wes Montgomery. LPs: w. Stephane Grappelly (Atl.), Gulda (Col.).

Addr: Rue Pepinet 5, Lausanne, Switzerland.

CAVANAUGH, WALTER PAGE,* *piano, singer;* b. Cherokee, Kans., 1/26/22. Led popular trio in Hollywood in 1940s. Worked local clubs with various small groups in 1950s. In 1962 he formed a seven-piece group, "The Page 7," which appeared on the Ed Sullivan and Johnny Carson TV shows and in person at Basin Street East in NYC, as well as in clubs in Studio City, Calif., with one of which he was active as co-owner. The group achieved a bright, cohesive sound that had an unusual instrumentation including two bass trumpets doubling on trombone. It is well represented in *Impact at Basin Street East* and *The Page 7* (RCA).

Addr: 11521 Moorpark St., No. Hollywood, Calif.

CAVE, JAY, *bass;* b. Altoona, Pa., 7/2/32. Mother taught piano, brothers are classical musicians. Studied woodwinds and piano before bass. First jazz gig w. Jon Eardley. Toured w. Ralph Sharon '54, Chris Connor '54-'55. W. Billie Holiday '57, Red Rodney '58, Nina Simone '58. Joined Al Hirt '65. Appeared on Hirt's TV series summer '65, Carnegie Hall concert May '65. Fav: Ray Brown. Infl: Rudy Black. LPs: w. Sharon (Beth.), Hirt (RCA); own fav. work on Rodney's *Red Rodney Returns* (Cadet).

Addr: 4030 Cortland Ave., Altoona, Pa.

CECIL, MALCOLM, *bass;* b. London, England, 1/9/37. Pl. w. Don Rendell, Ronnie Scott-Tubby Hayes Jazz Couriers, Dill Jones from '56, in R.A.F. '58-61. Then w. Vic Ash-Harry Klein '62, w. Jackie McLean and Freddie Redd in *The Connection.* '63-4 resident at Ronnie Scott's as member of Stan Tracey Trio, acc. Stan Getz, Johnny Griffin, Roland Kirk, J. J. Johnson, and many others. Left to join B.B.C. Radio Orch. Pl. in Sweden w. Dizzy Reece '56, w. Ronnie Scott '63. Has also been electronics consultant since '61. LPs w. Ash-Klein (Brit. Tempo), Ernest Ranglin (Brit. Island), Dick Morrissey (Brit. Fontana).

Addr: 125 Sutherland Ave., London W.9, England.

CEROLI, NICK, *drums;* b. Warren, Ohio, 12/22/39. Played in Youngstown and Cincinnati while in school before joining Ralph Marterie in '58. Bet. '59 and '65 worked in Chicago, Las Vegas and LA w. Marterie, Ray Anthony, Lionel Hampton, Gerald Wilson, Les Brown, Debbie Reynolds, Terry Gibbs, Stan Kenton. In LA Neophonic Orch. '66. W. Tijuana Brass from '65. Monterey JF '63 w. Wilson. Toured Mexico, S. America '63 w. Anthony. Favs: P. J. Jones, E. Jones, B. Rich. LPs: w. Kenton (Cap.), Ann Richards (VJ), Tijuana Brass (A & M).

Addr: 8126 Alcove, North Hollywood, Calif.

CHAMBERS, HENDERSON CHARLES,* *trombone;* b. Alexandria, La., 5/1/08. A prominent big band musician since the early 1930s, heard occasionally as a soloist with small recording combos such as Buck Clayton's (Col.) and Jimmy Rushing's (Vanguard). After free-lancing around NYC, joined Ray Charles ('61) and toured with him until Dec. '63. Joined Count Basie Jan. '64 and has worked with him mainly as a section member, not heard in recorded solos.

Addr: 246 W. 150th St., New York 39, N.Y.

CHAMBERS, JOSEPH ARTHUR (JOE), *drums;* b. Stoneacre, Va., 6/25/42. Brother a composer. Studied drums in Chester, Pa. First job w. Eric Dolphy Sept. '63-Feb. '64. Then w. Freddie Hubbard Mar. '64-May '65, L. Donaldson '65, Jimmy Giuffre and Andrew Hill from '65. W. Giuffre at Avant-Garde Festival, Judson Hall NYC Sept. '65; w. Hill at Toronto U. concert '65. Favs. and infl: M. Roach, E. Jones, K. Clarke, R. Haynes. Chambers is a sensitive and melodic drummer whose style is his own. LPs: w. Hubbard, Bobby Hutcherson (BN); Archie Shepp (Imp.).

Addr: 127 W. 82nd St., New York, N.Y.

CHAMBERS, PAUL LAURENCE DUNBAR JR.,* *bass;* b. Pittsburgh, Pa., 4/22/35. Combo work in Detroit 1949-54; NYC from '55, off and on w. Miles Davis. After leaving Davis in '63, teamed with two other former Davis sidemen, Wynton Kelly and Jimmy Cobb, to form trio, remaining with this group for 2½ years, then free-lancing and with Tony Scott at Dom, NYC, 1966. LPs w. Kelly (Verve), Davis (Col.).

Addr: 176 West 87th St., New York 24, N.Y.

CHARLES, RAY (Ray Charles Robinson),* *singer, piano, composer, organ, alto saxophone;* b. Albany, Ga., 9/23/32. Blind from age six, orphaned at 15, he worked with many bands around Fla. from 1947 and in Seattle from 1950, when he led a trio. Rec. for Atlantic in '52, with studio group; first rec. w. own band Nov. '54. From 1954-9 he turned out a steady flow of blues and gospel-style jazz hits and in May '59 made his first session with strings.

Charles began recording for ABC-Par. in 1960 and promptly produced what is known in the recording trade as a "smash hit single," *Georgia On My Mind.* Though he never renounced the blues, during the next few years he leaned more and more heavily on commercial backgrounds, popular songs and standards, with an occasional blues or blues-like popular song included for variety. His biggest hits included *Ruby, Hit the Road Jack, I Can't Stop Loving You, Born to Lose, Busted, Crying Time* and *What I Say.*

As had been the case with innumerable other artists who moved from simple, folk-derived beginnings to elaborate and lucrative ends and a mass popular following, Charles was harshly rebuked by jazz critics. He initiated a new trend by recording two albums entitled *Modern Sounds in Country and Western Music.* Pete Welding wrote that the songs provided Charles "mighty little to work with," had a "whimpering, lachrymose sameness" and were greatly disappointing. The records, however, were tremendously popular and sold in the millions.

Charles' great popularity overseas enabled him to play successful concerts in France, Belgium, Sweden, Germany and Switzerland in May-June 1962. He also took an acting role in a picture filmed in Ireland, *Ballad in Blue*, and sang the sound track theme for an American film, *The Cincinnati Kid*.

After six months of inactivity from August 1965, Charles organized a new big band and went on the road in March 1966. His accompanying vocal quartet, the Raelets, was also reorganized. In addition to the singing and playing he was by now involved in many business activities, including the operation of a record company, Tangerine, on which his new releases appeared as well as records by other artists under his sponsorship. Charles and the band travel in his own private plane. He has studied engineering extensively and has detected and fixed mechanical difficulties with the plane where sighted men have failed.

The tragedies of his personal life (which included, according to Charles' own statements, narcotics addiction from the age of 16 until he cured himself in 1965) lent a poignancy to his blues interpretations that had no equal in the jazz of the late 1950s and early '60s. Nevertheless, his uncanny faculty for choosing unlikely material and bringing new life to it has succeeded more often than not in justifying the diversification of his performances in the '60s. Whether judged as jazz or pop artist, singer or instrumentalist, bop pianist or funky blues soloist, Charles has maintained a rare level of authenticity and urgent honesty on these many levels.

LPs: All early albums on Atlantic. Best are *The Ray Charles Story*, two LPs spanning 1952-9 (Atl. 2-900) and *The Great Hits of Ray Charles Recorded on 8-Track Stereo* (SD 7101). *Genius + Soul = Jazz*, mainly instrumental with Charles playing organ, is on Impulse A-2. Among the many vocal LPs on ABC-Paramount are *Genius Hits The Road* (incl. *Georgia*) on 335, *Ingredients in a Recipe for Soul* (465) and *Ray Charles Live in Concert* (500).

Addr: RPM Enterprises, 2107 W. Washington Blvd., Los Angeles 18, Calif.

CHARLES, TEDDY (Theodore Charles Cohen), * *vibes, composer;* b. Chicopee Falls, Mass., 4/13/28. Worked with many combos and bands in New York, 1946 until mid-'50s; later became active as writer and recording combo leader in a series of projects he called "New Directions." Since 1956 has been a&r man for numerous record companies incl. Prestige, Warwick, Motown. Organized own record company, Polaris, '65. Semi-annual college concert tours throughout East and Midwest since '64 leading New Directions quintet.

Charles was one of the first important writers in a vein later known as third stream. Since 1961 has divided his professional life between music and sailing; he owns two schooner yachts and is dir. of a sailing club. Presented live jazz concerts under sail, summer '66. LPs: *Jazz at the Museum of Modern Art* (Warwick); *Russia Goes Jazz* (UA).

Addr: c/o Radio Registry, 850 7th Ave., New York City, N.Y. 10019.

CHERICO, EUGENE V. (GENE), *bass;* b. Buffalo, N.Y., 4/15/35. Started as drummer, pl. in Army band, but as a result of a train accident in Germany in 1955 took up bass as physical therapy for right arm. Stud. at Berklee Sch. Living in Boston, worked w. Toshiko Akiyoshi off and on from 1957, also Herb Pomeroy '57-9, Maynard Ferguson '59-60, Red Norvo '61, Benny Goodman '62, Geo. Shearing '63, Stan Getz '64-5, Peggy Lee '66. Favs: O. Pettiford, R. Mitchell, P. Chambers, Ray Brown. LPs w. Joe Morello, Gary Burton, Paul Desmond (RCA); Toshiko, Getz (Verve).

CHERRY, DONALD E. (DON), * *trumpet;* b. Oklahoma City, Okla., 11/18/36. First heard in New York in late 1959 as a front line associate of Ornette Coleman in the latter's quintet, Cherry recorded a series of albums with Coleman. They later broke up and Cherry left for Europe, where he has been active much of the time since Aug. 1964. Also pl. w. Sonny Rollins '63. For a while he was heard leading his own international quintet on the Continent. Although heard earlier playing a so-called "pocket trumpet," during his European travels he used this instrument less frequently, stating he preferred the cornet and was an admirer of the work of such earlier cornetists as Louis Armstrong and Bix Beiderbecke.

In his own playing Cherry remained firmly entrenched in the "new movement," expressing admiration for such musicians as Eric Dolphy and Albert Ayler, and for Indian music.

LPs w. Coleman, Coltrane (Atl.); Rollins (RCA); Steve Lacy (Pres.).

CHISHOLM, GEORGE, * *trombone, leader;* b. Glasgow, Scotland, 3/29/15. Despite the extraordinary Teagarden-like talent that had earned him a job with Benny Carter in the 1930s, Chisholm in the 1960s found himself working with a comedy-oriented vaudeville show. He was also active in TV, film and recording work, and in occasional BBC *Jazz Club* dates as soloist and with various groups. LPs: *Trad Treat* and *Music for Romantics* (Philips).

Addr: 5, Oakwood View, Southgate, London N. 14, England.

CHRISTY, JUNE, * *singer;* b. Springfield, Ill., 11/20/25. Sang with Stan Kenton band 1945-9 and has occasionally been reunited with him for concerts. Married in 1946 to saxophonist Bob Cooper, who accompanied her on overseas tours in the late '50s.

Miss Christy, one of the first and best band singers in a style originally associated with Anita O'Day, has continued to appear in night clubs intermittently. She visited Australia and played concerts in Japan in '64; England in '65 for a night club engagement. Among

79

her best LPs in recent years have been *Off Beat, Big Band Special* and *Do Re Me* (Cap.).

Addr: 3548 Stonewood Dr., Sherman Oaks, Calif.

CIRILLO, WALLACE JOSEPH (WALLY),* *piano, composer;* b. Huntington, N.Y. 2/4/27. Active as classical composer and pianist w. John La Porta and Charles Mingus through 1960. Settled in Florida in '60, taught in Palm Beach Co. public schools '61. Led own group Ft. Lauderdale-Miami area '62-'65. Guest soloist w. Flip Phillips, Phil Napoleon in Fla. Teaches privately and composes.

Addr: 480 N.E. 24th St., Boca Raton, Fla.

CLARE, ALAN, *piano;* b. London, England, 5/31/21. First professional mus. job on stage at age of eleven. Pl. w. Carlo Krahmer, Sid Phillips, and duets on piano and accordion w. George Shearing. Joined Sid Millward '42 in Army, pl. w. him until '49. Then w. Stephane Grappelly until '51. Since then worked as soloist in London clubs, making the Studio Club a leading London jazz center during a six-year engagement. Comp. background scores for films *Seven Keys, The Specialist.* Own LPs on Brit. labels—Dec., Pye.

Addr: 86a Holland Park, London W.11, England.

CLARKE, BUCK, *bongos, conga;* b. Washington, D.C., 1932. Began playing bongos at 16. After two years working in New Orleans and two years in the Army, pl. w. Arnett Cobb combo, then jobbed around Washington. Doubled as an artist, on the staff of the Smithsonian Institution; at a showing of his paintings, introduced his first trio. The next year, 1959, the group was enlarged to quintet size. Own LPs: *Drum Sum; Sound* (Cadet).

CLARK, CONRAD YEATIS (SONNY),* *piano;* b. Herminie, Pa., 7/21/31. The gifted Powell-influenced pianist was associated w. the Buddy De Franco Quartet for three years in the mid-1950s; also w. Wardell Gray, Oscar Pettiford and later with H. Rumsey's Lighthouse All Stars; free-lanced in NYC from 1957-62. Hospitalized late in '62 with a leg infection, he was released early in Jan. '63, but a few days later, 1/13/63, died of a heart attack in NYC. Own LPs: Time, BN. Also represented on LPs w. De Franco (Verve), Curtis Fuller, Clifford Jordan, Johnny Griffin (BN).

CLARKE, KENNETH SPEARMAN (KENNY, KLOOK),* *drums, leader, composer;* b. Pittsburgh, Pa., 1/9/14. Clarke, considered the first great pioneer of modern drums, was a close associate of Dizzy Gillespie in the '40s and a founder-member of the Modern Jazz Quartet, 1952-5. After frequent long visits to France he took up permanent residence there late in 1956, dividing most of his time between Paris and Figanieres, a small village in Southern France. Constantly in demand for a variety of studio and club engagements, Clarke achieved much prominence between 1960 and '66 through a series of six albums made in collaboration with pianist-arranger Francy Boland, under the name of the *Clarke-Boland Big Band.* He also did

combo work with Jimmy Woode, Ake Persson and Sahib Shihab, and occasionally played an executive role as a producer in Paris studios.

Ralph J. Gleason accurately assessed Clarke's contribution when he wrote, "I have a suspicion that Kenny Clarke, placed in the rhythm section of almost any group, is the equal of half a dozen poll winners, several thousand volts and the pocket history of jazz."

LPs with Clarke-Boland groups: Atl., Blue Note, Col.; also with Dizzy Gillespie and Double Six of Paris (Philips).

Addr: 142 bis Rue de Rosny, Montreuil sous bois, Seine, France.

CLARKE, TERENCE MICHAEL (TERRY), *drums;* b. Vancouver, B.C., Canada, 8/20/44. Played drums around Vancouver from 1959 with local groups and w. B. Kessel, V. Guaraldi. First U.S. appearance w. John Handy Quintet at Both/And Club in San Francisco and Monterey J. F. '65. LP: w. Handy (Col.).

Addr: 4027 W. 27th, Vancouver, B.C., Canada.

CLAYTON, WILBUR (BUCK),* *trumpet, composer;* b. Parsons, Kansas, 11/12/11. From 1936 to '43 Clayton was a mainstay of the Count Basie band. After Army service '43-6, he was a member of JATP for two years. Pl. w. Joe Bushkin's quartet in NYC '51-3. Since then he has free-lanced, mostly in NYC, and made many foreign tours beginning w. own combo as part of Newport JF show in Europe fall '59. In December '62 he ret. to France, where he had pl. in '49 and '53, to pl. at the 30th anniversary celebration of the Hot Club of France. In June '63 pl. at Britain's Manchester Jazz Fest., then concerts w. Humphrey Lyttelton in Switzerland. Pl. in Australia, Japan, winter '64. Clayton has often pl. in Toronto and ret. to England several times for engagements. His writings as well as his playing can be heard in a Nat Pierce album for RCA, *Big Band at the Savoy Ballroom,* rec. in '57 but released in the '60s. Other LPs on French Vogue and English Col.

Addr: 145-31 Glassboro Ave., Jamaica 35, N.Y.

CLEVELAND, JAMES MILTON (JIMMY),* *trombone;* b. Wartrace, Tenn., 5/3/26. One of most listened-to trombonists of the '50s, Cleveland continued his extensive NYC recording and free-lancing in a variety of fields. Played in TV and film soundtracks incl. *The Hustler, Mr. Broadway, East Side West Side, Kiss Her Good-By,* Quincy Jones' score for *A Man Called Adam.* In orch. for Broadway show *Funny Girl* '65-'66, some TV commercials. Own LP: Emarcy. Others: w. J. J. Johnson, K. Burrell, Jimmy Smith, Gil Evans, D. Byrd, S. Turrentine.

Addr: 618 Ashford St., Brooklyn 7, N.Y.

CLYNE, JEFFREY (JEFF), *bass;* b. London, England, 1/29/37. Pl. and rec. w. Ronnie Scott-Tubby Hayes Jazz Couriers, Vic Ash, Tony Kinsey, Gordon Beck successively since '58. Also free improvisation from '61 w. New Departures jazz and jazz-poetry gps., and currently w. Peter Lemer. Toured Europe w. Hayes '64 and '65, Israel w. Tony Crombie '63, TV w. Stan Tracey in Eng. and Germany '66. A skilled jazz bassist, and the most impressive British new-thing player on his instrument. Fav. LPs w. Stan Tracey (Brit. Col.), New Departures (Brit. Transatlantic).

Addr: 12 Hall Gate, Hall Rd., London N.W.8, England.

COBB, WILBUR JAMES (JIMMY),* drums; b. Washington, D.C., 1/20/29. Worked for several years with Dinah Washington, later with C. Adderley, S. Getz, D. Gillespie and from 1958-63 w. Miles Davis. He then joined forces with two other former members of the Davis group, bassist Paul Chambers and pianist Wynton Kelly. Under the name of the Wynton Kelly Trio they played night clubs and concerts. In 1965-6 they were jointly featured with guitarist Wes Montgomery. The trio was part of an all-star group led by J. J. Johnson that toured Japan in the summer of 1964.

LPs with Miles Davis (Col.), Wes Montgomery, Wynton Kelly (Verve).

Addr: 610 W. 150th St., Apt. 1A, New York City, N.Y.

COE, ANTHONY GEORGE (TONY),* alto sax, clarinet, composer; b. Canterbury, Eng., 11/29/34. Left Lyttelton to co-lead gp. w. John Picard '62-4, then rejoined Lyttelton. Invited to join Count Basie '65, but deal fell through. Also much arr. work for Lyttelton and commercial groups, and tutoring at teachers' training coll. Feat. soloist w. Birmington Symphony Orch. on Rhapsody in Blue '64. Toured Europe and U.S.A. w. Lyttelton. Pl. mainly tenor sax since '60, in style infl. by Paul Gonsalves, and treats other instruments similarly. Own LP on Brit. Fontana. LPs w. Lyttelton (Brit. Society, Brit. Col.) Also rec. w. Lenny Felix, Kenny Baker, Nat Gonella.

Addr: 17 Seymour Place, Canterbury, Kent, England.

COHN, ALVIN GILBERT (AL),* tenor sax, composer; also baritone sax, clarinets; b. Brooklyn, N.Y. 11/24/25. One of main exponents of swinging small band jazz during 1950s, esp. in quintet co-led with Zoot Sims. Played regularly from late '50s w. Sims, incl. 12-16 weeks per year at NYC Half Note; also other Eastern cities and London. Became more active as arranger. Arrs. include Lady Chatterley's Mother for Gerry Mulligan, Air Mail Special for Quincy Jones, an LP for Jimmy Rushing and others for Terry Gibbs. Played two seasons for Sid Caesar TV show and two Max Liebman TV specials. Own LP: w. Sims (Merc.); w. Brookmeyer, Gary McFarland (Verve). LPs as arr: w. Jones (Merc.), Mulligan (Verve), Rushing (Colpix).

Addr: 244 W. 48th St., New York 36, N.Y.

COHN, GEORGE THOMAS (SONNY), trumpet; b. Chicago, Ill., 3/14/25. Inspired by Roy Eldridge and Charlie Shavers, he started playing as a child and worked with many bands in Chicago including Walter Dyett 1943-5, Red Saunders off and on 1945-60.

Worked at Regal Theatre with many bands passing through Chicago. Also played with Louis Bellson, Erskine Hawkins. Left Chicago to join Count Basie band 1960. Has done mainly section work but is heard in occasional solos including Shanghaied in On My Way And Shoutin' Again (Verve), Amoroso in The Legend (Roul.), Meetin' Time in Kansas City Suite (Roul.). Many solos in Duke Jordan album on Charlie Parker label.

Addr: 225 So. Honore St., Chicago, Ill.

COKER, CHARLES MITCHELL (DOLO), piano; also alto sax; b. Hartford, Conn., 11/16/27. Raised in Florence, S.C.; first studied music there and at Mather Academy, Camden, S.C. First gigs as pianist around Philadelphia. W. Ben Webster '46, Kenny Dorham '55, S. Stitt '55-'57, G. Ammons '58, Lou Donaldson '58, E. Hawkins '59, Ruth Brown '59, Clyde McPhatter '59, P. J. Jones '59, Dexter Gordon '60-'61 incl. stage production of The Connection. Led own trio LA from '61. Although basically a product of the Bud Powell school, Coker lists as his favs. and influences Art Tatum, Hank Jones and Red Garland. LPs: w. Stitt (Roost), w. L. McCann (Pac. Jazz), w. Gordon, Junior Cook (Jazzl.) w. P. J. Jones (River.), w. Dorham (ABC-Par.). Own fav. work, Art Pepper's Intensity (Contemp.).

Addr: 2310 Cloverdale, Los Angeles 16, Calif.

COKER, HENRY,* trombone; b. Dallas, Texas, 12/24/19. With Benny Carter, Eddie Heywood in 1940s. Joined Count Basie '52 and remained for 11 years. Toured with new Ray Charles band 1966. LPs: see Basie (Verve, Roul., Reprise).

Addr: 116-12 Nashville Blvd., Gambria Heights 11, N.Y.

COKER, JERRY,* educator, arranger, tenor sax; b. South Bend, Ind., 11/28/32. Toured with Woody Herman orchestra 1953-4; later settled on West Coast, also played concert tour with Stan Kenton. Attended Yale U. in '58 on a composition scholarship.

In 1960s Coker became prominent as a jazz educator and leader of college bands. He headed the jazz program at Sam Houston State College in 1960, '61 and '62; Monterey Penisula Coll. '63 and '64; Indiana U. '65 and Miami U. in fall of '66. His jazz ensemble from Indiana U. took first place in the Intercollegiate Festival at Notre Dame in May '65.

From Jan.-May '66 Coker took the I.U. ensemble on a 15-week tour of the Near East under State Department auspices, visiting 12 countries and making a tremendous impact on audiences everywhere.

Coker's book, Improvising Jazz, was published by Prentice Hall in '64.

LP: Extension with Clare Fischer (Pacific Jazz).

Addr: 1310 N. Woodlawn, Bloomington, Ind.

COLE, EDWIN LE MAR (BUDDY),* piano, organ; b. Irving, Ill., 12/15/16. Best known as accompanist for many years to Bing Crosby, Judy Garland, Nat Cole

81

Hank Crawford *(Atlantic Records)*

David Newman *(Randi W. Hultin)*

Charles Lloyd

Sal Nistico *(Roberto Polillo)*

Joe Morello *(Columbia Records)*

Sonny Stitt *(Roberto Polillo)*

Clare Fischer *(William Claxton)*

Yank Lawson *(ABC-Paramount Records)*

Wynton Kelly (*MGM/Verve Records*)

John Tchicai (*Paul Minsart*)

Lambert, Hendricks and Ross

Johnny Lytle (*Al Benderson*)

Ray Brown (*Chuck Stewart*)

Illinois Jacquet and Leonard Feather (*Joe Alper*)

Ethel Ennis

Roy Eldridge (*Roberto Polillo*)

Billie Holiday

Earl "Fatha" Hines

Lee Morgan *(Francis Wolff-Blue Note Records)*

Charles Mingus (*Roberto Polillo*)

Shirley Scott *(Impulse Records)*

Kenny Clarke *(Roberto Polillo)*

Martial Solal *(Roberto Polillo)*

Oscar Brown, Jr.

Anthony Williams (*Francis Wolff-Blue Note Records*)   Gary Burton

Benny Carter (*Impulse Records*)   Paul Horn

John Patton *(Francis Wolff-Blue Note Records)*   Clara Ward *(Monte Kay)*

Bud Powell *(Randi W. Hultin)*

Cannonball Adderley *(Capitol Records)*

Birdland *(Leonard Feather)*

Igor Berukshtis and Boris Midney *(Impulse Records)*

Johnny Hodges

Clark Terry *(Impulse Records)*

Dizzy Gillespie (*Charles Frizzell*)

94

Cleo Laine *(Roy Burchell)*

Lou Rawls *(Capitol Records)*

Art Farmer *(Roberto Polillo)*

Charlie Byrd

Pepper Adams *(Francis Wolff)*

Karin Krog and Dexter Gordon *(Randi W. Hultin)*

Manny Albam *(Impulse Records)*

Stanley Turrentine *(Francis Wolff-Blue Note Records)*

Frank Sinatra and Count Basie

and other singers, Cole died of a heart attack 11/5/64 in No. Hollywood, Calif.

COLE, WILLIAM R. (COZY),* *drums;* b. East Orange, N.J., 10/17/09. One of most popular and most recorded swing drummers. First records w. Jelly Roll Morton 1930; then w. Calloway, Armstrong, Hines, Teagarden bands and radio, TV and movie work. Began leading own combos '58 after making hit single *Topsy.* Toured West Africa w. quintet for State Dept. cultural exchange '62-'63. Frequent appearances at NYC Metropole. Featured on A. Godfrey, G. Moore and S. Allen TV shows. Cole, adaptable to most musical situations, still puts on an exciting performance. Own LPs: Parker, Coral.

Addr: 1326 College Ave., Bronx 56, N.Y.

COLE, NAT "KING" (Nathaniel Adams Coles),* *singer, piano;* b. Montgomery, Ala., 3/17/17. Formed the original King Cole Trio in 1939 and made his first hit record, *Straighten Up and Fly Right,* in '43. Originally prominent as a pianist (he won the Esquire Gold award in this category 1946), Cole relegated his piano work and his trio into the background during the 1950s, when he was heard mainly as a singer of popular songs. He was featured in a number of movies, among them *St. Louis Blues,* in which he played the role of W. C. Handy. In the early 1960s, in addition to touring internationally as a solo artist, Cole from time to time presented his own musical revues, among them *Merry World of Nat King Cole* at the Greek Theatre in Los Angeles 1961 and *Sights and Sounds,* which toured in '63. In 1964 he completed what was to be his last motion picture, *Cat Ballou.* In December of that year he was operated on for a malignant tumor. He died in a Santa Monica hospital 2/15/65. Shortly after his death Mrs. Maria Cole, his widow, announced the formation of The Nat King Cole Cancer Foundation.

Though the tonal quality of Cole's voice lent a jazz character to some of his up-tempo songs, Cole in the later years was essentially a popular-music figure. His years as a jazz singer and/or Hines-influenced pianist are best represented by the following LPs: *Nat King Cole In the Beginning* (Decca 8260); *Nat Cole at JATP,* 1944 concert with Norman Granz (VSP 14); *The King Cole Trio* (Cap. 2311); *After Midnight,* in which the Trio is augmented by guest soloists Willie Smith, Stuff Smith, Harry Edison, Juan Tizol (Cap. 782); *The Swinging Side of Nat King Cole,* a vocal album in which he is accompanied by all the sidemen of the Count Basie band (Cap. 1724). On five tracks of another vocal album, *Let's Face The Music,* Cole briefly plays Hammond organ solos (Cap. 2008).

The Nat King Cole Story, a three-volume album and booklet, containing newly recorded versions of many of Cole's hits through 1960, is available on Cap. SWCL 1613.

COLEMAN, WILLIAM JOHNSON (BILL),* *trumpet, singer,* b. Paris, Ky., 8/4/04. With many bands overseas in 1930s; Teddy Wilson, Andy Kirk, John Kirby in NYC early '40s; living in France since Dec. '48, often touring around Continent. First British tour, acc. by Bruce Turner's English band, spring 1966. A greatly underrated soloist with warm tone and gently swinging style, he is widely respected in Paris jazz circles.

COLEMAN, EARL,* *singer;* b. Port Huron, Mich., 8/12/25. Sang w. Ernie Fields, Earl Hines, Jay McShann, King Kolax in '40s; Gene Ammons in '50s. Sporadically active in '60s: Robert's Show Lounge, Chi., Gerald Wilson band, LA '60; House of Jazz, Phila. '61; Ronnie Scott's in London and w. Don Byas in Paris '62; Sunday afternoons at Birdland and Monday nights at Village Gate from '62. App. at Synanon benefit at Village Gate '66. Television show w. Billy Taylor on Ch. 47, NYC '66. Sings in rich, ballad baritone orig. inspired by Billy Eckstine. LP: one track w. Elmo Hope (Aud. Fid.); own album for Atlantic, rec. Aug. '66.

COLEMAN, GEORGE,* *tenor sax, alto sax;* b. Memphis, Tenn., 3/8/35. Free-lanced around Chicago, then NYC in middle and late '50s, working w. B. B. King, John Gilmore, Max Roach. With Slide Hampton '59-'61, Wild Bill Davis '62. Joined Miles Davis early in '63 and remained through summer of '64. Led night club act w. Ossie Davis and Ruby Dee in autumn of '64. With Lionel Hampton from late '64. Played in Paris w. S. Hampton '61, Davis '64. Pl. NJF in house combo '65. Has also worked w. wife, organist Gloria Coleman. Played alto in soundtrack of Dick Gregory film based on life of Charlie Parker. LPs: w. Davis (Col.); S. Hampton (Atl., Epic); Chet Baker (Pres.); Herbie Hancock (BN).

Addr: 331 E. 14th St., New York 3, N.Y.

COLEMAN, ORNETTE,* *alto sax, composer, tenor sax, trumpet, violin;* b. Fort Worth, Texas, 3/19/30. Largely self-taught, Coleman played in rhythm and blues bands in the Southwest during the early '50s before settling in Los Angeles, where he studied theory and formulated much of his music, in 1954. In '58 he was heard by Red Mitchell, Don Payne and other LA musicians, and made his first recordings for Contemporary. He signed with Atlantic Records in '59 and was brought east under their sponsorship with the help of John Lewis and Gunther Schuller, so that he and his partner Donald Cherry might attend the Lenox, Mass. School of Jazz. In the autumn of '59 Coleman, playing a plastic alto, and Cherry opened at the NYC Five Spot with Charlie Haden and Billy Higgins, both from Los Angeles, and immediately became the center of heated controversy involving their music.

Between 1960 and '62 Coleman recorded seven albums for Atlantic, six of them with Don Cherry. They appeared around NYC with a quartet, and were also heard at the Newport and Monterey JFs. Coleman appeared at NYC Town Hall in late '62; after that he retired from public performing. In '63-4 he studied trumpet and violin. In 1965 he emerged from retirement, appeared at the Village Vanguard and later went to Europe with a trio featuring David Izenzon, bass, and Charles Moffett, drums.

Coleman's style is controversial because he does not usually employ the traditional concept of improvisation based on chord changes and because he often does not use a regular beat. He plays with a coarse, rushing intensity that reminds listeners of a human voice expressing emotions ranging from anguish to love.

Coleman, unlike Charlie Parker or John Coltrane, did not serve any apprenticeship in standard jazz bands. All of the compositions that he and his quartet played were his own, and they were sometimes as radical as his solos. When he arrived on the scene in New York, few musicians or critics had watched his development or prepared themselves for him—his music was already crystallized and was either to be accepted or rejected. Perhaps it was unfortunate that he was billed as "the change of the century" and "the shape of jazz to come," forcing listeners to consider him according to a non-musical criterion.

Nevertheless, by ignoring rather than modifying chord changes and regular meter, Coleman opened entire realms of possibility to jazz musicians in the '60s. By 1966 scores of saxophone players and composers had listed him as an influence and showed in their playing that they were making use of his style and of the freedom that he had first employed.

One of Coleman's most remarkable recordings was *Free Jazz*, in which a double quartet was used. Coleman, Cherry, Scott La Faro and Higgins were placed on one side of the studio while Eric Dolphy, Freddie Hubbard, Haden and Eddie Blackwell were placed opposite them. There followed 37 minutes of free and spontaneous improvisation in which soloists and accompanists were forced to use their wits in playing with or "against" one or more of the other musicians. The number of coherent musical ideas that were produced was considered amazing by some listeners, while others found the results frequently incoherent.

Many critics regarded Coleman's music as neither heretical nor radical, but as a variation of traditional blues and folk-forms. Richard B. Hadlock called it "emotionally direct, uncluttered and essentially simple . . . no harder to grasp than the free guitar improvisations of a good country blues player." Charles Mingus said that Coleman is "really an old-fashioned alto player" and added that "I'm not saying everybody's going to have to play like Coleman. But they're going to have to stop copying Bird."

The years following the arguments that surrounded Coleman have shown him to be an important soloist and a catalytic composer in the new jazz. His techniques and ideas have been applied by most of the young musicians who comprise the avant garde of the '60s.

LPs: On Contemporary: *Something Else* (3551), *Tomorrow is the Question* (3569). On Atlantic: *The*

Shape of Jazz to Come (1317), *Change of the Century* (1327), *This is Our Music* (1353), *Free Jazz* (1364), *Ornette!* (1378), *Ornette on Tenor* (1394), *John Lewis Presents Jazz Abstractions* (1365). The 1962 Town Hall concert is available on ESP-Disk 1006. Two LPs recorded at the Golden Circle in Stockholm, 1965, were released in '66 on Blue Note 4224 and 4225,

COLES, JOHNNY,* *trumpet;* b. Trenton, N.J., 7/3/26. Mainly self-taught; st. playing in 1939. Pl. with military band in '41; w. Slappy and His Swingsters '45-8; w. Eddie Vinson '48-51; formed group w. Philly Joe Jones et al '51, then w. Bull Moose Jackson '52. With James Moody 1956-58. Achieved wider recognition as member of Gil Evans band in club appearances and record dates from '59. In the '60s recorded as a leader, and pl. in small group w. George Coleman at NJF; also as sideman at Hunter Coll. jazz concerts. Plays in a warm, lyrical style comparable with one of his favorites, Miles Davis. Won New Star award DB Critics' Poll '65. Own LP on BN; LPs w. Evans (Pac. Jazz, Verve).

Addr: 708 High St., Newark, N.J.

COLLETTE, WILLIAM MARCELL (BUDDY),* *saxes, flute, clarinet, composer;* b. Los Angeles, Calif., 8/6/21. Worked with innumerable name bands in the 1940s and '50s, notably Benny Carter, Gerald Wilson, and the original Chico Hamilton Quintet. In the 1960s he expanded his activity as a composer, writing five fugues and scoring two educational motion pictures. In 1964 he wrote three arrangements for Thelonious Monk and played with Monk and Charles Mingus. He was a member of the house bands of the Monterey JF in '64 and '65. Played San Remo JF March 1961 and concerts in Milan and Florence. Member of LA Neophonic Orchestra during 1965 season. Featured on tenor sax in LP w. Benny Carter, 1966 (Impulse). Own LP: *Buddy Collette on Broadway* (Surrey).

LP as composer-arranger: *Jazz As I Feel It* with Earl Bostic (King). Flute and arr. on *Warm Winds* with Chas. Kynard (World Pacific). Played (and wrote 24 originals) for four LPs rec. in Italy but not released in U.S.

Addr: 5177 Pickford St., Los Angeles, Calif. 90019.

COLLINS, JOHN ELBERT,* *guitar;* b. Montgomery, Ala., 9/20/13. Early work w. Art Tatum, Roy Eldridge in Chicago; D. Gillespie, Slam Stewart, Billy Taylor in NYC. Joined Nat Cole Sept. '51 and remained until Cole's death. In 1965 he recorded for Lee Young's record production company and for Benny Carter, then joined the Bobby Troup Trio in Sept. and was still with Troup in '66, featured far more extensively than in any unit since his New York days, and revealing a style unspoiled by time and subtly effective in its melodic lines.

Though relegated to the background on almost all his LPs w. Cole, Collins is heard in a couple of tracks

on *The Nat Cole Story* and *After Midnight* (Cap.).
Addr: 2023 South Curson Ave., Los Angeles 16, Calif.

COLLINS, JOYCE (Joyce Collins Searle), *piano; also singer;* b. Battle Mountain, Nev., 5/5/30. Began playing in high school dance band. Studied piano and arranging at College of the Pacific, Stockton, Cal. In '55 w. Oscar Pettiford in San Francisco, '60 in LA w. Bob Cooper. Led own trio and duo from '60. Played in Paris '60, Mexico City '65. Served on AFM board of directors '60-'64; first woman to do so. Studies writing; plans to compose and orchestrate. Favs: Waller, John Lewis, Oscar Peterson, Herbie Hancock. Own LP: Jazzl.
Addr: 8734 Wonderland Ave., Los Angeles, Calif.

COLLINS, RUDOLPH ALEXANDER (RUDY),* *drums;* b. New York, N.Y., 7/24/34. Free-lanced around NYC during '50s, appearing w. Cootie Williams, Roy Eldridge, Austin Powell, Eddie Bonnemere, Cecil Taylor. With Herbie Mann '59-60, incl. tour of Africa. With Dizzy Gillespie from Dec. 1962 through Jan. '66. For tours, concerts, recordings etc. see Gillespie. LPs: w. Mann (Atl.), Gillespie (Phil., Lime.), Quincy Jones (Merc.), James Moody (Cadet), Leo Wright (Atl.), Dave Pike, Lalo Schifrin.
Addr: 1662 Rensselaer Rd., Teaneck, N.J.

COLTRANE, JOHN WILLIAM,* *tenor sax, soprano sax, composer, leader;* b. Hamlet, N.C., 9/23/26. First prominent in the bands of Dizzy Gillespie, Johnny Hodges and Earl Bostic, Coltrane began to gain widespread respect among musicians during his intermittent association with Miles Davis between 1955 and 1960. In 1960 he left Davis and formed his own quartet. That year he also recorded for Atlantic and won some public acceptance with his album *My Favorite Things.* By '61 Coltrane had begun a long association with Impulse Records and appeared with a combo that included McCoy Tyner, Elvin Jones and Reggie Workman or Jimmy Garrison, with Eric Dolphy frequently added. This was to be the format for many of his subsequent groups.

Coltrane's style of playing and group concepts underwent several important changes after leaving Davis. During the late '50s he played in a style involving so-called "sheets of sound," in which he employed not merely 16th and 32nd notes, but violent barrages of notes not mathematically related to the underlying rhythmic pulse, and not swinging in the traditional sense of the term. Many of the Atlantic recordings reflected an additional lyricism which he was to use in many later works. They were also the first in which he played the soprano sax. That instrument, rarely used successfully by modern jazzmen, gained a new quality in Coltrane's hands that Pete Welding described as "sinuous and serpentine," employing "a pinched, high-pitched near-human cry of anguish that is most effective . . . he used a device that sends chills along my

spine. He seems to be playing a slithering, coruscating melody line over a constant drone note."

Around '61 Coltrane became involved in the Indian improvisational concept, which entailed lengthy improvisations often based on a predetermined mode (scale arrangement) rather than on chords. Tremendous emotional vitality was transmitted on his recordings (particularly *Africa/Brass, At the Village Vanguard* and *Impressions*). Some critics attacked his use of harsh, human sounds and his often excessively long solos as "honking and bleating" and "anti-jazz," and claimed that his playing was sheer technical display that was without musical value and was destructive to jazz. Nevertheless, this innovation of Indian and modal ideas led to greater freedom for jazz soloists in the '60s, taking the music away from improvisations on songs or song patterns and allowing it to move toward a wholly new musical feeling. At the same time he recorded several blues numbers and two LPs devoted to ballads, with a combination of sensitivity and intensity that have come to characterize all of his efforts.

As a result of his use of these new concepts and the distillation of older forms of jazz, Coltrane's music in 1965 (on *A Love Supreme* and *Chim Chim Cheree*) reached a new synthesis of almost religious fervor, emotional force, and a nearly hypnotic tension. It was at this time that he also attained his greatest public acclaim, simultaneously winning the Hall of Fame, Record of the Year (*A Love Supreme*), Jazzman of the Year and tenor sax categories in the 1965 DB readers' poll.

From the late '50s Coltrane had a tremendous effect on younger saxophonists, both those who attempted to play in his style and those who used his expanded freedom to progress into music of their own.

Critical reaction, which had been mixed at the time of his early breakthrough, began to improve in 1961. In that year, though he had never before won a DB Critics' Poll award, he was a winner in three categories (tenor sax, miscellaneous instrument—soprano sax—and New Star combo) and thereafter was an annual winner in at least one category.

Nat Hentoff described Coltrane as having "the maturity and the degree of self-direction and self-knowledge to be basic," adding that "the only predictable assessment of Coltrane is that he will keep on changing." LeRoi Jones observed, "There is a daringly human quality to John Coltrane's music that makes itself felt wherever he records . . . He is a master, and the slightest sound from his instrument is valuable." Don DeMicheal, in 1962, found Coltrane "new and exciting" but speculated that his style might have become "a limited approach, stimulating as it may be. Certainly his work is of a high order, but even now much of what is played is similar in mood and effect." In a 1966 review of a reissue featuring some of Coltrane's work of the late 1950s, Dan Morgenstern commented, "This album evokes a feeilng of nostalgia in this admirer of 'middle' Coltrane. 'You can't go home again,' said Thomas Wolfe—but on hearing much of Coltrane's current work, one wishes that he could. Tension, after all, is most effective when contrasted with relaxation." As the above-cited poll results indicate, this was a minority view.

In 1965-6 Coltrane experimented more and more extensively in the instrumentation of his group. Sometimes he used two bassists, sometimes two drummers and one or two additional saxophonists. At the end of 1965 a radical change took place when Elvin Jones and McCoy Tyner both left the group. Tyner was replaced by Alice McLeod (Mrs. John Coltrane).

Fortunately Coltrane has been adequately recorded at all of the important stages of his career. Most of the numerous recordings with Miles Davis on Prestige and Columbia remained available, and the single example of the period with Monk was reissued on Riverside. Several tapes of the Prestige sessions under Coltrane's leadership were released during the '60s, including *The Believer* (7292), *Lush Life* (7188), *Black Pearls* (7316), *Settin' the Pace* (7213), *Bahia* (7353), *Dakar* (7280), *Traneing In* (7123), *Stardust* (7268), *Standard Coltrane* (7243), *Soultrane* (7142), *The Last Trane* (7378), *John Coltrane* (7105). Others from the same dates were issued under Red Garland's name.

The Atlantic recordings include *Giant Steps* (1311), *Coltrane Jazz* (1354), *My Favorite Things* (1361), *Ole Coltrane* (1373), *Coltrane Plays the Blues* (1382), *Coltrane Sound* (1419). He made one recording at about the same time entitled *Coltrane Time* with Kenny Dorham and Cecil Taylor on United Artists (14001).

Among the Impulse records are *Africa/Brass* (6), *At the Village Vanguard* (10), *Coltrane* (21), *with Duke Ellington* (30), *Ballads* (32), *with Johnny Hartman* (40), *Impressions* (42), *At Birdland* (50), *Crescent* (66), *A Love Supreme* (77), *Plays Chim Chim Cheree etc.* (85), *with Archie Shepp at Newport* (95), (95), *Ascension* (96), one track each on *The Definitive Jazz Scene* (99) and *The New Wave in Jazz* (90).

CONDON, ALBERT EDWIN (EDDIE),* guitar, leader; b. Goodland, Ind., 11/16/04. Early Chicago associate of Gene Krupa, Bud Freeman, Joe Sullivan and others who pioneered in the tightly-knit, sometimes tense form of group improvisation known as Chicago Style jazz. To NYC '28; partnership w. Red McKenzie in a group known as the Mound City Blue Blowers. Became focal point of a Dixieland jazz movement in the 1940s, presenting many concerts at Town Hall, opening own night club in '46 and launching own TV series in '48. Played first Newport JF '54. Club moved from Greenwich Village to midtown East Side in '58.

The early '60s found Condon no longer at the club, though it still bore his name. Early in '64 he assembled a combo for a successful tour of Australia, New Zealand and Japan. Soon after his return he was taken seriously ill. A "Tribute to Condon" concert was staged at Carnegie Hall and a TV program in his honor (with Condon himself seen briefly) was broadcast in '65.

The amazingly resilient Condon made a remarkable

comeback and in 1965-6 was back on the bandstand at Condon's Club.

Many Condon classics of the early days are in *Jazz Odyssey: The Sound of Chicago* (Col. C3L 32) and in *Eddie Condon: A Legend* (Mainstream 6024). Later recording: *Midnight In Moscow*, 1962 (Epic 17024).

Addr: 27 Washington Sq. North, New York 11, N.Y.

CONNOR, CHRIS,* singer; b. Kansas City, Mo., 11/8/27. In 1953 rose to prominence with Stan Kenton. After leaving the band in July of that year achieved popularity through her LPs for the Bethlehem label. In the '60s continued to appear at clubs, concerts and festivals. In 1966 she made a highly favorable impression at the Austin Jazz Festival. Own LPs: Atl.

CONNORS, CHARLES (CHUCK), bass trombone; b. Maysville, Ky. 8/18/30. With Dizzy Gillespie for nine months in 1957. After various jobs in music and day job working in sheet metal shop, joined Duke Ellington July 8, 1961 and toured internationally with him. Normally a section performer, but heard in solo on 1966 RCA version of *Perdido*.

COOK, HERMAN (JUNIOR),* tenor sax; b. Pensacola, Fla., 7/22/34. An important member of the Horace Silver quintet from May '58 to March '64, he has since worked with the group of his former Silver teammate Blue Mitchell. A strong, hot player, he has synthesized several post-bop tenor styles into a personal expression. Own LP: Jazzland; LPs w. Mitchell, Silver (BN).

Addr: 1331 Pacific St., Brooklyn 16, N.Y.

COOPER, BOB,* tenor sax, oboe, composer; b. Pittsburgh, Pa., 12/6/25. With Kenton 1945-'51, own combos and other West Coast groups, esp. Howard Rumsey's Lighthouse All-Stars, during '50s. Married singer June Christy 1946. During '60s appeared frequently with Rumsey, but devoted more time to composing and arranging. Completed *Music for Jazz Saxophones and Symphony Orchestra* '63, soundtracks for Ford film and TV special '64 and '65. Played on *Mr. Novak* TV show '65. Toured Japan with Christy '61; played and wrote for Japanese bands. Own LP: *Do Re Mi* w. June Christy (Cap.). Others: w. Laurindo Almeida (Cap.).

Addr: 3548 Stonewood Dr., Sherman Oaks, Calif.

COOPER, GEORGE (BUSTER),* trombone; b. St. Petersburg, Fla., 4/4/29. Three years with Lionel Hampton in mid-'50s; later lived in Paris. Joined Duke Ellington 1962 and made a strong impression with his peppery, volatile solos, especially on uptempo blues numbers. He can be heard in portions of the *Symphonic Ellington* and *Mary Poppins* (Reprise) and other Ellington LPs on Columbia and Reprise.

COPELAND, RAY M.,* trumpet, fluegelhorn, composer; b. Norfolk, Va., 7/17/26. Gigged around NYC from late '40s with numerous big band and bop groups, own band. In '61 left Roxy Theatre Orch. after 1½ years.

Free-lanced w. A. Kirk, R. Weston, V. Valdez, Machito, E. Hawkins, Lena Horne. W. Pearl Bailey and Louis Bellson '62-'64, incl. concert tour. Jack Paar TV show, Birdland, Metropole, Apollo. Back w. Weston for concerts in public schools. W. Ella Fitzgerald and N.Y. Philharmonic '65. Monterey JF '65 w. Gil Fuller. Member Long Beach, N.Y., concert band. Teaches privately. LPs: w. Machito (Roul.), D. Pike (Decca), J. Richards (Roul.), Weston (Bakton).
Addr: 110-91 195th St., St. Albans 12, N.Y.

CORB, MORTIMER G. (MORTY),* *bass;* b. San Antonio, Tex., 4/10/17. With L. Armstrong, B. Goodman, J. Teagarden, Bob Crosby during late '40s and '50s, then became active in Hollywood studio work. Has had several of own comps. recorded, incl. *Oasis, Goodbye My Love, Bayou Blues.* In '65 recorded for Marty Paich, Neal Hefti, Paul Smith. In soundtracks of films *Raisin in the Sun, The Family Jewels, Music Man.* LPs: w. Pete Fountain (Coral), Jack Jones (Kapp), Pearl Bailey (Roul.), Earl Grant (Decca).
Addr: 4343 Babcock, Studio City, Calif.

CORCORAN, GENE PATRICK (CORKY),* *tenor sax;* b. Tacoma, Wash., 7/28/24. With Harry James intermittently 1941-'57, then led own combo in Seattle. Rejoined James in '62. For itinerary see James, Harry. LPs: w. James (MGM). Still a first-class soloist in style influenced by C. Hawkins and other swing-era giants.
Addr: 1512 Hiawatha Rd., Las Vegas, Nev.

COREA, ARMANDO ANTHONY (CHICK), *piano;* b. Chelsea, Mass., 6/12/41. Studied music in Chelsea, Mass. from 1947 and obtained his first professional work through his father, who is also a musician. Worked with Mongo Santamaria for four months in 1962; Willie Bobo '63; Blue Mitchell '64-6, also off and on with Herbie Mann in '65. An able musician who has bridged the narrowing gap between jazz and Latin music, he names Tatum, Hancock, Tyner and Monk as his favorite artists and Bud Powell, Tyner and Bill Evans as major influences. LPs w. Mann, Hubert Laws (Atl.); Mitchell (BN); Sonny Stitt (Roost); Willie Bobo (Roul.); Mongo Santamaria (River.); Montego Joe (Pres.).
Addr: 18 No. Moore St., New York City, N.Y. 10013.

CORWIN, ROBERT (BOB),* *piano;* b. Hollis, N.Y., 10/2/33. Worked w. Don Elliott, Flip Phillips, Anita O'Day and as solo during '50s. W. Peggy Lee '62-'63, O'Day '61-'63, Louis Ney '61-'65, Ruth Price '65, Paul Horn '61. Some arranging for Ney. Toured Japan w. O'Day '63. Married to Amanda Mercer, daughter of Johnny Mercer, who inspired Mercer's song *Mandy is Two.*
Addr: 19836 Gilmore St., Woodland Hills, Calif.

COSTA, EDWIN JAMES (EDDIE),* *vibes, piano;* b. Atlas, Pa., 8/14/30; d. New York, N.Y., 7/28/62 in auto crash. A prolific recording artist, Costa was beginning to come into his own as a soloist and musical innovator before his death. An excellent reader, he was consistently in demand for studio work on both vibes and piano. Own LP: *In Their Own Sweet Way* w. Farmer. (Prem.). Others: *John Lewis Presents Jazz Abstractions* (Atl.), w. Woody Herman (Jazzl.), *Jazz Mission to Moscow* (Colpix).

COUNCE, CURTIS LEE,* *bass;* b. Kansas City, Mo., 1/23/26; d. Los Angeles, Calif., 7/31/63 of a heart attack. In LA from the late 1940s, Counce was one of the first Negroes to become involved in the West Coast jazz movement of the '50s. From '56 until his death he led his own trios and quintets around LA which at times included Carl Perkins, Jack Sheldon, Gerald Wilson and Harold Land. Counce's ideas and choice of musicians showed that he was on the verge of much greater individual expression. Own LPs: Contemp.

COVINGTON, WARREN,* *trombone, leader;* b. Philadelphia, Pa., 8/7/21. Led Tommy Dorsey Band after Dorsey's death 1956. Led same under own name since '61, feat. wife Kathee as vocalist. Active tours, studio, dances, etc. LPs: Decca.
Addr: 151 Fox Hollow Rd., Wyckoff, N.J.

CRANSHAW, MELBOURNE R. (BOB), *bass;* also *tuba, Fender bass;* b. Evanston, Ill., 12/10/32. Father was a drummer in KC, brother a pianist in Chi. and NYC. Piano lessons at age five. Studied drums from 4th grade until college; bass in high school and coll.; pl. tuba while in Army in Korea. First professional jobs in Chicago w. Eddie Harris and Walter Perkins in '50s. With Perkins he was charter member of the MJT+3, the Chicago-based group with whom he came to NYC '60. In the '60s has played with many combos incl. Sonny Rollins and Junior Mance. Also backed singers like Joe Williams, Josh White, Lesley Gore. Worked in England and Scotland with George Shearing-Joe Williams tour. Favs: Ray Brown, Percy Heath, Israel Crosby, Ron Carter, Scott La Faro, Bill Lee. Cranshaw is an extremely able player with a strong beat and a flexible style. His ambition is to be a musical therapist; has studied at Bradley, Roosevelt and Northwestern Univs. toward this end. LPs w. Rollins (RCA), MJT (Vee-Jay), Mance (River.), Count Basie-Sammy Davis (Verve), Joe Henderson, Lee Morgan, Donald Byrd, Grachan Moncur (BN), McCoy Tyner (Imp.), Carmen McRae, Paul Winter (Col.).
Addr: 320 W. 85th St., New York, N.Y.

CRAWFORD, BENNY ROSS JR. (HANK), *alto sax;* also *piano, tenor, baritone sax, composer;* b. Memphis, Tenn., 12/21/34. Started on sax 1948; stud. theory and comp. at Tenn. State U. Ray Charles heard him playing with a group of youngsters in Nashville, and a year later sent for him to join his small band on baritone sax.
Crawford joined Charles in 1958, switching to alto sax the following year. He acted as musical director for the group, and served in a similar capacity for the big band Charles fronted from 1961. He acquired

a substantial popular following both domestically and overseas (the band visited Europe in 1961, '62 and '63). As a result, he left Charles in June 1963 to form his own seven-piece band. Appeared at Monterey JF 1964.

The Crawford group, its character distinctly blues-textured, is an eloquent and intense medium for Crawford's imaginative writing, and a soulful setting for his own skillful work on alto and occasionally on piano. Comps. incl. *The Peeper, Stony Lonesome, Dig These Blues.*

Film: *Swingin' Along* w. Charles ('62). Favs: Ch. Parker, James Moody. Crawford has rec. many LPs for Atlantic as a leader; his personal favorites incl. *From The Heart* and *Soul of the Ballad.* LPs w. Charles: Atl., ABC-Par.

Addr: 2426 Hunter Avenue, Memphis, Tenn.

CRAWFORD, HOLLAND R. (RAY), *guitar;* b. Pittsburgh, Pa., 2/7/24. Brother played tenor sax. Studied piano, tenor in high school. First gig w. F. Henderson '40-42 as sax soloist. Guitar with Ahmad Jamal, Pittsburgh '48. To NYC w. T. Scott, Jimmy Smith, Gil Evans, Jamal. Moved to LA; some movie and concert work. Plans to teach music in LA schools. Ambition to record under own name, playing own music and w. own choice of musicians. Fav: Gil Evans. LPs: w. Jamal (Epic, Cadet), Smith, and own fav. work on Evans' *Out of the Cool.*

Addr: 4025 W. Adams Blvd., Los Angeles, Calif.

CRISS, WILLIAM (SONNY), * *alto sax;* b. Memphis, Tenn., 10/23/27. With early LA groups in late '40s, incl. H. McGhee, G. Wilson; toured w. B. Rich, led own LA combos during '50s. Moved to Europe 1962. In Paris played at Blue Note, Grand Severine and other clubs w. own groups, and in several films, one w. K. Clarke. In Germany and Belgium '62-'65 played concerts, TV, radio. Returned to U.S. '65 and played in LA. A superior soloist in the neo-Parker tradition. Own LPs: 2 for French Polydor. Others in U.S.: w. Onzy Mathews.

Addr: 10306 Mary Ave., Los Angeles, Calif.

CROMBIE, ANTHONY JOHN (TONY), * *drums, composer, leader;* b. London, Eng., 8/27/25. Own band in Israel '63; formed duo w. organist Alan Haven '64, which pl. in Las Vegas '65-6. Outstandingly imaginative drummer; talented leader, writer and pianist, but only works intermittently in pure modern jazz contexts. Own LPs on Brit. Tempo, Brit. Ember.

CROSBY, GEORGE ROBERT (BOB), * *singer, leader;* b. Spokane, Wash., 8/23/13. Bing Crosby's younger brother was best known in jazz as leader of a big band that pl. orchestrated Dixieland during the swing era, recording a series of durable performances between 1935 and 1942. Some of these records were made by the Bob Cats, a small contingent from the band.

In the 1960s, though virtually out of the music business and operating an automobile leasing agency

in Hawaii, Crosby occasionally returned for a reunion of the Bob Cats, featuring many members of the original personnel, usually for an engagement in Nevada. In the fall of 1964 he put together a nine-piece group for a month's tour of Japan, Okinawa and the Philippines. LPs: Decca, Coral, Dot.

Addr: 2562 Calle Del Oro, La Jolla, Calif.

CROSBY, ISRAEL, * *bass;* b. Chicago, Ill., 1/19/19. An important member of the Ahmad Jamal Trio from 1951, Crosby also played with Benny Goodman from '53-4, rejoined Jamal in '56 and on the breakup of Jamal's trio early in '62 joined George Shearing. A few months later he became ill and died in a Chicago hospital, 8/11/62.

Crosby, according to Shearing, "played bass parts that were so beautiful you could never write anything that good. He was one of the most inspiring musicians I played with." Crosby's best work can be heard on LPs with Jamal (Argo) and in a trio set with Shearing (Cap.).

CROW, WILLIAM ORVAL (BILL), * *bass;* b. Othello, Wash., 12/27/27. From early '50s, pl. w. with S. Getz, T. Gibbs, M. McPartland, G. Mulligan. In NYC w. A. Cohn and Z. Sims '60, Mulligan Concert Jazz Band and quartet '60-'61, Q. Jones '61, M. Allison '62, J. Raney and L. Konitz '61, B. Goodman tour of U.S.S.R. '62, Mulligan again '62-'65, B. Brookmeyer and C. Terry from '63. Toured Europe '63, Japan '64 w. Mulligan. Wrote articles and reviews for *Jazz Review* 1959-'60. LPs: w. Mulligan (Verve, Phil.), Brookmeyer (Verve), Brookmeyer-Terry (Main.), Goodman (RCA), Cohn (Colpix), Cohn-Sims (FM), M. Albam (Imp.), Brookmeyer-Raney-J. Hall (Pac. Jazz).

Addr: 261 W. 52nd St., New York, N.Y.

CULVER, ROLLAND PIERCE (ROLLIE), * *drums;* b. Fond du Lac, Wis., 10/29/08. With Red Nichols steadily from 1945; also played for several Hollywood films. On USIA tour of Europe and all of Asia '60, at World JF Japan '64. W. Five Pennies until Nichols' death '65. LPs: w. Nichols (Cap.), incl. own fav. *Old Time Blues and Rags.*

Addr: 4351 McConnell Blvd., Los Angeles 66, Calif.

CURSON, THEODORE (TED), *trumpet;* b. Philadelphia, Pa., 6/3/35. Studied with Jimmy Heath, played carnival gigs at age 12. Encouraged by Miles Davis, Curson worked in New York with Mal Waldron, Red Garland, Philly Joe Jones and Cecil Taylor before joining Charles Mingus' group, which included Eric Dolphy, for two years in 1959-60. Later played with Max Roach, Bill Barron and led his own groups. Several festivals and tours in Europe. Comps. include *Nosruc Waltz, Flatted Fifth, Straight Ice* and *Flip Top.* Cites Taylor, Mingus and Barron as influences. Favs: Dizzy Gillespie, Johnny Splawn, Miles Davis and Clifford Brown, but Curson plays with an intense style that is completely his own. Interested in encouraging jazz as a concert art and in exploring modern developments while maintaining traditional audience appeal. Own LPs: Old Town, Prestige, Aud. Fid., and favorite *The New Thing and the Blue Thing* (Atlantic). Others with Taylor (UA), Mingus (Candid) and Barron (Savoy).

Addr: 1549 S. Garnet, Philadelphia, Pa.

CUTSHALL, ROBERT DEWEES (CUTTY),* *trombone;* b. Huntington County, Pa., 12/29/11. Well known for his work w. Benny Goodman in '40s, he began a long association w. Eddie Condon in '49, pl. at Condon's NYC club and touring England and Scotland w. him '57. App. at Aspen JF, Colorado, '63-6. At Condon's w. Peanuts Hucko from Sept. '65. Took part in *Salute to Eddie Condon* filmed for TV '64. LPs w. Yank Lawson (ABC-Par.).

Addr: 93-29 86th Drive, Woodhaven 21, N.Y.

DAHLANDER, NILS-BERTIL (BERT),* *drums;* b. Gothenburg, Sweden, 5/13/28. A frequent visitor to the U.S. jazz scene since 1954, best known for his work with Terry Gibbs, Chet Baker and Teddy Wilson, Dahlander continued to divide his time between Sweden and America in the 1960s. In Sweden during 1965 he had his own TV show, worked with Earl Hines, made an album of old Swedish dances for the Fiesta label, and an LP of Swedish waltzes renovated with a beat which he described as "waltzanova" (bossa nova in ¾ time). An avocational painter, he had one showing in Uppsala during the year. Back in the U.S. in '66, he worked with Ralph Sutton in Aspen, Colorado.

DAILEY, ALBERT PRESTON (AL), *piano, composer;* b. Baltimore, Md., 6/16/38. Piano lessons at age six; piano and comp. at Morgan St. College '55-6, Peabody Cons., Balt. '56-9. Pl. in house band at Royal Theater in Balt. from age 15 for four years. On road w. Damita Jo '60-3. Own trio at Bohemian Caverns, Wash., D.C. '63-4. To NYC March '64 to play at Minton's w. Bill English. W. Dexter Gordon at Coronet, Bklyn. spring '65; Roy Haynes, Hank Mobley at Five Spot, Slugs' '65; Sarah Vaughan, Dave Pike, Art Farmer '66. All time favs.: Art Tatum, Bud Powell; current favs: Barry Harris, Tommy Flanagan. Thoughtful soloist who swings in a relaxed manner. Wrote arrs. for guitarist Sonny Forrest's Decca album. LPs w. Budd Johnson (Cadet), Frank Foster (Pres.).

Addr: 360 Central Park West, New York 25, N.Y.

DALEY, JOSEPH ALBERT (JOE), *tenor sax, clarinet, flute, composer;* b. Salem, Ohio, 7/30/18. Stud. saxophone w. Larry Teal in Detroit; arr. with Ray McConnell. BM in composition Chicago Musical College '53. Sideman with numerous bands in '40s and '50s incl. Woody Herman 1950-51. Worked for Judy Garland, Tony Bennett and many other top singers.

Formed own trio 1963 and generated a strong reaction with a free style of jazz. In a statement of his credo in '64 Daley said, "Mainstream jazz has reached an impasse . . . ever since I studied composition and the works of 20th-century composers, I have yearned to play in some sort of atonal and rhythmic manner that will be convincing." Daley has appeared in concerts at numerous colleges and high schools in the midwest and took part in the DB JF in Chicago August '65. Infls: Ch. Parker, S. Rollins. LP: *Joe Daley Trio at Newport '63* (RCA).

Addr: 1210 Astor, Chicago, Ill. 60610.

DAMERON, TADLEY EWING (TADD),* *piano, composer;* b. Cleveland, Ohio, 2/21/17. One of the first important arrangers of the bebop era, Dameron wrote for the first Dizzy Gillespie big band in the 1940s, led a bop quintet at the Royal Roost in NYC for most of 1948, and played with Miles Davis at the Paris JF in '49. His activity and influence waned during the 1950s. In '58, after a narcotics arrest, he was jailed, but from '61 became active again in jazz, writing record sessions for Blue Mitchell, Milt Jackson and Sonny Stitt. He also wrote two arrangements for the USSR tour of Benny Goodman's band.

Plagued by ill health, Dameron suffered a series of heart attacks and was frequently hospitalized in 1963. He made his final public appearance at a benefit held for him at the Five Spot in New York in Nov. '64. On March 8, 1965 he died in NYC of cancer.

Dameron was a valuable contributor in the evolution of modern jazz. Along with Gil Fuller and a handful of others he was among the first to incorporate the harmonic and rhythmic device of bop into the framework of big bands. In addition to the early Gillespie albums his work can be heard in several LPs under his own name: *The Magic Touch* (River.); *Tadd Dameron Band 1948* (Jazzland); *Dameronia* (Pres.).

D'AMICO, HENRY (HANK),* *clarinet;* b. Rochester, N.Y., 3/21/15. First prominent in the bands of Red Norvo, 1936-9, and Bob Crosby '40-41, d'Amico later became a studio musician at ABC network in NYC, '44-55. Later he returned to jazz, working at the Room at the Bottom in NYC, and in 1964 at the World's Fair with the Morey Feld Trio. Following a short hospitalization he died 12/3/65 in Queens, N.Y. Though he never enjoyed mass public recognition, he was one of the best and most fluent post-Goodman clarinetists of the swing years.

DAMITA JO (Damita Jo De Blanc), *singer;* b. Austin, Texas, ca. 1933. Raised in Santa Barbara, Calif., she began performing for friends and family at age five. Majored in music at Univ. of Calif. and Sam Houston St. Spent seven years as lead vocalist with Steve Gibson and the Red Caps. Later went out as a single, appearing in Nevada lounges, leading clubs and on TV. Using a repertoire of pop, blues and standard material, she displays what is unmistakably a jazz style although

she has been largely ignored by many jazz writers.
Own LPs: Epic.

Addr: 408 W. 57th St., New York 19, N.Y.

DANIELS, EDWARD KENNETH (EDDIE), *tenor sax, clarinet; also flute, trombone;* b. Brooklyn, N.Y., 10/19/41. Began studying alto sax at nine. Clarinet at 12; subsequent studies w. Daniel Bonade, Bernard Portnoy, Joe Allard. Attended High School of Performing Arts in NYC and played 1st clarinet in all-city high school orch. At 16-17 was a member of Marshall Brown's Newport Youth Band. B.A. from Brooklyn College '63; M.A. from Juilliard on clarinet '66.

First jazz job w. Tony Scott at Half Note, fall '65. With Thad Jones-Mel Lewis band from Jan. '66. Daniels, whose vigorous style seems to favor Sonny Rollins, received first prize on tenor at the Vienna International Jazz Competition, May '66. Rec. on trombone w. La Playa Sextet. LP w. Jones-Lewis (Solid State).

Addr: 702 44th St., Brooklyn 20, N.Y.

DANKWORTH, JOHNNY,* *alto sax, composer;* b. London, England, 9/20/27. One of the first British musicians to be infl. by Charlie Parker, whom he heard in NYC in '40s when Dankworth was pl. in bands on Cunard ocean liners. Own big band from '53; app. with it at NJF and Birdland '59.

Third-stream comp. *Improvisations,* co-authored w. Matyas Seiber, commissioned by Royal Phil. Soc. '59. Reverted to conventional big-band lineup '60. Wrote score of opera-ballet *Lysistrata* for Bath Fest. Soc. '64. Background scores for films: *The Servant* (in which he also app.), *The Criminal, Saturday Night and Sunday Morning, Darling, Sands of the Kalahari, Morgan, Return From the Ashes* and *Modesty Blaise.*

His orch. toured Ireland and Switzerland '63; Germany and Belgium '64. Visited U.S. briefly summer '65 to rec. part of his *Zodiac Variations* w. NYC jazzmen. Own LPs: *Shakespeare and All That Jazz* (w. his wife Cleo Laine), *What the Dickens, Zodiac Variations* (Fontana).

Addr: c/o Harold Davison, 235-241 Regent St., London W.1, England.

DAUNER, WOLFGANG, *piano, composer; also trumpet, valve trombone;* b. Stuttgart, Germany, 12/30/35. Studied w. aunt, a professional teacher, 1941. Did not take up music professionally until 1957 when, while working as a mechanic in Stuttgart, he was offered a tour with a commercial band. Studied trumpet, composition, at Stuttgart College of Music '58. During the '60s rose to the forefront among German jazzmen, taking part in festivals 1962 and '64 and gigging around Stuttgart w. Leo Wright, Benny Bailey, Attila Zoller. Composed music for commercial film, also arrs. for German TV show in '65. Worked w. own trio and w. Joki Freund Sextet. Fav: Bill Evans. According to German jazz critics, Dauner is the most important new German pianist since Horst Jankowski.

Comps.: *Dream Talk, Free Fall, A Long Night.* LPs: *Dream Talk* w. own trio; *Yogi Jazz* w. Freund Sextet (both CBS, not issued in U.S.).

Addr: 7 Stuttgart, Munster Elbestr. 131, Germany.

DAVIS, ARTHUR (ART),* *bass;* b. Harrisburg, Pa., 12/5/34. Studied at Juilliard and Manhattan Schools of Music and played in several classical orchs. before joining Max Roach '58. In Dizzy Gillespie band '60-'61; during that time also played w. John Coltrane, Gigi Gryce, Clark Terry-Bob Brookmeyer, Quincy Jones, Josh White, Leon Bibb, Frances Faye, Ahmad Jamal. W. Lena Horne London '61. NBC staff musician '62-'63. In NBC Symphony of the Air '61-'62, Westchester Symphony Orch., Radio City Symphony Orch., Symphony of the New World '65. Several jazz festivals incl. Randall's Island '59-'61, Newport '58-'61, '63. Films: *Let My People Go* w. Philharmonia Orch. of London, *The Pawnbroker* w. Quincy Jones. Teaches privately and gives numerous jazz and classical recitals and demonstrations. Toured Europe and N. Africa w. Gillespie '59, Europe w. JATP '60. Became increasingly active in TV work. Won DB New Star Award for bass '62.

Davis is a strong, melodic soloist and accompanist with a clear, resonant tone that fits into all of the varied situations in which he plays. LPs: w. Gillespie (Verve), Coltrane (Impulse), Roach (Jazzl., Impulse), Al Grey-Billy Mitchell (Cadet), Leo Wright (Atl.), numerous others.

Addr: 319 E. 25th St., New York, N.Y.

DAVIS, CHARLES, *baritone sax, soprano sax, composer;* b. Goodman, Miss., 5/20/33. Raised in Chicago, where he played dances after leaving high school. Sideman with Jack McDuff, 1954; Al Smith orch., backing Billie Holiday, '56; Sun Ra off and on, '54-6; septet backing Dinah Washington, '58; Kenny Dorham '59-60. Since then has free-lanced with I. Jacquet, L. Hampton, H. Crawford, J. Coltrane et al, and has led own quintet, '65-6, at club dates and concerts.

Davis is perhaps the most impressive of the handful of important new baritone saxophonists who have come to prominence during the 1960s. He feels his work can be heard to best advantage in a 1959 LP with Kenny Dorham on the Time label, and on Impulse and Atlantic LPs with Elvin Jones. Other LPs w. Jimmy Garrison (Imp.), Ronnie Mathews (Prestige), Julian Priester (River.). Among his compositions are: *Half & Half, Some Other Time, Turbo, Azan, Linda.*

Addr: 934 Carroll St., Brooklyn, N.Y.

DAVIS, EDDIE (LOCKJAW),* *tenor sax;* b. New York, N.Y. 3/2/21. The former soloist with name bands of the '40s led his own groups, often with organist Shirley Scott and tenor Johnny Griffin, around NYC during the '50s, then temporarily withdrew from active music in June '63 to work as a booking agent for Shaw Artists Corp. In Oct. '64 he returned as soloist and road manager for the Count Basie band. Davis plays a hard, funky tenor with strong roots in the older blues-jazz tradition. Own LPs: Pres., Roost; River. and Jazzl. w. Griffin.

Addr: 171-11 Foch Blvd., St. Albans, N.Y.

DAVIS, MILES DEWEY JR.,* trumpet, fluegelhorn, composer, leader; b. Alton, Ill., 5/25/26. First prominent in mid '40s as sideman with Ch. Parker, Coleman Hawkins and in Benny Carter and Billy Eckstine bands. Briefly led a nine-piece group that recorded for Capitol in 1949-50. Led own combo off and on from early '50s but achieved some of his most significant musical contributions in a series of albums featuring a large orchestra with Gil Evans as arranger and conductor.

In the 1960s Davis was considered by many jazz students to be the foremost trumpeter in the field (by now he was doubling frequently on fluegelhorn). He was the winner of jazz polls in DB, *Playboy*, etc. He continued to tour as leader of a quintet, and was responsible for bringing to prominence such important young musicians as Herbie Hancock, Ron Carter, Anthony Williams. He enjoyed phenomenal success on overseas tours, notably in Japan, where his group was the principal attraction in the World JF on a brief tour in the summer of 1964. For extended periods during the next two years he was sidelined by illness, but he continued to play intermittently at concerts and in night clubs. His association with Gil Evans was renewed occasionally; they worked together on music for a short-lived play, *Time of the Barracudas*, starring Laurence Harvey. It was presented in Los Angeles but never reached New York.

Davis' major contributions as soloist and as orchestral innovator were made in the 1950s. Though his performances during the '60s often reached magnificent peaks of brilliance, the historically meaningful work he has brought to jazz dates back to the Capitol band, to the later Evans collaborations, and to the combo in which Cannonball Adderley and John Coltrane were sidemen in 1957-9. Davis' own solo work, with its breathy, almost vocal quality, has retained a lyrical and sometimes jubilant character. His muted style particularly has been the source of inspiration for countless young trumpeters. His playing has remained virtually untouched by the defiantly angry aspects of the avant garde, most of whose practitioners he holds in great contempt. Although his combos in recent years have rarely produced any significant new group music, the solo contributions of leader and sidemen alike have assured their lasting importance.

LPs: Most of his best early work is on Prestige. *Birth Of The Cool*, with the nine-piece band, is on Capitol 1974. Almost all albums from the late 1950s are on Columbia, except a soundtrack LP, *Jazz on the Screen* (Fontana 67532). LPs with Gil Evans: *Miles Ahead* (8633); *Porgy and Bess* (8085); *Sketches of Spain* (8271); *Quiet Nights* (8906). Evans is also heard briefly on *Miles Davis at Carnegie Hall* (8612). Best LPs in '60s: *Miles Davis In Person* (C2S 820);

Someday My Prince Will Come (8456); *Miles & Monk at Newport* (8978); *Seven Steps to Heaven* (8851); *Miles Davis In Europe* (8983); *My Funny Valentine* (9106); *E.S.P.* (9150).

Addr: 312 West 77th St., New York City 24, N.Y.

DAVIS, NATHAN TATE, tenor, soprano sax, flute, clarinet, composer; b. Kansas City, Kansas, 2/15/37. Clar. at KC Cons. and U. of Kansas. After a period of Army service he went to Paris to join Kenny Clarke, working with him at the Club St. Germain, with Donald Byrd at the Blue Note and with Byrd and Eric Dolphy at the Chat Qui Peche. Toured Europe w. Art Blakey. Lugano JF with Kenny Clarke, Francy Boland. TV in Paris with own quintet and in Rome with Clarke. Movies incl. *Je Vous Salue Mafia*, for which he played most of the sound track. Favs: D. Gordon, Coltrane, Rollins, Getz. Infls: Dolphy, Byrd, Coltrane, Miles Davis, Wayne Shorter. LPs with own combos for French labels; also with Kitty White (Clover).

Davis points out that he is not an expatriate, just a "citizen of the world" who happened to find regular work in Europe.

Addr: 4138 W. 20th, Gary, Indiana.

DAVIS, RICHARD,* bass; b. Chicago, Ill., 4/15/30. Played in a variety of contexts during the '40s and '50s, incl. several Chicago classical orchestras, Benny Goodman, European tour w. Sarah Vaughan. With Orchestra U.S.A. 1961-64. Classical jobs w. Igor Stravinsky, Leonard Bernstein, '64. Visited Europe as member of Gunther Schuller Orch.

One of Davis' first jobs of importance in jazz was with the Eric Dolphy-Booker Little Quintet in 1961. He has become one of the most sought after modern bassists, having performed and recorded with Booker Ervin, Kenny Dorham, Charles Lloyd, Andrew Hill, Jimmy Giuffre, Bobby Hutcherson, James Moody, Roland Kirk, Maynard Ferguson, Barbra Streisand and others. Also played for three films and several TV shows.

Much of Davis' popularity among musicians is due to his amazing versatility. Andrew Hill, who calls him "the greatest bass player in existence," says, "Richard can do anything you demand of him. He has a lot of technique but his technique doesn't overpower his imagination." Although he has departed from the tradition of four-beat accompaniment, Davis places more emphasis on rhythmic implication, a strong tone and blues emotion than do many modern bassists. He won *Jazz* mag. readers' poll May 1966.

LPs: Best work on Ervin's *Space Book* (Pres.), Hutcherson's *Dialogue* (Blue.), Hill's *Black Fire* (Blue.), Dolphy's *Out to Lunch* (Blue.). Others w. Oliver Nelson (Impulse), Moody (Cadet), Kirk (Merc.), Dolphy (Pres.), Schuller (Cambridge), Tony Williams (Blue.), Ervin (Pres.), Hill (Blue.), Byard (Pres.).

Addr: 100-17 202nd St., Hollis, N.Y.

DAVIS, WILLIAM STRETHEN (WILD BILL),* *organ, piano, composer;* b. Glasgow, Mo., 11/24/18. Pioneer jazz organist since 1949; leader of own trio from '51. In the '60s Davis broadened his jazz audience through a series of recordings in collaboration with Johnny Hodges. Since 1950 he has worked annually every summer in an Atlantic City club. In addition to his musical interests he has become active in aviation and Calif. real estate.

Own LPs: Epic, Everest, RCA. LPs featuring Hodges: Verve, also RCA.

Addr: 4911 Valley Ridge Drive, Los Angeles, Calif.

DAVISON, WILLIAM (WILD BILL),* *cornet, leader;* b. Defiance, Ohio, 1/5/06. The veteran Dixieland cornetist, a prominent figure in early Chicago jazz, toured extensively in the midwest from 1960 to '66. In addition, he played for a year (1962-63) at Nick's in Greenwich Village. Toured England Jan., Feb. '64 as guest soloist with Freddie Randall band. Also visited Switzerland, West Germany, Austria. Soloist on syndicated Eddie Condon TV tribute '64. Davison also recorded his own album, *Swingin' Dixie,* for the Bear label. His big sound and confident Armstrong-inspired style never lost the colorful individuality he had established in the prohibition era.

Addr: 17 Park Ave., New York 16, N.Y.

DAWSON, ALAN,* *drums, vibes;* b. Marietta, Pa., 7/14/29. Studied in Boston, where he worked with many groups during 1950s; also toured w. Lionel Hampton '53.

Based at the Berklee School of Music in Boston, where he has been a teacher for the past decade, Dawson has also been active with the Boston Percussion Trio, playing concerts for young audiences. He has worked with Earl Hines, Booker Ervin, Teddy Wilson, Jaki Byard, Phil Woods, Sonny Stitt, Frank Foster et al while working regularly at Lennie's on the Turnpike.

Dawson is the author of *A Manual for the Modern Drummer.* In 1965 he tied with Dannie Richmond for first place in the new star division of the DB critics' poll. He played at the Berlin JF w. Sonny Rollins, Bill Evans, and while in Germany (10/27-11/4/65) rec. two LPs w. Booker Ervin, Dexter Gordon for Prestige. He is also heard on several other albums w. Ervin, Byard, Ch. McPherson (Pres.).

Addr: 157 Arlington St., W. Medford, Mass. 02155.

DEAN, DONALD WESLEY, *drums;* b. Kansas City, Mo., 6/21/37. Raised in Kansas City, Dean became active in the Los Angeles scene with Kenny Dorham in 1961. Since then with H. Land, G. Wilson, G. Shearing, D. Gordon, Jack Wilson, P. Newborn, M. Jenkins, H. Hawes. Favs: R. Haynes, M. Roach, A. Blakey. LPs with Carmell Jones and E. Anderza (Pac. Jazz).

Addr: 5552 Carlin St., Los Angeles 16, Calif.

DE FRANCO, BONIFACE FERDINAND LEONARDO (BUDDY),* *clarinet, bass clarinet, leader;* b. Camden, N.J., 2/17/23. A prominent name-band soloist in the '40s, De Franco played with Gene Krupa, Charlie Barnet, Tommy Dorsey, Boyd Raeburn and Count Basie. After leading his own big band in 1951 he formed a quartet, and led various small groups during the '50s. From 1961-4 he was frequently teamed as co-leader of a quartet with accordionist Tommy Gumina.

De Franco made guest appearances in 1965 with the Waukegan County Philharmonic, the Los Angeles Neophonic, and at the Kansas City JF. He also provided background music for a Nelson Riddle TV show *Profiles in Courage.* Throughout the 1960-65 period De Franco also appeared as a clinician at colleges in behalf of a musical instrument company.

In 1965 he began doubling on bass clarinet. His work on this instrument was widely acclaimed; some critics found that it had more warmth and strength of personality than his regular clarinet style. Nevertheless, from almost every standpoint De Franco remained the outstanding all-around clarinetist in jazz, technically impeccable and capable of extraordinary improvisational flights.

In Jan. 1966 De Franco replaced Ray McKinley as leader of the orchestra bearing the name of the late Glenn Miller, and controlled by the Miller estate. Touring and recording with this band, he modernized its personnel and style, using the traditional Glenn Miller sound in about half the repertoire.

LPs with Gumina: Merc., Decca. LP on bass clarinet: *Blues Bag,* in L. Feather's *Jazz of the '60s* Series (VJ); with Glenn Miller orch. (Epic).

Addr: 206 Bedford Pl., Thousand Oaks, Calif.

DE HAAS, EDGAR (EDDIE),* *bass;* also *guitar;* b. Bandoeng, Java, Indonesia, 2/21/30. Toured Europe, N. Africa with various groups before moving to U.S. '57, where he worked w. Goodman, Miles Davis, T. Gibbs, Toshiko-Mariano. Free-lanced NYC '60-'62 w. R. Haynes, K. Burrell, P. Nero, B. Dearie, Chris Connor. Co-led own quartet '62 w. Bobby Jaspar. Toured U.S. Europe w. folk group '63. With Gene Krupa '64-'65, incl. tours of S. America, Japan, Mexico. TV appearances incl. Al Hirt, Steve Allen, Tonight Show. LPs: w. Haynes (Pres.), S. Stitt (Verve), S. Hampton (Atl.).

Addr: 127 Nye Ave., Newark 12, N.J.

DENNIS, KENNETH CARL (KENNY), *drums;* b. Philadelphia, Pa., 5/27/30. After local work, pl. w. Earl Bostic '53; Jackie Davis '54; Erroll Garner '55; Sonny Stitt, '56; Billy Taylor '57. Also free-lanced in New York with Thelonious Monk, Charles Mingus, Miles Davis. After working with Phineas Newborn he came to Calif. in '60 to play with Lena Horne. From June '60 to Aug. '63 he was house drummer and entertainment director at the Rubaiyat Room in LA. In recent years he has appeared with his wife, singer Nancy Wilson, but has devoted most of his time to administrative work with a production company handling television shows, artist management, music publishing, etc. In 1965-6, busy with these enterprises, he rarely played drums ("I have found the administrative end of the entertainment field creative and challenging and look forward to much success in future years").

Addr: 9465 Wilshire Blvd., Beverly Hills, Calif.

DENNIS, WILLIE (William DeBerardinis),* *trombone;* b. Philadelphia, Pa., 1/10/26. After working with Benny Goodman and other name bands, also with Charles Mingus in the late '50s, Dennis was a prominent recording studio and TV station musician until his death in an automobile accident 7/8/65. U.S.S.R. tour w. Goodman '62. Pl. w. Gerry Mulligan Concert Jazz Band in '60s. LPs w. Mulligan (Verve), Buddy Rich (Emarcy), Goodman (RCA).

DE PARIS, SIDNEY,* *trumpet;* b. Crawfordsville, Ind., 5/30/03. Heard in 1930s w. McKinney's Cotton Pickers, Don Redman; w. Benny Carter 1940-41. Worked w. brother Wilbur's combo (see below) intermittently from 1943; still with him in '60s. LP: Atl.

DE PARIS, WILBUR,* *trombone;* b. Crawfordsville, Ind., 9/20/00. Started pl. w. father's band when a boy. With Orig. Blue Rhythm Band in '20s; Benny Carter, Noble Sissle, Teddy Hill, Louis Armstrong in '30s; Ella Fitzgerald, Duke Ellington in '40s. On leaving Ellington in '47 formed band w. brother Sidney De Paris (see above). They pl. at Child's Paramount restaurant for three years. Beginning in early '50s had house band at Jimmy Ryan's until that 52nd St. club moved to 54th St. in '62. Pl. at Broken Drum and Room at the Bottom, NYC '64; w. Guy Lombardo show at Jones Beach, summer '65; various gigs and one-nighters in midwest and Toronto '66.

De Paris, who visited Europe w. many of the bands in '30s, toured Africa for the State Dept. in '57, and had own band at Cannes Fest. '60, an event recorded on LP for Atlantic.

Addr: 55 West 19th St., New York 11, N.Y.

DEPPENSCHMIDT, BUDDY, *drums;* b. Philadelphia, Pa., 2/16/36. Father a bandleader in Philadelphia. First gig was w. Billy Butterfield '58-'59 on tour. Joined Charlie Byrd in Nov. '60 and remained with him until Feb. '62, including an extensive tour of South America. Returned to Pennsylvania '62 for further studies. Favs: L. Bunker, E. Thigpen, S. Manne, P. Motian, Tony DeNicola. LPs: w. Byrd (River., Everest, Verve), incl. the celebrated *Jazz Samba* LP w. Stan Getz, Byrd.

Addr: RD #2, River Rd., New Hope, Pa.

DESMOND, PAUL,* *alto sax;* b. San Francisco, Cal., 11/25/24. Desmond's partnership with Dave Brubeck, launched in 1951, continued through mid-1960s. He was a major contributor to Brubeck's perennial success in the early '60s as composer of *Take Five,* the first jazz work in 5/4 time to enjoy international acclaim.

Desmond also recorded occasionally as a leader with various groups featuring guitarist Jim Hall. In his own

albums as with Brubeck, his style has remained virtually unchanged despite the many new movements in the jazz of the '60s. Interviewed in 1965 he sardonically observed, "I've become an arch conservative. It is becoming fashionable to sound bad. I suspect that the only thing that will really save jazz . . . is the appearance of somebody who will make melodic jazz more fashionable than it seems to be now. A kid starting today finds it almost necessary to follow the avant-garde. But when the avant-garde is in a state of chaos, as it is nowadays, there's almost nowhere for him to go."

Desmond retained his firm popularity with jazz audiences, winning most of the annual readers' polls conducted by *Down Beat* and taking a place in the annual mythical "All-Star Jazz Band" elected by readers of *Playboy.*

Own LPs: *Glad To Be Unhappy, Bossa Antigua, Take Ten* (all RCA); *Desmond Blue* with strings arr. and cond. by Bob Prince (RCA); all LPs w. Brubeck (Col.).

DEUCHAR, JAMES (JIMMIE),* *trumpet, mellophone, composer;* b. Dundee, Scotland, 6/26/30. Pl. w. Ronnie Scott '60-2, '62-4 w. Tubby Hayes. From '66 w. Kurt Edelhagen as soloist and staff arr. Also w. Kenny Clarke-Francy Boland big band. Fav. own pl. on TV w. Benny Golson. LPs w. Hayes, Zoot Sims (Brit. Fontana).

Addr: Zulpicher Str. 39, Köln, Germany.

DICKENSON, VICTOR (VIC),* *trombone, composer;* b. Xenia, Ohio, 8/6/06. Prof. debut 1922 in Columbus. Prominent in '30s with Claude Hopkins, in '40s with Benny Carter, Count Basie, Sidney Bechet, Eddie Heywood et al. In '50s played mainly in Dixieland groups. Clubs with Wild Bill Davison '61-3. Since Feb. '63, featured with Saints and Sinners, playing and arranging. Overseas tours included Germany with George Wein in '61, South Pacific with Eddie Condon in '64, England and Continent in '65. TV tribute to Eddie Condon '64, Monterey JF '64, Columbus JF '65. Dickenson, wrongly identified with Dixieland, is one of the most fluent and versatile trombonists to have emerged during the swing era.

LPs with Claude Hopkins (Pres.); Wild Bill Davison (Bear); Buck Clayton and Odetta (River., RCA).

Addr: 774 East 225th St., Bronx 66, New York.

DICKERSON, WALT, *vibes, composer;* b. Philadelphia, Pa., ca. 1931. Older brother was classical violinist, another brother is singer. Mother pl. pno., sang in church choir. Pl. several other instruments before taking up vibes. Grad. '53 from Morgan State Coll. in Baltimore. After two yrs. in Army, lived on West Coast for four yrs. Sold real estate; worked his way across country and arrived in NY Jan. '60. Worked at Birdland, Village Vanguard, Five Spot, Minton's, Wells', Versailles. Later moved to Denmark for job at Montmartre Club in Copenhagen and remained in Europe for some time.

Dickerson is infl. more by pianists and saxophonists than by other vibes players, plays with a fine lyrical sense, a remarkable technique, sparing use of the motor that controls the vibrato, and a soft sound achieved by rubber rather than felt mallets. As Don DeMicheal has observed, "Instead of solos made up of one related note following another, Dickerson often blends areas of sound, placing them one on the other, creating a total effect. His solos have an asymmetrical shape, much like John Coltrane's . . . it well could be that Dickerson is the most important vibraphonist since Milt Jackson."

LPs: Prestige, Dauntless, Audio-Fidelity.

DI NOVI, EUGENE (GENE), * *piano, songwriter;* b. Brooklyn, N.Y. 5/26/28. With Chubby Jackson, Lena Horne, Buddy Rich, several others during '40s and '50s. Accompanied Horne in London '61, then settled in LA. Songs recorded incl. *Act Three* (Four Freshmen), *Nashville Blues* (Dinah Shore), *Summer Has Gone* (Doris Day), *Have A Heart* (Nancy Wilson), *Gal On The Move* (J. P. Morgan). Scored for films *Rendezvous Yugoslavia, The Cavern.* Played and wrote for Joey Bishop, Dick Van Dyke TV shows. Acc. Dinah Shore '66. Own LP: *Scandinavian Suite* (Roul.).

Addr: 4742 Heaven Ave., Woodland Hills, Calif.

DIXON, WILLIAM ROBERT (BILL), *composer, trumpet;* b. Nantucket, Mass., 10/5/25. Mother a writer and blues singer. Family moved to New York in 1933. Inspired by Louis Armstrong, Dixon acquired his first trumpet at 18; he also showed early talent for painting, which he studied at Boston University. After two years of Army service, including a year in Europe, he studied at the Hartnett School of Music 1946-51. He free-lanced as an arranger and trumpeter around New York. From the late '50s worked mostly as leader of his own group. After he met Cecil Taylor in 1959 they frequently worked together.

In 1961 Dixon began to concentrate on performing original music, and from '62 played his own works exclusively. He has written more than 400 compositions, recorded two albums for Savoy, and has become a central figure in (and tireless champion of) the avant garde, having taken part in organizing the "October Revolution" concert in 1964. He has also spent part of his time teaching trumpet and composition, painting (several one-man shows of his works have been seen in New York), and writing occasional articles. Ambition is "to write a short contemporary opera, and to collaborate closely with such musicians as Don Cherry, Archie Shepp and John Coltrane."

DIXON, ERIC, * *tenor sax, flute, clarinet, composer;* b. Staten Island, N.Y., 3/28/30. Worked with Johnny Hodges, Cootie Williams and various small groups in New York in middle and late '50s. From early '62 was prominent as a member of the Count Basie reed section, taking frequent solos and contributing to the orchestra's library. He is a strong-toned tenor soloist

and a first-rate flutist in a modern but non-avant garde style.

LP with Basie and The Kansas City Seven (Impulse). Other LPs with Basie (Verve, Reprise, etc.).

Addr: 12 Castleton Ave., Staten Island 1, N.Y.

DOGGETT, WILLIAM BALLARD (BILL), * *organ, piano, composer;* b. Philadelphia, Pa., 2/6/16. Very successful r&b artist during '50s, especially w. hit *Honky Tonk.* Continued to tour w. combo. At Juan-les-Pins JF '62. Arranged and conducted LP w. Ella Fitzgerald '63. Played numerous benefits for civil rights movement. Own LPs: Col., Warner Bros., ABC-Par., King. Others: w. Fitzgerald (Verve).

Addr: 120 W. Bayberry Rd., Islip, N.Y.

DODGION, JERRY, * *alto sax, flute;* b. Richmond, Calif., 8/29/32. Worked w. West Coast bands incl. Gerald Wilson and Benny Carter before joining Red Norvo in '58. Remained w. Norvo until '61, when he began free-lancing around NYC. Occasionally led own quartet w. wife, Dottie Dodgion, on drums. Toured S. America, '61; USSR '62 w. B. Goodman. W. "The Jazz Band," co-led by Mel Lewis and Thad Jones, 1966. LPs w. Goodman (RCA), Billy Byers (Merc.), Oliver Nelson (Pres.), Nelson-Stanley Turrentine (BN).

Addr: 436 W. 20th St., New York 11, N.Y.

DOLDINGER, KLAUS, *tenor and soprano sax;* b. Berlin, Germany, 5/12/36. Studied piano from 1947, clarinet from 1952, at the Robert Schumann Conservatory in Düsseldorf. Started as leader of an amateur Dixieland band but became professional musician in 1961. During the next five years he made rapid progress as a modern (but not quite avant garde) soloist. He was associated in 1963 in a Jazz Workshop with Don Ellis, Kenny Clarke and René Thomas, and in 1964 with Johnny Griffin, Sahib Shihab, Benny Bailey, Idrees Sulieman, Donald Byrd. Visited North Africa, the Middle East, and Scandinavia in 1964; played concert tour with his own quintet in '65 and visited South America, playing forty concerts under the sponsorship of the West German Government. The group also visited the U.S. briefly and played one concert in New Orleans. Doldinger, who says "I appreciate all good music, from Sidney Bechet to Coltrane," is one of the most impressive musicians to have emerged on the German jazz scene in recent years. Comps: *Jive Cats, Viva Brasilia, Bluesy Toosy.*

LPs: *Dig Doldinger* (Philips); *Doldinger in South America* (Emarcy).

Addr: Am Gengelsträschen 7, Düsseldorf, Germany.

DOLPHY, ERIC ALLAN, * *alto sax, bass clarinet, clarinet, flute, composer;* b. Los Angeles, Calif., 6/20/28; d. Berlin, Germany, 6/29/64. Raised in Los Angeles, Dolphy worked there with George Brown, Gerald Wilson, Eddie Beal and Buddy Collette, and gained some national recognition as a member of the Chico Hamilton quintet in '58-'59. In 1960 he settled in NYC and joined Charles Mingus, appearing regularly at the

Showplace with a quartet that included Ted Curson and Dannie Richmond. Dolphy and Booker Little fronted their own quintet at the Five Spot during 1961. In '61 Dolphy also began an association with John Coltrane that included tours, appearances in NYC and recording. In '62 he formed his own group with Freddie Hubbard, recorded with Ornette Coleman and a double quartet, and joined Orchestra U.S.A. Until '64 Dolphy free-lanced around NYC, recording with his own group for Prestige, Blue Note and FM and as a sideman frequently for Prestige and Impulse.

Early in '64 Dolphy rejoined Mingus for a European tour and, at the end of the tour, decided to remain in Europe and to live in Paris. He was recorded in concerts with Dutch and Scandinavian rhythm sections, and while in Berlin for a club date, died suddenly of diabetes and a possible heart attack.

Although Dolphy had earned the unqualified admiration of the musicians with whom he associated, his contributions to jazz and his importance as a soloist have yet to be understood by a majority of listeners. Although originating from the tradition of Charlie Parker, Dolphy's sound, especially on alto sax and bass clarinet, had a savage quality that recalled music of a much earlier era. During the brief years of his activity he was equally compelling as a performer of romantic ballads, blues and as a sideman in an orchestral setting. He was well schooled in a variety of musical styles, and voiced admiration for (or recognized as influences) such diverse sources as Parker, New Orleans marching bands, the sounds of birds (particularly in his flute playing) and contemporary European developments.

Dolphy was one of the few jazz musicians to use the bass clarinet successfully. Don Heckman wrote, "In Dolphy's hands the bass clarinet was never an awkward instrument; it possessed, instead, a serpentine aliveness that coiled with vitality." In comparing the bass clarinet with Dolphy's flute, Heckman adds that "his screamlike glissandos, the crisply articulated speech passages, and the blinding bursts of smeared notes were devices best expressed by single reeds."

Although by '63 Dolphy had come into some demand for a variety of recording dates, there were times during which he found work scarce, especially in situations in which he could express his own ideas. Critical controversy arose when John Tynan, in a review in *Down Beat*, described the music of Dolphy, John Coltrane and others as "anti-jazz."

Perhaps the words of the jazzmen who were closest to Dolphy best describe him as a musician and a person. Charles Mingus: "He was absolutely without a need to hurt . . . he had such a big sound, as big as Charlie Parker's . . . inside that sound was great capacity to talk in his music about the most basic feelings . . . we used to actually talk in our playing. He knew that level of the language which very few musicians get down to." John Coltrane: "My life was made much better by knowing him. He was one of the greatest people I've ever known, as a man, a friend, and a musician." Dolphy was a musician whose constant search encompassed a variety of sources and techniques, and who left in his recordings a great deal of inspiration for musicians of the future. He won the DB New Star Award for alto, flute and miscellaneous instruments in 1961 and was elected to the DB Hall of Fame in '65.

Most of the LPs which Dolphy recorded under his own name are on Prestige, including *Outward Bound* w. Hubbard (8236); *Out There* (8252); *At the Five Spot* Vols. 1 (8260), 2 (7294) and 3 (7394) and *Far Cry* (8270) w. Little; and *Dolphy in Europe* Vols. 1 (7304), 2 (7350) and 3 (7366). Others in own name are *Conversations* (FM) reissued as *Memorial Album* (VJ 2503); *Out to Lunch* w. Hubbard (BN 4163); *Last Date* (Lime. 82013).

The period with Mingus is best represented on *Mingus Presents Mingus* (Candid 8005), *Mingus* (Candid 8021) and *Town Hall Concert* (UA 14024). Others w. Mingus on Candid, Lime., Impulse. Dolphy is heard w. Coltrane on Impulse on *At the Village Vanguard* (10) and *Impressions* (42). Others most representative of his work are Mal Waldron *The Quest* (Pres. 8269), Andrew Hill *Point of Departure* (BN 4167), Ornette Coleman Double Quartet *Free Jazz* (Atl. 1364), Oliver Nelson *Blues and the Abstract Truth* (Impulse 5), Ron Carter *Where?* (Status 8265).

Others: w. Max Roach, Hubbard (Impulse); Ken McIntyre, Nelson, Latin Jazz Quartet (Pres.); Pony Poindexter (Epic); Orchestra U.S.A. (Colp., Col.), Gil Evans (Verve), Benny Golson (Aud. Fid.), John Lewis-Gary McFarland (Atl.), Teddy Charles (UA).

DONAHUE, SAM KOONTZ,* *leader, tenor sax, arranger, trumpet;* b. Detroit, Mich., 3/8/18. After leading his own band from 1957-9 Donahue worked as a sideman with Stan Kenton from Sept. 1960-Sept. '61. In Oct. '61 he was appointed leader of the Tommy Dorsey orchestra, a band organized with the cooperation of the late Tommy Dorsey's estate. The band was part of a show that included such associates of the early Dorsey band as Charlie Shavers and the Pied Pipers. The show gained popularity with the addition of Frank Sinatra Jr. as featured vocalist. Visited Japan as part of World JF summer '64; South American tour June '65, followed by a return to the Orient. Shortly afterward the Tommy Dorsey name was dropped and the same troup of performers appeared as the Frank Sinatra Jr. show. In '66 the band was reduced to octet size. LPs: RCA.

Addr: 312 North M. St., Lake Worth, Fla.

DONALDSON, LOU,* *alto sax;* b. Badin, N.C., 11/1/26. Began to make a name for himself in New York circles in the mid-1950s with a Parker-derived style, playing at The Five Spot, Half Note and other clubs. He has continued to work mostly around New York, but in Sept.-Oct. 1965 enjoyed a successful engagement at the Golden Circle in Stockholm. LPs: Blue Note and recent releases on Cadet.

Addr: 3124 Tiemann Ave., Bronx 69, N.Y.

DONATO, JOAO (Joao Donato de Oliveira), *piano, composer;* also *trombone, accordion;* b. Rio Branco, Acre, Brazil, 8/17/34. First instruments, in early 1940s, were cavaquinho (a type of ukulele) and accordion. First music lessons on piano. Won several radio amateur contests as accordionist while in early teens. This earned him a regular spot on a daily program in Rio.

From 1951-9 Donato worked very extensively in Rio and Sao Paolo as sideman, leader, soloist and writer. Many of these engagements, he says, were short-lived because of his insistence on a jazz-influenced approach toward the traditional Brazilian music, which was to be known as bossa nova and more recently as "MPM" (modern popular music). To U.S. Oct. '59. Pl. w. Mongo Santamaria '61. Wrote for Tito Puente and Herbie Mann '62. Back in Brazil '63, recorded two LPs with trio for Polydor. Back in U.S. '64, led trio for TV presenting A. C. Jobim, Joao and Astrud Gilberto. Arranger-conductor for Astrud Gilberto Jan. to Aug. '65; left to work with own trio.

Comps. incl. *Sambou, Sambou; Jodel; Aquarius, Caminho de Casa; Sugar Cane Breeze.* Own LPs: Pacific Jazz; also on *Bud Shank and His Brazilian Friends* (Pac. Jazz). LP of his comps.: *Bossa Nova Carnival* by Dave Pike (Pres.). Many other recordings not released in U.S.

Addr: 321 Sherman St., Healdsburg, Calif. 95448.

DORHAM, McKINLEY HOWARD (KENNY),* *trumpet, composer;* b. Fairfield, Texas, 8/30/24. One of the pioneers of modern trumpet during the bop era, he played with the bands of D. Gillespie, B. Eckstine, L. Hampton in the mid-'40s, also with Ch. Parker Quintet '48-50. Later worked with Art Blakey, Max Roach, and various groups of his own, also composed music for films.

In the '60s Dorham expanded his activities in many directions. From 1964 he was a consultant for the HARYOU-ACT anti-poverty program in NYC. He continued to work intermittently with groups of his own, visiting Scandinavia in the winter of 1963-4. In the spring of '66, at the Longhorn JF in Austin, Texas, he made a triumphant return to the city where he had attended high school in the 1930s. Early in '66 he was appointed a member of the board of the New York Neophonic Orch. Record reviewer for DB from '65.

LPs: Blue Note, Jazzland, Time, UA, Pac. Jazz.

Addr: c/o Lovette, 120 E. 56th St., New York 22, N.Y.

DOWDY, BILL,* *drums;* b. Benton Harbor, Mich., 8/15/33. Studied in Chicago and played with local blues bands. Founding member of The Four Sounds, formed in 1956 and reduced in 1957 to The Three Sounds. After playing in Washington, D.C., the trio went to

NYC Sept. '58. (For further details see Harris, Gene.) Dowdy left the group in March '66.

DRAPER, RAYMOND ALLEN (RAY),* *tuba, composer;* b. New York, N.Y., 8/3/40. With J. McLean, J. Coltrane, M. Roach during late '50s. Inactive in music due to illness '59-'64. Moved to LA, formed group w. Philly Joe Jones summer '64. Active in writing, co-led own quintet w. Hadley Caliman LA '65. In workshop w. pianist Howard Smalls. Comps. incl. *Tone Poem on the Watts Riots, Crisis in Algiers.* Ambition to have works performed in concert and on records, to make self an example to American youth of rehabilitation from narcotics. Fav: former teacher Henry Edwards. Infl: Miles Davis, Sonny Rollins. LPs: none since 1960; own on Josie, Pres. w. Coltrane.

Addr: 2331 Holgate Square, Los Angeles 31, Calif.

DREW, KENNETH SIDNEY (KENNY),* *piano, composer;* b. New York City, 8/28/28. A prominent figure in New York in the early 1950s, Drew worked with Lester Young and Charlie Parker. Later he settled in Calif., playing w. Buddy De Franco and his own trio. After returning to New York for a few years he took up residence in Paris in June 1961, having orginally come to Europe in an acting and playing role with the play *The Connection*. He took part in jazz festivals at Comblain-la-Tour and Bologna, 1962. In Jan. 1964 he moved to Copenhagen, working clubs and recording with Stuff Smith, Ben Webster and others. He studied extensively, took up writing for radio, commercials, etc. Own LP: *Undercurrent* (Blue Note), also *One Flight Up* w. Dexter Gordon (BN).

Addr: Forhaabningsholms Alle 17E, Copenhagen, Denmark.

DROOTIN, BENJAMIN (BUZZY),* *drums;* b. Russia, ca. 1920. Toured w. numerous swing bands during '40s, then free-lanced around NYC during '50s w. traditional groups incl. Condon, Braff, Hackett. With Dukes of Dixieland '62-'63. Played frequently at Eddie Condon's and other club dates. Several Newport JFs; toured Europe '61 w. Newport All-Stars. LPs: w. Dukes of Dixieland (Col.), Newport Band (Smash).

Addr: 5614 Netherland Ave., Riverdale 71, N.Y.

DUNLOP, FRANCIS (FRANKIE),* *drums, composer;* b. Buffalo, N.Y., 12/6/28. Pl. w. Ch. Mingus, Th. Monk, Sonny Rollins; Maynard Ferguson 1958-9; briefly with Duke Ellington '60. Rejoined Monk, with whom he toured Europe Oct. '61 and Japan April '63. Has since worked as songwriter and has appeared on concert tours performing a comedy, jazz and pantomime act. LPs with Monk (Col., River.).

Addr: 820 Gates Ave., Brooklyn, N.Y.

DU SHON, JEAN (Jean Atwell), *singer;* b. Detroit, Mich., 8/16/36. Youngest of 12 children whose parents died when she was five. Piano, voice, Detroit Cons. of Music. Prof. debut at age 15. To NYC 1960; worked w. Cootie Williams group at the Roundtable for several months. Later sang at concerts with Ramsey Lewis Trio, played Las Vegas Flamingo Hotel and many other night clubs and theatres. A superior, blues-conscious and definitely jazz-oriented performer.

Own LPs and LPs with Ramsey Lewis on Cadet.

Addr: 45 W. 132nd St., New York 37, N.Y.

DYLAG, ROMAN, *bass, composer;* b. Krakow, Poland, 2/22/38. Stud. Warsaw Acad. (piano, tpt., theory, harmony); also bass w. brother. Joined Hot Club of Melomani group '57. Pl. and rec. w. Stan Getz, Don Ellis in Poland, Bud Powell in Paris, innumerable U.S. and Swedish stars since moving to Stockholm Mar. '63. To U.S. summer '62 w. Polish group, the Wreckers, at festivals in Newport and Washington, D.C. Extensive TV and film recording. Co-composer w. Eje Thelin for film *Att Alska.* Fav. own recs. *Ballet Etudes: The Music of Krzysztof Komeda* (Metronome); *So Far* w. Thelin (Swed. Col.). Heard on *Stockholm Sojourn* w. Benny Golson (Pres.). Favs: La Faro, R. Brown, Pettiford, Heath, Chambers, Mingus.

Addr: c/o Beyer, Grandalstorpet, Tullinge, Sweden.

ECKSTINE, WILLIAM CLARENCE (BILLY), * *singer, trumpet, valve trombone;* b. Pittsburgh, Pa., 7/8/14. Rose to prominence as vocalist with Earl Hines' band 1939-43. From 1944-7 he led his own orchestra, which at one time or another included D. Gillespie, Ch. Parker and many of the bebop pioneers. Eckstine played valve trombone with this band. After its dissolution he worked as a single and moved out of the orbit of jazz into the pop music field. He occasionally doubles on trumpet, but is mainly known as a ballad singer with a strong affinity for jazz.

In recent years more than half his time has been spent at casinos throughout Nevada. The rest of each year is devoted to touring, much of it overseas. He entertains for the U.S. Forces regularly under official auspices; he has visited Europe and Australia every year and has appeared throughout Asia. Domestically, he has occasionally teamed up with orchestras for concert tours, including engagements in 1966 with Maynard Ferguson and Duke Ellington.

LPs: From 1960-64 he was heard in a series of albums on Mercury; later releases are on Motown. Among his most successful LPs in recent years have been *Billy Eckstine and Quincy Jones at Basin Street East* (Merc.) and *The Prime of My Life* (Motown).

Addr: 17010 Rancho, Encino, Calif.

EDISON, HARRY (SWEETS), * *trumpet;* b. Columbus, Ohio, 10/10/15. Worked with Count Basie 1937-50. From '52-8 mainly in Hollywood studios with Nelson Riddle, Lionel Newman, Benny Carter, Axel Stordhal. Later organized a quintet which accompanied Joe Williams on tour for 18 months 1960-61. To Europe '64. Many dates with F. Sinatra and Count Basie band '65-6.

In addition to his studio work, and assignments with Sinatra, Edison maintained a close association with the Memory Lane Club in LA, frequently leading a quartet there. His style, commonly associated with certain trademark phrases and with very personal bent-note effects, was molded in the swing era and is still among the most individual in the jazz of the '60s.

Own LPs: River., VJ, Sue. With Joe Williams: Roul. Many others w. Sinatra, Basie (Reprise, etc.).

Addr: 3754 Chesapeake, Los Angeles 16, Calif.

EDWARDS, EDWIN BRANFORD (EDDIE), * *trombone;* b. New Orleans, 5/22/1891. Earning international prominence as a member of the Original Dixieland Jazz Band, Edwards later led his own band in NYC. Inactive in later years, he died in NYC 4/9/63. His style, essentially rhythmic and contrapuntal, was typical of the earliest era of jazz trombone.

EDWARDS, THEODORE MARCUS (TEDDY), * *tenor sax, songwriter;* b. Jackson, Miss., 2/26/24. Prominent in West Coast jazz from the late '40s, Edwards worked frequently with Benny Goodman in '64-'65, appearing at the NY World's Fair, LA Melodyland and Disneyland and the SF Circle Star Theatre. Free-lanced around LA: concerts w. Shelly Manne, Gerald Wilson, Earl Grant, Nancy Wilson. Monterey JF '63 w. G. Wilson. On TV *Jazz Scene USA;* also several TV and radio commercials. In 1958 Chico Hamilton observed that Edwards was a highly original player, whose style may have preceded that of Coltrane and Rollins by several years. "Edwards plays a warm, manly brand of saxophone which . . . imparts an over-all feeling of rightness"—Ira Gitler. Own LPs: Contemp., Pac. Jazz. Others: w. G. Wilson (Pac. Jazz), Goodman (Cap.), Ray Charles (ABC-Par.). Also w. S. Vaughan, M. Torme, J. London.

Addr: 3103 S. Dalton Ave., Los Angeles, Calif.

ELDRIDGE, DAVID ROY (LITTLE JAZZ), * *trumpet, fluegelhorn, singer;* b. Pittsburgh, Pa., 1/30/11. With Zack Whyte, Speed Webb in '20s; Teddy Hill, McKinney's Cotton Pickers, Fletcher Henderson in '30s, during which time he became a dominant influence among jazz trumpeters; Gene Krupa, Artie Shaw, own bands in '40s; JATP in '50s.

From late '50s often associated in small group w. Coleman Hawkins; acc. Ella Fitzgerald '64-5; own quintet w. Richie Kamuca '65-6. App. Berlin Jazz Fest. '65. Joined Count Basie July '66.

Eldridge, who in the '60s divided his time almost equally between fluegelhorn and trumpet, is still a powerful, persuasive hornman and a singer of great heat and humor.

LPs: *Grand Reunion* (two vols.) w. Earl Hines (Limelight); *Alive at the Village Gate* w. Coleman Hawkins (Verve); *Coleman Hawkins and the Trumpet Kings* (Emarcy); *A Study in Frustration* w. Fletcher Henderson (Columbia).

Addr: 194-19 109th Ave., Hollis 12, N.Y.

ELGART, LARRY, * leader, alto, soprano saxes; b. New London, Conn., 3/20/22. Formed band with brother Les in which he toured 1953-8. Took over leadership until 1963, when the brothers were reunited and signed with Columbia Records. It was the first band to open a new NYC band location, The Mark Twain Riverboat, June '65. LPs: On Decca 1951-2; RCA '59-60; MGM '60-63; all others, in mid-'50s and since '63, are on Columbia.

Addr: 55 East 74th St., New York City, N.Y.

ELGART, LES, * trumpet, leader; b. New Haven, Conn., 8/3/18. Sideman with Bunny Berigan and other name bands in 1940s; then co-leader of band with brother Larry (see above). LPs: See Elgart, Larry.

ELLINGTON, EDWARD KENNEDY (DUKE), * composer, leader, piano; b. Washington, D.C., 4/29/1899. Stud. piano from 1906. First comp: *Soda Fountain Rag.* Local jobs as soloist, combo leader and commercial artist during World War I. To NYC briefly in 1922 and again, with more success, in '23, playing at Barron's in Harlem, Kentucky Club, and from 1927 the Cotton Club.

His band, now enlarged to ten men, made many recordings in the late 1920s and earned national prominence through network broadcasts. In the early '30s he became the first jazz composer to experiment successfully with extended comps. (*Creole Rhapsody,* 1931; *Reminiscing in Tempo,* '35). First pop melody hits: *Mood Indigo,* 1930; *Solitude,* '33; *Sophisticated Lady* '33; *In A Sentimental Mood* '35. First European tours: 1933, 1939.

Annual concerts at Carnegie Hall, 1943-50, produced a series of long works, notably *Black, Brown and Beige,* a "tone parallel to the history of the American Negro," in 1943. The 1950s saw the emergence of many other ambitious pieces, among them *Harlem,* which the band first played at the Met. Opera House 1951; *Night Creature,* 1955, since played by many symphonies in U.S. and abroad; *A Drum Is A Woman,* shown as color TV show on CBS, '57; and *Such Sweet Thunder,* an attempt to "parallel the vignettes of some Shakespearian characters in miniature," 1957, in collaboration with Billy Strayhorn (q.v.).

In 1959 Ellington was awarded the NAACP's coveted annual Spingarn Medal for outstanding achievement. During the same year the score for *Anatomy of a Murder,* his first assignment as a motion picture writer, won him three Grammy awards from NARAS.

Ellington later scored two more motion pictures: *Paris Blues,* 1961, recorded with an augmented band and nominated for an Academy Award; and *Assault on a Queen,* 1966, recorded with a band composed of some of his regular sidemen along with Hollywood studio jazzmen.

Tours: five consecutive European trips, 1962-6, arranged by Norman Granz; the 1966 tour also starred Ella Fitzgerald and was one of the most successful jazz shows ever to tour Europe. From 9/9 to 11/23/63 the band was on a State Department-sponsored tour of the Near and Middle East, cut short by the assassination of President Kennedy. The tour inspired a new extended work, *Impressions of the Far East.*

The band made its first tour of Japan in June-July, 1964. A new work that resulted from the trip was *Ad Lib on Nippon.* A visit by the band to the Virgin Islands in 1965 led to the writing of the *Virgin Islands Suite.*

In April 1966 Ellington and the band played four concerts at the first World Festival of Negro Arts at Senegal, Dakar, Africa under UNESCO auspices. The following month Ellington again toured Japan.

Television: *The Duke,* a Canadian CBS Special taped in summer '64, featured the band, Joya Sherrill and dancer Bunny Briggs. A CBS musical documentary produced by the news dept. during the first Japanese tour for the program *20th Century* was screened in 1964.

Two one-hour specials for Nat. Educ. TV network were filmed in SF and Monterey Aug.-Sept., '65 and released in Oct. '66.

As composer, Ellington scored an hour pilot show and wrote the theme for a year-long series, *Asphalt Jungle,* in 1961.

Festivals, concerts: Ellington appeared frequently at Monterey, Newport and many other jazz festivals. At Monterey in 1960 he performed a commissioned work, *Suite Thursday,* inspired by works of John Steinbeck. In 1965 he introduced *The Golden Broom and the Green Apple* with (and commissioned by) the N.Y. Philharmonic. In Dec. '65 a small group from the band premiered *Blue Mural* at NY Phil. Hall.

Perhaps the busiest period of Ellington's life was the summer of 1963. At this time, in addition to playing regular band dates, he was commuting to Canada in connection with the original music he wrote for the production of *Timon of Athens* at the Stratford Shakespearian Festival, and was involved in the formation of a "second Ellington orchestra," composed mainly of past and present members of his band, conducted by Jimmy Jones and supervised by Billy Strayhorn. This orchestra played for Ellington's stage production *My People,* commissioned by the Century of Negro Progress Exposition in celebration of the 100th anniversary of the Emancipation Proclamation. New material written for this show included the song *What Color is Virtue?*

On 9/16/65 Ellington, the band and a large company including a choir, singers and Bunny Briggs were presented in a sacred concert at Grace Episcopal Cathedral in San Francisco. The liturgical performance included a new Ellington work inspired by the first four words of the Old Testament, *In The Beginning God.* The service was heard again in other performances, one of them in Feb. 1966 at Coventry Cathedral in England.

In April 1966 Ellington made his official debut as

a lecturer, addressing students at the U. of Cincinnati.

The popularity polls won by Ellington and by his band during the past decade are too numerous to list here. Many will be found in the poll tabulation elsewhere in this book. They are, in any case, of no special significance; what is meaningful is the nature and durability of his talent. In the mid-1920s Ellington had the best orchestra in jazz and was its most talented composer. Four decades later the same evaluations held true and Ellington, far from tiring or growing stale, was busier than ever in a broader spectrum of activities than ever before. The initiatives he took, both during his pioneering years on records and in later ventures via the concert and festival stages, have been duplicated so often that few artists who imitate them today realize the source of their inspiration.

In May 1965 the Pulitzer Prize Advisory Board unanimously voted that either a long-term achievement award be presented to Ellington or no prize be given at all for that year. Ellington's comment, when the board finally decided against honoring him, was quoted around the world: "Fate's being kind to me. Fate doesn't want me to be too famous too young."

Ellington's orchestra, despite a number of brass section changes and an occasional shift in the rhythm section, retained its perennial ensemble quality and performance spirit. Principal trumpet soloists during the '60s were Ray Nance, Cootie Williams and Cat Anderson; chief trombone soloists were Lawrence Brown and Buster Cooper. The saxophone section was identical with that of the mid-1950s: Johnny Hodges, alto; Russell Procope, alto and clarinet; Jimmy Hamilton, clarinet and tenor; Paul Gonsalves, tenor; Harry Carney, baritone. The bassists included Aaron Bell and John Lamb; the drummers Sam Woodyard and Louis Bellson. Ellington's highly personal piano style was featured a little more often than in the past; he was even persuaded to give one recital in NYC as a pianist.

Following are the most important LPs released during the 1960s: *The Ellington Era* (Col., C3L 27) and *The Ellington Era* Vol. II (Col. C3L 39); each comprise three LPs and a booklet and include many of the definitive works recorded between 1927 and 1940. *Peer Gynt Suite* (Grieg) and *Suite Thursday* (Ellington & Strayhorn) (Col. 8397); *The Nutcracker Suite* (8341); *Piano in the Background* (8346); *Midnight in Paris* (8707); *Piano in the Foreground* (8829) (all Col.); *My People* (excerpts from Ellington musical show) (Contact CS 1); *Ellington & John Coltrane* (AS-30); *Ellington Meets Coleman Hawkins* (AS-26) (Impulse); *The Duke at Tanglewood* with Arthur Fiedler (RCA 2857); *Afro-Bossa* (6069); *The Symphonic Ellington* (6097); *Mary Poppins* (6141); *Ellington '65* (6122); *Ellington '66* (6154); *Will Big Bands Ever Come Back?* (6168); *Concert in the Virgin Islands* (6185) (all Reprise); *Money Jungle* with Charles Mingus, Max Roach (15017); *Paris Blues* (excerpts from sound track) (5092) (UA); *Back to Back* with Johnny Hodges (8317); *Side by Side* with

Johnny Hodges (6109); *Ella at Duke's Place* (4070) (Verve).

Addr: c/o Tempo Music, 52 W. 58th St., New York 19, N.Y.

ELLINGTON, MERCER KENNEDY, * *trumpet, composer, leader;* b. Washington, D.C., 3/11/19. Son of Duke Ellington. Bandleader off and on from 1939. Played E flat horn for a few months with his father's band in 1950.

In 1965, after three years as a successful disc jockey on WLIB, NYC, Ellington rejoined his father's orchestra, this time playing trumpet and doubling as band manager. A good example of his writing talent is the arrangement of *Jingle Bells* for the Ellington band in *Jingle Bell Jazz* (Col.). Own LPs: *Stepping Into Society; Colors in Rhythm* (Coral).

Addr: 180 West End Ave., New York 23, N.Y.

ELLIOTT, DON (Don Elliott Helfman), * *vibes, mellophone, trumpet, bongos, singer;* b. Somerville, N.J., 10/21/26. In a variety of jazz and studio gigs from mid-40s, incl. B. Goodman, G. Shearing, B. Rich, own groups. Composed and performed music for Broadway shows *A Thurber Carnival* '60, *Happiest Man Alive* '62, *The Beast In Me* '63. Composed and performed scores for several short films, incl. *Reflections of New York, I Wonder Why, Architecture USA, Reflections of Paris, Atoms on the Move, Tapline in Arabia.*

Addr: 241 Central Park W., New York, N.Y.

ELLIS, DONALD JOHNSON (DON), * *trumpet, composer, leader;* b. Los Angeles, Calif., 7/25/34. After earning B.M. from Boston Univ. in composition, worked w. Ray McKinley, Charlie Barnet, U.S. Army jazz bands and Maynard Ferguson during late '50s. In 1961 led own trio at NYC Village Vanguard and at Newport JF. At Wells' in Harlem '62 w. own quartet. With George Russell '61-'62. Appeared at First International JF in Washington D.C. Formed Improvisational Workshop Orch. in '63, making several live and TV appearances. Was soloist w. NY Philharmonic in Larry Austin's *Improvisations,* cond. by Leonard Bernstein, in '63. In '64 played in Gunther Schuller's *Journey Into Jazz.* To LA, began graduate studies at UCLA and formed Hindustani Jazz Sextet w. Hari Har Rao, and also new 23-piece band '64. Received Rockefeller Grant as creative associate at N.Y. State Univ. at Buffalo for academic year '64-'65, then returned to LA to reform above bands. Toured Poland '62, Scandanavia '63. Teaches privately and at UCLA. His articles and reviews have appeared in jazz magazines. Won DB New Star Award for trumpet in '62.

Ellis was one of the jazz innovators of the '60s whose experiments included contemporary "classical" music, unusual variations in time and, later, the influences of Indian music. His eclecticism, however, has not overshadowed a basic devotion to jazz forms and a strong sense of emotion in his playing.

Own LPs: *How Time Passes* (Candid), *New Ideas*

(Pres.), *Essence* (Pac. Jazz). Others: w. George Russell (Decca, River.), Charles Mingus (Col.).

Addr: 532 E. Hadley, Whittier, Calif.

ELLIS, MITCHELL HERBERT (HERB),* *guitar, composer;* b. Farmersville, Texas, 8/4/21. Toured with Oscar Peterson Trio 1953-8. Later accompanied Ella Fitzgerald and Julie London on night club and concert tours. A member of Donn Trenner's band on Steve Allen TV Show 1961-4; Terry Gibbs' combo on Regis Philbin Show '64-5. Best known comp. *Detour Ahead.* Like many of the Texas and Oklahoma guitarists, Ellis plays clean, fluent lines reminiscent of Charlie Christian and is a first-class blues soloist. LPs: *Softly, But With That Feeling* (Verve); *The Midnight Roll; Three Guitars in Bossa Nova Time; Herb Ellis & Stuff Smith Toether!; Herb Ellis-Charlie Byrd Guitar/Guitar* (Epic); *Man With a Guitar* (Dot).

ENEVOLDSEN, ROBERT MARTIN,* *valve trombone, tenor sax, bass, composer;* b. Billings, Mont., 1/11/20. In LA from 1951 with jazz and commercial groups. Las Vegas show and lounge bands '59-62; staff arranger and instrumentalist on Steve Allen nightly TV show, June '62-Oct. '64. Arrs. for Lionel Hampton, B. Eckstine. Arr. two Bobby Troup comps. for LA Neophonic Orch. '66. Wrote jingles for radio, TV. An accomplished, extremely versatile pop and jazz musician. LPs w. Ella Fitzgerald, Nancy Wilson, Marty Paich, Jennie Smith et al.

Addr: 20621 Aetna St., Woodland Hills, Calif.

ENNIS, ETHEL,* *singer;* b. Baltimore, Md., 11/28/34. After performing w. Benny Goodman in '58, Miss Ennis appeared in numerous night clubs across the country. Jazz club appearances included the NYC Village Gate and the Boston Jazz Workshop. Also appeared on several TV shows '64-'65. At Newport JF '64. Signed contract w. RCA records '63. A greatly matured performer, seemingly Fitzgerald-influenced but with an attractive personal timbre, Miss Ennis has made an unusually strong impression on jazz festival audiences. Her material is drawn from the current pop, standard and jazz repertoires and she occasionally indulges in superior scat-singing. LPs: RCA.

Addr: 3113 Leighton Avenue, Baltimore, Md.

ERICSON, ROLF,* *trumpet;* b. Stockholm, Sweden, 8/29/22. In U.S. since 1947, has worked with Benny Carter, Benny Goodman, Woody Herman, Stan Kenton and many other leading jazz and dance bands. Has returned intermittently to Sweden, playing with leading groups in both countries, incl. Ch. Mingus '62, Rod Levitt '62-5. Was member of Duke Ellington orchestra 1963-4. LPs w. Rod Levitt (River., RCA), Mingus, P. Gonsalves (Impulse).

Addr: Vita Liljansväg 62, Skarholmen, Stockholm, Sweden.

ERVIN, BOOKER TELLEFERRO JR.,* *tenor sax, composer;* b. Denison, Tex., 10/31/30. First prominent in 1958 when, shortly after arriving in NYC, he joined Ch. Mingus, with whom he worked at Newport 1960 and '62. Played concerts with Randy Weston, including Negro Arts Festival in Lagos, Nigeria '60. Toured Greenland with USO unit '62. Spent most of '64-6 in Europe, playing Scandinavian clubs late '64, then Blue Note in Paris. Most of '65 at club in Barcelona; '66 in Berlin and Munich. During those years he also played concerts in Italy and Norway, TV show in Amsterdam, etc. As Ira Gitler has written, Ervin is "a rugged individualist with an honest, forthright approach that is basic but is not so at expense of exploration . . . his sound is very much his own."

Own LPs: Prestige incl. fav. own LPs, *Freedom Book, Space Book.* Other LPs w. Weston (Bakton), Dexter Gordon, Don Patterson, Jaki Byard, Roy Haynes (Pres.).

ERWIN, GEORGE (PEE WEE),* *trumpet;* b. Falls City, Neb., 5/30/13. The veteran swing and dixieland revival trumpeter, who played with Benny Goodman and Tommy Dorsey during the '30s and led his own groups during the '40s and '50s, became increasingly active in radio and TV work after 1960. On the NYC staff of CBS, he played regularly for the Garry Moore, Carol Burnett, *Candid Camera* and Jackie Gleason shows. From '63 on a weekly radio jazz show with Ed Joyce. LPs: soloist for Gleason's recordings (Cap.).

Addr: 982 Boulevard, New Milford, N.J.

ESTES, SLEEPY JOHN, *singer, guitar;* b. Lauderdale County, Tenn., 1/25/04. One of 16 children, he moved with his family to the outskirts of Brownsville, Tenn., where he lives today. Father died in '20, and until he left for Memphis in '28 Estes helped run the cotton farm with his mother. Self-taught on guitar from age 12. He and harmonica player Hammie Nixon pl. in Memphis—streets, hotels, house parties, clubs incl. the Blue Heaven—'28-32. Ret. to Brownsville until '35 when he went to Chicago. Active on south side until '41 when he again ret. to Brownsville. Totally blind from '57, he was rediscovered in '62 by Chicagoan David Blumenthal in Tennessee to film a documentary, *Citizen North—Citizen South.* Brought to Chi. by Bob Koester for small concerts and reunion recordings w. Nixon.

Pete Welding describes Estes' work: "There is a strong feeling of intense anguish and inconsolable, piercing sorrow in Estes' singing . . . Yet there is no self-pity; rather the impression is that of a strong and proud man who is relating forthrightly the misfortunes that beset him and which, in large measure, hardened and shaped him."

Rec. for Victor in late '20s; Decca in '30s; Bluebird in '41. Own LPs on Delmark; two tracks incl. *Lawyer Clark Blues* on *Bluebird Blues* (RCA).

EVANS, WILLIAM JOHN (BILL),* *piano, composer;* b. Plainfield, N.J., 8/16/29. First prominent w. Tony Scott combo, then spent most of 1958 w. Miles Davis Quintet. LP debut as trio leader, Sept. '56, on Riverside.

In 1961-2 Evans made a series of extraordinarily

sensitive and lyrical albums for Riverside, with Paul Motian on drums and Scott La Faro (later Chuck Israels) on bass. By now he was widely respected among musicians and critics. The most personal characteristics of his work were his uniquely delicate articulation, his oblique harmonic approaches and manner of voicing chords, his occasional use of the left hand in rhythmic duplication of the right-hand line, and the ability to create a warm, beautiful mood within the framework of a popular song, a jazz standard or an original work. In the notes to one album, Evans commented, "There is in the trio's approach to all material a desire to present a *singing* sound."

Evans' career has been an erratic one, marked by protracted abscences due to personal problems. He has appeared in a few concerts, earned the enraptured attention of audiences at such clubs as the Village Vanguard in New York and Shelly's Manne Hole in Hollywood. He has won several awards, among them the DB Critics' poll as New Star, 1958, and a Grammy from NARAS for the album *Conversations With Myself* (Verve), on which he played two and three piano tracks by overdubbing.

LPs, in addition to those cited above, include *Interplay*, sextet w. Freddie Hubbard, Jim Hall (River.), *Undercurrent*, duo w. Jim Hall (United Artists), *Empathy*, trio w. Shelly Manne, *Trio '64, Trio '65* (Verve), *Trio w. Symphony Orch.* (arrs. by Claus Ogerman) (Verve), as sideman w. Oliver Nelson, *Blues & The Abstract Truth* (Impulse), *The Great Kai & J.J.* (Impulse).

Addr: c/o Creed Taylor, Verve Records, 1540 Broadway, New York 36, N.Y.

EVANS, GIL (Ian Ernest Gilmore Green),* *composer, piano;* b. Toronto, Canada, 5/13/12 of Australian parentage. Evans is best known for three phases in his career. During the first, from 1941-8, he was arranger for the Claude Thornhill band. The second phase was his close association with Gerry Mulligan, Miles Davis and John Lewis in the series of records made for Capitol in 1949-50 (see Davis, Miles). The third was his renewed association with Davis as head of a larger orchestra, usually around 20 pieces, that produced three memorable albums: *Miles Ahead* in 1957, *Porgy and Bess* in '59 and *Sketches of Spain* in '60. An unprecedented critical reaction greeted all three. Typical was the comment of critic-musician Bill Mathieu concerning *Sketches of Spain:* "This record is one of the most important musical triumphs that this century has yet produced. It brings together under the same aegis two realms that in the past have often worked against one another—the world of the heart and the world of the mind . . . what is involved here is the union of idea with emotion, precomposition with improvisation, discipline with spontaneity."

Evans occasionally led a band of his own in person in 1959 and '60. A band he led at the Jazz Gallery in NYC in late '60 was recorded in the album *Out of the Cool.* Another album under his name, *Into The Hot,* was released in '62, but Evans did not actually participate, except to sponsor the recording of three works by John Carisi and three by Cecil Taylor.

Evans was reunited with Davis once more when they made a rare personal appearance together, May 19, 1961 at Carnegie Hall. His activity during the next few years was sporadic. In 1963 he and Davis collaborated on music for a play that was to have been presented on Broadway, *The Time of the Barracudas.* The music was taped, used during the show's San Francisco run and dropped after a union dispute concerning its use in LA. The play never reached New York. *Quiet Nights,* a Davis-Evans album containing six short selections with the orchestra, was released in 1964. Evans' other activities during the next two years were confined to a few records: his own album, *The Individualism of Gil Evans;* five of the nine tracks in Kenny Burrell's *Guitar Forms;* and the vocal settings for Astrud Gilberto in *Look to The Rainbow.* These three were all on Verve; *Out of the Cool* and *Into the Hot* were on Impulse. Led MJF band Sept. '66.

André Hodeir has called Evans the most important figure in the field since Duke Ellington and stated flatly: "He is by far the finest arranger of his generation." The first three albums with Davis are indispensable to any jazz record collection: *Miles Ahead,* on Col. 8633, *Porgy and Bess* on 8085 and *Sketches of Spain* on 8271. *Miles Davis at Carnegie Hall,* with Evans' orchestra heard on several tracks, is on Col. 8612 and *Quiet Nights* on 8906.

Addr: Whitby Apts., 325 West 45th St., New York 36, N.Y.

EYDEN, BILL, *drums;* b. London, England, 5/4/30. From '51 pl. w. many Eng. bop groups, incl. Johnny Rodgers, Tubby Hayes, Vic Ash-Harry Klein, Vic Lewis, Ronnie Scott-Tubby Hayes Jazz Couriers, Dick Morrissey. Also w. Georgie Fame '63-5. From '66 w. Stan Tracey, and acc. Yusef Lateef, Lee Konitz, Sonny Rollins, Zoot Sims-Al Cohn. LPs w. Jazz Couriers, Hayes, Bogey Gaynair.

Addr: Flat 15, 29 Westbourne Terrace, London W.2, England.

FALAY, AHMED MUVAFFAK (MAFFY), *trumpet;* also *piano;* b. Izmir, Turkey, 8/30/30. Family musically inclined. Studied music first w. Izmir State Town Band '46, then at Ankara Cons. for seven years. Began pl. jazz at week-end private parties and balls. worked in Turkey '50-55; W. Germany '56-9; w. Harry Arnold, Arne Domnerus, Stockholm '60-1; Kurt Edelhagen, Clarke-Boland in Germany '62-5; Putte Wickman, George Russell in Sweden '65-6.

Falay also app. in Swedish movie *The Boy and the*

Tree w. Quincy Jones band, and played first Swedish jazz festival w. Jones '63. Occasionally he leads a group of Turkish-American and Swedish musicians in jazz combined with and inspired by Turkish folk music at Surbrun's Jazz Club in Stockholm. His ambition is to return to his native country and further pursue the welding of jazz and Turkish music. Favs: Gillespie, Davis, Clifford Brown, Dorham.

LPs w. Clarke-Boland (Atl., Col.).

Addr: 1715 Sokak No. 34, Karsiyaka, Izmir, Turkey.

FAME, GEORGIE (Clive Powell), *organ, singer, bandleader;* b. Leigh, Lancashire, England, 6/26/43. Started as rock 'n roll pianist '59, switched to organ and formed own Blue Flames '63. Band had hit single *Yeh Yeh* '65, toured Brit. w. Tamla-Motown Show same year. Many Brit. concerts and festivals, also solo singer w. all-star Harry South Big Band, regular TV and radio pop shows. TV and concerts in Paris, France, '65 and Scandinavia '66. Outstanding jazz-based r&b band, singer, organist, winner of '66 *Melody Maker* poll as singer. Largely responsible for mass popularity in Eng. of U.S. Negro pop styles. Infl. by Jon Hendricks, Ray Charles. Own LPs Brit. Col.

Addr: c/o Rik Gunnell, 47 Gerrard St., London W.1, England.

FARBERMAN, HAROLD, *percussion, composer, conductor;* b. New York, N.Y., 11/2/30. Studied percussion privately, then at Juilliard. Played club dates in NYC, then joined Radio City Music Hall orch. in '49. With Boston Symphony 1950-'62 as percussionist. Replaced Gunther Schuller as conductor of Orchestra U.S.A. '62. Compositions incl. *Then Silence* (dedicated to Eric Dolphy and Nick Travis); *Saxophone Concerto;* numerous others not related to jazz. Conducted several concerts of music of Charles Ives. Feels that any music reflecting contemporary America must be related to jazz. Favs: Max Roach, Louis Bellson. Own LPs: Cambridge. Others: w. Roach (Merc.), Orchestra U.S.A. (Col.).

Addr: 470 West End Ave., New York, N.Y.

FARLOW, TALMADGE HOLT (TAL),* *guitar;* b. Greensboro, N.C., 6/7/21. Prominent w. Red Norvo, Artie Shaw in the period from 1950-55, Farlow then went into semi-reitrement and by 1960 was completely inactive. In recent years he has played only occasionally for pleasure, usually sitting in at clubs near his home. Pl. weekends w. Don Friedman, Vinnie Burke in Asbury Park, N.J., for period in '65. His inactivity has been greatly regretted by those who knew him as one of the outstanding modern guitar artists of the '50s. LPs: Verve.

Addr: 16 Peninsula Avenue, Sea Bright, N.J.

FARMER, ADDISON GERALD,* *bass;* b. Council Bluffs, Iowa, 8/21/28. Twin brother of trumpeter Art Farmer, he free-lanced in New York with many groups in the 1950s and toured with the Art Farmer-Benny Golson

Jazztet 1959-60. Worked with Mose Allison et al 1960-62; died suddenly in NYC 2/20/63.

FARMER, ARTHUR STEWART (ART),* *fluegelhorn, trumpet;* b. Council Bluffs, Iowa, 8/21/28. To LA 1945; pl. w. Horace Henderson, Benny Carter. In '50s worked with Lionel Hampton; own quartet with Gigi Gryce; later pl. w. Horace Silver, Gerry Mulligan. Organized a sextet, known as the Jazztet, in coöperation with Benny Golson, Nov. 1959.

The Jazztet remained together, though with numerous personnel changes, until late 1962, when lack of work opportunities forced Farmer and Golson to disband. During the next two years Farmer, who by now had given up trumpet and was concentrating on the fluegelhorn, was heard most often in a quartet featuring Jim Hall on guitar, with various bassists and drummers. The Farmer-Hall team was one of the most memorable of the early 1960s. As Don DeMicheal wrote in DB: "Both are gentle players, their improvisations are lyrical, generally employing understatement . . . and often conjuring up an air of wistfulness; neither is a cliché player or musical trickster . . . each is a careful, musically economical musician—few notes are wasted by either."

With the departure of Jim Hall in 1964, Farmer formed a new group featuring pianist Steve Kuhn in his place. He spent the second half of 1965 working in Europe and returned there in summer of '66. In the interim, he appeared in clubs in the U.S. with a new group featuring saxophonist Jimmy Heath and a rhythm section.

Farmer, who was one of a handful of great jazz trumpeters to emerge in the 1950s, achieved even greater maturity and musical beauty as a fluegelhorn soloist in the '60s. His work in recent years has been well represented on records, notably the following: Jazztet (Cadet), *Jazztet Plays John Lewis* (Cadet), Farmer quartet (Cadet); later Jazztet sessions (Merc.); Farmer with Oliver Nelson Orchestra (Merc.), Farmer quartet with Jim Hall (Atl.), quartet with Steve Kuhn (Atl.), quintet w. Ch. McPherson (Scepter).

FATOOL, NICHOLAS (NICK),* *drums;* b. Milbury, Mass., 1/2/15. With swing and dixieland revival bands from mid-'30s, incl. Goodman, Shaw, Bob Crosby during '60s, incl. tour of Japan, Philippines, Okinawa '64. In Las Vegas w. Phil Harris, at Hollywood Palace w. Louis Armstrong, Hollywood Bow w. Pete Fountain. Marched in New Orleans Mardi Gras parade w. Fountain. LPs: w. Casa Loma Orch., Matty Matlock (Warn.).

Addr: 7003 Haskell Ave., Van Nuys, Calif.

FAWKES, WALLY, *clarinet;* b. Vancouver, British Columbia, Canada, 6/21/24. Pl. w. George Webb '43-8, Humphrey Lyttleton '48-56. Since then led own Troglodytes, until formed gp. w. Johnny Parker '65. Pl. season w. Sidney Bechet in Switzerland '54. Also pictorial half of *Trog,* whose nationally famous comic strip "Flook" appears in the *Daily Mail,* and political cartoons in the *New Statesman* etc. Fav. own solos w. Lyttelton *Fidgety Feet, Maryland, Trog's Blues, London Blues, Wally Plays the Blues.* Warm and accomplished traditional style clarinet.

Addr: Daily Mail, London E.C.4, England.

FELD, MOREY,* *drums;* b. Cleveland, O., 8/15/15. The well-known swing era drummer continued to work frequently in jazz, most often at the Eddie Condon Club; also appeared at Newport JF 1965. Started own school for drummers 1966.

Addr: 40-40 79th St., Jackson Heights, N.Y. 11373,

FELDER, WILTON LEWIS, *tenor saxophone;* b. Houston, Texas, 8/31/40. Brother, Owen, gave him his first saxophone. Started playing in high school; attended Texas Southern U. Joined The Swingsters in 1951, started playing professionally at age 12. The group evolved into the Jazz Crusaders, with which he has played on jobs since 1960. Felder played a bit role as a musician in the film *Sanctuary* in 1963. Compositions: *Turkish Black, Deacon Brown.* Favs: J. Coltrane, W. Shorter, S. Rollins, Joe Henderson. A superior, hard-driving tenor man, Felder says his best work is heard on *Freedom Sound* and *Chile Con Soul,* two of the many albums he has made with the Crusaders for the Pacific Jazz label.

FELDMAN, VICTOR STANLEY (VIC),* *piano, vibes, drums;* b. London, Eng., 4/7/34. A former British child prodigy, a U.S. a resident since '55, toured with Cannonball Adderley quintet 1960-61, then settled in Los Angeles. Studied film scoring with Leith Stevens. Worked mainly in Hollywood studios but also gigged with own jazz trio. Sev. months as accompanist to Peggy Lee, including London and Monte Carlo, '61. Toured USSR on vibes with Benny Goodman band, '62. Accompanied June Christy in London, '65.

Equally fluent on piano and vibes, Feldman has continued to mature and is greatly respected by jazz musicians, including Miles Davis, for whom he has gigged and recorded, and who wanted Feldman as a permanent member of his group. He is also a composer of several attractive themes, notably *Seven Steps To Heaven,* for Davis.

Own LPs: *World's First Album of Soviet Jazz Themes* (Ava); *Stop The World I Want To Get Off* (Pacific Jazz); others on Contemporary, Riverside, VJ. Film scores: Two science and art films for UCLA.

LPs as sideman with Miles Davis (Columbia), C. Adderley, Wes Montgomery, James Clay (all Riverside), *Blues Bag* for L. Feather (VJ). TV shows, records, with Marty Paich, H. Mancini, Lalo Schifrin, et al. Movie sound tracks: *Sandpiper, Harlow,* etc.

Addr: 22662 Califa St., Woodland Hills, Calif.

FELIX, LENNIE, *piano;* b. London, England, 8/16/20. Pl. w. Freddy Randall '50, Harry Gold '53-4, but mainly heard as soloist or leader of own trio, heavily infl. by Earl Hines and Art Tatum. Toured Far East '54, Europe '55, pl. in Paris '56 and Vienna '59. Many

radio and TV shows since '61. LPs on Brit. Col., Brit. Nixa, but doesn't feel well represented on records.

Addr: 233 Lauderdale Mansions, London W.9, England.

FERGUSON, ALLYN M.,* *composer, piano;* b. San Jose, Calif., 10/18/24. Stud. w. Nadia Boulanger in France, at Berkshire Sch. w. Aaron Copland; Ph.D. from Stanford, where he was Prof. of Mus. and organized jazz sextet. Conducted symphony orch. for four years. Active mainly in pop music, writing and cond. for Johnny Mathis, King Sisters, movies, TV, radio commercials. A rehearsal group which he organized in Hollywood in the 1960s made an unusual album of jazz-oriented treatments of the Moussourgsky *Pictures at an Exhibition* themes, released in 1964 on the since-defunct Ava label.

Addr: 5657 Round Meadow Road, Calabasas, Calif.

FERGUSON, MAYNARD,* *trumpet, leader, baritone horn, valve trombone;* b. Montreal, Canada, 5/4/28. In U.S. permanently from 1949; best known as featured high-note trumpet specialist w. Stan Kenton 1950-53.

Ferguson free-lanced in LA for three years, led pick-up bands briefly in NYC and LA, then in March 1957 started his own touring 13-piece orchestra. The band enjoyed fair commercial success and produced a series of soloists and composers who were later to earn individual prominence, among them Rolf Ericson, Rufus (Speedy) Jones, Don Ellis, Bill Chase, Slide Hampton, Frankie Dunlop, Willie Maiden, Jaki Byard, Don Sebesky, Don Rader, and singer Anne Marie Moss.

The economic problems of the big band business finally convinced Ferguson that he could no longer retain the band on a full-time basis. In 1965 he began accepting engagements with a sextet.

As a soloist, he contributed some interesting work on baritone horn and valve trombone, and a great deal of spectacular bravura on the trumpet.

LPs: Many by the big band on Roulette; later albums by band and sextet on Mainstream.

Addr: P.O. Box 175, Millbrook, N.Y.

FISCHER, CLARE, *composer, piano, organ;* b. Durand, Mich., 10/22/28. Raised in Michigan, Fischer obtained a Master's Degree in music at Mich. State before moving to L.A. in 1957. Prominent for several years as mus. dir. of Hi-Los, incl. Europe 1958. His first recorded work of importance was as conductor-arranger for Dizzy Gillespie's *A Portrait of Duke Ellington.* Since then, several widely heralded recordings and appearances have established Fischer as a leader in the rejuvenation of West Coast jazz and as an innovator of great interest.

Fisher's first recording under his own name, *First Time Out,* startled listeners with a trio that, although heavily influenced by Bill Evans and Scott La Faro (the bassist was Gary Peacock), seemed to fulfill much of the life, emotion and excitement through the playing of fast and complicated lines that Evans and La Faro had implied.

Fischer lists as his influences Earl Hines, Art Tatum, Bud Powell, Lee Konitz and, especially in writing, Duke Ellington. His compositions and later recordings show intimate knowledge of the essences of those musicians and interest in newer ideas from Brazilian music, the contemporary avant-garde and older forms. Another trio, *Surging Ahead,* and a large orchestral recording featuring Jerry Coker, *Extensions,* were followed by several bossa nova albums, some featuring Bud Shank and Joe Pass. Fischer worked as a sideman with Cal Tjader in 1964, has accompanied singers occasionally and played on South American and European tours.

Says Fischer, "I would like to be free of having to consider 'what will sell a record' and be able to play what I consider to be my sincerest product."

Own LPs: Pac. Jazz. Others w. Gillespie (Verve), Tjader (Verve) and George Shearing (Capitol).

Addr: 2202 Sunset Crest Dr., Hollywood 46, Calif.

FITZGERALD, ELLA,* singer; b. Newport News, Va., 4/25/18. Sang with Chick Webb's band 1935-9; after Webb's death in '39, led the band herself for a year. First hit recording: *A-tisket, A-tasket* with Webb '38. From '46 toured regularly with the Jazz At The Philharmonic unit assembled by Norman Granz, who later became her manager. Occasional film appearances, including *Pete Kelly's Blues* and *Let No Man Write My Epitaph.*

In the early 1960s Miss Fitzgerald, internationally accepted by the general public, did not play in jazz clubs but was heard at such locations as The Flamingo in Las Vegas, The Fairmont Hotel in San Francisco and The Americana in NYC. She toured Europe annually in a show that usually included the Oscar Peterson trio. In the winter of '65-'6 she was reunited with Duke Ellington for the first time in eight years. Her new album with the Ellington band, *Ella At Duke's Place* (Verve) and a European tour with the Ellington band in Jan. of '66 were acclaimed by the public, and by most critics, as her most successful endeavor in many years.

Other overseas tours included trips to Latin American in 1960 and to Japan and Hong Kong in '64. She also gave numerous major concerts in the U.S., including an appearance at the Hollywood Bowl in '65 backed by Nelson Riddle's orchestra.

Though there was occasional disagreement among critics concerning her qualifications as a jazz singer (Nat Hentoff has classified her as a "peerless popular singer" rather than a great jazz artist), there was virtually no doubt in the minds of musicians, fellow singers and the public. Miss Fitzgerald continued to win both the Critics' and Readers' polls annually in DB. Some of her albums clearly were aimed at the popular market while others placed greater stress on the jazz aspects of her singing.

Among her outstanding LPs in recent years are *A Swinging Christmas* (64042); *Ella in Berlin* (6163); *Ella in Hollywood* (4052); *Clap Hands Here Comes Charlie!* (4053); *Ella Swings Brightly with Nelson* (4054); *Ella Swings Gently with Nelson* (4055); *Rhythm is My Business* (4056); *EF Sings the Harold Arlen Song Book Vol. 1* (4057); *Harold Arlen Song Book Vol. 2* (4058); *Ella Sings Broadway* (4059); *Jerome Kern Song Book* (4060); *Ella and Basie* (4061); *These are the Blues* (4062); *The Best of EF* (4063); *Hello, Dolly* (4064); *Ella at Juan-les-Pins* (4065); *Tribute to Cole Porter* (4066); *Ella in Hamburg* (4069); *Ella at Duke's Place* (4070); all on Verve.

Addr: c/o Salle Productions, 451 N. Canon Dr., Beverly Hills, Calif.

FLANAGAN, TOMMY LEE,* piano; b. Detroit, Mich., 3/16/30. Played with best bop groups during late '40s and '50s, incl. Miles Davis, J. J. Johnson, K. Burrell, O. Pettiford. W. Coleman Hawkins '61. Later w. Jim Hall. Accompanist for Ella Fitzgerald Feb. '63 until Jul. '65; Tony Bennett '66. Toured England and S. America w. Hawkins, Europe twice and Japan once w. Fitzgerald. Juan-les-Pins JF '64. A fine pianist in bop-swing tradition. LPs: w. Johnson (Col.), Milt Jackson, Wes Montgomery (River.), John Coltrane (Atl.), Roy Haynes (Imp.), Booker Ervin, Lucky Thompson (Pres.), Art Farmer (Scepter).

Addr: 547 Riverside Dr., Apt. 1C, New York 27, N.Y.

FLORENCE, ROBERT C. (BOB), composer, piano; b. Los Angeles, 5/20/32. Stud. w. Robt. MacDonald at L.A. City Coll. Pl. concert piano, later took up jazz. Further studies with Dr. Wesley LaViolette. Organized rehearsal band in Hollywood and soon earned local reputation as writer. Came to prominence as arr. for Si Zentner band from 1959 and wrote arr. of *Lazy River* which became award-winning hit for Zentner in 1961.

A highly skilled arranger, Florence names Bob Brookmeyer, Bill Holman, Bill Finegan and Al Cohn among his favorites, but says he is less influenced by other arrangers than by soloists, among them saxophonist Bill Perkins and trombonist Bob Edmondson.

Own LP: *Here and Now!* (Liberty).

Addr: 3363 Bennett Dr., Hollywood 28, Calif.

FONTANA, CARL CHARLES,* trombone; b. Monroe, La., 7/18/28. With Woody Herman, Lionel Hampton, Stan Kenton in '50s. Settled in Las Vegas, playing in local show bands and occasionally with jazz combos. Took part in Las Vegas JF '62. With Benny Goodman in LV '66; rejoined Herman in spring of '66 for European tour. Though not well known to present-day audiences, Fontana is a modern trombonist with exceptional technique and ideas.

Addr: 1705 Willowbrook, Las Vegas, Nev.

FOSTER, FRANK BENJAMIN,* tenor sax, composer; b. Cincinnati, Ohio, 9/23/28. Tenor and arranger for

Count Basie from 1953. With Basie through '64. Toured Europe '62, Japan and Hawaii '63, Europe '63 w. Basie. Newport '60-'61, '63; Antibes JF '61. Soundtrack w. Basie for film *Sex and the Single Girl*. With Woody Herman briefly '65. Formed own 18-piece band '65, made debut at Birdland. Town Hall concert feat. Ernestine Anderson, vocalist. Arr. and conducted Sarah Vaughan LP Aug. '65. Own LP: *Basie is Our Boss* (Cadet). Others: as arr. and tenorist w. Basie, *Easin' It* (Roul.); as arr. w. Vaughan, *Viva Vaughan* (Merc.).

Addr: 117-23 134th St., South Ozone Park 20, N.Y.

FOSTER, GEORGE MURPHY (POPS),* *bass;* b. outside New Orleans, La., 5/19/1892. Left home in 1914, played on riverboats. Well known via tours and records w. Luis Russell and Louis Armstrong in 1930s. In the 1960s, after an up-and-down career, he was still prominent in traditionalist circles, playing in Britain with the New Orleans All Stars in 1966. Foster was the first jazz string bass player to gain prominence as a soloist on records, playing in a basic walking style.

FOUNTAIN, PETER DEWEY JR. (PETE),* *clarinet, leader;* b. New Orleans, La., 7/3/30. Played with local groups, then earned national popularity on weekly Lawrence Welk TV show April '57 to Jan. '59. Signed Coral recording contract '59. His first two albums, *Pete Fountain's New Orleans* and *The Blues*, were immediate best sellers and established Fountain's combo as one of the most commercially successful in jazz. He has since established his own club, The French Quarter Inn on Bourbon St. in New Orleans, where he plays most of each year. He has given concerts at the Hollywood Bowl and in 1966 played a highly successful engagement in Las Vegas. After his national success, Fountain broadened his base; with Bud Dant as musical director and conductor, he recorded in many settings from big band to Dixieland combos, string ensembles and vocal groups. With Godfrey Hirsch on vibes and either a New Orleans or Hollywood rhythm section, he has revitalized both the clarinet and combo style of the Benny Goodman swing-era small groups.

Own LPs: Coral.

Addr: 31 Swan St., Lake Vista, La.

FOURNIER, VERNEL ANTHONY,* *drums;* b. New Orleans, 7/30/28. Best known as Ahmad Jamal Trio drummer from 1956. A tasteful, exceptionally discreet performer, he also toured with Geo. Shearing, 1962-4. Larry Novak house band at Mr. Kelly's, Chi., '64-5; rejoined Jamal, '65-6, then toured w. Nancy Wilson. LPs: *Extensions* w. Jamal (Cadet); *Jazz Moments, Rare Form* w. Shearing (Cap.)

Addr: 11554 So. May, Chicago 43, Ill.

FOWLER, WILLIAM L., *guitar, educator;* b. Salt Lake City, Utah, 7/4/17. Parents both musicians. Self-taught on banjo and guitar; formed own combo after graduating high school. Led groups around Utah, Nevada and Idaho, then directed stage shows and bands for the military during World War II. Studied music at American Conservatory; Eastman School of Music; Academia Chigiana in Siena, Italy. Earned Ph.D. in composition from Univ. of Utah 1954. Now an associate professor of music at Univ. of Utah. Directed univ. jazz workshops '61 and '62 which included George Shearing and other groups. Director of public relations for National Stage Band Camps. Was co-inventor of ceramic classic guitar pickup and ceramic bass pickup, both used by several noted performers. Ambition is to teach musicians to be at home in both classical and jazz music. Favs. and infl: on playing—Reinhardt, Segovia, Jim Hall, Johnny Smith; on writing—Leo Sowerby, Leroy Robinson, Prokofiev, Russ Garcia. LPs: Several w. Utah Symphony (Vang., West.).

3546 Apollo Dr., Salt Lake City, Utah.

FOWLKES, CHARLES BAKER (CHARLIE),* *baritone sax;* b. Brooklyn, N.Y., 2/16/16. A member of the Count Basie orchestra since Apr. '51, Fowlkes continues as an anchor man of the band during the '60s. Though rarely heard on his own, he was featured to advantage in a solo performance of *Misty* on the album *Dance Along With Basie*. Other LPs: see Basie.

Addr: 120-68 200th St., St. Albans, N.Y.

FRANKLIN, ARETHA, *singer;* b. Memphis, Tenn., 1942. Raised in Detroit; daughter of the pastor of that city's New Bethel Baptist Church. She sang in choirs from early childhood, and from the age of 14 was a featured soloist with her father's touring gospel troupe.

After extensive travels on the gospel circuit she made the change to secular music at the age of 18, encouraged by a friend of the family, bassist Major Holley. The latter recommended her to John Hammond of Columbia Records, who recorded her first album in August 1960. The following year she won the new star award in the female vocal division of the DB Critics' Poll.

The victory was a surprise to Miss Franklin, who said she does not consider herself a jazz singer. Nevertheless, Barbara Gardner of DB called her "the most important female vocalist to come along in some years" and other jazz critics were equally enthusiastic. She was frequently compared with Ray Charles and Dinah Washington.

Pete Welding paid tribute to Miss Franklin's "impressive vocal equipment and ability to use her voice to best advantage in projecting conviction and honest direct emotion." Equally at home in gospel-oriented material, blues and pop songs, she has worked mainly in night clubs during the 1960s.

Among her best Col. LPs are *Aretha*, w. Ray Bryant combo; *The Electrifying Aretha Franklin; Unforgettable*, a memorial album of Dinah Washington's hits; and *Yeah!*

FREEMAN, LAWRENCE (BUD),* *tenor sax;* b. Chicago, Ill., 4/13/06. Freeman, who with Coleman Hawkins was one of the two completely original tenor sax voices of the 1920s, continued to develop his style and maintained his integrity of personality in the 1960s. He played at the Newport, Monterey, *Down Beat* (Chicago), Pittsburgh and many other jazz festivals. Toured Australia, New Zealand, Japan, 1963; Europe, Intl. Jazz Fest., '64. Comp. music for NBC spectacular, *Making of a Pro,* '63; also several instrumentals feat. on *Tonight* TV show. Started work on book, *Three Little Words,* 1965. Own LP w. two guitars, United Artists; *That Newport Jazz* (Col.).

Addr: 65 East 96th St., New York City.

FREEMAN, RUSSELL DONALD (RUSS),* *piano, composer;* b. Chicago, Ill., 5/28/26. Best known as regular pianist with Shelly Manne's group (incl. European tour for Norman Granz in 1960), Freeman in 1962 started his own publishing firm and became increasingly active as a writer of both popular songs and jazz instrumentals. He became a member of Board of Dirs. of Local 47 in 1965. LPs w. Manne (Contemp., Cap.), Vi Redd (UA) et al.

Addr: 22296 Cass Ave., Woodland Hills, Calif.

FRIEDMAN, DONALD ERNEST (DON),* *piano, composer;* b. San Francisco, Calif., 5/4/35. First prominent in the mid-50s w. West Coast jazz groups, and from 1958 with various combos around New York, Friedman made significant progress during the 1960s as a composer and occasional leader of his own trio. In 1965-6 he and Attila Zoller were co-leaders of a quartet and appeared together at Newport.

The lyrical and highly original character of Friedman's writing can be discerned in his various Riverside albums, and in their title numbers: *Day In The City, Circle Waltz, Flashback.* Although at first he was frequently compared with Bill Evans, it soon became evident that both as instrumentalist and composer Friedman had his own identity. In Dan Morgenstern's words, "Even in his most challenging work he always seems in full command of musical fundamentals; he knows that all real music rests, firmly and finally, on the ability to order sounds in a way that communicates sensibly to the listener." Own LPs: River. LPs with Zoller (River., Philips); Booker Little (Pres.), John Handy (Roul.), Herbie Mann (Atl.), Charles Lloyd (Col.).

Addr: 1541 First Ave., New York, N.Y.

FRIGO, JOHN VIRGIL,* *bass, violin, composer;* b. Chicago, Ill., 12/27/16. Member of Soft Winds Trio with Herb Ellis and pianist Lou Carter 1947-52. Later freelanced in Chicago and in recent years has been in constant demand for recordings. He has composed and arranged many jingles. Since 1962, has led his own trio at Mr. Kelly's Club. Has also collaborated with singer Mara Lynn Brown, his wife, directing band for her in Puerto Rico engagement, 1965, also arranging and playing on her Decca album *My Way,* for which he also wrote words and music of two tunes. Frigo has also been active in art, having given one-man shows of his pastel drawings and paintings.

Addr: 2801 Sheridan Rd., Chicago 14, Ill.

FRISHBERG, DAVID L. (DAVE), *piano, composer;* b. St. Paul, Minn., 3/23/33. Lessons briefly when a child but self-taught on piano from age 15 when Pete Johnson-Joe Turner records interested him in boogie-woogie. Started playing prof. in St. Paul while in high school and cont. while studying journalism at the U. of Minn. After AF service '55-7, came to NYC. Acc. Carmen McRae, pl. w. Kai Winding '58-9. W. Dick Haymes, Odetta in early '60s; Gene Krupa '60-1. Then he pl. w. Wild Bill Davison and Peanuts Hucko at Nick's and Condon's; also w. Bud Freeman; Ben Webster summer '63; Al Cohn-Zoot Sims from that year. As a song writer, Frishberg is represented by *Peel Me a Grape, I'm Hip, Wallflower Lonely, Cornflower Blue,* rec. by such singers as Anita O'Day, Cleo Laine and Blossom Dearie. Early imp. infl.: Al Haig. Favs: Ellington, Rollins, Armstrong, Holiday, Young. A vigorous, two-handed player, at home in many styles, he is yet to be feat. in solo on LP.

Addr: 190 Waverly Pl., New York 14, N.Y.

FULLER, CURTIS DUBOIS,* *trombone, composer;* b. Detroit, Mich., 12/15/34. Came to NYC in 1957, worked with Lester Young, Dizzy Gillespie, Gil Evans; toured w. Art Farmer-Benny Golson Jazztet '59-60. Led own quartet; toured for almost a year w. Quincy Jones' band, incl. European tour. He then joined Art Blakey's Jazz Messengers, taking leave of the group to join Coleman Hawkins for a South American tour in the summer of 1961.

After rejoining Blakey, Fuller remained with the sextet until Feb. 1965. Back in the U.S., he free-lanced in NYC.

Fuller is not an avant-gardist, nor can he be classified as a soul trombonist or a hard bopper. Obviously inspired by J. J. Johnson, he is known for his technical facility, yet on occasion plays with great restraint and a beguiling lyricism. An early winner in the new star division of the DB Critics' poll, he has fulfilled the promise shown in his first New York engagements and is one of the most flexible trombonists in the jazz of this decade.

Own LPs: Blue Note, Savoy, Impulse, Epic, Status, Smash. Also on *Meet the Jazztet* (Cadet) and many w. Blakey on Blue Note, Colpix, United Artists, Riverside.

FULLER, WALTER GILBERT (GIL),* *composer, leader;* b. Los Angeles, Calif., 4/14/20. Father an engineer. Raised in Calif. and Newark, N.J. As teen-ager, wrote for Nina Mae McKinney, Floyd Ray, Tiny Bradshaw. Bachelor's degree in engineering. Back in Calif., arr. for Les Hite band 1940-42. Army, '42-5. Returned to NYC, wrote for Herman, Barnet, Basie, Shaw, Carter, but was best known as pioneer arranger-composer, in the then burgeoning bebop idiom, for the Billy Eckstine and Dizzy Gillespie bands.

After an erratic career in the '50s, much of it spent in music publishing, real estate and engineering, Fuller returned to Calif. in 1957. He did film underscoring, briefly had his own record label (Orovox) in 1960-61, wrote for Ray Charles' first country-and-western LP in '62.

Fuller returned to jazz prominence early in 1965, when he wrote music for Gillespie's appearance with the Neophonic Orch., directed by Stan Kenton, for whom he had worked in 1955. In Sept. '65 he was musical co-ordinator and leader of the house orchestra at the Monterey JF. With Gillespie as featured soloist he rec. an LP for World Pacific, his first as a leader. Later made another with James Moody as soloist.

Fuller is a far more important figure in jazz history than most students have acknowledged. When jazz was shaken out of its swing-era complacency by Gillespie and Parker, the orchestral counterpart for their improvisational contribution was provided more effectively by Fuller than by any other writer. His outstanding early arrs. for Gillespie incl. *Manteca, Swedish Suite, One Bass Hit* and esp. his own comp. *Things to Come*, rank as modern jazz classics.

Fuller also anticipated by several years the amalgamation of jazz and Afro-Cuban elements, writing for Machito and Tito Puente in the 1940s. He wrote many backgrounds for singers and perhaps a hundred stock arrs. for mus. publishers. Despite his unquestionable versatility, he says, "Everywhere I went they tagged me as a bebop writer. The fact that I was a trained, experienced, all-around musician meant nothing to them. Being a pioneer has its disadvantages."

Addr: P.O. Box 8403, Los Angeles 8, Calif.

GALBRAITH, JOSEPH BARRY,* *guitar;* b. Pittsburgh, Pa., 12/18/19. With Claude Thornhill orchestra in '40s, studio staff work in NYC since '47. Participated in innumerable record dates in '50s. Continued to play in studio in '60s. Featured on *Barry's Tune* in Gil Evans' *Into the Hot* (Impulse). LP w. Willie Rodriguez (River.).

Addr: 15 Alta Vista Circle, Irvington, N.Y.

GALES, LAWRENCE BERNARD (LARRY), *bass;* b. New York City, 3/25/36. At age 11 studied privately with third cousin, George Duvivier. Played bass in high school band, also cello. Att. Manhattan School of Music '56. Pl. w. Steve Pulliam '59, J. C. Heard '60, Eddie Lockjaw Davis-Johnny Griffin '61, Herbie Mann '62, Junior Mance trio '63, w. Mance trio as acc. to Joe Williams '64, Mary Lou Williams '64, Thelonious Monk from '65. Orig. infl.: Duvivier, Pettiford; favs.: Paul Chambers, Wilbur Ware, Ron Carter. Comp. *Filet of Soul* (rec. by Mance) and *Grab Your Hat* (rec. by Willie Bobo). LPs w. Davis-Griffin, Mance (Jazzl.), Clark Terry-Buddy Tate (Pres.), Mary Lou Williams (Mary), Monk (Col.).

Addr: 659 E. 165th, Bronx 56, N.Y.

GANLEY, ALLAN, *drums;* b. Tolworth, Surrey, England, 3/11/31. Pl. w. Tubby Hayes '63-5; w. Stan Tracey '65; acc. Art Farmer, Freddie Hubbard, Roland Kirk, and on TV Clark Terry-Bob Brookmeyer, Benny Golson, Maynard Ferguson. Also toured Eng. giving drum demonstrations, broadcast w. own gp. Frequent *Melody Maker* poll-winner. LPs w. Hayes (Brit. Fontana), Joe Harriott-John Meyer (Brit. Col.).

Addr: 296 Dollis Hill Lane, London N.W.2, England.

GARCIA, RUSSELL (RUSS),* *composer, trumpet, French horn;* b. Oakland, Calif., 4/12/16. Active in Hollywood studio work during the '50s, Garcia was a&r man for Verve Records '60-61. In Munich, Germany '62-'64 writing for films, TV, radio, JFs. Returned to LA, soundtracks for TV shows *Laredo, The Virginian*, films *Time Machine, Atlantis*. Comp. *Adventure in Emotions* performed and recorded by LA Neophonic Orch. '65; comp. *Abstract Realities* performed at Monterey JF '65. Also taught at Kenton summer jazz clinics. LPs: w. O. Peterson, E. Fitzgerald, A. O'Day, M. Torme, L. Armstrong (Verve).

Addr: 7436 Mulholland Dr., Hollywood 46, Calif.

GARLAND, WILLIAM M. (RED),* *piano;* b. Dallas, Tex., 5/13/23. Became widely known and influential while a member of the Miles Davis group '55-7, '58. Rec. series w. own quintet feat. Coltrane, Donald Byrd in late '50s for Prestige. Formed own trio '59 and toured U.S. To Philadelphia in mid-'60s, pl. weekends. When mother died in '65, ret. to Dallas. Pl. in LA spring '66 at Memory Lane, It Club. Own LPs: Pres., Jazzl.; LP w. Phil Woods (Status).

GARNER, ERROLL LOUIS,* *piano, composer;* b. Pittsburgh, Pa., 6/15/23. Self-taught; does not read music. To NYC 1944. Made innumerable records in late '40s. Won *Esquire* New Star Award in '46, DB poll in '49 and several other popularity polls in late '50s.

In 1963 Garner completed his first assignment as a film writer, composing four main themes for the film, *A New Kind of Love*. He toured England and the Continent in 1962, '64 and '66. Appeared on TV for Eurovision Network. He was the only American to star in a gala and Eurovision TV show in Montreux, Switzerland, April 1966. Recorded live concert at Amsterdam, Concertgebouw April '66. In recent years he has also taken part as guest soloist with several symphony orchs. in Lexington, Ky., and Kalamazoo, Mich., etc.

Because of the unusually melodic and commercially assimilable nature of his playing, Garner has enjoyed more television exposure in the U.S. than most jazz artists, appearing on the Ed Sullivan, Jackie Gleason, Perry Como, Merv Griffin, Ernie Ford shows, etc. as well as the *Bell Telephone Hour, Today* and *Tonight* shows, and frequently on radio as well as TV with Arthur Godfrey. His best-known original tune is *Misty*, composed in the late '50s and later established as one of the most recorded popular compositions of this decade.

In the early '60s Garner produced his own recordings, among them *Dreamstreet, Closeup in Swing* (released on ABC-Para.) and *One World Concert* (Reprise). He signed with MGM Records in '65. Many earlier albums are available on Col., Merc., and other labels.

Addr: 520 Fifth Ave., New York 36, N.Y.

GARRISON, JAMES EMORY (JIMMY),* *bass;* b. Miami, Fla., 3/3/34. Raised in Philadelphia, where he played with local groups until 1958, when he moved to NYC. From 1961-6 he was a fundamental force in the John Coltrane combo, with which he toured internationally and recorded on Impulse. Other record dates with J. R. Monterose, Pete La Roca, Eddie Harris.

Garrison has developed in recent years into a powerful, technically formidable bassist whose improvisations have a strong emotional impact and whose work in the rhythm section is an urgent, driving factor in Coltrane's group. He is a master of double and multiple stopping, bringing to the instrument at times a melodic quality almost comparable with that of a guitar.

Addr: 132 Lafayette St., Brooklyn, N.Y. 11238.

GASKIN, RODERICK VICTOR (VIC), *bass;* b. Bronx, N.Y., 11/23/34. Father played flute in NYC Latin bands. Studied with him, guitar 1941, later piano and various other instruments at N.Y. School of Music. After service in Marines, joined rock 'n' roll group in San Diego, first on guitar, then switched to bass. Moving to LA in 1962, Gaskin worked with the Paul Horn Quintet for a year, also gigged w. the Jazz Crusaders and Harold Land. Later played w. Buddy Collette, Shelly Manne, Bud Shank, Phineas Newborn Jr., Curtis Amy, Oscar Brown Jr., Lou Levy, and other local combos. Joined Les McCann Trio February 1964.

Favs: Ray Brown, Israel Crosby, and Scott La Faro, although he was influenced by direct association with Leroy Vinnegar, Al McKibbon, Red Mitchell and Ralph Pena.

LPs with most of above groups, also with Gerald Wilson, Monty Alexander (Pac. Jazz), and Roy Ayers (United Artists).

Gaskin is a dependable modern bassist, not in the "freedom bag" but capable of fluent solos and reliable section work. Is also photographer, has done album cover pictures for Pac. Jazz.

Addr: 2452 Horseshoe Canyon Road, Los Angeles 46, Calif.

GASLINI, GIORGIO, *piano, composer;* b. Milan, Italy, 10/22/29. Studied piano as a child. Later studied composition at Milan Conservatory of Music. Made first major appearance at Florence JF in 1947 with own trio. In '48 was heard on Italian radio and in concerts with duo. Premiered own composition *Tempo e Rela-*

zione at San Remo JF w. chamber octet in '57. Between 1958 and '60 conducted a symphonic orchestra in concerts. In '60 composed and played music for Antonioni's film *La Notte.* From '63 appeared and recorded w. own quartet composed of Gianni Bedori, Bruno Crovetto and Franco Tonani. Appeared w. Bill Smith at the Hanover, Germany, Jazz Workshop '65. In '65 also did music for Vermuccio film *Un Amore.*

Although barely known outside of Europe, Gaslini is one of the most promising of European jazz innovators. He was one of the first Europeans to use the twelve-tone row in jazz, and his compositions reflect a sophisticated use of rhythmic variation and careful juxtaposition of soloists in addition to a strong loyalty to communication and swing. As a soloist, using simplicity and heavy rhythm, he is similar to Mal Waldron and Lennie Tristano, his style perhaps originating from Tatum and Monk. He was friendly with the late Eric Dolphy, for whom he wrote a tribute entitled *I Remember Dolphy.* Favs: Hines, Monk, Tristano, Coltrane; Schoenberg, Varese, Webern, Ives. LPs: *Oltre, Dall' Alba All' Alba* (RCA Ital.).

Addr: Via Caminadella 9, Milan, Italy.

GAUDRY, MICHEL, *bass;* b. Normandie, France, 9/23/28. Stud. bass at Geneva Cons. From 1957 acc. many artists at Mars Club, Paris, incl. B. Holiday. C. McRae. 1961 at Nancy Holloway Club w. Art Simmons. From 1962, several years at Blue Note, Paris, w. Bud Powell, Kenny Clarke et al. Frequent commercial studio work by day, jazz club jobs at night. LPs w. Quincy Jones, Andre Previn, Phil Woods, many other U.S. jazzmen in Paris. Favs: Red Mitchell, Ray Brown, Scott La Faro, Paul Chambers. One of France's most supple and adaptable bassists.

Addr: 34 Rue Ste. Anne, Paris 1, France.

GELLER, HERBERT (HERB),* *alto sax;* b. Los Angeles, Calif., 11/2/28. Played with several big bands from '46 incl. Joe Venuti, Claude Thornhill, Lucky Millinder, Billy May. Mainly small combo work in LA '52-58, incl. H. Rumsey, S. Rogers, C. Baker. After working in the East w. Benny Goodman and Louis Bellson, he took up residence in Europe and settled in Berlin as member of the SFB Broadcast house band in Berlin. In August '65 he was a member of Friedrich Gulda's international big band. Co-owner of the Jazz Gallery, a club in Berlin, '64-5. Moved to Hamburg to play on the air with another big band, for Norddeutscher Rundfunk, 1966.

GETZ, STANLEY (STAN),* *tenor sax;* b. Philadelphia, Pa., 2/2/27. With name bands from age 16, when he joined Jack Teagarden. Pl. w. Stan Kenton, Randy Brooks, B. Goodman. First nationally known as member of Woody Herman "Four Brothers" band '47-9. Led own quartet; staff work at NBC; seen in film *The Benny Goodman Story* '56.

Leaving with JATP on a European tour in '58, Getz remained abroad for three years, making his headquarters outside Copenhagen. After playing various night clubs and concerts in Scandinavia and elsewhere in Western Europe, he returned to the U.S. in January 1961.

During the next year Getz led a quartet in clubs around the country, but his success was not commensurate with his talent, for during his absence from the U.S. the more aggressive tenor sax sound of John Coltrane had taken hold of the jazz public's interest. Getz, instead of modifying his style to accommodate himself to the prevalent attitudes, continued to play in the comparatively gentle style with which he had been associated ever since *Early Autumn*, his best-remembered solo with the Herman band.

His first major artistic achievement after his return home was the recording of an album featuring the writing of Eddie Sauter, with Getz improvising over several pieces written for strings. Released in January 1962, the album, entitled *Focus*, was widely praised by critics and enjoyed a fair sale.

The major breakthrough that launched another successful career for Getz, establishing him permanently with mass audiences as a superb artist, was the result of a collaboration with the guitarist Charlie Byrd. Intrigued by some songs he had heard during a tour of Brazil, Byrd suggested to Getz the idea of recording them. On Feb. 13 1962, at All Souls Unitarian Church in Washington, D.C., they recorded the album *Jazz Samba*. Two of the tunes included were *Desafinado* (*Slightly Out of Tune*) and *Samba De Una Nota So* (*One Note Samba*), both composed by Antonio Carlos Jobim. The tunes became nationally popular and were recorded by scores of other artists, but the Getz-Byrd album of these and five other tunes far outdistanced the rest and became one of the biggest-selling LPs in jazz history.

Oddly enough, the phrase "bossa nova" was nowhere used in the title or liner notes, but this phrase, the Brazilians' term for new wrinkle or new wave, soon came into wide use in association with the melodically and rhythmically charming music it denoted. Getz was established as the first American soloist to incorporate the idiom effectively into American jazz and to enrich it with rhythmic improvisational qualities that created a perfect musical marriage.

During the next year innumerable jazz, pop and Latin artists in the U.S. made bossa nova albums in an attempt to jump aboard a potentially lucrative bandwagon. Some of the albums were musically successful, but many were transparently insincere, and bossa nova was soon in danger of being played into the ground through brutal commercial exploitation. Meanwhile Getz produced two more splendid albums: *Big Band Bossa Nova*, with arrangements by Gary McFarland, in late '62, and *Jazz Samba Encore*, with the Brazilian guitarist-composer Luiz Bonfa, in 1963.

By the spring of 1963 the bossa nova craze seemed to be fading, but Getz was determined to try a new combination of talents, this time employing the voice and guitar of Joao Gilberto, well known for some years as Brazil's most talented singer of bossa nova, along with the piano of Jobim. Because Gilberto only sang in Portuguese, Getz asked Astrud Gilberto, then Joao's wife, to perform a couple of numbers in English. Though she had never sung professionally, her version of *The Girl From Ipanema* in this album became a hit, and the album again brought Getz and bossa nova to a high place in the best-seller charts after its belated release in 1964.

Since 1964 Getz has been involved in many musical activities other than bossa nova. Among them was the soundtrack for a film, *Mickey One*, which marked a reunion with composer-arranger Eddie Sauter; and appearances in two other films, *Get Yourself A College Girl* and *The Hanged Man*. He was also seen on many major TV shows, some of them commercial programs of the kind not normally receptive to jazz.

During these years of phenomenal success Getz continued to mature as a peerless melodist, a sensitive artist whose languid sound and occasional contrasting moments of firm, solid swinging were responsible for his breaking down of barriers so often set up against jazz performers. He won numerous awards from the time bossa nova was established. *Desafinado* and *The Girl From Ipanema* earned him Grammy awards from NARAS in 1962 and '64, the latter as record of the year; the Getz-Gilberto LP was voted the best jazz performance of 1964. An annual *DB* poll winner throughout the 1950s, Getz also won many more such awards in the '60s from *DB*, *Playboy* etc. (see poll tabulations).

LPs: *Mickey One* soundtrack is on MGM; all others on Verve, except a date as sideman on *Bob Brookmeyer and Friends* (Columbia); JATP in Europe (Verve). Some reissues of earlier material on Prestige, Roost.

Addr: 15 South Broadway, Irvington, N.Y.

GIBBS, TERRY (Julius Gubenko),* *vibes, leader;* b. Brooklyn, N.Y., 10/13/24. Established in the 1940s, along with Milt Jackson, as one of the first two vibes representatives of the modern jazz (bop) generation, Gibbs in the late 1950s and early '60s continued his efforts to front a big band whenever possible. Working early 1959 at the Seville Club in Hollywood, and recording for Mercury, he led an excellent ensemble that provided a suitable backdrop for his always exciting solo work, using arrangements by Manny Albam, Bob Brookmeyer, Al Cohn, Bill Holman, Marty Paich and others. He also led a similar big band at the MJF in 1961.

During the next four years Gibbs continued to appear and record intermittently with the big band, taping several LPs for Mercury and Verve. He spent most of 1963 and '64 in and around N.Y., again alternating between quartet and big band work. Late in 1964 he returned to the West Coast to front the staff orchestra, a sextet, on the Regis Philbin Show, a nightly syndicated TV series. Gibbs wrote all original music played by this group.

Steve Allen, a friend and admirer of Gibbs, appeared with him at Shelly's Manne Hole, and employed him as musical director for Allen's show in Las Vegas Aug.-Sept. 1965.

Gibbs' band won the 1962 DB Critics Poll as the best new big band of the year.

In addition to the big band LPs listed above, Gibbs had several excellent combo albums on Mercury, Limelight, Impulse, Mainstream, Verve.

Addr: 22220 Marlin Pl., Canoga Park, Calif.

GILBERTO, ASTRUD, *singer;* b. Bahia, Brazil, 1940. Family moved to Rio when she was two. Father, German-born, is a painter, teacher, and prof. of languages.

Mrs. Gilberto's professional debut came about by accident when, through her then husband, Joao Gilberto, she met Stan Getz and was hired to sing the English lyrics to *The Girl From Ipanema,* which her husband sang in Portuguese. She subsequently toured with the Getz combo. Her timbre and phrasing are exceptionally light and gentle. She is not a jazz singer but became popular through her association with bossa nova. Own LPs: Verve; w. Getz (Verve).

Addr: c/o Verve Records, 1540 Broadway, N.Y. 36, N.Y.

GILBERTO, JOAO, *singer, guitar;* b. Juaseiro, Bahia, Brazil, June, 1931. First became interested in music at boarding school, where he heard a vocal group rehearsing. Later, back in Juaseiro, played drums in a local band. Self-taught on guitar, he developed into a solo performer. A member of the Garotos da Lua, a well-known vocal group, heard him, and he joined them, remaining until the unit broke up. Gilberto resumed working as a single and evolved the style of singing and guitar rhythms that came to be associated in the late 1950s (and from 1962 in the U.S.) with the movement known as bossa nova (new wave).

Though Gilberto is not strictly a jazz artist, his influence was very deeply felt in American jazz circles, particularly when he came to the U.S. and recorded an album with Stan Getz, which remained a best seller for several years. His ex-wife, Astrud Gilberto (q.v.), enjoyed a comparable recording career. Own LPs: Atl., Cap. LP w. Getz: *Getz/Gilberto* (Verve).

Addr: c/o Verve Records, 1540 Broadway, New York 36, N.Y.

GILLESPIE, JOHN BIRKS (DIZZY), * *trumpet, composer, singer, leader;* b. Cheraw, S.C., 10/21/17. Studied trombone at 14, trumpet at 15; harmony, theory at Laurinburg Inst., N.C. Toured with Teddy Hill band '37-9; many other bands during next five years including Earl Hines, Billy Eckstine. After leading his own combo, Gillespie took a big band on a short tour in '45. He organized a new band in '46 and retained it until 1950. Fronted combo from '50; toured internationally in '56 with new large orchestra assembled for a State Department-sponsored tour, the first of its kind ever

initiated by the U.S. Government. Since the band broke up in Jan. '58 Gillespie has led a quintet, except for special occasions when big bands were formed for concerts or recording.

In 1960 Gillespie's group included Leo Wright and Junior Mance. During the next year Lalo Schifrin replaced Mance and began to make important contributions as composer. In '61 Gillespie made a tour of Argentina, played long engagements at the Jazz Workshop in San Francisco, and enjoyed a great musical and popular success at the Monterey JF, where he played Schifrin's *Gillespiana,* J. J. Johnson's *Perceptions,* and *Tunisian Fantasy,* an extension by Schifrin of the early Gillespie composition *Night in Tunisia.* For this occasion he fronted a specially assembled large orchestra.

An annual favorite at Monterey, Gillespie scored another outstanding success there in 1962 when he presented Lalo Schifrin's work *The New Continent* with a large orchestra conducted by Benny Carter. During the same year an improvised, totally unaccompanied soundtrack recorded by Gillespie for a documentary film about the Dutch painter Karel Appell won first prize at the Berlin Film Festival.

A unique venture undertaken in the summer of 1962 was Gillespie's appearance at the Juan-les-Pins Festival, for which his quintet was augmented by a big brass section composed of American and European musicians. This short-lived venture drew high praise from critics.

That Gillespie's popularity extended beyond the boundaries of music was illustrated in 1963, when more than a thousand signatures were obtained for a petition to the California Secretary of State to put his name on the ballot as an independent candidate for President of the U.S. The tongue-in-cheek campaign earned international publicity for him during the next year.

By now, changes in the quintet had brought in James Moody on saxes and flute, and Kenny Barron in place of Schifrin. His rhythm section remained the same for several years (Rudy Collins on drums and Chris White on bass) until Jan. 1966, when Candy Finch and Frank Schifano joined the group.

Gillespie's 1965 appearance at Monterey was the occasion of a reunion with Gil Fuller, chief arranger for the early Gillespie big band, who on this occasion was leader of the festival orchestra. A recording of *The Shadow of Your Smile* by Fuller's festival personnel, with Gillespie as guest soloist (World Pacific), won a NARAS award nomination in March 1966.

In addition to frequent overseas tours, festival and night club appearances and occasional films (notably *The Hole,* in which he did not play but simply took part in an ad lib comedy dialogue), Gillespie was seen on educational television shows, in the company of such jazz critics as Ralph Gleason and Martin Williams.

Gillespie's role in jazz history is not fully understood nor adequately acknowledged by the younger jazz students, many of whom see him as a clown, a humorous singer and monologist whose trumpet playing sometimes seems secondary to his role as entertainer. Though he is among those who feel that art and entertainment are compatible, and that communication with his audiences is vitally important, Gillespie remains first and foremost a musical giant.

As a trumpeter, composer and documenter of the new music known in the mid-1940s as bebop, he played a role at least as important as that of John Coltrane or Ornette Coleman in the '60s. Two decades after the first impact of his innovations, he was still not content to coast along on the strength of past achievements.

In an interview with Gene Lees published in *Down Beat* in 1960, Gillespie said: "What I want to do now is extend what I've done. When an architect builds a building, you know, and decides he wants to put on some new wings, it's still the same building. He keeps on until it's finished, and when he dies, somebody else can do it."

In the mid-1960's Gillespie was still adding new wings. Whether he won the jazz polls (as he continued to at times) or finished second to Miles Davis was of no consequence, though he has confessed occasionally to a feeling of having been overlooked by some of the less mature jazz audiences. He has remained, in the opinion of most trumpet players and many music experts, the greatest living jazz trumpet player, a composer of superb melodies (of which *Con Alma* is a striking example), and one of the four or five most important figures in the entire history of jazz.

Own LPs on Philips: *At The French Riviera* (200-048); *Dizzy With The Double Six of Paris* (200-106); *Dizzy Goes Hollywood* (200-123); *New Wave!* (200-070); *Something Old, Something New* (200-091). On Verve: *Carnegie Hall Concert* (8423); *Ebullient* (8328); *Electrifying Evening* (8401); *Essential* (8566); *Gillespiana* (8394); *Perceptions* (8411); *Portrait of Duke Ellington* (8386). On Limelight: *Jambo Caribe* (82007); *New Continent* (82022). On RCA: *The Greatest* (2398).

GILMORE, JOHN, *tenor sax;* b. Summit, Miss., 1931. Moved to Chicago while still an infant. Studied music under Capt. Walter Dyett at Du Sable High. Played solo clarinet in Air Force band while in service '48-52. Tenor w. Earl Hines as part of a show for nationwide tour w. Harlem Globetrotters. With Sun Ra in Chi. during late '50s and NYC in '60s; also pl. w. Art Blakey '64-5. Gilmore, who has absorbed from both Rollins and Coltrane, is capable of working in either avant garde or modern-mainstream contexts with equal zest and drive. LPs w. Blakey (Lime.), Sun Ra (ESP, Saturn); *Blowing in From Chicago* w. Clifford Jordan (BN).

Addr: 62 E. 7th St., New York 3, N.Y.

GILSON, JEF (Jean-Francois Quievreux), *piano, composer, leader;* b. Guebwiller, France, 8/25/26. Stud.

clarinet in Paris 1942; piano '48; harmony with Andre Hodeir. Led own bop quintet 1950-51. Worked as sound engineer '51-7. From 1960 became active again as leader of own combos and orchestras. In 1965 joined the Double Six of Paris as singer and arranger.

Gilson has recorded several albums released in France on the CED label. One, *Oeil-Vision*, is an essay in free-jazz with a quintet feat. Jean-Luc Ponty. Another, *Jef Gilson A Gaveau*, introduces a 13-piece band feat. Nathan Davis and Woody Shaw.

Gilson, though well known in France as one of the country's best sound engineers, has a variety of other activities. He has written reviews for *Le Jazz Hot*, has performed concerts in many cities, and has collaborated on many ventures with composer-arranger Claude Lenissois. Favs: H. Hancock, T. Monk; Gil Fuller, C. Mingus, E. Dolphy.

Addr: 35, Boulevard Serurier, Paris 19°, France.

GIUFFRE, JAMES PETER (JIMMY),* *composer, clarinet, tenor* and *baritone sax;* b. Dallas, Texas, 4/26/21. Giuffre, who had earned great popularity as a clarinetist in the late 1950s, gave up playing saxophone in 1960 in order to concentrate on playing clarinet. He toured Europe with a trio in JATP show, played with a new trio at the Five Spot, then later in 1960 formed an abstract-jazz trio with Paul Bley on piano and Steve Swallow on bass. Toured Germany, Austria, 1961; visited Finland, '62 in "Program For Young American Culture" project. Formed new trio in 1964 with Don Friedman and Barre Phillips. Resumed private teaching of instruments and composition. Toured England, France, and Switzerland with trio in '65.

Changing the format of his trio, Giuffre used bass and drums (Richard Davis and Joe Chambers) for an avant garde festival at Judson Hall in N.Y. After several years of working in a framework almost entirely outside jazz, Giuffre decided late in 1965 to re-orient his group, composition and playing, and to resume doubling on tenor sax: "We will now use the vocabulary of the more established jazz world . . . meter, chords, keys, and time-keeping rhythm-section, standard tunes and in general a more definitive framework. Yes, it feels good to play the blues again; however, my private composition and concert work will go on."

During the abstract period several Giuffre works were performed at concerts, among them *Composition for Trio and String Orchestra*, with N.Y. Chamber Orch. at Town Hall '61; *Piece for Clarinet and String Orchestra* '61, *Clarinet Quintet #1*, commissioned for International Jazz Festival at Wash. D.C. '62; *Hex*, premiered by Orchestra USA at Carnegie Hall '65.

During the years 1960-66 Giuffre greatly extended his technical capacity as a clarinetist and broadened his scope as a composer. His work both as combo leader and composer has established him as a major talent with almost limitless potential; his only problem seems to have been lack of definite direction. This may have been due largely to economic problems faced by his abstract group, and its impatience with the perennial traditions of jazz. By 1966, however, it seemed certain that Giuffre would leave a permanent and important mark.

LPs with trio: *Fusion* and *Thesis* (Verve); *Free Fall* (Col.); *Hex* was recorded by Orchestra USA (Col.) in *Sonorities* album. *Piece for Clarinet and String Orchestra* and *Mobiles* were recorded w. Giuffre as soloist with the Sudwestfunk Orch. of Baden Baden (Verve).

Addr: 149 E. 97th St., New York 29, N.Y.

GLENN, EVANS TYREE,* *trombone, vibes;* b. Corsicana, Texas, 11/23/12. Played with name bands in swing era incl. Benny Carter, Cab Calloway. Later with Don Redman, Duke Ellington. From 1953 he worked for ten years on a daily radio show in New York, also played clubs with his own quartet. In 1965 he joined Louis Armstrong.

Addr: 308 W. Englewood Ave., Englewood, N.J.

GOYKOVICH, DUSKO (Dusan Gojkovic),* *trumpet, composer;* b. Jajce, Yugoslavia, 10/14/31. Worked with Yugoslav and German bands; with International Youth Band at Brussels and Newport '58. Kurt Edelhagen band in Cologne '60. Stud. comp. and arr. at Berklee School in Boston '61-3. Toured with Maynard Ferguson band '63-4, Woody Herman '64-5. Formed quintet with Sal Nistico, touring the Continent in '65. Rejoined Herman in London March '66 for tours of England, Spain, Germany, Africa and Eastern Europe through June '66. An all-around modern-jazz trumpeter and writer of exceptional ability. LPs with Kenny Clarke-Francy Boland (Blue Note); *Jazz in the Classroom* (Berklee); Maynard Ferguson (Cameo); Woody Herman (Col.).

Addr: 105 Moltkestrasse, Cologne, West Germany.

GOLDBERG, RICHARD (RICHIE), *drums;* b. New Orleans, La., 10/22/28. Prof. start w. Amos Milburn and Lightnin' Hopkins in mid-'40s. Pl. w. Eddie Vinson '47; to NYC w. I. Jacquet '52. Later worked w. Bennie Green, Jimmy Smith, Dinah Washington; Mary Lou Williams 1956. On the road w. Ray Charles '57-'58. Settled in LA and free-lanced locally until 1965, when he and his wife, alto saxophonist Vi Redd, moved to San Francisco and co-led a quartet.

LPs: *Bird Call* with Vi Redd (UA); *Ray Charles at Newport* (Atl.).

Addr: 2118 Spaulding Ave., Berkeley, Calif.

GOLDKETTE, JEAN,* *leader, piano;* b. Valenciennes, France, 3/18/99. Best known as a band organizer and booker, Goldkette was associated with McKinney's Cotton Pickers and the original Casa Loma orch. He also led his own band in Detroit in the late 1920's and occasionally recorded with prominent New York stars added to his personnel, among them Bix Beiderbecke. Goldkette lived in retirement in Detroit until 1961, when he moved to Santa Monica, Calif. He died of a heart attack 3/24/62 in Santa Barbara, Calif.

Goldkette was important not as a musician or leader but mainly as a focal figure with a good ear for talent who was able, during the early years of jazz, to give occasional solo prominence to several important musicians.

GOLDSTAIN, GENNADY, *alto saxophone, flute, composer;* b. Moscow, USSR, 1/25/38. Studied clarinet in Leningrad School for Children.

In 1958 made his professional debut with a big band led by Yusef Vainstain, and since that time has worked regularly as soloist with this orchestra, as well as in small-combo settings. Appeared at Leningrad JF spring 1965; television appearances in jazz programs on Leningrad and Tallinn stations, Dec. 1965.

Goldstain (or Golstain) has absorbed a variety of influences through Voice of America and through recordings he has heard, as well as through occasional personal contact with musicians such as Phil Woods. He names Charlie Parker, Cannonball Adderley, Woods, Sonny Rollins and Ornette Coleman as his preferred saxophonists and Gil Evans, Count Basie and Al Cohn among the orchestral influences. In 1965 an album featuring him in a quintet with trumpeter Constantin Nosov, as well as with Vainstain's orchestra, was released under the title *Leningrad Jazz Festival* on Vee Jay Records. Though a totally individual style had not yet matured, the recordings revealed him as a musician of exceptional promise with technique, a fine beat and remarkable fluency.

Addr: Flat 26, Vladimirsky Square, 10, Leningrad, USSR.

GOLSON, BENNY,* *tenor sax, composer;* b. Philadelphia, Pa., 1/25/29. After three years spent mainly as co-leader with Art Farmer of the Jazztet, Golson in 1963 began to become more active as a writer. In 1964-6 he visited Europe several times for writing assignments. Conducted twenty-five piece international band for Prestige LP, *Stockholm Sojourn*, February '64. Two TV shows in London '64; many festival appearances; wrote sound track for film in Munich, October '65.

Golson has gained a substantial reputation as a writer of melodies that have become jazz standards, the best known being *Whisper Not* and *I Remember Clifford*. Others include *Just By Myself, Little Karin* and *Are You Real*.

Golson's personal favorites among his own many admirable LPs are *Free* (Cadet) and *Turning Point* (Mercury). Other LPs with Jazztet (Mercury) and with various groups of his own on Audio Fidelity, Jazzland, Prestige, and Cadet.

Addr: 865 West End Ave. #7-C, New York 10025, N.Y.

GOMEZ, EDGAR (EDDIE), *bass;* b. Santurce, Puerto Rico, 10/4/44. Began to play bass at age of 11; was in Marshall Brown's Newport Youth Band '59-'61. Studied at Juilliard from '63. W. Rufus Jones '63, Marian McPartland '64, Paul Bley '64-'65, Gary McFarland '65. At *Down Beat* JF w. McFarland '65. Favs and infl: R. Brown, R. Davis, Peacock, Swallow, Mingus. Also lists experience w. Marshall Brown as invaluable. By 1965 Gomez was one of the more able exponents of the new music of the '60s. W. Bill Evans '66. LPs: w. Montego Joe (Pres.), Giuseppi Logan (ESP), own fav. w. Bley, *Barrage* (ESP).

Addr: 86-11 34th Ave., Jackson Heights, N.Y.

GONSALVES, PAUL, * *tenor sax;* b. Boston, Mass., 7/12/20. After working with Count Basie and Dizzy Gillespie, joined Duke Ellington 1950. Categorized at first as a virtual carbon copy of Ben Webster, Gonsalves slowly emerged in the Ellington context as a soloist of great individuality with a unique warmth and intimacy of sound, especially on ballads. Though he made a reputation as a generator of excitement through his long solos on *Diminuendo and Crescendo In Blue,* Gonsalves is best represented by such ballads as *Chelsea Bridge* in *The Virgin Islands Concert* album; *So Little Time* in *Ellington '65; Days of Wine and Roses* in *Ellington '66* (Reprise).

Own LPs: *Gettin' Together* (Jazzland); *Cleopatra; The Way It Is;* also featured on *Everybody Knows Johnny Hodges; Inspired Abandon* w. Lawrence Brown (Impulse); etc. For other LPs see Ellington, Duke.

Addr: 117-27 Francis Lewis Blvd., Cambria Heights 11, N.Y.

GOODE, COLERIDGE, *bass;* b. Kingston, Jamaica, B.W.I., 11/29/14. Went to Eng. '34, stud. engineering at Glasgow U., took up bass '40. Pl. w. Johnny Claes, Harry Hayes; '46 rec. and pl. w. Django Reinhardt-Stephane Grappelly; '47-51 rec. and pl. w. Ray Ellington. Pl. w. Joe Harriott since '58. LPs w. Harriott (Jazzland, Capitol), David Mack, Michael Garrick.

Addr: 32 Elgin Crescent, London W.11, England.

GOODMAN, BENJAMIN DAVID (BENNY), * *clarinet, leader;* b. Chicago, Ill., 5/30/09. A child prodigy, he made his professional debut at 12, worked with Ben Pollack's band 1926-9, then free-lanced in NYC radio and recording. Organized his first band 1934 for radio series; took a band on the road '35. Until 1944, when he disbanded for the first time, Goodman reigned as King of Swing, the best known instrumentalist-leader of the era in which big band jazz flourished.

Goodman continued to front a band off and on, assembling a special all-star group for the 1955 film *The Benny Goodman Story.* In the 1960s he led groups of various sizes and was often in the news in connection with his appearances as both classical and jazz soloist.

From May 30 through July 8, 1962, under the State Department's Cultural Exchange Program, Goodman toured the USSR with a band specially assembled for the occasion. It was the first genuine jazz orchestra from the U.S. ever to make such a tour. Goodman's Moscow premiere was attended by Premier Khrushchev. The band comprised John Frosk, Jimmy Maxwell, Joe Newman, Joe Wilder, trumpets; Jimmy Knepper, Willie Dennis, Wayne Andre, trombones;

Jerry Dodgion, Phil Woods, Tommy Newson, Zoot Sims, Gene Allen, saxophones; John Bunch, piano; Turk Van Lake, guitar; Mel Lewis, drums; Bill Crow, bass; Joya Sherrill, vocalist; Teddy Wilson, pianist with sextet only; Victor Feldman, vibes, with sextet only.

Other overseas trips: Mexico City, 1963; Japan, '64. His domestic appearances included a Poulenc concert at Carnegie Hall, April '63; a classical concert at Hollywood Bowl August '63; classical music and jazz at the Stratford Shakespearean Festival in Ontario, '65.

On the local level, Goodman in 1963 instituted a series of yearly festivals under the auspices of the Rockrimmon Festival Foundation, at which he presented classical and jazz artists.

A special TV program, *The World of Benny Goodman,* was presented a few months after his USSR tour.

In May '66, Goodman signed a long-term contract with Decca. LPs of recent years include *Benny Goodman Quartet—Made in Japan* (Cap. 2282), *Benny Goodman in Moscow* (RCA 6008); *Together Again!,* reunion of original Goodman quartet (RCA 2698); *Meeting At The Summit,* playing works by Bernstein, Copland, Gould, Stravinsky (Col. 6805).

Addr: 200 E. 66th St., New York, N.Y. 10021.

GOODWIN, WILLIAM R. (BILL), *drums;* b. Los Angeles, Calif., 1/8/42. Father was well-known actor of same name. Piano lessons 1947-54, then studied saxophone w. Frank Chase; mainly self-taught on drums. First prof. job w. group led by Ch. Lloyd. Worked with Mike Melvoin off and on, 1961-5, Bud Shank, '61-3; Frank Rosolino, '62; five months w. H. Rumsey at Lighthouse, '64; Art Pepper, '64; Paul Horn, '65-6, and many other Hollywood combos. Contemporary fav. is Pete La Roca. LP: *Jazz' Great Walker* w. L. Vinnegar (VJ).

Addr: 5220 Riverton Avenue, North Hollywood, Calif.

GORDON, DEXTER, * *tenor sax, composer;* b. Los Angeles, Cal., 2/27/23. A leading name-band musician in the '40s and combo leader in the '50s, Gordon in Sept. 1960 joined the West Coast company of the stage play *The Connection,* for which he wrote music, led a quartet and took an acting role. In Oct. 1960 he recorded an album, *The Resurgence of Dexter Gordon* (Jazzland); thereafter he recorded for Blue Note.

Moving to NYC, Gordon left for Europe in Sept. '62. For the next four years he made Copenhagen his home, returning to the U.S. only for the first half of '65, when he played a series of night club dates. Working in Berlin, Stockholm, Paris, London etc., he also took part in the Danish version of *The Connection* and was featured in a Danish film. He appeared at jazz festivals in Molde, Norway; Malmo, Sweden; Berlin, San Remo and Lugano.

Gordon's comeback during the '60s was an encouraging indication that the virile bop-derived style with which he was associated when he worked with Billy Eckstine and Charlie Parker can still find a wide audience. Ira Gitler has called him "a highly important player; the first man to synthesize the Young, Hawkins and Parker styles in translating the bop idiom to the tenor saxophone . . . he is a melodist and can also contrast rhythmic figures effectively . . . his big sound and declarative attack command attention."

LPs: *Doin' All Right, Dexter Calling, Go, A Swingin' Affair, Our Man in Paris, One Flight Up* (all Blue Note); w. Booker Ervin (Pres.); Herbie Hancock (BN), Pony Poindexter (Epic).

Addr: Andreas Bjørnsgd. 22/5, Copenhagen K, Denmark.

GORDON, JOSEPH HENRY (JOE),* trumpet; b. Boston, Mass., 5/15/28. Worked with Charlie Parker, Lionel Hampton, Dizzy Gillespie, Herb Pomeroy, before moving to Los Angeles in 1958. Played many gigs with Harold Land, Benny Carter and others; principally with Shelly Manne Quintet 1958-60. After being severely burned in a fire, Gordon died in Santa Monica, Calif. 11/4/63. A highly rated jazz trumpeter, inspired by Gillespie, he never achieved the recognition that was due him. He is well represented on his own LP, *Looking Good* (Cont.). Other LPs w. Manne, Jimmy Woods (Cont.); Th. Monk (River.).

GOURLEY, JAMES PASCO JR. (JIMMY),* guitar; b. St. Louis, Mo., 6/9/26. Played in various groups in Chicago in 1940s and '50s but lived in Paris from '51-54 and again took up residence there Dec. '57. Played with Kenny Clarke at Blue Note in Paris '59-63. Toured Switzerland and Italy with own quartet '64. Back at Blue Note '64-5. Own quartet at the Chat Qui Peche Nov. '65 to Jan. '66. Rejoined Kenny Clarke in trio with organist Lou Bennett Feb. '66.

Gourley recorded with Lester Young for Verve just before Young's death. He also worked as consultant and recorded for the films *Paris Blues* with Duke Ellington and *Ballade Pour un Voyou*. LPs with Kenny Clarke, Lou Bennett and other groups on French labels. Featured on *Americans in Europe Vol. 1* (Impulse).

Addr: 53 rue de Ponthieu, Paris, France.

GOZZO, CONRAD JOSEPH,* trumpet; b. New Britain, Conn., 2/6/22. Heard in the 1940s with the bands of Claude Thornhill, Benny Goodman, Woody Herman and Boyd Raeburn, Gozzo later settled in Los Angeles, where he played radio shows with Bob Crosby and later became a highly valued studio man. He was considered one of the outstanding lead trumpeters on the West Coast. Gozzo died of a heart attack in Los Angeles 10/8/64.

GRAAS, JOHN,* French horn, composer; b. Dubuque, Iowa, 10/14/24. Originally a classical musician with extensive training, Graas free-lanced in Hollywood in the 1950s and earned some prominence as a jazz French horn soloist and as a composer both of straight jazz works and of third stream compositions such as *Jazz Symphony No. 1* and *Jazz Chaconne No. 1*; he recorded both for the since defunct Andex label.

In 1961 he worked with singer Eddie Fisher in Las Vegas, and was busy as a studio musician and teacher. He died suddenly of a heart attack 4/13/62 in Van Nuys, Calif.

The musical conceptions of John Graas knew no geographical boundaries. He was determined to stretch the borderlines of jazz while keeping faith with its origins. In effect, he was a third stream musician years before that catch phrase became popular. Some of his best work can be heard on two albums entitled *Jazz Lab* (Decca) and on *Coup de Graas* and *John Graas!* (Merc.).

GRANELLI, GERALD JOHN (JERRY), drums; also vibes, piano; b. San Francisco, Calif. 12/30/40. Father and uncle both drummers. Studied violin for a year, later studied drums with Joe Morello, his main influence. After club dates in S.F. area joined Vince Guaraldi in 1962. Formed own group, the Jazz Ensemble, '64. Worked with Jon Hendricks, John Handy, Martial Solal, Jack Sheldon and Jimmy Witherspoon; also records and clubs with Denny Zeitlin from summer of '64. In '65 completed movie score with own group for story by Herbert Gold called *Jim The Man* premiered at San Francisco Film Festival.

Favs: Philly Joe Jones, Roy Haynes, Buddy Rich, Max Roach and Joe Morello.

LPs with Guaraldi (Fantasy), Zeitlin (Col.). Granelli, particularly in his work with Zeitlin, showed exceptional aptitude for sympathetic small combo work.

Addr: 168 Westlake Ave., Daly City, Calif.

GRANZ, NORMAN,* producer; b. Los Angeles, Calif., 8/6/18. Started producing concerts at LA Philharmonic Auditorium in 1944. From the mid-'40s his concerts, in the U.S. and also later overseas, set a pattern for informal jazz stage shows and earned tremendous international popularity. Granz also pioneered the concept of recording "live" at actual performances instead of in recording studios. After his last U.S. tour in '57 he continued to take jazz shows abroad, making his own residence in Switzerland.

In Jan. 1961 Granz sold his Verve Record company to MGM for $2,500,000. Though no longer in the record business he became very active in the importing of various artists to Europe for extended tours, and acted as manager for Ella Fitzgerald, Oscar Peterson and Duke Ellington. Maintaining homes in Paris and Geneva, he returned to the U.S. from time to time, usually to supervise Miss Fitzgerald's recordings and to negotiate tours.

Addr: c/o Salle Productions, 451 N. Canon Drive, Beverly Hills, Calif.

GRAPPELLY, STEPHANE,* violin; b. Paris, France, 1/26/08. First came to public attention with Django Reinhardt in the Quintet of the Hot Club of France in 1934. In the 1960s he was still on tour in France and recorded occasionally with visiting U.S. musicians who have been among his admirers for many years,

John Lewis *(Roberto Polillo)*

Freddie Hubbard *(Francis Wolff-Blue Note Records)*

George Braith *(Blue Note Records)*

Tubby Hayes

Eraldo Volonte *(Roberto Polillo)*

Lars Gullin *(Randi W. Hultin)*

Don Cherry (*Francis Wolff-Blue Note Records*)

J. J. Johnson

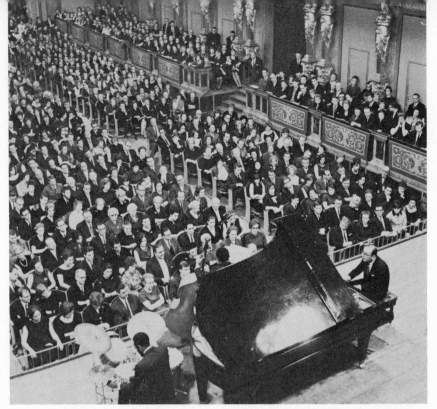

Gulda Jazz Trio. L. to R.: Albert Heath, Ron Carter, Friedrich Gulda (*Votava*, Vien

Thelonious Monk

Louis Bellson (*Impulse Records*)

Hank Mobley (*Francis Wolff-Blue Note Records*)

Stan Kenton (*Capitol Records*)

Giorgio Gaslini (*Roberto Polillo*)

Cootie Williams (*Don Schlitten*)

Oliver Nelson (*Chuck Stewart*)

Esther Phillips (*Charles Frizzell*)

135

Bill Evans

Jaki Byard *(Don Schlitten)*

Booker Little (*Don Schlitten*)

Donald Byrd (*Roberto Polillo*)

Eric Dolphy (*Roberto Polillo*)

Carmen McRae *(Charles Stewart)*

Tyree Glenn and Aretha Franklin

Dexter Gordon *(Randi W. Hultin)*

Gilbert Rovère *(Roberto Polillo)*

Dave Brubeck and Jimmy Rushing
(Columbia Records)

Cal Tjader *(MGM/Verve Records)*

Ray Charles *(ABC-Paramount Records)*   Wild Bill Davis

Elvin Jones *(Roberto Polillo)*

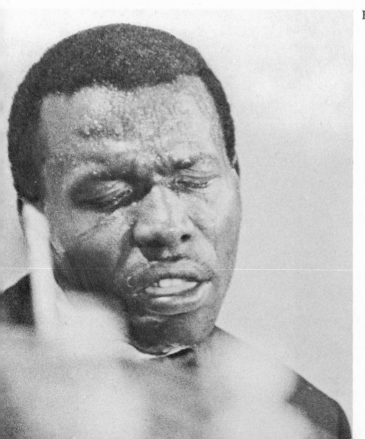

Sonny Rollins

Gary McFarland *(MGM/Verve Records)*

Lennie Tristano *(Roberto Polillo)*

L. to R.: Dizzy Gillespie, Gil Fuller, Dick Bock

Antonio Carlos Jobim *(MGM/Verve Records)*

Abbey Lincoln and Max Roach *(Bob Thiele)*

Larry Young *(Francis Wolff-Blue Note Records)*   Eddie Harris *(Atlantic Records)*

Grant Green *(Francis Wolff-Blue Note Records)*   Herbie Hancock *(Blue Note Records)*

incl. Duke Ellington, Oscar Peterson, John Lewis, Stuff Smith.

According to Frank Tenot of the French magazine *Jazz*, Grappelly has the style of "a sensitive and refined musician who is both a sentimentalist and an artist. He likes elegant, well-balanced and melodic phrases and his improvisations are constructed with the logic of a person who thinks clearly and knows exactly where he wants to go."

Though these characteristics are best displayed in his ballad work, Grappelly can swing forcefully at times and ranks among the handful of genuine masters of jazz violin.

LP: *Feeling + Finesse = Jazz* (Atl.).

Addr: 10 Rue d'Orchampt., Paris 18, France.

GRAVES, MILFORD, *drums, percussion;* b. Jamaica, N.Y., 8/20/41. Self-taught during childhood. Came to prominence at various N.Y. avant-garde events: October Revolution w. Giuseppi Logan, N.Y. Arts Quartet, 10/64; w. Jazz Composers' Orch, New Music Concert at Town Hall, 12/64, 1/65; Newport '65; *Down Beat* concerts, N.Y. Museum of Modern Art, 7/65. Plays drums as part of total ensemble rather than as an accompanist. Taught music at Black Arts Repertory Theater, Harlem. Studied North Indian music w. Wasantha Singh. Regarding his radical departure from conventional drumming, Graves says, "When I was born there were drums in my house. No one was a musician and I was the only child, so there was no one to distort my mind toward hearing the drum as a drum—I had no bias as to what came out of the drum."

Own LP: ESP. Others w. Logan, Paul Bley, N.Y. Arts Quartet, Lowell Davidson (all ESP); Montego Joe (Pres.); Miriam Makeba, Hugh Masekela (RCA).

Addr: 287 New Lots Ave., Brooklyn 7, N.Y.

GRAY, JOHN W. (JOHNNY), *guitar;* b. Vinita, Okla., 6/2/24. Stud. in Washington, D.C. 1944. Toured w. Ray McKinley band '47-8. Staff musician at ABC in Chicago 1952-60. Since then has free-lanced in Hollywood, also toured six months w. Geo. Shearing '62. Gray says, "I should have been a horn player; I was influenced primarily by Lester Young, Charlie Parker and Dizzy Gillespie." He is a fluent modern soloist along lines patterned after Charlie Christian. Own LP: *The New Wave* (Cap.); others w. Shearing, Nancy Wilson (Cap.), Julie London (Lib).

Addr: 11261 Otsego St., North Hollywood, Calif.

GRAY, GLEN (SPIKE) (Glen Gray Knoblaugh),* *leader;* b. Roanoke, Ill., 6/7/06. Leader of the Casa Loma Orch., a band of the '30s stated by some experts to have been the first large white orchestra with a jazz policy, Gray retired in 1950 but from 1956 began making records again, using specially assembled groups of studio musicians. He died in Plymouth, Mass. 8/23/63. After his death, records continued to appear under his name, dedicated to revivals of the sounds and tunes associated with various big bands in the swing era.

GREEN, BERNARD (BENNY),* *composer, critic, baritone sax;* b. Leeds, Yorkshire, England 12/9/27. Book *The Reluctant Art—Five Studies in the Growth of Jazz* pub. by Horizon Press. Wrote book and lyrics of opera-ballet *Lysistrata* by Johnny Dankworth '64. Regular TV apps. as commentator on events from '64, own current affairs and conversation show for *Rediffusion '66.*

Addr: 6 Barn Rise, Wembley, Middlesex, England.

GREEN, VERNICE JR. (BUNKY), *alto sax;* also *tenor, flute, baritone, clarinet;* b. Milwaukee, Wis., 4/23/35. Several church singers but no prof. mus. in family. Mainly self-taught; infl. by Charlie Parker. Played variety of jobs in Milwaukee, from jazz clubs to strip show, until 1960, except for an interlude of two months in 1960 when, recommended by Lou Donaldson, he worked in NYC and LA w. Ch. Mingus. Moved to Chicago 1960; worked there w. Nicky Hill, Ira Sullivan, Andrew Hill, Red Saunders, Louis Bellson. Started stud. at Roosevelt U. for music degree, 1963; in '64 was a winner at Notre Dame Intercoll. Jazz Fest. and won trip to Algiers under U.S. Govt. sponsorship for World Intl. Trade Fair. Led pit band at Gai Paris, Chi., '65. LPs w. Paul Serrano (Riv.), MJT Plus 3 (VJ); own LPs on VJ, Argo.

Though influenced by the directions of the new school, Green essentially is a product of the Parker school. He is one of the most consistently swinging performers in this class to have come to prominence in the 1960s.

Addr: 2646 N. Hoyne Ave., Chicago, Ill.

GREEN, FREDERICK WILLIAM (FREDDIE),* *guitar;* b. Charleston, S.C., 3/31/11. Except for a brief interlude in 1950, has been a member of Count Basie's rhythm section since 1937. His steady strumming on an unamplified guitar has been an invaluable component of the group's sound. Green's has long been considered the definitive rhythm-guitar style. Very rarely heard in solo work, he may be heard individually in a few passages on *Memories Ad Lib* with Basie and Joe Williams (Roulette). Other LPs: see Basie, Count.

Addr: 2171 Madison Avenue, New York 37, N.Y.

GREEN, GRANT, *guitar;* b. St. Louis, Missouri, 6/6/31. Began studying guitar while in grade school, and played with local groups from 1944. After dividing his time between jazz and rhythm and blues groups, including Jimmy Forrest combo, Jack Murphy, Sam Lazar, Green moved to New York in 1960. A few months later, through the intercession of Lou Donaldson, he made his debut on Blue Note Records. His work was warmly received by the critics. In 1962 he won the New Star guitar category in the DB critics' poll. Green has led his own groups in clubs, mostly in and around New York, and has been featured in a wide variety of contexts on his albums. Robert Levin observed that Green "is particularly concerned with the guitar's horn-like possibilities, and has reduced certain elements of Charlie Christian's approach to their basics." Nat Hentoff wrote: "Though technically assured, Green avoids bravura displays of digital expertise. With maximum economy of means, he drives into the core of whatever tune he's enlivening, and unravels a series of uncommonly uncluttered variations."

Though many of Green's albums have featured him in settings including an organist, and frequently playing blues, he is by no means limited to this type of context, as is illustrated in such albums as *The Latin Bit* and *Idle Moments* (both Blue Note). In 1966 he began recording for Verve.

GREEN, URBAN CLIFFORD (URBIE), * trombone; b. Mobile, Ala., 8/8/26. Earned jazz reputation with Woody Herman band 1950-52. Later pl. w. Benny Goodman (incl. film, *The Benny Goodman Story*) but has worked mainly as studio musician in New York. In '65 he was with Elliot Lawrence's house band on Les Crane's *Nightlife* TV show. Led Tommy Dorsey orch. for four weeks at Riverboat in NYC '66; later formed his own band to play at the same location. Avocationally is a farmer, raising cattle outside Phila.

Own LPs: Command.

Addr: 35-05 163rd St., Flushing, N.Y. 11358.

GREEN, WILLIAM EARNEST, *saxophones, woodwinds;* b. Kansas City, Kans., 2/28/25. Stud. clarinet. Pl. w. WPA band in K.C. Settling in LA, became one of the city's busiest free-lance musicians. Worked as sideman and soloist w. Nelson Riddle from 1960; led group at Marty's Club in LA. TV: *M Squad* show '64. Gil Fuller Orch. at Monterey JF '65. Clarinet with Highland Park Symphony. Has also been teaching for several years. Favs: Benny Carter, Lucky Thompson, Ch. Parker, Don Byas.

Own LP: *Shades of Green* (Everest). LPs w. Gil Fuller (Pac. Jazz); Benny Carter (Impulse); *Golden Boy* with H. B. Barnum (Cap.).

Addr: 4526 Don Miguel Dr., Los Angeles, Calif.

GREER, WILLIAM ALEXANDER (SONNY), * drums; b. Long Branch, N.J., 12/13/03. With Duke Ellington from 1919 to March '51, Greer established himself as one of the premier percussionists in jazz. Pl. w. Johnny Hodges, Red Allen, Tyree Glenn in '50s. Free-lance in NYC in '60s. App. at Ellington Jazz Society concert at Town Hall '63. LP w. Earl Hines (Impulse).

Addr: 1029 College Ave., Bronx 56, N.Y.

GREY, ALBERT THORNTON (AL), * trombone; b. Aldie, Va., 6/6/25. Played in 1940s and '50s with Benny Carter, Jimmie Lunceford, Lionel Hampton, Dizzy Gillespie. Joined Count Basie 1957 and remained until early 1961.

During most of the next three and a half years, while he was away from the Basie band, Grey became co-leader with another former Basie orchestra member, tenor saxophonist Billy Mitchell, of a combo that enjoyed some success playing nightclubs and concerts. Grey rejoined Basie in Oct. 1964 and became one of the most prominently featured soloists in the band,

specializing in a modern equivalent of the old rubber plunger technique originated in Duke Ellington's band by the late Tricky Sam Nanton.

Own LPs: *Shades of Grey* (Tangerine) and several earlier albums on Cadet, including those featuring Billy Mitchell. Many LPs with Basie (Roul., Verve, Reprise).

GRIFFIN, JOHN ARNOLD III (JOHNNY), * tenor saxophone; b. Chicago, Ill., 4/24/28. Prominent in the groups of Art Blakey, Thelonious Monk and others in the late '50s, Griffin formed a quintet with Eddie (Lockjaw) Davis, playing at Birdland March, 1960. The combo remained together until July 1962, recording two albums for Prestige and six for Jazzland. In Dec. '62 Griffin left for Europe, working the Blue Note in Paris, The Golden Circle in Stockholm, Ronnie Scott's club in London. He returned to New York in March '63 but was back on the Continent two months later. During the next three years he played concerts in France, Italy, Germany, Switzerland, and Belgium as well as club dates in Paris, Brussels, Berlin and Copenhagen, etc. Living in Paris 1966. Among the many excellent LPs by this hard-driving soloist are: *Change of Pace* (River.), *Tough Tenor Favorites* w. Davis (Jazzland), *Night Lady* (Emarcy); also *Full House* w. Wes Montgomery (River.), *Four Seasons* w. Raymond Fol (Philips).

Addr: 432 East 46th St., Chicago, Ill.

GRIMES, HENRY ALONZO, * bass; b. Philadelphia, Pa., 11/3/35. From 1957 active in the east w. groups of Gerry Mulligan, Tony Scott, Sonny Rollins, Grimes in the '60s moved more into the area of the avant garde, app. w. Cecil Taylor and Perry Robinson, among others; also worked w. Mose Allison. LPs w. Taylor in *Into the Hot* Gil Evans (Imp.); Don Cherry (BN); Robinson (ESP), Allison (Alt.), Rollins (RCA).

Addr: 272 East 7th St., New York 9, N.Y.

GROVE, RICHARD DEAN (DICK), *piano, arranger;* b. Lakeville, Ind., 12/18/27. From a musical family, Grove began playing with local bands while attending high school. Majored in comp., minored in piano at Denver U. Music School. Began leading own band in LA '62, playing at colleges, the Lighthouse through '64. Piano w. John Graas quintet. Staff arranger for *King Family* TV show. Grove is an eclectic and talented performer and composer. Favs. and infl: O. Peterson, B. Evans, P. Jolly; Gil Evans. Own LP: *Little Bird Suite* (Pac. Jazz). Others: arr. and cond. for Pete Jolly *Hello Jolly* (Ava).

Addr: 8239 Webb Ave., No. Hollywood, Calif.

GRUNTZ, GEORGE, * piano; b. Basel, Switzerland, 6/24/32. After part-time free-lancing in Switzerland and Sweden during the '50s, Gruntz returned to professional music in '63. Comps. incl. several jazz symphonies and chamber pieces, and a film soundtrack w. Donald Byrd. Accompanied several top U.S. artists on European tours, incl. Byrd, R. Kirk, L. Konitz, Dexter Gordon. Appeared at all major European jazz festivals.

Toured Japan w. Helen Merrill as pianist and band-leader '63. W. Flavio Ambrosetti's All-Stars from '65. Led own trios in Switzerland and throughout Europe. Feels that European tradition of music as an art has helped jazz to become an established art form there. In '65 began forming a jazz workshop in Switzerland. LPs: numerous releases under own name in Europe. One available in U.S. is *Bach Humbug!* (Phil.).

Addr: 4123 Allschwil-Basel, Weiherweg 1, Switzerland.

GRUSIN, DAVE, *composer, piano;* b. Denver, Colo., 6/26/34. Stud. U. of Colo. Pl. w. visiting musicians incl. Terry Gibbs, Johnny Smith. After Navy service in '56 went to NYC to continue studies. Pl. w. Andy Williams 1959 and remained with him off and on as musical director to '66. TV shows with Benny Goodman '62. Since 1960 Quincy Jones has been close associate and strong influence. Settled in LA '62. Arrs. for Peggy Lee, Mel Torme. Pl. w. Ruth Price at Shelly's Manne Hole '66. To Amsterdam to write TV shows for Caterina Valente May '66. A highly capable pop and jazz writer, he began to move into the area of motion picture composing in '66.

LPs: Epic, Col.

Addr: 8657 Wonderland Ave., Los Angeles 46, Calif.

GUARALDI, VINCENT ANTHONY (VINCE), *piano, composer;* b. San Francisco, Calif., 7/17/28. Worked during 1950s with Cal Tjader, Woody Herman. In 1960s was heard chiefly around San Francisco, leading his own trio and teaming up frequently from '63 with guitarist Bola Sete. In 1962 Guaraldi won a Grammy award from NARAS for the best jazz composition of the year, *Cast Your Fate To The Wind.* He was featured at Monterey JF '64. Wrote and performed *Charlie Brown's Christmas* for TV '65 and an original jazz mass heard at Grace Cathedral in San Francisco, 5/21/65.

Guaraldi has revealed an adaptable talent, specializing in bossa nova but by no means limited to this idiom. According to John S. Wilson, "He distinguishes himself not by undertaking stylistically identifying mannerisms but simply by digging in and playing strong, melodic, and rhythmic piano. He has an exceptional knack for catching and projecting the spirit of a tune, for finding the essence of the piece and bringing strength and validity to his exposition of it." LPs: *Vince Guaraldi Trio; Black Orpheus; Bola Sete & Friends; Flower is a Lovesome Thing; Jazz Impressions; Latin Side* (all Fant.).

Addr: 31 Millay Pl., Mill Valley, Calif.

GUARNIERI, JOHN A. (JOHNNY), *piano, composer;* b. New York City, 3/23/17. Came to prominence with Benny Goodman 1939-40 and Artie Shaw '40-41. Was one of the most prolific recording artists in jazz in the '40s.

Leaving NYC in '62, Guarnieri settled in Hollywood and worked from 1963-5 as soloist at the Hollywood Plaza Hotel. He also worked on the perfection of what he called "multiple sounds—a modern take-off on Bach but with a French Impressionistic approach." He also specialized in playing in 5/4 time.

Guarnieri also wrote a musical show, *What A Perfect Business,* with librettist Martin Silberston.

Own LP: Dot. Early LPs with Goodman combos (Col.).

Addr: 10425 Sarah St., No. Hollywood, Calif.

GUERIN ROGER, *trumpet;* b. Saarebruck, Saar, France, 1/9/26. Prominent from 1947; pl. w. Django Reinhardt, many other French groups and U.S. expatriates. To Newport w. International Band '58.

After touring w. Quincy Jones' band, Apr.-Sept. 1960, Guerin free-lanced in Paris doing TV, radio and recording work, but leaving when special occasions arose. Antibes JF '61; also in '62 w. D. Gillespie big band. Recklinghausen JF Workshop '61-3-5. Hamburg Jazz Workshop '62, '65. Soundtrack w. Ellington, Armstrong for *Paris Blues;* stage music for *Monsieur Turcaret* w. Ellington. Lugano JF and several LPs w. Kenny Clarke-Francy Boland big band (Atl.). Other albums w. Andre Hodeir, *Jazz et Jazz* (Phil.), Pierre Michelot, Martial Solal.

Addr: 33 Rue Poussin, Paris 16, France.

GUILBEAU, PHILLIP (PHIL), *trumpet;* b. Lafayette, La., 1/16/26. Began playing when he entered high school 1939. Served in Navy 1942-5. Worked rhythm and blues bands, incl. three years with Paul Williams, on whose hit record *The Hucklebuck* he played a solo (1949), and two years with Big Joe Turner.

Guilbeau is best known for his 4½ years with Ray Charles, 1960-65. He played all the trumpet solos on Charles' album *Genius Plus Soul Equal Jazz* (Imp.). He was also featured along with other members of the Charles band under the leadership of Hank Crawford in several albums on Atlantic. In 1965-6 he toured with the Count Basie band.

Comps: *Blues for Helen, Please Send My Lover Back To Me.*

Addr: 4723 8th S. NW, Washington, D.C.

GULDA, FRIEDRICH, *piano, composer;* b. Vienna, Austria, 5/16/30. The dual career of Gulda, originally a classical pianist but well known also as a jazzman after he played Birdland in 1956, continued to expand in the early 1960s. In 1961, in addition to appearing as soloist under numerous conductors at Salzburg, etc., he was heard in a jazz workshop performance in Hamburg. In 1963 his *Music for Three Soloists and Band* and *Music No. 1 for Piano and Band* appeared on record. The latter was described by critic Joachim Berendt as "a concerto of brilliant solidity . . . no experiments . . . the big form swings."

In 1964 Gulda made a combined classical and jazz tour of South America, using bassist Jimmy Rowser and drummer Albert Heath for the jazz portions. During that year an all-star international band, which he called the Euro-jazz Orchestra, was introduced in TV shows in Germany and Austria as well as on records.

Gulda continued to activate this idea from time to time, using a personnel composed of musicians from all over Europe, American expatriates and a few musicians flown specially from the U.S.

In 1965 Gulda appeared as guest soloist with the Los Angeles Neophonic Orchestra, performing his *Music for Piano and Band No. 2*. The work, a maturely effective amalgamation of classical and jazz forms, established Gulda more firmly than ever as one of the musical phenomena of the 20th century.

As a jazz pianist, Gulda extended himself far beyond the Powell-influenced style he had displayed in the 1950s. As a composer he brought to his work an unusual scope of knowledge due to his background, combined with a keen awareness of the need to retain all the essential elements of the jazz traditions.

LPs: *From Vienna With Love* with International Orchestra (Col.), *Ineffable*, piano trio (Col.).

Addr: c/o Loew, Riemergasse 14, Vienna I, Austria.

GUMINA, THOMAS JOSEPH (TOMMY), *accordion;* b. Milwaukee, Wis., 5/20/31. Began studying accordion at age 11 in Milwaukee, then from '44-9 under Andy Rizzo in Chi. Discovered by Harry James at Tic-Toc in Milwaukee in Late '51, he remained w. James band for three years before going out as a single. Own combo, mainly in Las Vegas, until he joined Buddy De Franco in 1960, app. w. him intermittently until '65.

Gumina, who has made extensive and effective use of polytonality, also plays an instrument called the accordio-organ, which combines the characteristics of Hammond organ and accordion. LPs w. De Franco (Merc., Decca).

Addr: 3361 Manning Ct., Los Angeles 64, Calif.

GWALTNEY, THOMAS O. (TOMMY), *clarinet, vibes;* b. Norfolk, Va., 2/28/21. Learned clarinet from E. Caceres, P. Hucko and some private instruction. Played in college bands during early '40s, w. Sol Yaged NYC '46-'47. W. Bobby Hackett '56-'57, appearing with him at Newport, Randall's Island JFs. With B. Butterfield '58-'59, Charlie Byrd '62. Led own groups around Norfolk and Washington, D.C. '59-'61 and '65. Produced and promoted successful Virginia Beach JF in '59, '60, '61 and again in '65.

In Jan. '65 Gwaltney opened his own jazz club, Blues Alley, in Washington, D.C., which attracted many of the top swing-era musicians, incl. Butterfield, Maxine Sullivan, Hackett and Bud Freeman. He also appears there regularly with his own group. Favs: on clarinet, Hucko, Goodman, Fazola; on vibes, Hampton, Gibbs, Tjader. Lists most of the greats of the swing era as influences.

Own LPs: Laurel; his own fav. is on Riverside, *Goin' to Kansas City*. Others w. Hackett (Cap.), Butterfield (Epic) and Buck Clayton-Nancy Harrow (Candid).

Addr: 1073 Wisconsin Avenue N.W., Washington, D.C.

HACKETT, ROBERT LEO (BOBBY), * *cornet, trumpet;* also *guitar;* b. Providence, R.I., 1/31/15. Acquired early association with Dixieland style and was often compared with Bix Beiderbecke. After working with jazz groups, he played in Glenn Miller band as guitarist and occasional cornetist 1941-2. Has since led jazz combos from time to time but is best known for his recordings, lightly touched with a jazz quality, in the commercial Jackie Gleason series on Capitol. To Mexico w. Benny Goodman, 1963. In the mid-'60s he was frequently heard in person and on records with singer Tony Bennett, playing in a melodic, legato style with a superbly gentle tone.

Own LPs: Col., Epic, Pick., Cap.

Addr: 34-21 84th St., Jackson Heights 72, N.Y.

HADEN, CHARLES EDWARD (CHARLIE), *bass;* b. Shenandoah, Iowa, 8/6/37. No formal musical training, but all of Haden's family active in Midwestern folk music since 1930s. Played with Art Pepper '57, Paul Bley '57-59, Hampton Hawes '58-59, Ornette Coleman '59-62, Denny Zeitlin '64-66. Haden plays bass as a participating, rather than accompanying, instrument. Has wide range, plays in emotional modern idiom. Several American festivals with Coleman and Zeitlin. Active since 1963 at Synanon, the narcotics rehabilitation center, which he says saved not only his career but his life. Favs: J. Blanton, W. Ware, Scott La Faro, Ornette Coleman.

Denny Zeitlin said of Haden: "We immediately got a groove going together. He has radar ears like no other bass player, warmth of sound, and a basic strength that so many of the modern bassists lack." Four LPs w. Coleman (Atlantic); others w. Zeitlin (Col.).

Addr: 110 Lombard, San Francisco, Calif.

HAFER, JOHN RICHARD (DICK), * *tenor sax;* also *other reeds, flute, oboe, English horn;* b. Wyomissing, Pa., 5/29/27. From 1949 played w. Charlie Barnet, Woody Herman, Claude Thornhill, Bobby Hackett, Nat Pierce. With Elliot Lawrence '58-'60; Charles Mingus at NYC Village Vanguard '62; Benny Goodman at Disneyland '62. Appeared on Merv Griffin TV show from Apr. '65. LPs w. Mingus, Johnny Hartman (Impulse).

Addr: 64 Schley Ave., Staten Island 8, N.Y.

HAGGART, ROBERT SHERWOOD (BOB), * *bass, composer;* b. New York City, 3/13/14. Prominent with Bob Crosby band from 1935, he won several magazine polls as No. 1 jazz bassist between 1937 and '44. In the '60s has been heard as TV staff musician, occasionally reviving his early hit *Big Noise From Winnetka*. Other comps: *What's New?*, *South Rampart Street Parade*.

Addr: 20 Ridge Dr., Port Washington, N.Y.

HAHN, JERRY DONALD, *guitar;* b. Alma, Neb., 9/21/40. Father a guitarist. Stud. at Wichita (Kan.) U., played first jobs there. To San Francisco '62, played hotel and studio bands, joined John Handy '64. Appeared w. Handy, Monterey JF, '65. Early big infl.:

Barney Kessel; other favs.: Wes Montgomery, Kenny Burrell, Howard Roberts. LP w. Handy (Col.).

Addr: 540 Rutland Dr., Pacifica, Cal.

HAIG, ALAN W. (AL),* *piano;* b. Newark, N.J., 1923. One of the first bop pianists, he played with Dizzy Gillespie, Ch. Barnet, Ch. Parker in '40s; later with Stan Getz, Chet Baker. Though no longer prominent in jazz, he has continued to work in cocktail lounges and clubs mostly in New York and New Jersey.

Own LP on Mint; also *Jazz Will-O-The-Wisp,* on Counterpoint. Earlier performances as sideman have been reissued on Mainstream, Savoy, Verve, etc.

HAKIM, SADIK (Argonne Dense Thornton),* *piano;* b. Duluth, Minn., 7/15/22. An influential early bebop pianist, Hakim played w. C. Parker, L. Young, S. Stewart. In 1960 left Buddy Tate's band after 5 years to form own group. At Birdland w. S. Rollins Oct. '64. Free-lanced around NYC w. trios and quartets. Own LP: Parker.

Addr: c/o Stein, 533 W. 45th St. Apt. 3D, New York, N.Y.

HALL, EDMOND,* *clarinet;* b. New Orleans, 5/15/01. Toured w. New Orleans bands in '20s. To NYC '28. In '30s pl. w. Claude Hopkins and other big bands; '40s w. Red Allen, Teddy Wilson combos and own groups. Condon's club '50-55, with Louis Armstrong '55-8; later free-lanced in NYC.

In '62 Hall toured England and Scandinavia for three weeks. In '64 he was a feat. soloist w. the Dukes of Dixieland on a tour of Japan. Since 1958 he has been feat. at annual JF in Milton, Mass. and since '62 JF at Aspen, Colo. He was back at Condon's in '62, has also pl. TV shows w. Yves Montand, *Today* show, etc. and recorded w. H. Belafonte (RCA). Hall has an unusually personal tone and sound and is probably the most proficient and convincing of all the pioneer New Orleans clarinetists still active in jazz.

Addr: 889 Stebbins Ave., Bronx 59, N.Y.

HALL, JAMES STANLEY (JIM),* *guitar;* b. Buffalo, N.Y., 12/4/30. Hall moved to LA from Cleveland in 1955 and made his recording debut w. Chico Hamilton. W. Jimmy Giuffre trio '59, duo w. Lee Konitz '60-'61, Sonny Rollins '61-'62. Feature w. Art Farmer quartet Nov. '62-May '64. Led own trio w. Percy Heath or Ron Carter and Tommy Flanagan in '62 and '63, and w. Red Mitchell and Colin Bailey '65. Newport '62, '63. Toured South America w. Ella Fitzgerald and Roy Eldridge '60, Europe w. Farmer '64. Appeared on Ralph Gleason TV show '62 and '63, BBC-TV w. Farmer '64. Also interested in private teaching, writing.

Hall's influence, both as a traditional and an innovating musician, has probably been felt more since 1960 than that of any guitarist since Charlie Christian and Django Reinhardt. In fast tempos his technique is faultless, with an emotional drive that lifts his music far above conventional standards. In slower tempos, however, his basic blues origins are more keenly felt through a resonant tone and intricately constructed lines. Rollins, Bill Evans and Farmer each teamed with Hall in LPs that show him more as a partner than an accompanist. His melodic contrapuntal lines alongside their solos may have been an example for similar new freedom in other rhythm instruments.

Of Hall's duo recording with Evans, *Undercurrent,* Pete Welding said in DB, "There are any number of moments of glowing, unalloyed beauty. Two of jazz's foremost lyrical players respond to each other in a powerful rush of extemporization." Hall has received similar accolades from scores of critics and musicians. Won DB critics' poll '63-5; readers' poll '65-6.

Own LP: Pac. Jazz. Others: w. Hamilton, *Modest Jazz Trio* (Pac. Jazz), Paul Desmond (RCA), Farmer (Atl.), Giuffre (Atl., Verve), Red Mitchell (Pac. Jazz), Evans (River., UA), Rollins (RCA), *John Lewis Presents Jazz Abstractions* (Atl.).

Addr: 49 W. 12th St., New York 11, N.Y.

HAMILTON, FORESTSTORN (CHICO),* *drums, composer;* b. Los Angeles, Calif., 9/21/21. Sideman with Lionel Hampton and many other West Coast bands in '40s. Frequently accompanied Lena Horne from 1948. Member of original Gerry Mulligan Quartet '52. From 1956-60 he led an unusual quintet featuring cello and flute. In '60 he formed a new group featuring Charles Lloyd, Gabor Szabo and Albert Stinson. During the next few years he led quintets and quartets, toured Japan; music for film *Repulsion* in 1965. In 1965 his group was reorganized to accompany Miss Horne for engagements in London and U.S.

Own LPs: Columbia, Reprise, Impulse.

Addr: 3788 6th Ave., Los Angeles 18, Calif.

HAMILTON, JAMES (JIMMY),* *clarinet, tenor sax, composer;* b. Dillon, S.C., 5/25/17. Played with Teddy Wilson, Benny Carter et al until 1942. Since then has been member of Duke Ellington orchestra. Hamilton, like Buddy De Franco, plays with a pure, legitimate clarinet sound, and has impeccable technique along with a strong personal style. He is also a capable tenor saxophonist, as can be heard in such records as *The Brown Skin Gal* in *Ella At Duke's Place* (Verve) and *Hello Dolly!* in *Ellington '65* (Reprise). His innumerable clarinet solos with Ellington include portions of the *Virgin Islands Suite; Moon River* in *Ellington '66,* and *The Perfect Nanny* in *Mary Poppins;* also portions of *The Symphonic Ellington* (all Reprise). Won DB critics' poll as new star '62. Own LP: *Swing Low* (Everest). Other LPs: See Ellington, Duke, and Ellington, Mercer.

Addr: 26 Hunter Ave., New Rochelle, N.Y.

HAMMER, HOWARD ROBERT (BOB), *composer, piano;* b. Indianapolis, Ind., 3/3/30. Stud. Mich. St. Univ., Manhattan Schl. Music. Local jobs in Mich. at 15. Later worked as sideman for Gene Krupa, Sauter-Finegan, L. Hampton, Ch. Mingus, J. Knepper, J. Dorsey, Red Allen, W. Herman. Wrote arrangements for Mingus album (Impulse). Arr. for W. Herman:

Mingus' *Better Get It In Your Soul,* and originals, *Dear John C, Doin' The Snake.* Arr. two albums for Johnny Hartman. Wrote *Hammerhead Waltz* for Clark Terry (heard in *The Definitive Jazz Scene,* Vol. 1—Impulse). Influences as pianist: Bud Powell, Nat Cole, Art Tatum, Horace Silver; as writer: Ellington, Ch. Mingus, Bill Holman, J. Carisi, Eddie Sauter.

Hammer is a very capable modern (but not avant garde) writer, most of whose best work can be heard in his various assignments on Impulse albums.

Addr: 19 Wiles Dr., Stony Point, N.Y.

HAMMER, JAN JR., *piano;* b. Prague, Czechoslovakia, 4/17/48. Mother a singer, father a composer, singer and vibist. Member Czech jazz group The Junior Trio. Trio won Czech youth band competition '63; at Prague JF '64, West Berlin Blue Note '64, Yugoslav JF '65 w. mother as vocalist. Film w. J. Berendt *Jazz in Czechoslovakia.* Favs: Evans, Bley, Friedman. LPs: Phil., Supraphon.

Addr: Vladislavova 13, Prague, Czechoslovakia.

HAMMOND, JOHN HENRY JR.,* *critic;* b. New York City, 12/15/10. Hammond's reputation as a discoverer of major musical talents, established in the 1930s through his association with Benny Goodman, Count Basie, Billie Holiday and innumerable others, was maintained in the 1960s in his work as an executive at Columbia Records in New York. Among the artists with whose recordings he has been associated in recent years are: Denny Zeitlin, Bob Dylan, Aretha Franklin, Bobbie Norris, Friedrich Gulda, Ray Bryant, Marlowe Morris, Illinois Jacquet, Herb Ellis, Roy Gaines, Stuff Smith, John Handy.

Addr: c/o Columbia Records, 51 West 52nd St., New York, N.Y. 10019.

HAMMOND, JOHN PAUL, *singer, guitar, harmonica;* b. New York City, 11/13/42. Father is the noted talent scout and writer (see above). Self-taught; studied the work of Robert Johnson, Muddy Waters, Bo Diddley, Elvis Presley and others to develop a style and technique based on traditional folk blues. Appeared at Newport Folk Festival 1963-4; Village Gate, Village Vanguard '64; Carnegie Hall '65. Toured England 1965. Comps: *Lonesome Sundown Blues, Bad Luck Games.*

LPs: Vanguard.

Addr: 86 MacDougal St., New York City.

HAMPTON, LIONEL,* *vibraharp, drums, piano, leader;* b. Louisville, Ky., 4/12/13. Started as drummer in Chicago. Picked up vibes at 17, when he was a member of the Les Hite band supporting Louis Armstrong. Led own band in LA until Benny Goodman hired him 1936. After four years as member of Goodman quartet, formed own band and was best known for his exciting version of *Flying Home,* first recorded May 1942.

In the 1960s Hampton continued to lead a big band despite the problems presented by a diminution of available clubs and dance halls in which to play.

Many of his greatest successes were scored overseas. He has been received with great enthusiasm in Israel, where he toured in 1954 and '57. In 1961 the band undertook a six-week tour of Europe. In '63 a seven-week tour was arranged throughout Japan, the Philippines and Formosa. In '64 the band appeared in the Antibes Music Festival.

After numerous personnel changes, Hampton finally acknowledged the economic impossibility of sustaining a big band on a full-time basis. In July 1965 he formed a sextet known as the "Jazz Inner Circle" featuring organ, trumpet, two saxophones and drums. This group played at the London House in Chicago, Al Hirt's club in New Orleans, etc. Hampton left March 1966 with this group on a tour of Japan, the Philippines, Okinawa, etc.

Hampton's reputation, which established him in the late 1930s as the first vibraharpist to play genuine jazz on this instrument (Adrian Rollini, his only predecessor of any consequence, used the vibes mainly for cocktail-lounge style music), has been sustained throughout the years. His style has never become old fashioned; it is sophisticated, melodic and buoyant, making frequent use of double-time passages and invariably swinging with a compellingly energetic rhythmic sensitivity. Though his drum playing, singing and entertainment values are rarely of much consequence in terms of his merit as a jazz musician, they have helped to establish him as a popular personality.

Hampton and his wife, Gladys, have their own record label, Glad-Hamp Records. In addition to several albums on this label Hampton has been featured in recent years on the following: *Together Again,* reunion of original Goodman Quartet (RCA 2698); *You Better Know It!* (Impulse 78); *The Great Hamp and Little 'T'* (w. Charlie Teagarden) (Coral 757438); *Many-Splendored Vibes* (Epic 16027). His earlier performances have been released on RCA, RCA Camden, MGM, Verve, GNP, Decca. His first Carnegie Hall concert, for *Esquire* Magazine in 1945, is on Decca DL 8088.

Addr: 337 W. 138th St., New York 30, N.Y.

HAMPTON, LOCKSLEY WELLINGTON (SLIDE),* *trombone, tuba, composer;* b. Jeannette, Pa. 4/21/32. Raised in Indianapolis. Pl. w. Buddy Johnson, Lionel Hampton, Maynard Ferguson in '50s. Formed own octet '59 and app. w. it for several years before joining the Lloyd Price band as musical director. Worked w. quartet at benefit for radio station WBAI at Village Gate Dec. '65. Own LPs: Atl., Epic.

Addr: 214 E. 25th St., New York 10, N.Y.

HANCOCK, HERBERT JEFFREY (HERBIE), *piano, composer;* b. Chicago, Ill., 4/12/40. Both parents, sister and brother musically inclined. Piano lessons from 1947. In Dec. 1960 Donald Byrd heard Hancock in Chicago and the following month he went to NYC with Byrd. Worked with Phil Woods, Oliver Nelson, then joined Miles Davis combo May 1963. He also remained active as recording bandleader and composer. His best-known work was a simple, gospel-influenced tune, *Watermelon Man*, popularized by Mongo Santamaria. Hancock's main interests, however, both as pianist and composer, are of a far more adventurous nature. Many of his works are rhythmically, harmonically and metrically complex; he reflects the influence of the free music to which he was exposed while working briefly in 1962-3 with Eric Dolphy. He has also been influenced by Davis and Anthony Williams.

Own LPs: Blue Note. LPs with Davis (Col.); LPs with D. Byrd, Anthony Williams (Blue Note).

Addr: 202 Riverside Dr., New York 25, N.Y.

HANDY, GEORGE (George Joseph Hendleman),* *composer, piano;* b. Brooklyn, N.Y., 1/17/20. The highly talented comp. of several progressive works, assoc. w. B. Raeburn in '40s, continued to write jazz and semi-classical works during the '60s. Wrote three saxophone quartets and *New York Suite* for the NY Saxophone Quartet '64 and '65. Works performed at NY Town Hall and Carnegie Hall. Also wrote for Kay Thompson. Began writing record reviews for DB '65. LP: *Sax. Quartet No. 1* recorded by NY Sax. Quartet (20th Cent. Fox).

Addr: 126 MacDougal St., New York 12, N.Y.

HANDY, JOHN RICHARD III,* *alto sax;* also *soprano, tenor and baritone saxes, clarinets, flute;* b. Dallas, Tex., 3/2/33. Active in San Francisco-Oakland jazz from late '40s as teacher and musician. To NYC in '58. W. Charles Mingus '58-'59, Randy Weston '59. Formed own group '59, played at Five Spot, Birdland, Jazz Gallery, concert at U.N. Building. On U.S. Govt. tour of Europe '61. Went to Sweden and Denmark as single, did radio, concert work there. In soundtrack for Swedish film *Boo's Up and Down*. W. John Mehegan quartet in concert w. NY Little Symphony. Back to West Coast, jazz soloist w. Santa Clara Symphony Orch., SF State College Symphonic Band '63. Soloist w. Mingus at Monterey JF '64. Organized own quintet in SF '65, with Michael White on violin, and received one of biggest ovations at Monterey '65.

Handy was noted during his stay with Mingus for his strong, biting alto work, especially in duets with tenor Booker Ervin. Mort Maizlish describes his playing as possessing "a unique sound, reminiscent of Parker and Dolphy in its round, melodic vitality, and an exciting technique at fast tempos." His appearance at Monterey in '65 showed that he had departed from the bop influences that had characterized his playing. His extended composition *Spanish Lady*, the highlight of his performance, was a fascinating display of new rhythms and use of the violin in an avant-garde setting. Other comps. incl. *Tears for Ole Miss, If Only We Knew,* work for symphonic band. Own LPs: Col., Roul., Pac. Jazz. Others: w. Mingus; best solos on *Wonderland* (UA), *Mingus Ah Um* (Col.), also Atl., Col., with Mingus.

Addr: 454 29th Ave., San Francisco, Calif.

HANNA, JAKE, *drums;* b. Roxbury, Mass., 1931. At eight, pl. w. church band. School band in Dorchester, Mass. Local gigs at 18. Spent 3½ yrs. in Air Force band, pl. bass drum. Toured w. Tommy Reed band for a year; three yrs. stud. and gigging in Boston. House drummer for long period at Storyville; few months on road w. Maynard Ferguson '58. Spent most of '59-61 w. Marian McPartland Trio. Also worked w. Toshiko Akiyoshi and briefly w. Duke Ellington, Bobby Hackett, Harry James, Herb Pomeroy.

Hanna is best known for a long intermittent association with Woody Herman, and particularly for the tremendous drive and fire generated by his work in the band led by Herman in 1962-4. As Miss McPartland has written, Hanna "uses his technique logically —no unnecessary pyrotechnics—and he has the good judgment and the power necessary to hold and control the rhythm at all times."

The best of his many LPs include *Herman '63; Herman '64; Encore; Woody's Goodies* (all Philips).

HANNA, ROLAND,* *piano;* b. Detroit, Mich., 2/10/32. Free-lanced locally from late 1940s; Army band 1950-52; later stud. at Eastman Sch. and Juilliard. Toured internationally w. Benny Goodman 1958; w. Ch. Mingus '58; own trio at Five Spot '59. Had own duo and trio at new Five Spot location several times in early '60s. Heard occasionally w. Thad Jones-Mel Lewis band 1966. LPs w. Mingus (Merc.), Goodman (Col.).

Addr: 88 Shepard Ave., Teaneck, N.J.

HARDEE, JOHN, *tenor sax;* b. Texas, ca. 1920. Enjoyed a brief period of recognition and activity in NYC in the mid-'40s when upon his discharge from the Army in '45 he began to play on 52nd St. and at sessions in NYC. Inspired by Chu Berry, Hardee was a hard-driving Texas tenorman, capable of bringing his strongly swinging solos to heated climaxes without artifice. His slow blues playing was particularly moving as well. Reported to be teaching school and gigging occasionally in Dallas in the '60s. Recorded w. Tiny Grimes for Atl., and his own for Blue Note and Sittin' In, in the '40s. Unfortunately, these are not available on LP.

HARDING, LAVERE (BUSTER),* *composer;* b. Cleveland, Ohio, 3/19/17. Arranged for Teddy Wilson, Artie Shaw, Larry Clinton, Dizzy Gillespie, Cab Calloway, Roy Eldridge, Glenn Miller, Tommy Dorsey, Earl Hines, also frequently for Count Basie, and for Billie Holiday's record dates. A first-class swing-oriented arranger, Harding did his last work for Jonah Jones. After a long illness he died in NYC 11/14/65.

HARDY, HAGOOD, *vibes;* b. Angola, Indiana, 2/26/37. Studied piano in Oakville, Ontario, 1946-53. Started playing vibes in clubs and on TV while at the U. of Toronto 1956-8. Led own group in Toronto 1956-8; Gigi Gryce Sextet Mar.-Apr. '61; Herbie Mann May '61-July '62. After almost two years with the Martin Denny group he joined George Shearing Quintet Aug. '64. In addition to the above regular engagements,

Hardy had his own group at Birdland for one-night stands and gigged in NYC with Sol Yaged, Mal Waldron, Ted Curson, Marty Napoleon.

Hardy who earned his BA and took graduate courses in political science while in Toronto and New York, is a promising and intelligent musician. Inspired by Milt Jackson and Cal Tjader, he says, "I prefer the linear, melodic school of thought rather than the vertical, angular concept, as I feel the vibraphone is very well suited to it."

LPs with Herbie Mann (Atl.); Shearing (Cap.).

Addr: 22943 Enadia Way, Canoga Park, Calif.

HAREWOOD, ALPHONSE (AL), *drums;* b. Brooklyn, N.Y., 6/3/23. No formal training; learned to play by watching his brother, also a drummer. Played with many jazz combos in New York including J. J. Johnson 1954-6; Gigi Gryce, Art Farmer, Dave Amram-George Barrow in mid-'50s; Curtis Fuller, Benny Golson '58-9; Lou Donaldson '59-61; Mary Lou Williams '62; Stan Getz '62-4. Member of Play House Four at Minton's in early '60's. TV shows with Getz, also Monterey JF '63. A dependable, tasteful drummer, he names Chick Webb, Philly Joe Jones, Art Blakey, Max Roach, Kenny Clarke as influences. LPs with Lou Donaldson, Horace Parlan, Stanley Turrentine, Ike Quebec, Dexter Gordon, Shirley Scott, Grant Green, DoDo Greene, Gene Harris (Blue Note); Kai Winding-J. J. Johnson (Beth.); Dave Amram-George Barrow (Decca); Curtis Fuller-Benny Golson (Savoy, Pres.); Ahmed Abdul-Malik (RCA).

Addr: 523 Crown St., Brooklyn, N.Y. 11213.

HARRIOTT, ARTHURLIN (JOE), * *alto, baritone, tenor sax, leader, composer;* b. Jamaica, B.W.I., 7/15/28. After emigrating to England in 1951, pl. in many small groups. Formed his own combo in 1960. That year, while hospitalized, reviewing the jazz scene, he decided that jazz had exhausted itself and something new had to be found. It was then that he began experimenting, breaking away from conventional melodic and harmonic restrictions. Though Ornette Coleman had just begun to be heard, Harriott says that Coleman never influenced him and that his innovations are all his own. An album he made entitled *Abstract* (Cap.) received enthusiastic reviews both in England and the U.S. Harriott's alto sax work, and his free form compositions, are among the most interesting experiments produced by the British avant garde. An LP attempting to blend the traditions of jazz and Indian classical music was issued on Brit. Col.

His group has appeared at many British and Continental jazz festivals from 1958.

HARRIS, BARRY DOYLE, * *piano;* b. Detroit, Mich., 12/15/29. Developed a fine reputation around Detroit through his backing of visiting hornmen as house pianist at Blue Bird and Rouge Lounge. Taught his own jazz theory '58-60. Left Detroit in '60 w. Cannonball Adderley; then settled in NYC, pl. w. Yusef Lateef

and with own trio. Some jobs in '60s w. own quintet; w. Coleman Hawkins '65-6. Inspired by Charlie Parker and Bud Powell, his style is faithful to the articulation and spirit of the latter but with own touch. Own LPs: River.; LPs w. Lateef, Charles McPherson, Carmell Jones (Pres.); Lee Morgan, Hank Mobley, Dexter Gordon (BN); Hawkins (Imp.).

HARRIS, WILLARD PALMER (BILL), * *trombone;* also *guitar;* b. Philadelphia, Pa., 10/28/16. One of the most popular and original trombonists of the 1940s, best known for *Bijou* and other records with Woody Herman '44-6. In '50s toured with JATP, also with Benny Goodman '59.

In recent years Harris has been living in Las Vegas, working first with Charlie Teagarden, later with Red Norvo in local lounges. He has taken to doubling on guitar. Not to be confused with guitarist Willie (Bill) Harris (see below). LP: *Out of the Herd* (Emarcy), Woody Herman (VSP).

Addr: 1414 Silver Mesa Way No. 3, Las Vegas, Nevada.

HARRIS, WILLIE (BILL), * *guitar;* b. Nashville, N.C., 4/14/25. Established as an accomplished jazz, r&b and classical guitarist during the '50s, Harris led his own group at Village Vanguard, '60; pl. w. J.F.K. Quintet '62; Society of Classical Guitar, N.Y. '62. Graduate Washington Junior College of Music, plays in Washington and teaches own method, "The Harris Touch." Own LP: *Great Guitar Sounds* (Merc.).

Addr: 2021 Hamlin St. N.E., Washington, D.C.

HARRIS, EDDIE, *tenor sax;* also *piano, vibes, composer;* b. Chicago, Ill., 10/20/34. Studied piano with a cousin; sang with choirs and gospel groups in Baptist churches throughout Chicago. While at DuSable High School, began playing vibes; soon after, played clarinet and tenor sax. He made his professional debut as a pianist, playing a one-nighter with Gene Ammons' band.

In the service, Harris was with the 7th Army Symphony Orchestra, touring all over France and Germany and sitting in with local jazz combos. Soon after returning to civilian life in Chicago, he made his record debut on Vee-Jay. A single release of the Ernest Gold movie theme *Exodus* became a national hit. This performance was also included in Harris' album *Exodus to Jazz*. During the '60s Harris worked as leader of various small combos. Though the great commercial success of *Exodus* was not followed up by other major hits, his talent both as saxophonist and composer maintained a high level. He names an interesting variety of musicians as influences on his playing: "I like Miles for choice of notes, Milt Jackson for feeling, Stan Getz for timbre and sound, Charlie Parker and Clifford Brown for smoothness and articulation, Rollins and Coltrane for their skips and intervals."

Harris' later LPs appeared on Columbia and Atlantic. Among the best are *Cool Sax From Hollywood to*

153

Broadway; Cool Sax, Warm Heart (Col.); *The In Sound* (Atl.).

Addr: 363 East 90th Place, Chicago, Ill.

HARRIS, GENE, * *piano;* b. Benton Harbor, Mich., 9/1/33. Formed The Three Sounds (originally The Four Sounds) in 1956; came to New York in '58 and built up a following in the early '60s, playing in an uncluttered, generally blues-directed style. The group enjoyed excellent acceptance among night club audiences despite mixed reactions among the critics. After a series of albums for Blue Note that were substantial sellers, the group transferred to the Verve label in 1963 and to Mercury's Limelight jazz subsidiary in '65. In '65-66 they began to record with large groups featuring arrangements by Julian Lee. Among the Sounds' best LPs are *Black Orchid; Feelin' Good; Moods* (Blue Note); *Anita O'Day and The Three Sounds* (Verve); *Three Moods; Beautiful Friendship* (Limelight).

HARRIS, TASSO, *trombone, educator;* b. Pittsburgh, Pa., 11/8/18. Played as sideman in numerous swing bands incl. Artie Shaw, Tommy Dorsey, Bunny Berigan, C. Thornhill, Ina Ray Hutton, Red Norvo, G. Krupa, S. Donahue, V. Monroe, Alvino Rey, Axel Stordahl. From early '50s taught music at Univ. of Denver, incl. course in "Brass and the Jazz Band." Also teaches privately in own studio, and at National State Band Camp summer jazz clinics. Trombonist w. Denver Symphony. Favs: J. Teagarden, T. Dorsey, J. J. Johnson, Carl Fontana.

Addr: 9950 W. 17th Ave., Denver, Colo.

HARTE, ROY, *drums;* b. New York, N.Y., 5/27/24. Cousin of Dave Pell. Began study of drums at age 10; became a protege of Dave Tough at 13. While in high school worked simultaneously w. Muggsy Spanier and Dizzy Gillespie. Later w. B. Sherwood, B. Raeburn, L. Millinder, V. Musso. On West Coast got several studio gigs, incl. Disney soundtracks and Capitol pop recordings. One of founders of World Pacific records. From 1950 was president of Hollywood Drum City. Published several drum instruction books. Appears frequently around LA w. Harry Babasin. Favs: Tough, Buddy Rich. LPs w. L. Almeida (Pac. Jazz), B. Shank (Noct.), H. Geller (Imp.), Babasin (Noct.).

Addr: 16343 Celinda Pl., Encino, Calif.

HASAAN (Hasaan Ibn Ali), *piano, composer;* b. Philadelphia, Pa., 5/6/31. Stud. from age 13. Gained much early encouragement from Elmo Hope. Went on the road with Joe Morris' band 1946. Starting in 1950 he appeared locally in concerts with Clifford Brown, Max Roach, Miles Davis, J. J. Johnson and many others. After many years of obscurity he was brought to public attention while on a visit to New York, when Roach arranged to record him in a set of original compositions. Though Hasaan acknowledges a debt to Hope, Art Tatum, Thelonious Monk and Bud Powell, his playing and writing both have an original quality that is well represented in the album *The Max Roach Trio Featuring the Legendary Hasaan* (Atl.).

HAVENS, ROBERT L. (BOB), *trombone;* b. Quincy, Ill., 5/3/30. Parents both played instruments; studied trombone from age of 7. Joined Ralph Flanagan when band passed through town '55. W. George Girard, New Orleans '56-'57, Al Hirt '57-'60, Lawrence Welk as jazz soloist from '60. On weekly Welk TV series. Occasionally led own dixieland groups, incl. at Disneyland '65. Favs: Jack Teagarden, Miff Mole, Abe Lincoln. Ambition is to keep Teagarden style alive, lead own band. Own LPs: Dot, South. Others: w. Girard (Vik, GTJ); Hirt (Aud. Fid., South., Verve, Metrojazz); J. Caprano, A. Hug, S. Bonano (South.); Welk, Frank Scott (Dot); P. Fountain (Coral).

Addr: 8101 Glade Ave., Canoga Park, Calif.

HAWES, HAMPTON, * *piano, composer;* b. Los Angeles, Cal., 11/13/28. Prominent in 1950s w. Shorty Rogers, Howard Rumsey, Red Mitchell. Won new star division of DB critics' poll 1956; selected as "Arrival of the Year" by *Metronome* '56.

After several years of irregular activity Hawes returned to the scene in 1963, appearing on the Steve Allen TV show. He took part in John Hendricks' *Evolution of the Blues Song* concert at UCLA, Feb. '64; was the opening attraction at Basin Street West in SF, Sept. '64; also worked w. Jackie McLean, Harold Land and other small groups.

In June 1965 Hawes and Red Mitchell were reunited. With a drummer, they worked at a restaurant coincidentally known as Mitchell's Studio Club in Los Angeles and remained there regularly for the next year.

As Lester Koenig wrote, "Hawes is young enough to be responsive to the winds of change which have swept the jazz world in recent years, and old enough to be fully a part of the jazz tradition." Originally inspired by Bud Powell and others of the bop era, Hawes has developed a strongly original style and is, in John A. Tynan's words, "one of the foremost jazz piano talents of our generation."

Own LPs: many on Contemp., incl. *Green Leaves of Summer*, 1964; *Here and Now*, '65.

Addr: 19307 Broadacres, Compton, Calif.

HAWKINS, COLEMAN (HAWK or BEAN), * *tenor sax;* b. St. Joseph, Mo., 11/21/04. The first prominent tenor saxophone soloist of jazz history, Hawkins played with Fletcher Henderson's band from 1923-34, then spent five years in Europe. His best known and most successful record, *Body and Soul*, was recorded soon after his return to the U.S. in 1939. After a year leading a big band he fronted various small combos, toured with Norman Granz's JATP and free-lanced around New York.

The advent of such new tenor styles as those of Sonny Rollins and John Coltrane were a challenge to Hawkins, for unlike most veteran jazzmen he continued to evince a lively interest in new styles and trends. During the early 1960s, in addition to appearing with small combos at numerous night clubs and jazz festivals, he was in constant demand for LPs and became one of the most prolific recording artists on the jazz scene.

An album entitled *Body and Soul*, including this tune and 15 others reissued from sessions with various groups spanning 1927-63, provides the best illustration of the course followed by Hawkins through the years (RCA LPV-501). Other reissues, comprising various sessions recorded during the 1940s, can be found on *Classic Tenors* (Contact CM3), *Coleman Hawkins and the Trumpet Kings* (Emarcy 66011), *Meditations* with the Esquire All Stars and others (Mainstream 6037) and *On The Bean* (Continental 16006).

Hawkins has also been co-starred with various other jazz artists, including Duke Ellington (Impulse 26), Milt Jackson, *Bean Bags* (Atl. 1316), Eddie (Lock-jaw) Davis in *Night Hawk* (Pres. 2016), Sonny Rollins (RCA 2712), Roy Eldridge and Johnny Hodges (Verve 8504), The Earl Hines Trio (Limelight 86020 and 86028), Clark Terry (Col. 1991).

Accompanied by various small groups, he is also heard in *The Hawk Relaxes* (Pres. MV15), *Good Ole Broadway* (MV23), *No Strings* (MV25), *Desafinado* (Impulse 2), *Today and Now* (Impulse 34), *Wrapped Tight* (Impulse 87), *Live At The Village Gate* (Verve 8509).

Addr: 445 W. 153rd St., New York 31, N.Y.

HAYES, LOUIS SEDELL,* *drums;* b. Detroit, Mich., 5/31/37. Toured with Horace Silver 1956-9, then joined Cannonball Adderley and remained with him six years. Joined Oscar Peterson Trio, replacing Ed Thigpen, July 1965, playing his first date w. Peterson at Newport JF.

During his years with Adderley, Hayes played in Europe six times. He was heard on numerous record dates with other groups, most notably *A Touch of Satin* w. J. J. Johnson (Col.), *A World of Piano* w. Phineas Newborn (Contemp.), *The Artistry of Freddie Hubbard* (Impulse), *Undercurrent* w. Kenny Drew (Blue Note). Own LP for VJ; many w. Adderley for Riverside, Capitol.

Hayes is a seasoned, mature drummer who lays down a firm, authoritative beat. Though an admirer of Philly Joe Jones, he tends toward a less explosive style that fits admirably into a trio context.

Addr: 929 Park Place, Brooklyn 13, N.Y.

HAYES, EDWARD BRIAN (TUBBY),* *tenor sax;* also *vibes, flute, baritone and alto saxes;* b. London, England, 1/30/35. Led own groups in England, incl. w. Ronnie Scott, during '50s. First U.S. appearance was at NYC Half Note Sept. '61; there again in '62 and '64. At Boston Jazz Workshop '64, LA Shelly's Manne-Hole '65. In London formed own big band, appeared on own TV series there '61-'62 and '63. Played w. Ellington Orch. at London Royal Festival Hall Feb. '64. Films incl. *All Night Long* w. C. Mingus, D. Brubeck; *The Beauty Jungle, Dr. Terror's House of Horrors* w. own quintet. At Washington, D.C. JF '62,

Antibes JF '62, Lugano JF '63. International appearances incl. Brussels '62, Oslo '63, Vienna w. Friedrich Gulda '64 and '65, Berlin '64.

Clark Terry, Ronnie Scott and other leading U.S. and British musicians have expressed high praise for the work of Hayes, esp. on tenor. Influenced by Parker and Coltrane, he plays with vitality, fluency and an evident respect for the traditions of the 1940s and '50s.

Own LPs: *Tubby the Tenor*, rec. in NYC w. Clark Terry et al (Epic), *Introducing Tubbs* w. British groups (Epic), others on Smash, Jazzland.

Addr: 2-25 Putney Hill, London S.W. 15, England.

HAYNES, FRANK, *tenor sax;* b. San Francisco, 1931. Moved to New York in 1960 and worked with Randy Weston, Walter Bishop and others at various Manhattan clubs. Haynes, who never attained prominence, was a driving tenor player whose career was cut short when he died 11/30/65 of cancer. His work can be heard in a few recordings, notably with Dave Bailey on *Two Feet in the Gutter* (Epic), *Bash!* (Jazzline) and in Les McCann's *Live at the Village Gate* (Pacific Jazz).

HAYNES, ROY OWEN,* *drums;* b. Roxbury, Mass., 3/13/26. Pl. w. combos in Boston; later toured with Lester Young, Ch. Parker, and for five years with Sarah Vaughan. Led own trio in '58; quartet with Phineas Newborn in '60s. Has also worked off and on with Stan Getz since 1950. After spending most of 1960-65 leading a quartet, Haynes rejoined Getz Dec. '65 but continued to work occasionally as a leader. He is a masterful technician who has moved continuously with the times. Won DB critics' poll as new star '62.

Own LPs: Pres., Imp., Pac. Jazz. LPs with J. Mc-Lean (Blue Note), Oliver Nelson (Impulse), Eric Dolphy (Pres.).

Addr: 194-24 Hollis Ave., Hollis 12, New York.

HAZARD, RICHARD P. (DICK), *composer, piano;* b. Trenton, N.J., 3/2/21. Studied piano 1929-32, but later took up engineering professionally. After living in Philadelphia 1943-45 was sent to Salinas, Calif. on research project and it was there that he started writing and playing. Moved to Hollywood 1946 and played on Hoagy Carmichael radio series. Worked intermittently as an accompanist and conductor for Herb Jeffries 1950-58. Has written arrangements for Peggy Lee, Judy Garland and many other singers. Though not principally associated with jazz, Hazard is greatly respected by Benny Carter and other arrangers, especially for his ballad work and his writing for strings.

LPs: *So Pretty* featuring Herb Steward (Ava); arranged others for Harry Edison (VJ) et al. Favorite arranger: Robert Farnon. Influenced most strongly by Ravel and Delius.

Addr: 1541 Oriole Lane, Los Angeles 69, Calif.

HEATH, ALBERT (TOOTIE),* *drums;* b. Philadelphia, Pa., 5/31/35. Younger brother of Percy and Jimmy (see below). Pl. w. J. J. Johnson 1958-9; later with various groups in NY incl. trio with Cedar Walton and

Reggie Workman at Five Spot. Emigrated to Stockholm Jan. 1965, working with Geo. Russell. Pl. concerts w. Friedrich Gulda. LP w. Ch. McPherson (Pres.), Jimmy Heath (River.), Kenny Dorham (BN).

HEATH, JAMES EDWARD (JIMMY),* *flute, composer, tenor sax;* b. Philadelphia, Pa., 10/25/26. Veteran of many of best bop groups from late '40s, incl. McGhee, Gillespie, Dorham, Miles Davis. Switched from tenor to flute and became increasingly active as writer in '60s. Tunes recorded by J. Mance, Blue Mitchell, Milt Jackson, F. Gulda, M. Santamaria, Eddie Harris. Played w. Donald Byrd '64. Helped M. Jackson w. vibraharp book. With Art Farmer at Half Note, '65. LPs: River. Others w. Jackson (Lime.), Cal Tjader (Verve), Carmell Jones (Pres.).

Addr: 112-19 34th Ave. #1-C, Corona 68, N.Y.

HEATH, PERCY,* *bass;* b. Wilmington, N.C., 4/30/23. Pl. w. Howard McGhee, Miles Davis and other early bop groups; Dizzy Gillespie 1950-52. Founder-member of Modern Jazz Quartet, with which he began touring in 1954. In addition to his work with John Lewis and the MJQ, Heath occasionally has made record dates with other groups, incl. Riverside albums led by his brother Jimmy and also feat. the youngest brother, Tootie.

LPs with Paul Desmond-Jim Hall (RCA); also see Lewis, John.

Addr: 175-02 139th Rd., Springfield Gardens, L.I., N.Y.

HEATH, EDWARD (TED),* *leader, composer, trombone;* b. Wandsworth, London, England, 3/30/00. Pl. w. many British big bands in '20s and '30s incl. Jack Hylton, Ambrose, Geraldo. Left latter in '44 to form own band of BBC series. Gained great popularity in England through regular Sunday concerts at the London Palladium inaugurated in '45. Toured U.S. '56 and on several other occasions. In '60s continued to lead band. LPs: London.

HEATLEY, SPIKE, *bass;* b. London, England, 2/17/33. Started in India '55-7 w. Alan Ross. Ret. to Eng. and pl. w. Vic Ash, Dill Jones, Ronnie Scott-Tubby Hayes Jazz Couriers, Tubby Hayes. Pl. w. Eddie Thompson '59-60, Johnny Dankworth '60-2. Since then w. Tony Coe, Ronnie Ross, Danny Moss. Impressive bassist in Pettiford tradition. LPs w. Tony Coe and Bill LeSage (Brit. Philips); Dankworth (Brit. Fontana), *Strike Up the Bard,* Ken Jones (Brit. Col.), LeSage (Brit. World Record Club).

Addr: 20 Park Rd., London W. 7, England.

HECKMAN, DONALD J. (DON), *critic, alto saxophone, clarinet, composer;* b. Reading, Pa., 12/18/32. Studied clarinet in late '40s in Miami, Florida; never studied alto formally. Pl. w. Univ. of Miami bands 1948. Toured Venezuela in '51 with college jazz band. Club dates with various groups in mid-50s, then out of music until 1960, when he joined John Benson Brooks trio for two years. Off and on with Don Ellis groups '62-3. Co-leader of group with Ed Summerlin '63-6.

Led own group in series of live FM radio shows for Pacifica Network '63.

Inspired by L. Konitz, E. Dolphy and O. Coleman, Heckman says, "I am most influenced by the concept of the playing composer who shapes and molds his music through actual participation in its creation. My current interests are directed toward music and theatre." Heckman has made an important contribution as a critic, writing a series of analytical articles for such publications as *Down Beat* on Ornette Coleman and others. Jazz reviewer for *American Record Guide.*

Addr: 275 W. 4th St., New York City, N.Y.

HEFTI, NEAL,* *composer;* b. Hastings, Nebr., 10/29/22. Trumpeter and/or arranger in '40s for many bands incl. Charlie Barnet, Earl Hines, Woody Herman, Harry James. Best known as composer of *The Good Earth* and *Wildroot* for Herman. In 1950s wrote many originals for Count Basie band, also led own orchestras off and on from '52, playing trumpet and sometimes piano.

Hefti moved from NYC to LA in summer of '60. Recording executive and artist for Reprise Rec. '61-2. Returned East '62-3, writing series of band arrangements for school and college youths. Back in LA from late '63, he soon built a reputation as composer of music for motion pictures. His film credits include *Sex and The Single Girl* (in which Basie's band appeared), *How To Murder Your Wife, Synanon, Harlow, Boeing Boeing, Lord Love A Duck, Duel at Diablo.* Hefti earned even greater success as writer of the music for the *Batman* TV series in '66 and for another TV series, *Green Hornet,* later in '66. Though the *Batman* music had a tongue-in-cheek, rock 'n' roll flavor, occasional jazz elements were still discernible in some of his film and TV work. His most popular compositions are the ballad *Li'l Darlin',* introduced by Basie, and the rock-blues known as *Batman Theme.*

LPs: *Jazz Pops, Themes From TV's Top 12, Sinatra-Basie* (Reprise); *Li'l Darlin'* (20th-Fox); *Lord Love A Duck* (UA); *Batman* (RCA). *On My Way and Shoutin'* w. Count Basie (Verve); earlier Basie albums on Roulette.

Addr: 15917 Valley Vista, Encino, Calif.

HENDERSON, WILLIAM RANDALL (BILL),* *singer;* b. Chicago, Ill., 3/19/30. First prominent in jazz as vocalist on Horace Silver record, *Senor Blues,* 1958 (BN). Continued to work night clubs as single in '60s, also toured as vocalist w. Count Basie band '65-6. LPs in early '60s on VJ; later LPs (incl. album w. Oscar Peterson Trio) on Verve.

HENDERSON, JOSEPH A. (JOE), *tenor sax, composer;* b. Lima, Ohio, 4/24/37. Brother also plays sax. Began professional playing in show bands. Worked w. Sonny Stitt '59. Led own group Detroit '60. Jack McDuff '62. Co-led group w. Kenny Dorham '62-'63. W. Horace Silver '64-April '66. Toured world '60-'62 with special service unit of U.S. Army. Juan-les-Pins, Monterey JFs '64. Recorded w. Andrew Hill '65. Basically a soul tenorman, Henderson's work with Hill shows the further influence of Rollins, Coltrane and Ornette Coleman. Hill predicted that he "is going to be one of the greatest tenors" because "he has the imagination to make it in the avant-garde camp, but he has so much emotion too." Other favs and infl: Parker, Tatum, Stitt, Powell; Bartok, Hindemith, Stravinsky. Would like to become better known as a composer. Own LPs: *Page One, In 'n Out, Our Thing* (BN). Others: w. Hill, Dorham, Pete La Roca (BN).

Addr: 108 Montague, Brooklyn, N.Y.

HENDERSON, SKITCH CEDRIC,* *leader, piano;* b. Halstad, Minn., 1/27/18. Led dance band 1947-9. NBC staff musician since '51. Came to prominence on *Steve Allen Show* '55-6.

From 1962 Henderson led an excellent and highly versatile orchestra on *Tonight,* the TV show starring Johnny Carson. A strong jazz element could frequently be detected in the arrangements. The soloists included such first-class jazz musicians as Doc Severinsen, Clark Terry, Snooky Young, trumpets; Tom Newsom, tenor sax and arranger; Tony Mottola, guitar; Bobby Rosengarden or Ed Shaughnessy, drums. The band's library included arrangements by Neal Hefti, Walt Levinsky, Torrie Bito, Ernie Wilkins and Henderson. Left NBC Sept. 1966.

LPs: Col.

Addr: c/o National Broadcasting Co., New York 20, N.Y.

HENDERSON, WAYNE MAURICE, *trombone, euphonium, composer;* b. Houston, Texas, 9/24/39. Stud. trombone from sixth grade. From his early teens he has been a part of the group known in recent years as the Jazz Crusaders. Has played many college campuses, radio and TV shows, clubs throughout the Southwest, several Eastern tours, and *Jazz Scene U.S.A.* TV show produced by Steve Allen. Like the other members of this group, Henderson is a highly capable and greatly underrated musician. Fav: Slide Hampton. Infl: J. J. Johnson. Comps: *Young Rabbits, Congolese Sermon, In A Dream, Scratch, M. J. S. Funk.*

LPs with Jazz Crusaders (Pac. Jazz). Also dates with Ray Brown, Monk Montgomery, Les McCann, Mongo Santamaria.

Addr: 416 N. Maie Ave., Compton, Calif.

HENDRICKS, JOHN CARL (JON),* *songwriter, singer;* also *drums;* b. Newark, Ohio, 9/16/21. Moved to New York '52 and teamed with Dave Lambert in '57 for vocal recording of *Four Brothers.* In '58 Lambert and Hendricks joined with Annie Ross to form a unique vocal trio, most of whose repertoire was based on well-known instrumental jazz records, for which Hendricks set lyrics not only to the melodies but also to the original solo improvisations.

Lambert, Hendricks & Ross won a series of DB and *Playboy* polls as the No. 1 vocal group in jazz. Illness forced Miss Ross out of the trio in 1962 and Yolande Bavan took her place. In '64 Dave Lambert left, and

by the fall of that year Hendricks had given up the trio and was working as a single.

In addition to his knack for fitting lyrics to extremely complex melodic lines, Hendricks has written some delightful original compositions, notably *Gimme That Wine* and *Yeh! Yeh!.* The latter became a rock 'n' roll hit when it was recorded by Georgie Fame.

One of Hendricks' outstanding achievements was the creation of a musical presentation, *Evolution of the Blues Song,* for which he served as narrator and was assisted by several singers. Presented at the Monterey JF 1960, it was recorded on Col. 8383. Other solo Hendricks LPs: *Fast Livin' Blues* (Col.), *Salute to Joao Gilberto* (Reprise); *In Person at the Trident* (Smash). LPs by Lambert, Hendricks & Ross: Roul., Col., Wor. Pacific. By Lambert, Hendricks & Bavan: RCA.

Addr: 68 Cloudview Rd., Sausalito, Calif.

HENDRICKSON, ALTON REYNOLDS (AL),* *guitar, singer;* b. Eastland, Texas, 5/10/20. A leading studio guitarist, well known for his work on the early recordings by Artie Shaw's Gramercy 5, Hendrickson was heard in a number of bossa nova albums, 1962-5. Pl. w. D. Gillespie, Monterey Jazz Festival '62. Records and movies with John Mandel, Neal Hefti, Bill Holman, Nelson Riddle.

LPs: *New Continent* w. Gillespie-Schifrin (Limelight); Louis Bellson-Schifrin (Roulette).

Addr: 2801 Belden Dr., Hollywood 28, Calif.

HERBERT, MORT (Morton Herbert Pelovitz),* *bass, composer;* b. Somerville, N.J., 6/30/25. With Gene Krupa in '57 and Louis Armstrong '58-61. Passed bar exam and became deputy district attorney, Los Angeles County 1962, practicing lawyer 1964. Still active in free-lance playing and writing, esp. w. Herb Ellis.

Addr: 8915 Swinton Ave., Sepulveda, Calif.

HERMAN, WOODROW CHARLES (WOODY),* *clarinet, alto sax, singer, leader;* b. Milwaukee, Wis., 5/16/13. Pl. w. Isham Jones band 1934-6; led own band from '37 and with the exception of a seven-month hiatus in 1947 has been on tour continually since then. From 1955-59 he alternated between a big band and small combos.

In Feb. 1960 Herman launched a new orchestra, with a strong personnel incl. lead trumpeter Bill Chase. The band played many colleges, concerts and festivals, and on one occasion joined forces with the Connecticut Symphony. By 1962 a new upsurge in the band's reputation was observed as such soloists as Sal Nistico, tenor sax, Phil Wilson, trombone, and the drums of Jake Hanna strengthened the personnel.

The excitement of the Herman bands of the 1940s was recaptured in the next two years. Herman won a NARAS Grammy award for *Encore* as the best big-band jazz album of '63. In 1965 the orchestra was received with wild enthusiasm at the Antibes JF. By now the sidemen included Andy McGhee, tenor sax, and Ronnie Zito on drums. Similar reaction greeted

Herman in 1966 during tours of Western Europe, North Africa and Eastern Europe.

Much of the success of the band was attributed to Herman's popularity among his men and the resultant team spirit, as well as to the knack shown by Herman and Nat Pierce, his invaluable musical director and pianist-arranger, in selecting musicians.

A three-LP album comprising reissues of the classic performances by the 1945-7 bands is available on Col. C3L 25. Other releases in the '60s: *Swing Low Sweet Clarinet* (004), *Herman 1963* (065), *Encore* (092), *Herman 1964* (118), *Woody's Big Band Goodies* (171), all Philips; *My Kind of Broadway* (Col. 9157), *Woody's Winners* (Col. 9236), *Herman & The Fourth Herd* (Surrey 1032).

Addr: c/o Abe Turchen, 200 West 57th St., New York 19, N.Y.

HEYWOOD, EDDIE JR.,* *piano, composer;* b. Atlanta, Ga., 12/4/15. Prominent as a jazz pianist with Benny Carter 1939-40 and as leader of sextet in mid-'40s. His performances and recordings in recent years have receded from jazz and are conceived in terms of popular success rather than jazz content. Best known comp. *Canadian Sunset.* A sextet LP representative of his best jazz phase is available on Mainstream 6001; he also can be heard to advantage w. Shelly Manne (Contact).

Addr: 170 Oxford Rd., New Rochelle, N.Y.

HIGGINBOTHAM, JACK (J.C.),* *trombone;* b. Social Circle, Georgia, 5/11/06. The pioneer swing era trombonist, best known for his big band work in the '30s and sextet partnership with Red Allen in the '40s, began an association with the Metropole in NYC, 1956, and played there frequently until the early 1960s. He visited Scandinavia in 1963. During the same year he appeared in an all-star group at the NJF, and in a festival in Norfolk, Va. Reunited briefly with Louis Armstrong in 1964; returned to Copenhagen November '65. Except for a session with Tiny Grimes, Higginbotham was inactive on records during most of this period.

Addr: 152 W. 118th St., New York, N.Y.

HIGGINS, BILLY,* *drums;* b. Los Angeles, Calif., 10/11/36. A member of the original Ornette Coleman quartet that played at the Five Spot in '59, Higgins has free-lanced extensively in NYC in the '60s at Slugs', etc. with a variety of groups represented in his recording credits below. A highly sensitive, musical drummer who is at home in many settings, he won a new star award in the DB Critics' poll '60. LPs w. Sonny Rollins (RCA), Jackie McLean, Sonny Clark, Dexter Gordon, Herbie Hancock, Hank Mobley (Blue Note), Coleman (Atl.).

HIGGINS, HAYDN (EDDIE),* *piano;* also *organ, vibes;* b. Cambridge. Mass., 2/21/32. Mother a classical pianist, brother an authority on Indian music. Attended Northwestern U. School of Music during early '50s; remained in Chicago and became active in several facets of music scene there. With Jimmy Ille's Dixie- land group '52-'54. Formed own trio '57, playing Blue Note, Playboy Club, Cloister, other Chicago clubs; house band intermittently at London House from '57. Traveled w. Jack Teagarden for six months '62-63. Comps. incl. *Expoobident, Wayning Moments, Tango Africaine.* Recording engineer for Universal Studios from '64. Favs: Oscar Peterson; also Bill Evans, Wynton Kelly, Hank Jones. Own LPs: *Ed Higgins Trio* (Replica), *Eddie Higgins* (VJ), *Soulero* (Atl.). Others: w. Lee Morgan, Wayne Shorter (VJ); own fav. Al Grey, *Thinking Man's Trombone* (Cadet).

Addr: 1360 Standburg Terr., Chicago 10, Ill.

HILL, ANDREW, *piano, composer;* b. Port au Prince, Haiti, 6/30/37. His family, whose name originally was Hille, came to the U.S. in 1941 and soon settled in Chicago. Hill started in music as a boy soprano, singing, playing accordion and tap dancing. He appeared in local talent shows from 1943-7. In 1950 he learned to play blues on the piano. His teacher was a baritone saxophonist. On his early jobs he played baritone as well as piano. He worked with Paul Williams' r&b at 15, later coming into contact with many name jazzmen at Joe Segal's jam sessions.

During his Chicago years Hill came to know Barry Harris, who became an influence along with Powell, Tatum and Monk. After traveling to New York as Dinah Washington's accompanist, he settled there in '61, playing with singers and small combos. Lived in Los Angeles in '62, working with Lighthouse group and Roland Kirk quartet. Returned to NYC '63 with his wife, organist Laverne Gillette.

Hill came to prominence when he was signed by Blue Note Records. His first album, *Black Fire,* showed an astonishing maturity both of technique and ideas. His original works lacked the chaotic quality sometimes found in the more aggressive members of the avant garde. As A. B. Spellman wrote, "he seemed to feel that he could create his own music without beating down all the shibboleths singlehandedly to the accompaniment of the derision of his peers."

Hill's work is unconventional in conception, structure, phrasing and in the unusually sensitive collaboration with his sidemen. The latter included Bobby Hutcherson on his second album, *Judgement;* Eric Dolphy and Kenny Dorham on the third album, *Point of Departure.*

Hill, who has also appeared successfully in Europe, has shown unmistakable signs of developing into one of the important pianists and composers of the *cosa nova* trend in the jazz of the '60s.

Own LPs: Blue Note; also with Roland Kirk (Mercury); *Conflict* with Jimmy Woods (Cont.).

Addr: 212 West 102nd St., New York 25, N.Y.

HILL, FREDERICK ROOSEVELT (FREDDY), *trumpet, composer;* also *piano, cello;* b. Jacksonville, Fla., 4/18/32. Stud. privately with Percy Mills. Attended Fla. A&M Coll. and from 1949-53 pl. in the college band, of which Nat and Cannonball Adderley were also members. U.S. Army 1953. String teacher in Fla. publ. schools 1955-7. Settling in LA, he worked off and on with the Gerald Wilson band from 1957-66 and with Earl Bostic 1959-60. Favs: Fats Navarro, also Gillespie, M. Davis. Ambition: to develop as prof. arr. LPs w. Gerald Wilson, Gil Fuller (Pac. Jazz), Lou Blackburn (Impulse), L. Vinnegar (Contemp), Marvin Jenkins (Palomar).

Addr: 1717 So. Fairfax Ave., Los Angeles 17, Calif.

HILLYER, LONNIE, *trumpet;* b. Monroe, Ga., 3/25/40. Family moved to Detroit when he was three. Picked up older brother's trumpet when his brother went into the Army '51. Pl. in elementary school band. While in high school studied at Larry Teal's music studio. Studied w. Barry Harris from age 14; w. trumpeter Bill Horner Jr. for a year '58. Jammed at World Stage —a musicians' organization—sessions '55-7. Pl. w. Yusef Lateef at Half Note, NYC, Minor Key in Detroit '59; w. Joe Henderson at Bluebird, Detroit '60. Taught trumpet in Detroit '59-60. To NYC late summer '60. Worked w. Slide Hampton '60, Barry Harris at Minton's '62-3, Charles Davis '66. From '60 Hillyer has pl. off and on, with Charles Mingus' groups incl. the MJF '64-5. In '66 he and Charles McPherson formed their own quintet. First infl. by his brother's Louis Armstrong and Harry James records, Hillyer names Gillespie, Davis, Navarro and Freddie Webster as his favs. As one of the few young trumpeters to have been strongly influenced by Gillespie, he shows in his playing a great understanding of Dizzy's style. LPs w. Mingus (Candid, Mingus), Harris (River.), Lateef (Pres.).

Addr: 203 W. 103rd St., New York, N.Y.

HINES, EARL KENNETH (FATHA),* *piano;* b. Duquesne, Pa., 12/28/05. After several years of comparative obscurity in the San Francisco area, Hines appeared in 1964 in three concerts at The Little Theatre, NYC. Enthusiastic critical reaction to these concerts enabled him to begin working more regularly in trio or quartet contexts, often using his former arranger, Budd Johnson, on tenor sax.

In 1965 Hines enjoyed tremendous ovations at the Newport and Monterey Jazz Festivals. He also appeared at a Berlin Jazz Festival, following which he made a European tour. He soon found himself in demand for many engagements around the Continent in 1965-6. He made TV appearances, incl. a series of five half hour shows for French National Broadcasting System. Toured USSR w. combo summer '66.

Hines was elected in 1965 to DB Hall of Fame. The honor was long overdue. His style was almost exactly the equivalent of what had been heard on his classic performances with Louis Armstrong's Hot Five in the 1920s, and with his own big band in the '30s and '40s. Without any of the harmonic complexities or over-technical linearity of younger pianists, Hines continued in his 60s to outswing most men of half his age.

LPs: *The Grand Terrace Band,* reissues of 1939-40 big band performances (RCA); *Oh, Father!,* reissues of 1933-8 big band (Epic); also a new and inferior set with Hollywood studio big band (Cap.). Combo LPs: *Grand Reunion* (two volumes), with Roy Eldridge, Coleman Hawkins (Lime.); Little Theatre Concert (Focus); others on Col., RCA, River. Solo LP: *Spontaneous Explorations* (Contact).

Addr: 815 Trestle Glen Rd., Oakland 10, Calif.

HINTON, MILTON J. (MILT),* *bass;* b. Vicksburg, Miss., 6/23/10. Originally known as key sideman in Cab Calloway orchestra from 1936-51. In '50s toured for a year with Louis Armstrong, also worked with Teddy Wilson, Benny Goodman. For more than a decade Hinton has been in constant demand for both commercial and jazz work in the New York studios. He has recorded with L. Hampton, K. Burrell, J. Dankworth, Sammy Davis Jr. and hundreds of other artists. Has also appeared on innumerable TV shows. Concerts with Ben Webster, Sammy Davis, Judy Garland. SNCC shows with H. Belafonte '65-6. Active in church youth work, lecturing and playing. Wrote background music for Urban League movie, *Outskirts of Hope.* Film Festival in Cannes, France in '65 with Diahann Carroll.

Addr: 173-05 113th Ave., St. Albans, N.Y., 11433.

HIRSCH, GODFREY M., *vibes,* also *drums, piano;* b. New Orleans, La., 2/2/07. Both parents musicians. Started on drums in high school 1922. Percussionist at Saenger Theatre, NO, 1932-7, then a year with Louis Prima, three years with Richard Himber. Dave Roberts Trio, 1943, followed by service in U.S. Navy '43-5. Member of WWL-CBS staff band 1945-60. In 1960 he joined Pete Fountain's combo; has since been seen with him in night clubs, TV, etc., and has served as deputy leader at Fountain's own club. Early records with Prima; many LPs with Pete Fountain, and on his own LP (Coral). A capable vibraphonist inspired by Red Norvo and Lionel Hampton, he says his aim is "to style his playing with the cycle of time and not get stagnant."

Addr: 2509 Tulane Ave., New Orleans, La.

HIRT, ALOIS MAXWELL (AL), *trumpet;* b. New Orleans, La., 11/7/22. Father a policeman. Al took up trumpet at age six and played in the Sons Of The Police Department Junior Police Band. He studied extensively with many teachers until 1940, then attended Cincinnati Conservatory. After Army service, 1943-6, toured with big bands led by Jimmy and Tommy Dorsey, Ray McKinley (with whom he toured Europe for a year) and Horace Heidt. He spent the next eight years on staff at a New Orleans radio station, playing mainly lead trumpet.

After leaving the radio station Hirt formed a combo, which included Pete Fountain. They went to work at Dan Levy's Pier 600 Club, and during this time began recording Dixieland albums.

Around 1960 Hirt's startling bravura style and impressive physical stature (almost 6½ ft. tall, he then weighed 300 lbs.) attracted increasing attention. During the next two years he became a national name and a best-selling recording artist on RCA Victor. Touring occasionally, he played in Las Vegas with his own Dixieland group, but more and more frequently in 1963-6 he was featured as a personality in TV shows, including his own network TV series in the summer of 1965. He appeared as soloist with New Orleans Symphony, '63 and Boston Pops Orchestra, '64. Films: *Rome Adventure* and *World By Night*.

Hirt is a musical anomaly. In '61 Bill Coss said: "His group is really a Dixieland deception. He and his musicians are far more flexible than that. At his worst there are the dance steps, the pat music, the sloppy playing from one who has no excuse for such . . . he is thoroughly capable of transmitting power and glory into the trumpet. Thus far he has allowed only a glimpse of what he can do."

During the years since then Hirt has moved even further away from jazz, to exploit his tremendous economic potential as personality and virtuoso. His principal influences were Harry James and Ziggy Elman, and his current favorite is Dizzy Gillespie; but little of his former good taste is allowed to penetrate to the public. He is greatly admired by fellow-trumpeters for his phenomenal technique and power.

From the jazz standpoint his best albums are two early Coral sets co-starring Fountain; also *Al Hirt in New Orleans* (Coral) and *Our Man In New Orleans* (RCA). His own preferences include *Horn A Plenty, Pops Goes the Trumpet* w. Arthur Fiedler and Boston Pops, and *Trumpet and Strings* with Marty Paich (all RCA).

In recent years Hirt has spent much of his time playing at his own club in New Orleans. He appeared at Carnegie Hall in 1965 with a big band, arranged and conducted by Gerald Wilson, recorded for an RCA album.

Addr: 7540 Canal Blvd., New Orleans, La.

HIRT, GERALD P., *trombone;* b. New Orleans, La., 7/29/24. Started gigging with local groups 1939; lead trombone with New Orleans Symphony 1941-2. Army Bands, '42-6. After a year with Louie Prima, 1947, and three years with various local groups, Hirt gave up music. He was a police detective for the New Orleans police department 1951-61, then returned to music and joined combo led by his brother, trumpeter Al Hirt. Has appeared with him on many TV shows, RCA LPs, etc. Names Joe Howard as important influence.

Addr: 8508 Palm St., New Orleans, La.

HITE, LES,* *leader, alto sax;* b. DuQuoin, Ill., 2/13/03. Prominent in Los Angeles in the 1920s and '30s, Hite led the band fronted by Louis Armstrong for long periods from 1930-32. His band was heard in the east in 1940-42, when its personnel briefly included Dizzy Gillespie. Hite retired from the band business in 1945. In 1957 he became a partner in an artists' agency. He died of a heart ailment in Santa Monica, Cal. 2/6/62.

Hite's band was heard backing Louis Armstrong in Vol. 4 of *The Louis Armstrong Story* (Col.), but the excellent series of records made by his band of the early '40s for RCA (incl. the hit *T-Bone Blues*) had not been reissued by 1966.

HODEIR, ANDRÉ,* *composer, critic;* b. Paris, France, 1/22/21. Came to prominence in mid-'50s as author of *Jazz: Evolution & Essence*. Hodeir's multiple career has taken him into the areas of classical and jazz criticism and composing. His work *Around the Blues* was recorded by MJQ, 1960. Other works: *Détails*, played at Washington Fest. '62, *Transplantation I* for big band '64, *Anna Livia Plurabelle* for voice and orchestra. Concerts in Paris '64 with new big band. Books: *Toward Jazz* and *Since Debussy* (both Grove Press). Hodeir is an extremely skilled comp.-arr. who reflects a variety of classical and jazz infls. As an author he is responsible for some of the most provocative and profound analyses of jazz now available.

LP: *Paris Scene* (Savoy); *Jazz et Jazz* (Philips).

HODES, ARTHUR W. (ART),* *piano;* b. Nikoliev, Russia, 11/14/04. Played with best Chicago musicians during '20s; later a writer, disc jockey, lecturer and spokesman for traditional jazz. During '60s toured numerous colleges with "Sound of Jazz," a lecture-concert program on jazz and its history, which also appeared on Chicago educational TV. Teaches piano privately. Writes regular column "Sittin' In" for *Down Beat;* "Jazz Junction" for newspaper *The Reporter*. Own LPs: *Summit Meeting* (Jazzol.), *Cat on the Keys* (Con. Disc). Others w. Albert Nicholas (Delm.), tracks on *Plain Old Blues, Meet Me in Chicago* (Merc.).

HODGES, JOHN CORNELIUS (JOHNNY or RABBIT),* *alto sax, composer;* b. Cambridge, Mass., 7/25/06. A member of Duke Ellington's orchestra from 1928-51 and again since 1955, the pioneer alto saxophonist continued to tour with Ellington in the 1960s but also engaged in several musically rewarding side ventures. Most notably, from 1961 he was teamed with organist Wild Bill Davis in a consistently attractive series of albums with a variety of small group accompaniments. These included *Blue Hodge, Mess of Blues, Blue Rabbit, Joes' Blues, Wings and Things* (Verve), and *Con-Soul Sax* (RCA). Hodges was also heard with the Billy Strayhorn orchestra (actually Ellington's band with minor personnel changes), and in *The Eleventh Hour*, arr. and cond. by Oliver Nelson (both Verve). Another big band date composed mainly of Ellington men was *Everybody Knows Johnny Hodges* (Impulse). In '66 he recorded with Lawrence Welk's orch. for Dot. As Duke Ellington has said, "Johnny Hodges has complete independence of expression. He says what he wants to say on the horn, and that is *it*. He says it in *his* language, from *his* perspective, which is specific, and you could say that his is pure artistry."

Addr: 555 Edgecombe Ave., New York 32, N.Y.

HOFFMAN, INGFRIED, *organ;* b. Stettin, Germany, 1/30/35. Studied piano as child. Got into professional music after winning an amateur concert. From '63 a sideman w. Klaus Doldinger; toured S. America, N. Africa, played one concert in New Orleans. Favs: Jimmy Smith; also Parker, Gillespie, Monk. Own LP: *Hammond Tales* (Phil.). Others: w. Doldinger (Phil., D. Gram.)., *International Jazz Workshop* (Emarcy).

Addr: Severinstrasse 92-96, Cologne, Germany.

HOLLEY, MAJOR QUINCY JR. (MULE),* *bass;* b. Detroit, Mich., 7/10/24. Worked in Detroit with Ch. Parker; lived in England 1954-6, later pl. w. Woody Herman, Kenny Burrell Trio, C. Hawkins, R. Eldridge, Q. Jones, Cohn-Sims and in 1964 w. Duke Ellington. Active as teacher in recent years, also gave series of open air concerts for handicapped children. Much TV, radio work; in pit bands of several B'way shows.

LPs w. Q. Jones, Cohn-Sims (Merc.); C. Hawkins (Verve, Impulse); *Ellington '65* (Reprise).

Addr: 640 Riverside Dr., New York, N.Y. 10031.

HOLLOWAY, JAMES L. (RED), *tenor sax;* b. Helena, Ark., 5/31/27. Mother plays piano, father plays violin. Stud. at Chicago Conservatory. First gig w. Gene Wright, Chicago '43-'46. W. 5th Army band '46-'47. W. Roosevelt Sykes '48, N. Towles '49-'50, own quartet '52-'61 except for brief stints w. L. Hampton, B. Webster. W. Lloyd Price '61-'63, B. Doggett '63, J. McDuff from '63. In Europe '64 at Antibes JF, Golden Circle in Stockholm. Favs. and infl.: G. Ammons, Webster, Ellington. Also trains horses, teaches horseback riding. Own LP: *Sax, Strings and Soul* (Pres.). Others: w. McDuff (Pres.), Doggett (Col.), Price (ABC-Par.), The Coasters (L.L.), The Flamingos (Chess), The Moonglows (Change), Bobby Bland and Little Junior Parker (Duke, Peacock), Johnny Davis (Univ.).

Addr: 7210 S. Evans Ave., Chicago 19, Ill.

HOLMAN, WILLIS (BILL),* *composer, tenor sax;* b. Olive, Calif., 5/21/27. Prominent in the 1950s with the Charlie Barnet and Stan Kenton bands, later in combos with Shorty Rogers and Mel Lewis. In 1960 Holman worked with Gerry Mulligan writing the library for the latter's concert jazz band. He continued to arrange for various other big bands, notably Terry Gibbs and Stan Kenton, '61-2, and Woody Herman from '63. His arr. of *After You've Gone,* heard in *Woody Herman: 1964* (Phil.) is one of Herman's most popular items of recent years and illustrates Holman's exceptional gift for revitalizing old material.

He wrote a jazz sequence for the Jerry Lewis film *Three On A Couch* in 1966. He composed *Trilogy,* introduced by LA Neophonic in 1965, and was co-composer with Gerry Mulligan of *Music for Baritone Saxophone and Orchestra,* premiered by Mulligan with the Neophonic Orch. in Jan. 1966.

Holman has also done extensive vocal background work, for Judy Garland's TV series as well as for albums by Anita O'Day, Ella Fitzgerald, June Christy, Peggy Lee and Sarah Vaughan.

Holman was a faculty member at the Summer Jazz Clinic held in 1965 at the U. of Utah. He also played with the faculty band, revealing a driving, compelling style that has all too seldom been heard since the demands on him for writing assignments limited his playing time.

Own LP: Capitol.

Addr: 444 S. California St., Burbank, Calif.

HOLMES, RICHARD ARNOLD (GROOVE), *organ;* b. Camden, New Jersey, 5/2/31. No formal musical training. Worked for several years in small clubs and in 1960 was discovered by Les McCann in Pittsburgh. McCann recommended him to Richard Bock of Pacific Jazz Records. Starting in 1961 Holmes recorded a series of albums for this label and worked mainly in clubs in the Southern California area.

Though he names Jimmy Smith as his favorite blues organ artist, Holmes states that he has been influenced by no other organist: "I listen to none of them—nothing they do interests me; I play completely differently. I listen to bass men." Holmes himself also plays bass; a valuable aspect of his style is his bass pedal line, which more closely resembles that of a string bass than the bass lines of most organists. He plays in a straightforward blues-rooted style and is not given to the over-busy technical excursions of which some of his contemporaries are guilty.

Own LPs with trio (Pres.), with Onzy Mathews Big Band (War. Bros.), also small group sessions featuring Ben Webster, Gene Ammons, Les McCann, Joe Pass, on various Pac. Jazz albums. His most impressive LP is *You Better Believe It!* (Pac. Jazz) in which he is heard as a featured soloist with the Gerald Wilson big band.

Addr: 721 Ferry Ave., Camden, N.J.

HOLT, ISAAC (RED),* *drums;* b. Rosedale, Miss., 5/16/32. Began association with Ramsey Lewis and El Dee Young when they were teenagers; in '56 they formed the Ramsey Lewis Trio and by '65 had achieved national prominence. Left Lewis summer '66.

LPs: Cadet, Merc.

HOOD, WILLIAM H. (BILL), *baritone sax, composer;* b. Portland, Oregon, 12/13/24. Stud. piano; self-taught on saxes, flute, clarinet, and as a writer. Toured Pacific after World War II as conductor for G.I. show. Sideman w. Freddie Slack 1946-7. Attended college in Mexico City 1951-2, appearing locally on weekly jazz radio show. Free-lanced with many groups in Calif. Appeared at Monterey JF 1958, '62 and '65. Worked with Benny Goodman '61 and '65; Terry Gibbs '65. Favs: H. Carney, Ch. Davis; infls.: Coleman Hawkins, Ch. Parker, D. Ellington.

LPs: Best solo work on *I Get A Boot Out of You* w. Marty Paich (War. Bros.). Others: *The New Continent* w. Dizzy Gillespie (Limelight); *Explosive Side of Sarah Vaughan* (Roul.); *Jazz Wave* with Med

Flory (Jubilee); and dates with Chet Baker (Pac. Jazz), Benny Carter (Impulse).

Addr: 5727 Fulcher Ave., No. Hollywood, Calif. 91601.

HOOPER, NESBERT (STICKS or STIX), *drums, leader, composer;* b. Houston, Texas, 8/15/38. Educ. E. O. Smith Jr. High; Wheatley High; Texas Southern U. Formed his own band in 1952.

Hooper's original unit was known as The Swingsters. Later it was billed as the Modern Jazz Sextet and as The Nite Hawks, and finally as the Jazz Crusaders. After several years of successful local work the group moved to the West Coast, playing major colleges there as well as many night clubs. TV appearances on Steve Allen's *Jazz Scene USA,* etc. Hooper names Max Roach as his most important influence but is also an admirer of Elvin Jones, Billy Higgins, and Philly Joe Jones. His compositions include *Blues for Ramona, Stix March, Sinnin' Sam, Para Mi Espoza.*

All the recording work of Jazz Crusaders has appeared on the Pacific Jazz label. Among the group's most representative albums are *Heat Wave, Tough Talk, Freedom Sound, Chile con Soul.*

Addr: 1232 W. 91st St., Los Angeles, Calif.

HOPKINS, SAM (LIGHTNIN'), * *singer, guitar;* b. Centerville, Texas, 3/15/12. A farm worker who drifted into music and began playing on a full-time basis in 1946, Hopkins remained an itinerant singer, working mainly in Texas, until his rediscovery by a folklorist, Mack McCormick. Hopkins came to New York in Oct. 1960 and during the next few years was exposed to audiences entirely different from those for whom he had been accustomed to play. Many of them were white college students or sophisticated audiences at such night clubs as the Village Gate in NYC. He took part in a CBS-TV workshop program, *A Pattern of Words and Music.*

Hopkins' work has a unique and lyrical beauty that reaches deep into the roots of the folk blues idiom from which his style sprang. McCormick once wrote, "Lightnin' stands among the great whirlpool of the blues, drawing upon it at random, bending it to suit a mood, taking impish pleasure in creating surprises, constantly shaping and shattering and remaking the blues in his own image." Own LPs: Candid, Time, Verve, World Pacific, Mainstream, VJ, Pres.

HORN, PAUL, * *flute, alto sax, clarinet, composer, leader;* b. New York City, 3/17/30. Came to prominence as soloist with Chico Hamilton Quintet 1956-8. In the 1960s, while active in commercial studio work in Hollywood, Horn also played clubs with his own quintet and began recording as a leader for Columbia in 1962. He was featured in a half-hour TV documentary by Wolper Productions, *The Story of a Jazz Musician;* also in a movie, *Wild and Wonderful,* with Tony Curtis. His group played college concerts, was seen on Steve Allen and *Tonight* TV shows, etc.

Both as soloist and composer Horn grew immensely

in stature during the early 1960s. His flute work, probably as individual as that of any performer in jazz, was doubly effective on the strength of the settings provided by his writing, and occasionally by that of others, notably Lalo Schifrin. The latter's composition, *Jazz Suite on The Mass Texts,* with an enlarged ensemble, was recorded in 1965, a year after Horn had signed with RCA Victor. This composition, which earned national publicity, was later performed in churches and at concerts. In '65-66, he was also associated with singer Tony Bennett in acc. role on many occasions.

As a composer and leader Horn was among the first in jazz to make valuable use of modal devices, which form the basis for many of the quintet's interpretations. He was also one of the first, along with Dave Brubeck, to devote a substantial proportion of his writing and playing to unusual time signatures. In 1966 he recorded an album for RCA based on the newly imported 5/4 bossa nova beat from Rio, the Jequibau. Own LPs: Columbia, RCA.

Addr: 2452 Horseshoe Canyon Rd., Los Angeles 46, Calif.

HORN, SHIRLEY, *singer, piano;* b. Washington, D.C., 5/1/34. Four years of study at Howard University Jr. School of Music; six years of private study. Through the interest and help of such musicians as Miles Davis, Jimmy Jones, John Levy and Quincy Jones, she came to prominence in the early 1960s. Has led her own trio since 1954, working in recent years at the Village Vanguard and other clubs as well as TV commercials, concerts in New York and Washington, D.C. She has an attractive style as pianist and an unusually gentle and appealing vocal timbre. Favs: Billie Holiday, Peggy Lee, Ray Charles; Oscar Peterson, Bill Evans. LPs: Mercury.

Addr: 824 Burns St. S.E., Washington, D.C.

HOUSE, SON (Eddie James House, Jr.), *singer, guitar;* b. Lyon, Miss., 3/21/02. Father played trombone. Lived in New Orleans from about 1906-26, then returned to Miss., where he started to play the guitar around 1927 in Mattson. Played at country dances, then on weekends in small bars and levee camps in northwest Miss.

House traveled to Grafton, Wisc. in August 1930 to record for Paramount. During most of the '30s he worked as a tractor driver. In 1942, while at home in Robinsonville, Miss., he was recorded by Alan Lomax for the Library of Congress. From 1943 he lived in Rochester, N.Y., working as porter and chef. By the time he was rediscovered in 1964 he had given up music completely. He came out of retirement for what turned out to be a new career, appearing at Philadelphia Folk Festival Aug. '64; Newport, UCLA, Mariposa, Swarthmore and New York Folk Festivals '65; also at Carnegie Hall in a reunion with other early blues artists in Nov. '65.

House, whose main influence was the late Ch. Patton, has had two separate careers, the first playing for and with Negroes, the second almost entirely before predominantly white college and festival audiences. In Dick Waterman's words, "His music truly lives the Delta. Calm and soft spoken offstage, he becomes harsh, guttural, driving, intense and a throbbing melancholy figure when he begins to sing."

Own LP: Col. Library of Congress recordings were issued on Folkways. Early 78s were reissued on Orig. Jazz Library.

Addr: 61 Greig St., Rochester, N.Y.

HOUSTON, JOHN CHARLES, *piano* and *trombone;* b. Philadelphia, Pa., 3/22/33. Started on trombone with private teacher, then played local jobs in Philadelphia as house pianist in various groups. After moving to LA, gigged with Harold Land, Curtis Amy and many other combos. Influenced orginally by Bud Powell but later by Bill Evans, Barry Harris, Wynton Kelly, McCoy Tyner, Red Garland and others. Houston has been heard on albums with Sonny Stitt (Prestige), Harold Land (Imperial), Curtis Amy (Pac. Jazz).

Addr: 2337 West Blvd., L.A., Calif.

HOWARD, AVERY (KID), *trumpet;* b. New Orleans, 4/22/08; d. New Orleans, 3/28/66. Started as drummer, then took up cornet under influence of Chris Kelly. Led own band from late '20s and reached his peak as a soloist during early '30s. His brass band played for Buddy Petit's funeral in '31. Howard recorded with George Lewis in '44 for Climax Records but lapsed into obscurity from '46 and played only occasionally in the '50s with George Lewis and others. Later made a comeback and gained wide respect among New Orleans jazz students.

HUBBARD, FREDERICK DEWAYNE (FREDDIE), *trumpet;* also *fluegelhorn, piano;* b. Indianapolis, Ind., 4/7/38. Sister sang and played classical music, spirituals; brother played piano. Studied mellophone while in high school. First gigs were with the Montgomery brothers in Indianapolis. With Sonny Rollins for 4 months in 1960. Then joined Slide Hampton, J. J. Johnson, Quincy Jones. Came into public light as member of Art Blakey's Jazz Messengers, which he joined in 1961. After leaving Blakey led own groups for a year, then joined Max Roach. Toured Europe w. Jones, Europe and Japan w. Blakey, Austria '65 w. Friedrich Gulda. In Berlin JF '65. Played w. Jones in soundtrack for film *The Pawnbroker.* Won DB New Star Award for trumpet 1961.

Within a relatively short time, Hubbard gained a large following among the jazz audience as one of the most skilled, original and forceful trumpeters of the '60s. Technically, he resembles Dizzy Gillespie and Fats Navarro in that he has the ability to develop delicate and complicated lines at a rapid pace. To quote Mort Maizlish: "Stylistically, Hubbard is an eclectic musician with a strong basis in bop and an openness of melody and rhythm, especially in his recordings

with Eric Dolphy and Ornette Coleman; reminiscent of Booker Little."

Own LPs: Blue Note, Impulse. LPs w. Blakey (UA, BN, River.), O. Nelson (Imp.); Bill Evans (River.); Coleman (AH.), Dolphy, Hutcherson (BN); Coltrane (Imp.).

Addr: 919 Park Pl., Brooklyn, N.Y.

HUBBLE, JOHN EDGAR (ED), * *trombone;* b. Santa Barbara, Calif., 4/6/28. Swing and dixieland trombonist from early 40s. W. Billy Maxted '59-'61, Phil Napoleon '62-'64, Don Ewell '63, own quartet '64. Taught privately, had son of Jack Teagarden as pupil. Member Jackie Gleason band '64-'65. '65 free-lanced in NYC w. Max Kaminsky, Johnny Windhurst, Sal Pace. LP: w. Maxted (K&H).

Addr: 222 W. 23rd St., New York, N.Y.

HUCKO, MICHAEL ANDREW (PEANUTS), * *clarinet, tenor sax;* b. Syracuse, N.Y., 4/7/18. Heard with many name bands in '40s and '50s including Glenn Miller AAF orch., Jack Teagarden, Louis Armstrong. Played Newport JF 1963-4; Aspen JF '64-6. Led quintet at Eddie Condon's Nov. '63-Jan. '65 and again Sept. '65 through '66. Has also toured extensively in Far East; his record of *Suzukake No Michi* with Shoji Suzuki Rhythm Aces has been a top seller since 1960 on RCA-Japan. Also pl. w. Roman New Orleans Rhythm Kings for RCA Italia.

LPs: *Midnite in Moscow* with Eddie Condon, 1962 (Epic); *Great Moments in Jazz Re-created at the Newport Jazz Festival* (RCA); *If the Big Bands Were Here Today* (Avant Garde).

Addr: 230 East 15th St., New York, N.Y. 10003.

HUGHES, WILLIAM HENRY (BILL), *bass trombone;* b. Dallas, Texas, 3/28/30. Father played tbn. Violin at Armstrong High, Washington, D.C., 1946. Stud. pharmacy, Howard U., '48-52. Sideman w. Andy Kirk, '49; Frank Wess, '50-52. Worked with Count Basie, 1953-7; rejoined the band '63. Favs: J. J. Johnson, Urbie Green, Geo. Roberts, Dick Hixson.

LPs w. Basie (Verve, Roulette, Reprise). Fav. own solo: *Magic.* Other LPs w. Osie Johnson, Q. Jones, Ray Anthony.

HUMAIR, DANIEL, *drums;* b. Geneva, Switzerland, 5/23/38. Clarinet, drums from age 7. Entered music after winning jazz competition for amateurs. Poll winner as best drummer in France annually from 1962. Inspired by Elvin Jones, Roy Haynes, and Philly Joe Jones. Humair is best known as the drummer with the Swingle Singers, with whom he has toured the Continent and the U.S.

Own LPs: Vega. Several as sideman with Martial Solal since 1962; others with Chet Baker, Jean-Luc Ponty, Lucky Thompson, Swingle Singers, Attila Zoller, George Gruntz.

Addr: 3 Muller Brun, Geneva, Switzerland.

HUMES, HELEN, * *singer;* b. Louisville, Ky., 6/23/13. Best known as Count Basie's band singer 1938-42 and for her hit recording *Be-baba-leba* in 1945. Toured

Australia with Red Norvo in 1950s and appeared with him in clubs.

Living in Calif., Miss Humes worked at Shelly's Manne Hole in Hollywood April to Dec. 1961, then spent several months in Honolulu. Toured Australia March-June '62. After playing at Monterey JF she went to Frankfurt, Germany with the Blues Festival in Sept. '62. Inactive during most of '63, she worked nightclubs in Spokane, San Francisco, Chicago '64, then opened 6/15/64 in Sydney, Australia for a 10-month stay. After returning to the U.S. she found little work; the interest in and appreciation for her uniquely charming, high-timbred blues and ballad sound seemed to be limited to areas outside the U.S. Own LPs: Contemporary.

Addr: 607 Iowa Ave., Louisville, Ky. 40208.

HUMPHREY, PAUL NELSON, drums; b. Detroit, Mich., 10/12/35. Stud. piano as child. Played drums w. Detroit groups. W. Wes Montgomery '61; Gene Ammons, Lee Konitz, Ernie Andrews '62. Led own trio '62 and own group in San Francisco production of *The Connection*. W. Les McCann from '63. Newport '65 w. McCann. World tour '55-'57 w. U.S. Navy band. Favs: Roach, Haynes, Elvin Jones. LPs: w. McCann, Monty Alexander, McCann-Gerald Wilson (Pac. Jazz); Montgomery (Fant.).

HUMPHREY, PERCY G.,* trumpet; b. New Orleans, 1/13/05. Leader of Eureka Brass Band since 1947; concerts for NO Jazz Club, Mardi Gras Parade. Has been to Calif. w. several groups to play at Disneyland. Educ. TV jazz show rec. by WYES. Often at Preservation Hall, Dixieland Hall since 1960. Favs: Joe Oliver, Louis Armstrong. Has rec. w. Paul Barbarin, own groups etc. for Good Time Jazz, Atlantic, Southland, GHB, Jazzology, Folkways.

Addr: 4519 So. Robertson, New Orleans, La.

HUMPHREY, WILLIAM J. JR. (WILLIE),* clarinet, saxophone; b. New Orleans, 1901. Brother of trumpeter Percy and trombonist Earl. Entire family musical. Has fronted many bands; pl. w. Paul Barbarin at Dixieland Hall, Sweet Emma Barrett at Preservation Hall. Career in recent years has run parallel to that of Percy Humphrey (see above). Favs: B. Goodman, Ed Hall, J. Dodds, I. Fazola.

Addr: 2315 Cadiz St., New Orleans, La.

HUMPHRIES, ROGER, drums; b. Pittsburgh, Pa., 1/30/44. Nephew of well-known trumpeter Frank Humphries. Studied from age 3. First major job leading own group at Carnegie Music Hall in Pittsburgh '60. Joined Horace Silver Quintet 1964, touring w. Silver in U.S., Europe, and appearing at Monterey and Antibes Festivals. Favs: Roach, Blakey. One of the most promising young drummers, he is featured in *Song For My Father* and other of Silver's Blue Note LPs; also w. Carmell Jones (Pres.).

Addr: 319 Jacksonia St., Pittsburgh, Pa.

HUTCHENRIDER, CLARENCE BEHRENS,* clarinet; b. Waco, Texas, 6/13/08. Best known through his 1931-

1943 work in the Glen Gray Casa Loma Orchestra. Own trio since 1958 at the Gaslight Club in NYC, also rec. LP, *Music from the Gaslight Era*.

HUTCHERSON, ROBERT (BOBBY), vibes, marimba; b. Los Angeles, Calif., 1/27/41. Raised in Pasadena. Sister is singer Renee Robin. Took a few piano lessons ca. 1950 but became interested in music at 15 after hearing a Milt Jackson record. Bought a set of vibes while at school and was soon playing local dances and concerts. A pianist, Terry Trotter, helped him expand his harmonic knowledge and he studied vibes informally with Dave Pike.

Hutcherson worked around Los Angeles with Curtis Amy, Charles Lloyd and others, then joined the Al Grey-Billy Mitchell combo. With this group he worked in SF; then, in 1961, at Birdland in NYC. After leaving the Grey-Mitchell unit he worked off and on for a year in Brooklyn and New York clubs with Jackie McLean. During this time he met Eric Dolphy and played on the latter's Blue Note LP *Out to Lunch*.

He remained in New York for another year, playing with combos led by Archie Shepp, Hank Mobley, Charles Tolliver, Grachan Moncur III and McLean. Returning to the West Coast, he free-lanced with small groups, also played in Gil Fuller's big band at the Monterey JF, Sept. 1965.

Hutcherson won the 1964 DB Critics' Poll award as new star; *Jazz* mag. poll as overall best vibraphonist, May 1966. He was widely acclaimed for his fresh, free style, bearing less resemblance to Milt Jackson than that of any other vibraphonist in recent years. In addition he began in 1965 to make a unique contribution on the marimba, of which he said: "It's such a basic instrument, and it's not really been brought out in jazz."

Hutcherson, in both his vibes and marimba work, shows exceptional imagination and fluency. His use of four mallets in his vibes performances has often been a notable characteristic.

Own LPs on Blue Note. Others incl. *Life Time* w. Tony Williams, *Idle Moments* w. Grant Green (both BN).

Addr: 2905 Sterling Place, Altadena, Calif.

HYMAN, DICK,* piano, composer, organ; b. New York City, 3/8/27. After three years as musical director for the Arthur Godfrey radio show, Hyman became increasingly active as arranger-conductor for recordings in 1961-6. Much of his work was in the pop and commercial area, but his talent as a writer could be observed in his work for Ethel Ennis, Ada Lee, Cozy Cole, J. J. Johnson, Jonah Jones, Joe Puma, Bobby Hackett, Al Hirt, Pee Wee Spitelara. As composer: Settings of Shakespearean lyrics, rec. by Earl Wrightson as *Shakespeare's Greatest Hits*, 1964. Publication: *Duets in Odd Meters and Far-Out Rhythms*, '65.

Own LPs: Command, also co-featured with Mary Mayo on *Moon Gas* (MGM), in which he played Lowrey organ. *Cleopatra* w. P. Gonsalves (Impulse).

Theme and underscoring for two TV specials featuring Sir John Gielgud's Shakespearean recitations, 1966. Hyman continued to appear occasionally as jazz pianist, subbing at Eddie Condon's and gigging with Tony Scott in '65.

Addr: 176 S. Mountain Ave., Montclair, N.J.

IND, PETER, * *bass;* b. Oxbridge, Middlesex, England, 7/20/28. Pl. w. Coleman Hawkins-Roy Eldridge '60-1 in NYC. '63 moved to Big Sur, Calif., unacc. solo concerts and clubs in San Francisco. '66 returned to Eng. doing solo dates and freelancing. Book *Cosmic Metabolism and Vortical Accretion* based on ideas of Wilhelm Reich pub. Ziegenhaus '65. Exhibition of his paintings Monterey, Calif., '64. Own LP on Wave, LPs w. Konitz (Pres., Verve).

Addr: 11 Swakeleys Drive, Ickenham, Uxbridge, Middlesex, England.

ISRAELS, CHARLES H. (CHUCK), * *bass;* b. New York, N.Y. 1936. Studied music at MIT, Brandeis; played w. B. Holiday, D. Staton, M. Roach in late '50s. Toured Europe w. Ballet USA summer '61. Joined Bill Evans trio autumn '61 after death of Scott La Faro. With Evans steadily from that time except for brief gigs w. Stan Getz '64 and J. J. Johnson. Toured U.S., Europe '64 and '65 with Evans. Began doing A & R work for new jazz line for Vanguard Records and recording there with own group '65. Teaches summers at Indian Hill Music Workshop, Stockbridge, Mass.

Israels filled the virtuoso position left by La Faro remarkably well. His playing is equally complex and intense, and if anything more emotional. A fiercely demanding musician, he draws feelings from the bass that complement Evans' melodic inventions. LPs w. Evans (River., Verve); Getz (Verve); Gary Burton (RCA).

Addr: c/o Indian Hill, Stockbridge, Mass.

IZENZON, DAVID (DAVE), *bass;* b. Pittsburgh, Pa., 5/17/32. Studied bass from '56; Master's degree '63. After working with various local groups including that of pianist Dodo Marmarosa '58, he moved to New York in 1961 and was soon swept into the new wave of jazz of the '60s, playing with Paul Bley, Archie Shepp, Sonny Rollins, Bill Dixon, as well as with non-avant gardists such as Mose Allison. Played off and on with Ornette Coleman in 1962, and in '65-6 played concerts with him in England and on the Continent.

Izenzon has occasionally taught other bassists, including Gary Peacock. He believes that the era when a bassist's main function was to keep time has come to an end. "So many musicians," he has said, "are afraid of disorder that they forget to be afraid of slavery. The bassists can no longer be tied down; we must have freedom to establish communication."

Exceptionally fine arco improviser.

LPs w. Bill Dixon, Joe Scianni (Savoy), Archie Shepp (Impulse), Sonny Rollins (RCA), Ornette Coleman (ESP, Blue Note).

JACKSON, CALVIN, * *composer, piano;* b. Philadelphia, Pa., 5/26/19. Late '40s and early '50s own TV and radio shows with 21-piece jazz orch. in Canada. In '60s settled on West Coast, appearing as soloist in both classical and jazz concerts in LA '61-2. Scored film *Blood and Steel* for 20th Cent. Fox '61, and TV score for MGM TV series, *The Asphalt Jungle* '62. Appearances on Steve Allen shows, TV series, *The Detectives;* film, *Three On a Couch.* Starred in NBC special *Rehearsing With Calvin* '62. Acad. Award nomination for scoring *Unsinkable Molly Brown;* had own KBCA radio show *At Home With Calvin Jackson,* '65. Kansas City JF. Led big band at Carousel Theatre, W. Covina, Calif. March '66.

Comps: *Profile of An American,* dedicated to John F. Kennedy, performed by Hollywood Symphony in June '66.

Own LPs: Reprise.

Addr: c/o CA1-A1 Productions, 7264 Melrose Ave., Hollywood 46, Calif.

JACKSON, GREIG STEWART (CHUBBY), * *bass, songwriter;* b. New York City, 10/25/18. Pl. w. many dance bands from 1937; won *Esquire* and DB awards in mid-'40s while with Woody Herman band. Lived in Chi. 1953-8. Back in NYC, he moderated children's TV shows, leading 18-piece band in one such series. Many recordings as sideman; led own trio in clubs '64-'66. Taught on faculty of Stan Kenton Summer Jazz Clinic '64. Also appeared and recorded with his teenage son, a drummer. Has collaborated with Steve Allen on several songs.

Own LPs: Cadet, Everest; on Woody Herman *The Thundering Herds* (Col.).

Addr: 543 Ivy Ave., Palm Beach Gardens, Fla.

JACKSON, CLIFTON LUTHER (CLIFF), * *piano;* b. Washington, D.C., 7/19/02. He earned great popularity as house pianist at Cafe Society from 1943-51; subsequently worked at Lou Terrasi's and other NYC clubs. From '64 was heard at Jimmy Ryan's in that establishment's new home on West 54th St. LP: one-half of *Uptown and Lowdown* (Pres.).

Addr: 818 Ritter Pl., New York 59, N.Y.

JACKSON, FRANZ, * *tenor sax, clarinet, leader, arranger;* b. Rock Island, Ill., 1912. Played with Noone, Eldridge, Waller, Henderson and Hines during '30s and early '40s, formed Original Jass (*sic*) All-Stars in '56. In 1960 acquired own recording co., Pinnacle Records; recorded own band, other traditional jazz. Ran Chicago Red Arrow Jazz Club. Band also appeared weekly at Chicago Jazz Ltd. '60-'63, Chicago Old Town Gate from '64. Since 1951 pl. first bassoon in De Paul U. Community Symphony. Concerts at Indiana U., Purdue U., Chicago Pub. Lib., *Down Beat* JF '65. LPs: Pinn., Phil., River.

Addr: 5358 S. Wells St., Chicago 9, Ill.

JACKSON, MAHALIA,* *singer;* b. New Orleans, 10/26/11. To Chicago at 16. Sang in churches. Began recording in '45 and within a few years acquired an international following, touring Europe in '52. Sang at Newport JF '57 and '58; recorded *Black, Brown and Beige* with Duke Ellington '58.

During the 1960s Miss Jackson reached an unprecedented level of world acceptance. A favorite of royalty and of many foreign chiefs of state, she was received by the Pope, sang several times for President Kennedy and became a friend and favorite performer of President Johnson.

Musically she expanded her repertoire and her settings. As a result of the Ellington initiative she went on to sing with other large orchestral backgrounds supplied by Percy Faith, Johnny Williams and others. No longer limiting herself to gospel material, she sang popular songs that seemed suited to her style. She continued to maintain that she is not a jazz singer and regarded her Newport and Ellington associations as exceptions to a rigid rule of disassociation from jazz. Her billing as "The World's Greatest Gospel Singer" was justified by her fervent, stirring performances.

Miss Jackson was married in 1964 to Sigmund Galloway, a saxophonist. Later in '64 she became seriously ill with a heart ailment and was almost totally inactive for a year and a half. She did no recording in '65. In early 1966 she resumed touring and returned to the recording studios.

LPs: Col.

Addr: 8358 So. Indiana Ave., Chicago 19, Ill.

JACKSON, MILTON (MILT or BAGS),* *vibraharp;* also *piano, singer, guitar;* b. Detroit, Mich., 1/1/23. Stud. in Detroit. To NYC w. D. Gillespie; later pl. w. Monk, Woody Herman. Best known as founder-member of Modern Jazz Quartet. For details of MJQ's activities see Lewis, John.

During the '60s, in addition to touring and recording with the Quartet, Jackson occasionally formed groups of his own during the MJQ's summer vacation. He was often heard in a quintet feat. Jimmy Heath. In Aug. '65 he gave a concert at the Museum of Modern Art in NYC. The recording was released on Limelight. He rec. a vocal LP in Italy in '64.

Regarded as the definitive modern jazz vibes stylist of the 1950s, Jackson has continued to play in the gentle, subtle style that established him as a poll winning favorite of jazz audiences. He has been an annual winner of DB Readers' and Critics' polls and of the *Playboy* All Stars' All Stars.

Own LPs: Impulse, River., Atl., Limelight. LPs w.

MJQ (Atl.); Coleman Hawkins (Atl.); Ray Brown, Oscar Peterson (Verve).

Addr: 192-12 105th Ave., Hollis, N.Y.

JACKSON, OLIVER JR.,* *drums;* b. Detroit, Mich., 1934. Known earlier for his work with Yusef Lateef and other groups in Detroit, Jackson has been active in the 1960s mainly with swing-style groups in NYC, among them Buck Clayton, with whom he toured Europe in 1961; Lionel Hampton, with whose band he visited Africa in '63; Charlie Shavers, Earl Hines, Conrad Janis, Teddy Wilson and Junior Mance. LPs with Billy Mitchell (Smash), Earl Hines (Focus), Morris Nanton (Pres.).

Addr: 395 Riverside Dr., Apt. 9E, New York City, N.Y. 10025.

JACKSON, PRESTON,* *trombone;* b. New Orleans, La., 1903. One of earliest Dixieland trombonists; played w. Erskine Tate, Louis Armstrong, led own groups in Chicago. Largely inactive in music since late '50s. One LP w. Lil Armstrong (River.).

Addr: 325 W. 59th Pl., Chicago, Ill.

JACQUET, JEAN BAPTISTE ILLINOIS,* *tenor sax, bassoon;* b. Broussard, La., 10/31/22. Played famous *Flying Home* solo in Lionel Hampton band of early '40s. Later worked with Cab Calloway, Count Basie, own band; many JATP tours. Associated originally with freak high note effects, he played in a more conservative and attractive style in the '50s, usually leading a quartet. In '59 he bought a bassoon, studied with Manuel Zegler of N.Y. Philharmonic. By Dec. '65, when Jacquet introduced his bassoon to New York audiences, he revealed a facility that according to DB writer Burt Korall indicated this might eventually be an extremely expressive vehicle for him.

LPs: *JATP-All Stars; Nat Cole at JATP* (VSP); others on Cadet, Verve, Epic.

Addr: 112-44 179th St., St. Albans, N.Y. 11433.

JACQUET, ROBERT RUSSELL,* *trumpet, singer;* b. Broussard, La., 12/3/17. Stud. at Wiley Coll., TSU and USC. Brother of Illinois Jacquet, with whom he has worked off and on since '41. 1960: Pl. w. other brother Linton Jacquet, in Oakland, Calif. and with Gerald Wilson in LA. 1961: concerts w. Benny Carter. 1962: stud. at USC, pl. w. Hide-Away All Stars, LA, and with I. Jacquet. '64: house band at It Club, LA. '65-6: w. Cedric Haywood band in Houston, Tex.

LPs w. I. Jacquet (Cadet, RCA).

Addr: 2006 Ruth, Houston, Texas.

JAMAL, AHMAD,* *piano, composer;* b. Pittsburgh, Pa., 7/2/30. Among many notable performances in the U.S. and abroad, Jamal appeared with the Cleveland Summer Symphony in 1965. His trio included Jamil Nasser, bass, and Vernel Fournier, drums. Fournier was replaced by Frank Grant '66.

Ralph J. Gleason, in a 1965 column, wrote: "A very great deal of the current style adopted by piano-bass-drums trios in jazz is a result of the explorations of Ahmad Jamal. I was struck by the subtle way in which he has clothed the very avant-garde things he does that entice the average jazz listener rather than making him uncomfortable, as many avant-garde things do."

Jamal's compositions include *One for Miles, Minor Moods* and *Extensions.* LPs: Cadet.

Address: 55 Liberty St., New York 5, N.Y.

JAMES, WILLIAM (BILLY), *drums;* b. Pittsburgh, Pa., 4/20/36. First job w. Lionel Hampton '54. W. Booker Ervin '56-'57, J. Moody '60-'61, Candido '61, S. Stitt and G. Ammons '61-'62, E. Davis '62-'63; most often w. Don Patterson in mid-'60s. Favs: Blakey, P. J. Jones, E. Jones, F. Butler, Roach. Ambitions are to do own big band date, study drums in Africa. LPs: own fav. Ammons-Stitt *Boss Tenors in Orbit* (Verve); others w. Stitt (River.), Patterson (Pres.).

JAMES, ROBERT (BOB), *piano, composer;* b. Marshall, Mo., 12/25/39. Started playing 1944 and studied extensively, receiving his Masters degree in composition from the Univ. of Michigan in 1962. His trio was a prizewinner at the intercollegiate jazz festival heard at Notre Dame in '61. James moved to New York in '63, worked for Maynard Ferguson for three months and then became pianist and arranger for Sarah Vaughan. Though his writing for Miss Vaughan is aimed at the popular audience, James' main musical interests lie in a more adventurous direction. He has been closely associated with bassist Chuck Israels and other members of the new school.

James says his goal is "to form a concert improvising group with electronic music and visual events, both cinematic and live."

LPs: Merc., ESP; others w. Chet Baker (Lime.) and Vaughan (Merc.).

Addr: 418 Central Park W., Apt. 81, New York 25, N.Y.

JAMES, HARRY HAAG, * *trumpet, leader;* b. Albany, Ga., 3/15/16. Despite the shrinking of the big-band scene, the James orchestra remained continuously active during the 1960s and enjoyed unprecedented musical success. In 1960 James undertook a concert and dance tour of Mexico in August; shortly afterward he toured South America for the first time. On January 25, 1964 he celebrated his 25th anniversary as a bandleader. In April he took the band on its first tour of Japan, and the following September made his first and very successful appearance at the Monterey JF, to which he returned the following year.

James maintained a high standard for his band and a style that was more consistently jazz-oriented than that of the groups he had fronted in earlier years. Most of his arrangements were written by men who had previously worked for Count Basie, notably Neal Hefti, Ernie Wilkins and Thad Jones. James' own trumpet style, which in the '40s was inclined toward sentimentality and bravura, achieved a more jazz-routed groove, reflecting such influences as Roy Eldridge and Harry Edison. Soloists in his band included Corky Cor-

coran, tenor sax; Jack Perciful, piano; Ray Sims, trombone; and most notably Buddy Rich on drums.

After more than twenty years of marriage, James was divorced in 1965 from actress Betty Grable.

LPs: MGM, Dot.

Addr: 1606 Vista Del Mar, Hollywood 28, Calif.

JAMES, PERCY EDWARD JR., *bongo, conga drums;* b. St. Louis, Mo., 3/6/29. Played in school band while attending Lincoln U. in Jefferson City, Mo. W. Quartette Tres Bien in St. Louis and on tour of Midwest and West Coast. QTB was well received at Lighthouse LA '65. Comps. for QTB incl. *Master Charles, Brother Percy.* Favs: Chano Pozo, other Afro drummers. LPs: w. QTB (Decca).

Addr: 2720A Sheridan Ave., St. Louis, Mo.

JAMES, CORNELIUS (PINOCCHIO), *singer;* b. Macon, Ga., 12/23/27. Father, Cornelius Sr., and mother, Mattie Henderson, both musicians. Studied piano and voice at Cosmopolitan School of Music in Cincinnati. Vocalist with Jack Jackson and His Jumping Jacks 1945. After various jobs as a single he was discovered by Lionel Hampton in Cincinnati in April, 1957 and began a long-lasting association with him, including a European tour, '57-8; visit to Buenos Aires in '60, Essen JF in Germany '61, seven-week tour of Far East 1963.

A raw, earthy blues stylist combining elements of the country and urban traditions, James has been featured in some twenty performances on Hampton's own label, Glad-Hamp Records.

Addr: 5214 Ebersole Ave., Cincinnati, Ohio.

JAMES, NEHEMIAH (SKIP), *singer, guitar, piano;* b. Yazoo County, Miss., 1902. Father a Baptist pastor. Started playing guitar 1912. After high school, while working in a saw mill in Arkansas, picked up knowledge of piano. Played many house parties around Jackson and Vicksburg. Recorded 17 tunes for Paramount in 1930 in Grafton, Wisc. In 1932, discouraged by lack of work, he gave up music. He resumed again from 1938-40, traveling with a gospel group in which he preached, played and sang. He then drifted away again, working various odd jobs until 1964, when a group of young folk blues enthusiasts discovered him in a hospital in Tunica, Miss. He appeared at the Newport Folk Festival in '64 and soon was in demand for appearances before a new generation of blues students. James, who writes most of his own material, is a compelling performer in the basic early blues tradition.

JANIS, CONRAD, * *trombone, leader;* b. New York, N.Y., 2/11/28. Led own groups and acted in Broadway, TV shows during '50s. In '63-'64 acted in, wrote some of music for and led own band in Actors' Studio Broadway production of *Marathon '33* with Julie Harris. Appeared on Steve Allen, Les Crane TV shows and at Stratford (Conn.) Shakespeare Festival. Also acted in Broadway show *Sunday in New York* and TV *The Untouchables, Stoney Burke, The Nurses, Get Smart.* Co-directs Janis Gallery of Modern Art with father in NYC. Played at various times in Spain and Paris.

Addr: 12 E. 72nd St., New York, N.Y.

JANKOWSKI, HORST,* *piano, composer, leader;* b. Berlin, Germany, 1/30/36. After considerable jazz experience, incl. work w. Tony Scott in Yugoslavia and Benny Goodman in Brussels, Jankowski reached the mass audiences of Europe and the U.S. in 1965 with his strictly commercial recording of his own composition *A Walk in the Black Forest* (Mercury). Visiting the U.S. late in '65, he appeared on TV shows in several cities. He told a reporter, "It's funny that after all my years as a concert and jazz pianist, I get a hit record playing with two fingers."

JARRETT, KEITH, *piano, composer;* b. Allentown, Pa., 5/8/45. Eldest of five brothers, all musically inclined. Studied piano from age three and made rapid progress; gave first solo concert when he was seven and from then on played professionally; also took up drums, vibes, soprano. In June 1962 played a two-hour solo concert of his own compositions. Went to Boston for three years, spent a year studying at Berklee School on a scholarship; led his own trio and appeared on local TV. Moved to New York, where he worked with Roland Kirk, Tony Scott and others; joined Art Blakey Dec. 1965. To Europe w. Ch. Lloyd spring '66.

Jarrett is a technically phenomenal performer who, despite his youth, shows extraordinary maturity and seems destined for great accomplishments in the years to come. He states that he has no favorites but admires "anyone who is sincere as an artist and as a person." His performances have indicated an understanding of much of piano jazz history, taking in elements of Art Tatum and Bud Powell as well as Bill Evans and McCoy Tyner.

LP w. Blakey (Limelight).

Addr: 635 E. 11th St., New York City, N.Y. 10009.

JASPAR, ROBERT B. (BOBBY),* *flute, tenor sax, clarinet, composer;* b. Liège, Belgium, 2/20/26. Prominent in the U.S. after immigrating in 1956, he played with groups led by J. J. Johnson, Miles Davis and Donald Byrd. Hospitalized in Sept. 1962, he underwent serious heart surgery and died in NYC 2/28/63. He was survived by his widow, singer Blossom Dearie. A mature and dependable musician in the bop idiom, he was greatly respected by musicians associated with him.

JAZZ CRUSADERS. See Hooper, Stix.

JENKINS, MARVIN LEE, *piano;* also *organ, flute, clarinet;* b. Aultman, Ohio, 12/8/32. Mother plays piano, brother Obie leads band in Canton, Ohio. Studied music from age of 10. Played in brother's band '46-'54, in Army band '54-'56. To West Coast, won Intercollegiate JF w. LA State College Quintet '59. W. Barney Kessel on piano and flute '59-'61, Gloria Lynne '62-'64. Led own trio at The Scene LA '64-'65. Taught privately at own studio from '57. Comps. incl. *Big City, Rainy Day in L.A., Next Spring.* Favs: O. Peterson, A. Jamal. Own LPs: Orovox, Palomar, Reprise.

Own fav. *Marv Jenkins at the Rubaiyat Room* (Reprise). Others: w. Kessel (Contemp.).

Addr: 1619 Burnside Ave., Los Angeles, Calif.

JOBIM, ANTONIO CARLOS (pron. zho-beem), *composer, guitar, piano;* b. Rio de Janeiro, Brazil, 1927. Music director at Odeon Records in mid-50s. Around 1957 he persuaded the executives at this company to record his friend Joao Gilberto, singing two tunes, Jobim's *Chega de Saudade* and Gilberto's *Bim Bam.* The record was a surprise hit and Gilberto was permitted to cut an album. Jobim described the music on the record as "bossa nova," meaning new wrinkle or new wave.

Though Jobim is not a jazz performer, he and Gilberto, along with a nucleus of other composers, are considered to have been the founders of the bossa nova movement in Brazil, which spread to the U.S. in 1962. Jobim's best-known compositions are *Desafinado* (*Slightly Out of Tune*), *One Note Samba* and *The Girl from Ipanema.* Others included *Corcovado* (*Quiet Nights*), *Meditation* and *Jazz Samba* (*So Danco Samba*). Jobim's music (along with music by Luiz Bonfa) was heard in the Brazilian film *Black Orpheus.*

Jobim spent most of 1965 in Los Angeles, writing songs and appearing on TV shows.

Own LP: Verve. Many of his comps. are heard in various LPs by Stan Getz and in countless other bossa nova albums. Jobim also plays in the best-selling album *Getz/Gilberto* (Verve).

JOHANSSON, JAN,* *piano, guitar, composer;* b. Soderhamm, Sweden, 9/16/31. Worked w. Stan Getz, Oscar Pettiford in Scandinavia in late '50s. Big band writing in '60s: *Mobil '66,* commissioned by symphony orchestra for combined symphony group and jazz band; many big band works commissioned by Radio Sweden, combo pieces for Arne Domnerus. Pl. at concert with combos and Domnerus septet. Movies: *Barnvagnen, Nattlek.* LPs for Swedish label, one of which, *Sweden Non Stop,* came out in U.S. on Dot.

Addr: Fritjofs Väg 35, Upplands Visby 2, Sweden.

JOHNSON, ALBERT J. (BUDD),* *tenor sax, composer;* b. Dallas, Texas, 12/14/10. Best known as a key figure in the Earl Hines band, 1934-42, he was later associated with Billy Eckstine, Woody Herman, Dizzy Gillespie and other innovators of the '40s. During 1950s he free-lanced in NYC with Benny Goodman and others.

Johnson toured Europe with the Quincy Jones band in 1960, also worked with Count Basie in 1961, playing jazz festivals in France and at Newport. From 1962-5 he was in NYC writing, playing club dates and making many records. In addition, he rejoined Earl Hines for combo work in '65. Worked with Tommy Dorsey band under direction of Urbie Green '66.

A major figure in the swing era, Johnson was one of the few who made the transition from earlier styles to a modern approach.

Own LPs with small combos: Cadet, Swingville;

others w. Earl Hines (RCA, Focus), Booker Pittman (Col.).

Addr: 60 Carolina Ave., Hempstead, N.Y.

JOHNSON, GUS,* *drums;* b. Tyler, Texas, 11/15/13. Colleague of Ch. Parker in Jay McShann band in early '40s. Later played with Earl Hines; Count Basie 1948-54. After touring with Ella Fitzgerald '57-9, he spent about a year with Woody Herman's band, worked frequently with Gerry Mulligan's combo and band, and has been back with Miss Fitzgerald on several occasions. When not playing he is an auxiliary policeman with the 47th Precinct. Johnson is in constant demand for record dates and is one of the most adaptable of modern drummers.

LPs with Mulligan, Fitzgerald (Verve) etc.

Addr: 1057 E. 219th St., Bronx, N.Y.

JOHNSON, JAMES LOUIS (J.J.),* *trombone, composer;* b. Indianapolis, Ind., 1/22/24. Pl. w. Benny Carter 1942-5; Count Basie '45-6; Illinois Jacquet '47-9; teamed with Kai Winding in quintet '54-6. First prominent as composer when his works were presented at Monterey JF '59. Teacher at Lenox Summer Jazz School, 1960.

After touring internationally with a sextet, Johnson disbanded the group in 1960. From Sept. '60 to Mar. '61 he worked on an extended composition, *Perceptions.* The six-part work was recorded in May 1961 with a large orchestra conducted by Gunther Schuller. The performance was repeated in Sept. '61 at Monterey. Johnson then spent more than a year on the road as a member of Miles Davis' combo. In '63 he again took time out from playing in order to prepare the arrangements for his album *J. J.'s Broadway.* He then formed a new quartet to play clubs and concerts. In July 1964 he headed an all-star sextet, with Clark Terry and Sonny Stitt, for a tour of Japan.

Though internationally acknowledged as the first and greatest trombonist of the bop generation, Johnson is less widely known as a composer and arranger of extraordinary merit. As Schuller observed in his comments on *Perceptions,* "His compositional abilities and his range of expression . . . have expanded with each new work through the years. Beyond all externals of form and technique, this music combines an eloquent musical imagination with a strongly disciplined mind, producing an enjoyable music of depth, pulsating warmth and infectious spirit."

LPs: *J. J. Johnson, Trombone and Voices; J. J. Inc.* (sextet) and *A Touch of Satin* (quartet) are on Columbia; *Proof Positive* and *The Great K and J. J.* on Impulse; *J. J.'s Broadway* on Verve; all later albums, incl. *Goodies* and *J. J.!* (big band) are on RCA. *Perceptions,* with Gillespie and the 21-piece orchestra noted above, is on Verve.

Addr: 1365 St. Nicholas Ave., New York, N.Y. 10033.

JOHNSON, JAMES OSIE,* *drums, composer, singer;* b. Washington, D.C., 1/11/23. First heard with the Harlem Dictators and Sabby Lewis, later with the Navy band at Great Lakes, Chicago, Johnson toured with Earl Hines 1952-3. From 1954 he was a prominent free-lance musician in NYC and was also on staff at NBC and CBS for extended periods. After a long illness he died of a kidney ailment in New York, 2/10/66.

JOHNSON, LONNIE,* *singer, guitar;* b. New Orleans, 2/8/1889. From 1925 was heard on hundreds of records, including guitar duets wtih Eddie Lang and a few sides with Louis Armstrong, Duke Ellington. Popular again in '40s, but lapsed into obscurity in '50s until he was rediscovered in Philadelphia and brought back to records in 1960. He subsequently appeared with success at numerous clubs. LP: *Blues and Ballads* with Elmer Snowden (Pres.); tracks in *Bluebird Blues* (RCA).

JOHNSON, PETE,* *piano;* b. Kansas City, Mo., 3/25/04. In the '20s pl. in KC clubs w. own band and w. singer Joe Turner; app. w. him in *Spirituals to Swing* at Carnegie Hall '38. Highly successful boogie-woogie duos and trios w. Albert Ammons and Meade Lux Lewis at Cafe Society in late '30s-early '40s. In '50s pl. in his home city of Buffalo, N.Y. App. NJF '58. Since suffering a heart attack in Dec. of that year he has been inactive musically. In '65 a book entitled *The Pete Johnson Story,* edited by German discographer Hans J. Mauerer, was published by the U.S. and Europe Fund Raising Project for Pete Johnson. Proceeds from the book go to Johnson to help defray hospital and living expenses. The book can be ordered in the U.S. from James Wertheim, 248 E. 10th St., New York, N.Y. 10009.

In '66 a benefit session for him was held at the Palm Garden, NYC, and on his 62nd birthday a special concert honoring him was performed at Buffalo's Kleinhan's Music Hall with the Buffalo Phil. pl. arrs. of his *Wee Baby Blues* and *Roll 'Em Pete.* LPs w. Turner on Arhoolie.

Addr: 171 Broadway, Buffalo 4, N.Y.

JOHNSON, PLAS JOHN JR.,* *tenor sax;* b. New Orleans, La., 7/21/31. Active mainly on rock and roll dates in the West Coast during the 1950s, Johnson rose to prominence in the pop and jazz fields in 1960-66. He is best known as the featured soloist in the movie *The Pink Panther* with Henry Mancini's orch. and on Mancini's sound track album (RCA). Also recorded a theme for TV series *Honey West.* Featured in series of Glen Gray LPs on Cap. 1960-65; Earl Grant combo recordings '60-'66; Mancini recordings and appearances since '62.

In addition to the above, Johnson recorded two albums, *Sax Fifth Avenue* and *Johnny Beecher on The Scene,* under the pseudonym Johnny Beecher, on Charter label 1962-3, and *Blue Martini* on Ava.

Addr: 3903 Burnside Ave., Los Angeles, Calif.

JOHNSON, REGINALD VOLNEY (REGGIE), *bass;* b. Owensboro, Ky., 12/13/40. After playing trombone at jr. high school spent six years in various Army bands. Started playing bass professionally Nov. 1961. Jobs w. Archie Shepp, Bill Barron, 1964-5; Burton Greene, Roland Kirk, Warren Covington, Sun Ra, 1965. Pl. w. Bill Dixon at "October Revolution" avant garde concert at Cellar Cafe in NYC Oct. '64. Joined Art Blakey Nov. '65. Influenced by Ray Brown, Ron Carter and Paul Chambers, Johnson also names Reggie Workman, Charlie Haden and Gary Peacock among his favorites.

LPs w. G. Logan, Marion Brown (ESP); A. Shepp (Impulse); A. Blakey (Limelight).

Addr: 78 Manhattan Ave. Apt. 4-G, New York City, N.Y. 10025.

JOLLY, PETE (Peter A. Ceragioli),* *piano, accordion;* b. New Haven, Conn., 6/5/32. W. Shorty Rogers, B. De Franco, G. Auld and own groups in LA during '50s. On concert tour of New Zealand '60. Returned to LA to become active in studio work. Comps: *Little Bird,* a substantial seller as a single record; *El Yorke,* others. TV shows incl. *Get Smart, I Spy.* Signed w. Columbia Records '65. Own LPs: Col., Ava.

Addr: 11936 Hesby St., North Hollywood, Calif.

JONES, BURGHER WILLIAM (BUDDY),* *bass, tuba;* b. Hope, Ark., 2/17/24. After 14 years with the Jack Sterling morning radio show at CBS, NYC, Jones freelanced with Johnny Richards and others. He then joined the Nitelife Show, 1965, in a group led by Elliot Lawrence, in whose big band he had played in 1950.

Addr: RD1, Mt. Bethel, Pa.

JONES, CARMELL, *trumpet, composer;* b. Kansas City, Kans., 1936. After attending Kansas U. 1958-60, played with combo in Kansas City, Mo. and was heard there by the German jazz critic Joachim Berendt, who was the first to draw attention to his talent. Gigging in LA from 1961-4 Jones worked frequently with Harold Land. After touring with the Horace Silver Quintet for a year, he moved to Europe in Aug. '65 and joined the SFB Orchestra in Berlin. A strong, mature trumpeter who has progressed beyond his neo-bop origins.

LPs: Pac. Jazz, Pres.; LPs w. Charles McPherson, Booker Ervin (Pres.), Gerald Wilson (Pac. Jazz), Harold Land (Imp.), Red Mitchell-Land (Atl.).

JONES, CLAUDE,* *trombone;* b. Boley, Okla., 2/11/01; d. NYC, 1962. Worked with Fletcher Henderson, Cab Calloway, Duke Ellington; out of music from 1952.

JONES, CURTIS, *singer, piano;* b. Naples, Texas, 1906. Worked on farm as a child; later moved to Dallas, where he played guitar, organ and piano. He was also heard in Kansas City and Chicago in the '30s. Sank into obscurity in '40s but was rediscovered in Chicago in 1958 by two Calif. blues students. In the '60s he has made occasional records and appeared in Chicago coffee houses, also toured abroad from 1962. Folk music student Robert G. Koester has called him "a man reborn of the blues revival."

Own LP on Delmark.

JONES, ELVIN RAY,* *drums;* b. Pontiac, Mich., 9/9/27. Younger brother of Hank and Thad Jones, he played in Detroit bands from 1952-6, then moved to NYC, where he worked with the Pepper Adams-Donald Byrd quintet and other combos. In 1960 he joined the John Coltrane Quartet and during the next five years became the most important new influence among jazz drummers, as revolutionary and important in the '60s as were Philly Joe Jones in the '50s and Max Roach in the '40s.

Jones' main achievement was the creation of what might be called a circle of sound, a continuum in which no beat of the bar was necessarily indicated by any specific accent, yet the overall feeling became a tremendously dynamic and rhythmically important part of the whole sound of the group. Jones moved away from the old concept of swinging toward a newer freedom analogous with that established by Coltrane himself. As Don DeMicheal pointed out in DB, "He has an ability to construct drum solos of sometimes amazing complexity and rhythmic daring that nonetheless retain form, and form is the ingredient often missing from most drummers' solos." Jones has indicated that he is interested in broadening his musical scope by changing meters, by using accelerandos and decelerandos in his solos, and sometimes by employing the concepts of African and Indian drummers.

After leaving Coltrane, Jones flew to Europe early in '66 to join Duke Ellington, but left him after four days. Back in NYC, he worked briefly with Tony Scott, then free-lanced with his own group.

Own LPs: Atl., River. LPs with Coltrane (Atl., Impulse).

Addr: 151 West 16th St., New York, N.Y. 10011.

JONES, ETTA, *singer;* b. 11/25/28. Professional debut at 16, going on the road with Buddy Johnson's band. With J. C. Heard in '48, Earl Hines Sextet '49-52. Received Gold Record for hit, *Don't Go To Strangers,* on Prestige, 1960. Favs. and infls.: Billie Holiday, Thelma Carpenter.

Own LPs: *Etta Jones & Sylvia Syms* (Grand Prix); *Don't Go To Strangers; Hollar!; So Warm; Something Nice* (Pres.).

Addr: 1027 East 217th St., Bronx, N.Y.

JONES, HENRY (HANK),* *piano, composer;* b. Pontiac, Mich., 7/31/18. Prominent in N.Y. from '44. Toured w. JATP '47; pianist for Ella Fitzgerald '48-'53, then became NYC studio musician.

Hank Jones is one of the most active and versatile jazz musicians of the '60s. Playing modern jazz, ragtime, pop music and acc. innumerable singers, he has taken part in dozens of major TV shows, mainly on CBS, and has played on so many records that a complete listing would fill several pages. He has worked with his younger brothers Elvin (on Atlantic LP) and Thad (with the Thad Jones-Mel Lewis Orch. 1966). Small acting role, background music for Sammy Davis film *A Man Called Adam* '66. TV shows: *Strollin' '20s* w. H. Belafonte; *Telephone Hour* w. B. Goodman; B. Streisand, Carol Burnett specials; Al Hirt, J. Gleason shows. Radio: *Jazz and Dixieland* '61-'64. Own LP: *Here's Love* (Argo). LPs with Pepper Adams (Motown), B. Brookmeyer (RCA), Ray Brown (Verve), Chet Baker (Merc.), K. Burrell (Col.), Nat Cole (Cap.), B. Eckstine (Merc.), V. Feldman (River.), L. Hampton (Imp.), Milt Jackson (Atl., Imp.), J. J. Johnson (Col., MGM, RCA), Gary McFarland (Imp.), Wes Montgomery (River.), Oliver Nelson (Pres.), Johnny Smith (Roul.), J. Teagarden (Verve), Clark Terry (Verve, RCA, River.), B. Webster (Imp., Col.), Joe Williams (RCA).

Addr: 39 7th St., Cresskill, N.J. 07626.

JONES, HERBERT ROBERT (HERB), *trumpet;* also *arranger;* b. Miami, Fla., March 1923. Father plays drums. Played in local bands while studying at Florida A & M. Free-lanced in NYC from 1953 w. L. Millinder, A. Kirk, Budd Johnson. '56-'58 w. Cab Calloway in Miami. Became member of Ellington's trumpet section Sept. '63, in Ceylon. Arr. for Ellington incl. *El Busto, Cootie's Caravan, The Prowling Cat, The Opener.* On all tours, festivals, recordings w. Ellington Sept. '63. Infl. on playing: Armstrong, Gillespie; on writing: Dameron, E. Barefield. Would like to continue arranging, do works of his own.

Addr: 957 Anderson Ave., Bronx 52, N.Y.

JONES, JAMES HENRY (JIMMY), *composer, piano;* b. Memphis, Tenn., 12/30/18. Family moved to Chicago 1921. First prominent as pianist with Stuff Smith, J. C. Heard, Sarah Vaughan; from late 1950s devoted most of his time to arranging and conducting. Arr. for H. Belafonte TV shows, incl. *The Strollin' '20s,* 1965; Duke Ellington TV appearances, '62-6; led band for Ellington's *My People* show in Chi. '63. Cond. for Lena Horne, Nancy Wilson at Waldorf-Astoria, NYC. App. as pianist w. own trio several times on *Today* TV show. European tour as mus. dir. for Ella Fitzgerald with Ellington band, '66. A skilled, serious and imaginative writer.

LPs as arr: *Fusion* w. Wes Montgomery (River.), *Broadway My Way* w. Nancy Wilson (Cap.), *Ella at Duke's Place* (Verve); *Loads of Love* w. Shirley Horn (Merc.), many others w. Joe Williams, Billy Taylor, Chris Connor et al.

Addr: 792 Columbus Ave., New York 25, N.Y.

JONES, ROBERT ELLIOTT (JONAH), *trumpet, leader;* b. Louisville, Ky., 12/31/09. A name-band musician since the early 1930s, Jones, after some years of relative obscurity, came to national prominence with his quartet in the late 1950s, playing in a commercialized style of mild jazz interest. He continued to enjoy similar success in the 1960s, playing major locations and setting a precedent by playing in the Rainbow Grill of the New York RCA Building, where no jazz combo had been previously heard. He also visited Australia and Mexico.

Own LPs: Cap. LP featuring his quartet with Glen Gray and Casa Loma Orch. (Cap.); 1955-6 LPs on Dec.

Addr: 4 Washington Sq. Village, New York, N.Y.

JONES, JOSEPH RUDOLPH (PHILLY JOE), * *drums;* b. Philadelphia, Pa., 7/15/23. Best known through his intermittent association with Miles Davis, starting in 1952. Also worked '50s with Tony Scott, Tadd Dameron, Gil Evans. In 1962 he rejoined Davis, but the reunion was short-lived. He spent much of 1964 and part of '65-6 free-lancing in Los Angeles and San Francisco. He visited Japan in Jan. '65 with a show featuring four drummers.

Though at times a very heavy drummer who has tended to dominate many groups in which he has played, Jones is a master of every aspect of jazz percussion. He is as effective playing brushes with a pianist as he is when involved with a larger combo in the most oblique rhythmic cross-rhythms on cymbals, snare and bass drum. Along with Elvin Jones, he is one of the most electrifying drummers to have influenced jazz in the 1958-65 period.

Own LPs: *Philly Joe's Beat; Philly Joe Jones & Elvin Jones Together!* (Atl.); others on Riverside.

JONES, QUINCY DELIGHT JR., * *composer, leader;* b. Chicago, Ill., 3/14/33. After touring Europe with his own big band during 1960, Jones settled in New York, became increasingly active as an arranger, and entirely inactive as a trumpet player. In May 1961 he was appointed to an a&r job at Mercury Records. He continued to front a big band from time to time, appearing in theatres and clubs. In Nov. 1964 he was appointed vice president of Mercury Records.

In 1964-6 Jones continued to record as a leader, but also served as mus. director and arr. for many singers, notably Peggy Lee, Frank Sinatra and Billy Eckstine. He made numerous appearances as conductor of the Count Basie orchestra during its joint engagements with Sinatra.

Concurrently with his other careers, Jones in the 1960s began to earn recognition as a writer of motion picture scores. His first film, *The Boy and The Tree,* a Swedish production, was followed by a series of American movies: *The Pawnbroker, Mirage, The Slender Thread, Walk Don't Run.*

Jones was presented with a "Grammy" award by NARAS in 1963. In 1964, in Holland, he received the Thomas Edison award at the Grand Gala du Disque.

While the nature of his associations gradually took him further away from the core of jazz, and even led to his recording quasi-rock 'n' roll instrumentals, Jones continued to bring to his work a high degree of craftsmanship, developed during his associations in the 1950s with Lionel Hampton, Dizzy Gillespie and others. Own LPs: Mercury. LPs of own arrangements for Basie: Reprise, Verve. Many other LPs as arranger and musical director for Sinatra (Reprise), Peggy Lee (Cap.), Sarah Vaughan (Merc.), et al.

Addr: c/o Mercury Records, 35 E. Wacker Dr., Chicago 1, Ill.

JONES, REUNALD SR.,* *trumpet;* b. Indianapolis, Ind., 12/22/10. The veteran big band trumpeter left Basie in '59 after six years and free-lanced around NYC until joining Nat King Cole in Jan. '61. W. Cole until Cole's death in '65, touring Japan, Europe, Pacific, Australia w. him. '65 w. Nancy Wilson, Vic Damone, Diahann Carroll. In France w. Carroll. LPs: w. Cole, but not featured on any.

Addr: 64 W. 108th St. #3A, New York, N.Y.

JONES, RUFUS (SPEEDY), *drums;* b. Charleston, S.C., 5/27/36. Pl. trumpet in elementary school band. Took up drums at 13 and worked first prof. job w. local 15-piece band led by Brant Bassell. Att. Florida A&M on scholarship. To NYC where he pl. w. Lionel Hampton '58, Red Allen and Sol Yaged at Metropole '59. With Maynard Ferguson '59-'63 and then led own quintet '63-4. Joined Count Basie Jan. '64, remaining until '66. Own group again '66; also w. Reuben Phillips house band at Apollo Theater. First inspired by Gene Krupa and Max Roach, he names Roach, Rich, Bellson, Philly Joe Jones and Art Blakey as favs. Jones, whose nickname derives from his exceptional technique, is a hard-driving player who is an exciting soloist. Own LP on Cameo; LPs w. Ferguson (Roul., Cameo), Basie (Verve). Joined Woody Herman June '66.

Addr: 131 Moore St., Brooklyn 6, N.Y.

JONES, SAMUEL (SAM),* *bass, cello, composer;* b. Jacksonville, Fla., 11/12/24. Came to prominence in NYC with Les Jazz Modes, Kenny Dorham, Illinois Jacquet, Cannonball Adderley, then with Dizzy Gillespie through 1958. After eight months with Thelonious Monk, Jones rejoined the Adderley combo in Nov. 1959 and remained for six years. During that time he was featured on many records with Adderley's group and others, including two for which he served as leader: *The Chant* and *Down Home* (River.).

In Feb. 1966 Jones became a member of the Oscar Peterson Trio, replacing Ray Brown.

As Harvey Pekar commented, "Jones in the rhythm section makes an interesting choice of notes and is a powerful walker with a huge tone . . . his 'cello approach is similar to his bass concept—he must be one of the most percussive of jazz 'cellists." Own LPs: River. LPs with Adderley (River., Cap); Ray Brown (Verve); Milt Jackson, Wes Montgomery (River.).

Addr: 1 Lerome Pl., Teaneck, N.J.

JONES, THADDEUS JOSEPH (THAD),* *cornet, trumpet, composer;* b. Pontiac, Mich., 3/28/23. Worked in Detroit with brothers Hank and Elvin, also with own band in Okla. City and w. Billy Mitchell in Detroit. Toured w. Count Basie band from May 1954 until Jan. '63. In Feb. '63 worked on movie, *Asphalt Girl,* with Roland Hanna Quartet, in Japan. To Las Vegas summer '63 to write album for Harry James band. In '64 pl. concert w. Th. Monk at Carnegie Hall; worked w. G. Mulligan small group and big band; Newport

JF and European tour w. Geo. Russell Sextet summer '64. Wrote album of arrs. for Basie. Staff musician at CBS-TV Nov. '64. Started quintet w. Pepper Adams, heard at many clubs in NY area in '65. In Dec. '65 Jones and Mel Lewis formed an 18-piece band, for which Jones did most of the writing. They played to capacity audiences at concerts in NYC clubs during '66. Jones, one of the finest soloists to emerge from the Basie band of the '50s, is an inspired and consistently interesting writer.

Own LP w. Lewis (Solid State).

LPs w. Basie (Roul., Reprise, etc); arrs. for H. James (MGM, Dot); pl. w. Th. Monk (Col.), James Moody (Scepter).

Addr: 170 Intervale Rd., Teaneck, N.J. 07666.

JORDAN, CLIFFORD LACONIA,* *tenor sax;* b. Chicago, Ill., 9/2/31. Played w. r & b, visiting jazz bands in Chicago during mid-'50s, then on West Coast and in NYC w. Horace Silver, Max Roach. Formed quintet w. Kenny Dorham '61-62, touring NY area and West Coast. 1962 led own quartet w. Andrew Hill, J. C. Moses, Eddie Khan. Rejoined Roach '63, toured Europe, Japan and U.S. On European tour w. Charles Mingus '64, w. Roach again '65. In '64 wrote, arranged and played an album of Leadbelly's tunes entitled *These Are My Roots* (Atl.). Although Jordan is basically a blues-tinged, bop musician, his powerful solo ability and his work w. Roach and Mingus have earned him respect among the avant-garde of the '60s. Own LPs: BN, River., Jazzl., Atl. Others: Lee Morgan (VJ, River), J. J. Johnson (Col.), Roach (Impulse, Fantasy), P. Poindexter (Epic), C. McPherson (Pres.).

Addr: 275 Willoughby Ave., Brooklyn, N.Y.

JORDAN, IRVING SIDNEY (DUKE),* *composer, piano;* b. Brooklyn, N.Y., 4/1/22. Studied privately from 1930 until '38, playing in school band at Brooklyn Automotive High. After graduation in '39, joined Steve Pulliam combo, playing at NY World's Fair. During the 1940s Jordan became well known in modern jazz circles as one of the first bebop pianists, playing with Charlie Parker and others. Later worked for Stan Getz, Roy Eldridge, Oscar Pettiford.

In 1959 Jordan went to Paris and worked as both composer and pianist. He was co-writer with Jacques Marray of the sound track music for the French motion picture *Les Liaisons Dangereuses.* On the French sound track LP, issued in the U.S. first on Epic and later on Philips, Jordan can be heard playing piano on the *Prelude In Blue* side. He also recorded an LP of his own, leading a quintet that played the same music, on the short-lived Charlie Parker Records label. Another excellent example of his work as pianist and composer is *Flight to Jordan* (Blue Note). Heard at Open End club, NYC, in '60s.

JORDAN, JAMES TAFT,* *trumpet, singer;* b. Florence, S.C., 2/15/15. Attained prominence w. Chick Webb band, and Webb band under Ella Fitzgerald's leadership 1933-42. Pl. w. Duke Ellington '43-7, Benny

Goodman in late '50s. In '60s free-lancing in NYC. App. at Ellington Jazz Society concert at Town Hall '63. Own LP: Pres.; LP w. Fitzgerald (Verve).

Addr: 270 Convent Ave., New York 31, N.Y.

JORDAN, LOUIS,* *singer, alto sax. leader;* b. Brinkley, Ark., 7/8/08. After two years w. Chick Webb, formed own quintet 1938 and recorded many major hits during the 1940s, one of which, *Choo Choo Ch'Boogie,* sold over a million.

For three years, 1960-62, Jordan worked as a single. In Dec. 1962 he toured England, playing concerts with Chris Barber. He reorganized his group, known as the "Tympany Five," with a new instrumentation, now featuring an organist, in '63. The group played leading night clubs, Nevada lounges and service clubs throughout the U.S.

Jordan is generally considered to be the progenitor of the small-group rhythm-and-blues idiom that led, during the 1950s, to the rise of rock 'n' roll, though his own group stayed much closer to jazz. In 1964 Jordan returned to records after a long absence, cutting singles and an album for Ray Charles' company, Tangerine Records. Earlier LPs: Decca, Mercury.

Addr: 6011 Buckler Avenue, Los Angeles 43, Calif.

JORDAN, SHEILA, *singer;* b. Detroit, Michigan, 11/18/29. Raised in Summerhill, Pa. From the age of three she was eager to sing, and all through her school years appeared in numerous recitals. Later, during her second high school year, she stopped singing and moved back to Detroit. Later she resumed performing, sometimes as part of a vocal trio that was a precursor of Lambert, Hendricks & Ross. She moved to NYC in 1950. Married pianist Duke Jordan '52 (since divorced). Worked at various day jobs through the '50s, but for several years sang off and on at clubs in Greenwich Village and was heard there by George Russell, through whom she was brought to Blue Note Records. She made her album debut in 1963, and was praised by critics for her lyrical, emotional style. In Don DeMicheal's words, "she has an excellent jazz feel, a style that is buoyant, with time sense, projection of emotion, and a rare sensitiveness which gives her singing a poignancy that can be moving." Own LP: Blue Note. Also feat. w. George Russell singing *You Are My Sunshine* in the *Outer View* (River.).

KAMINSKY, MAX,* *trumpet;* b. Brockton, Mass., 9/7/08. Perennial Dixieland favorite; played with most important bands and own groups from 1924. Led Jackie Gleason's personal band for several seasons, playing warm-up sets for TV series. W. own group at Metropole, Condon's, Newport J.F. '64-'65, N.Y. World's Fair '64-'65. In 1963 published *My Life in Jazz* w. V. E. Hughes, a breezy, highly readable but

somewhat incomplete autobiography. LPs: West., UA, Seeburg.

Addr: c/o Hotel Bristol, 129 W. 48th St., New York 36, N.Y.

KAMUCA, RICHARD (RICHIE),* *tenor sax;* b. Philadelphia, Pa., 7/23/30. Worked with Stan Kenton, Woody Herman, Maynard Ferguson in '50s. Member of house band at Shelly Manne's club 1960-61, then moved to New York, where he played with Gerry Mulligan band, Gary McFarland combo, and formed a quintet co-led by Roy Eldridge. Also appeared on Merv Griffin TV Show.

LPs with Shelly Manne (Cont.); McFarland (Imp.).

Addr: 780 Greenwich St., New York City, N.Y. 10014.

KATZ, RICHARD AARON (DICK),* *piano, composer;* b. Baltimore, Md., 3/13/24. Educated at Manhattan and Juilliard Schools of Music, Katz free-lanced in NYC during the '50s, with innumerable musicians incl. O. Pettiford, K. Dorham. With Philly Joe Jones in '60. In '61 at NYC Jazz Gallery w. Jim Hall, then w. Nancy Harrow. In concert w. Gunther Schuller and Delaware Symphony Orch., then w. A. Cohn-Z. Sims, Don Ellis, P. Woods-G. Quill. Europe w. Helen Merrill; Paris Blue Note w. own quartet. Orchestra U.S.A. '64. On board of directors of NARAS. In '65 continued work w. Orchestra U.S.A. and Helen Merrill, and worked w. Roy Eldridge. LPs: w. Benny Carter (Impulse), Orchestra U.S.A. (Col.), Harrow (Atl.).

Addr: 15 W. 11th St., New York 11, N.Y.

KATZ, FREDERICK (FRED),* *composer, cello, piano;* b. Brooklyn, N.Y., 2/25/19. Originally a classical musician, he later worked in the pop and jazz fields, touring with Chico Hamilton quintet 1955-6. His comps. include *Cello Concerto* '61, *Toccata* '63. In 1964 he wrote a Jewish liturgical service for cantor, choir and jazz group performed on CBS in various temples and at Redlands U. Also music for several art films incl. *The Sorcerer.* Katz is assistant professor of anthropology at Valley State College.

LPs with Hamilton (Wor. Pac., Decca); *Poitier Meets Plato* (War. Bros.).

Addr: 3701 Loadstone Dr., Sherman Oaks, Calif.

KAY, CONNIE,* *drums;* b. Tuckahoe, N.Y., 4/27/27. Early work with Miles Davis, Cat Anderson, Lester Young, Ch. Parker, Stan Getz. Joined Modern Jazz Quartet 1955.

For details of Kay's activities during more than a decade with the MJQ, see Lewis, John. Recordings with various John Lewis groups (Atl.), Orchestra USA (Colpix, Col.); C. Hawkins, R. Eldridge, J. J. Johnson, S. Getz (Verve); Bill Evans (River., UA); Mike Zwerin's sextet of Orchestra USA (RCA); Ray Charles, Joe Turner, Ruth Brown (Atl.); Paul Desmond (RCA); Jimmy Heath, Bobby Timmons, Milt Jackson, C. Adderley (River.), Lucky Thompson (Pres.).

During the MJQ's two-month vacation every summer Kay occasionally worked with other groups. He was heard with Milt Jackson and Clark Terry at the Village Vanguard in 1964; also briefly with Bud Powell at the Blue Note in Paris.

Addr: 431 Bronx Park Ave., Bronx 60, N.Y.

KEANE, ELLSWORTH McGRANAHAN (SHAKE), trumpet, fluegelhorn; b. St. Vincent, B.W.I., 5/30/27. Taught music by father from age of 5. While schoolteacher in St. Vincent had poems broadcast in Eng. by BBC, and pub. two collections of verse. Came to Eng. '52, joined Mike McKenzie's Harlem Allstars w. Joe Harriott, and pl. w. many groups while spending two years stud. Eng. Lit. at London U., and contributing frequently to BBC literary programs. '59-65 pl. w. Joe Harriott, mostly free form jazz from '60, and often app. as feat. soloist w. commercial bands on TV and radio. Made several European tours w. Harriott, also made commercial recs. under own name. Joined Kurt Edelhagen Orch. as feat. soloist in Cologne, Germany, '65. Highly distinctive and talented trumpet and fluegelhorn, with powerful and oblique style, equally at home in conventional and avant garde settings. LPs w. Harriott (Capitol, Jazzland).

Addr: 32 Elgin Crescent, London W.11., England.

KEATING, JOHNNY,* leader, composer, trombone; b. Edinburgh, Scotland, 9/10/27. With Ted Heath as trombonist, later arranger, in '50s, Keating has led a big band in the '60s, incl. a series of LPs for London Records.

KELLAWAY, ROGER, piano, composer; b. Waban, Mass., 11/1/39. Began studying classical piano at age seven, continuing until 1959 when he went on the road. Bass in high school; also dabbled in percussion, and wrote and orchestrated first comp. at that time. Majored in comp. and minored in piano at New England Cons. '57-9. While in high school pl. w. Dick Wetmore. Left Cons. to join Jimmy McPartland on bass, then pl. bass w. Ralph Marterie. To NYC early '60s, he worked as pianist at Jilly's; w. Kai Winding '62; Mark Murphy '63. Attracted wider attention w. Al Cohn-Zoot Sims. From '64 w. Terry-Brookmeyer, in band at Eddie Condon's, and w. own trio.

Kellaway is a versatile pianist who is not bound to any one style; his two-handed chordal attack can generate much excitement. As a comp. he has written a number of attractive originals, and many arrs. for singers. Early infl.: Oscar Peterson, Billy Taylor. Own LPs: Pres., Regina. LPs w. Terry-Brookmeyer (Main.), Terry (Cameo, Imp.), Russian Jazz Quartet (Imp.).

KELLY, THOMAS RAYMOND (RED),* bass; b. Shelby, Montana, 8/29/27. The former Woody Herman and Stan Kenton bassist joined Harry James' band Sept. 1961 and remained with him for the following five years, including a three-week trip to Japan in May, 1963.

LPs: all Harry James albums since he joined band

(MGM, Dot); also session with Modest Jazz Trio (Pac. Jazz).

Addr: 994 King Richard, Las Vegas, Nevada.

KELLY, WYNTON,* piano, composer; b. Brooklyn, N.Y., 12/2/31, of West Indian parentage. Prominent in 1950s with Lester Young, Dizzy Gillespie. Toured with Miles Davis 1959-63. With his associates in the Davis rhythm section, bassist Paul Chambers and drummer Jimmy Cobb, he formed his own trio. This group was featured in the World JF in Japan in summer of '64 and played many clubs in U.S., later adding a featured soloist, guitarist Wes Montgomery.

Though sometimes associated with the "funky" blues approach that has been heard on some of his recordings, Kelly is an all-around modern pianist whose intense drive and ability to create excitement have provided some of the most impressive moments at various jazz festivals in recent years.

Own LPs: Verve, VJ. LPs with Davis: Col.

Addr: 586 Lincoln Pl., Brooklyn, N.Y.

KENNEDY, JOSEPH J. JR. (JOE), violin, composer, conductor; b. Pittsburgh, Pa., 11/17/23. His grandfather, Saunders Bennett, introduced him to violin in McDonald, Pa., '33. Entered music professionally through encouragement by his family; the late Jimmie Lunceford gave him incentive to pursue his arranging activities.

Led Four Strings in Pitts. '48; Ahmad Jamal became the group's pianist in '49. From '50-8 app. as soloist in colleges and universities throughout Virginia. Rec. Master's in Music from Duquesne Univ. '60, and began to teach in the Richmond, Va. school system. Kennedy is chairman of music department at Maggie L. Walker High School and a resident member of the Richmond Symphony Orch.

Since 1959 he has been Jamal's chief arr., app. w. him in arranging, conducting and playing roles for Cadet Records. Pl. at Arts Festival, Birmingham, Mich. '60-1. Conducted the Cleveland Summer Symphony in premiere of his own work Suite for Trio and Orchestra incl. Jamal, July '65. Other comps. incl. Tempo for Two, Surrealism, You Can Be Sure. Favs: Jascha Heifetz, Yehudi Menuhin, Art Tatum, Charlie Christian, Duke Ellington, Jimmie Lunceford. Rec. w. Four Strings for Asch '48. Own LP on Red Anchor; LPs w. Jamal (Cadet).

An excellent all-around musician, Kennedy is a fine jazz soloist. His son, Joseph Kennedy III, a French hornist, pianist and arranger, was a member of the prize-winning Duquesne Univ. band at the Villanova Jazz Fest. '63.

Addr: 2007½ Barton Ave., Richmond, Va. 23222.

KENTON, STANLEY NEWCOMB (STAN),* leader, composer, piano; b. Wichita, Kansas, 2/19/12. Raised in LA. Started first band at Balboa Beach in '41. Acquired national reputation after recording of his theme, Artistry in Rhythm. Band broke up in '47; Kenton continued to lead various groups during the next decade, including a 40-piece unit with strings in 1950 and a more conventional swinging band in the mid-'50s.

From 1959-63 Kenton was head of the Stan Kenton Clinics, a series of courses in jazz offered each summer under the auspices of the National Stage Band Camps. These annual summer clinics involved Kenton as head of a faculty that included many leading jazz and popular musicians. The students came to facilities at camps around the U.S. for instruction in all phases of modern music. Kenton withdrew from the camps in '63.

In 1960 Kenton led a band with regular instrumentation, arrs. by Johnny Richards and Gene Roland. Early in '61 he launched a new venture, a 27-piece ensemble featuring a section of four mellophoniums, a specially devised instrument.

Still on the road in '62 and '63, Kenton won Grammy awards from NARAS for his albums of *West Side Story* and *Adventure in Jazz*. Throughout '64 he was off the road without a band and spent some time writing. A new project was launched in Jan. 1965 when a group known as the Los Angeles Neophonic Orchestra, which included many members of former Kenton orchestras, gave a series of concerts at the Los Angeles Music Center. A second series was given in '66. Though technically Kenton was not the leader of this orchestra, his was the guiding force behind it and much of the music played was of the ambitious, symphonic-jazz nature associated with much of his work through the years.

Through the Neophonic Orchestra Kenton introduced and conducted new works by many important composers, writing for the most part in the so-called third stream idiom. He also brought in guest soloists such as Friedrich Gulda, Dizzy Gillespie, Buddy De Franco, Gerry Mulligan, Cal Tjader.

LPs: Many on Cap., including *Artistry in Voices and Brass* (2132); *Adventures in Blues* (1985); *Greatest Hits* (2327); *Kenton/Wagner* (2217); *Artistry in Bossa Nova* (1931); *Stan Kenton Conducts The Los Angeles Neophonic Orchestra* (2424).
Addr: 8467 Beverly Blvd., Los Angeles 48, Calif.

KESSEL, BARNEY,* *guitar;* b. Muskogee, Oklahoma, 10/17/23. Though mainly busy in the Hollywood studios doing commercial record dates, Kessel led his own combo for occasional night club work in the early 1960s and continued to record as a leader. He is the author of an instruction book, *The Guitar*. In the mid-60s he played regularly on such television shows as *Hollywood Palace, I Spy, Man From UNCLE,* etc. Own LPs: Contemp., Reprise.
Addr: 1727 Las Flores Dr., Glendale, Calif. 91207.

KIEFER, RICHARD (RICK), *trumpet;* b. Cleveland, Ohio, 5/24/39. Professional debut 1955. Pl. w. Buddy Morrow '57; Benny Goodman, Urbie Green, Maynard Ferguson '57-'63, then worked in Germany; jazz festivals in Berlin '64, Recklinghausen '65. Pl. in Munich w.

Max Greger Orchestra. LPs with Ferguson (Roul., Cameo).
Addr: 17314 Riverway Dr., Lakewood, Ohio.

KINCAIDE, DEANE,* *composer, saxophones, clarinets;* b. Houston, Tex., 3/18/11. Veteran arranger for Pollack, Bob Crosby, Dorsey bands in 1930s and '40s. Member NBC *Tonight* Orch. '63-'65, arranger for Jackie Gleason TV series '64-'65. LP: arr. for Muggsy Spanier, *Columbia, Gem of the Ocean* (Ava).
Addr: 44 Kent Rd., Glen Rock, N.J.

KING, RILEY B. (B.B.), *guitar, singer;* b. Itta Bena, Miss., 9/16/25. Cousin is blues singer Bukka White. Began teaching self guitar in 1943; later studied Schillinger System. First job as disc jockey and singer on Memphis radio. One of the most popular and widely heard blues singers, King has recorded 200 singles and over 20 LPs. Favs. and infl: Django Reinhardt, T-Bone Walker. Would like to see Negroes become unashamed of blues, their music. LPs: RPM, Crown, Bullet, Kent, ABC-Par.
Addr: c/o R. C. Haskin, 565 Fifth Ave., New York, N.Y.

KING, BERTIE, *alto sax;* b. Colon, Panama, 6/19/12. Brought up in Jamaica, B.W.I., came to England '36. Pl. and rec. w. Benny Carter, Ken "Snakehips" Johnson, Leonard Feather's Olde English Swing Band, Una Mae Carlisle. Brit. Navy '39-'43, since then w. Leslie "Jiver" Hutchinson, and freelancing and touring in Europe, Australia, India, Caribbean, U.S.A. Infl. by Benny Carter. Own LP on Brit. Nixa.
Addr: 18a Haverstock Hill, London N.W.3.

KING, MORGANA,* *singer;* b. Pleasantville, N.Y., 6/4/30. NYC clubs from 1956. Originally a jazz-oriented singer, she later adopted a highly dramatic and technically remarkable style almost totally removed from jazz and achieved commercial success with an album entitled *With a Taste of Honey* (Mainstream).

KING, PETER, *tenor sax, alto sax;* b. Kingston-on-Thames, Surrey, England, 8/11/40. Started as professional on clarinet w. Dixieland bands '56; pl. w. Dick Morrissey and Gus Galbraith after changing to alto and modern jazz '58. Led own group at Ronnie Scott's '59-'60, then pl. w. J. Dankworth for a year. Since then w. Tony Kinsey, also w. own group at Annie's Room, pl. mainly tenor from '62. Also many arrs. for Annie Ross and Joy Marshall, and comp. *Sasa-Hivi* rec. by Tubby Hayes big band. Fiery and fluent saxist. LPs w. Kinsey (Brit. Dec.), Dakota Staton (Brit. HMV).
Addr: 2 Fairmead, Tolworth, Surrey, England.

KIRK, RONALD T. (ROLAND), *flute, tenor sax, manzello, stritch, slidesophone, clavietta, composer,* etc. b. Columbus, Ohio, 8/7/36. Educated at Ohio State School for the Blind. Kirk says that at the age of six he tried to get music out of a water hose. His parents were counselors at a summer camp outside Columbus, where he wanted to be the bugle boy. He took up trumpet at 9, but a doctor advised him that the pressure would strain his eyes (since infancy he had been able to see nothing but light); as a result, he switched to saxophone and clarinet, which he played with a school band from 1948. Soon he was working weekend gigs with professional groups, and by 1951 was heard with well-known bands around Ohio and leading his own group for dance dates.

While on tour with the Boyd Moore band, Kirk began experimenting with the idea of playing two instruments at once. He was 16 years old when, he says, "One night I dreamed I was playing *three* instruments at once. Next day I went to a music store and tried out all the reed instruments. Eventually they took me to the basement, to show me what they called the scraps. That is where I found the manzello and the stritch." These two instruments are of obscure origin. The manzello is constructed somewhat like an alto sax, with a large, flat bell, but its sound is more like that of a soprano sax. The stritch, though it resembles a longer soprano sax, is in effect a straight alto.

Kirk worked out a technique for holding the tenor sax, stritch and manzello and playing three-part harmony through the use of trick fingering. In 1960 Ramsey Lewis introduced Kirk to Jack Tracy, recording director at Cadet (formerly Argo) Records. Kirk made a record date 6/7/60 in Chicago and immediately was the subject of extensive controversy. Some listeners felt that his effects, such as the playing of two or three horns at once and the use of a siren whistle for a climactic sound at the end of a solo, were gimmicks. But Kirk protested, "Nothing is a gimmick. I do everything for a reason. I hear sirens and things in my head when I play." During the next year Kirk made another album, for Prestige. In 1961 he was a member of Charles Mingus' group for four months and traveled with him as far as Calif., where he also worked with a group of his own.

International interest in Kirk soon spread. He made his first trip to Europe that year, traveling alone to play the Essen JF in Germany. In 1963 he played a month at the Ronnie Scott club in England, followed by clubs or concerts throughout the Continent, at some of which he worked with Dexter Gordon and Johnny Griffin. In 1964 he again toured the Continent for two weeks with the European JF, followed by another month at the Scott club. For most of his engagements since 1962 Kirk has used his own rhythm section, though on records he has been teamed with a variety of small and large groups.

Kirk's acceptance by the critics, despite a little skepticism at first, was affirmed in 1962 when he won the DB International Critics Poll. Since then he has won many polls annually in the "Miscellaneous Instrument" and flute categories, including the *Melody Maker* poll in England and others in Germany and Poland.

Kirk's unique qualities lie not only in the variety of instruments he has played (he claims to have used a total of 45), but also in the comprehensive nature of his repertoire, in the flexibility of his style, and in his entire attitude toward music. He has written many attractive original works, but has also played conventional standard and pop tunes, occasional adaptations of classical works, and even such songs as *Trees* and *The Skater's Waltz*. The extent of his musical interests can be gauged from the titles of some of his compositions. One is called *From Bechet, Byas & Fats;* others are *A Quote From Clifford Brown, Mingus-Griff Song* and *No Tonic Pres.*

Though he is given to avant garde explorations that are as abstract as any of Coleman and Coltrane, he may switch unpredictably to a relatively conventional tonal solo based on a familiar melody. He is an artist of seemingly limitless ambition, eager to play as many different forms of music as he can through as many different media as possible. He could not be classified either as an avant gardist or as a traditionalist; he is a completely original performer, a category in himself, and in the opinion of many who have heard him the most exciting new jazz instrumentalist of the 1960s.

Among Kirk's many compositions are *Three for Dizzy; Three For the Festival; You Did It, You Did It; A Stritch In Time; E. D.; Lonesome August Child; April Morning; Narrow Bolero; Hip Chops, The Business Ain't Nothin' But The Blues; Mystical Dreams.*

LPs: *Introducing Roland Kirk* (Cadet); *Kirk's Works* (Pres.); *We Free Kings; Domino; Reeds & Deeds; Roland Kirk Quartet Meets the Benny Golson Orchestra; Kirk in Copenhagen; Gifts & Messages* (all Merc.); *I Talk With The Spirits; Rip, Rig & Panic; Slightly Latin* (Lime.).

Addr: 415 Central Park West, New York 25, N.Y.

KLINK, AL, * *tenor sax, flute;* b. Danbury, Conn., 12/28/15. Soloist w. G. Miller, B. Goodman, T. Dorsey, Sauter-Finegan bands; w. NBC staff from 1954. On Steve Allen, Eddie Fisher, Johnny Carson TV shows. LPs: w. Enoch Light (Command), w. Carol Sloane, w. Don Lamond, w. Bob Haggart.

Addr: 31 Elton Rd., Stewart Manor, Garden City, N.Y.

KNEPPER, JAMES M. (JIMMY), * *trombone;* b. Los Angeles, Calif., 11/22/27. Worked in a variety of big bands during early '50s. Began playing with Charles Mingus in 1957, and appeared with him intermittently through '61. Joined Benny Goodman for Russian tour '62. At NYC Basin Street East '60, '63. In orch. of Broadway show *Funny Girl* '64-'66.

Knepper's recorded work attests to the fact that he was one of the most inventive and most emotionally satisfying trombonists of his time, bridging the chronological gap between the similarities of Lawrence Brown and Dickie Wells, and the new trombonists of the '60s. His solos with Mingus were intricate, beautifully structured and complete statements combining hard blues, Mingus' drive and a sound suggesting the human voice. A musician of impeccable taste, he never employs gimmicks or spectacular technique, of which he is capable, but relies solely on expressive musical ideas and a warm and personal tone.

Own LP: w. Pepper Adams, *The Pepper-Knepper Quintet* (Metrojazz). Others: On most of Mingus' recordings bet. '57 and '61; best solos on *Tijuana Moods* (RCA), *The Clown* and *Tonight at Noon* (Atl.); w. Mingus on Atl., Col., Candid, Beth., Lime.; w. Clark Terry (Candid), Gil Evans (Impulse).

Addr: 11 Bayview Pl., Staten Island, N.Y.

KONITZ, LEE,* alto sax; b. Chicago, Ill., 10/13/27. First prominent as member of Claude Thornhill band '47-8, and as one of several Thornhill musicians involved with Miles Davis' Capitol recording group, '49-'50. During the '50s, except for a year with Stan Kenton ('52-3), Konitz led various small groups and was closely associated with Lennie Tristano. First heard on records with Tristano in 1949, he was reunited with him for night club work in '59 and again in '64. From 1962-4 he was in relative obscurity, teaching and occasionally playing in the Monterey Peninsula area in Calif. In '65-6 he toured Europe on his own, working with local rhythm sections in London and on the Continent. In '64, Don Heckman observed in DB, "Konitz has quietly become—within the tonal style of improvisation—one of the most consistently creative alto players on the scene . . . that his star should have been eclipsed for so many years seems little short of astonishing."

Own LPs: Pres., Atl., Verve, Wor. Pac.; two tracks in *Charlie Parker 10th Memorial Concert* (Limelight).

KRAL, IRENE,* singer; b. Chicago, Ill., 1/18/32. Sister of Roy Kral. Began w. Woody Herman, Maynard Ferguson bands. Also appeared on several Steve Allen TV shows as pop-jazz soloist, and w. Stan Kenton and Herb Pomeroy bands. W. Shelly Manne, '62-'63. Appeared on Laurindo Almeida's Grammy award-winning LP *Guitar from Ipanema*. Married to trumpet-fluegelhornist Joe Burnett. In the words of songwriter Tommy Wolf, Miss Kral is "an impeccable musician with a unique sound, remarkable timing, sensitive phrasing and lyric interpretation."

Addr: 27 N. East Ave., Oak Park, Ill.

KRAL, ROY JOSEPH,* singer, piano, composer; b. Chicago, Ill., 10/10/21. First prominent in vocal team with Jackie Cain in Charlie Ventura combo 1948-9 and again in '53. Married to Miss Cain since '48. They have worked night clubs and lounges with their sophisticated act, which has a light and attractive jazz flavor. Seen most often in Las Vegas, where they lived in the late 1950s, they moved to New York in 1962. Many TV shows with Steve Allen, Andy Williams, Dinah Shore, Johnny Carson, Ernie Ford, Mike Douglas, Soupy Sales. They have also recorded more than 20 TV and radio commercials.

LPs: *Like Sing*, songs by André Previn (Col.); *By Jupiter* and *Girl Crazy* (Roul.); album of Beatle tunes (Atl.).

Addr: 4715 Independence Ave., New York City, N.Y. 10471.

KRAUTGARTNER, KAREL, leader, alto sax, composer; b. Mikulov, Czechoslovakia, 7/20/22. From a musical family. Sideman in Czech dance orchs. '40-'55. Soloist and leader of own groups on Czech radio from '55, playing jazz and classical works. Comps. incl. *The Students' Suite,* suite from the play *The Family Gathering.* Festivals: Bled '62, Munich '64, Prague '64-'65. Favs and infl.: Parker, Konitz, Ellington.

Addr: Prague 5, Zborovská 62, Czechoslovakia.

KRESS, CARL,* guitar; b. Newark, N.J., 10/20/07. A pioneer jazz guitarist, Kress recorded on many of the early Red Nichols collectors' items, as well as with Miff Mole, the Dorsey Bros. et al in 1927-9. He was part owner of the original Onyx Club in NYC. In later years he appeared and recorded with Geo. Barnes. Their guitar duets were successful renovations of a style of an earlier era which Kress had originated in tandem with Eddie Lang in 1932.

While appearing with Barnes in a Nevada casino, Kress died of a heart attack 6/10/65 in Reno, Nev. LP: *Town Hall Concert—George Barnes and Carl Kress* (UA). Also w. Bud Freeman (UA).

KROG, KARIN (Karin Krog Bergh), singer; b. Oslo, Norway, 5/15/37. From a musical family, began to appear in Oslo and Stockholm in early '60s. At Antibes JF '64. Heard and admired by Donald Byrd. Several TV, radio and other festival appearances. Favs: Billie Holiday, Betty Roche, Jimmy Scott, Eddie Jefferson. Own LP: Phil.

Addr: Nobels Gt. 35, Oslo 2, Norway.

KRUPA, GENE,* drums, leader; b. Chicago, Ill., 1/15/09. Came to New York in 1929; worked with Red Nichols and several name bands, achieving national prominence in the Benny Goodman orchestra 1935-8. Leader of a big swing band '38-'43 and again (after a few months with Tommy Dorsey) from '44-'51. During the '50s he led his own trio or quartet and toured several times with the JATP unit.

In 1960 Krupa played the *Daily News* jazz concert in Madison Square Garden. He was part of the special TV program *Chicago And All That Jazz,* Nov. '61. He has made many other TV appearances on *The Lively Ones, Tonight,* and the Merv Griffin, Al Hirt, Mike Douglas and Sammy Davis shows.

Though Krupa has continued to lead a quartet, playing frequently at the Metropole in NYC, there was a nostalgic revival of his big band when an orchestra of local musicians was assembled for him to front at a Disneyland concert in June 1963.

Krupa's quartet, featuring Charlie Ventura on tenor saxophone, toured Japan in June 1964 and visited Mexico City the following month.

Krupa's role as the first internationally celebrated jazz drummer, and his contribution as a bandleader, can be studied in a comprehensive album, *Drummin' Man* (Col. C21-29), which covers recordings from

Thelonious Monk (*Roberto Polillo*)

Joe Henderson *(Francis Wolff-Blue Note Records)*

Sarah Vaughan

Gerald Wilson

Junior Mance (*Capitol Records*)

Bud Freeman (*Columbia Records*)

Kenny Burrell (*Chuck Stewart*)

Henry Mancini (*RCA Victor Records*)

David Izenson *(Paul Minsart)*

Art Taylor *(Roberto Polillo)*

Staple Singers

Dave Brubeck and sons *(Columbia Records)*

Archie Shepp Sextet. L. to R.: Archie Shepp, Alan Shorter, Roswell Rudd, John Tchicai
(Impulse Records)

Art Blakey (*Show Artists Corp.*)

Jimmy Cobb and Miles Davis

Tony Scott and Shinichi Yuize of Japan
(*Farkas Studios*)

Swingle Singers (*Philips Records*)

Wayne Shorter *(Francis Wolff-Blue Note Records)*

Joe Williams

Ben Webster

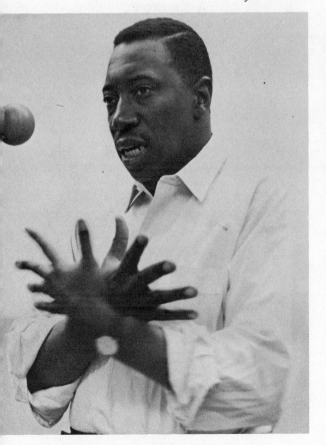

Ornette Coleman *(Bob Thiele)*

Helen Arlt and Louis Armstrong

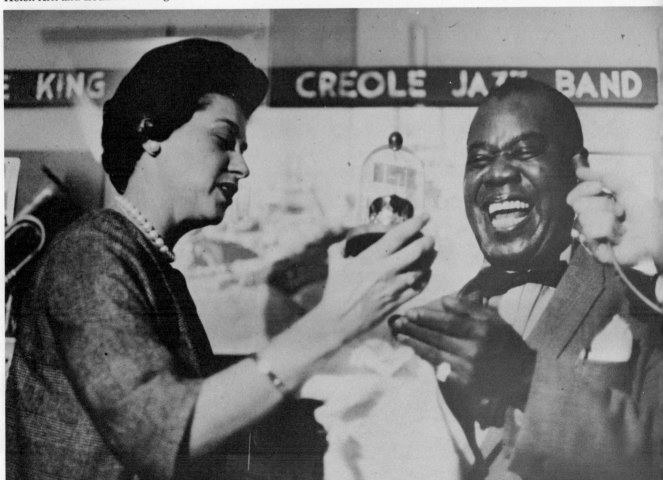

Cab Calloway

Maynard Ferguson *(Charles Stewart)*

Les McCann Ltd. L. to R.: Les McCann, Victor Gaskin, Paul Humphrey
(Limelight Records)

Eddie Costa *(Impulse Records)*

Pee Wee Russell and Bud Freeman *(Roberto Polillo)*

Toshiko Akiyoshi *(Leonard Feather)*

McCoy Tyner and John Coltrane (*Impulse Records*)

Bobby Hutcherson (*Francis Wolff-Blue Note Records*)

Gunther Schuller *(Monte Kay)*

Booker Ervin *(Don Schlitten)*

Mal Waldron *(Don Schlitten)*

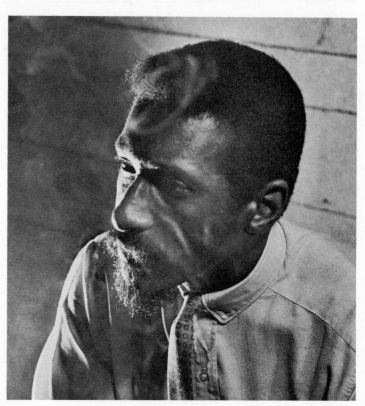

Andrew Hill *(Francis Wolff-Blue Note Records)*

Terry Gibbs *(Impulse Records)*

193

LA FARO

1938 to 1949. Most of his recordings in recent years, featuring the quartet, are on Verve.

Addr: 10 Ritchie Dr., Yonkers, N.Y. 10705.

KUHN, ROLF, * clarinet; b. Cologne, Germany, 9/29/29. After extensive touring in the U.S. during the late '50s and appearances here w. Benny Goodman, Urbie Green and Warren Covington, Kuhn returned to Germany in 1961. Organized and led a 16-piece orchestra appearing regularly on North German radio. Also led numerous smaller combos, many of which included younger brother Joachim on piano, for radio appearances. In Stockholm for *Jazz Under the Stars* w. Arne Domnerus '63 and '64. Own LPs: Bruns., Phil., Amiga, Col.

Addr: Kollanstrasse 10, Hamburg 54, Germany.

KUHN, STEPHEN LEWIS (STEVE), piano; b. Brooklyn, N.Y., 3/24/38. Began playing and studying piano at age of 5; at 13 played dance band gigs in Boston. Obtained B.A. degree from Harvard '59. With K. Dorham '59-'60, J. Coltrane '60, S. Getz '61-'62 and '62-'63, Art Farmer from July '64 and w. own trios intermittently. At Newport '63 w. Getz, Monterey '64 w. Farmer. On Steve Allen TV show w. Getz '63; also many college concerts. Favs: Waller, Tatum, Powell, Evans; Parker, Coltrane, Miles Davis. Hopes to do more work with own groups, increase composing activities. Own LPs: Dauntless, Contact. Others: w. Dorham (Time), Getz (Verve), P. La Roca (BN), Farmer (Atl.), John Rae (Savoy), G. Burton (RCA).

Addr: 901 Eighth Ave., New York 19, N.Y.

KYLE, WILLIAM OSBORNE (BILLY), * piano; b. Philadelphia, Pa., 7/14/14. Rose to prominence with the John Kirby Sextet, with which he played from 1938-42 and again briefly in '46. After several long engagements with Broadway show bands he joined Louis Armstrong in 1953 and during the next 13 years gained great popularity during his travels all over the world with Armstrong. After being hospitalized with an ulcer attack he died in Youngstown, Ohio, 2/23/66.

Kyle was an important pianist in that he was one of the first to break away into an individual style during the stage in jazz (the late 1930s) when virtually every new pianist on the scene reflected the influence of Teddy Wilson. His style was basically simple, moving most often in single-note lines, but with a swinging quality that was unmistakably his own. LPs with Armstrong on Cap., Decca, Col., etc.

KYNARD, CHARLES E., organ; also piano, tuba; b. St. Louis, Mo., 2/20/33. Mother played piano, father played alto sax. Studied piano in Kansas City from 1942. In 1956-'57 toured world with US Army show. Holds B.A. in music education from U. of Kansas. Appeared on Ed Sullivan TV show '56, w. Kansas City Philharmonic '61. To LA, worked in studio orchestras for Columbia and Warner Bros., appeared regularly around town. Also a teacher of mentally retarded children for LA County public schools. Kynard is an exciting, driving organist in the tradition of Jimmy Smith

and Jack McDuff. Favs: Smith, M. Buckner, Wild Bill Davis, B. Doggett, McDuff. Infl: Oscar Peterson. Own LPs: Pac. Jazz. Others: w. Sonny Stitt, Les McCann, Clifford Scott (Pac. Jazz), Howard Roberts (Cap.), Marvin Jenkins (Palomar).

Addr: 802 N. Burris Ave., Compton, Calif.

LACY, STEVE (Steven Lackritz), * soprano sax; b. New York, N.Y., 7/23/34. One of the few musicians to devote all of his playing time to the soprano sax, Lacy pl. w. a variety of Dixieland and mainstream groups, then w. Cecil Taylor, Gil Evans during the '50s. In '59 app. at the Five Spot w. Jimmy Giuffre; then worked 16 weeks w. Thelonious Monk, '60. Led own quartet around NYC w. Roswell Rudd and Dennis Charles, devoting repertoire to Monk compositions. Europe in '63; pl. at Cafe Montmartre in Copenhagen w. Kenny Drew, and at the Bologna (Italy) Jazz Fest. Went to Europe again in '65 w. Carla Bley in Jazz Realities, remaining to lead his own group w. trumpeter Enrico Rava.

As a soprano saxophonist and as an interpreter of Monk, Lacy is one of the most original performers in jazz. Said to have interested John Coltrane in the instrument, he has a tone that reflects neither Coltrane's nor Sidney Bechet's; he plays with a rough and biting sound that fits well into the feeling of Monk's tunes. Since leaving U.S. he has changed his style to include themeless free improvisation. Own LPs: Pres.; Italian GTA, Ital. RCA; LPs w. Gil Evans (Pres., Pac. Jazz), Jazz Realities (Dutch Fontana).

Addr: Fermo Posto, Turin, Italy.

LA FARO, SCOTT, * bass; b. Newark, N.J., 4/3/36. First prominent in Southern California with Chet Baker, Barney Kessel, Howard Rumsey, La Faro settled in NYC in '59, led his own trio and worked with Stan Getz and Bill Evans. He was only 23 when he won the New Star Award in the DB Critics' Poll. La Faro recorded with Bill Evans late in June of 1961. A couple of weeks later, after visiting his mother in Geneva, N.Y., he was killed instantly when his car crashed into a tree near that town, 7/6/61.

La Faro's development as a bassist had astonished his contemporaries as well as bassists representing earlier schools. As Ray Brown remarked on hearing of his death, "He was one of the most talented youngsters to come up in years. He wasn't a powerful bassist, but he had a different style going. I was amazed by his facility, his intonation, and his ideas."

La Faro was the first of a line of bassists in the '60s who began to free the instrument of its long accepted restrictions. He was less interested in playing "time" (i.e. a steady series of pulsations) than in creating stimulating, rhythmically original and often melodic lines, even during the ensemble passages, in any group in which he played. The direction in which his work pointed led to similar developments among innumerable other bassists of the '60s such as Gary Peacock, Steve Swallow and Albert Stinson. La Faro's best work on records can be heard in *Sunday At The Village Vanguard* and *Explorations*, both with the Bill Evans Trio on Riverside, as well as with other small group dates incl. *The Arrival of Victor Feldman* (Cont.).

LAFITTE, GUY,* *tenor sax;* b. St. Gaudens, France, 1/12/27. Began playing clarinet in 1945. First gig w. a gypsy combo in Toulouse. On concert tours of Europe and Africa w. Big Bill Broonzy '50, Mezz Mezzrow '51, Bill Coleman '52. In Paris '54 w. Andre Persiany. Organized own Paris Jazz Trio '57 w. Christian Garros, Georges Arvanitas. Led own groups from '57. In concert w. L. Hampton '59; film *Paris Blues* w. Armstrong and Ellington '62; Cannes, Antibes, Juan-Les-Pins JFs. Favs. and infl.: C. Hawkins, H. Evans, Gonsalves, Rollins. Ambition is to play with more simplicity.

LPs: Under exclusive contract for Columbia-Pathe Marconi from '54; recorded over 50 LPs, incl. w. Hampton, L. Thompson, Coleman, Mezzrow, E. Berry, B. Clayton. Won Grand Prix du Disque for *Les Classiques du Jazz* '57.

Addr: 14 rue Boulle, Paris, France.

LAINE, CLEO, *singer;* b. Southall, Middlesex, England, 10/27/27. Started career '53 in cellar club w. Johnny Dankworth. App. w. him at Royal Festival Hall, London, two weeks later. Consistent *Melody Maker* poll-winner since '56. Left Dankworth '58 to work as single. West End stage roles in *Flesh to a Tiger* (which won Moscow Arts Theatre Gold Medal), Sandy Wilson musical *Valmouth*. Lead role in Kurt Weill's *The Seven Deadly Sins* at '61 Edinburgh Festival; Royal Variety Performance '62; sang w. Scottish National Orchestra in Glasgow '64; and recited Poulenc's *Babar, The Little Elephant* w. London Philharmonic Orchestra. Has given lieder recitals. Sang in *Freedom Road*, which won Berlin TV Festival Grand Prix '64, and theme song of film *The Servant*. Continued activity as jazz singer, w. frequent TV appearances. Outstanding jazz singer, w. fine technique, whose distinctive sound and style are still underrated due to her success in other fields. Married to Johnny Dankworth. Own LPs inc. *Shakespeare and All That Jazz, Woman Talk*, both on Brit. Fontana.

Addr: c/o Harold Davison, 235-241 Regent St., London, W. 1, England.

LAMARE, HILTON (NAPPY),* *guitar, banjo, singer;* b. New Orleans, La., 6/14/10. Worked with Ben Pollack and Bob Crosby band in 1930s. Since then, free-lancing in Los Angeles, has frequently been reunited with some of his ex-Crosby colleagues. Played at Roaring 20s in LA 1960-61; Crosby in Las Vegas '62; Eddie Miller in Cleveland, Ohio '63; jazz concerts in LA and New Orleans. Also teaching in LA '66.

LPs with Bob Crosby (Decca, Coral).

Addr: 14251 Cohasset St., Van Nuys, Calif.

LAMB, JOHN LEE, *bass;* b. Vero Beach, Fla., 12/4/33. Started on drums. Studied at Lincoln Park Academy 1948. Classically trained, he attended Air Force School of Music and spent eight years with USAF dance band and combos; also attended Phila. Musical Academy, studied composing and arranging. Six months with Red Garland, 1954-5; two years leading own sextet in Phila. '57-9, later played with Paul Currey Trio '60-'62, Johnny Walker Trio '62-4. Joined Ellington 1964 and toured with him internationally. First infl.: Ed Safranski. Fav: Ray Brown. Lamb is one of the stablest and best-trained bassists heard with Ellington in many years.

LPs w. Ellington on Reprise, etc.

Addr: 2707 54th Dr., Philadelphia, Pa.

LAMBERT, DAVID ALDEN (DAVE),* *singer, vocal arranger;* b. Boston, Mass., 6/19/17. After more than six years as a member of the poll-winning vocal trio originally known as Lambert, Hendricks & Ross (later Lambert, Hendricks & Bavan), Lambert left the group in Feb. 1964. He settled in New York and became active in his old role of vocal group organizer, also as master of ceremonies and disc jockey. LPs: see Hendricks, Jon.

LAND, HAROLD DE VANCE,* *tenor sax;* b. Houston, Tex., 12/18/28. In late '50s pl. w. Max Roach-Clifford Brown Quintet, Curtis Counce. Monterey JF with Gerald Wilson '63; July '65 own quartet at Club Blue Horn in Vancouver with Philly Joe Jones. Has led own group at It Club, Living Room and many other clubs in LA and San Francisco. Worked with underscore groups on various movies incl. *The Manchurian Candidate, Flower Drum Song*, etc. Co-led quintet w. Red Mitchell '61-2.

Though he has impressed those who have heard him in Calif., Land is one of the most underrated tenor saxophonists on the contemporary jazz scene. His style in the '50s had a drive and virility that was rare in the somewhat cool circles of West Coast jazz in those days. In recent years, as Ira Gitler commented, he has played "better than ever in his lyrical, connective style that flows with grace and rhythmic heat."

Own LP: *Jazz Impressions of Folk Music* (Imperial); *West Coast Blues* with Wes Montgomery (Jazzland); *Soviet Jazz Themes* with Victor Feldman (Ava); *Moment of Truth; On Stage* with Gerald Wilson (both Pac. Jazz); *The Young Savages* (Col.).

Addr: 5106 4th Ave., Los Angeles, Calif. 90043.

LANG, MICHAEL ANTHONY (MIKE), *piano;* b. L.A., Calif. 12/10/41. Father is well-known motion picture executive Jennings Lang; step-mother is singer Monica Lewis. Began piano 1946, composition 1953. Piano studies with Pearl Kaufman, B.M. from University of Michigan '63. Won award as best pianist at Intercollegiate Jazz Festival, Notre Dame '63, with Bob Pozar Trio; prize was three-week engagement at Village Vanguard. Pianist with LA Neophonic Orchestra early 1965. With Paul Horn Quintet '64-5. A fast-maturing musician whose many influences range from James P. Johnson and Art Tatum to Clare Fischer and Paul Bley. LPs w. Paul Horn (RCA).

Addr: 606 Mountain Dr., Beverly Hills, Calif.

LA PORTA, JOHN D.,* *composer, saxophones, clarinet;* b. Philadelphia, Pa., 4/1/20. An important figure both as musician and composer during the '50s, La Porta played with Woody Herman, Leonard Bernstein, Igor Stravinsky, Charles Mingus and Teo Macero before joining the faculty of the Berklee School of Music as Supervisor of Instrumental Ensembles. Has written numerous music instruction books. Active in youth band movement, incl. director of Boston Youth Band from '64; faculty of Summer Stage Band Clinics from '59; touring clinician in high schools across the country.

La Porta is still an active musician, performing with his own quartet around Boston, and as a member of the Berklee Saxophone Quartet, which includes Charlie Mariano. He has also written several stage band arrangements and has recorded both jazz and a Brahms chamber work with his own groups. Own LPs: Everest, Fantasy. Others: w. Herman (*Ebony Concerto,* Everest); w. Mingus (*Jazz Composers' Workshop No. 2,* Savoy); *Jazz Compositions of the 20th Century* (Col.).

Addr: 34 Maple St., South Hamilton, Mass.

LA ROCA, PETE (Peter Sims),* *drums, composer;* b. New York City, 4/7/38. Recommended by Max Roach to Sonny Rollins, he pl. w. Rollins, as well as w. Tony Scott and Slide Hampton, in '50s. W. John Coltrane '60; own group in NYC intermittently '61-2. House drummer at Jazz Workshop in Boston, fall '63-April '64; Art Farmer quartet '64-5; Charles Lloyd '66.

Originally infl. by Philly Joe Jones and Elvin Jones, La Roca's pl. typifies the best of the new drumming style which states and implies the beat all over the set. As a comp. he has written a series of intriguing originals. Interested in Indian music, Sanskrit, yoga, and James Joyce. Own LP: *Basra* (BN); LPs w. Farmer (Atl.), Joe Henderson (BN), *Night of the Cookers,* vols. 1 & 2, (BN).

LA ROCCA, DOMINICK JAMES (NICK),* *cornet, leader;* b. New Orleans, 4/11/1889. La Rocca was famous as the founder of the Original Dixieland Jazz Band, which in 1917 made what was often called the first jazz record. The band broke up in 1925; La Rocca reorganized it briefly in 1936 but did very little professional playing after '37. Though out of the limelight, he continued, through letters to newspapers and magazines, to claim credit as a founder of jazz. He bitterly denounced those who belittled his contribution and who pointed out that jazz was essentially of Negro origin. Shortly before his death, Southland Records issued an LP under La Rocca's name, though he ac-

tually did not play on it. La Rocca died in New Orleans 2/22/61.

LASHA, WILLIAM B. (PRINCE) (Pron. rhymes w. Bechet), *flute, composer;* b. Fort Worth, Texas, 9/10/29. A childhood companion of Ornette Coleman, with whom he learned music informally. The two led a band professionally while still in high school. Lasha and Coleman continued to work together off and on during most of the late 1940s. After touring the South for a while, playing baritone and alto saxes, Lasha lived in New York. In 1954 he moved to Calif. and met Sonny Simmons, the alto saxophonist. Lasha and Simmons worked together intermittently and went together to Ft. Worth in '62. Shortly afterward they went to Los Angeles and made their joint record debut on an LP entitled *The Cry* (Contemp.). Lasha, though not one of the most revolutionary of the new wave, clearly is dedicated to the same musical principles as Coleman. He says that both he and Coleman were inspired by Red Conner, a tenor saxophonist from Ft. Worth who died in the 1950s.

Heard in Europe during most of the latter half of 1965, Lasha recorded in England. He has also been featured on *Illuminations* w. Elvin Jones (Impulse).

Addr: c/o Moffett, 65 Pike St., New York 2, N.Y.

LATEEF, YUSEF,* *flute, tenor sax, oboe, composer, leader;* b. Chattanooga, Tenn., 1921. After working in Detroit during the 1950s, Lateef moved to NYC in Jan. 1960 and led his own quartet. Later he was featured w. Ch. Mingus, 1960-61; Babatundi Olatunji, '61-2. He then joined the Cannonball Adderley combo, touring with the group for two years incl. Europe, Japan. On leaving Adderley he resumed his career as combo leader, first with a quintet and later a quartet.

During this period Lateef was active in several other areas. He played on the soundtracks of such films as *The Cool World* (Mal Waldron's score) and Charles Mills' *Tracks in the Sand.* Studied with Dr. Allen Kimbler, a student of Karlheinz Stockhausen; later stud. flute w. Harold Jones. Taught saxophone at Stan Kenton Summer Jazz Clinics '63; lectured at colleges.

Publication: *Yusef Lateef's Flute Book of the Blues.*

In addition to developing new sounds and ideas on flute and oboe, Lateef added new instruments to his media of expression, the Taiwan flute and the Shanni, an Indian wind instrument. Also made two instruments himself, a bamboo flute in F and a pneumatic bamboo flute.

Middle Eastern and other extra-European influences became increasingly apparent in Lateef's work during the 1960s, especially in his flute and oboe improvisations and in many of his compositions. His work retained its great sense of authority and strength of emotion along with remarkable displays of virtuosity on the many instruments at his command.

Lateef is a talented painter whose abstracts have

been exhibited by Fine Arts Committee of Teaneck, N.J.

Own LPs on Impulse, and earlier sets on New Jazz, Prestige. Many others as sideman incl. w. Adderley (River.).

Addr: 129 Circle Driveway, Teaneck, N.J.

LAWRENCE, ELLIOTT,* *leader, composer, piano;* b. Philadelphia, Pa., 2/14/25. Leader of swinging dance band from late 1940s. Mus. dir. and arr. for B'way shows *Bye Bye Birdie* '61; *How To Succeed in Business Without Really Trying* '62 (won Tony award); *Here's Love* '64; *Golden Boy* '65; TV series *Nightlife* '65. Comp.-arr. for NBC documentaries; comp.-cond. for films *Screaming Wheels* '64, *Hot Rod Hullabullo* '66.

LPs: Original cast recordings of B'way shows.

Addr: 30 Central Park West, New York 24, N.Y.

LAWS, HUBERT, *flute;* also *saxes, guitar, clarinet;* b. Houston, Tex., 11/10/39. Studied sax while in jr. high school. First job was w. Jazz Crusaders '54-'60. Soloist in Houston Youth Symphony '57. W. Mongo Santamaria '63, Orchestra U.S.A. '64, Sergio Mendes '65. Other playing and recording gigs incl. Lena Horne, J. Moody, J. J. Johnson, C. Terry, J. Hall, B. Golson, J. Cleveland, E. Hawkins, R. Davis, A. Prysock, T. McIntosh. In Berkshire Festival Orch. '61. In film *Made In Paris* w. Santamaria '65. Stud. at Juilliard. Fav: Julius Baker of N.Y. Philharmonic. Infl. on playing: Herbie Hancock, Coltrane, Miles Davis, Wes Montgomery; on writing: McIntosh, Gil Evans. Own LP: (Atl.). Others: w. Moody (Cadet), Orch. U.S.A. (Col.), Mendes (Atl.), Jazz Crusaders (Pac. Jazz), Santamaria (Col.).

Addr: 102 W. 93rd St., New York, N.Y.

LAWSON, JOHN R. (YANK),* *trumpet;* b. Trenton, Mo., 5/3/11. A prominent swing band soloist in the 1930s and early '40s, Lawson in recent years has done staff work on TV (Johnny Carson show, 1965) but has also continued to work frequently in jazz. Played NJF w. Louis Armstrong, '62; toured Japan, Okinawa, Phillipines w. Bob Crosby '64. Worked in NYC at Eddie Condon's '63-5. Own LPs for ABC Paramount, also feat. on several Cap. albums w. Jackie Gleason, and on ABC-Paramount w. Clancy Hayes.

Addr: 105 East 10th St., New York 3, N.Y.

LEE, JEANNE, *singer;* b. New York City, 1/29/39. Father was a concert singer. Piano lessons for seven years. Pl. in junior high orch. Stud. modern dance, choreography in college. Entered music through association w. pianist Ran Blake, w. whom she formed trio playing Monterey JF '62 and touring Europe '63. If such a phrase can have validity, Miss Lee may be termed an avant garde singer. Recently she has been performing experimental poetry: "I am concerned with the music in the sound of the word or in abstract speech sounds. I believe this concept has possibilities for vocal improvisation far beyond the traditional imitation of instrumental sounds."

LP with Ran Blake: *The Newest Sound Around* (RCA).

Addr: 1370 Prospect Ave., Bronx 59, N. Y.

LEE, JULIAN, *arranger, piano;* b. Dunedin, New Zealand, 11/11/23. Educ. at N.Z. Foundation for Blind and Univ. Coll. in Auckland; stud. piano, organ, brass, woodwinds, harmony. Played tenor sax and trumpet in dance band. From 1947-56 wrote for house band at N.Z. Broadcasting Corp. Moved to Sydney, Australia, '56 and during the next seven years enjoyed great success as pianist, arranger, writing for large orchestras, 20-voice choir, etc., and running his own jingle company. Immigrated to Calif. '63 as protegé of Geo. Shearing. Free-lanced as pianist, occasionally as trumpeter, but worked mainly as arranger, collaborating with Shearing for some of the latter's Capitol LPs, and writing arrangements for two orchestral albums featuring The Three Sounds (Limelight) and Gerry Mulligan's album *Feelin' Good* (Limelight).

Addr: 900 Ford St., Burbank, Calif.

LEE, PEGGY,* *singer, composer;* b. Jamestown, N. Dak., 5/26/22. Sang with Benny Goodman band 1941-3. Later worked as single and achieved national popularity in late '40s. Acad. Award nomination for film role in *Pete Kelly's Blues* 1956.

Since the late '50s Miss Lee has extended her activities as songwriter, composing lyrics and sometimes music. She has collaborated with Duke Ellington (*I'm Gonna Go Fishin'*), Quincy Jones (*New York City Blues*), Milton Raskin (*Fisherman's Wharf*), Lalo Schifrin (*Theme From Joy House*), Cy Coleman (*Then Was Then*).

Working in person and on records with such conductor-arrangers as Benny Carter, Quincy Jones and Lou Levy, she has achieved an incomparable level of beauty in her ballad performances and of jazz-influenced conviction in her blues and up-tempo numbers. She made her first trip to Europe in 1961, playing in London and Monaco. In addition to TV shows with Jack Paar, Andy Williams, Dean Martin, Judy Garland et al, she enjoyed phenomenal popular success in her appearances at Basin Street East, The Americana and The Copa in NYC, The Diplomat in Hollywood, Fla., etc.

Outstanding among her LPs (all on Cap.) are *Blues Cross Country* with Quincy Jones Orch., *Pass Me By* with Lou Levy Orch., *Sugar and Spice* with Benny Carter Orch.

Addr: c/o Ludwig Gerber, 9229 Sunset Blvd., Hollywood 69, Calif.

LEEMAN, CLIFFORD (CLIFF),* *drums;* b. Portland, Maine, 9/10/13. In many of best swing bands of '30s and '40s, incl. Shaw, Barnet, both Dorseys. 1960 in Las Vegas w. Bob Crosby. Appeared on TV w. Red Nichols and on *Chicago and All That Jazz* '61. W. Wild Bill Davison at NYC Nick's '62, Dick Haymes '63, Dukes of Dixieland in Las Vegas and Mexico City '63-'64, P. Hucko at Eddie Condon's NYC '64. In several all-star jazz concerts at Aspen, Colo. '63-'65. Toured Australia, New Zealand, Japan '64 w. large traditional group incl. Condon, Rushing, Clayton. Columbia, S.C. JF '65 w. T. Parenti, A. Hodes. LPs: w. Joe Turner (Atl.), B. Crosby (Dot), Condon (Col.), Steve Allen (Decca), B. Butterfield (Essex).

Addr: 21-04 154th St., Whitestone, N.Y.

LEGGE, WADE, * *piano;* b. Huntington, W. Va., 2/4/34. Raised in Buffalo, Legge came to prominence as pianist with Dizzy Gillespie 1952-4. Later worked with Johnny Richards orchestra; returned to Buffalo and free-lanced. Died Buffalo, N.Y., 8/15/63.

LEGRAND, CHRISTIANE, *singer;* b. Aix Les Bains, France, 8/21/30. Miss Legrand is a member of a noted French musical family: her uncle is Jacques Hélian, her father Raymond Legrand and her brother the noted contemporary arranger Michel Legrand. She studied piano in Paris from the age of 5 and made her professional debut singing with her brother's orchestra. In addition to working as featured soloist with him from 1954-8 she was the lead soprano in the Blue Stars, a pioneer modern jazz vocal group, from 1955-7, and in The Double Six of Paris from '58-'60. Since 1962 she has been the soprano soloist with the Swingle Singers. Her film work has included *La Parisienne,* in which her voice was used to underline Brigitte Bardot's role. The sound track of this picture was a great success in Paris. She was also heard in *The Umbrellas of Cherbourg,* for which her brother wrote the music and Miss Legrand sang the role of the mother.

Christiane Legrand is one of the most remarkable singers in her field, that of group vocal jazz. Because of her extraordinary range and purity of sound she has often been compared with Annie Ross. Her ambition is to sing and act in musical comedy. She names Ella Fitzgerald and Michel Legrand as her chief musical influences.

Addr: 8, rue de Lorraine, Asnieres (Seine) France.

LE SAGE, WILLIAM (BILL), * *vibes, composer, piano, accordion;* b. London, Eng., 1/20/27. Much arranging for films and TV since '61. Co-led quartet w. Ronnie Ross in early '60s. Formed own Directions in Jazz unit, inc. four cellos, '63, wh. app. at Eng. concerts, and at Hamburg Jazz Workshop '64. Also led own bands at Hamburg Workshop '62 and '66. Own LPs w. Directions in Jazz on Brit. Philips; others on Brit. World Record Club.

Addr: 21 Park Road, London W.7., England.

LESBERG, JACK, * *bass;* b. Boston, Mass., 2/14/20. Alternating between commercial and jazz work, Lesberg worked on film underscores, commercial jingles and record dates in NYC. Visiting Paris and Strasbourg in October 1962 he played with Georgie Auld and Doc Severinsen. Toured Australia, New Zealand, Japan with Eddie Condon March-April '64. Iceland w. L. Armstrong Feb. '65. Newport JF w. Geo. Wein '65.

LPs w. Bud Freeman (Cap.); J. Teagarden (Cap.); *Midnight in Moscow* w. E. Condon (Epic).

Addr: 21 Northfield Rd., Glen Cove, N.Y.

LESTER, KETTY (Revoyda Frierson), *singer;* b. Hope, Ark., 8/16/34. Moved to San Francisco in '52, studying voice there w. Myrtle Leonard and at City Coll. First appearance in *Straw Hat Revue* in Berkeley. Sang at Purple Onion clubs in SF and LA; after Dorothy Shay heard her at the Los Angeles club, became a protege of Miss Shay. Settled in LA 1955. App. in Ziegfeld Follies tour '57; toured South America with Cab Calloway in Cotton Club revue '58.

In 1962 her record of *Love Letters* on the Era label became a hit; she was subsequently signed by RCA Victor and appeared on *Tonight,* the Vic Damone show and other major TV programs. From 1962 she made several successful appearances in England and on the Continent.

Influenced by Billie Holiday, Tony Bennett, Sarah Vaughan and the music of Miles Davis, Miss Lester is an exceptional singer with strong projection, a huskily attractive timbre and a sense of phrasing that reveals her knowledge of the blues and her roots in jazz.

LPs: RCA, later releases on Tower.

Addr: 5931 Comey Avenue, Los Angeles, 34, Calif.

LETMAN, JOHN BERNARD (JOHNNY), * *trumpet;* b. McCormick, S.C., 9/6/17. With Cab Calloway, Basie, other important bands during '40s; free-lanced around NYC w. own groups during '50s. Became active in Broadway, TV work. In plays *Marathon '33* and *Never Live Over a Pretzel Factory* '64, on Phyllis Diller, Mike Douglas TV shows '65. Played at Cincinnati JF '63, Connecticut JF '65. Did studio recording for several major companies. Own LP: *Many Angles of John Letman* (Beth.).

Addr: 111-41 139th St., Jamaica 37, N.Y.

LEVEY, STAN, * *drums;* b. Philadelphia, Pa., 4/5/25. One of the most influential of early bop drummers; worked w. Gillespie, Pettiford, Parker during '40s, Kenton and Rumsey during '50s. Accompanied Peggy Lee '62 incl. trip to England, Ella Fitzgerald '63 incl. three European tours. Toured Japan w. Pat Boone '64. Played in tracks for numerous films and TV shows. Became very successful as a photographer, doing several album covers in addition to fashion and industrial work. Began studying mallet and keyboard instruments 1965. LP: *Arrival of Victor Feldman* (Contemp.)

Addr: 12742 Cohasset, North Hollywood, Calif.

LEVITT, RODNEY CHARLES (ROD), *trombone, composer;* also *piano, recorder;* b. Portland, Ore., 9/16/29. Parents amateur pianists. Studied trombone while in grade school. Joined Dizzy Gillespie big band '56-'57, incl. tour of Mideast and S. America. With NYC Radio City Orch. from '57 until '63. Played w. Gil Evans at Birdland '59. Led own orch. from '60; in concerts at Judson Hall '63, Carnegie Hall '64 and '65, Newport JF '60 and '64. Favs: Jack Teagarden,

Bill Harris, Lawrence Brown, Joe Nanton, Kai Winding; composers: Ellington, Gil Evans, Stravinsky. Own LPs: *Dynamic Sound Patterns* (River.); *Insight, Solid Ground* (RCA). Others: w. Gillespie (Verve), Evans (Wor. Pac.).

Addr: 11 Riverside Dr., New York, N.Y.

LEVY, LOUIS A. (LOU),* *piano;* b. Chicago, Ill., 3/5/28. In LA jazz from late '40s, incl. w. Raeburn, Chubby Jackson, Herman, acc. for Peggy Lee, Ella Fitzgerald. Rejoined Fitzgerald '60-'61, incl. JATP. W. Lee again '61. Also free-lanced from '60, incl. w. T. Gibbs, S. Getz, Z. Sims at Shelly's Manne Hole. Toured Pacific, Europe, Israel w. Fitzgerald. Has acquired an excellent reputation as accompanist. Own LPs: RCA, Phil. Others: w. Fitzgerald (Verve), Lee (Cap.), B. Holman (Coral), Nancy Wilson (Cap.), Shorty Rogers (Reprise).

Addr: 4222 Rhodes Ave., Studio City, Calif.

LEWIS, GEORGE,* *clarinet;* b. New Orleans, La., 7/13/00. Pl. w. Black Eagle band, Buddy Petit, Earl Humphrey early in career. Own band w. Red Allen for a year '23. W. WPA as stevedore, etc. and virtually out of music in '30s. Rediscovered along w. Bunk Johnson in '42, he pl. and rec. w. him. In '50s led own group of NO veterans, touring England in '57, and England and the Continent in '59. App. NJF '57. In '60s made similar trips to Japan enjoying great popularity there at clubs, concerts and festivals. Own LPs: GHB; *Jazz at Preservation Hall* (Atl.).

LEWIS, JOHN AARON,* *composer, piano, leader;* b. La Grange, Ill., 5/3/20. Extensive music studies 1927-42. First prominent in jazz as pianist and arranger with Dizzy Gillespie '46-7. Key figure in Miles Davis Capitol recording group in '49. Founded Modern Jazz Quartet 1952. From late '50s was also active as teacher, writer of motion picture music, performer with symphony orchs., and, from 1958-64, musical director at Monterey JF. His film scores include *Odds Against Tomorrow, No Sun in Venice, A Milanese Story.*

Lewis has written and performed in a great variety of orchestral contexts. He played with and conducted a brass ensemble in *The Golden Striker* (the album's title number was a theme from his score for the film *One Never Knows*). He wrote a ballet, *Original Sin,* first produced for the SF Ballet Mar. 1961; augmented the Modern Jazz Quartet with a string quartet, and later with a big jazz ensemble; assembled an album (*Jazz Abstractions*) in which Ornette Coleman was featured in a Gunther Schuller composition; and was instrumental in bringing to the attention of U.S. audiences a series of European artists whom he discovered or sponsored, among them Albert Mangelsdorff, Svend Asmussen and The Zagreb Jazz Quartet. All the above can be heard in Atlantic albums either under Lewis' name or that of the MJQ.

During the 1960s Lewis, who maintains homes in Nice and New York, took the MJQ on a European tour once a year. The group visited Czechoslovakia and Yugoslavia in '65, Japan and Australia in '66. Though rarely seen on commercial U.S. television, the Quartet was assigned special programs of its own in Sweden and England. Lewis' best known U.S. television credit was the writing of music for a Harry Belafonte special, *New York 19.* In 1963 he composed the music for William Inge's play *Natural Affection,* presented on Broadway.

From 1962 Lewis also organized and presented several seasons of concerts by a large ensemble of leading jazz and classical musicians under the name of Orchestra USA. Its repertoire included Lewis' own music; works by Gunther Schuller and Gary McFarland, who were his close associates in the venture; by Harold Farberman, who replaced Schuller as conductor, and by several other Third Stream writers.

In 1966 Lewis was appointed to the Board of Trustees of the Manhattan School of Music, where he had earned his MA in music in 1953.

In his multiplicity of undertakings during the past decade Lewis has become a symbol of the great diversification of music, and of the elimination of artificial barriers between so-called classical music and jazz, between bop and the avant garde, and between the musics and musicians of various nations. Jazz students concerned with an investigation of the overall developments in music since the late 1950s may gain a comprehensive insight by studying the various LPs released under the names of the Modern Jazz Quartet (Atl.); John Lewis (Atl.) and Orchestra USA (Col., Colpix).

Addr: c/o Paul Schwartz, MJQ Music, 200 W. 57th St., New York 19, N.Y.

LEWIS, MEADE LUX,* *piano;* b. Louisville, Ky., 1905. Discovered by John Hammond in the mid-'30s and famous for his *Honky Tonk Train Blues,* Lewis achieved prominence in the late '30s and early '40s, recording for various labels and appearing at Carnegie Hall and Cafe Society. He later moved to Los Angeles, playing clubs there and in other cities. He was returning from an engagement in Minneapolis when he was fatally injured in an automobile accident 6/7/64. LPs: Verve, River.

LEWIS, MEL (Melvin Sokoloff),* *drums;* b. Buffalo, N.Y., 5/10/29. Own group w. Bill Holman during '50s, in LA from '57. Member G. Mulligan Concert Jazz Band from 1960. Bet. '60 and '63 worked w. Mulligan and Dizzy Gillespie in NYC, toured w. B. Goodman and F. Sinatra, appeared in Gibbs and G. Wilson bands on West Coast. In '63 moved from LA to NYC, joined ABC radio and TV staff. Tours: Europe w. Mulligan '60; England and Europe w. Gillespie '61; U.S.S.R. w. Goodman '62; European concerts w. Friedrich Gulda from '64. House drummer Monterey JF '59-'62; in first jazz concert at Vienna Int'l. Music Festival '65. Clubs and concerts in NYC 1966 as co-leader w. Thad Jones of a swinging big band. Lewis, who won the DB New Star Award '62, is one of most gifted drummers in a style often recalling the late Tiny Kahn.

LPs: Jones-Lewis (Solid State); w. Mulligan (Verve, UA); Gibbs (Merc., Verve); Kenton (Cap.); Gillespie (Lime.); Gulda (Col.); G. McFarland (Impulse); Goodman (RCA), and many others.

Addr: 28 Alta Vista Circle, Irvington, N.Y.

LEWIS, RAMSEY E. JR.,* *piano, composer;* b. Chicago, Ill., 5/27/35. Formed trio 1956; first played in New York '59. For several years the group continued to work with moderate success in night clubs, in Chicago and on the road. In 1964 one of Lewis' records, *Something You Got,* enjoyed a fairly substantial popular reaction.

In the summer of 1965 the trio at last achieved national acclaim on the strength of its recording of *The In Crowd.* The single record sold well over a million copies and during the next year Lewis' albums had a total sale of well above the million mark. Commercially, his group had suddenly become the most popular jazz combo in the U.S.

Like many jazz artists who have gained mass popular appeal, Lewis has been criticized by some jazz writers and has sustained his reputation without their help. The trio broke attendance records in every club it played for many months after its recording success. A Carnegie Hall concert at which Lewis was the sole attraction was sold out in advance.

Barbara Gardner has said that Lewis' approach "incorporates the hint of Old World dynamics and progression to a climax. Still, underlying all is the consistent fusing of powerful, contrasting dynamics, and earthy, straightforward projection . . . this quality has earned the trio a reputation as a 'Soul Group.' "

The In Crowd was awarded a Grammy by NARAS as the best small-group jazz record of 1965.

LPs: *Down To Earth* (Merc.); all others on Cadet.

LINCOLN, ABBEY,* *singer;* b. Chicago, Ill., 8/6/30. Worked in Calif. and Hawaii in early '50s using name Gaby Lee. Changed name to Abbey Lincoln in '56. Played night clubs; toured in road company of stage show, *Jamaica.* In 1960 she took part in the recording *We Insist! (Freedom Now Suite),* composed by Oscar Brown Jr. and Max Roach. She has since occasionally given public performances of the work in collaboration with Roach, to whom she is married. During the '60s Miss Lincoln developed from a synthetic "intimate" club singer into a far more individual performer, proud of her racial heritage and frequently singing material related to her background. Her LPs unfortunately are on the long-defunct Candid label. She is also an actress of great sensitivity, her best-known film being *Nothing But A Man.*

LINDBERG, NILS,* *piano, composer;* b. Uppsala, Sweden, 6/11/33. Worked w. Benny Bailey, Anders Burman, Ove Lind and Putte Wickman. Infl. by Swedish

folk music in his jazz writing. LP incl. own comps.: *Trisection* on Capitol.

LINGLE, PAUL,* *piano;* b. Denver, Colo., 12/3/02. This legendary pianist, well known among fellow musicians for many years in San Francisco and greatly admired by such local associates as Turk Murphy, moved to Honolulu in 1952. After playing and teaching there he became seriously ill and died in a Honolulu hospital in 1962. He was one of the most dedicated of the pianists inspired by Jelly Roll Morton and Scott Joplin.

LISTON, MELBA DORETTA,* *trombone, composer;* b. Kansas City, Mo., 1/13/26. A prolific recording artist and arranger during the '40s and '50s, associated w. Billie Holiday, Basie, Gillespie, Quincy Jones and Randy Weston. From the late '50s she expanded her composing and arranging activities, concentrating less on the trombone. Comps. incl. *Just Waiting, All Deliberate Speed, Melba's Blues.* Organized Pittsburgh JF Orch. '64. Arr. for Charles Mingus Town Hall Concert NYC '62, Duke Ellington Jazz Society Orch. concert NYC '63, mus-dir. for Eddie Fisher '64. Award-winning TV commercial for Rock Wine Co. '65. Appeared as trombonist w. Budd Johnson, Lincoln Center NYC '64; and *Instant Jazz* at NYC Town Hall '65. Numerous LPs as arranger or conductor incl.: J. Mance (Jazzl.), J. Griffin (River.), The Metronomes (Jazzl.), Weston (Roul., Colpix), D. Burns (Van.), Staton (UA), Q. Jones (Merc.), Elvin Jones (Atl.), M. L. Williams (Mary).

Addr: 644 Riverside Dr. #86, New York 31, N.Y.

LITTLE, BOOKER JR.,* *trumpet;* b. Memphis, Tenn., 4/2/38; d. New York, N.Y., 10/5/61 of uremia. Toured and recorded with Max Roach in '58, then appeared in NYC '59-'60 with Mal Waldron, John Coltrane. Most important job was in quintet co-led with Eric Dolphy at NYC Five Spot in summer of '61 which also included Waldron, Richard Davis and Eddie Blackwell.

In addition to having an extremely impressive technique, Little by the time of his death had already become one of the most promising trumpet innovators of the '60s. In the recordings of the Five Spot dates he showed that he was taking his instrument away from the influences of Miles Davis and Clifford Brown and was employing dissonance and unusual melodic ideas. He told Robert Levin of *Metronome,* "I can't think in terms of wrong notes—in fact I don't hear any notes as being wrong. It's a matter of knowing how to integrate the notes and . . . how to resolve them . . . More emotion can be expressed by the notes that are played flat." Own LPs: With Dolphy *At the Five Spot* Vols. 1-3 (Pres.), *Booker Little* (Time) *Booker Little Quartet Plus Max Roach* (UA). Others: Dolphy *Far Cry* (Pres.), Roach *We Insist* (Candid), *Award Winning Drummer* (Time), *Conversations* (Jazzland).

LITTLE, DUDLEY (BIG TINY), *piano, leader, singer;* b. Worthington, Minn., 8/31/30. Professional debut 1945 with local group in Mankato, Minn. In Tokyo 1952-4, led own Japanese jazz group. Piano with Irving Ashby Trio, Long Beach, Cal., '55. Joined Lawrence Welk band '55, and during the next four years of constant television exposure with Welk gained enough prominence to leave in '59 and organize his own six-piece combo. He has recorded more than 20 albums (Coral), mostly in a honky tonk or psuedo-ragtime vein. However, Nat Cole and many others were aware of his jazz ability, evidence of which can be found in his *Movin' On* album. Favs: Fats Waller, Oscar Peterson. Compositions include *Sidewalk Serenade, Last Call, Nashville Blues.*

Addr: 2400 Michael Dr., Carson City, Nevada.

LLOYD, CHARLES, *tenor saxophone, flute, composer, leader;* b. Memphis, Tenn., 3/15/38. Lloyd's father was a pharmacist. Inspired by a local big bop band, Lloyd acquired his first saxophone around 1948. Self-taught at first, he later studied with Irving Reason. His schoolmates included Frank Strozier, Booker Little and George Coleman.

While still in Memphis, Lloyd gained early experience playing alto with local rhythm and blues groups such as those of B.B. King and Bobby Bland. After graduating from high school he moved to Southern California in 1956 and went to college at USC to major in dentistry, but switched to composition in his second year. While at college he gigged on alto with Gerald Wilson and others. After graduating, he taught music for a while, then joined Chico Hamilton's group in 1961. The following year he switched to tenor sax and became increasingly active on flute, which he had taken up in 1958.

Leaving Hamilton in 1964, Lloyd toured with the Cannonball Adderley combo. He formed his own quartet in July, 1965 and during the next few months came to prominence via his Columbia albums and a cross-country tour of nightclubs.

Lloyd's liberal musical philosophy has established him as one of the most important and successful figures in the avant garde. While still in Memphis he listened to the records of Coleman Hawkins, Ben Webster and Lester Young; his influences have also included Sonny Stitt, Sonny Rollins and John Coltrane. As he says, "The younger musicians should be well grounded in all the basics of music, as well as equipping themselves with new tools. The people I like to surround myself with, the ones I consider my peers, can play simple 32-bar choruses as well as our more complex works; we all try to function as complete musicians."

Lloyd's tenor work reflects this catholic attitude; his flute playing has arrived closer to a completely original sound than that of almost any other jazz flutist. He uses a broad range of devices to obtain a variety of sounds on both instruments, and has ex-

traordinary equipment from a technical standpoint.

Own LPs: Col. Several LPs w. Hamilton on Col., Reprise, Impulse.

Addr: 1 Sheridan Sq., New York 14, N.Y.

LOCATELLI, JOSEPH J. (JOE), *drums;* b. Boston, Mass., 6/5/34. Played w. several dance bands, then w. Billy May in 1960. W. Jackie Cain-Roy Kral '62; Warren Covington, Vido Musso '62; R. Norvo, B. Holman, Johnny Smith, C. Mariano '65. Taught at summer jazz clinics at Reno, Salt Lake City. Favs: Clarke, Blakey, P. J. Jones, Roach, Manne.

Addr: 6252 Parsifal Pl., Las Vegas, Nev.

LOCKWOOD, ROBERT JR., *guitar, singer;* b. Marvell, Ark., 3/27/15. Influenced by his stepfather, he began pl. the blues at age 19. Worked in St. Louis for a while, then in Chi. from '39. Rec. for Bluebird in early '40s. In '50s pl. w. Little Walter, Willie Mabon, Eddie Boyd, Roosevelt Sykes and Muddy Waters. LP w. Otis Spann for defunct Candid label in 1960.

LOFTON, LAWRENCE (TRICKY), *trombone;* b. Houston, Texas, 5/28/30. Began playing in high school; early experience with rhythm and blues artists including T-Bone Walker, Bill Doggett, Joe Liggins, Joe Turner. Moved to Los Angeles in 1946, working there mainly with small combos. After Army service, returned to LA in '53 and has been featured in various small group sessions, club and record dates. Favs: J. J. Johnson, J. Cleveland, C. Fuller, B. Harris. LPs w. Richard "Groove" Holmes (Pac. Jazz) et al.

Addr: 2644 S. Raymond Ave., Los Angeles 7, Calif.

LOGAN, GIUSEPPI, *alto and tenor saxophones, Pakistani oboe, composer;* b. Philadelphia, Pa., 5/22/35. After singing in choirs and playing in school band, made professional debut at 15. Studied with Dennis Sandole and others, also at New England Conservatory. Played with string ensemble in concert at Town Hall, NYC. Logan, who has stated that politics, religion and philosophy play an active role in all arts, is a prominent figure in New York avant garde circles. His ambition is to write a symphony.

Own LPs: ESP.

Addr: c/o ESP Disk, 180 Riverside Drive, New York 24, N.Y.

LOWE, MUNDELL,* *guitar, composer;* b. Laurel, Miss., 4/21/22. Played with name bands and jazz combos in '40s; NBC staff musician 1950-58. Later concentrated mainly on writing. Wrote scores for NBC including *Castro's Year of Power* 1960, *The Marriage Racket* '62, and *The Poor People of Mexico* '62; this last won an award. Producer of jingles and underscores for radio and TV commercials. In Dec. '65 Lowe moved to Calif., where he occasionally played guitar with Peggy Lee and others but became almost a full-time writer, notably as regular composer for the ABC-TV series *Love On A Rooftop.*

LPs: *Satan in High Heels,* sound track album (Ch. Parker Records); *After Hours* with Sarah Vaughan (Roul.); *Bittersweet* with Carmen McRae (Focus);

Mood to be Wooed with Sammy Davis Jr. (Reprise).

Addr: 5233 Lemona Ave., Van Nuys, Calif.

LUCRAFT, HOWARD,* *composer, guitar;* b. London, England, 8/16/16. Musician, commentator for BBC. To Calif. 1950. Prod. radio, TV shows. Commissioned to comp., arr. and perform *LA Jazz Suite* for festival at H'wood Bowl, 1960. Comps. and arrs. for Stan Kenton, Anita O'Day, Vic Lewis; syndicated radio backgrounds for commercials. (Some were rec. in England by Ted Heath.) Articles in London *Melody Maker*, *LA Times* etc.

Addr: Box 91, Hollywood 28, Calif.

LYONS, JAMES (JIMMY), *alto saxophone;* b. Jersey City, N.J., 12/1/32. Raised mainly in NYC. In 1941 went to live with his grandfather, who had purchased the restaurant at the Woodside Hotel in Harlem, where Count Basie and many other jazzmen often made their headquarters. Raised in this atmosphere, and frequently visiting the Apollo Theatre and Savoy Ballroom, he became interested in music and was given a saxophone for his 15th birthday. Took a few lessons but was mainly self-taught. To Korea with U.S. Army; after three years in service, returned to New York but made little musical progress until 1960, when he met Cecil Taylor, whose group he joined soon afterward. They worked together at the Five Spot, also on location in Copenhagen.

Lyons says that he refuses to label his music. Though associated with the avant garde, he shows a strong Charlie Parker influence combined with many qualities of the freedom inherent in the new wave. In 1965 he appeared at the Newport and *Down Beat* JFs.

LPs: *Into The Hot* with Gil Evans (Impulse); *Cecil Taylor At The Montmartre Cafe* (Fantasy).

LYTLE, JOHN DILLARD (JOHNNY), *vibes;* b. Springfield, Ohio, 10/13/32. From a musical family; played in father's band at age of 9. Drummer for Ray Charles '50, Jimmy Witherspoon '50, Gene Ammons '53, then switched to vibes. W. Boots Johnson '55-'57. Formed own trio in '57; has toured most of East Coast. Also made several appearances w. Springfield Symphony. Favs: Jackson, Hampton. Own LPs: numerous releases on River., Jazzl.

Addr: 3000 W. State, Springfield, Ohio.

LYTTELTON, HUMPHREY,* *trumpet, leader;* b. Windsor, England, 5/23/21. The former traditionalist trumpeter, first heard in the U.S. in 1959, graduated through the 1950s toward a swing-era style. His group accompanied Buck Clayton at the International Jazz Festival in Manchester, June, 1963. The partnership was so successful that it developed into a regular association. Lyttelton toured Britain and Europe with Clayton in '64, '65 and '66; Britain with singer Joe Turner in May, 1965.

Popular on the continent, Lyttelton worked in Germany and/or Switzerland annually from 1961. He acted as master of ceremonies for BBC *Jazz Club* program from 1952, and for other BBC shows from 1964.

Own LPs on British labels: Society; 77; World Record Club.

Addr: Alyn Close, Barnet Rd., Arkley, Herts, England.

MABERN, HAROLD, *piano;* b. Memphis, Tenn., 3/20/36. Took up music at 16; mainly self-taught. Moved to Chicago in 1954, gigging w. Morris Ellis and other bands until 1958. He then joined a combo led by Walter Perkins known as the MJT Plus Three; the group recorded three albums for Vee Jay. Played New York clubs in 1960. Recorded w. Jimmy Forrest for Delmark. A NYC resident from 1959, Mabern worked for a year w. Lionel Hampton, then joined the Art Farmer-Benny Golson Jazztet, recording for Merc. Later pl. w. Donald Byrd and in Calif. with Miles Davis. Joined J. J. Johnson August 1963 and during the next two years pl. with him in major clubs around the country. Acc. Joe Williams '66. Names Tatum, P. Newborn, Chris Anderson, A. Jamal, Billy Wallace, Bud Powell as influences. LPs w. Hank Mobley, Freddie Hubbard (BN).

MADI, KALIL, *drums;* b. Cleveland, O., 12/13/26. Self-taught. Brother was drummer with local groups. Played in grade and high schools. Worked locally with Caesar Dameron (Tadd Dameron's brother) and Jimmy Hinsley. Came to NYC in late '40s. Worked with Earle Warren, Erskine Hawkins, Cootie Williams, Lucky Thompson. In Philadelphia with Red Garland. In many groups accompanying singers, including Dakota Staton, Carmen McRae, Chris Connor. Later worked with Randy Weston and other modern groups. Joined the Three Sounds 1966. Favs: Jo Jones, Sid Catlett, C. Webb, Z. Singleton, M. Roach, many others.

LPs with Hasaan (Atl.), Three Sounds (Limelight).

MAINI, JOSEPH JR.,* *alto sax, tenor sax;* also *clarinet, flute;* b. Providence, R.I., 2/8/30. Prominent in the late '50s and early '60s in Southern Calif., Maini was frequently heard with Shelly Manne, Gerald Wilson and Terry Gibbs. In March of 1964 he played lead alto w. Louis Bellson's big band at Shelly's Manne Hole in Hollywood.

A few weeks later, in a bizarre shooting accident at a friend's house, Maini placed the muzzle of a revolver to his head and pulled the trigger, shooting himself fatally. He died 5/8/64 in Los Angeles.

Best known as an alto saxophonist, Maini was widely respected in jazz and undoubtedly had great potential when his career was tragically ended.

MAINIERI, MICHAEL JR., *vibes;* b. Bronx, N.Y., 7/24/38. Father in vaudeville, grandfather a guitarist. Stud. vibes at 12; at 14 app. w. own group on Paul Whiteman TV show. As a protege of Buddy Rich, he toured and soloed with Rich's band until 1962, incl. S. America '61 and Asia '62. Won DB New Star Award '61. Was inactive in music due to illness '62, then began to free-lance w. own groups in '63. Played in NY *Daily News* Concert, Madison Square Garden; Stoney-brook Festival, Mike Wallace TV show. '65 formed trio w. Joe Beck, Midge Pike. Mainieri, who plays with a fast, exciting technique, is something of a modern Terry Gibbs. Favs: Milt Jackson, Dave Pike, Gary Burton, Charlie Parker, Debussy. Own LP: Cadet. Others: w. Rich (Merc., Cadet, MGM).

Addr: 21 Morsemere Ave., Yonkers, N.Y.

MAKEBA, MIRIAM, * *singer;* b. Johannesburg, S. Africa, 3/4/32. Member of Xosa tribe. To U.S. 1959 as protegée of Harry Belafonte. Has app. in England, France, Denmark, Italy; sang for Pres. Kennedy at Mad. Sq. Garden birthday party. Invited by Emperor Haile Selassie to sing at OAU Conference in Ethiopia '63; app. before UN Special Committee on Apartheid '64, and before many African heads of state in Ghana Oct. '65.

At leading clubs and concert halls in the U.S., Miss Makeba has revealed a greatly matured style with power, beauty, emotional range, accurate pitch and a unique multilingual repertoire. Though not basically a jazz artist, when she wishes she can outswing almost any singer on the jazz scene.

LPs to early 1966 on RCA. Later LPs on Merc.

Addr: 472 N. Woodlawn, Englewood, N.J.

MANCE, JULIAN C. JR. (JUNIOR), * *piano;* b. Chicago, 10/10/28. The ex-Dizzy Gillespie pianist toured with the Eddie Davis-Johnny Griffin quintet, 1960-61. Formed own trio, spring '61, touring as acc. to Joe Williams August 1962-May 1964. After leaving Williams, continued to tour w. own trio. He also recorded in big-band settings for Capitol LPs, in contexts that did less than justice to his honest blues-rooted style. The latter is more appropriately represented in a trio set, *That's Where It Is* (Cap.). Overseas tour: Sept.-Oct. '62 w. Joe Williams & G. Shearing. Own LPs: River., Cap.

Addr: 94-01 25th Ave., East Elmhurst, Flushing, N.Y.

MANCINI, HENRY (HANK), * *composer, conductor;* b. Cleveland, Ohio, 4/16/24. After playing piano with Tex Beneke 1945-6, free-lanced in Hollywood. Wrote for motion pictures 1951-7 but came to prominence as writer for *Peter Gunn* TV series, in which he set a precedent by using modern jazz backgrounds for a dramatic show. By 1960 Mancini had returned from TV to film work. His scores and recordings during the next few years earned him innumerable awards, among them the following from NARAS: In 1960, *Blues and The Beat* (Best Jazz Performance); *Mr. Lucky* (Best Arrangement). In '61 *Breakfast at Tiffany's* (Best Orchestral Performance and Best Sound Track album) and three awards for the song from that picture, *Moon River* (as Record of the Year, Song of the Year and Best Arrangement). In '63 *The Days of Wine and*

Roses was voted Song of the Year and Record of the Year. In '65 *Pink Panther* and the theme from that film earned him three awards.

In addition, Mancini was voted leader of the mythical all-star band in the annual *Playboy* Jazz Poll 1964, '65 and '66.

Though much of Mancini's work did not attempt to qualify as jazz, occasional albums provided reminders of his skill as a writer for a big, swinging band. Notable among them were *Blues and The Beat, Uniquely Mancini* and *Turtles* (RCA). LPs of Mancini's compositions have also been recorded by Quincy Jones, Sarah Vaughan, Jack Wilson and many other artists.

Addr: 911 Gateway West, Los Angeles, Calif., 90067.

MANCUSO, RONALD BERNARD (GUS), * *baritone horn, bass;* b. Rochester, N.Y., 1933. West Coast innovator on baritone horn. Carl Fontana 1961-'63, own group '64-'65. Some festival, TV appearances. LPs: Fantasy.

Addr: 2216 S. 6th St., Las Vegas, Nev.

MANDEL, JOHN ALFRED (JOHNNY), * *composer;* b. New York City, 11/23/25. Best known for his brilliant underscoring for the 1958 movie *I Want To Live,* Mandel in the 1960s was active in arranging field and songwriting. His movie credits include *The Americanization of Emily* and *Harper.* Composed Academy Award winning song, *The Shadow of Your Smile,* for *The Sandpiper,* '66.

Among his arranging credits on records were *Ring A Ding Ding* for Frank Sinatra, *I Like The Duke I Like The Count* for Mel Torme, *Jo Plus Jazz* for Jo Stafford and the sound track albums of the movies. He also wrote TV underscore music for the *Mr. Roberts* and *Ben Casey* shows, and special arrangements for the Andy Williams show.

Addr: 8552 Appian Way, Los Angeles 46, Calif.

MANGELSDORFF, ALBERT, * *composer, trombone;* b. Frankfurt am Main, Germany, 9/5/28. First heard in U.S. as a member of the Newport International Band in 1958, Mangelsdorff returned to Germany and consolidated his already unique reputation. In 1960 he pl. w. a specially organized group, The European All Stars. During the next five years he played hundreds of concerts with his own group all over Europe, as well as TV shows in Germany, Italy, Yugoslavia and Belgium. In addition, he was commissioned by the German Goethe Institute to play an Asian tour, Jan.-March 1964. Traveling in Turkey, Iraq, Iran, India, South Vietnam, Ceylon, Hong Kong etc., he was impressed by the diversity of musical traditions in these countries and later incorporated in his own work some of the Asiatic ragas; he also recorded a work by Ravi Shankar.

In 1962 John Lewis, who regards Mangelsdorff as the greatest trombonist since J. J. Johnson, recorded an album with him, *Animal Dance* (Atl.). Mangelsdorff can also be heard with his own quintet on *Now, Jazz Ramwong* (Pac. Jazz).

In July 1965 Mangelsdorff appeared with an excellent group at the Newport JF, impressing listeners with his originality of concept and extraordinary facile technique. Joachim E. Berendt, the German jazz critic, who accompanied Mangelsdorff's quintet through Asia, considers him one of the most resourceful and inspiring jazz instrumentalists of the '60s.

Addr: 45 Fichardstr, Frankfurt, Germany.

MANGIONE, CHARLES FRANK (CHUCK), *trumpet, composer;* b. Rochester, N.Y., 11/29/40. Father an avid jazz fan, introduced Chuck to several prominent jazzmen, incl. D. Gillespie, A. Blakey, H. Silver, K. Winding. After hearing him play, Gillespie presented him with a tilted-bell trumpet. Studied at Eastman School of Music. Made recording debut 1960 as protege of Cannonball Adderley. Co-led Jazz Brothers 1960-64 with brother Gap, feat. Jimmy Garrison and Sal Nistico. To New York in '65, played with Winding, M. Ferguson, Blakey. Critics considered him an outstanding soloist. Favs: Gillespie, Miles Davis, Clifford Brown. LPs: River., Jazzland; w. Blakey (Lime.).

Addr: 160 E. Third St., New York 9, N.Y.

MANGIONE, GASPARE CHARLES (GAP), *piano, composer;* b. Rochester N.Y., 7/31/38. Brother of Chuck Mangione (see above). Mainly self-taught until 1961, then stud. w. Geo. Pappa-Stavrou. BA in Mus. and liberal arts, Syracuse U., 1965. Worked way through school playing; Salt City Six 1958-9, then co-led group with Chuck which evolved during 1959-61 into the Jazz Brothers, membership at times incl. Ron Carter, Roy McCurdy, Sal Nistico. House pianist at club near University, '61-2; re-formed Brothers combo '63 and kept group very active until Chuck left for NYC March '65. Formed own trio w. conga, bass; since June '65, also teaching piano in Rochester. Concerts of orig. mus. by the Mangione Bros. were performed by Syracuse Symph., Rochester Phi., Eastman Orch. Most important work is *Amore E Tristezza* pl. at Syr. U. Arts Fest. '62.

LPs: Salt City Six (Roul.); three w. Jazz Bros. on Riverside.

Addr: 5 Norran Drive, Rochester, N.Y.

MANN, HERBIE (Herbert Jay Solomon),* *flute, composer, leader, tenor saxophone;* b. Brooklyn, N.Y., 4/16/30. First prominent in 1953-4 as member of Mat Mathews Quintet. Formed his own Afro-Jazz sextet June '59. Early in 1960 this group, blending jazz and African music, undertook an extensive State Department-ANTA tour of 15 African countries.

In July of 1961 Mann played in Brazil. On returning from this trip he changed instrumentation of his group, replacing one of his drummers with a guitar and adding more lyrical and sensitive arrangements to his repertoire. When the bossa nova craze spread to the U.S. he played many tunes in this idiom.

In 1962 Mann enjoyed a major popular success with a best-selling record, *Comin' Home Baby.* Written by (and featuring) bassist Ben Tucker, it was included in the best selling album *Herbie Mann At the Village Gate.* Mann visited Brazil again in 1962-3, and toured Japan in '64. He continued to expand the scope of his performances by incorporating the ethnic music of many countries.

In 1964 Mann decided to change instrumentation of his combo by adding two trombones and a fluegelhorn, playing arrangements by Oliver Nelson, Johnny Carisi and others. Established by now as the most popular flutist in jazz and winner of many polls, he began doubling on tenor sax, which he had not played in many years.

Mann scored another major commercial success when his group enjoyed a phenomenally enthusiastic reaction at the Newport JF in 1965. The performance was recorded live (see below).

LPs: *Sound of Mann* (Verve); *Brazil, Bossa Nova & Blues* (UA); *The Family of Mann; Right Now; Herbie Mann at the Village Gate; Herbie Mann Returns to the Village Gate; Herbie Mann Live at Newport; Latin Fever; Nirvana* with Bill Evans; *My Kinda Groove; Standing Ovation at Newport; Today* (all Atl.); *Latin Mann* (Col.).

Addr: 300 Central Park West, New York 24, N.Y.

MANNE, SHELDON (SHELLY),* *drums, leader, composer;* b. New York City, 6/11/20. With name bands from 1939. Best known for work with Stan Kenton, Woody Herman in late '40s. Extensive club, TV, movie and recording work in LA from '52. In Nov. 1960 Manne opened his own club in Hollywood, Shelly's Manne Hole. Using local musicians at first, he later enlarged the club and brought in name combos and occasionally big bands. He frequently worked there himself, leading a quintet that often included Conte Candoli, trumpet; Frank Strozier, alto; Russ Freeman, piano; Monty Budwig, bass. He toured Europe in Feb.-Mar. '61 and played concerts in Japan in Feb. '64 in a show featuring four drummers. Manne has also made second career out of breeding show horses.

Although much of his time is devoted to commercial studio work, Manne remains one of the best and most sensitive, adaptable drummers on the West Coast. Own LPs: Cont., Imp., Cap., Contact; *Empathy* w. Bill Evans (Verve). He was also featured on the first Ornette Coleman LP on Cont.

Addr: 18024 Parthenia, Northridge, Calif.

MANONE, JOSEPH (WINGY),* *trumpet, singer;* b. New Orleans, 2/13/04. First prominent through his swing combo recording of *The Isle of Capri* in 1935. Moved from NYC to Calif., made film and radio appearances with Bing Crosby in '40s. Moved to Las Vegas in '54; Florida '55-7. Played at Roundtable NYC '60. In recent years was seen at Newport JF, New York World's Fair, TV tribute to Eddie Condon, and casino dates in Nevada. The original *Isle of Capri* can be heard in

Swing Street (Epic); a new version was heard in *Great Moments in Jazz Recreated at the Newport Jazz Festival* (RCA).

Addr: 3821½ Daisy St., Las Vegas, Nev.

MANTLER, MIKE, *trumpet, composer;* b. Vienna, Austria, 8/10/43. Began playing when 12 years old. Studied at Academy of Music in Vienna. Left for U.S. in fall of 1962 and spent two years in Boston, where he played with pianist Lowell Davidson. Moving to New York in Sept. 1964, he played with Davidson at the Cellar Cafe, worked for six months with Cecil Taylor, including concerts at Judson Hall and Town Hall. Also appeared in concerts with Paul Bley. In July, 1965, as a member of the Jazz Composers' Guild, he joined with Carla Bley in introducing the Jazz Composers' Orchestra at the Newport JF. In Sept. '65 he returned to Europe with Carla Bley, working in Germany and Austria before returning to U.S.

Mantler, whose compositions include *Communications III, IV,* has stated that "music need not be understood intellectually but must be felt emotionally. Innovation is a natural source that can be found in every area of creation, and which must continue to penetrate in our new music."

MARIANO, CHARLES HUGO (CHARLIE),* *alto sax;* b. Boston, Mass., 11/12/23. W. big bands during '50s, incl. S. Kenton, H. Pomeroy, S. Manne. Began to receive recognition as inventive and forcefully emotional soloist beginning with formation of own quartet w. wife, Toshiko Akiyoshi '60. Toured Japan '61 and '63, Europe '64 with quartet, lived in Japan '63-'64. Teaches at Berklee School of Music; also several summer jazz clinics. John S. Wilson, who called his work on Charles Mingus' *Black Saint and the Sinner Lady* "a brilliant combination of authority, virtuosity and inspiration," hails him as a saxophonist of "impassioned drive and emotional power who digs into his lines with perceptive deliberation." Own LP: *A Jazz Portrait* (Regina). Others w. Toshiko (Candid), Mingus (Impulse), Elvin Jones (Impulse), McCoy Tyner (Impulse). Has written many excellent arrs. for Toshiko et al.

Addr: c/o Berklee School of Music, 284 Newbury St., Boston 15, Mass.

MARKEWICH, MAURICE (REESE),* *piano, flute;* b. Brooklyn, N.Y., 8/6/36. Led own groups in New York from 1957 with Nick Brignola, Eddie Khan. Played in Army Reserve Band, received M.S. in social work from Columbia U. Studying medicine with psychiatry as goal. Has written book on harmony. Favs: Bill Evans, Denny Zeitlin, Walter Norris.

Addr: 30 E. 95th St., New York 28, N.Y.

MARSALA, JOSEPH (JOE),* *clarinet;* b. Chicago, Ill., 1/4/07. A greatly underrated clarinetist, Marsala, leader of his own combo from 1936-45, later went into music publishing and record production. Since 1962 he has been producing records for Seeburg Corp.

In June, 1965 he made a brief return to records in *Sweet Lorraine* on Tony Bennett's album *Songs For The Jet Set* (Col.).

Addr: 360 N. Michigan Ave., Chicago, Ill.

MARSALA, MARTY,* *trumpet, drums;* b. Chicago, Ill., 4/2/09. The career of this excellent musician was limited during the 1960s by long periods of serious illness. He led a group at the Club Hangover in San Francisco Feb. to April 1962 and at Jazz Ltd., Chicago, May to July '62.

Addr: 3605 N. Bell Ave., Chicago, Ill.

MARSH, WARNE MARION,* *tenor sax;* b. Los Angeles, Calif., 10/26/27. Met Lennie Tristano while stationed in N.J. w. Army '47. Settled in NYC '48 and began studying and pl. w. him. Worked in music sporadically since early '50s always w. Tristano such as app. at Half Note in NYC in mid-'60s. At his best, a brilliant improviser who has deepened within his own highly personal expression.

MARSHALL, JACK WILTON,* *composer, guitar;* b. El Dorado, Kans., 11/23/21. Marshall in recent years occupied himself not only with playing and writing, but also as producer of albums for Howard Roberts, Jack Sheldon and other jazz artists. He has been associated with many TV series as composer-conductor, has written music for TV commercials, and has given regular monthly jazz concerts at a San Francisco club. He has also written comedy material and magazine articles on subjects other than music.

His most interesting LP was a duo album with Shelly Manne, *Sounds Unheard Of* (Cont.); also arranged *Guitars-Bossa Nova* (Cap.) and *Softly* with Wanda De Sah (Cap.).

Addr: 121 Waziers, Newport Beach, Calif.

MARSHALL, WENDELL,* *bass;* b. St. Louis, Mo., 10/24/20. The former Lionel Hampton and Duke Ellington sideman has taken little part in jazz in recent years, having worked chiefly in the pit bands for such music shows as *A Funny Thing Happened On The Way To The Forum* and *Fiddler On The Roof.*

Addr: 186-01 Hilburn Ave., St. Albans, N.Y.

MARX, WILLIAM WOOLLCOTT (BILL), *composer, piano;* b. Los Angeles, Calif., 1/8/37. Father was the celebrated comedian and harpist Arthur (Harpo) Marx. Studied piano first; then comp. at Juilliard 1955-57. Active mainly in Hollywood leading a trio and writing arrangements for his own and other albums. Artists for whom he has written include Wynton Kelly, Lorez Alexandria, and Peter, Paul and Mary. His trio accompanied Ann Richards on *Live at the Losers* (VJ); two albums with his father for Mercury. Own LPs: *Jazz Kaleidoscope* and *My Son The Folkswinger* (VJ). Has also comp. music for many TV shows and two scores for independent movies.

Favs. include Carl Perkins, Hank Jones; Samuel Barber, Charles Ives, Gershwin, Schoenberg.

Addr: 8448 Ridpath Dr., Hollywood 46, Calif.

MASEKELA, HUGH RAMAPOLO, trumpet, composer; b. Witbank, South Africa, 4/4/39. St. playing in high school at 14 after seeing film *Young Man with a Horn.* Worked w. dance bands and shows. To Britain '59 on scholarship to Guildhall Sch. of Mus. Protege of John Mehegan. To Manhattan Sch. of Mus. '60 on Belafonte Foundation Scholarship. Many appearances, concerts and arrs. for his wife, Miriam Makeba. Formed own group 1964. Began to gain general popularity through MGM records and concerts w. quartet '66.

MATHEWS, MAT, accordion; b. The Hague, Holland, 6/18/24. Although in the early 1950s he was hailed by Ralph Gleason, John S. Wilson and most other leading critics as an outstanding jazz accordionist, Mathews failed to make commercial headway in jazz and receded into the field of pop music. In the mid-1960s, having returned to the Netherlands, he was active as producer-arranger, made occasional solo appearances on TV, and wrote arrangements for films in France and Germany. He also produced and performed for several European record companies.

Addr: Haverkamp 73, The Hague, Holland.

MATHEWS, RONALD ALBERT (RONNIE), piano, composer; b. Brooklyn, New York, 12/2/35. Studied locally in 1946 and again, with Hall Overton, in '54. Graduated from Manhattan School of Music '59. Has worked off and on with Max Roach since 1963, including sound track for Japanese movie '63; *Freedom Now Suite* on educational TV. Fav: Art Tatum. Comps: *Ichi-Bahn, Dorian, Honey Dew, The Thang.*

Own LP: *The Thang* (Pres.); others with Roy Haynes (New Jazz) and *Breaking Point* with Freddie Hubbard (Blue Note). He considers this last the best recorded example of his work.

Addr: 117 St. James Place, Brooklyn 38, N.Y.

MATLOCK, JULIAN CLIFTON (MATTY),* clarinet; b. Paducah, Ky., 4/27/09. Played with Ben Pollack and Bob Crosby bands in '30s. Resident of LA since '43, has broadcast and recorded with Crosby, Red Nichols and many other traditionalist combos. Led own quartet at Page Cavanaugh's, Studio City, summer '61; 14-month engagement at New Frontier in Las Vegas from Dec. '62. Has since led other groups in San Fernando Valley, also rejoined Crosby dates in Lake Tahoe and tour of Orient in '64. In Fla. with Billy Maxted '65; Red Nichols May-July '65; Phil Harris in Las Vegas '65-6.

LPs: *Dixieland Left to Right* (Merc.); *Double Dixie* with Harry James (MGM); *My Wife The Blues Singer* with Beverly Jenkins (Impulse).

Addr: 4431 Simpson Ave., No. Hollywood, Calif.

MATSUMOTO, HIDEHIKO (SLEEPY),* tenor sax, soprano sax, flute; b. Japan 10/12/26. Popular tenor man infl. by G. Ammons, S. Rollins and S. Stitt. App. as musician and/or actor in several films in '50s. In early '60s, under infl. of John Coltrane, he broadened his style and took to doubling on soprano. Led own quartet as supporting act in concerts starring Miles Davis

at World Jazz Festival, touring Japan in summer of '64.

LP w. Toshiko Akiyoshi Mariano, *Jazz in Japan* (VJ).

MATTHEWS, ONZY D. JR., arranger, leader, piano, singer; b. Fort Worth, Tex., 1/15/36. In LA from age of nine. Stud. voice Westlake Coll. of Music, Hollywood, 1952. Organized an 18-piece band which included Dexter Gordon, Sonny Criss and Frank Butler in 1961, and played most jazz and night clubs in LA area, incl. Lighthouse, Renaissance, Cocoanut Grove, Palladium, Summit, Adams West. Recorded w. own band and also arranged and conducted appearances and recordings for Ray Charles, Lou Rawls, Lionel Hampton, Della Reese, Richard "Groove" Holmes. Played dramatic roles on *Kraft Theater,* stage play *The Last Mile.* Favs: John Lewis, Ray Charles, George Shearing; infl. on writing: Ellington, Strayhorn, Mundy. LPs w. own band: *Blue With a Touch of Elegance, Make Someone Happy* (Cap.); w. Rawls (Cap.), Curtis Amy (Palomar). As arranger: w. Holmes (Warner Bros.), Judy Henske (Elek.), *Charles R & B Meets Country & Western* (ABC-Par.).

Addr: 3913 W. 27th St. #2, Los Angeles, Calif.

MATZ, PETER, composer, piano; b. Pittsburgh, Pa., 11/6/28. Stud. flute, reeds in Chicago '42. Piano w. Maynard Ferguson '51. In 1952 started arranging; accompanied and conducted for Kay Thompson. To NYC '54. Became prominent as arranger and pianist with Broadway shows.

Though he has arranged and conducted for many pop artists including Noel Coward, Diahann Carroll, Andy Williams, Perry Como, Matz made his first major national impact as writer for Barbra Streisand from 1962. When required, a jazz feeling has been evident in his writing; his ballad arrangements are among the most colorful and effective in the field of modern vocal accompaniment. Favs: Bill Evans, Tristano, O. Peterson; Fav. writers: Gil Evans, E. Sauter, N. Hefti, H. Mancini.

LPs w. Barbra Streisand (Col.); Carmen McRae (Mainstream); Ruth Brown (Mainstream); Georgia Brown (Cap.).

Addr: 2 W. 67th St., N.Y.C.

MAY, E. WILLIAM (BILLY),* composer; b. Pittsburgh, Pa., 11/10/16. The celebrated arranger of Charlie Barnet's version of *Cherokee* occupied himself chiefly in the 1960s with television and recording work. He was responsible for a swinging instrumental album *Bill's Bag* (Cap., 1962). Arr. for many Reprise LPs incl. Sinatra. TV work for *Naked City* series, jingles for Stan Freberg. Sidelined by serious illness 1963-4, but gradually returned to activity in '65.

Addr: P.O. Box 537, Cathedral City, Calif.

MAY, EARL CHARLES BARRINGTON,* bass; b. New York City, 9/17/27. After four years as leader accompanying singer Gloria Lynne, May left Miss Lynne in 1963 and worked with many other artists in the NYC area. He has frequently worked with other singers, among them Carmen McRae and Sarah Vaughan. LP w. Coltrane (Pres.).

Addr: 41-25 Kissena Blvd., Flushing, N.Y.

McBROWNE, LEONARD LOUIS (LENNY), * *drums;* b. Brooklyn, N.Y., 1/24/33. Worked in early '50s with Pete Brown, Buster Bailey; later, with Paul Bley as part of first mixed trio to play many midwestern schools which were just beginning to desegregate. Led own combo, The Four Souls, 1959-61. Remaining in New York, he worked with Sal Salvador; Chris Connor; Sarah Vaughan; Lambert, Hendricks & Bavan; Carmen McRae. Between 1964 & '66 mainly with Randy Weston, Walter Bishop Jr., Ray Bryant, Teddy Wilson, Toshiko Akiyoshi. Own LPs: World Pacific, River.; others with Randy Weston (Bakton); Paul Bley (GNP); Sonny Stitt (Verve); Fred Katz (Decca); Sal Salvador (Roul.).

Addr: 4 Downing St., Brooklyn, N.Y.

McCANN, LESLIE COLEMAN (LES), *piano, singer, composer;* b. Lexington, Ky., 9/23/35. McCann says: "Almost all my relatives sang in the church choir. When I was six, I had piano for just a few weeks. My teacher died. In high school I played tuba, also drums." After Navy service (won Navy talent contest as singer, 1956), he returned to school. McCann secured his first job at the Purple Onion in Hollywood. Led trio acc. singer Gene McDaniels, 1959; arr. LP for Lewis Sisters (Liberty); cut first LP with own trio, *The Truth* (Pac. Jazz), April 1960, and during the next year or two built a strong following as a purveyor of gospel-influenced "soul music."

McCann's reputation reached international proportions by 1962, when the trio played the Antibes Festival and proved to be the major hit in a show that also included Ray Charles and Count Basie. In 1963, toured Europe w. Zoot Sims and Ch. Byrd.

McCann has been the subject of critical controversy. Ira Gitler, in a one-star review of his initial LP, wrote: "Essentially McCann is working out of a cocktail bag, but he has brought a brand of homogenized funk into the lounge with him. His routines are so contrived that any swinging he does is negated." John Mehegan, on the other hand, once wrote: "I think McCann is an exciting, fresh and honest jazz pianist. He deserves every opportunity to aspire to the piano Valhalla of Waller, Tatum, Powell and Peterson. Part of this opportunity has been denied him by a segment of the critic fraternity in openly accusing him of plagiarism and cynical contrivance."

In addition to many LPs with his trio on Pac. Jazz (and from 1965 on Limelight), McCann rec. as sideman on many Pac. Jazz dates w. Groove Holmes, Clifford Scott, Jazz Crusaders et al., and as a competent singer. Pl. on Stanley Turrentine date for Blue Note.

Films: rec. soundtrack for *The Great Dream* with his trio. Orig. inspired by E. Garner; other favs. O. Peterson, Dwike Mitchell, Ray Bryant. "I have been influenced by life itself and also by the music of the Baptist Church. My ambition is to be the best performer possible in every way I can, mainly to make people happy." McCann's philosophy is reflected in his simple, sometimes blues-rooted but often pretty, ballad-inclined performances.

A talented photographer, McCann has a studio in Hollywood at which he works on album covers and display books for actors and models.

Compositions: *The Truth, Pretty Lady, The Shampoo, It's Way Past Suppertime, The Shout.*

Addr: 6248 Scenic Avenue, Hollywood 28, Calif.

McCLURE, RONALD DIX, *bass;* b. New Haven, Conn., 11/22/41. Accordion at five; piano in school band, bass drum in marching band, then bass, which he stud. w. Joe Iadone. Grad. in '62 from Julius Hartt Cons. in Hartford, Conn. Pl. w. Joe Porcaro, Buddy Rich, off and on w. Maynard Ferguson band, also w. Herbie Mann, Don Friedman. In '65-6 worked often w. Marian McPartland Trio. Replaced Paul Chambers in Wynton Kelly Trio April '66. Miss McPartland wrote in DB: "He has a most unusual technique . . . often uses double-stops, triple-stops, and what sound like quadruple-stops. Such is his ability, he apparently can play anything he hears in his head." LPs w. Ferguson (Roul.).

Addr: 18 West 71st St., New York, N.Y. 10023.

McCOY, FREDERICK ALLAN (FREDDIE), *vibes;* b. New York, N.Y., 11/29/32. Self-taught; played drums before switching to vibes. Worked as a flight instructor before deciding to devote full time to music in 1961. Sideman w. Kenny Burrell, Johnny Smith, Philly Joe Jones, Doug Watkins before forming own group for recording with Prestige. Plays in the modern swing-soul idiom. Fav: Lionel Hampton. Own LPs: *Lonely Avenue, Spider Man* (Pres.).

Addr: 29-16 Humphreys St., East Elmhurst 69, N.Y.

McCRACKEN, ROBERT EDWARD (BOB), * *clarinet, tenor sax;* b. Dallas, Texas, 11/23/04. Prof. from 1921. Worked w. Willard Robison in '27-8; F. Trumbauer, J. Venuti in '30s; B. Goodman, Russ Morgan in '40s; L. Armstrong, '52; later in Cal. w. Kid Ory, Ben Pollack, J. Teagarden. England and Continent w. Ory, Red Allen in '59, then free-lanced in LA, w. own group; also TV work on *The Untouchables* '63-4; club in Palm Springs w. Dave LeWinter, '65; w. Doc Cenardo in El Monte, '66. LP w. Ory (Verve).

Addr: 11021½ Otsego St., North Hollywood, Calif.

McCURDY, ROY WALTER JR., *drums;* b. Rochester, N.Y., 11/28/36. Father, uncles and grandfather were all amateur musicians. Studied at Eastman School from age of ten. In Air Force Band for four years. Joined Mangione Bros. Sextet, playing upstate N.Y. and NYC. Asked by Art Farmer to join Jazztet '61. Mitchell-Ruff Trio '62, B. Timmons '62, Betty Carter '62-'63, S. Rollins '63-'64, C. Adderley from '65. Newport '63 w. Rollins. Toured Europe '62 w. Mitchell-Ruff, Japan w. Rollins '63. Favs: K. Clarke, M. Roach, P. J. Jones,

E. Jones. Plans to return to school to study percussion; would like to do studio work. McCurdy is a dependable, knowledgeable, swinging, modern performer. LPs: w. Mangione Bros. (River.), Farmer-Golson (Merc.), Timmons (River.), Rollins (RCA), Carter (UA); own fav. work on Farmer's *Perception* (Cadet).

Addr: 176 Shelter St., Rochester, N.Y.

McDUFF, BROTHER JACK (Eugene McDuffy), *organ, composer;* also *bass, piano;* b. Champaign, Ill., 9/17/ 26. Self-taught. Later, after becoming a professional, studied at New York Tech. in Cincinnati, Ohio. Own group in Midwest in early '50s. With Porter Kilbert, Eddie Chamblee in Chicago '57; Willis Jackson '57-8. Formed own group October '59. Played at Nice JF, France '64-5; Golden Circle in Stockholm, Sweden March '65. Fav. organist: Jimmy Smith; fav. composers: Tadd Dameron, Horace Silver. His own compositions include *Rock Candy, Sanctified Waltz, Dink's Blues*. Dan Morgenstern, reviewing one of McDuff's albums, wrote: "He is a robust, swinging player, capable of setting and sustaining a rocking groove, but he can also play with surprising delicacy. He can construct agile single-line solos or dig in with all registers wide open, but his sound never becomes cloying or unmusical."

Own LPs: Prestige, Atlantic. LPs w. Roland Kirk, Willis Jackson, Sonny Stitt, Gene Ammons, Bill Jennings, Betty Roche (Prestige).

Addr: 45 W. 132nd St., New York, N.Y.

McFARLAND, GARY, *composer, vibes;* b. Los Angeles, Calif. 10/23/33. McFarland's background is unusual; he is, in Gene Lees' words, an adult prodigy. Until he was 24, he could scarcely read music, though he came from a family in which both parents and three brothers were all musically inclined. The family moved to Grants Pass, Ore., in 1948. McFarland became interested in music while in the Army in Oklahoma, but, he says, had no self-discipline. He briefly tried playing trumpet, trombone and piano, but lost interest. He then took up vibes and started playing in service clubs in 1955.

After brief attendance at two Los Angeles colleges he completed a semester at San Jose C. C. in '57-'58. A flutist, Santiago Gonsalez, praised one of his tunes and encouraged him to study composing. McFarland then obtained a scholarship to Berklee School in Boston, where he spent a semester in '59.

In September 1960 McFarland moved to New York. His first recorded arrangements were *Weep* and *Chuggin'*, pl. by G. Mulligan band on *Concert in Jazz* (Verve), July '61. Also in '61 he wrote his first album for a singer, *All The Sad Young Men* for Anita O'Day, and his first instrumental album as a leader, a jazz version of the score of the Broadway show *How To Succeed in Business Without Really Trying* (Verve). The latter stirred great critical interest and within a year McFarland was established as an important new jazz writer.

His other albums have included a superb set with Bill Evans, strings and woodwinds (Verve); *Big Band Bossa Nova* with Stan Getz (Verve) and *Point of Departure,* with a textet (Impulse). All these were in 1962-3. In October 1964 a John Lewis ensemble recorded an album, *Essence,* comprising six McFarland originals (Atl.). This set showed the great variety of tone colors and textures at McFarland's command, as well as his sense of continuity and great melodic originality.

In February 1964 McFarland wrote a two-act jazz ballet with choreographer Donald McKayle. It was performed at Hunter College in NYC. The following November he recorded a commercial album, *Soft Samba.* Though of minor musical interest, featuring McFarland whistling and humming, it was a commercial success and enabled him to take his own quintet on the road in the summer of 1965. He also led the house orchestra for the first *Down Beat* Jazz Festival in Chicago, July '65.

Among his musical preferences McFarland cites Ellington, Strayhorn, Gil Evans, Ravel, Debussy, A. C. Jobim, and some of Burt Bacharach's movie score writing; favs. on vibes: Gary Burton, Milt Jackson.

By 1966 McFarland had earned the admiration of many fellow writers. His future as a major force in jazz depended on whether he decided to write up to the highest possible standards or restrict himself to simpler material that would have a better chance of commercial success. As an instrumentalist, though not technically formidable, he is a capable and tasteful soloist.

Addr: 244 W. 48th St., New York 36, N.Y.

McGARITY, ROBERT LOUIS (LOU),* *trombone;* also *violin;* b. Athens, Ga., 7/22/17. Played with Benny Goodman, Raymond Scott bands in 1940s. Later entered the New York studio field and did extensive radio, TV and recording, including regular job with group on Arthur Godfrey CBS radio show. Toured Japan with Bob Crosby Oct. '64. Though not often prominent in jazz circles in recent years, McGarity is one of the best soloists in a style reminiscent of Jack Teagarden.

Addr. 322 E. 19 St., New York City 3, N.Y.

McGHEE, ANDY, *tenor sax, flute, clarinet, composer;* b. Wilmington, N.C., 11/3/27. Started in high school band. Attended New England Conservatory in Boston and played local night clubs. After graduating from Conservatory played briefly with Roy Eldridge, 1949. Played with various local groups, then joined Lionel Hampton orchestra in 1957 and remained with the band for six years, touring Europe in '57, '58 and '61; also Far East in '63. From '63 w. Woody Herman.

McGhee names Paul Gonsalves as his most important influence, though he was an admirer of Lucky Thompson, Sonny Rollins and the early John Coltrane. LPs: with Hampton, including his original comp. **and** arr., *McGhee* (Glad-Hamp), also *Golden Vibes* **on** clarinet with Hampton (Col.); several with Herman on Phil., Col.

Addr: 15 Devon St., Roxbury, Mass.

McGHEE, WALTER (BROWNIE), * singer, guitar; b. Knoxville, Tenn., 11/30/15. Continuing his partnership with Sonny Terry which had begun in 1939, McGhee in 1960 toured India for the State Department. The duo also enjoyed great success in England and in Germany 1962-64, and in Australia in 1965. McGhee in 1959 began an intermittent association with Harry Belafonte; toured with the latter's company in 1964-65. Frequent appearances at colleges throughout USA, clubs in Canada, and many engagements at the Ash Grove in LA, where the duo has been very popular since 1958. Sang at Newport Folk Festival 1961 and '62.

McGhee writes 99% of the material he performs. Comps. incl. *My Fault, Walk On, Living With The Blues, Corn Bread Peas,* and *Sporting Life Blues.* TV appearances with Pete Seeger, Belafonte and others.

LPs with Terry: Mercury, VJ, Fantasy, Savoy, Smash, Verve, etc.

Addr: 540 37th St., Oakland, Calif.

McGHEE, HOWARD, * trumpet, composer; b. Tulsa, Okla., 3/6/18. Pl. w. Lionel Hampton, Andy Kirk, Ch. Barnet in early '40s; later with C. Basie, C. Hawkins, JATP, Oscar Pettiford.

After remaining in virtual obscurity during most of the 1950s, McGhee, one of the first major bop trumpeters, returned to prominence in the '60s and was frequently heard in various concert groups organized by George Wein as well as at Wein's Newport JF. He worked in a group featuring J. J. Johnson and Sonny Stitt which toured Europe and played Newport.

As Nat Hentoff observed in 1961, "Howard McGhee is a unique example of a jazzman who has spanned several stylistic eras, adapting himself to each while retaining an intensely personal tone and conception."

Though he organized a 16-piece band in the spring of '66, McGhee's best work on records in recent years features him with small groups.

Own LPs: Cont., UA, Beth. Also heard on *That Newport Jazz* (Col.) and with Joe Williams (RCA); Lorez Alexandria (Cadet). Arrs. for Dakota Staton (UA).

Addr: 106 W. 69th St., New York 23, N.Y.

McGRIFF, JIMMY, organ; b. Phila., Pa., 4/3/36. Father a pianist, brother plays drums. McGriff played bass with several groups in Phila. area before switching to organ, which he learned through studying the fundamentals with Jimmy Smith. Formed own trio and toured, playing many domestic clubs and appearing successfully at Antibes Jazz Festival.

One of the better organists of the post-Jimmy Smith school, McGriff names Smith and Richard "Groove" Holmes among his favs. He says, "What I play isn't really jazz . . . it's sort of in between. Just old time swing with a jazz effect to it." Own LPs: Sue.

McINTOSH, THOMAS S. (TOM), composer, trombone; b. Baltimore, Md., 2/6/27. Stud. voice at Peabody Conserv. '44; trombone in US Army band; later at Juilliard, grad. in '58. Started playing around NYC '56. Worked with James Moody, '59; Art Farmer-Benny Golson Jazztet '60; rejoined Moody in '62 and wrote *Great Day* album for him (Cadet). Wrote *Something Old, Something New* LP for D. Gillespie '63 (Philips). Arr. Wiltwyck Sch. Concert under direction Lionel Hampton, Carnegie Hall, May '64 (60-piece orch.). Writer and soloist from 1964 with New York Jazz Sextet, also in '66 with Mel Lewis-Thad Jones big band. Favs: Lawrence Brown, J. J. Johnson; playing infls.: Gillespie, Miles Davis. Writing infls.: Ellington, J. Lewis, Geo. Russell, Ch. Mingus. McIntosh, one of the most skilled jazz writers to come to prominence in the '60s, says: "Since 1959 my interest in jazz has been secondary to studying and teaching the Bible."

LPs: *The Jazztet and John Lewis* (Cadet); *Cup Bearers* (River.); *New Jazz on Campus* for Paul Winter (Col.); *Running the Gamut, New York Jazz Sextet* (both Scepter). He considers this last to be his best work.

Addr: 200 West 108th St., New York, N.Y.

McINTYRE, KENNETH ARTHUR (KEN), alto sax; also flute, oboe, bass clarinet, bassoon, piano; b. Boston, Mass., 9/7/31. Father was mandolin player. Stud. South End Music School 1940. Worked locally in Richie Lowry Orch., Rodney Smith combo. Played piano while in U.S. Army in Japan 1953. B.M. and M.M. in composition and Cert. in flute from Boston Conserv. of Music. Taught in public schools in NYC as music director and vocal teacher. Led own groups at Storyville, Birdland, Coronet, Five Spot, other clubs. Made record debut in 1960 for Prestige-New Jazz. Other LPs for UA, 1961-2. Soloist at NJF '63; sideman with Composers' Orchestra, NJF '65. In 1965-6 McIntyre was a full-time student at Boston U. of Fine and Applied Arts working toward Doctorate of Mus. Arts Degree. Has also been active in the field of social work.

McIntyre is a highly original and sensitive performer and composer. His infls. are C. Parker, J. Coltrane, O. Coleman and E. Dolphy. Some of his best work both as composer and soloist, feat. unusual construction and time signatures as well as ideas that rarely sound derivative, can be found in the album *'Way, 'Way Out* (UA), also on *Year on the Iron Sheep,* (UA), *Looking Ahead* w. Dolphy (Pres.).

Addr: 334 E. 108th St., New York, N.Y. 10029

McKENNA, DAVID J. (DAVE), * piano; b. Woonsocket, R.I., 5/30/30. Known for his work in the '50s with Woody Herman, Charlie Ventura and Bobby Hackett, McKenna continued to work intermittently with Hackett and has also been heard with the Buddy Morrow band from time to time during the past few years. Own LP: Realm.

Addr: 360 W. 21st St., New York, N.Y. 10011.

McKIBBON, ALFRED BENJAMIN (AL),* *bass; also conga;* b. Chicago, Ill. 1/1/19. Best known through his association with Dizzy Gillespie in 1948-9 and his seven years with George Shearing Quintet in the '50s. After a year and a half with Cal Tjader in '58-9, McKibbon settled in Los Angeles. Free lanced extensively, appearing often with Calvin Jackson Duo, and many record dates with Neal Hefti, Ray Charles, Ernie Freeman. Staff musician at NBC in Burbank, Cal. during '65. LPs w. Tjader (Fant.), Jack Wilson (Atl.), Neal Hefti (Reprise).

Addr: 6904 Woodrow Wilson Dr., Hollywood, Calif.

McKINLEY, RAY,* *drums, singer, leader;* b. Fort Worth, Texas, 6/18/10. After working with Jimmy Dorsey band 1935-9, co-led band with trombonist Will Bradley '39-'42, then led own band '42. Played in Glenn Miller's AAF band, taking over leadership jointly with Jerry Gray after Miller's death. Organized new band in Miller style, sponsored by Miller estate '56; toured Iron Curtain countries '57. Conducted and co-hosted *Glenn Miller Time* on CBS-TV summer '61. Toured Japan Feb.-Mar. '64 and again in April '65, enjoying one of the greatest successes scored by any group in that country. McKinley resigned as leader of the Glenn Miller band 1/5/66 to go into semi-retirement.

LPs: *Borderline* (Savoy); *Authentic Sound; Glenn Miller Time; Miller Sound; New Miller Orch.; On Tour* (all RCA); *Glenn Miller Time; Great Songs of the '60s* (both Epic); *Swinging '30s* (Grand Award).

Addr: 568 Pepper Ridge Road, Stamford, Conn.

McKUSICK, HAROLD WILFRED (HAL),* *saxophones, clarinet, flute, composer;* b. Medford, Mass., 6/1/24. Sideman with name bands in the 1940s and early '50s (Herman, Raeburn, Rich, Thornhill, Lawrence), McKusick became a CBS staff musician in 1958 and has since combined this regular work with considerable free-lance recording activity in NYC.

Own LPs: Beth., Coral, Decca, Prestige, Jubilee.

Addr: 30 East 49th St., New York City, N.Y. 10017.

McLEAN, JOHN LENWOOD (JACKIE),* *alto sax, composer;* b. New York City, 5/17/32. Heard during the 1950s with Charles Mingus, Art Blakey and many other combos in NYC, McLean in 1959 began a two-year run as player and actor in Jack Gelber's play, *The Connection.* In early '60s toured Germany and Belgium with own band, returned to U.S. '63 and played major jazz clubs. In '65 McLean toured Japan with all star group. Has recorded on Prestige and Blue Note. During '60s his style evolved impressively under infl. of Ornette Coleman and the avant garde; also developed as composer.

Own best LPs: *Destination Out, A Fickle Sonance, Let Freedom Ring* (all Blue Note). Many others on Blue Note; earlier LPs on Status, Josie.

Addr: 20 Avenue D, New York City 9, N.Y.

McLEOD, ALICE, *piano;* b. Detroit, Mich., 8/27/37. From a musical family (her half-brother is bassist Ernie Farrow), she stud. w. private teachers. Worked locally w. trio, also gigged w. Terry Pollard. Spent a year on the road with Terry Gibbs Quartet 1961-2. Originally a post-bop pianist who had been strongly under the influence of Bud Powell, she later moved closer to the modal style of McCoy Tyner and in Jan. 1966 replaced Tyner in the John Coltrane combo. Married to Coltrane '66. Harmonically advanced and technically an accomplished musician, she ranks with Toshiko Akiyoshi among the most modern-oriented girl jazz pianists.

McNAIR, HAROLD, *flute, alto sax, tenor sax;* b. Kingston, Jamaica, 5/11/31. Went to Europe '59, pl. in France w. Kenny Clarke, '60-1 own gp. in Eng., then in France w. Quincy Jones. Ret. to Bahamas '62, rec. in Europe '65, then moved to N.Y.C. Warm and fluent flute-player. Own LPs on Rank (U.S.), Island (Brit.) LPs w. Martial Solal (French Barclay), Arne Domnerus (Swedish Philips).

McPARTLAND, JAMES DUGALD (JIMMY),* *cornet;* b. Chicago, Ill., 3/15/07. Member of the original "Austin High School Gang." Played in Ben Pollack band 1927-9, later with Broadway pit bands and touring dance bands. While in service, met and married pianist Marian Page, 1945. Has appeared with her occasionally, also led own Dixieland groups.

In 1965, in addition to co-starring with Marian McPartland at London House and other clubs, he appeared at the DB JF. Joined Tony Parenti at Jimmy Ryan's Club 1965-6. McPartland still plays the instrument given him by Bix Beiderbecke, when he replaced Bix in the Wolverines in 1925. At Condon's '66.

LPs: *Chicago and All That Jazz,* based on TV show (Verve); *Meet Me In Chicago* (Merc.); *Jazz at Carnegie Hall* (Forum); *Music Man Goes Dixieland* (Epic); *That Happy Dixieland* (Camden).

Addr: 41 Webster St., Merrick, L.I., N.Y.

McPARTLAND, MARIAN,* *piano, composer;* b. Windsor, England, 3/20/20. Early experience in pop music. While with USO met Jimmy McPartland, whom she married in Aachen, Germany. After working with him in U.S. '46-'50, formed own trio in '51 and worked frequently at Hickory House, NYC.

Mrs. McPartland has diversified her activities considerably in the 1960s. She wrote the soundtrack for an art film, *Mark,* which won awards at Edinburgh and Venice Festivals. Wrote song *There'll Be Other Times,* recorded by Sarah Vaughan. Her *Twilight World* was featured by Doc Severinsen on the *Tonight* TV show. She toured the country as member of Benny Goodman Sextet, fall '63, playing major concert halls. Worked for a year with British musical revue *The Establishment* at Strollers Club, NYC. Returned to England in '61 and '63 for TV and radio work and in '66 to play Ronnie Scott's Club.

She has been active in radio, as disc jockey on

WBAI; also in journalism, writing features and record reviews for DB.

LPs: *West Side Story; Bossa Nova Plus Soul* (Time); others on Argo, Cap., Savoy, and with her husband on Brunswick and Epic.

Addr: 41 Webster St., Merrick, L.I., N.Y.

McPHERSON, CHARLES, *alto sax;* b. Joplin, Mo., 7/24/39. Family moved to Detroit when he was nine years old. Got an alto when he was 13 and studied w. private teacher for six months. Pl. in band at Northwestern High. Started gigging around Detroit when he was 17 with Barry Harris, Lonnie Hillyer et al. Studied w. Harris. To NYC '59. Through Yusef Lateef joined Charles Mingus and has pl. with the bassist's groups off and on since then incl. app. at MJF '64-5. During the '60s also worked w. Barry Harris at Minton's several times. Formed own group w. Hillyer '66, pl. at Slugs' and a concert at the Harlem YMCA. Movie: sound track for *Night Song.* Orig. infl.: Johnny Hodges, Charlie Parker. McPherson is one of the closest in style to the late Parker but he is no mere imitator. As Ira Gitler has written: "McPherson has really grasped the rhythmic nuances inherent in Parker's phrasing, and his sound is one of the most vital to be heard in some time." Own LPs: Prestige; LPs w. Harris (River.), Mingus (Candid, Mingus), Art Farmer (Scepter).

McRAE, CARMEN,* *singer, piano;* b. New York City, 4/8/22. Band singer in mid-'40s with Benny Carter, Mercer Ellington. Played piano and sang at Minton's Play House. Prominent as solo vocalist from '54; nationally known by late '50s.

As Ralph J. Gleason, one of her foremost advocates, has observed, "Carmen makes lyrics live and throb and breathe with meaning . . . she makes tragedies and celebrations of life out of every song . . . to hear her sing is one of the great experiences in jazz." Around 1960 Miss McRae's work matured conspicuously as she broadened the scope of her material and interpretations. Appearing at night clubs and in concerts and festivals throughout the U.S. and abroad, she enjoyed particular success in the Northern California area and was a regular favorite at the Monterey JF. It was there that she played a role opposite Louis Armstrong in the Dave and Iola Brubeck musical presentation *The Real Ambassadors* in 1962. In '64 she took part in the World JF that toured Japan. On her night club appearances she has been accompanied by the Norman Simmons Trio, though she often replaces Simmons at the piano for part of each set.

LPs: *The Real Ambassadors* (Col.); *Something Wonderful,* with Buddy Bregman orch. (Col.); *Lover Man,* tunes associated with Billie Holiday (Col.); *Take Five* with Dave Brubeck (Col.); *Bittersweet* (Focus); *Live at Sugar Hill* (Time); *Second to None, Haven't We Met?, Woman Talk, Live at the Village Gate* (Mainstream).

Addr: 160 West End Ave., New York 23, N.Y.

McSHANN, JAY (HOOTIE),* *leader, piano;* b. Muskogee, Okla., 1/12/09. The veteran pianist and bandleader, in whose orchestra Charlie Parker played in the late 1930s and early '40s, continued to appear in Kansas City jazz spots. He was heard with a big band on a local TV show, October '63, and at the Kansas City Jazz Festival March '64. At the '65 festival he led a five piece combo. Big band at First Annual Camdenton, Mo. music festival August '65.

Addr: P. O. Box 4841, Kansas City, Mo.

MEHEGAN, JOHN F.,* *piano, teacher, writer;* b. Hartford, Conn., 6/6/20. Has gained most prominence as teacher at Juilliard from 1947 and other schools, and as critic and columnist. Instructor at Columbia Teacher's College '57-'60. Founded own jazz studio NYC '63. Regular critic NY *Herald Tribune* '57-'60. Lecture and concert tour of South Africa '59 was cut short when asked to leave for "fraternizing" with African musicians. In Europe on State Dept. tour '61. Has published numerous instructional books for young people, four volumes on jazz improvisation. Reviews have appeared in *Down Beat, Jazz* and other periodicals, in which Mehegan is outspokenly critical of some aspects of contemporary jazz. Books: *Jazz Improvisation* Vols. I, II et seq. Publ. Watson-Guptill.

Addr: 354 W. 11th St., New York, N.Y.

MELDONIAN, RICHARD A. (DICK),* *alto sax, soprano sax, tenor sax, flute;* b. Providence, R.I., 1/27/30. In late '40s and early '50s pl. w. major jazz bands incl. Shorty Rogers, Charlie Barnet, Stan Kenton. Since 1953 has lived in NYC working as free-lance musician and leader of jazz groups, notably 1964 Newport JF. Sideman on record dates with Benny Goodman, Woody Herman, Elliot Lawrence, Gerry Mulligan, Bill Russo, Neal Hefti, Dave Brubeck. Also jingles, TV shows and concerts. With own quintet, concerts in NYC area. LPs w. Russo (Roul.), Nat Pierce (RCA).

Addr: 200 Franklin St., Haworth, New Jersey.

MELVOIN, MICHAEL (MIKE), *piano, organ;* b. Oshkosh, Wisc., 5/10/37. Started to play at age three in Chicago; studied piano for fifteen years in Milwaukee. B.A. in English, grad. Dartmouth U. '59. Worked in New York area '59-'61, then moved to west coast and was heard with Frank Rosolino and Leroy Vinnegar combos on various gigs 1962-5; Gerald Wilson band '63; Paul Horn Quintet '64; Terry Gibbs combo and band '64-5.

Has also been accompanist and/or musical director for many singers, including Gene McDaniels, with whom he toured New Zealand '64; Marian Montgomery, Fran Jeffries, Joe Williams, Peggy Lee. Names Hank Jones, Monk, Powell, Evans, also Miles Davis and Charlie Parker as influences on his fluent, adaptable modern playing.

LPs with G. McDaniels (Lib.); L. Vinnegar (Contemp. and VJ); P. Lee (Cap.); M. Montgomery (Cap.).

Melvoin, who had his own teen DJ show at age 16

in Milwaukee and subsequently worked various radio jobs in Wisconsin and NYC, says his ambition is to conduct orchestras for TV and records and to play clubs regularly with his own trio.

Addr: 7935 Shadyglade Ave., No. Hollywood, Calif.

MEMPHIS SLIM (Peter Chatman), * *piano, singer, songwriter;* b. Memphis, Tenn. 9/3/15. Worked in Chicago in comparative obscurity for many years but emerged with a reputation of his own after his blues composition *Every Day* was recorded by Joe Williams. During the '60s, along with many other authentic blues artists, he earned greater acceptance both at home and abroad and began to consolidate his already strong reputation in England when he played concerts there in 1961. To Kenneth Allsop his performance was "an exciting glimpse of the submerged seven-eighths of the jazz iceberg—the kind of rolling barrelhouse piano that has been played, irrespective of pop fads, in the colored ghettos for the past 40 years."

Own LPs: Folkways, Pres., Vee, Disc, Chess, UA, Verve.

MENDES, SERGIO, *piano, composer;* b. Niteroi, Brazil, 2/11/41. Stud. at Niteroi Cons. of Mus. 1950. An early participant in the bossa nova movement, he toured several Latin American countries in 1960 and '61, played jazz festivals in France and Italy in '63 and Japan in '64. Settled in U.S., toured w. *Brasil '65* combo. *Brasil '66* toured w. Tijuana Brass show.

Own LPs: Philips, Atl., also with Brasil '65 (Cap. and Atl.); w. Herbie Mann (Atl.), Cannonball Adderley (River.).

Addr: 4463 Laurel Canyon, #20, Studio City, Cal.

MERRILL, HELEN, * *singer;* b. New York City, 7/21/29. Worked in nightclubs from late 1940s, also toured with Earl Hines Sextet in '52. Left for Europe in summer of '59 and since then has spent most of her time touring in various countries, meeting with greater successes in Japan and Italy than she ever enjoyed at home. She is heard on two numbers in the sound track album of a film entitled *Smog* (Italian RCA) not released in the U.S. Also *Helen Merrill in Tokyo* (King-Tokyo); *The Artistry of Helen Merrill* (Mainstream).

MERRITT, JAMES (JYMIE), * *bass;* b. Philadelphia, Pa., 1926. Worked w. Bull Moose Jackson, Chris Powell, B. B. King before going to NYC '57. W. Art Blakey late '58-'63; Max Roach '66. LPs w. Blakey (BN, UA, Imp.).

METTOME, DOUGLAS VOLL (DOUG), * *trumpet;* b. Salt Lake City, Utah, 3/19/25. Played with Billy Eckstine, Herbie Fields, Woody Herman, Tommy Dorsey, Pete Rugolo, Johnny Richards in '40s and '50s. Best known for his work w. Benny Goodman's '49 bop-influenced big band, Mettome was inactive in late '50s for a year due to illness. In early '60s free-lanced in NYC incl. own quartet at Roundtable '63. Returned to Salt Lake City, where he died, 2/17/64, reportedly from an allergic reaction to medication at a local hospital.

MIDDLEBROOKS, WILFRED ROLAND, * *bass, tuba;* b. Chattanooga, Tenn., 7/17/33. Played w. B. Collette, E. Dolphy, E. Fitzgerald in LA during '50s. W. Fitzgerald thru '62, then w. Carol Lawrence, Kay Starr, B. Troup, T. Scott. With Paul Smith from Oct. '63. Toured world w. Fitzgerald and JATP. LPs: w. Smith (Cap., War. Bros.).

Addr: 5519½ Ruthelen St., Los Angeles, Calif.

MIDDLETON, VELMA, * *singer, dancer;* b. St. Louis, Mo., 9/1/17. A featured performer with Louis Armstrong from 1942, Miss Middleton was on tour with the Armstrong show in Africa when she died in Freetown, Sierra Leone, 2/10/61.

MIDNEY, BORIS, *clarinet, saxophones, composer;* b. Moscow, USSR, 10/22/37. Father a conductor and pianist, mother a classical singer. While studying at music institute, formed jazz quartet. Studied classical composition and clarinet; self-taught on sax. Played with many groups in hotels and clubs in USSR, also with state orchestra. Visited Japan; while there defected to West and was brought to NYC. Midney, who had some experience in Moscow composing background music for films, recorded several of his original works with a group formed in New York, the Russian Jazz Quartet, on LP entitled *Happiness* (Impulse). Favs: George Russell, Gil Evans; Ornette Coleman. Chief ambition is to create a new form of music "which could not be described as classical music utilizing jazz forms or vice-versa but will represent a new, distinct dimension."

Addr: 324 East 52nd St., New York, N.Y.

MILES, LIZZIE (Elizabeth Mary Landreaux), * *singer,* b. New Orleans, La., 3/31/1895. A leading blues singer and recording artist from the 1920s, Miss Miles retired from music in 1959. She died in New Orleans 3/17/63.

In later years Miss Miles seemed primarily concerned with performing as an entertainer rather than with maintaining her early reputation as a blues singer in the Bessie Smith tradition. She can be heard, singing in English and Cajun French, on *A Night In Old New Orleans,* with Sharkey's Kings of Dixieland (Cap.).

MILES, LUKE (LONG GONE), *singer;* b. Lachute, La., 5/8/25. As a teenager he was influenced by Sonny Boy Williamson, whom he heard on records, and later by Lightnin' Hopkins, who, he says, "taught me just about everything about blues singing."

After working around home as a cotton picker, Miles left for Houston, Texas in 1952 and it was there, with Hopkins, that he made his professional debut as a singer. Hopkins gave him his nickname. After working around Texas, Miles moved to Los Angeles in May 1961 and sang in a club at Hermosa Beach. In 1964 he made his record debut. Miles sings with much of the power and emotional conviction of the earlier blues artists such as Blind Lemon Jefferson and Leadbelly.

Own LP: *Country Born* (Wor. Pac.).

MILLER, CLARENCE H. (BIG),* *singer, bass;* b. Sioux City, Iowa, 12/18/23. With Jay McShann '49-'54. Scored success at Great South Bay Fest. '57. Took part in Jon Hendricks' *Evolution of the Blues Song* presentation at Monterey JF '60. In '60s pl. clubs in Calif. incl. Shelly's Manne Hole. Living in Honolulu '64-5 as singer and manager of club. App. in *Evolution of the Blues Song,* Vancouver, B.C. '66. LPs: Col., incl. *Evolution of the Blues Song.*

MILLER, EDDIE,* *tenor sax, clarinet;* b. New Orleans, 6/23/11. The veteran tenor saxophonist, a distinguished soloist in the Bob Crosby band of the swing era, continued to make occasional appearances with Crosby in the '60s. Played Japan with Crosby during 1964 Olympics.

Addr: 4904 Ben Ave., No. Hollywood, Calif.

MILLS, JACKIE,* *drums;* b. Brooklyn, N.Y., 3/11/22. A drummer with many leading name bands from 1941 to '58, notably with Harry James several years off and on from 1949, Mills in 1960 began doubling as a recording director. From 1960-65 he served as A&R man for Ava Records. During much of this time he was also active as a song writer and continued to play drums, with Harry Edison combo, at Memory Lane in Los Angeles. From Feb., 1965 he served as west coast director for Mainstream Records.

Addr: 4920 Oak Lane Drive, Encino, Calif.

MINGUS, CHARLES,* *bass, composer, arranger, leader, piano;* b. Nogales, Ariz., 4/22/22. Raised in the Watts district of Los Angeles, Mingus played there and in San Francisco during the '40s before moving to New York in '51. With Red Norvo, Billy Taylor, Charlie Parker, Stan Getz and Art Tatum before establishing himself as a prominent combo leader during the mid-'50s. His first important groups of that period, which often included J. J. Johnson, Kai Winding, John La-Porta, Thad Jones, Teo Macero, Mal Waldron and Teddy Charles, reflected a heavy European influence, especially in experiments with counterpoint and atonality. In 1957 Mingus hired drummer Dannie Richmond, who was to remain with him from that time, and led a group that included Shafi Hadi, Clarence Shaw and Jimmy Knepper. By this time Mingus was involved in an attempt to return blues-shouting elements to instrumental jazz.

Mingus' "Jazz Workshop" bands around '59-'60 (incl. John Handy III, Booker Ervin, and Knepper) appeared regularly around New York. In '60 he led a quartet with Eric Dolphy and Ted Curson for an extended appearance at the NYC Showplace. The music performed at that time was of a much freer nature, and included some near-verbal "conversations" between Mingus and Dolphy. In 1960 he also recorded a date with full orchestra, entitled *Pre-Bird,* for Mercury, consisting of several extended compositions written during the '40s. At the 1960 Newport JF Mingus, after a dispute with the management, led a splinter group in a rival festival at a Newport hotel, Cliff Walk

Manor. This led to the formation of the Jazz Artists Guild, one of Mingus' many attempts to establish a cooperative recording company among musicians.

During the '60s Mingus appeared regularly at the NYC Five Spot, Half Note and other jazz clubs with a large group that included Jerome Richardson, Dick Hafer, Charlie Mariano and Jaki Byard. In '63 that group recorded two albums for Impulse, including *The Black Saint and the Sinner Lady,* one of the outstanding achievements of Mingus' career.

Early in 1964 Mingus took a group that included Dolphy and Clifford Jordan on a tour of Europe that was cut short after friction between Mingus and business agents. At the '64 Monterey JF Mingus performed his extended composition *Meditations on Integration,* which he recorded and released on his own label, Charles Mingus Records, and which was acclaimed as one of the high points of the festival. He continued to play in NYC and in '65 performed there and in Los Angeles with a group that included Julius Watkins, Jimmy Owens, Eddie Preston, Lonnie Hillyer and Charles McPherson.

Mingus' over-all style encompasses the rhythmic call-and-response prayers of the Pentecostal and Holiness Churches, New Orleans collective improvisation, the ensemble sound of the Ellington band, horn solos in the Charlie Parker vein and a strong dose of European impressionism in addition to the constant use of Mingus' own ideas. This eclecticism has been a strong influence on younger musicians and has made Mingus an important link between older, half-forgotten styles and the free improvisation of the '60s.

Mingus was also one of the first bassists to exploit that instrument to its full potential, both as a solo medium and as a backing for hornmen. With a rich tone, a deep understanding of rhythms even in seemingly a-rhythmic pieces and a perpetually amazing technique, Mingus' bass innovations have been copied by literally hundreds of modern bassists.

As a teacher Mingus has had a lasting effect on dozens of the leading musicians of the '60s. A leader who frequently demands the almost-impossible from his men, his recordings reflect musical thought and talent in his soloists that is often absent in their independent efforts. Describing Mingus' leadership, Nat Hentoff said, "Mingus hovers over his men like a brooding Zeus making up the final score card for eternity. His own moods are unpredictable. When he is buoyant, the bandstand becomes a picnic ground in Elysium. When he is angry, the room contracts and is filled with the crackling tension of an impending storm. At those times, Mingus' bass begins to mutter like a thunderbolt on the way. This huge cauldron of emotions at the center of a band can be taxing to a sideman; but if the latter has his own center of emotional and musical gravity, he can survive—and grow."

Mingus has always listed Duke Ellington as one of his primary influences, and has on several occasions recorded excellent interpretations of Ellington's tunes.

He also performed on a trio date with Ellington in '62 for United Artists, released as *Money Jungle.*

Outspoken on musical, racial, social and other matters, Mingus has been one of the musicians to advocate that jazz is basically a Negro music, and has attempted to return it to its folk Negro roots. A volatile personality in both business dealings and racial confrontations has made him the center of several misunderstandings. His long autobiography, *Beneath the Underdog,* was written during the early '60s, but was not published as of 1966.

Mingus' motion picture work included the John Cassavetes picture *Shadows* and a British production, *All Night Long.*

Regardless of the frequent tempests surrounding him, Mingus by 1966 had established himself as one of the great soloists, leaders and innovators of American music. His profound ability to embrace all of the varied concepts of jazz, including deep personal expression and a pervasive feeling of truth in his music, have made him a giant of immeasurable stature.

Several of Mingus' earliest records under his leadership were originally issued on his own label, Debut, and have been reissued by Fantasy on their Debut Series: *Chazz* (6002), *Mingus Quintet w. Max Roach* (6009), *Four Trombones* vols. 1 (6005) and 2 (6010), *Right Now* (6017). Others on the same series in which Mingus participated are Miles Davis *Blue Moods* (6001), Charlie Parker *Jazz at Massey Hall* (6003), *Fabulous Thad Jones* (6004), Oscar Pettiford *My Little Cello* (6008), *Bud Powell Trio* (6006).

Other early works include Charlie Parker *The Happy Bird* (Parker), Red Norvo *Move* (Savoy), *Jay and Kai* (Savoy), Teddy Charles *Evolution* (Pres.) and Mingus' *Jazz Experiment* (Jazztone 1271) and *Jazz Composers' Workshop No. 2* (Savoy 12059).

Those after 1957 are *Tijuana Moods* (RCA 2533); *Mingus Three* (Jub. 1054); *East Coasting,* reissued as *The Genius of Charlie Mingus* (Beth. 6019); *Jazz Symposium* (Beth 6026); *Pithecanthropus Erectus* (Atl. 1237); *Blues and Roots* (Atl. 1305); *Tonight at Noon* (Atl. 1416); *The Clown* (Atl. 1260); *Oh Yeah* (Atl. 1377); *Jazz Portraits,* reissued as *Wonderland* (UA 14005); *Mingus Ah Um* (Col. 1370); *Mingus Dynasty* (Col. 1440); *Pre-Bird,* reissued as *Mingus Revisited* (Limelight 82015); *Mingus Presents Mingus* (Candid 8005); *Mingus* (Candid 8021); *Newport Rebels* (Candid 8022); *Jazz Life* (Candid 8019); Duke Ellington *Money Jungle* (UA 14017); *Town Hall Concert* (UA 15024); *The Black Saint and the Sinner Lady* (Impulse 35); *Mingus Mingus Mingus Mingus Mingus* (Impulse 54); *Mingus Plays Piano* (Impulse 60); *Mingus at Monterey* (Mingus 001 and 002).

MITCHELL, BILLY,* *tenor sax;* b. Kansas City, Mo., 11/3/26. Worked with Lucky Millinder, Gil Fuller, Woody Herman in '40s; various Detroit clubs and Dizzie Gillespie band in mid-'50s. Toured with Count Basie 1957-61, then led own group jointly with trombonist Al Grey; won DB New Star award for small combo in '62. Recorded in Europe in '63 with Clarke-Boland orchestra. Own LPs on Smash; w. Clarke-Boland (Atl.).

Addr: 407 Yale Ave., Rockville Centre, N.Y.

MITCHELL, RICHARD ALLEN (BLUE),* *trumpet;* b. Miami, Fla., 3/13/30. Toured w. Horace Silver Quintet 1958-64. Concert tour in Japan w. Geo. Wein show Jan. '65. Free-lance work in New York, and toured U.S. with own quintet. Own LPs: Riverside (to 1963); since then with Blue Note. LPs w. Silver (Blue Note).

Addr: 25 W. 132nd St., New York City, N.Y.

MITCHELL, DWIKE,* *piano;* b. Jacksonville, Fla., 2/14/30. Pl. w. Lionel Hampton in mid-'50s; then formed unit w. Willie Ruff. As Mitchell-Ruff Duo they gained international publicity as the first modern jazzmen to play in the Soviet Union. In the '60s they app. mainly at their own club in New Haven, Conn., also at Hickory House, NYC. In '66 were official participants in President Johnson's goodwill trip to Mexico City. This marked the first time jazz musicians served in this diplomatic capacity. LPs w. Mitchell-Ruff Trio on Atlantic.

Addr: 1150 Chapel St., New Haven, Conn.

MITCHELL, GROVER, *trombone;* b. Whatley, Alabama, 3/17/30. Started playing at school in Pittsburgh, 1943. Worked with midwestern territory bands out of Indianapolis '47-8. Subbed occasionally with Duke Ellington 1959-61, also worked briefly with Lionel Hampton '60. Joined Count Basie Oct. 1962 and toured internationally with him, including three visits to Europe and one to Japan. Mitchell is a find lead trombonist, not principally known as a jazzman, but he is heard in a solo on the Al Grey album, *Shades of Grey* (Tangerine).

Addr: 1244 Burnett St., Berkeley, Calif.

MITCHELL, KEITH MOORE (RED),* *bass;* also *piano, 'cello, bass guitar;* b. New York City, 9/20/27. Mitchell's association with Hampton Hawes, which began in 1956, continued off and on during the next decade. They worked reg. at Studio Club, Hollywood, 1955-6. Mitchell has also appeared and rec. w. Andre Previn since '56; co-led own group with Harold Land 1961-2. Much studio work, incl. permanent position as 1st bass at MGM. Though most of his time was devoted to commercial work, Mitchell was still rated among Hollywood's top bassists and has been called by John S. Wilson "a tremendously strong guiding force in the rhythm section."

Best LP as bassist: *Hear Ye!* w. Mitchell-Land Quintet (Atl.); as 'cellist, *Rejoice!* w. own combo (Pac. Jazz); as pianist w. the Modest Jazz Trio on *Good Friday Blues* (Pac. Jazz).

Addr: 4803 Cromwell Avenue, Los Angeles 27, Calif.

MITCHELL, GORDON B. (WHITEY),* *bass;* b. Hackensack, N.J., 2/22/32. Brother is Red Mitchell. Played with various swing and mainstream bands, headed own groups in NYC during '50s. Toured w. Benny Goodman summer '63. In Broadway show *Fade Out-Fade In '64-'65, Bell Telephone Hour* TV w. Andre Previn '64, '65. Moved to Los Angeles in '65. Worked in studios as musician, comedy writer. LP w. Red Mitchell and Blue Mitchell (Metro.).

Addr: 4527 Calhoun Ave., Sherman Oaks, Calif.

MOBLEY, HENRY (HANK),* *tenor sax, composer;* b. Eastman, Ga., 7/7/30. Pl. around Newark, N.J. in early '50s when he joined Max Roach; also w. Dizzy Gillespie, Horace Silver, Art Blakey, T. Monk in '50s; Miles Davis in early '60s; own groups and free-lance in mid-'60s. Mobley, in his solid but unspectacular way, has continued to grow both as a saxophone stylist and composer. This is graphically illustrated by a series of excellent LPs rec. for Blue Note. Others LPs w. Davis (Col.), Freddie Roach (BN).

MODERN JAZZ QUARTET.* Instrumental group founded by John Lewis in 1951 and permanently organized from '54. See Lewis, John.

MOER, PAUL,* *piano, composer;* b. Meadville, Pa., 7/22/16. This versatile and facile pianist, whose modern style belies his age, visited Australia with Benny Carter in 1960, and during that year began a valuable association in Hollywood with the Paul Horn Quintet which lasted until 1963. He has also been heard in recent years w. Buddy De Franco and Ruth Price. His compositions inc. *Tall Polynesian* which he rec. w. Horn (HiFiJazz), *Short Politician,* also w. Horn (Col.)

Addr: 9323 Kester Avenue, Van Nuys, Calif.

MOFFETT, CHARLES MACK, *drums, trumpet, orchestra bells, composer, educator;* b. Fort Worth, Tex., 9/11/29. Stud. trumpet, piano privately. Pl. w. r&b combo at age 13; trumpet in high school band. At 19 he was welterweight boxing champion, Pacific Fleet, US Navy. Drums in dance band at college in Austin; BA in music educ. Taught high school in Texas for eight years, leading school band to first place in state festivals. In NYC pl. w. Ornette Coleman '61, S. Rollins '63; music dir. for recreation center on lower East Side. Instructor for Presbyterian Church Drum and Bugle Corps. Toured Europe w. Ornette Coleman from '65-6. Pl. concerts and festivals in France, Germany, Scandinavia, Italy. Comps: *Yelvihs Overture, Komonjet, Adnerb, Last Night and Tomorrow.* One of the most respected drummers in the new wave of the '60s. Film: *Who's Crazy?* with Coleman (Paris, Mar. '66).

LPs w. Coleman (Blue Note, ESP), A. Shepp (Impulse), Chas. Tyler (ESP).

Addr: 65 Pike St., New York, N.Y. 10002.

MOLE, IRVING MILFRED (MIFF),* *trombone;* b. Roosevelt, L.I., N.Y. 3/11/1898. Mole was the first musician ever to achieve international prominence as a jazz trombone soloist. Best known for his work with the Original Memphis Five and with various Red Nichols groups, he later played with Paul Whiteman and Benny Goodman; spent five years in Chicago from 1948-53. During the next few years he became less and less

active as illness limited his work. After it was learned that he had been reduced to working as a street vendor in New York, some friends arranged for a benefit to be held for him, but the gesture came too late. Mole suffered a stroke and died in NYC, 4/29/61.

Tommy Dorsey once called Miff Mole the Babe Ruth of the trombone. Certainly he was the first jazzman to draw attention to the instrument's potential as a medium for melodic playing at a time when it was largely limited to rhythmic punctuations, glissandi and crude obbligatos. His role in the history of jazz is at least as important as that of better-known artists who came to prominence a few years later, notably Jack Teagarden, J. C. Higginbotham and Dorsey.

MONCUR, GRACHAN III, *trombone, composer;* b. New York City, 1937. His father was a bandleader in Newark, also played bass with The Savoy Sultans. Grachan III was raised in NYC and Newark, then attended Laurinburg Institute in Laurinburg, No. Carolina, well known for its music department (Dizzy Gillespie had studied there). After graduating from school Moncur worked in Nat Phipps' band in Newark, of which Wayne Shorter was a member. He extended his studies by attending Manhattan School of Music and Juilliard, then spent 2½ years with the Ray Charles band. After a period with the Art Farmer-Benny Golson Jazztet, he returned to the Ray Charles band for six months, then settled in NYC, working with Jackie McLean, Herbie Hancock and others. App. in Broadway show, *Blues for Mr. Charlie.*

Moncur was the first outstanding young trombonist to be identified with the new music of the 1960s. Both as soloist and composer he has shown great promise. Own LPs on Blue Note including *Evolution, Some Other Stuff;* also LPs w. McLean (BN).

Addr. 117 So. Elliott Pl., Brooklyn 17, New York.

MONK, THELONIOUS SPHERE,* *piano, composer;* b. Rocky Mount, N.C. 10/10/20. First important at Minton's, Monroe's Uptown House and other Harlem clubs in early '40s as an innovator of the new jazz that was to be called bebop. Led his own small groups from the mid-'40s but did not work regularly until he began to receive due acclaim in the mid and late '50s. In the 60's he has led a quartet featuring Charlie Rouse, tenor sax, in clubs, concerts and major festivals all over the world. Monk also appeared with a large ensemble interpreting his compositions at Town Hall '59; Philharmonic Hall '63; Carnegie Hall '64.

Some musicians, notably pianists such as Oscar Peterson, have criticized Monk's technique and touch while acknowledging his value as a composer. On the other hand, pianist Bill Evans has written of him: "Make no mistake. This man knows exactly what he is doing in a theoretical way—organized, more than likely in a personal terminology, but strongly organized nevertheless. We can be further grateful to him for combining aptitude, insight, drive, compassion, fantasy, and whatever makes the total artist, and we should also be grateful for such direct speech in an age of insurmountable conformist pressures."

Own LPs on Columbia: *Monk's Dream* (8765); *Criss-Cross* (8838); *Big Band & Quartet in Concert* (8964); *Miles & Monk at Newport* (8978); *It's Monk's Time* (8984); *Monk* (9091); *Solo Monk* (9149); *Monk Misterioso* (9216). LPs on Riverside: *Monk & Coltrane* (9490); *Monk in France* (9491).

Addr: 243 W. 63rd St., New York 23, N.Y.

MONTGOMERY, CHARLES F. (BUDDY),* *piano, vibes, composer;* b. Indianapolis, 1/30/30. Brother of Wes and Monk (see below). Worked with Slide Hampton in local club. Toured with the Mastersounds 1957-60, spent several months with M. Davis Quintet. Formed Montgomery Brothers Quartet in SF; played many clubs, Monterey JF '61, rec. w. George Shearing '62. For next few years pl. cocktail piano jobs, acc. singers, and early in '65 wrote material for a short-lived re-organization of the original Mastersounds.

LPs: The Mastersounds (Fant.); Montgomery Brothers (Pac. Jazz, Riverside, Fant.); George Shearing and Montgomery Bros. (Jazzland), Johnny Griffin (Riv.)

MONTGOMERY, MARIAN (Marian M. Runnels Holloway), *singer;* b. Natchez, Miss., 11/17/34. Self-taught; debut on television show in Atlanta, Ga. Played Chicago clubs under name of Pepi Runnels. First prominent in 1963, when she signed a Capitol Records contract; appeared at numerous clubs throughout U.S. In 1965 she visited England, where she met and married pianist-arranger Laurence Holloway. Has since divided her time between England and U.S., taking part in BBC shows, etc. A very capable singer with a distinctive jazz timbre, sensitive phrasing and fine projection. Her favs. and influences: C. McRae, Peggy Lee, Ray Charles, Joe Williams, et al. LPs: Cap.

Addr: c/o L. Holloway, 36 Grosvenor St., London W1, England.

MONTGOMERY, WILLIAM HOWARD (MONK),* *bass;* b. Indianapolis, Ind., 10/10/21. First prominent as a member of the Mastersounds, a group that made its debut in Seattle in 1957 and remained together until Jan. 1960. After the dissolution of this group Montgomery, who doubles on Fender electric bass and regular bass, formed a combo with his brothers Buddy and Wes. He later worked with various small groups in LA and SF. In April 1965 the Mastersounds were reorganized in Seattle, but the reunion did not last long. Montgomery worked in LA with Jack Wilson Quartet in late '65. Early in '66 he became a member of the Cal Tjader Quintet.

LPs: See Montgomery, Buddy.

MONTGOMERY, JOHN LESLIE (WES),* *guitar;* b. Indianapolis, Ind., 3/6/25. Came to prominence 1958-9 as a member of the Mastersounds. Worked with brothers Buddy and Monk, then with trio feat. organ and drums. Teamed up with the Wynton Kelly Trio for nightclub and concert work 1965-6. Nominated for two Grammy awards by NARAS '65; voted top jazz

guitarist by fellow musicians in *Playboy* "All Stars' All Stars" jazz poll for five successive years. Has appeared at concerts in San Remo, Brussels, Lugano, Madrid and London.

Montgomery, who does not read music, is a stunning, self-taught musician whose sense of swing and improvisation have been excellently presented in recent LPs on Verve with orchestral settings. A number of earlier LPs, some of them with his brothers Monk and Buddy, are on Riverside.

Addr: c/o Verve Records, 1540 Broadway, New York 36, N.Y.

MOODY, JAMES,* *alto and tenor sax, flute, composer;* b. Savannah, Ga., 2/26/25. First prominent with D. Gillespie in '47. Gained popular recognition through his own record of *I'm In The Mood for Love*. He led a small group off and on for some years, also for a while in 1962 joined forces with Gene Ammons and Sonny Stitt in a "Battle of the Saxophones" group. Not long afterward he rejoined Gillespie and impressed listeners throughout the U.S. and on overseas tours with his exceptional fluency as a soloist on flute and saxophones.

Own LPs: Cadet, Scepter, Pres.; LPs with Gillespie (Philips, Limelight).

Addr: 61-65 97th St., Forest Hills, N.Y.

MOONEY, JOE,* *singer, Hammond organ, accordion, piano;* b. New Jersey, 1911. Wrote many vocal arrangements in '30s. Took up accordion '35. Enjoyed brief surge of popularity in jazz circles in mid-'40s leading his own quartet. Later played Hammond organ and worked in nightclubs in NYC and Florida.

After he had been absent from the recording studios for some years, a company of Mooney's admirers was formed to back the production of an album, which he recorded in July 1963. During the next two years he worked at a series of New York clubs, appeared in concerts with Stan Getz, wrote and played radio and TV commercials, and appeared at the New York World's Fair. In 1966 he returned to Florida to work at Julius La Rosa's club.

Mooney's quiet, gentle style, both instrumentally and vocally, is well represented in his Columbia LPs: *The Greatness of Joe Mooney* and *The Happiness of Joe Mooney*.

Addr: 12801 N.W. First Ave., Miami, 68, Fla.

MOORE, DUDLEY, *piano;* b. England, 4/19/35. Pl. w. Vic Lewis '58-9, Johnny Dankworth '59-'60. Led own trio since '61. A star of *Beyond the Fringe*, which opened in London '61, and ran on Broadway '62-4. Has had TV comedy series w. Peter Cook since ret. to England. Comp. background scores for film *The Most*, several plays at the Royal Court Theatre (London), six ballets, and documentaries and TV plays. Fluent pianist infl. by Peterson, Garner. Comedy LPs are *Beyond the Fringe* on Dec., and own on Brit. Parlophone. Trio LPs on Atl., Brit. Dec.

Addr: 102 Cheyne Walk, London S.W.10., England.

MOORE, RUSSELL (BIG CHIEF),* *trombone;* b. Komatke, Ariz., 8/13/13. Played with Harlan Leonard, Noble Sissle and other bands in '40s, including Louis Armstrong big band '43-5.

In 1964 Moore rejoined Armstrong, played with his combo for the next year and visited Bermuda, Ontario, New Zealand, Australia, Japan, Formosa, Okinawa, India, Iceland, Nova Scotia, Virgin Islands. A member of the Pima tribe, he participated in the National Congress of American Indians, Washington, D.C. and the American Indian Festival in Boston in 1965.

LP: *Hello Dolly!* w. Armstrong (Kapp).

Addr: 32-37 71st St., East Elmhurst, N.Y. 11370.

MOORE, WILLIAM JR. (BILLY),* *composer, piano;* b. Parkersburg, W. Va., 1916. In 1960 the brilliant ex-Lunceford arranger ended his seven years on tour as pianist-arranger with the Peters Sisters. He lived in Berlin for 3½ years, 1960-63, as staff arranger for Berliner Rundfunk Radio. Joined Delta Rhythm Boys January, 1964 as pianist-arranger and toured with them throughout Europe '64-'66.

Addr: 20A-Amerikavej, Copenhagen V, Denmark.

MOORE, MILTON A. (BREW),* *tenor sax;* b. Indianola, Miss., 3/26/24. In NYC in '40s, pl. w. C. Thornhill, G. Mulligan. Clubs in San Francisco '55-60. To Europe, '61; 6 mos. w. K. Clarke at Blue Note, Paris; most of '62 at Jazzhus Montmartre, Copenhagen, also clubs in Sweden, Norway, Germany. Back to SF, also acc. Buddy Greco in Reno, '64. Returned to Copenhagen Mar. '65; clubs throughout Scandinavia, Germany, Poland. Several TV shows; working on weekly series *Weekend '66* in mid-'66. LPs: Debut, Fantasy. Several w. Cal Tjader (Fant.).

Addr: Prinsessegade 52, Copenhagen K, Denmark.

MOORE, MELVIN (MEL), *trumpet;* also *violin;* b. Chicago, Ill., 6/15/23. Professional debut w. Jimmie Lunceford band. After touring with Lunceford 1943-1946, he spent a year with Lucky Millinder, and was with Duke Ellington briefly in 1948 and 1950. Various free-lance jobs, rock 'n' roll dates, etc.; returned to jazz prominence at the Monterey Festivals in 1964, with Charles Mingus and Thelonious Monk, and '65 with Gil Fuller.

LPs w. Lunceford, (Decca), Gerald Wilson, Gil Fuller (World Pacific).

Addr: 4045 W. 28th St., Los Angeles, Calif.

MOORE, OSCAR FRED,* *guitar;* b. Austin, Texas, 12/25/16. As a member of the original Nat King Cole Trio from 1937-47, he was one of the best known and most talented exponents of modern jazz guitar, harmonically ahead of his time. Since then he has worked sporadically in Los Angeles. After a long absence from records he returned with an album dedicated to Nat Cole, released in 1966 on Surrey. Comps: *Tell Me You'll Wait For Me, Beautiful Moons Ago.*

Addr: 7641 Beck Ave., No. Hollywood, Calif.

MOORE, PHIL III (George Philip Moore), *piano, composer;* b. 6/8/39. Father, Phil Moore Jr., is the celebrated composer and vocal coach. Studied with mother in San Francisco from '45. While attending Berklee School, led own group on Boston TV show. Began working with Los Angeles combos in early '60s and with Gerald Wilson band '65-6. Has also served as musical director for singer Gene McDaniels. Favs: Herbie Hancock, Andrew Hill. LPs with Gerald Wilson (Pac. Jazz).

Addr: 1250 So. Arlington Ave., Los Angeles, Calif.

MORELLO, JOSEPH A. (JOE),* *drums;* b. Springfield, Mass., 7/17/28. Worked with Stan Kenton, Marian McPartland. Joined Dave Brubeck Quartet 1956. Became one of the most respected and inventive percussionists in modern jazz history. For details of his work with the Quartet, see Brubeck, Dave. Morello won the DB Readers' Poll 1962, '63 and '64 as the most popular jazz drummer.

Own LP: RCA. LPs with Brubeck (Col.).

Addr: 14 Marshall St., Irvington 11, N.J.

MORGAN, HAROLD LANSFORD (LANNY), *alto sax;* also *flute, clarinet;* b. Des Moines, Iowa, 3/30/34. Father played alto w. own band, Ted Weems; mother a singer. Studied violin from age of six. First important gig was in award-winning LA City College Stage Band '53; then w. Charlie Barnet and other bands incl. S. Zentner, T. Alexander, T. Gibbs, B. Florence, K. Hanna, F. Carle, E. Grady. Joined Maynard Ferguson 1960. In '65 formed own quintet at Cork & Bib, Westbury, N.Y. Toured Germany and Low Countries w. US Army jazz show '57-'58, Sweden w. Ferguson '62. W. Ferguson at Newport '60, '61, '63, Ohio Valley JF '63. Favs: Parker, Mariano, Woods, Adderley, Pepper, Konitz. Major infl: Coltrane. Hopes to record own group. LPs: w. Ferguson (Roul., Cameo, Main.), Alexander (Lib.), Zentner (Lib.), R. De Michel (Chall.), J. Witherspoon (Reprise).

Addr: 10 E. Garfield St., Bayshore, N.Y.

MORGAN, LEE,* *trumpet, composer;* b. Philadelphia, Pa., 7/10/38. Toured with Dizzy Gillespie 1956-8; Art Blakey Jazz Messengers '58-'61, then pl. w. Jimmy Heath and other small groups, mainly in Philadelphia.

Back in NYC in summer of '63, Morgan resumed recording as a leader for Blue Note. He was again on tour with the Blakey combo in 1964-5. During this time his Blue Note album and its title number, a blues called *The Sidewinder*, established him as a hit composer and reached the best seller lists. It later was used as a background for a TV commercial. Morgan in recent years developed an attractive tone and his style was rounded out from the synthesis of early influences (Clifford Brown, D. Gillespie, F. Navarro). His other compositions include *Desert Moonlight, Totem Pole* and *Hocus-Pocus.* Own LPs: Blue Note, Jazzl., VJ. LPs w. Blakey (Blue Note, Limelight); w. G. Moncur, H. Mobley (BN).

Addr: 372 Central Park West, New York, N.Y. 10025.

MORR, SKIP (Charles Wm. Coolidge),* *trombone; also drums;* b. Chicago, Ill., 3/28/12. Heard with several popular dance bands in the 1930s and in the Hollywood studios from 1942, Morr moved to San Francisco in the 1950s, working there with Marty Marsala, Joe Sullivan, Muggsy Spanier. He died in Ross, Calif. in Dec. 1962.

MORRIS, MARLOWE,* *organ, piano, composer;* b. Bronx, N.Y., 5/16/15. Early experience in 1940s with Coleman Hawkins, Sid Catlett and many other small groups as pianist. Later took up Hammond organ.

In 1962 Morris signed with Columbia Records and made an album entitled *Play The Thing,* which in '63 was awarded the Grand Prix du Disque from the Hot Club of France. He has continued to play at various clubs incl. the Showcase, Shalimar and Bourbon Street West in NYC, Tic Toc in Boston, Little Belmont in Atlantic City, etc. Engaged in writing music and instructing, 1966.

Addr: c/o Lee, 238 W. 138th St., New York, N.Y.

MOST, ABRAHAM (ABE),* *clarinet, alto sax, flute;* b. New York, N.Y., 2/27/20. An LA studio musician and occasional leader from 1950, Most continued to be active in film and TV work. On regular staff at 20th Century Fox; also *Dick Van Dyke, Gomer Pyle, Get Smart, Peyton Place, Long Hot Summer* TV shows. Played in film *Mirage* w. Quincy Jones. Studied counterpoint and composition from '62; plans to expand into writing for films. LPs: w. Glen Gray (Cap.).

Addr: 17030 Otsego St., Encino, Calif.

MOST, SAMUEL (SAM),* *clarinet, alto sax, flute;* b. Atlantic City, N.J., 12/16/30. Brother is Abe Most. One of the earliest jazz flutists, he pl. with M. Mathews, T. Wilson and T. Charles in the '50s. In '59-61 he was with B. Rich, touring the Far East under State Department auspices. Also played with Louis Bellson's band in LA and Las Vegas and led own quartet at Shelly's Manne Hole in Hollywood. From 1963-6 he was a member of Red Norvo's group, playing mainly alto flute and working most frequently at the Sands in Las Vegas.

LPs with Buddy Rich (Cadet).

Addr: 17030 Otsego St., Encino, Calif.

MOTEN, CLARENCE LEMONT (BENNY),* *bass;* b. New York City 11/30/16. After working with Dakota Staton 1961-63 and free-lancing in NYC, Moten returned to Red Allen's combo in 1964.

Addr: 208-03 47th Ave., Bayside, 11361, N.Y.

MOTIAN, STEPHEN PAUL,* *drums;* also *guitar;* b. Providence, R.I., 3/25/31. After discharge from service in '54 came to NYC and worked w. George Wallington, Oscar Pettiford, Lennie Tristano, and Al Cohn-Zoot Sims in '50s. Joined Bill Evans '59 and remained w. the pianist's trio into '63. W. Paul Bley '64; free-lanced in NYC '65-6. Also pl. a month in Hawaii '65. LPs w. Evans (River.), Mose Allison (Atl.), Joe Castro (Clover).

Addr: 14 West 71st St., New York 23, N.Y.

MOULE, KEN, *arranger, composer, piano;* b. Barking, Essex, England, 6/26/25. Toured and rec. w. own Seven '54-6. Arr. for Ted Heath '56-9, freelance arr. since. Arr. and cond. Lionel Bart's *Twang* '65. Own LPs: Brit. Decca.

Addr: 41 Ewhurst Ave., Sanderstead, Surrey, England.

MULLIGAN, GERALD JOSEPH (GERRY or JERU),* *baritone sax, composer, piano;* b. New York City, 4/6/27. First prominent with Gene Krupa band '46-7 and with Miles Davis band (mainly on records) '48-'50. Best known for the pianoless quartet he organized in Calif. 1952. He has since led many similar small groups.

In the 1960s Mulligan alternated between leading a 13-piece band, which he took on a European tour in 1960, and a variety of small combos. He toured Japan in 1964. In '66 he organized a new group featuring piano, guitar, bass and drums.

Though he has been well known as a composer and arranger since 1947, when his *Disc Jockey Jump* was recorded by Krupa, Mulligan has been virtually inactive as an arranger for several years, preferring to leave the orchestration of his works to others. He has continued, however, to make valuable contributions as a composer. In 1966 he collaborated with Bill Holman on *Music For Baritone Saxophone and Orchestra,* which he introduced as featured soloist with the LA Neophonic Orch. Mulligan was married in 1965 to actress Sandy Dennis.

Deservedly, Mulligan has retained the esteem of jazz enthusiasts everywhere as an instrumentalist who played a vital part in the evolution of modern jazz, notably in the phase represented by the Miles Davis nonet records, and later by demonstrating the advantages inherent in freeing the rhythm section of the piano. Nevertheless, he has retained a casual pleasure in playing in any context and has frequently appeared at jazz festivals during the 1960s working with Dixieland, swing and bop groups, sitting in with big bands, and generally showing a lust for playing and a rare enthusiasm and communication with his audiences.

Mulligan has been an annual winner of the *DB* and *Playboy* polls on baritone sax, and of countless other polls. Pl. clarinet occasionally '65-6.

Outstanding LPs: *Mulligan Meets Johnny Hodges* and several featuring his 13-piece band (Verve); *Two Of A Mind* with Paul Desmond (RCA); *Night Lights* with Art Farmer, Bob Brookmeyer (Philips); all 1965-6 LPs on Limelight. Early LPs by Quartet with Chet Baker, etc. are on Pac. Jazz.

Addr: c/o Pryor, 640 5th Ave., New York 19, N.Y.

MURANYI, JOSEPH PAUL (JOE),* *clarinet;* b. Martins Ferry, Ohio, 1/14/28. After free-lancing with various traditional groups in N.Y. (among them Conrad Janis, Red Allen and Max Kaminsky at the Central Plaza) Muranyi played with the groups of Yank Lawson, Bobby Hackett, Jimmy McPartland and Eddie Condon as well as gigging with various groups of his own. From 1963 he was leader of a commercially successful traditionalist group known as the Village Stompers. Though of limited musical sophistication the Stompers played to enthusiastic audiences throughout the U.S. and did particularly well in Japan in 1964.

Addr: 643 Hudson St., New York 10014, N.Y.

MURPHY, MARK HOWE, *singer;* also *piano;* b. Syracuse, N.Y., 3/14/32. Entire family musical. Studied piano at age of seven, played and sang w. older brother's dance band. Began extensive touring and recording in U.S. during late '50s, incl. NYC Village Gate and Village Vanguard. Appeared on Steve Allen's *Jazz Scene USA, Tonight,* other TV shows. At Newport JF '62, Ohio Valley JF '63. In Europe during early and mid-'60s made numerous TV, radio and personal appearances in Britain, Scandinavia, the Netherlands and Yugoslavia, and placed second in the *Melody Maker* poll for male vocalists '65. Although not primarily a jazz singer, Murphy has gained considerable popularity with the jazz audience. Gene Lees said of him, "More and more Murphy is being recognized as a genuinely original performer." Favs: Lee Wiley, Peggy Lee, Lou Rawls, Matt Monroe et al. LPs: Decca, Cap., Fontana, River. incl. own fav. *That's How I Love the Blues* (River.).

Addr: c/o O'Sullivan, 40 Cornwall Gardens, London S.W.7, England.

MURPHY, LYLE (SPUD),* *composer, saxes;* b. Salt Lake City, Utah, 8/19/08. Murphy's most important work has been writing, editing and teaching. He is the author of a 12-volume text on composing and arranging. He has written the music scores for two pictures, *The Tony Fontane Story* and *God's Country.* The former won an award in 1963 for best movie score for a film with a religious background. In June, 1965 Murphy was elected president of Amer. Soc. of Mus. Arrs.

Own LPs: GNP, Decca, Contemp., Liberty. Many jazz and modern classical works as composer-conductor for RCA and others.

Addr: 1837 Whitley, Hollywood, Calif.

MURPHY, MELVIN E. (TURK),* *trombone, composer, leader;* b. Palermo, Calif., 12/16/15. In Sept. 1960 Murphy established his own nightclub, Earthquake McGoon's, in partnership with Peter Clute, in San Francisco. He worked there regularly during the next six years and continued to enjoy a strong following among lovers of the revivalist brand of traditional jazz. Compositions: *Something for Annie, Ballad of Marie Brizzard.* Recorded portion of sound track for Columbia Pictures *The Interns;* appeared in *Good Neighbor Sam* for Columbia Pictures. Played MJF Sept. 1963; other appearances at Disneyland, Ed Sullivan TV Show, etc. LP: *Let The Good Times Roll* (RCA).

Addr: 729 Chestnut St., San Francisco, Calif.

MURRAY, JAMES ARTHUR (SUNNY), *drums;* b. Philadelphia, Pa., 9/21/37. Began studying with brother at age nine. Moved to New York 1957. After working with traditional jazz artists such as Willie The Lion Smith and Red Allen, began a long association with Cecil Taylor. During the 1960s he collaborated with many artists of the new generation, among them Ornette Coleman, Don Cherry, Archie Shepp, Roswell Rudd, Gary Peacock, Albert Ayler. One of the rising drummers of the new school, he has stated that one of his main ambitions is to perform solo, "on an instrument I will build myself, with a natural sound."

Own LP: Debut; other LPs w. Albert Ayler (ESP), Gil Evans (Impulse), Cecil Taylor (Fantasy), Archie Shepp (Savoy).

MUSSO, VIDO WILLIAM,* *tenor sax;* b. Carrini, Sicily, 1/16/13. After free-lancing for several years in California, leading his own group, the former Goodman and Kenton tenor star took up residence in Las Vegas in 1957 and has worked there regularly in lounges. Featured at Sands Hotel 1962-6.

Addr: 3355 Natahan Way, Las Vegas, Nevada.

MUTCHLER, RALPH D., *educator, arranger, saxes, clarinet, piano;* b. 11/20/29. BS No. Dakota State U., grad. U.S. Naval School of Music; BM and MM Northwestern U.

Active as arranger for various Chicago and road bands; also wrote for Willis Conover's "The Orchestra" in 1953 in Washington, D.C. In recent years has been head of music department at Olympic College, Bremerton, Wash., and has taught at summer Jazz Clinics for National Stage Band Camps.

Favs. and infls: Joe Theimer (director of The Orchestra), Dick Marx, Bill Holman, Dave Pell. Fav. own comp: *A La Mode* recorded by Art Van Damme (Col.).

Addr: Dept. of Music, Olympic College, Bremerton, Wash.

NANCE, WILLIS (RAY),* *cornet, violin, singer;* b. Chicago, Ill., 12/10/13. Played with Earl Hines, Horace Henderson in late '30s. Joined Duke Ellington 1940. Left in '44 but returned after less than a year and remained until 1963. In '64 and '65 he played with Paul Lavalle's orchestra at the New York World's Fair. He has also rejoined Ellington's band several times for brief periods. During the years with Ellington he lent a uniquely personal touch with his swinging violin technique, highly individual trumpet sound (he later switched to cornet) and humorous contributions as dancer and singer. Recent solos of interest have included the following: On cornet, *Angu* in *Afro Bossa, Sleepy Time Down South* in *Will Big Bands Ever Come Back?* and *Harlem* in *The Symphonic Ellington.* On violin, *Sempre Amore* in *Afro Bossa, Artistry in Rhythm* and *Woodchoppers' Ball* in *Will Big Bands Ever Come Back?, Fiddler on The Diddle* in *Virgin*

Islands Concert and *Night Creature* in *The Symphonic Ellington* (all Reprise); also feat. w. Abdul-Malik (Status).

NANTON, MORRIS P.,* *piano;* b. Perth Amboy, N.J., 9/28/29. Continued to work clubs with own trio in New Jersey, and also played numerous college concerts. LPs: Pres.

Addr: 219 Grant St., Perth Amboy, N.J.

NAPOLEON, MARTY,* *piano;* b. Brooklyn, N.Y., 6/2/21. Nephew of veteran Dixielander Phil Napoleon. Played with Louis Armstrong 1952-4, then with various small groups in NYC, sometimes forming his own trio. In March 1966, on the death of Billy Kyle, he replaced Kyle in Armstrong's group.

Addr: 1937 West 11th St., Brooklyn 23, N.Y.

NAPOLEON, PHIL,* *trumpet, leader;* b. Boston, Mass., 9/2/01. Leader of the Original Memphis Five in the 1920s; later worked in commercial pop bands. Living in Fla. in recent years. In mid-'60s, played for entr'actes at tapings of Jackie Gleason television shows. In Feb. 1966 he opened his own club, Phil Napoleon's Retreat, near Miami, featuring his own sextet.

NAPOLEON, TEDDY GEORGE,* *piano;* b. Brooklyn, N.Y., 1/23/14. Featured on and off with Gene Krupa between 1944 and '58, Napoleon later confined his activity to NYC. After a long illness he died of cancer, 7/5/64 in Elmhurst, N.Y.

NASSER, JAMIL SULIEMAN,* *bass, composer;* b. Memphis, Tenn., 6/21/32. With B. B. King in mid-'50s; then to NYC w. Phineas Newborn '56; later w. Teddy Charles, S. Rollins, S. Stitt. Europe, N. Africa and Middle East Feb. '59-Feb. '62. Pl. on Lester Young's final rec. date, Paris '59. Living in Milan, '61, wrote TV commercials, pl. concerts, acted in movies, comp. & arr. acc. for Tennessee Williams play *Blues* at Teatro San Marco. Formed trio w. bass, drums, dancer. Back in U.S., own trio 1962-4; then w. Ahmad Jamal Trio '64-6. LPs w. Jamal (Cadet).

Addr: 45 West 89th St., New York 24, N.Y.

NEIDLINGER, BUELL,* *bass;* b. Westport, Conn., 3/2/36. Free-lanced NYC from 1955, began playing w. Cecil Taylor '57. Played w. Taylor in stage production of *The Connection* '60. W. Jimmy Giuffre, Freddie Redd, Don Cherry, Alan Francis and Taylor '60-'62. Member Houston Symphony Orch. '62-'64. Awarded two year Rockefeller grant in '64 to study new music at NY State U. at Buffalo. W. Budapest Quartet at Tanglewood '65. Gave several solo bass recitals in NYC of works by Bussotti, Kagel. LPs: w. Taylor (Contemp., Candid).

Addr: Essex, Conn.

NELSON, OLIVER EDWARD,* *composer, saxophones, flute;* b. St. Louis, Mo., 6/4/32. Best known in the 1950s as a saxophonist with Wild Bill Davis, Louis Bellson and others, Nelson later acquired a distinguished reputation as a composer-arranger in both jazz and classical music. His works include a wood-

wind quintet, 1960; a song cycle for contralto and piano '61; *Dirge for Chamber Orchestra,* '62; *Soundpiece for String Quartet and Contralto,* '63. Played and conducted with large orchestra in concert at Lincoln Center in '63. Commissioned to write a new work, *Soundpiece for Jazz Orchestra,* which he played and conducted for the Light Music Week in Stuttgart, Germany, 1964. He also wrote scores for a CBS-TV series, *Mr. Broadway,* and for an educational film, *Encounter and Response.*

Nelson's writing employs a broad canvas, but in his jazz albums there is a clear indication both of his versatility and of his origins. Though not strictly classifiable as an avant gardist, he was one of the most mature and compelling writers to emerge during the early 1960s. This can be clearly discerned in his albums *Blues and The Abstract Truth* and *More Blues And The Abstract Truth* (both on Impulse). Other orchestral LPs: *Afro-American Sketches* (Pres.); *Full Nelson* (Verve); *Fantabulous* (Argo). He is also heard playing tenor and alto, leading a sextet feat. Eric Dolphy in *Screamin' the Blues* (Pres.).

Addr: 110-05 173rd St., Jamaica, N.Y.

NERO, PETER BERNARD, *piano;* b. NYC 5/22/34. Stud. from age 7 w. priv. teacher. Appeared as soloist sev. times w. Paul Whiteman, sev. symphony orchs. During late '50s, when he was still known as Bernie Nierow, appeared at Hickory House in NYC. Formed own trio '61 and very shortly, helped by powerful management and record promotion, rose to nat'l. popularity, playing in a commercial style that bordered on jazz and sometimes showing the influence of his favorites: Tatum, Peterson, Wynton Kelly, Bill Evans. First American artist to appear at the Grand Gala du Disque, Amsterdam, Oct. '64. Concerts and TV in London, Paris, Rome, etc. Ambition: To write an extended work for trio and orch., "communicable to mass audience yet still musically valid"; also to "experiment with complex forms in which musicians can improvise in stimulating, organized framework, yet actually freer than the so-called Freedom Bag."

LPs: Many on RCA, his own pref. being The *Colorful Peter Nero, Sunday in New York, Reflections, Songs You Won't Forget, Career Girls, The Best of Peter Nero, Nero Goes Pops.*

Addr: 4 E. 52nd St., NYC.

NEWBORN, PHINEAS JR.,* *piano, composer;* b. Whiteville, Tenn., 12/14/31. Father was drummer. As a result of enthusiastic reports by Count Basie and John Hammond, Newborn came to NYC in 1956 and was hailed by some critics as a genius, with greater technical command of the piano than any other jazz soloist since Art Tatum. He later worked with Charles Mingus and was in Europe for brief periods in '58 and '59.

During the 1960s Newborn's career went into a decline as a consequence of emotional illnesses. He was confined to Camarillo State Hospital intermittently, but when in better health was heard mainly around Los Angeles, leading a trio in night clubs, such as the Living Room, '66.

Reviewing one of his albums in 1962, Pete Welding noted "Newborn's assured and mature conception, the deepened emotional thrust of his playing, and the un-failing sense of ordered direction that course through his work. . . . His playing is marked by a passionate intensity and a healthy emotional spontaneity that were too often absent in his earliest work. As a result, his playing now has a *total* human quality, with heart and mind in balance."

Newborn's compositions include *New Blues* and *Theme for Basie*. Both are heard on one of his most remarkable LPs, *The Great Jazz Piano of Phineas Newborn Jr.* (Contemp.). Other LPs on Contemp. incl. *A World of Piano* and, as sideman with Howard McGhee, *Maggie's Back In Town*.

Addr: c/o Contemporary Records, 8481 Melrose Place, Hollywood 69, Calif.

NEWMAN, DAVID (FATHEAD), * *alto and tenor saxophone;* b. Dallas, Tex., 2/24/33. A member of the Ray Charles organization from 1954-64, Newman was heard on many of Charles' records and made a movie in Ireland in '64. He visited Europe four times and made a world tour in '64. He had an individual con-tract as a leader on Atlantic Records from 1960 and recorded one album for Riverside.

Addr: 2623 Downing Ave., Dallas 16, Texas.

NEWMAN, JOSEPH DWIGHT (JOE), * *trumpet;* b. New Orleans, 9/7/22. Worked with Count Basie intermit-tently 1943-6 and again from Jan. '52 until 1961, when he settled in NYC. Led own combos in clubs off and on during next five years. Toured Soviet Union with Benny Goodman, '62. Concerts with Orchestra USA, '63; Oliver Nelson, '64; Gary McFarland, '66. From March '64 he played in the orchestra of the Broadway show *What Makes Sammy Run?* for 18 months.

Newman is vice president of Jazz Interactions Inc., an organization designed to promote jazz education-ally and musically. Since 1964, he has appeared at churches, theological schools and colleges performing a jazz religious service with pianist Roger Kellaway, under the sponsorship of Rev. John Gensel. Newman has also played such TV shows as *Mr. Broadway, The Reporter, East Side West Side,* and *The Sammy Davis Show.*

LPs: *Joe Newman at Count Basie's* (Merc.); *Joe Newman Good N' Groovy* (Pres.); *Benny Goodman in Moscow* (RCA); *Quincy Jones Plays Hip Hits* (Merc.).

Addr: 202 Riverside Dr., New York, N.Y. 10025.

NEWSOM, THOMAS PENN (TOMMY), *tenor sax, flute, clarinet, composer;* b. Portsmouth, Va., 2/25/29. BA from Peabody Conserv., MA from Columbia Teachers Coll. Extensive N.Y. studio work. Toured Europe, No. Africa, Saudi Arabia 1955 w. USAF dance band. W. Benny Goodman, toured Latin Amer. '61 and USSR

'62. Joined NBC staff Oct. '62; tenor, woodwinds, writer w. Skitch Henderson on *Tonight* show from Apr. '63. Arrs. for many albums incl. Billy Butterfield LP of Bix tunes (Epic). *Hello Benny* for Goodman (Cap.). Best recorded work are arrs. on Col. album *Brazilian Byrd* for Charlie Byrd. Fav. own tenor solo: *Goin' To Kansas City* w. Buck Clayton (River).

Addr: 444 Palmer Ave., Teaneck, N.J.

NICHOLS, HERBERT HORATIO (HERBIE), * *piano, com-poser;* b. New York City, 1/3/19. Introduced to jazz audiences in 1955 through a Blue Note album, Nichols was belatedly recognized as a writer and soloist who had pioneered in modern jazz. After an erratic career marked by bad luck, obscure jobs backing singers and playing in groups unworthy of him, he died of leuke-mia in NYC, 4/12/63.

NICHOLS, ERNEST LORING (RED), * *leader, cornet;* b. Ogden, Utah, 5/8/05. An important figure in early jazz history, Nichols was best known for a series of recordings he made from 1926 to '31 under the name of Red Nichols and His Five Pennies. These groups varied in personnel and often included such men as Jimmy Dorsey, Miff Mole, Joe Venuti, Benny Good-man, Glenn Miller.

After the appearance in 1959 of a motion picture entitled *The Five Pennies,* there was a revival of in-terest in Nichols. He continued to front his own group, touring Japan with the World JF in 1964. He was working at a casino in Las Vegas when he died of a heart attack, 6/28/65.

Opinions differ greatly on Nichols' talent as a cor-netist. Some critics found in his work a pure, light quality reminiscent of Bix Beiderbecke; others felt he lacked a deep jazz feeling. Whatever his value as solo-ist, he made a unique contribution in bringing together on records some of the best-remembered small groups of the first so-called Golden Age of Jazz.

NIEHAUS, LEONARD (LENNIE), * *composer, alto sax;* b. St. Louis, Mo., 6/11/29. Worked w. Kenton in 1950s. Since leaving the band in '59 has done very little playing; worked mostly on TV writing; publ. works for stage bands, books of exercises, etudes. Con-certs and records with Lalo Schifrin. Jazz clinics at U. of Utah, etc. Wrote most arrangements for Jean Turner LP (Cap.); arrangements for Kenton's *Sophisticated Approach* (Cap.).

24201 Gilmore St., Canoga Park, Calif.

NIMITZ, JACK JEROME, * *baritone sax;* also other *saxo-phones, clarinets;* b. Washington, D.C., 1/11/30. Mem-ber of Stan Kenton Orchestra in late '50s. Has done much movie work, incl. w. David Amram and John Mandel. Formed quintet with co-leader Bill Hood, spring '64, utilizing combinations of tenor, baritone and bass saxes; and bass and contra-bass clarinets, working at several LA clubs. Sideman w. Charles Mingus, Thelonious Monk, Gerald Wilson, Terry Gibbs. Member Neophonic Orch. '65 and Monterey

J.F. Orch. '64-'65. LPs: w. Wilson (Pac. Jazz), Shelly Manne (Cap.), Gil Fuller (Pac. Jazz), Kenton (Cap.), Mingus (Mingus).

Addr: 12250 La Maida St., North Hollywood, Calif.

NIMMONS, PHILLIP RISTA (PHIL),* *composer, clarinet; also alto sax, piano;* b. Kamloops, Brit. Columbia, Canada, 6/3/23. Originally intended to be a doctor after grad. from U. of Brit. Col. but instead went into music full-time. Studied clarinet at Juilliard, NYC, and comp. at Royal Cons., Toronto. Wrote scores for Canadian radio and TV from '50; own group on CBC '57. Many app. at Canadian fest. and concerts. From '60-4 operated Advanced School of Contemporary Music w. Oscar Peterson in Toronto. LPs w. own tentet on Canadian RCA; Verve.

NISTICO, SAL, *tenor sax;* b. Syracuse, N.Y., ca. 1937. Pl. w. R&B bands in upstate N.Y. in '50s; then w. Mangione Bros. '60-1. Featured soloist w. Woody Herman '62-5; w. Count Basie for five months '65. Living in Sweden for some time, he rejoined Herman for State Dep't.-sponsored tour '66.

Nistico is an extremely hard-driving saxophonist influenced first by Charlie Parker, then by Gene Ammons and Sonny Rollins. Although he is capable of negotiating the fastest tempos with ease and great fire, he is also able to impart a thoughtful, unsaccharine lyricism to his ballad performances. Own LPs: Jazzland; LPs w. Herman (Philips, Col.); Mangione Bros. (Jazzland).

NORVO, RED (Kenneth Norville),* *vibraharp, xylophone, leader;* b. Beardstown, Ill., 3/31/08. To Chi. at 17; pl. w. Paul Ash, worked as single in vaudeville, later w. Victor Young and Paul Whiteman on NBC radio. Led pianoless swing combo in NYC '35; own 12-piece band from 1936 w. wife Mildred Bailey as vocalist. Switched from xylophone to vibes '43; led various small combos. Pl. w. Benny Goodman, '45; Woody Herman, '46. Settled in Calif. '47; from 1950-58 led own trio w. guitar, bass.

A respected musician whose light, subtle style established him as the first nationally known jazz figure on a mallet instrument, Norvo continued in the 1960s to play the type of gentle, swinging music always associated with him. He confined his sphere of activity mainly to the state of Nevada, working lounges there and often serving as leader of a house group at the Sands Hotel. He also worked often in association with Frank Sinatra. For his lounge work he was teamed for several years with singer Mavis Rivers. Occasionally he was reunited with Goodman. Unfortunately, except for one LP on VJ acc. Miss Rivers, he has been almost entirely inactive on records in the '60s.

Addr: 420 Alta Avenue, Santa Monica, Calif.

NOSOV, CONSTANTIN GEORGIEVITCH, *trumpet, fluegelhorn;* b. Leningrad, U.S.S.R., 7/24/38. Studied music from childhood. Attended Children's Sch. of Music, Rimsky-Korsakov Music College. Started play-ing professionally in Leningrad '56. From 1960 appeared regularly w. Joseph Weinstein Orch. and Gennady Golstein quintet. Made several TV appearances in Moscow, Leningrad TV, and at Tallin JF. Favs: Miles Davis, Freddie Hubbard LP: *Leningrad JF* (VJ).

Addr: Fontanka 85 Apt. 103, Leningrad, U.S.S.R.

NOTO, SAM,* *trumpet;* b. Buffalo, N.Y., 4/17/30. W. Kenton, Bellson big bands during '50s. In Count Basie band Sept. '64-Jan. '65. Formed own quintet w. Joe Romano Feb. '65; played around Buffalo and Western N.Y. state. LPs: w. Basie (Verve).

Addr: 502 Prospect, Buffalo 1, N.Y.

NOTTINGHAM, JAMES EDWARD JR. (JIMMY),* *trumpet;* b. Brooklyn, N.Y., 12/15/25. The former name-band sideman divided his time between commercial and jazz work in the 1960s. In addition to playing many TV shows at CBS with Jackie Gleason, Ed Sullivan, Al Hirt, he formed a quintet in 1962 with Budd Johnson as co-leader, playing night clubs in NYC area. To France 1962, pl. Antibes Festival w. D. Gillespie. Lincoln Center concert with Oliver Nelson; lead trumpet w. Q. Jones on Limelight LP and with Ray Charles on Impulse LP. W. Thad Jones-Mel Lewis band '66.

LPs as jazz soloist: *Boss of the Blues* with Joe Turner (Atl.); *Music of Rodgers and Hart* (RCA).

Addr: 80 Carolina Ave., Hempstead, L.I., N.Y.

O'DAY, ANITA,* *singer;* b. Chicago, Ill., 12/18/19. First prominent as a vocalist with the Gene Krupa and Stan Kenton bands in the early 1940s, Miss O'Day in the '60s was still singing in the same highly personal style that had established her voice as one of the most original sounds to emerge from the swing era. During the 1960s, in addition to nightclub work, she appeared at many concerts and festivals in the U.S. and overseas, visiting Sweden almost annually. She toured Japan in Dec. 1963. In 1965 she appeared in England at Annie Ross' club and on BBC.

As Barbara Gardner pointed out in *Down Beat,* Miss O'Day is "superb in the art of phrasing . . . she exhibits excellent comprehension of the lyric as well as the melody without becoming a slave to either. She handles the lyrics and changes with that very difficult deceptive looseness and freedom . . . a result of great conceptual and technical control. She sings smoothly without panic or strain at either extreme of her range and remains consistently impressive in projection, phrasing and flexibility."

Among Miss O'Day's many successful LPs, most of them on Verve in the 1960s, are *Anita Sings the Most* with the Oscar Peterson Trio, *All The Sad Young Men* with Gary McFarland, *Incomparable!* arr. by Bill Holman, *Time For Two* with Cal Tjader, *Anita O'Day &*

The Three Sounds (all Verve). Also rec. for Clover 1965.

Addr: 23758 Malibu Rd., Malibu, Calif.

ODETTA,* *singer, guitar, actress;* b. Birmingham, Ala., 12/31/30. Heard mainly in San Francisco clubs from early '50s; frequent concerts in East from 1958. Since '59 she has appeared regularly at the Newport Folk Festival; also at Monterey JF, and hundreds of concerts in public and college concert halls from coast to coast and around the world. The countries visited on her many overseas tours have included Italy, Sweden, Germany and Belgium in '63-4; Japan, Africa and Istanbul in '65; Australia in '65 and '66; England '64 and '66. In 1965, in a ceremony in her home town, she was presented with the key to the city in Birmingham, Ala. Films: *Sanctuary; Cinerama Holiday.* TV: *Belafonte Special,* '62; *CBS Easter Special; Nightlife; Kaleidescope,* '65. Odetta's performances of work songs, ballads and blues are clearly related to jazz, though she is usually classified as a folk artist.

LPs: Fantasy, River., RCA.

Addr: Albert B. Grossman, 75 E. 55th St., New York City 22, N.Y.

O'FARRILL, ARTURO (CHICO),* *composer;* b. Havana, Cuba, 10/28/21. To NYC '48; wrote for Benny Goodman and Dizzy Gillespie bands. Led own band in '53. Lived in Mexico from late '50s, gave jazz concerts in Mexico City 1962-3; TV series with own orchestra; premiere of Wind Quintet in Mexico City '63. Back to USA April '65, working briefly in Las Vegas before returning to NYC. Wrote arrs. for Count Basie LPs, *Basie Meets Bond,* Dec. '65 (UA); *Basie Plays the Beatles,* May '66 (Verve).

Addr: 574 West End Ave., New York, N.Y. 10024.

OGERMAN, CLAUS, *composer, piano;* b. Ratibor, Poland (formerly Germany), 4/29/30. Studied piano, theory, conducting in Germany. Pianist and arr. w. Kurt Edelhagen in 1952 at Baden-Baden radio station, and '53-7 w. Max Greger band in Munich. Wrote scores for fourteen feature films and worked as arranger-conductor for almost all labels in Germany before emigrating to USA Nov. '59.

In New York Ogerman rose swiftly to the top ranks as an arranger in both pop and jazz fields. His influences on piano were Tatum, Bill Evans, Herbie Hancock; in writing, he names Gil Evans and Marty Paich. Among the dozens of LPs for which he has arranged are sessions by Cal Tjader, A. C. Jobim, Bill Evans, Stan Getz, Jimmy Smith, Wynton Kelly, Johnny Hodges, Astrud Gilberto, Kai Winding, Donald Byrd (all Verve); Dinah Washington (Mercury), Betty Carter (Atco).

Own LPs on United Artists and RCA.

Addr: 160 E. 84th St., New York City, 28, N.Y.

OLIPHANT, GRASSELLA, *drums;* b. Pittsburgh, Pa., 9/1/29. Brother a vibist. Gigged around Pittsburgh with Ahmad Jamal, Tommy Turrentine, Joe Kennedy. First important job was w. Jamal in '52. In Washington be-

came musical director of a jazz club, Abart's-International, where he also led a house group. With Sarah Vaughan '58-'60, Gloria Lynne as drummer and manager '60-'63. At Newport JF w. Lynne '61. Comp. special music, *The Clock,* for General Time Corp. '66. Fav: Charlie Persip. Infl: Jo Jones. Own LP: *The Grass Roots* (Atl.). Others: w. Lynne (Everest).

Addr: 42 W. 94th St. #2A, New York 25, N.Y.

OLIVER, MELVIN JAMES (SY),* *composer, leader, singer, trumpet;* b. Battle Creek, Mich., 12/17/10. Pl. trumpet w. Zack Whyte. Rose to prominence as trumpeter, vocalist and chief arranger w. Jimmie Lunceford band, 1933-9, and as arr. for Tommy Dorsey 1939 through late 1940s. One of the most influential writers of the swing era, he worked as a musical dir. for Decca and other record companies from 1947. From late 1950s, free-lanced as successful arranger, mainly in recording studios, writing backgrounds for leading singers. Own LPs: Decca, Dot. Early LPs w. Lunceford: Dec., Col.

Addr: 1619 Broadway, New York 19, N.Y.

ORANGE, JOSEPH, *trombone;* b. New York, N.Y., 11/11/41. Uncle is J. C. Higginbotham. Others in family are also musicians. Studied w. Higginbotham, Carmine Caruso, Al Grey. First job was w. Marshall Brown's Newport Youth Band in '60; appeared at Newport, Pittsburgh JFs. With Lloyd Price '63, Lionel Hampton '64, Archie Shepp '65, Herbie Mann '65-6. Infl: on playing, Higginbotham, J. J. Johnson; on writing, Gil Evans, Shepp. Ambition is to return trombone to swing-era conception while assimilating styles of Johnson school. LPs: w. Shepp *Fire Music* (Impulse), Mann *Today* (Atl.).

Addr: 1319 Prospect Ave., Bronx 59, N.Y.

ORE, JOHN THOMAS,* *bass;* b. Philadelphia, Pa., 12/17/33. Played w. Bud Powell, Ben Webster, George Wallington, others around NYC during '50s. Joined Thelonious Monk in spring of '60; with him until spring '63. W. Teddy Wilson '64-'65, Powell late '65. Appeared in Montreal and Quebec City '64 in concert w. the Double Six. In NYC Jazzmobile and Black Arts Theatre concerts summer '65. Toured Europe twice w. Monk '61 and '63; also Newport JF w. Monk '62. On *Tonight* TV show w. Wilson '65. A fine, rhythmic bass player with an exceptionally strong tone. LPs: w. Monk *Monk's Dream, Criss Cross* (Col.); w. Powell (Roul.).

Addr: 1379 St. Johns Pl., Brooklyn 13, N.Y.

ORSTED PEDERSEN, NIELS-HENNING, *bass;* b. Osted, Denmark, 5/27/46. Mother is a church organist. Stud. piano but began gigging as bassist in early '60s, soon attracting the attention of visiting American musicians. Pl. w. Bud Powell, Quincy Jones '63, Roland Kirk '64; jazz festivals in Germany '65, also w. Sonny Rollins, Bill Evans, John Lewis, Dexter Gordon, Johnny Griffin '65; Kenny Drew '66.

An extraordinarily precocious youngster, Orsted Pedersen was only 17 when he was offered a job with Count Basie's band. Because of problems presented by his age he was unable to accept it. He has an exceptional sound and phenomenal facility and ideas. He has recorded with a wide range of artists, incl. Albert Ayler (Fant.), Roland Kirk (Merc.), Dexter Gordon (BN), and with small groups led by Stuff Smith, Ben Webster, Alex Riel and the Danish Radio Jazz group. He names many U.S. bassists as influences and stated in '66 that he hoped to eventually settle in the U.S.

Addr: Osted Pr. Roskilde, Denmark.

ORTEGA, ANTHONY ROBERT (TONY or BATMAN),* *saxophones, clarinet, flute;* b. Los Angeles, Calif., 6/7/28. Heard in numerous jazz and Latin bands during '50s, incl. Lionel Hampton, Luis Rivera, Dizzy Gillespie. Joined Quincy Jones '60. Free-lanced in Lake Tahoe, Cal., also worked there w. own quartet, incl. wife Mona Orbeck. In LA w. Don Ellis; Gerald Wilson band. With Q. Jones in soundtrack of film *The Pawnbroker.* LPs w. Rivera (Imp.), J. Cain-R. Kral (Col.), Wilson (Pac. Jazz), Jones (Merc.).

Addr: 5445 Conwell Ave., Azusa, Calif.

ORY, EDWARD (KID),* *trombone, composer;* b. La Place, La., 12/25/1886. Best known as composer of *Muskrat Ramble* and soloist on Louis Armstrong records in 1920s. In 1960s Ory has been in complete retirement except for a few appearances at the annual Dixieland Jazz nights at Disneyland.

LPs: Contemp., Verve.

Addr: 327 Medio, Los Angeles 49, Calif.

OUSLEY, HAROLD LOMAX, *tenor sax;* b. Chicago, Ill., 1/23/29. Studied piano as a child, then switched to reed instruments when in high school. Gigs as sideman in Chicago included w. King Kolax, Miles Davis. To NYC in '59, worked w. Machito, H. McGhee, Benny Green, C. Terry, J. Newman. Led own groups at Birdland, Count Basie's Lounge. Toured Europe w. a show in '59, then played in Paris w. Terry, Bud Powell. Main infl: Gene Ammons. Other infl and favs: Parker, D. Gordon, Rollins, Young. Comps. incl. *Haitian Lady, Minor Revelation.* Own LP: Beth. Others: w. McGhee (UA), Machito (Roul.), Dinah Washington (Merc.); best work w. Grasella Oliphant *Grass Roots* (Atl.).

Addr: 875 Amsterdam Ave. Apt. 7-E, New York 25, N.Y.

OVERTON, HALL F.,* *composer, piano, teacher;* b. Bangor, Mich., 2/23/20. Writer of many classical works and teacher of numerous jazzmen. Arranged Thelonious Monk's compositions for orchestral performances in NYC concerts 1959 & '63. Teacher at Juilliard School of Music since 1960; courses in jazz and composition at New School since 1962. His symphonic works include *Symphony For Strings,* '56, and *Second Symphony* '62. Wrote *Dialogues for Chamber Orch.,* commissioned by Clarion Orch., performed on State Department sponsored tour of USSR '64. Received

Academy of Arts & Ltrs. award '64. Commissioned by John Lewis to write *Sonorities* for Orchestra USA '64 (recorded on Col.). His work for Monk is represented in *Monk Orchestra at Town Hall* (River.) and *Monk Big Band and Quartet in Concert* (Col.).

Addr: 67-38 108th St., Forest Hills 75, N.Y.

OWENS, JAMES ROBERT (JIMMY), *fluegelhorn, trumpet;* b. New York City, 12/9/43. Stud. w. Donald Byrd. Pl. in Newport Youth Band 1959-60, later w. Slide Hampton, Ch. Mingus at Monterey '65, L. Hampton, Hank Crawford; Herbie Mann '66. Favs: Miles Davis, D. Gillespie, Art Farmer. Though not yet widely exposed via records, Owens by 1966 showed signs of developing into the most important new fluegelhornist since Art Farmer.

Addr: 236 Park Ave. South, New York 3, N.Y.

PAICH, MARTIN LOUIS (MARTY),* *composer;* b. Oakland, Calif., 1/23/25. Formerly an active member of the West Coast jazz clique as pianist and arranger, Paich in the 1960s rose to eminence as one of the most skillful writers in the Hollywood studios. In '63 he was staff arranger at NBC for the Dinah Shore and Andy Williams shows. In '64 he recorded a full length feature cartoon, *Hey There It's Yogi Bear.* Arranged and conducted *Alice in Wonderland* for TV show 1965. Composed or orchestrated several works for LA Neophonic Orchestra, 1965-6, incl. *Color It Brass, Neophonic Impressions 65,* and Mel Torme's *California Suite,* for which he was guest conductor. Arranged and conducted award winning backgrounds for Ray Charles and Sammy Davis Jr., also wrote albums for Lena Horne and Astrud Gilberto and many other singers.

Addr: 24157 Lupin Hill Rd., Hidden Hills, Calif.

PALMER, EARL C. SR., *drums;* b. New Orleans, La., 10/25/24. Parents were vaudevillians. Studied piano and percussion 1948-52 at Gruenwald's School of Music in New Orleans. Toured for many years as dancer, with mother and aunt in vaudeville team. To Los Angeles in 1957 and during the '60s was in demand for a tremendous number of TV, movie and record sessions. Although he has gained an identification with rock 'n' roll, Palmer is an all-around drummer who feels that his extensive work with Buddy Collette, Red Callender and Benny Carter has been most important to his career as sideman and soloist. Fav: Vernel Fournier. Main infls: Sid Catlett, Buddy Rich, Louis Bellson. Motion picture work with Neal Hefti in *Harlow, Boeing Boeing.* Has played with Monterey Jazz Festival house orchestra every year since the festival's inception.

Outstanding LPs include: *Swinging Brass* with Frank Sinatra, Neal Hefti, (Reprise), *Jazz Pops* with Hefti

(Reprise), *Harlow* with Hefti (Col.), and literally hundreds of other albums. His own personal favorite is *Explosive Sarah* with Sarah Vaughan and Benny Carter (Roulette).

Addr: 4505 Don Pablo Pl., Los Angeles 8, Calif.

PARENTI, ANTHONY (TONY),* *clarinet, saxes;* b. New Orleans, La., 8/6/00. From 1927 appeared w. numerous traditional bands, incl. Pollack, T. Lewis, Dukes of Dixieland, Joe Sullivan, own combos; also did extensive radio and concert work around NYC. Led own Deans of Dixieland '62-'63 at Eddie Condon's. From '63 appeared regularly at NYC Jimmy Ryan's. Guest shot on *Al Hirt's Fanfare* TV show '65. Own LPs: River., Jazzt., Jazzol., South., Con. Hall, Melodisc.

Addr: 83-06 Vietor Ave. Apt. 6-M, Elmhurst, N.Y.

PARIS, JACKIE,* *singer, guitar;* b. Nutley, N.J., 9/20/26. Heard with many 52nd St. combos in late 1940s; w. Lionel Hampton band '49-'50. Won DB critics' poll as New Star male singer '53. Best known for his early record of *Skylark*, Paris in the '60s was heard at Playboy Clubs etc. in vocal-team performances with his wife, the Canadian-born singer Anne Marie Moss.

LP: *The Song is Paris* (Impulse).

Addr: 245 East 62nd St., New York 21, N.Y.

PARKER, LEO,* *baritone sax;* b. Washington, D.C., 1925. One of the first baritone saxophonists to come to prominence during the bebop years, Parker played in the mid-'40s with Billy Eckstine, Benny Carter and Dizzy Gillespie. After 1948 he was only intermittently active, plagued by personal problems. In 1961 he began to make a comeback, recording two albums for Blue Note. The comeback was short-lived; on Feb. 11, 1962 Parker died suddenly of a heart attack in NYC.

PARLAN, HORACE LOUIS,* *piano;* b. Pittsburgh, Pa., 1/19/31. First prominent in New York as a sideman with Charles Mingus from 1957, Parlan in 1960-61 was a member of a cooperative group, the Play House Four, with Booker Ervin, Al Harewood and George Tucker. He then played with the Eddie Davis-Johnny Griffin Quintet until it disbanded in July 1962. After freelancing with own and other combos in NYC, he joined Roland Kirk Nov. '63 and toured with him through March '66.

Parlan, who names Ahmad Jamal and his teacher, James Miller, among his own main influences, has been heard in many LPs on Blue Note with his own group and with Stanley Turrentine and Dexter Gordon. Other LPs with Dave Bailey, Tubby Hayes (Epic), Booker Ervin, Eddie Davis (Pres.), Slide Hampton (Atl.), Davis-Griffin (River.), Babs Gonzales (Audio Fid.), R. Kirk (Merc., Limelight).

Addr: 758 E. 168th St., Bronx, N.Y. 10456.

PASS, JOE (Joseph Anthony Passalaqua), *guitar;* b. New Brunswick, N.J., 1/13/29. Studied with Nick Gemus in Johnstown, Pa. 1939-40. Local gigs, and tour with Tony Pastor Orch., while still in school.

According to Pass, "I left school and got a Local 802 card; gigged around Long Island and Brooklyn, and started goofing—pot, pills, junk. Traveled around the country with different tours. Spent a year in the Marine Corps. Meantime had been in and out of hospitals. After getting arrested, I moved to Las Vegas and worked the hotels there. Busted again. After that I spent three years and eight months at the U.S. Public Health Service Hospital in Fort Worth, Texas. Back in Vegas, I did commercial work. Still in and out of jails for narcotics violations. Then I came to Synanon."

Pass' story is a striking illustration of how careers and even lives have been saved by the Synanon Foundation in Santa Monica, Calif., where former narcotics addicts have helped one another to stay clean. Since he first entered the Foundation in 1961, Pass has been active in bringing groups to play for the members there and has also helped and brought in other musicians with similar problems. The post-Synanon stage of his life has not only been musically busy but has also established him belatedly as possibly the most exciting new talent on jazz guitar to emerge since Wes Montgomery came to prominence in the late 1950s. Since 1962 he has worked with many West Coast groups including those of Bud Shank, Gerald Wilson, Bobby Troup, Julie London, Clare Fischer, Bill Perkins, Earl Bostic, Les McCann, Groove Holmes, Carmell Jones, Page Cavanaugh. In 1955-6 he toured and recorded with George Shearing.

Pass' first LP was *Sounds of Synanon* in 1962 (Pac. Jazz). He has since recorded many albums of his own for the same label and has been featured with other Pac. Jazz and World Pacific artists including Les McCann, Gerald Wilson. Fav. own album: *For Django.* He names Django Reinhardt, Dizzy Gillespie, Charlie Parker and Coleman Hawkins as his main influences. Won *Down Beat* New Star Award 1963. Appeared at Monterey JF '63.

Addr: 5645 Vesper Ave., Van Nuys, Calif.

PATTERSON, DON, *organ, composer;* b. Columbus, Ohio, 7/22/36. Started as pianist and was originally impressed by Carmen Cavallaro, later by Erroll Garner.

After listening to Jimmy Smith in 1956 Patterson decided to take up the organ, on which he made his professional debut in '59. He gigged and recorded with Sonny Stitt, Gene Ammons, Eddie (Lockjaw) Davis, Kenny Burrell, Wes Montgomery and others, but in the '60s was frequently heard in clubs accompanied simply by a drummer, Billy James.

Patterson says of his organ work, "I try to keep the piano sound—play piano licks, and the organ helps my piano playing too." Own LPs: Prestige; w. Ammons-Stitt (Verve).

PATTON, "BIG" JOHN, *organ;* b. Kansas City, Mo., 1936. Mother, a pianist, played in churches. Patton took up piano in 1948 and gained extensive professional experience in the band of singer Lloyd Price. After leaving Price in 1961 he took up organ. Two years later, on the recommendation of Lou Donaldson,

Erroll Garner

Teddy Wilson (*Columbia Records*)

Oscar Peterson Trio. L. to R.: Louis Hayes, Oscar Peterson, Ray Brown *(Limelight Records)*

Richard Davis *(Charles Stewart)*

Jimmy Smith (*Chuck Stewart*)

Coleman Hawkins and Duke Ellington (*Impulse Records*)

Oscar Peterson (*Limelight Records*)

Woody Herman (*Roberto Polillo*)

Herbie Mann's group at Shelly's Manne Hole. L. to R.: Joe Orange, Jack Hitchcock, Jimmy Owens, Herbie Mann, Bruno Carr, Reggie Workman, Patato Valdes (*Fred Seligo*)

Coleman Hawkins

Ramsey Lewis Trio. L. to R.: Red Holt, El Dee Young, Ramsey Lewis

Kai Winding (*MGM/Verve Records*)

Pete Jolly

Duke Ellington

Blue Mitchell *(Francis Wolff-Blue Note Records)*   Paul Desmond

L. to R.: Clark Terry, Bob Brookmeyer, John Dankworth

Paul Gonsalves *(Roberto Polillo)*

Percy Heath *(Roberto Polillo)*

Joe Turner

Bill Smith *(Roberto Polillo)*

Sam Rivers
(Francis Wolff-Blue Note Records)

Red Norvo

Mel Torme

Horace Silver *(Francis Wolff-Blue Note Records)*

L. to R.: Dave Bailey, Gerry Mulligan, Bill Crow, Art Farmer

Chico Hamilton (*Impulse Records*)

Nina Simone

Wes Montgomery *(Roberto Polillo)*

Albert Ayler *(Bernard Gidel)*

Buddy De Franco

Modern Jazz Quartet. L. to R.: standing, Connie Kay
and John Lewis; sitting, Percy Heath and Milt Jackson

Chris Barber *(Roberto Polillo)*

Gil Cuppini *(Roberto Polillo)*

Bola Sete

Miles Davis (*Roberto Polillo*)

Lionel Hampton *(Roberto Polillo)*

Joe Pass *(Woody Woodward-Pacific Jazz Records)*   Oscar Valdambrini and Gianni Basso

he made his record debut. Don Nelsen wrote in DB: "Patton possesses a creditable array of equipment: a crisp articulation, a light but not limp touch, a rather fertile imagination . . . an approach that is less orchestral than many of his fellow organists." Though he is a most effective blues soloist Patton is by no means restricted to the blues. LPs: Blue Note.

PAYNE, CECIL McKENZIE,* *baritone, alto saxes;* b. Brooklyn, N.Y., 12/14/22. W. Gillespie, Dameron, Moody, other bop groups during '40s and early '50s, Randy Weston '58-'60. Acted, played and wrote some of music for NYC play *The Connection* '61. Went to Europe '63, again in '64 w. Lionel Hampton. Toured S. America '63 w. Machito. Paris JF '64. W. Weston again '66. Own LP: Parker; *Dakar* w. Coltrane (Pres.).

Addr: 1009 Sterling Pl., Brooklyn 13, N.Y.

PAYNE, DONALD RAY (DON),* *bass;* b. Amarillo, Tex., 1/7/33. W. Herbie Mann, Tony Bennett during late '50s. W. Mann through '62, Bennett through '63, then free-lanced around NYC. Began to play new style of bass, influenced by friend Scott La Faro. Led own trio NYC for 18 months '63-'64. Became interested in Brazilian music and recorded w. several bossa nova artists. Studied writing, wrote some TV commercials. Toured Africa '60 w. Mann, Brazil '61 w. Bennett. LPs: w. Mann (Atl.), Bennett (Col.), L. Bonfa-S. Getz (Verve), Bobby Scott (Merc.), A. Gilberto (Verve).

Addr: 3511 Cambridge Rd., Bronx 63, N.Y.

PAYNE, PERCIVAL (SONNY),* *drums;* b. NYC, 5/4/26. A popular member of the Count Basie orchestra since early 1955, Payne left after just ten years with the band. He formed his own trio, also worked as part of Frank Sinatra's accompanying group during much of 1965. Rejoined the Basie band 12/28/65. LPs: see Basie. Also played four tracks (including own composition, *Jilly's Honey*) on Al Grey album (Tangerine).

PEACOCK, GARY, *bass, composer;* b. Burley, Idaho, 5/12/35. Studied piano during school years in Washington and Oregon. Played piano in Army band in Germany in 1956. After discharge, began to concentrate on jazz. Lived for a while in Germany and played there with Hans Koller and Attila Zoller, also with Tony Scott and Bud Shank. Later, in Los Angeles, worked with Shank, B. Kessel, P. Horn, Jimmy Woods, Terry Gibbs, Shorty Rogers. Late in 1962 he moved to New York and soon became an important figure in avant garde circles, gigging with Paul Bley, Jimmy Giuffre, Roland Kirk, George Russell, Don Ellis, Bill Evans. Worked in Europe with Albert Ayler, Don Cherry in 1965.

Peacock revealed early in his career a tendency to extend his role as a bassist beyond the normal concepts heard in the bop and post-bop eras. His exceptional technical facility and wealth of ideas militated against his adhering to the old method of "walking" or time-keeping and established his style as an integral part of the overall sound of many musical experiments in which he participated. Many LPs with Don Ellis, Clare Fischer, Carmel Jones, Bud Shank (Pac. Jazz); Barney Kessel, Prince Lasha (Contemp.); Bill Evans (Verve); Anthony Williams (Blue Note); Albert Ayler (ESP).

PEARSON, COLUMBUS CALVIN JR. (DUKE),* *piano, composer;* b. Atlanta, Ga., 8/17/32. Appeared w. John Peck, own trio, Donald Byrd during '50s. Continued association w. Byrd during '60s, incl. arranging. Comps. incl. *Noah, March Children, Cristo Redentor, Chant,* all recorded by Byrd; and *Jeannine,* rec. by numerous groups. W. Golson-Farmer Jazztet '60, incl. Newport JF. Accompanist for Nancy Wilson '61, incl. tours of U.S., Canada, S. America, Mexico. Also acc. Dakota Staton. Appeared w. Thad Jones-Pepper Adams '65. A&R assistant to Alfred Lion at Blue Note Records from '65. A strong, skilled pianist with religious origins. Own LPs: *Profile, Tender Feelings, Wahoo* (BN); *Hush* (Jazzline); *Honey Buns* (Atl.). Others: w. Byrd, Grant Green, Johnny Coles (BN).

Addr: 451 E. 165th St. Apt. 1-D, Bronx 56, N.Y.

PECK, NAT, *trombone;* b. New York City, 1/13/25. Pl. w. Glenn Miller '44, Don Redman '47. '47-'51 pl. and rec. in France w. Coleman Hawkins, Roy Eldridge, Kenny Clarke, Don Byas, and stud. at Paris Conservatory. Ret. to U.S. '51-8, freelancing on TV in NYC. Back to France, pl. and rec. w. Michel Legrad, André Hodeir, Christian Chevalier, Duke Ellington. '62 to Germany, where he pl. w. Quincy Jones and rec. w. Francy Boland-Kenny Clarke. Freelancing in England since '64.

Addr: 70 Hamilton Terrace, London N.W. 8., England.

PEDERSEN, GUY, *bass;* b. Grand Fort Philippe, France, 6/10/30. Stud. at Roubaix Cons. Prof. debut at Tabou 1952. Pl. w. Bobby Jaspar '54, Stephane Grappelly; five years with Michel Legrand, four years with Martial Solal trio; also extensive studio work; joined Swingle Singers 1964 and toured internationally (see Swingle, Ward). Favs: Scott La Faro, Ray Brown, Chuck Israels. LPs w. Swingle Singers (Philips); many others, most of them released only in Europe, with B. Jaspar, Don Rendell, Lionel Hampton, Michel Legrand, Jean-Luc Ponty, Memphis Slim, Martial Solal.

Addr: 35 Rue Gallieni, Malakoff, Seine, France.

PEIFFER, BERNARD,* *piano, composer;* b. Epinal, France, 10/23/22. A U.S. resident since 1954, Peiffer worked mostly in Philadelphia during the 1960s, also played concerts at numerous colleges, incl. complete tour of the U.S. in 1964. He pl. the Montreal JF in 1962 and made many other appearances in Canada. Became U.S. citizen 1965.

Though he has appeared occasionally at the Village Vanguard, Basin St. East and other leading jazz clubs,

Peiffer has remained virtually unrecognized by the jazz public at large despite his extraordinary talent. He is, however, well represented on records by some admirable LPs on Decca, Laurie and Merc.

Addr: 133 W. Upsal, Philadelphia, Pa.

PEÑA, RALPH RAYMOND, * *bass;* b. Jarbidge, Nev., 2/24/27. Heard during '50s with numerous top West Coast groups incl. Shorty Rogers, J. Giuffre, own combos; increased activity in recording and composing during '60s. In duo w. Pete Jolly Feb. '58 until Jan. '62. W. Ben Webster in appearances in LA, Phoenix in '60; G. Shearing European tour '62. W. Frank Sinatra in appearances and recordings from 1960. Toured world w. Sinatra '62. Led own 9-piece band around LA '63. Comps. incl. *Serendipity.* Also designed and built walking aid for severely handicapped. LPs: w. Jolly (Ava); Sinatra (Cap., Rep.); C. Fischer, J. Pass, B. Shank, D. Grove (Pac. Jazz); A. O'Day, E. Fitzgerald (Verve); N. Wilson, B. May (Cap.).

Addr: 12961 Archwood St., North Hollywood, Calif.

PEPPER, ARTHUR EDWARD (ART), * *alto, tenor saxes;* b. Gardena, Calif., 9/1/25. Well known through his intermittent association with Stan Kenton from 1943 to '52, Pepper in later years was beset by narcotics problems. After serving a long jail sentence he returned to the Los Angeles scene and played at Shelly's Manne-Hole in 1964, revealing a style in which the main influence clearly had changed from Charlie Parker to John Coltrane. He was away from the scene again in much of '65-6, serving another prison sentence. Own LP: Cont.

PERAZA, ARMANDO, * *bongos, conga drum;* b. Havana, Cuba, 5/30/24. Best known as featured soloist with George Shearing quintet 1954-64. When Shearing's group was disbanded, Peraza joined the combo of Cal Tjader, with whom he had worked previously in the early '50s. LPs with Shearing (Cap., MGM); Tjader (Verve).

PERCIFUL, JACK T., * *piano;* b. Moscow, Idaho, 11/26/25. Featured with Harry James since April 1958. Toured with him in Mexico and South America 1961 and Japan '64; two appearances at Monterey JF. Movie: *Ladies' Man* with Jerry Lewis. TV: *Hollywood Palace, Jerry Lewis, Tonight Show,* etc. all with James. LPs with James on MGM, Dot.

Addr: 2416 Hassert, Las Vegas, Nev.

PERKINS, WILLIAM REESE (BILL), * *saxophones, flutes, piccolo;* b. San Francisco, Calif., 7/22/24. Prominent with Woody Herman and Stan Kenton in the 1950s, Perkins concentrated mainly on studio work in the 1960s. Though employed as a recording engineer in a Hollywood studio, he has continued to work as a musician, specializing in piccolo, flutes and tenor. Own LP: *Bossa Nova With Strings* (Liberty). Other LPs w. Terry Gibbs, Louis Bellson, Victor Feldman, LA Neophonic Orch., Bob Florence, Allyn Ferguson.

Addr: 12147 Miranda St., No. Hollywood, Calif.

PERKINS, WALTER, *drums;* b. Chicago, Ill., 2/10/32. Stud. w. Oliver Coleman 1949. Local groups around Chicago in '50s incl. Ahmad Jamal for a year '56-7. Formed own combo, known as MJT + 3, with which he made his NYC debut in '60. After the group disbanded he worked w. Carmen McRae '62-3, incl. Army camp tour in Germany; also w. Sonny Rollins, '62; Art Farmer, Teddy Wilson, '64. Fav: Sid Catlett.

LPs w. MJT + 3 (VJ); Clark Terry (Impulse); C. McRae (Col.); Billy Taylor (Merc.); A. Jamal (Cadet). Fav. own LP, *Lucky's Back* w. Lucky Thompson, 1966 (Rivoli).

Addr. 115-21 167th St., Jamaica, N.Y.

PERRIN, JEANNINE (MIMI), *singer, piano;* b. Paris, France, 2/2/26. Studied w. private teacher. Pl. gigs w. own trio as pianist, later as singer. Sang with vocal group, the Blue Stars of France, 1956-8. Background work with various vocal groups on records '58-'60. Organized her own sextet, The Double Six of Paris, in 1960. The Double Six, which was so-called because 12 voices were heard on the records (via overdubbing), employed the technique initiated by Lambert, Hendricks & Ross, namely the setting of lyrics to well-known jazz recordings, including the improvised solos. Miss Perrin's French lyrics to these solos frequently dealt with science fiction subjects.

The Double Six played a two-month tour of Canada in 1961, including Montreal JF. San Remo JF '62; concert at Town Hall, NYC, '63. Subsequently played numerous other festivals, concerts, TV shows throughout Western Europe. The group broke up in April 1965, but later that year Miss Perrin organized a new sextet, along similar lines, for a debut early in 1966.

Miss Perrin's background includes an English degree at the Univ. of Paris and three years spent as an English teacher in Paris high schools. A pioneer on the French vocal scene, she says her ambition is to form "the ideal and most swinging vocal group, with Annie Ross, Joe Williams, Jon Hendricks, two of the Double Six and myself." Favs: Billie Holiday, Joe Williams, Sarah Vaughan; Russ Freeman, T. Monk, B. Powell, H. Silver. She also names Charlie Parker and the big jazz bands as major influences.

LPs: *The Double Six Meet Quincy Jones* (Cap.); *Swingin' and Singin', Dizzy Gillespie and The Double Six, The Double Six Sing Ray Charles* (all Philips).

Addr: 31 Rue Jouffroy, Paris, 17, France.

PETERSON, OSCAR EMMANUEL, * *piano, singer;* b. Montreal, Quebec, Canada, 8/15/25. Popular in mid-'40s as sideman with Canadian band. Came to U.S. in '49 for Norman Granz concert and toured with Granz's JATP throughout 1950s, leading a trio.

Peterson continued to tour internationally with great success in the '60s, visiting Europe annually, usually as part of a concert package with Ella Fitzgerald. His trio from 1959-65 included Ed Thigpen on drums and bassist Ray Brown, who had joined him in '51. Thigpen was replaced in the summer of '65 by Louis Hayes.

In Jan. of '66 Ray Brown left; his place was taken by Sam Jones.

Peterson has continued to win innumerable popularity polls. His talent as a phenomenally endowed pianist in a tradition stemming from Art Tatum, Earl Hines and Nat Cole has been supplemented by a growing reputation as a composer. His *Canadiana Suite* won a NARAS nomination as one of the best jazz comps. of 1965. Other comps. include *Hallelujah Time, Children's Tune, The Smudge, Lovers' Promenade*.

After a silence of many years, Peterson resumed singing in 1965, recording an album, *With Respect to Nat*, in a voice very similar in timbre to that of the late Nat King Cole.

LPs: *My Fair Lady* (8581); *The Trio* (8420); *Trio W. Milt Jackson* (8429); *Bursting Out* (8476); *The Sound of the Trio* (8480); *West Side Story* (8454); *Affinity* (8516); *Oscar Peterson & Nelson Riddle* (8562); *Swinging Brass* (6119); *The Trio Plays* (8591); *We Get Requests* (8606); *The Trio and Gerry Mulligan Quartet at Newport* (8559) (all Verve); *Trio + One* with Clark Terry (Merc. 60975); *Canadiana Suite* (86010); *Eloquence* (86023); *With Respect to Nat* (86029) (Limelight).

Addr: 640 Roselawn Ave., Toronto 5, Ontario, Canada.

PETTIFORD, OSCAR,* *bass, cello, composer;* b. Okmulgee, Okla., 9/30/22. Prominent during the 1940s in the bands of Charlie Barnet, Duke Ellington and Woody Herman, Pettiford free lanced in New York in the 1950s but made his home base in Europe from 1958. Hospitalized late that year in Vienna, after an automobile accident, he recovered and continued to work, mainly in Copenhagen, where he played frequently with Stan Getz. After a short illness he died 9/8/60 in Copenhagen.

Pettiford's best work can be heard in some of the RCA Ellington LPs of the mid-'40s; also w. Coleman Hawkins on Contact. As a leader he is featured on *Oscar Pettiford Orchestra in Hi-Fi* (ABC Para.), *My Little Cello* (Fant.), and in an album under his own name recorded in Copenhagen and released on Jazzland. He was also well known as the composer of several popular instrumentals such as *Swingin' Till The Girls Come Home, Black-eyed Peas and Collard Greens, Tricrotism*.

Pettiford's role in bass history is a significant one. He was the successor to Jimmy Blanton in the evolution of modern jazz; in addition, he pioneered in the successful use of pizzicato jazz cello. His style, unprecedentedly fluid in its day, was the inspiration for many leading musicians of his era.

PHILLIPS, BARRE, *bass;* b. San Francisco, Cal., 10/27/34. Began playing in Dixieland band at Stanford U. when he was 15. Did not begin to emerge in modern jazz circles until the early 1960s, when he was a sideman with Don Ellis, Don Heckman, Geo. Russell, Jimmy Giuffre, Archie Shepp, Don Friedman-Attila

Zoller, Bob James, Ken McIntyre. Toured with Peter Nero 1965-6. Soloist with New York Philharmonic in Jan. '64. Visited Europe Sept.-October '64 with Geo. Russell and Feb.-Mar. '65 with J. Giuffre. With Archie Shepp at Newport '65.

Phillips, a bassist of the new wave, says "I feel that every serious player has something to offer and something to learn from. My favorite bass players are Wilbur Ware, Steve Swallow and Richard Davis."

LPs w. Shepp (Impulse), Bob James (ESP), Leonard Bernstein (Col.).

Addr: 290 Wardwell Ave., Staten Island, N.Y.

PHILLIPS, ESTHER (Esther Mae Jones), *singer;* b. Galveston, Tex., 12/23/35. Started singing in church. At 13 won an amat. show in LA; Johnny Otis heard her and she toured w. his band 1949-52 as "Little Esther." Hit record, *Double Crossing Blues,* '49; several more hits before the band broke up. Out on her own for a while, she became ill and was out of music for several years, living in Houston. Rec. a country music song, *Release Me,* for small firm in '63; it became her biggest hit and was followed by top-selling version of *And I Love Him*. Sang w. Beatles on BBC-TV Nov. '65. NJF, '66. She has a mordant sound, slightly reminiscent of Dinah Washington (whom she names as fav. and main infl.), but with a quality of phrasing and articulation all her own. LP: *Esther* (Atl.).

Addr: 76 Norwood Av., Elberon, N.J.

PHILLIPS, JOSEPH EDWARD (FLIP),* *tenor sax;* b. Brooklyn, N.Y., 2/26/15. Popular as leading soloist with Woody Herman 1944-6; later toured frequently with JATP. To Europe with Benny Goodman, fall '59. Leading own quartet in Pompano Beach, Fla. in mid-'60s. Own LP: Sue; also on *Out of the Herd* (Emarcy).

Addr: 310 S.E. 12th St., Pompano Beach, Fla. 33060.

PICOU, ALPHONSE FLORISTAN,* *clarinet;* b. New Orleans, La., 10/19/1878. Picou, whose early work unfortunately was never preserved on records, recorded in 1940 with Kid Rena and in 1947 with Papa Celestin. After earning an almost legendary reputation in New Orleans jazz, with a background of 65 years in music, he died 2/4/61 in New Orleans.

PIERCE, BILLIE, *piano, singer;* b. Pensacola, Fla., ca. 1905. Younger sister of Sadie Gootson who was w. Buddy Petit in '31. At age 16 once pl. for Bessie Smith when Bessie's accompanist became ill. Pl. tent shows w. Ma Rainey. To New Orleans '30; worked in French Quarter w. her husband DeDe and George Lewis during depression years. Later she and DeDe worked together in Decatur St. clubs until both were stricken with severe illnesses in mid-50s. They app. in ABC-TV special *The Anatomy of Pop* '66. Samuel Charters described her in his *Jazz: New Orleans* as "one of the last of the 'classic' style blues singers and a fine band pianist." LP, *Blues and Tonks from the Delta,* in Riverside's "Living Legends" series.

PIERCE, JOSEPH DE LACROIS (DEDE), *trumpet, cornet;* b. New Orleans, La., 2/18/04. Husband of Billie Pierce (q.v.). Infl. by Louis Armstrong, Kid Rena and Chris Kelly. The latter showed him fingering and he had some formal training from Prof. Chaligny. Own band for dances. Pl. w. Paul Barnes '33, Albert Burbank '47. He and Billie toured in unit acc. Ida Cox. Pl. lead in Young Tuxedo Brass Band until he became blind in mid-50s. LP: Riverside.

PIERCE, NAT,* *piano, composer;* b. Somerville, Mass., 7/16/25. Pierce's association with the Woody Herman band (from 1951-5) was renewed when he joined Herman in June, 1961 as chief arr. and road mgr. He played an important part in the resurgence of the orchestra, discovering and hiring many new soloists, writing such original material as *Tunin' In, Dr. Wong's Bag, Poor House Blues, Stingray, Kissin' Cousins.* Also wrote exceptionally attractive arrangements of standards including *Days of Wine and Roses, Body and Soul, Jazz Me Blues, Blue Monk.*

In addition, Pierce wrote arrs. for Carmen McRae and others. An album he recorded in Feb. '57 at the Savoy Ballroom in Harlem (his was the last big band to play there before it was torn down) was released by RCA Victor in '62. Other LPs w. Herman (Phil., Col.).

Pierce is an arranger of exceptional talent, in a tradition drawing directly from the best elements established by big band styles such as those of Count Basie, Duke Ellington and the earlier Herman bands.

Addr: 127 W. 82nd St., New York City, N.Y. 10024.

PIERSON, ROBERT MOREY (BOB), *tenor sax;* b. Detroit, Mich., 11/30/30. Father a musician. Studied clarinet w. Albert Luconi. Won contest at Detroit theatre while Lionel Hampton's band was playing there; joined Hampton band briefly 1949. Pl. w. Ralph Marterie, Dean Hudson, Johnny Long in '50s. Alto sax w. Neal Hefti; Quincy Jones '62-3; Buddy Morrow '65. Flute w. Paul Winter sextet '65, touring Brazil for State Department. Toured w. Woody Herman 1965-6. Early record w. Don Jacoby College All Stars (Dec.); more recently w. Herman (Col.).

Addr: 8744 Shari Drive, Garden City, Michigan.

PIKE, DAVID SAMUEL (DAVE),* *vibes, marimba;* b. Detroit, Mich., 3/23/38. Worked with many leading LA musicians from '57, incl. Paul Bley, Dexter Gordon, Harold Land and own groups. To NYC in '60; led own quartet, then joined Herbie Mann in '61. Toured Japan w. Mann '64. Favs: Milt Jackson, Lionel Hampton. Infl: Bud Powell, Sonny Rollins, foreign and classical music. Own LPs: River., Epic, Pres., Decca. Others w. Mann (Atl.).

Addr: 34 W. 65th St., New York 23, N.Y.

PLATER, ROBERT (BOBBY),* *alto sax, clarinet, flute;* b. Newark, N.J., 5/13/14. After spending 18 years almost continuously with the Lionel Hampton orchestra, Plater left Hampton in Sept. 1964 to join Count Basie.

Replacing Frank Wess in Basie's sax section, he was heard in occasional solos including *Happy House.* Plater is mainly known as an excellent section man.

PLUMMER, WILLIAM (BILL), *bass;* b. Boulder, Colo., 3/27/38. Raised in LA. Mother played piano, trumpet. Played w. high school jazz group. Studied bass w. Monty Budwig, Herman Reinshagen, sitar w. Hari Har Rao. Free-lanced in LA from '56: jobs incl. H. Geller, F. Ortega, T. Ortega, B. De Franco, G. Shearing, P. Jolly, Nancy Wilson; most important w. The Jazz Corp and w. Paul Horn '61. Rejoined Horn '63. Monterey JF w. M. Makeba '60. Favs: Peacock, Mingus, Budwig, Mitchell, R. Brown, Chambers, G. Karr. LPs: w. De Franco-Gumina (Merc.), Roy Ayers (MGM), Wilson (Cap.); best work w. Horn (Col., RCA).

Addr: 11210 Christy St., Lake View Terrace, Calif.

POINDEXTER, NORWOOD (PONY),* *soprano sax;* also *alto, tenor, clarinet;* b. New Orleans, La., 2/8/26. Prof. debut in New Orleans 1940; later toured with Billy Eckstine and worked with various groups in San Francisco. Joined accompanying group of Lambert, Hendricks & Ross in the summer of '61, remaining until summer of '63. Formed his own quartet, working clubs on East Coast. Left for Europe, Aug. '64, and has appeared in festivals in Berlin and Bologna, clubs in Paris, Copenhagen, Milan, Madrid. One of the most impressive of the numerous saxophonists who took up soprano during the 1960s. Own LPs: Epic, Prestige; also *Lambert, Hendricks & Bavan at Basin Street East* (RCA).

Addr: Lista de Correos, Ibiza, Spain.

POLLACK, BEN,* *leader, drums;* b. Chicago, Ill., 6/22/03. Leader of a popular band in the 1920s and '30s; members at one time incl. Benny Goodman, Glenn Miller, Harry James, Muggsy Spanier. In the early '60s Pollack appeared occasionally in Hollywood and Palm Springs leading small combos; by 1965 he had virtually given up playing and was running a restaurant in Palm Springs, Calif.

POLLARD, TOMMY, *vibraphone, piano;* b. London, England, 1923; d. London, 10/7/60. Pl. w. Johnny Claes '41, and same year replaced George Shearing w. Harry Parry. '42-'45 in R.A.F. Then w. Harry Hayes and B. Featherstonhaugh. '47 transatlantic crossings in ship bands, and took up vibes. '49-'51 pl. w. Ronnie Scott at Club Eleven, later free-lance. Inactive due to ill health for last five years of his life. Pollard was among the earliest British bebop mus., and probably the most accomplished soloist at first. LPs w. Ronnie Scott, Victor Feldman (Brit. Tempo).

POMEROY, HERB,* *trumpet, composer, leader, educator;* b. Gloucester, Mass., 4/15/30. Extensive experience with jazz groups in 1950s including Ch. Parker, Lionel Hampton, Stan Kenton. Taught at Lenox School of Jazz 1959-60. Specialized in music for Cultural Exchange Program, U.S. State Department, working in Malaysia in 1962 as director of Radio Malaya Orch. Member of Orchestra USA '62-3. Director MIT

Concert Jazz Band since '63. Host on jazz TV show in Boston '65-6. Instructor at Summer Jazz Clinics '63-'66. Along with all these activities, Pomeroy has been a permanent resident instructor at the Berklee School of Music since '55.

Own LP: *Band in Boston;* LPs w. John Lewis (Atl.); Anita O'Day, Gary McFarland (Verve); Orchestra USA (Colpix). Conductor of all albums in series of LPs by students on Berklee label.

Addr: 258 Commonwealth Ave., Boston 16, Mass.

PONTY, JEAN-LUC, *violin;* b. Arranches, Normandy, France, 9/29/42. Father a violin teacher, mother piano teacher. Stud. at five; at 16, to Cons. Nat. Superieur de Musique, where he won prize. Two years w. Concerts Lamoureux classical orchestra. Sideman w. Jef Gilson band 1961-4. After scoring big hit at Antibes JF, July '64, decided to stay in jazz full time. TV in Stockholm, radio concerts in Germany and Belgium; club in Madrid '65.

Ponty, who also plays saxophone and other instruments, says, "When I play, I don't think of the violin, but of jazz, of music. I don't especially want to be a violinist, but a jazzman." He names Miles Davis, Clifford Brown, Parker, Rollins, Coltrane, Monk, Bill Evans and Ornette Coleman among his favorite musicians.

Stuff Smith, hearing Ponty, said "Keep your eye on this youngster. He is a killer! He plays on violin like Coltrane does on sax."

Own LPs: Philips. LPs w. Jef Gilson (CED, French label).

Addr: 52 Rue des Trois Freres, Paris 18, France.

PORCINO, AL,* *trumpet;* b. New York City, 5/14/25. Many years of big band exp. w. Krupa, T. Dorsey, Kenton, Basie, Chubby Jackson, several times w. Woody Herman. Settled in LA '57. Clubs, LPs w. Terry Gibbs, '59-'62. In '62, contracted 25-piece band for Dizzy Gillespie and Lalo Schifrin to play *New Continent* at MJF and on LP Tours: Australia, 1960 w. Sinatra; Hawaii, '63 w. Vic Damone; Mexico, '64 w. Eddie Fisher. Exceptional lead trumpeter.

LPs w. Gibbs (Verve); Shelly Manne (Cap); Gillespie (Limelight).

Addr: 4447 Morse Avenue, Studio City, Calif.

POTTER, CHARLES THOMAS (TOMMY),* *bass;* b. Philadelphia, Pa., 9/21/18. Well known through his association with Charlie Parker and others in the bebop era, Potter played with Tyree Glenn in early 1960, then worked with Harry Edison combo May 1960-Jan. 1961. Gigs with Buck Clayton Quintet '63. Duo with Jamaican pianist Cecil Lloyd, '64. Toured Europe with George Wein's Charlie Parker Memorial Group. Pl. w. Al Cohn-Zoot Sims '65.

LPs with Harry Edison, Joe Williams (Roul.), Gil Evans (Pac. Jazz), Jimmy Forrest (Pres.).

Addr: 314 Jefferson Ave., Brooklyn, N.Y. 11216.

POWELL, BENJAMIN GORDON (BENNY),* *trombone;* b. New Orleans, 3/1/30. After almost twelve years

with the Count Basie orchestra, Powell left Basie 8/29/63 and settled in New York. Led various combos 1963-6; also gigged as sideman with Grant Green, Roland Kirk et al. Began subbing in Broadway shows Nov. '63; joined trombone section in pit band of *Funny Girl* Mar. '64; joined *Golden Boy* show orch. Oct. '64. President of Ben-G Enterprises, Inc., producers of jazz concerts, including NAACP benefit at Birdland, May '65. TV shows with Billy Taylor, Sammy Davis. Stud. bass trombone, singing, acting; took acting role in Sammy Davis film *A Man Called Adam.* Led various groups in "Jazzmobile" concerts heard in streets of Harlem summer '65. Many record dates w. N. Adderley, D. Byrd, S. Davis, C. Basie, Tony Bennett, Lucky Thompson.

Addr: P.O. Box 39, Radio City Sta., New York 19, N.Y.

POWELL, EARL (BUD),* *piano, composer;* b. New York City, 9/27/24. Powell is considered the virtual founder of modern jazz piano. He was associated with the early experiments at Minton's Play House in NYC that led to the evolution of bebop. After playing w. Cootie Williams' big band, 1943-4, and w. combos led by Dizzy Gillespie, Don Byas and others, he worked intermittently, troubled by emotional illnesses.

Sporadically active in New York through the 1950s, he took up residence in France in 1959. He worked there regularly, his health somewhat improved, until 1962, when he was stricken with tuberculosis. After a long period of convalescence he returned to activity almost two years later and arrived back in the U.S., 8/16/64 for what was supposed to be a brief visit. However, after working briefly at Birdland, he disappeared, and his projected return to Paris never materialized. Seriously ill and almost entirely inactive for the rest of his life, he died 7/31/66 in a Brooklyn hospital.

Powell's recordings of later years offer little evidence of the great power and confident flow of ideas that marked his earlier work. His last few LPs appeared on Roul. and Reprise, but the jazz student interested in evaluating his tremendously important place in jazz history is advised to study his earlier albums on Blue Note and Verve.

Other LPs from the '60s: *A Portrait of Thelonious* (Col.), *Essen Jazz Festival* (Fant.), *Dizzy Gillespie & the Double Six* (Phil.), Art Blakey (Epic), *Americans in Europe* (Imp.).

POWELL, EVERARD STEPHEN SR. (RUDY) (Moh. name Musheed Karweem),* *clarinet, alto sax;* b. New York City, 10/28/07. Prominent with many name bands during swing era including Fats Waller, Teddy Wilson, Fletcher Henderson, Cab Calloway. Frequently worked with Jimmy Rushing during '50s. Toured U.S. and Europe with Ray Charles band 1961-2. Played in orchestra for Duke Ellington's *My People* show in Chicago '63. LP: *Buck Jumpin'* with Al Casey (Pres.).

Addr: 102 West 138th St., New York, N.Y. 10030.

POWELL, SELDON,* *tenor sax, flute;* b. Lawrenceville, Va., 11/15/28. Big-band experience w. Lucky Millinder, Sy Oliver, Erskine Hawkins, Neal Hefti, Louis Bellson, Johnny Richards. Benny Goodman in '50s. Buddy Rich Quintet, spring '60; ABC-TV studio work June-Oct. '60; commercial TV shows through mid-'65. With Clark Terry '63; rejoined Bellson '62 and '64. Free-lancing in NYC '66. LPs w. Ch. Rouse, 1961 (Epic); w. Bill English, '62 (Vanguard); Willie Rodriguez, '63 (River.). Movie: *A Man Called Adam* w. Sammy Davis, '66.
Addr: 89 Carolina Avenue, Hempstead, L.I., N.Y.

PREVIN, ANDRE,* *piano, composer, conductor;* b. Berlin, Germany, 4/6/29. To U.S. 1939; record debut '45; staff conductor at MGM film studios from '48. Though mainly active as studio writer, Previn frequently appeared and recorded as a jazzman during the '50s; his 1957 LP of *My Fair Lady* with Shelly Manne was a best seller.

In the '60s, Previn devoted his time increasingly to classical music and to conducting symphony orchestras. In the early '60s he recorded a series of popular albums with string ensembles, and a few jazz albums. His relationship with jazz was also maintained in occasional TV appearances.

The album *Andre Previn Plays Harold Arlen* (Cont.) won a Grammy as the Best Solo Jazz Performance of 1961. Actually there have been several Previn albums during the '60s of far greater interest to jazz students. Among them are the following, all featuring Previn's trio with Red Mitchell and Frankie Capp: *Like Previn!* (Cont.), *Light Fantastic* (Col.); trio augmented by J. J. Johnson in a set of Kurt Weill tunes (Col.) and by Herb Ellis in a new version of *My Fair Lady* (Col.). The pop albums with orchestra, containing many passages of jazz interest, include *A Touch of Elegance* (Ellington compositions) and *Thinking of You* (Col.).

Previn has also been successful as a writer of popular songs in collaboration with his wife, lyricist Dory Langdon. An LP of their songs, *Like Sing,* was recorded by Jackie and Roy Kral (Col.). Recordings since 1965 were on RCA.
Addr: 1454 Stone Canyon, Los Angeles 24, Calif.

PRICE, RUTH, *singer;* b. Phoenixville, Pa., 4/27/38. Self-taught as a singer; was originally a dancer, taking up ballet as a child and attending ballet school in 1952 on a scholarship. Inspired by Charlie Parker, she decided to try singing; joined Charlie Ventura's combo summer 1954. After leaving Ventura, free-lanced in Phila. clubs where acc. often included Red Garland and other modern jazzmen. Later, in NYC, spent several months at Village Vanguard. When singing jobs were scarce she continued to work as a dancer.

Moving to Hollywood in 1957, she sang at Jazz City, returned to dancing in a stage production *Vintage '60.* After working at Shelly's Manne-Hole and many other clubs in the area, she joined Harry James'

band in the summer of 1964 and remained until Dec. '65, visiting Japan with the band.

Miss Price has inherent good taste in her style and her choice of material, a natural sense of phrasing and an individual sound, as well as a sure sense of intonation. She did not record with James and her earlier albums are no longer available; her best work can be heard on an LP recorded with Shelly Manne's group at his club (Contemp.)
Addr: 875 N. Beverly Glen, Los Angeles 24, Calif.

PRINCE, ROBERT,* *composer;* b. New York City, 5/10/29. The writer of *New York Export: Opus Jazz* composed a second ballet, again for Jerome Robbins, entitled *Events,* which was performed by Ballets USA in NYC and throughout Europe, as well as on RCA LP, 1961. Comp. incidental music for *Oh Dad, Poor Dad . . .* off and on B'way and on tour, '62. Wrote *Meet The Band* for Benny Goodman's USSR tour, '62. Dance and instrumental music for *Something More, Dr. Faustus,* '64; *Half a Sixpence,* '65. TV and film scoring work, '64-5.
LPs: *Events* and *Opus Jazz* (RCA); arr. & cond. *Desmond Blue* for Paul Desmond (RCA).
Addr: 127 Audley St., Kew Gardens, N.Y. 11418.

PROCOPE, RUSSELL,* *alto and soprano sax, clarinet;* b. New York City, 8/11/08. With Chick Webb, Fletcher Henderson and other swing bands in '30s. After seven years with John Kirby sextet, joined Duke Ellington in 1945 and has since been a mainstay of the Ellington reed section, featured only occasionally in alto solos and more frequently in recent years on his Albert System clarinet, notably in *La Scala* and *Harlem* on the *Symphonic Ellington* album and *More* in *Ellington '65* (Reprise); *Sleepy Time Down South* in *Will Big Bands Ever Come Back?* (Reprise).
LPs: See Ellington, Duke, and Ellington, Mercer. Own LP: Dot.
Addr: 870 St. Nicholas Ave., New York 32, N.Y.

PROHASKA, MILJENKO, *bass, composer;* b. Zagreb, Yugoslavia, 9/17/25. Began playing violin at age of nine. Graduated Zagreb Musical Academy 1956. From late '30s led own combos and large bands in Yugoslavia, making numerous TV, radio and personal appearances, including numerous European JFs. Comps. incl. *Intima, Concertino for Jazz Quartet and Strings, Concerto.* Became friend of John Lewis, who recorded some of Prohaska's comps. with Orchestra U.S.A. Did scores for several films, radio dramas and one ballet. Favs: Ray Brown, Richard Davis, Ron Carter; Glenn Miller, Stan Kenton, Dizzy Gillespie. Infl: Ellington, Quincy Jones, Gil Evans, Yugoslav folk music. Comps. can be heard on *Jazz Journey* and *Sonorities* by Orchestra U.S.A. (Col.).
Addr: Bogoviceva I/VI, Zagreb, Yugoslavia.

PRYSOCK, ARTHUR, *singer;* b. Spartanburg, So. Carolina, 1/2/29. Came to prominence with Buddy Johnson orchestra 1945, playing Harlem ballrooms and clubs. After many years working as a single he began to attain recognition in 1964-5, appearing several times on the *Tonight* TV show. He was also featured in concerts at the Academy of Music, Philadelphia, Symphony Hall in Newark, and in Feb. 1966 sang before a capacity audience at Carnegie Hall.

A jazz-influenced pop singer, Prysock names F. Sinatra, S. Vaughan, T. Bennett, Gloria Lynn; Count Basie, L. Hampton as influences.

LPs: *Arthur Prysock-Count Basie* (Verve); many solo LPs (Old Town).

Addr: 255 I.U. Willets Road, Searingtown, L.I., N.Y.

PURNELL, WILLIAM (KEG),* *drums;* b. Charleston, W. Va., 1/7/15; d. 1965. Was best known as drummer with Benny Carter in 1939-41 and Eddie Heywood off and on from '42 to '52.

QUARTETTE TRES BIEN. An instrumental combo formed in 1959. For details see James, Percy; St. James, Albert; Simmons, Richard; Thompson, Jeter. LPs: Decca.

QUEBEC, IKE ABRAMS,* *tenor sax;* b. Newark, N.J., 8/17/18. A warm-toned tenor man in the Coleman Hawkins-Ben Webster manner, Quebec was heard in the 1940s with Roy Eldridge, Benny Carter and Coleman Hawkins. From 1944-51 he was frequently heard with Cab Calloway, but during the 1950s he was virtually inactive in jazz. In 1961-2 he recorded a series of albums for Blue Note. Stricken with lung cancer, he died in NYC, 1/16/63.

QUILL, DANIEL EUGENE (GENE),* *alto sax, clarinet;* b. Atlantic City, N.J., 12/15/27. With many bands incl. Claude Thornhill, Buddy De Franco, Gene Krupa in '50s, he teamed w. Phil Woods in a twin-alto combo in NYC '57-8; then w. Johnny Richards. W. Gerry Mulligan Concert Jazz Band in early '60s, then freelance NYC. In '66 feat. in Monday night sessions at Kenny's Pub; own quartet for engagement at Embers West. Hot, jagged style on alto, orig. inspired by Charlie Parker; also an excellent jazz clarinetist as demonstrated by his work on *Gerry Mulligan '63* (Verve); other LPs w. Mulligan (Verve).

RADER, DONALD ARTHUR (DON), *trumpet, fluegelhorn, composer;* b. Rochester, Pa., 10/21/35. Father pl. trombone, bass; stud. w. him from age five. After pl. in Navy and college bands, left college to join Woody Herman in Oct. 1959. After year and a half with Herman, pl. w. Maynard Ferguson, May '51-Mar. '63; Count Basie Mar. '63 to Aug. '64. Later free-

lanced w. Louis Bellson, Frank Foster Quintet, Della Reese, Harry James, Terry Gibbs. During most of these jobs he played the jazz trumpet chair, also wrote arrangements for Ferguson, Herman, Basie, Gibbs.

A competent, swinging trumpeter, inspired by Miles Davis, Rader also admires Gillespie, F. Hubbard, J. Sheldon, Lee Morgan and Clifford Brown. His writing influences were Bill Holman, Shorty Rogers, Willie Maiden and Quincy Jones. He feels his best playing and writing can be heard in the more recent Woody Herman albums on Col., esp. *My Funny Valentine.* His ambition is to work as a studio composer and arranger.

LPs with Ferguson (Roul., Mainstream), Basie (Verve), etc. Fav. own solos: *Hey Jealous Lover* on *Hits of '50s and '60s* with Basie (Reprise), *Three More Foxes* in *Color Him Wild* w. Ferguson (Mainstream), *Fox Hunt* in *Maynard '63* (Roul.).

Addr: 7702 Starfire Drive, Anaheim, Calif.

RAE, JOHN (John Anthony Pompeo),* *drums;* also *vibes, timbales;* b. Saugus, Mass., 8/11/34. With many well-known combos during '50s, incl. G. Shearing, C. Cole, R. Sharon, H. Mann. W. Peter Appleyard in '60-'61, then w. Cal Tjader from May '61 as drummer. Also w. own quartet summer '63 and Vince Guaraldi summer '64. Part-time disc jockey for KJAZ, San Francisco. LPs: all of Tjader's from '61 (Fantasy, Verve). Others w. Stan Getz (Verve), Bola Sete (Fantasy), Buddy Collette (Pac. Jazz).

Addr: 2654 Webster St., San Francisco, Calif.

RAEBURN, BOYD ALBERT, *leader, composer, saxophones;* b. Faith, S.D., 10/27/13. Best known for the progressive band he led in the mid-1940s, Raeburn died 8/2/66 in Lafayette, Ind.

RANDI, DON (Don Schwartz), *piano;* also *harpsichord, organ;* b. New York City, N.Y., 2/25/37. Father was active with Hebrew Actors' Union, directed Jewish films. Raised in Catskill Mountains, where he studied piano. Concentrated on classical music for 13 years. While studying at Los Angeles Conservatory, became interested in jazz. Worked in Hollywood clubs off and on for 10 years, also record dates with singers. Led own trio in album, 1962. In '66 his composition *Mexican Pearls* enjoyed popular success. An enthusiastic, technically able pianist, influenced by O. Peterson, Nat Cole, H. Silver, Al Haig, Monk, Tatum. Own LPs: Verve, World Pacific. The single record of *Mexican Pearls* is on Palomar.

Addr: P.O. Box 48712, Hollywood 48, Calif.

RANEY, JAMES ELBERT (JIMMY),* *guitar, composer;* b. Louisville, Ky., 8/20/27. Worked with Woody Herman, Buddy De Franco, Artie Shaw, Terry Gibbs, Stan Getz in late '40s and early '50s, later with Red Norvo and Jimmy Lyon trio. Worked with Don Elliott quartet in Broadway show *A Thurber Carnival*, 1960. Rejoined Stan Getz 1962-3. Since then has been doing TV jingles, recordings and private teaching. LPs with

Jim Hall, Zoot Sims (Main.), Gary McFarland (Imp.); Getz on reissues from '50s (Pres. Roost, Main.).

Addr: 141-40 84th Dr., Briarwood 35, N.Y.

RANEY, SUE (Raelene Claire Claussen), *singer, songwriter;* b. McPherson, Kansas, 6/18/40. Studied with mother, who had voice and piano studio in Albuquerque, New Mex. Was prof. singer from age eight. Early band singing experience with Ray Anthony. Worked with Nelson Riddle for BBC in London and for Kennedy's Inaugural Ball. Numerous TV shows with Stan Kenton et al. A charming jazz-influenced singer who names Ella Fitzgerald, Sarah Vaughan as favs.

LPs: Philips, Capitol. Songs: *No Place To Go, Burnt Sugar, Statue of Snow.*

Addr: 9465 Wilshire Blvd., Beverly Hills, Calif.

RASKIN, MILTON WILLIAM (MILT), * *composer, lyricist, piano;* b. Boston, Mass., 1/27/16. Played in Gene Krupa, Tommy Dorsey bands; studio musician in LA since 1944. In the 1960s he conducted and orchestrated for Nancy Wilson, George Shearing, George Chakiris. Lyric for *Naked City* theme (*Somewhere In The Night*) and *The Fugitive* theme for TV. Wrote lyrics to a series of instrumental numbers associated with the Stan Kenton band, which Kenton recorded as *Artistry in Voices and Brass* (Cap.). Raskin also is a talented painter and has had several showings in Southern Calif.

Addr: 24352 Las Naranjas Dr., Laguna Niguel, So. Laguna, Calif.

RAWLS, LOU, *singer;* b. Chicago, Ill., 12/1/35. Gained early experience in a junior choir in church. Later toured with Sam Cooke and with a leading gospel group known as the Pilgrim Travelers. After two years in U.S. Army as parachute jumper, settled in Hollywood in 1958, appeared at Hollywood Bowl with Dick Clark show, and worked local clubs. His first album, *Stormy Monday,* recorded with the Les McCann Trio, was composed mainly of blues and made a big impression on jazz audiences.

Rawls, who also studied dramatics, was seen in acting roles on such TV shows as *Bourbon Street Beat* and *77 Sunset Strip.* Also sang on the *Steve Allen Show,* Johnny Carson's *Tonight Show.*

He has a vigorous, confident style, a strong affinity for the blues and a personal sound. Later albums were conducted by Onzy Matthews (*Black and Blue, Tobacco Road*) and by Benny Carter (*Nobody But Lou, Lou Rawls and Strings*). All are on Capitol.

Addr: 1120 So. Gramercy Pl., Los Angeles, Calif.

RED, SONNY (Sylvester Kyner), * *alto sax;* b. Detroit, Mich., 12/17/32. Pl. w. Barry Harris in Detroit, early '50s; to NYC w. Curtis Fuller '57. Returned to Detroit, then pl. in Canada. Came back to NYC '59 and has been part of local scene since as free-lance. Jobs w. Donald Byrd in early '60s; Kenny Dorham '66. Own LPs: Jazzland; *A Story Tale* w. Clifford Jordan (Jazzland).

REDD, FREDDIE, * *piano, composer;* b. New York City, 5/29/28. Best-known for his score for the off-Broadway production of Jack Gelber's *The Connection,* he app. on stage as player and actor '59-'60, and also in same capacity in film. Free-lanced around NYC w. own group in '60s, then to SF where he pl. w. own trio, John Handy and others. LPs: *Shades of Redd* and *The Connection* (BN).

REDD, VI (Elvira Redd Goldberg), *singer, alto sax, soprano sax;* b. Los Angeles, Calif., 9/20/28. Her father, Alton Redd, a veteran drummer from New Orleans, played with Les Hite, Kid Ory. Brother Buddy and husband, Richard Goldberg, are also drummers. Studied with her great-aunt, Mrs. Alma Hightower, who also taught Melba Liston. Played local dance dates while at high school and at LA City and State colleges, where she majored in social science. Pl. w. Dick Hart and other local groups, 1954-6. Retired from music to join Board of Education, as social worker '57-'60. Returning to music in '61, she played Shelly's Manne-Hole and other LA clubs; Las Vegas JF 1962. Sang and pl. w. Earl Hines at Birdland, NYC, and other clubs in U.S. and Canada 1964. In 1965 she settled in San Francisco, leading a quartet with her husband.

As a singer, Miss Redd has an exceptionally rich, warm and personal timbre and a deep blues feeling. As an alto saxophonist, she is also extraordinarily effective as a blues performer. Originally inspired by Charlie Parker, she also names Sonny Stitt and Phil Woods as her favorites.

Own LPs: *Bird Call* (UA); *Lady Soul* (Atco); also with Al Grey on *Shades of Grey* (Tangerine).

Addr: 2118 Spaulding Ave., Berkeley, Calif.

REDMAN, DONALD MATTHEW (DON), * *composer, leader, saxes;* b. Piedmont, W. Va., 7/29/00. Prominent as saxophonist and arr. w. Fletcher Henderson, 1923-26; McKinney's Cotton Pickers '27-'31, and leader of his own big band '31-'40. Redman also organized the first band to tour Europe after World War II (1946-7). In the 1950s and '60s he was almost entirely inactive as an instrumentalist, worked most frequently as mus. director and arr. for Pearl Bailey. Redman died of a heart attack in NYC, 11/30/64.

A schooled musician in an era when most jazzmen had a limited musical education, Redman played a role of incalculable value in the development of arranged jazz. Though others have been more widely publicized, he certainly was the first musician to make completely successful use of jazz orchestration. His sectionalized concepts, as demonstrated in the early records by Henderson, show that the effective use of brass, reeds and rhythm both in section and ensemble work took a tremendous step forward when Redman began writing regularly. In effect, he was the first real jazz arranger; in addition, during the early days he was an alto (and occasionally soprano) saxophonist with a light, charmingly swinging style, and a vocalist whose recitatif choruses became jazz classics. Among the most famous examples of his talking-singing was the original record of his own composition *Gee Ain't I Good To You* with McKinney's Cotton Pickers. Redman's other well-known compositions were *Cherry, How'm I Doin'*, and *Chant of the Weed*, which he used as the radio theme of his orchestra in the '30s.

An excellent example of Redman's work can be found in an RCA album, *Don Redman—Master of the Big Band*, one side of which is divided to 1929-30 tracks by McKinney's Cotton Pickers while the other side offers eight examples (incl. *Chant of the Weed*) of his 1938-40 band.

REECE, ALPHONSO SON (DIZZY), * *trumpet;* b. Kingston, Jamaica, 1/5/31. Migrated to Europe in '48, pl. w. Don Byas et al. Moved to London '54 and established himself as a leading jazzman in British Isles; also pl. w. Jaques Hélian's big band in Paris. To NYC Oct. '59. Own group at Village Vanguard May '60. Free-lance since then as sideman and occ. leading his own combo as w. experimental films at Bridge Theater '66. Own LPs: Blue Note, New Jazz.

REICHENBACH, WILLIAM FRANK (BILL), *drums;* b. Washington, D.C., 12/18/23. Stud. privately from 1939. Started playing while in service and continued prof. on discharge. Worked w. name bands incl. Art Mooney, 1948, T. Dorsey '51. Acc. Georgia Gibbs 1958-9. Joined Charlie Byrd Trio 1961 and was heard on the celebrated Byrd-Stan Getz album *Jazz Samba* which triggered the bossa nova craze in the U.S. Feat. on all Byrd LPs from 1961 (River., Col., Epic). Favs: S. Manne, Connie Kay, B. Rich.
Addr: 7603 Wildwood Dr., Takoma Park, Md.

REID, IRENE FRANCES, *singer;* b. Savannah, Georgia, 9/23/30. Self-taught. Started as prizewinner in amateur night at Apollo Theatre in Harlem in 1948. After numerous appearances as a single during the 1950s she joined the Count Basie band in Oct. '62 and toured with the orchestra in the U.S. and Europe. Miss Reid was heard (but not credited) in the Basie band's performance of Bessie Smith's *Backwater Blues* in the album *Basie in Sweden* (Roul.). After leaving the band she earned some prominence on her own and made two excellent albums: *It's Only The Beginning*, arr. by Geo. Siravo (MGM), *Room for One More*, arr. Oliver Nelson (Verve). Also sang *Once A Thief* and *The Right To Love* in Lalo Schifrin album (Verve).

Miss Reid names no favorites, believing that there is much to be gained by listening to all the singers, "not copying any style but watching such pointers as diction, delivery, and conception of rhythm." A first-class performer of both ballad and blues, she is a greatly underrated artist.
Addr: 2166 Clinton Ave., Bronx, N.Y.

RENAUD, HENRI, * *piano, composer;* b. Villedieu, Indre, France, 4/20/25. One of the most adaptable free-lance musicians in Paris, Renaud worked in 1961 with Kenny Clarke's quintet at the Blue Note. From '62-

'64 he was house pianist at the Trois Mailletz. From '64-6 played concerts, radio, one nighters with own band as well as with S. Grappelly and others. Movie with Zoot Sims. Composed TV theme for daily show 1964. LPs with Z. Sims, Sonny Criss, own septet and trio for European labels. Also active from 1962 as disc jockey, Radio Monte Carlo, and from '64 as a&r man at CBS Records in Paris.
Addr: 87 Ae. Victor Hugo, Boulogne, 75, France.

RENDELL, DON PERCY, * *tenor sax, clarinet;* b. Plymouth, Eng., 3/4/26. Led own quintet since '60, coinciding with change from Lester Young infl. to more extrovert style. Still among most respected British mus. TV in Belgium '62, Lugano, Switzerland, Jazz Festival '63. Also engaged in voluntary Bible teaching. Own LPs on Jazzland, Brit. Col.
Addr: 23 Weir Hall Gardens, London N.18., England.

RICH, BERNARD (BUDDY), * *drums, singer;* b. Brooklyn, N.Y., 6/30/17. Returning to activity in 1960 after a heart attack, Rich concentrated briefly on singing. He then returned to full-time instrumental work, leading a small combo, and for six months in 1960-61 was part of a show that toured the Far East under the auspices of the U.S. State Department. In 1961 he rejoined the Harry James band, with which he had worked intermittently since 1953. Although still occasionally sidelined by illness, Rich was the vital generating force of the James orchestra and has continued to amaze musicians with his technique, imagination and uniquely propulsive beat. He also made occasional individual appearances away from the band on various TV shows. App. NJF '65. Left James April '66 to form own big band.
Own LPs: Argo, Verve, Mercury. LPs w. James: MGM, Dot.
Addr: 1734 Sombrero Drive, Las Vegas, Nev.

RICHARDS, ANN, * *singer;* b. San Diego, Calif., 10/1/35. Sang with Charlie Barnet, Geo. Redman. Joined Stan Kenton 1955. She was married to Kenton '55-'61. Heard in Playboy clubs and many LA night spots during '60s. A strongly jazz-rooted singer with excellent projection and control.
LPs: *Ann, Man!* (Atco); others on VJ, Cap.

RICHARDS, EMIL (Emilio Joseph Radocchia), * *vibraphone; composer;* also *xylophone, piano, tympani;* b. Hartford, Conn., 9/2/32. The former Geo. Shearing soloist was feat. w. the Paul Horn quintet from 1960-1963. He was also part of a group that went on a world tour accompanying Frank Sinatra, May to July '62. In addition to innumerable studio dates, TV and movie work, he played w. Don Ellis' Hindustani Jazz Sextet, '64-6; worked with Harry Partch from '63 and pl. concerts w. Stan Kenton's Neophonic Orch. '65-6. Richards is the author of a book of original compositions inspired by Indian music, all in unusual time signatures.

LPs w. Horn (Col.), Dizzy Gillespie (Merc.), Kenton (Cap.).

Addr: 4124 Sunswept Dr., No. Hollywood, Calif.

RICHARDS, JOHNNY (John Cascales),* *composer;* b. Schenectady, N.Y., 11/2/11. Wrote and arranged for Boyd Raeburn, Stan Kenton and Charlie Barnet in '40s; string date for Dizzy Gillespie, '50. In '50s continued to contribute to Kenton book, also many freelance dates in NYC from '52. Formed own big band '58 and appeared with it throughout the East, most often at Birdland. In the '60s, Richards busied himself for the most part with writing but did re-form his band for a brief period in '65 with jobs at the Birdland and the Village Gate. Music for film *Kiss Her Goodbye*. LP: *My Fair Lady* Roul.).

RICHARDS, CHARLES (RED),* *piano;* b. Brooklyn, N.Y., 10/19/12. Has played with many traditionalist groups incl. Bobby Hackett, Sidney Bechet, Jimmy McPartland, Muggsy Spanier, Wild Bill Davison. In recent years has led his own all-star group, a sextet praised highly by critics and using a traditional and mainstream repertoire. Known as the Saints and Sinners, the group features Herman Autry, trumpet; Vic Dickenson, trombone; Rudy Powell, clarinet. Feat. regularly at Colonial Tavern in Toronto four times a year, and in hotels and clubs in several U.S. cities. Appeared at Ohio JF Aug. '65. Album released in England: *Saints and Sinners* (Dobell).

Addr: 3944 Paulding Ave., Bronx, N.Y. 10466.

RICHARDSON, JEROME C.,* *saxophones, woodwinds, singer;* b. Oakland, Calif., 12/25/20. With San Francisco bands in 1940s; Lionel Hampton, Earl Hines, Lucky Millinder and many others in NYC in '50s. Frequently w. Quincy Jones from 1960, incl. European tour; subbed as director of the band acc. Tony Bennett.

Richardson has been one of the most active and versatile New York jazzmen of the 1960s. He has continued to lead his own group occasionally (at Minton's, also the Jazz Gallery); gigged w. Kenny Burrell, pl. night clubs w. Peggy Lee, Billy Eckstine, Brook Benton, Julie London, Oliver Nelson; led own band at Basin Street East 1964. TV work w. Sammy Davis.

Own LP: *Going to the Movies* (UA). Many others w. Quincy Jones (Merc.), Leroy Holmes (MGM) et al.

Addr: 250 West 94th St., New York 25, N.Y.

RICHMOND, DANNIE,* *drums;* also *tenor sax;* b. New York City, 12/15/35. This impeccable drummer continued his activities as a member of Charles Mingus' various groups. In 1963 he took part in the poll-winning Impulse album, *Black Saint and Sinner Lady* with Mingus. Appeared at Monterey festivals with Mingus '64-5. Tied for first among new drummers w. A. Dawson in 1965 DB critics' poll.

Own LP: Impulse; LPs with Mingus: Impulse, Atlantic, etc.

Addr: 60 West 142nd St., New York, N.Y.

RIDLEY, LAURENCE HOWARD JR. (LARRY), *bass;* b. Indianapolis, Ind., 9/3/37. Brother plays trumpet. Studied music at Indiana Univ., Lenox Sch. of Jazz; violin w. Michael Krasnopolsky. First gigs were in Indianapolis w. Freddie Hubbard, James Spaulding, Montgomery Bros. Bet. 1960 and '65 toured and worked w. Slide Hampton, P. J. Jones, L. Donaldson, R. Weston, D. Washington, C. McRae, R. Garland, Barry Harris, Josh White, C. Hawkins, J. McLean, R. Haynes, Art Farmer-Jim Hall, Hubbard, S. Rollins, H. Silver. Played two NYC Town Hall concerts w. McLean '63. Newport JF '65. A strong, firm bass player. Favs: Brown, Heath, Pettiford, Chambers, Ware; Ellington, Parker, Rollins, Coltrane, T. Flanagan, W. Montgomery. LPs: w. Hampton (Atl.), B. Barron-B. Ervin (Savoy), Hubbard (BN), Garland (Jazzl.), H. McGhee (UA), Haynes (Pres., Pac. Jazz), McLean (BN).

Addr: 1048 Union St. Apt. 1D, Brooklyn 25, N.Y.

RIGGS, JOE GORDON, *alto sax, clarinet, flute, oboe;* b. Bosworth, Missouri, 1/16/36. Father pl. sax; mother a singer and dancer. Started on sax in 1946 in St. Louis; pl. dance gigs while in high school; stud. George Russell's Lydian Concept with Ed Summerlin at North Texas State Coll. After three years with Ted Weems orch. and later work with Dean Hudson and Charlie Barnet, he joined Harry James and has been featured soloist with him in recent years. Favs: Ch. Parker, P. Woods, C. Adderley, J. Hodges, M. Royal. LPs with James (MGM, Dot).

Addr: c/o Harry James, 1606 Vista Del Mar, Hollywood 28, Calif.

RILEY, BENJAMIN A. JR. (BEN), *drums;* b. Savannah, Ga., 7/17/33. Studied with Cecil Scott in NYC. Played in high school, Air Force bands before first professional job, w. Bobby Brown, in 1956. Between '56 and '65 gigged with Gene Rodgers, R. Weston, N. Simone, K. Burrell, E. Davis-J. Griffin, J. Mance, S. Stitt, S. Getz, W. Herman, P. Winter, A. Jamal, R. Bryant, S. Rollins, D. Katz, R. Hanna, W. Bishop Jr., B. Taylor, K. Winding. With Thelonious Monk from 1964. Toured Europe '64, Europe and Asia '65. At Newport JF '59, '64, '65, several smaller JFs incl. Chicago, Cincinnati, Pittsburgh, Randalls Island. TV appearances w. Simone, Rollins, Monk, Winter. An excellent drummer whose work has complemented Monk's admirably. Favs: Clarke, Roach, Blakey, P. J. Jones, Haynes, Jo Jones. LPs: w. Rodgers (Merc.), Griffin-Davis (River., Pres.), J. Steig (Col.), Rollins (RCA), Monk (Col.), Simone (Colpix), Sam Jones (River.), Winter (Col.).

Addr: 200 State Ave., Wyandanch, N.Y.

RIVERS, SAMUEL CARTHORNE (SAM), *tenor sax;* also *soprano sax, piano, bass clarinet, flute, viola;* b. El Reno, Okla., 9/25/30. Mother a pianist, father a member of Fisk Jubilee Singers and Silvertone Quartet. Raised in Little Rock and Chicago, played in school and local bands. To Boston Conservatory of Music, '47; later attended Boston U. Pl. w. Jaki Byard, Joe

Gordon, Herb Pomeroy, Gigi Gryce in Boston. Two month w. Miles Davis, incl. tour of Japan, summer '64. First recording w. own group, '65.

Rivers, although he received little national attention before the release of his recordings, is known to musicians for his distinctive modern style, derived partly from John Coltrane and Charlie Parker, combined with a warm, personal tone reminiscent of Ben Webster and Lester Young, but with little vibrato. Also influenced by Coleman Hawkins and Sonny Rollins; interested in the new works of Albert Ayler, Archie Shepp. Own LP: *Fuchsia Swing Song* (BN). Others, all on Blue Note, w. Tony Williams, Bobby Hutcherson, etc.

Addr: 310 S. Main St., Randolph, Mass.

ROACH, FREDDIE, *organ, composer;* also *vibes, flute, piano, bass, drums;* b. Bronx, N.Y., 5/11/31. Mother was a church organist; grandmother a concert pianist and choir director. Stud. piano w. uncle. Began playing a pipe organ in the home of an aunt with whom he was living in White Plains, N.Y., in 1939. He also studied at Newark Conservatory but was mainly self-taught as an organist. In 1949 made professional debut with The Strollers, led by Grachan Moncur Jr., the bassist. Played in Marine Corps band 1951-3. Later worked as pianist and/or organist with Chris Columbus, Cootie Williams, Lou Donaldson. Has played bit parts (not as musician) in several movies. Favs: Tatum, Powell, Hank Jones, John Lewis; Jackie Davis, Jimmy Smith, Shirley Scott. Roach has been called by Nat Hentoff "an unusually judicious organist who makes many others sound by contrast as if they are singlemindedly trying to blow down the walls." He is also a composer of some talent, as can be observed on his own LP, *Down To Earth* (Blue Note). Other LPs, as leader, and as sideman with Ike Quebec, all on Blue Note.

ROACH, MAXWELL (MAX), * *drums, composer;* b. Brooklyn, N.Y., 1/10/25. Early associate of Ch. Parker and Dizzy Gillespie; he and Kenny Clarke were first outstanding drummers in the bebop phase of jazz. He has continued to lead small groups during the 60s, was a pioneer in the use of modern choral backgrounds, and has occasionally performed, in concerts and clubs, his *Freedom Now Suite,* written in collaboration with Oscar Brown Jr., and featuring Roach's wife, actress-singer Abbey Lincoln. An Italian film short, based on the suite, was issued in '66.

LPs: *Best of Roach & Brown* (GNP); *It's Time; Percussion Bitter Sweet* (Impulse); *Legendary Hasaan* (Atl.); *Many Sides of Max Roach; Moon-Faced & Starry-Eyed* (Merc.); *Max* (Argo); *Max Roach* (Time); *Speak, Brother, Speak* (Fant.).

Addr: 788 Columbus Ave., New York, N.Y.

ROBERTS, HOWARD MANCEL, * *guitar;* b. Phoenix, Ariz., 10/2/29. Prominent in LA since 1950 as freelance studio musician. In the 1960s he branched out as leader of his own recording groups. Was also heard

in all guitar solo work on the soundtrack of the motion picture *The Sandpiper* with Johnny Mandel on Mercury. Has made occasional personal appearances with own group. LPs: Cap.

Addr: 5002 Wilkinson Ave., No. Hollywood, Calif.

ROGERS, MILTON M. (SHORTY), * *composer, trumpet, fluegelhorn, leader;* b. Great Barrington, Mass., 4/14/24. Played with Red Norvo, Woody Herman in '40s; Stan Kenton, Howard Rumsey in '50s. Later known as composer-arranger for films and albums. In the '60s Rogers has occasionally appeared leading small groups but has confined his work largely to the studios and chiefly to commercial backgrounds for popular singers, etc. Visited London spring '66 in connection w. *That Certain Girl,* a show for which he had written the music.

Own LPs: Atl., Reprise, War. Bros., Cap.

Addr: c/o R. Ginter, 120 El Camino Dr., Beverly Hills, Calif.

ROKER, GRANVILLE WILLIAM (MICKEY), *drums;* b. Miami, Fla., 9/3/32. While in Army 1953-55, began playing drums in drum and bugle corps. After his discharge played w. rock and roll groups in Philadelphia and studied formally at Music City for a few months '56. In Philly until '59 w. Jimmy Heath, Jimmy Oliver, etc. To NYC, Nov. '59 to play w. Gigi Gryce at Five Spot. With Gryce until '61; Ray Bryant '61-3; Joe Williams '63-5 as part of Junior Mance acc. trio. Freelance in NYC '65 w. Milt Jackson, Clifford Jordan, Hank Mobley, Sonny Rollins, Mary Lou Williams. W. Art Farmer from early '66. Favs: Roach, P. J. Jones, Elvin Jones. A tasteful, adaptable, hard-driving drummer. LPs w. Gryce (Pres.), Rollins (Imp., RCA), Bryant (Col.), J. Williams (RCA), Mance (River.), McCoy Tyner (Imp.), Nat Adderley (River.), Duke Pearson, Art Farmer (Atl.).

Addr: 320 West 85th St., New York 24, N.Y.

ROLAND, GENE, * *composer, trumpet, trombone, mellophonium, soprano saxophone;* b. Dallas, Tex., 9/15/21. From 1944 associated w. Stan Kenton as player and writer off and on; also has written for many bands incl. Hampton, Barnet, Thornhill, Shaw, James, Herman. Pioneered "Four Brothers" sound in mid-'40s. In 1960 traveled w. Kenton for five months pl. solo mellophonium. Wrote entire album for Kenton on which he also pl. mellophonium and soprano sax: *Adventures in Blues* (Cap.). Own LP: *Swingin' Friends* (Bruns.).

ROLLINS, THEODORE WALTER (SONNY), * *tenor sax, composer;* b. New York City, 9/7/29. Came to prominence w. Miles Davis and Max Roach groups in mid-'50s. Own group, usually a pianoless trio, from summer of '57 to *Playboy* Festival, Chicago, summer '59. Although he was then at a height of popularity with the jazz public and a powerful influence on his fellow musicians, Rollins then entered a period of self-imposed exile during which he re-assessed his values, investigated Rosicrucianism, and practiced assiduously, most often in the solitude of the pedestrian walk of the Williamsburg Bridge, high above the East River. In late '61 he returned to public playing at the Jazz Gallery, NYC, with a quartet featuring guitarist Jim Hall. His playing had not changed drastically but seemed a refinement and deepening of the kind of melodic theme development he had been identified with in the '50s.

When he replaced Hall with trumpeter Don Cherry in '63, Rollins entered a short period of dabbling in the extreme avant garde but later returned to a style more typical of that associated with him. For a time, he presented his music in an unusual manner by strolling around a club while playing, a set of Indian bells hanging from his neck. In '66 he began using a piano in his group again. His typical club and concert sets are notable for the absence of any pause between selections. Rollins goes through an assortment of standards and originals, varying their length as fits his mood, sometimes returning to the same song several times during the course of a performance. Pl. in Japan '63; Berlin JF '65; Ronnie Scott's, London '65. While in England did score and soundtrack for film, *Alfie*. Won DB critics' poll '62-3; *Playboy* All-Stars' All Stars '63. Among his comps. that have become standards are *Oleo, Airegin, St. Thomas* and *Doxy*.

LPs for RCA: *The Bridge* (2527); *What's New* (2572); *Our Man in Jazz* (2612); *Now's the Time* (2927); *The Standard Sonny Rollins* (3355); *Sonny Meets Hawk* (2712); for Impulse: *Sonny Rollins on Impulse* (91).

Addr: 195 Willoughby Ave., Brooklyn 5, N.Y.

ROSE, WALTER (WALLY),* *piano;* b. Oakland, Calif., 10/2/13. This excellent ragtime revivalist continued working as soloist in various nightclubs and hotels in San Francisco during the early 1960s. During most of 1965 he was at the Fairmont Hotel, SF.

LP: *Blues Over Bodega* w. Lu Watters (Fant.).

Addr: 40 White St., San Francisco, Calif. 94109.

ROSOLINO, FRANK,* *trombone, singer;* b. Detroit, Mich., 8/20/26. First prominent in jazz circles as soloist and bop singer with Gene Krupa 1948-9; also worked with Stan Kenton '52-4; Howard Rumsey at Lighthouse '55-'60.

From summer '62 to fall '64 Rosolino was with Donn Trenner house band on *Steve Allen* TV show, frequently doubling as comedian. Although he was one of the first important trombone soloists produced by the bebop era and is still an exceptionally gifted instrumentalist, Rosolino's only album as a leader features him mainly as a comedy singer: *Turn Me Loose!* (Reprise). Other LPs with Steve Allen (Dot).

Addr: 11651 Paloma St., Garden Grove, Calif.

ROSS, ANNIE (Annabelle Short Lynch),* *singer, songwriter;* b. Mitcham, Surrey, England, 7/25/30. Came to prominence in 1952 with her vocal version of *Twisted*, for which she composed lyrics to a Wardell Gray saxophone improvisation. Achieved international recognition with the formation of the Lambert, Hendricks & Ross Trio in 1958 (see Lambert, Dave; Hendricks, Jon). In April, 1962, while the trio was touring Europe, Miss Ross became ill and was forced to leave the trio. During the next four years she free-lanced extensively with great success in Britain, playing numerous television shows, singing with bands, and working as a single in nightclubs. She was married to British actor Sean Lynch '63. In 1965-6 she was a partner in a club known as Annie's Room. She sang there occasionally herself, but the club usually featured well-known American jazz singers. Recent LP on Brit. Ember. Miss Ross' solo LPs of the 1950s are still available on World Pacific and Prestige; her work with Lambert and Hendricks is on ABC Para., Roul., World Pacific and Col. Festival apps: Warsaw, Bologna '65; Frankfurt '66.

Addr: 12a Douglas Court, West End Lane, London, N.W. 6, England.

ROSS, ARNOLD,* *piano, composer;* b. Boston, Mass., 1/29/21. A member of Glenn Miller's Army band and subsequently prominent in Hollywood with leading bands, combos, and singers, Ross had serious problems with narcotics in the 1950s. His career became erratic. After he entered the Synanon Foundation in Santa Monica, Calif. in July 1960, he not only was cured but became active in the organization of Synanon. He has since worked studio dates from time to time, also toured Australia with Jane Russell '63 as her musical director and accompanist, but is mainly active as a Synanon executive (member of Board of Directors since '64) and has been helpful to musicians and the many non-musicians who have experienced similar difficulties. Played piano and portrayed himself in film *Synanon,* '64. LP: *Sounds of Synanon* (Pac. Jazz).

Addr: Synanon House, 1351 Ocean Front, Santa Monica, Calif.

ROSS, RONALD (RONNIE),* *baritone saxophone;* b. Calcutta, India, 10/2/33. Well known in England during the 1950s through his work with Don Rendell, Ted Heath and others, Ross visited the U.S. with the Newport International Band in '58 and with his own combo the following year. He also toured England with an Anglo-American band led by Woody Herman in '59. In recent years he has played at Jazz Workshop in Hamburg two or three times a year; co-led a band w. Bill Le Sage; jazz festival in Lugano, with Kenny Clarke's big band Sept. '65; also rec. film music w. Benny Golson, Bob Farnon. LPs w. Le Sage on Brit. World Record Club, Brit. Phil.

Addr: 6, Irvine Way, Orpington, Kent, England.

ROUSE, CHARLES (CHARLIE),* *tenor sax;* b. Washington, D.C., 4/6/24. With Eckstine, Gillespie, Ellington bands in '40s; also rec. and pl. w. Tadd Dameron. Co-led Les Jazz Modes w. Julius Watkins '56-8. With T. Monk from '59, he has app. w. him in U.S., Asia and Europe. Rouse is an exuberant bop-derived soloist who well understands Monk's music and delivers it in a personal, immediately recognizable style. Won DB critics' poll as new star '61. Own LPs: Blue Note, Jazzland, Epic; for other LPs see Monk.

ROVÈRE, GILBERT, *bass, cello;* b. Toulon, Var, France, 8/29/39. Brother, Paul, is bassist. Studied at 15; prof. debut with jazz combo in Cannes. Sideman at Blue Note in Paris with Bud Powell, Kenny Drew, Johnny Griffin, Dexter Gordon, Kenny Clarke and others, 1962-3. Replaced Ernie Shepard in Duke Ellington band when Shepard became ill in '64. With Art Simmons 1964-5 at Living Room in Paris; member of Martial Solal trio since Mar. '65. Has also worked with Clark Terry, Sonny Stitt, Stephane Grappelly, Barney Wilen. Many recordings with Wilen, Powell, Lou Bennett, Solal, Jean-Luc Ponty et al. Has played at most Continental jazz festivals. Favs: J. Blanton, C. Mingus, S. La Faro, O. Pettiford, R. Brown; Duke Ellington. Rovère is highly regarded among French and visiting American musicians as a strong section and solo bassist. LP w. Powell (Reprise).
Addr: 6 Rue Bleue, Paris 9, France.

ROWLES, JAMES GEORGE (JIMMY),* *piano, singer;* b. Spokane, Wash., 8/19/18. Played with Benny Goodman, Woody Herman, Tommy Dorsey, Bob Crosby in '40s. Hollywood small combo and studio work in '50s. Regular recordings with Henry Mancini, Neal Hefti for records, films etc. in '60s; staff musician for three years at NBC. Has continued to accompany Peggy Lee occasionally. A tasteful, technically admirable jazz soloist, strongly influenced by Ellington and originally introduced in jazz circles by Ben Webster. Own LP as singer: Capitol. LPs with Billy May, Bill Holman (Cap.); Mancini (RCA); Hefti (various labels); *BBB & Co.* with Benny Carter (Status).
Addr: 638 N. Bel Aire Dr., Burbank, Calif.

ROWSER, JAMES EDWARD (JIMMY),* *bass;* b. Philadelphia, Pa., 4/18/26. With Dinah Washington, Maynard Ferguson in late '50s, free-lancing in New York in '60s. To Mexico with Benny Goodman Sextet June '63. Brazil and Argentina with Friedrich Gulda April-May '64.
LP with Gulda (Col.).
Addr: 595 E. 167th St., Bronx 56, N.Y.

ROYAL, ERNEST ANDREW (ERNIE),* *trumpet;* b. Los Angeles, Calif., 6/2/21. Worked with Les Hite, Cee Pee Johnson in '30s; Lionel Hampton, Woody Herman in '40s. Toured Europe w. Duke Ellington summer '50; then two years w. Jacques Hélian on continent and No. Africa. Pl. w. Stan Kenton, Neal Hefti in '50s. Has been a member of the staff at ABC from '57. A fine jazzman and all-around musician, Royal was once well-known only for his high-note work. LP: *The Thundering Herds* w. Herman (Col.).
Addr: 116-03 128th St., South Ozone Park 20, N.Y.

ROYAL, MARSHALL,* *alto sax, clarinet;* b. Sapulpa, Okla., 12/5/12. Pl. w. Les Hite in '30s; Lionel Hampton in early '40s. Musical director and lead alto player

with the Count Basie orchestra since 1951. For details of his activities in recent years see Basie, Count.
Addr: 5326 Onacrest Dr., Los Angeles 43, Calif.

RUDD, ROSWELL HOPKINS JR., *trombone, composer;* b. Sharon, Conn., 11/17/35. Parents both amateur musicians. Studied French horn as a child. Graduate of Yale Univ. To NYC w. Eli's Chosen Six '54-'59, Herbie Nichols '60-'63; also Wild Bill Davison, Bud Freeman, Ed Hall, Eddie Condon. The value of his experience with traditional groups was apparent later when he graduated into avant garde music. W. Herbie Nichols '60-'62, Steve Lacy '61-'63, NY Art Quartet w. John Tchicai and Milford Graves from Mar. '64. In Denmark and Netherlands Oct.-Nov. '65, making radio, TV and personal appearances. Newport '65 w. Jazz Composers' Orch.
Rudd plays the trombone with a rough urgency that makes him one of the leading spokesmen for the revolution of the '60s. LeRoi Jones, in assessing him as "a gifted arranger and exciting instrumentalist," says that "he is especially a pleasure with his big, muscular trombone sound. The horn sounds, for a change, like there's a human agency behind it. Rudd [is one of] a few musicians trying to restore some humanity to that horn, instead of, say, continuing to imitate J.J.'s automatons." Won DB New Star Award for trombone '63. His arr. of J. Coltrane's *Niema* for an Archie Shepp LP was voted best of year in *Jazz* magazine critics' poll 1966. Favs: Ellington, Monk, and "aboriginal music of the world." LPs: NY Art Quartet (ESP, Phil.), Archie Shepp *Four for Trane* (Impulse).
Addr: 124 Chambers St., New York 7, N.Y.

RUFF, WILLIE,* *bass, French horn;* b. Sheffield, Ala., 9/1/31. Gigged w. Benny Goodman '54, then worked w. Lionel Hampton '55. As Mitchell-Ruff Duo, he and pianist Dwike Mitchell (q.v.) pl. clubs like Birdland. After triumphant impromptu app. at Tschaikovsky Cons. in Moscow '59, they returned to U.S. for concerts, lectures and TV. Adding drummer Charlie Smith, they worked at own club in New Haven, Conn. In '66, w. drummer Helcio Milito as their third man, they pl. at Hickory House, NYC. Ruff and Mitchell also were part of President Johnson's goodwill visit to Mexico in April '66, marking the first time jazzmen took part in a diplomatic mission of this kind. LPs w. Mitchell-Ruff Trio on Atlantic.
Addr: 87 Kensington St., New Haven, Conn.

RUGOLO, PETER (PETE),* *composer;* b. San Piero, Patti, Sicily, 12/25/15. Best known as arranger for Stan Kenton 1945-9 and free lance writer for many jazz and pop dates in the 1950s. Rugolo, who won several magazine polls between 1947 and '54 as the No. 1 jazz arranger, withdrew almost entirely from this field in the 1960s as he became a highly successful writer of musical scores for television, including *The Thriller* series 1962, *Fugitive* '63-5, *Run For Your Life* '65-6 and many others. Briefly reunited with

Kenton in '65 when he wrote an original work for the LA Neophonic Orch.

Addr: 1335 No. Doheny Dr., Los Angeles, 69, Calif.

RUMSEY, HOWARD,* *bass, leader;* b. Brawley, Calif., 11/7/17. Played in original Stan Kenton band 1941-2. Inaugurated jam session policy at The Lighthouse, Hermosa Beach, Calif., 1949 and has remained there ever since, leading various groups composed of outstanding Los Angeles musicians. Since 1962, as musical director of the club, Rumsey has brought in big-name combos and large orchestras. His own group has continued to play there two or three nights a week. By 1966 the Lighthouse was the oldest surviving jazz club in the U.S. Many albums were recorded there by Ramsey Lewis, Art Blakey, The Jazz Crusaders and other groups.

Own LPs: Contemporary.

Addr: The Lighthouse, 30 Pier Ave., Hermosa Beach, Calif.

RUSHING, JAMES ANDREW (JIMMY),* *singer;* b. Oklahoma City, Okla., 8/26/03. Affectionately known as "Mister Five By Five" because of his size, Rushing sang w. Walter Page's Blue Devils and Bennie Moten in the '20s, then rose to fame w. the Count Basie band from '35-'50. Own group until June '52 when he began to work as a single. His robust blues shouting found a new popularity from '57 and he has app. at major festivals and on foreign tours since. With Eddie Condon All Stars in Australia, Japan '64. In '65-6 he played many weekend engagements at the Half Note, NYC, backed by Al Cohn and Zoot Sims, singing in old-time form to the delight of the younger blues-oriented generation as well as his long-time fans. Won DB critics' poll '58-'60. Own LPs: Colpix; LPs w. Basie: reissues on Decca, RCA.

Addr: 32-17 110th St., Corona 69, N.Y.

RUSHTON, JOSEPH AUGUSTINE JR. (JOE),* *bass sax;* b. Evanston, Ill., 4/19/07; d. San Francisco, 3/2/64. Best known for his work with Red Nichols, with whom he played from 1947-63. He and Adrian Rollini are regarded as pioneers of the bass saxophone.

RUSSELL, GEORGE ALLAN,* *composer, piano, leader;* b. Cincinnati, Ohio, 6/23/23. First came to the attention of jazz audiences through the premiere of his work *Cubana Be-Cubana Bop*, introduced by Dizzy Gillespie's band in 1947. From 1953 he spent most of his time formulating the principles upon which, he says, the contemporary jazz of the 1960s is based. His thesis, the *Lydian Concept of Tonal Organization*, has been revised periodically since then and is correctly claimed by Russell to have been "jazz's first major theoretical contribution to the entire world of music."

In 1960 Russell formed his own sextet, which pl. at Five Spot Cafe, Birdland, Museum of Modern Art, Lincoln Center, the 1962 Washington Jazz Festival, later performing throughout the Midwest and playing at Newport in '64.

The sextet toured Europe in Sept.-Oct. '64 with George Wein's History of Jazz package show. Russell and most of his men remained in Europe; the sextet played clubs and TV in Scandinavia and Germany. Toured Swedish schools, '65; Molde, Norway JF, summer '65. Russell also taught his Lydian Concept in Stockholm and was interviewed with Karlheinz Stockhausen at a concert that featured the music of both.

Russell became in the 1950s, and has remained, one of the few scholarly musicians with firm bases in both classical music and jazz and the rare ability to fuse the idioms with complete success. As Pete Welding wrote in DB, "Russell's success on records has been due as much to his having been able to attract and stimulate men sympathetic to his musical goals and to draw the utmost from them as it has been to his brilliant gifts as a composer. Russell's music demands much of its participants; they must . . . respond to it . . . to a degree rarely demanded of jazzmen. For his is first and foremost a collective music."

LPs: *The Stratus Seekers, Ezzthetic, Stratusphunk, The Outer View* (River.); *Russell Sextet at the Five Spot, Russell Sextet in Kansas City* (Dec.); *Jazz Workshop* (RCA); *Russell Sextet at Beethoven Hall,* w. Don Cherry, for German label (SABA).

Addr: 10 Hillside Avenue, New York 40, N.Y.

RUSSELL, LUIS CARL, *leader, composer, piano;* b. Careening Cay, Panama, 8/5/02. Prominent as leader of his own band in Chicago and of the band that accompanied Louis Armstrong from 1935-43, Russell was an active bandleader until 1948 but spent most of the 1950s in retirement. He died of cancer, 12/11/63 in NYC. Russell's band can be heard in a few tracks with Armstrong (Col.), but some of the excellent sides he made under his own name have long been unavailable.

RUSSELL, CHARLES ELLSWORTH (PEE WEE),* *clarinet;* b. St. Louis, Mo., 3/27/06. Prominent with small jazz groups on records and in clubs from 1927, Russell frequently worked with Eddie Condon in the 1930s and '40s and also with various groups organized by George Wein in the '50s.

During the 1960s Russell's reputation as a unique voice in jazz grew substantially on an international level. He toured Europe with George Wein's All Stars in the spring of 1961; Australia, New Zealand and Japan with Eddie Condon in early '64; visited Europe again with Wein in fall of '64, and soon afterward paid an individual visit to England for concert appearances.

In the U.S. Russell played the Newport and Monterey JF; DB JF in Chicago '65. Played in Museum of Modern Art concert taped and televised by NBC July '65. Played radio commercial for American Motors in '65. He was almost invariably a winner of the annual critics' poll conducted by DB.

Russell, not content to settle for the harmonic and melodic limitations of the Dixieland repertoire, began to experiment in the '60s with new material, recording compositions by Thelonious Monk, Ornette Coleman, and others representing post-Dixieland schools of jazz. His basic improvisational style, however, retained its own attractively individual coarseness and achieved frequent moments of warm intensity. Recent LP: *New Groove* (Col.). Also available is an LP of reissues from the Commodore catalog of the 1930s and '40s, *Pee Wee Russell—A Legend* (Mainstream).

Addr: 345 8th Ave., New York, N.Y. 10001.

RUSSELL, TONY, *trombone, leader, composer;* b. Wanstead, Essex, England, 5/24/29. Pl. w. George Webb's Dixielanders '47, army '47-9, then toured and rec. w. Vic Lewis, Jack Parnell, Tony Crombie, and many others. '56-'65 w. Johnny Dankworth. Stud. composition w. Richard Rodney Bennett and Bill Russo, joined Russo's London Jazz Orch. '63, took over leadership of London Jazz Orch. '64, and heard with them since on Eng. concerts and broadcasts. Comp. score of musical *The Matchgirls* '66. LPs w. Dankworth (Roulette, Brit. Col., Brit. Fontana), London Jazz Orchestra (Brit. Col.). Fav. own solos on own comps. *Joe and Lol's Blues* w. Dankworth, *Loves Labour* w. London Jazz Orch.

RUSSO, WILLIAM JOSEPH JR. (BILL), * *composer, trombone;* b. Chicago, Ill. 6/25/28. Early jazz experience with Lee Konitz, Lennie Tristano. Played with several name bands and was arranger and occasional trombonist with Stan Kenton 1950-55. Later lived in Chicago, New York and Europe, devoting much of his time to writing symphonies and ballet music.

In 1961-2 Russo was in Rome completing an opera. From 1962-5 he was based in London, where his writing included *The Island,* presented on BBC, and *The English Concerto* for Yehudi Menuhin. Other works included the TV opera or jazz musical, *Land of Milk and Honey,* presented on BBC TV in '64. In '65 he was director of the Center for New Music at Columbia College in Chicago. Still interested in jazz, he organized a local jazz ensemble. In Mar. 1966 he appeared as guest conductor of the Los Angeles Neophonic Orch., introducing his own work *In Memoriam (To The Memory of Philip Ball).* LPs: *The Seven Deadly Sins* (Roul.); own British big band (FM).

Addr: 260 E. Chestnut St., Chicago, Ill. 60611.

RUTHER, WYATT (BULL), * *bass;* b. Pittsburgh, Pa., 2/5/23. Pl. w. Brubeck, Garner, Ottawa Symphony, Chico Hamilton, Shearing in '50s. Buddy Rich '60-'61 incl. overseas tours. In '62 he worked w. Cohn-Sims, G. Mulligan, A. Jamal. Acc. C. McRae and other singers '63-4, also pl. w. Mary Lou Williams, Chuck Wayne. Worked w. Count Basie band (incl. dates with Sinatra), Sept. '64-April '65. Free-lanced in SF with John Handy, Chris Ibanez '65-6.

LPs w. B. Rich, Basie (Verve); Al Grey, Ray Charles (Tangerine).

Addr: 208 Cardinal Rd., Mill Valley, Calif. 94941.

SAFRANSKI, EDWARD (EDDIE), * *bass;* b. Pittsburgh, Pa., 12/25/18. In the 1940s played with Hal McIntyre for four years, then rose to prominence w. Stan Kenton '45-8, winning numerous polls and awards. After working w. Charlie Barnet '48-9, he became a staff member of NBC in NYC. App. in the TV series *The Subject is Jazz* '58; *Dial M for Music* '66.

Addr: 53 Coolidge Ave., Rye, N.Y.

ST. CYR, JOHN ALEXANDER (JOHNNY), * *banjo, guitar;* b. New Orleans, La., 4/17/1890. A veteran of many pioneer bands including Fate Marable, St. Cyr remained active during the 1960s with a group of veterans known as the Young Men From New Orleans, heard every summer season from 1960 on a riverboat in the New Orleans quarter at Disneyland until his death in L.A. on 6/17/66. TV appearances: Red Rowe, Ed Sullivan; *Chicago and All That Jazz,* NBC special 1961.

ST. JAMES, ALBERT, *drums;* b. St. Louis, Mo., 8/15/34. Largely self-taught. First gig w. Jimmy Forrest. Played w. Charlie Parker summer '54. W. Dick Gregory '63, Quartette Tres Bien in concert w. Nancy Wilson St. Louis '64, tour of Midwest, West Coast '64-'65. Comps. for QTB incl. *Blues for the Congo, I Remember Jamie.* Favs: Blakey, Haynes, P. J. Jones. Infl. on writing: T. Dameron, H. Silver. LPs: w. QTB (Decca), incl. own fav. *Steppin' Out.*

Addr: 5937 Page, St. Louis, Mo.

SALOMON, HANS, * *tenor sax, composer;* also *alto sax, clarinet;* b. Vienna, Austria, 9/10/33. Appeared around Austria and Germany from '54; also active in film, TV and concert work. Joined Johannes Fehring's big band in '56, and appeared regularly with him from that time. Began to play bass clarinet '63. Also played and recorded w. Friedrich Gulda. LPs: w. Fehring, Gulda.

Addr: Treustrasse 92, Vienna 20, Austria.

SALVADOR, SAL, * *guitar, leader;* b. Monson, Mass., 11/21/25. With Stan Kenton in '50s, then led own combo. Formed big band in late '50s and continued to lead it intermittently in the '60s. In mid-'60s cut down to small group again. Own LPs: Roulette, Golden Crest.

Addr: 136 W. 46th St., New York 36, N.Y.

SAMPLE, JOSEPH LESLIE, *piano;* b. Houston, Tex., 2/1/39. Studied piano while in grade school. A member of the Jazz Crusaders since 1954. In LA also worked with Roy Ayers, Curtis Amy, Philly Joe Jones, Frank Butler, Don Wilkerson. In '65 accompanied Johnny Hartman, Bill Henderson. Appeared w. Jazz Crusaders on TV *Jazz Scene USA.* Favs. and infl: Oscar Peterson, Phineas Newborn, Fats Waller, Art Tatum; Debussy, Stravinsky, Webern. LPs: w. Jazz Crusaders (Pac. Jazz).

Addr: 2112 W. 76th St., Los Angeles, Calif.

SANDERS, FARRELL (PHARAOH), *tenor saxophone;* b. Little Rock, Ark., 10/13/40. In 1959 he moved to Oakland, Calif., where he stud. locally and worked w. Hughie Simmons and other groups. Moving to New York in 1962, he pl. w. Rashied Ali, Don Cherry, Sun Ra, John Gilmore and many other small groups mostly composed of avant gardists. He showed a strong link to John Coltrane but his later style and sound have had much in common with the work of Albert Ayler. He is not concerned with a conventional use of the saxophone as a melodic medium, but has achieved some extraordinary sounds, many of them the result of considerable technical virtuosity, in which two or three tones can sometimes be heard simultaneously. Own LP: ESP; also feat. w. John Coltrane (Impulse).

SANTAMARIA, RAMON (MONGO), *leader, Latin percussion instruments;* b. Havana, Cuba, 4/7/22. Raised in the Jesus Maria district of Havana, Santamaria was exposed from childhood to a variety of Afro-Cuban rhythms. His grandfather had come to Cuba directly from Africa. As a child he studied violin but soon switched to drums and by the early 1940s was well established as a conga and bongo expert. He toured internationally during three years with Perez Prado. Later spent seven years with Tito Puente, three years with Cal Tjader and led his own group from 1961. Scored big commercial success with his version of Herbie Hancock's composition *Watermelon Man.* Much of his later work skirted the boundary line between Latin popular music and Afro-Cuban-tinged jazz.

Santamaria's main influence was Chano Pozo. His ambition, he says, is to establish all over the world an effective combination of Afro-Cuban and Latin concepts with rhythm-and-blues and jazz.

Concerts w. D. Gillespie, J. McDuff, et al; TV w. Andy Williams; movie, *Made In Paris,* released 1966.

LPs: Eleven early albums for Fantasy; five for River. in early 1960s; more recently with Col.

Addr: 304 West 89th St., NYC, N.Y.

SAUTER, EDWARD ERNEST (EDDIE),* *composer;* b. Brooklyn, N.Y., 12/2/14. A veteran arranger, Sauter came to prominence w. Red Norvo and Benny Goodman in the '30s and '40s. Co-led popular jazz band w. Bill Finegan '52-'57. Arranged *Joy of Christmas* for N.Y. Philharmonic and Tabernacle Choir, 1963. Movie: *Mickey One* w. Stan Getz, '65. LP: *Focus* w. Getz (Verve).

Addr: 10 Wheeler Pl., West Nyack, N.Y.

SCHIFANO, FRANK, *bass;* also *Fender bass;* b. Brooklyn, N.Y., 12/19/27. Studied bass at High School of Performing Arts, NYC, and began taking local jobs while still in school. Worked as sideman in 1948 with Kenny Drew, Allen Eager. Joined Buddy Rich, 1949. During '50s worked with many pop and jazz groups including Herbie Fields 1954, Kai Winding '58. In early '60s worked in Latin bands including Machito

'62, Tito Puente '64. Switched to Fender electric bass and joined Dizzy Gillespie combo Jan. 1966.

Addr: 255-55 148 Ave., Rosedale, N.Y. 11422.

SCHIFRIN, BORIS (LALO), *piano;* b. Buenos Aires, Arg., 6/21/32. Father was concertmaster of Buenos Aires Philharmonic. Studied piano from '40; harmony at 16; sociology, law, at Univ. of Buenos Aires. After Argentine army service, went to Paris on scholarship. Stud. w. disciple of Maurice Ravel, meanwhile playing with local jazz combos. Represented Argentina at Internat'l Jazz Festival, Salle Pleyel, '55.

Returning home, Schifrin formed a 16-pc. band, the first Argentine group in what he calls "the Basie-Gillespie tradition." Gillespie, visiting Argentina in '56, heard this band and expressed hope Schifrin would write something for him.

In '57 he began writing for films. A jazz score for *El Jefe* won an Argentine Academy Award. A non-jazz, 12-tone score the following year won him another award. In '58 Schifrin moved to NYC. Worked with jazz trio, wrote many arrangements for X. Cugat. In '59 he took a sketch of his *Gillespiana Suite* to Gillespie. The latter, impressed with the youngster's playing as well as his writing, hired him for his quintet in 1960.

Schifrin toured with Gillespie for three years. His most important contributions as writer are *Gillespiana,* introduced Nov. '61 at Carnegie Hall, and *New Continent,* presented at Monterey Jazz Festival in '62. In '62 he was commissioned by the Washington Jazz Festival to write a ballet, *Jazz Faust.*

Leaving Gillespie in Nov. '62, Schifrin played gigs and records with Quincy Jones, then returned to writing on an almost full-time basis. Within the next couple of years he had made so much headway, with constant demands for his services as a writer of TV and movie scores, that he moved to Bev. Hills, Calif. and soon had almost a dozen film scores to his credit. Films include *Rhino, Joy House, Once A Thief, Blindfold, The Black Cloak, See How They Run, Cincinnati Kid, The Liquidator.* TV scores for *Chrysler Theater.*

As pianist, Schifrin names T. Monk, Bill Evans, Peterson and Bud Powell as influences. His writing influences, he says, have been Dizzy Gillespie and Igor Stravinsky.

Schifrin has continued to record frequently as a jazz artist, most often as composer and conductor, occasionally also as pianist. In addition to his own LPs on Roulette and Verve, he is best known for the brilliant original *Jazz Suite on the Mass Text,* recorded by Paul Horn (RCA). Other albums: *Sweet Sass* for Sarah Vaughan (Roulette), *Reflections* for Stan Getz (Verve) and *The Cat* for Jimmy Smith (Verve). This last won him a NARAS award for best orginal jazz composition of '64.

In bringing Lalo Schifrin to the attention of the American public, Dizzy Gillespie performed a major service for music. Schifrin, an extraordinarily gifted pianist and an eclectic writer, names as his goal the integration of classical music and jazz. To a greater extent than most others who have stated this aim, he has already succeeded.

Addr: 213 El Camino, Beverly Hills, Calif.

SCHULLER, GUNTHER,* composer; b. Jackson Heights, N.Y., 11/11/25. Began his association with jazz as sideman on Miles Davis record, 1950. Originally a classical musician and French horn player with the Metropolitan Opera for 10 years, Schuller during the '50s became interested in jazz and was the first classical figure prominently identified with the synthesis of forms known as Third Stream music.

In 1961 he served as acting music director at the Monterey JF. He was musical director for the first International JF held in Washington, D.C. in '62. In 1963-4, continuing a long association with John Lewis, he was conductor of Orchestra U.S.A. Also in 1963 he presented the first full-fledged jazz concert ever held at Tanglewood, Mass., and went on a State Department-sponsored visit as American music specialist, lecturing in Poland, Yugoslavia and Germany on new developments in jazz.

As a composer, Schuller is well known for his jazz ballet *Variants,* commissioned and presented by the City Center Ballet with choreography by Geo. Balanchine in 1961. Also comp. *Concertino for Jazz Quartet & Orch.* rec. w. MJQ (Atl.), *Abstraction* and *Variants on a Theme of Thelonious Monk* w. John Lewis (Atl.), *Conversation* w. MJQ et al. in *Third Stream Jazz* (Atl.), *Journey Into Jazz* w. Orch. U.S.A. (Col.); conducted Orch. U.S.A. on Colpix LP.

Addr: 610 West End Avenue, New York 24, N.Y.

SCHUTT, ARTHUR,* piano; b. Reading, Pa., 11/21/02. Heard on innumerable significant jazz records of the late 1920s and early '30s with Frank Trumbauer, Bix Beiderbecke, Red Nichols, Joe Venuti, the Dorsey Bros., Benny Goodman et al, Schutt later worked as a Hollywood studio musician. According to John Hammond he was one of the most important pianists of his era. After a long period of inactivity and illness, Schutt died in San Francisco 1/28/65.

SCOBEY, ROBERT (BOB),* trumpet, leader; b. Tucumcari, N. Mex., 12/9/16. A traditionalist veteran well known for his association with Lu Watters in the 1940s, Scobey later formed his own Frisco Jazz Band, which enjoyed musical and commercial success during the '50s, mainly in and around San Francisco. Later moved to Chicago, where he played clubs off and on. He was at Bourbon St. during most of 1961-2 and briefly in '63, despite serious illness. He died of cancer in Montreal, Can., 6/12/63.

SCOTT, BOBBY,* composer, leader, piano, singer; b. Bronx, N.Y., 1/24/37. A child prodigy; made prof. debut at age 11 and while in teens pl. w. Louis Prima, Tony Scott, Gene Krupa. By late 1950s had begun to concentrate on composing. During 1960s worked closely w. Quincy Jones as pianist, arranger and re-

cording supervisor at Mercury Records. Scored major popular hit w. title song from his score for *A Taste of Honey.*

Own LP: Merc. LPs w. Q. Jones (Merc.), Chet Baker (Lime.).

Addr: c/o Mercury Records, 745 Fifth Avenue, New York 22, N.Y.

SCOTT, CLIFFORD, saxes, flute, clarinet; b. San Antonio, Tex., 6/21/28. Studied clarinet in high school. First gig was w. Lionel Hampton big band on long European tour '53. Joined Bill Doggett r & b combo in '56 and performed on Doggett's million-selling single *Honky Tonk.* Appeared on Steve Allen TV show w. own group '64; also *Kraft Theatre* and *Alfred Hitchcock,* and MGM film *Drums of Africa.* Scott has become an increasingly popular performer in the r & b tradition. Favs: Coltrane, Hodges, Young, Ammons, Adderley, Parker. Infl: Ammons, Hodges. LPs: King, Cap., Pac. Jazz, Inf., Class.

Addr: 6423 3rd Ave., Los Angeles, Calif.

SCOTT, RONNIE,* tenor sax; b. London, England, 1/28/27. Pl. w. many British bands incl. Ted Heath, Jack Parnell to '53 when he formed own group. Jazz Couriers w. Tubby Hayes '56. Pl. in U.S. '55. Continent '56, '59. Opened own club '59, which has since presented visiting American groups and soloists as well as English musicians incl. Scott. Pl. a week at Half Note in NYC w. Jimmie Deuchar, Ronnie Ross in '63. Virile soloist w. affinity for Rollins, Stitt, Mobley.

Addr: Ronnie Scott Club, 47 Frith St., London W.I., England.

SCOTT, SHIRLEY,* organ; b. Philadelphia, Pa., 3/14/34. In '60, after a four-year association w. Eddie "Lockjaw" Davis, she left to form own trio. Soon after, joined forces w. Stanley Turrentine (q.v.), whom she later married. A hard-driving, blues-rooted player, Miss Scott has continued to record on her own as well as with her husband. Own LPs: Imp., Pres.; w. Turrentine (BN).

Addr: 183 Stuyvesant Road, Teaneck, N.J.

SCOTT, TONY (Anthony Sciacca),* clarinet, saxes, piano, composer; b. Morristown, N.J., 6/17/21. Played in many small combos in 52nd St. clubs during 1940s and early '50s also with big bands of Buddy Rich, Charlie Ventura, Claude Thornhill; briefly with Duke Ellington '53. Worked mainly with own groups 1954-9.

From Dec. 1959 until July 1965 Scott remained outside the U.S. touring the Far East. He visited Japan, Formosa, Okinawa, Hong Kong, Korea, the Philippines, Indonesia, Bali, Singapore, Malaya, Thailand and Saigon. He was the first modern American jazz musician to make extensive visits to these areas. He recorded classical folk music of the Far East and made concert appearances with players of Oriental instruments. In addition to appearing at the first Hong Kong JF Jan. 1961 and first Japan JF in '62, he made several tours of U.S. bases in Japan, took part in jazz clinics, and was the featured performer in several TV programs in Japan. He played one concert for and with the King of Thailand; played with a traditional Balinese orchestra in Bali, and with a noted Indian classical singer at Hindu and Sikh Temples in Hong Kong in '64. He recorded frequently for Japanese labels.

Returning home, Scott appeared at the Newport JF in 1965. He subsequently played clubs and concerts in NY, most notably a long engagement at a new club, The Dom, where he led a quartet with which many leading NYC musicians sat in. He incorporated folk songs of the Far East in his repertoire.

LP: *Music for Zen Meditation* (Verve).

Addr: 587 W. Merrick Rd., Valley Stream, L.I., N.Y.

SEAMEN, PHILLIP WILLIAM (PHIL), *drums;* b. Burton-on-Trent, Staffordshire, England, 8/28/26. Since '45 pl. and rec. w. Nat Gonella, Tommy Sampson, Paul Fenoulhet, Jack Parnell, Ronnie Scott, Don Rendell, Kenny Graham, Tubby Hayes, Joe Harriott, Scott-Hayes Jazz Couriers, Dick Morrissey, and own gps. Aggressive player with exceptional technique and invention, the most prominent modern jazzman in Eng. on his instrument. LPs w. Dizzy Reece, Tubby Hayes, Jimmie Deuchar, Ronnie Scott (all Brit. Tempo), Joe Harriott (Jazzland), Dick Morrissey, Harry South (both Brit. Mercury), among others.

Addr: 46a Glebe Rd., London S.W.13., England.

SEBESKY, DONALD J. (DON), * *composer, trombone;* b. Perth Amboy, N.J. 12/10/37. Studied drums, accordion, trumpet, bass, piano and arranging. Prof. debut through help of Warren Covington, with whom he studied at high school. Played trombone in the Commanders and the Tommy Dorsey bands, both under Covington's leadership; also with Kai Winding, Stan Kenton, Claude Thornhill and Maynard Ferguson. He then gave up playing to concentrate on arranging and conducting. Already well known for his writing with Ferguson, he arranged albums for Carmen Mc-Rae, Astrud Gilberto, Wes Montgomery and Charles Mariano. Conductor and arranger on *Jimmy Dean Show* ABC-TV; has also written large orchestral symphonic work, violin sonata and trumpet concerto.

As a soloist Sebesky was heard to advantage in *Frame For The Blues* with Ferguson (Roulette); as a writer he contributed to many Ferguson albums on Roul., Cameo, and Mainstream.

Fav. trom.: B. Harris, B. Brookmeyer, J. J. Johnson.

Fav. arr.: Bill Holman, Al Cohn, Johnny Mandel, Bill Finegan, Marty Paich and Gerry Mulligan.

Sebesky is a colorful writer whose skill has been shown to great advantage in all the above contexts.

Addr: 58 Stonybrook Rd., Somerville, N.J.

SEDRIC, EUGENE HALL (GENE or HONEY BEAR), * *clarinet, tenor;* b. St. Louis, Mo., 6/17/07. Prominent as an associate of Fats Waller in many of his combo recordings in the middle and late 1930s, Sedric later

worked with Jimmy McPartland and Bobby Hackett. After visiting France and playing there with Mezz Mezzrow, he joined Conrad Janis' traditional combo in NYC. After a long illness he died in NYC, 4/3/63. His sharp, piercing and often hard swinging clarinet, as well as his warmer tenor saxophone style, can be heard in various Fats Waller reissues on RCA and Camden.

SETE, BOLA (Djalma De Andrada), *guitar;* also *lute, composer;* b. Rio de Janeiro, Brazil, 7/16/28. Father played guitar in Rio; sister was pianist and music teacher. Studied theory and harmony at National School of Music in Rio.

Sete made his prof. musical debut playing with a Brazilian folk music group; later became interested in jazz and went on to the conservatory to learn more about music. He was a staff musician on three radio stations in Rio before moving to the U.S. in 1960. For a long while after his arrival here he played, unrecognized by jazz fans, as a featured soloist in lounges of hotels on the Sheraton chain. Heard by Dizzy Gillespie in such a lounge, he made his first jazz impact when he appeared at the Monterey Jazz Festival in Sept. 1962, playing solo and with Gillespie. After recording w. Gillespie, he signed w. Fantasy records. From 1963-6 Sete was heard both in person and on records as a featured soloist with the Vince Guaraldi trio. Together they have worked on motion pictures and TV sound-tracks, also six shows for National Educational Television. Sete has also toured Europe and appeared on BBC programs. Formed own group '66.

Of the innumerable guitarists spawned by the bossa nova movement Bola Sete almost beyond question is the most versatile and talented. Inspired by Andres Segovia, he has shown himself capable of unaccompanied, unamplified performances in the classical guitar tradition; yet his jazz work—inspired by George Van Eps, B. Kessel, Tal Farlow—has an authenticity and a swing rare in guitarists of any nationality. His bossa nova performances, of course, have evidenced a sensitive amalgamation of Brazilian and U.S. rhythmic values. Sete's ultimate aim, he says, is to write more original music for TV, motion pictures and records, and to give frequent concerts at colleges.

Despite the extraordinary quality and considerable quantity of his LP output, Sete says, "I still have not made a record that really captures all I am trying to say."

Own LPs: *The Incomparable Bola Sete, Tour de Force, Bossa Nova* (all Fant.); others include *From All Sides* w. Guaraldi (Fant.), *New Wave* w. Gillespie (Phil.).

Addr: 22-2nd St., Sausalito, Calif.

SEVERINSEN, CARL H. (DOC), * *trumpet;* b. Arlington, Ore., 7/7/27. Sideman with several leading swing bands in the 1940s and a staff musician at NBC throughout the '50s, Severinsen rose to national prominence from October 1962 as a member and assistant conductor of the Skitch Henderson orchestra on the nightly NBC program *Tonight,* with Johnny Carson. Severinsen, a very capable jazz soloist and a trumpeter with all-around command of the instrument, has also made frequent appearances around the U.S. as brass clinician and consultant for a musical instrument company. He has been seen as guest artist on the Perry Como show and other programs, and as soloist with the Amarillo, Minneapolis and other symphony orchestras. Led own band, Basin St. E., '66.

In a sideline that has taken up his spare time in recent years he has operated Harmony Farms Inc., breeding registered quarter horses.

Severinsen has recorded a series of LPs of a pop nature for the Command label, but has also been heard in such jazz LPs as Stan Getz's *Big Band Bossa Nova,* Bob Brookmeyer's *Gloomy Sunday* and some of Gerry Mulligan's big band sessions (all Verve).

Addr: RFD 1, Box 85, Bellvale Road, Warwick, N.Y.

SHANK, CLIFFORD EVERETT JR. (BUD),* *alto sax, baritone sax, flute, composer;* b. Dayton, Ohio, 5/27/26. An important figure in West Coast jazz from 1947, Shank continued to develop his talents and move into more areas of music during the '60s. Active in the studios, Shank wrote the music for the films *Barefoot Adventure* and *War Hunt* in '61 and '62. Recorded with Japanese kotoist Kimio Eto '60, Indian sitarist Ravi Shankar '62, w. several Brazilian musicians '65. International appearances incl. Mexico City Palacio de Bellas Artes '62; 1st S. American JF, Argentina '63; concerts in Rio de Janeiro and Buenos Aires '63 and '64; JFs in France, Switzerland and Sicily '63; TV and concert appearances in Rome and Yugoslavia '63. Own LPs: Pac. Jazz; w. Brasil '65 (Cap.), Gerald Wilson (Pac. Jazz), Julie London (Lib.). Others w. Kenton et al. Hit pop LP, *Michelle,* '66.

Addr: 12347 Valleyheart Dr., Studio City, Calif.

SHAUGHNESSY, EDWIN THOMAS (ED),* *drums;* b. Jersey City, N.J., 1/29/29. Played with most of the major bands and as prominent studio musician from 1948. Small group jobs w. Eddie Condon, Joe Newman, Charles Mingus, Don Ellis, Teddy Charles, Oliver Nelson, Stan Getz, Skitch Henderson, Mundell Lowe. Member Orchestra U.S.A. from '62. Has published book on jazz drumming and had own comps. recorded by Clare Fischer, Teddy Charles. LPs: w. Nelson (Pres.), Newman (Merc.), Gary McFarland (Verve), Gary Burton (Vict.), Jimmy Smith (Verve).

Addr: 325 West End Ave., New York 23, N.Y.

SHAVERS, CHARLES JAMES (CHARLIE),* *trumpet, singer, composer;* b. New York City, 8/3/17. Shavers' long association with the original Tommy Dorsey orchestra in the 1940s and '50s was renewed in the '60s when he joined a band under Dorsey's name, actually conducted by Sam Donahue. He remained with this unit when its name was changed late in 1965 to the Frank Sinatra Jr. Show. Presented as a featured vocalist and instrumentalist, Shavers enjoyed favorable reactions as the band toured Canada, the U.S., Latin America, and in the summer of '64 made an extensive tour of Japan and other Pacific areas.

Shavers' other activities in recent years have included record dates in NYC and a brief engagement with Benny Goodman. He has retained the clean, clear sound that established him as one of the most original trumpet soloists of the swing years.

Own LPs on Everest and Capitol; also with Dorsey on RCA; T. Dameron on River.

Addr: 31-28 101st St., E. Elmhurst 69, N.Y.

SHAW, ARTIE (Arthur Arshawsky),* *clarinet, composer, leader;* b. New York City, 5/23/10. After several years playing with dance bands and working on radio shows, Shaw became a bandleader in 1935 and enjoyed his peak years of success shortly after his record of *Begin The Beguine,* made in 1938, became a best seller. He continued to lead bands off and on through the '40s and formed a small combo with which he worked in 1953-4, but from 1956-60 he was in retirement in Spain.

Now completely retired from music, Shaw has been occupied with his position as president of Artixo Productions, a film distribution and production company. He is also the author of two books. One, *The Trouble With Cinderella,* a semi-autobiographical work, was published in the 1950s; the second, a novel entitled *I Love You, I Hate You, Drop Dead!* appeared in 1965.

Addr: c/o Artixo Productions, Ltd., 575 Lexington Ave., New York, N.Y. 10022.

SHAW, ARVELL, *bass;* b. St. Louis, Mo., 9/15/23. Shaw's association with Louis Armstrong, which began in 1945 when Armstrong was still fronting a big band, was renewed in 1964. He toured the Iron Curtain countries, the Far East and Australia, also played on Armstrong's *Hello Dolly* album. Benny Goodman, with whom Shaw had toured Europe in 1958, hired him again in '62 for a trip to Latin America. Shaw also recorded with Lionel Hampton in '62. Free-lance work in New York City '65-'66.

Addr: 1580 President Street, #20, Brooklyn, New York 11213.

SHAW, CLARENCE EUGENE (GENE), *trumpet;* b. Detroit, Mich., 6/16/26. Took piano lessons at four, switched to trombone at six; later returned to studying classical piano for two years. After Army service, was convalescing in an Army hospital in Detroit when he developed an interest in the trumpet. Inspired by Dizzy Gillespie's record of *Hot House* and helped by a friend, Allan Bryant, he made rapid progress on trumpet and within a few weeks was playing his first job at a Detroit club. He later studied harmony, theory, and composition at Detroit Inst. of Music. After working around Detroit he played jobs with Lester Young, Wardell Gray, Lucky Thompson, also worked for a while with Charles Mingus. In 1957 he recorded the album *Tijuana Moods* with Mingus (RCA). It was not issued until five years later, but Mingus observed: "If this album had been released in 1957, Shaw would be a star today." Own LPs: Cadet.

SHEARING, GEORGE ALBERT,* *piano, composer;* b. London, England, 8/13/19. Discovered by this writer at a Rhythm Club jam session in London, Shearing made his record debut at 19 and for many years was Britain's most popular jazz pianist. After settling in the U.S. in Dec. '47 he formed his quintet, with the aid of the writer, in Jan. '49 and enjoyed tremendous popular success with it throughout the '50s.

In Oct. 1961 Shearing moved from NYC to No. Hollywood, Calif. His quintet at that time included Israel Crosby and Vernel Fournier. Late in '62 Shearing broke up the quintet and formed a West Coast group with a similar sound. Its members during the next few years included Gary Burton, Joe Pass, Bob Whitlock, John Guerin and other West Coast musicians.

After disbanding this group, Shearing spent virtually all of 1964 in retirement, studying classical piano with Jakob Gimpel. He also acted as disc jockey on a local radio series 1963-4. In '65, reorganizing a quintet, he played clubs and concerts, appeared with increasing frequency as guest soloist with symphony orchestras, and headed his own weekly television program, *The George Shearing Show.*

Shearing, who has continued to enjoy international popularity, toured Europe in 1962 and Japan in '63. He was continuously active as a writer of songs and arrangements. (Most of his albums feature Shearing's own arrs., though they were transcribed and orchestrated by others.) He also wrote the music for a cartoon film, *Dangerous Dan McGrew,* in '65. In 1961 Shearing was teamed with the Montgomery Brothers for a Riverside album. Though most of his own LPs (on Cap.) are extremely pop-oriented, they frequently include passages that demonstrate Shearing's undiminished ability as a highly skilled improvising jazz pianist. From the jazz standpoint, his best albums in recent years are *San Francisco Scene; Live Concert* (these are both in-person albums), *Shearing Bossa Nova;* and *Jazz Moments* featuring the trio with Crosby and Fournier (all Cap.).

Addr: 4233 Navajo, No. Hollywood, Calif.

SHELDON, JACK,* *trumpet, singer;* b. Jacksonville, Fla., 11/30/31. A Los Angeles resident since 1947, Sheldon played with many small groups in the 1950s, also Stan Kenton '58; Benny Goodman in '59 and again in '66 in Las Vegas.

During the 1960s, while continuing to play admirable trumpet in a style sometimes reminiscent of Miles Davis, Sheldon expanded his activities. He became a professional actor, playing a major role on the *Cara Williams Show* in 1965. He was also featured on several other programs, incl. *Steve Allen Show, Edie Adams Show, Talent Scouts, I Spy,* and *Nut*

House. Own TV show: *Run Buddy Run,* 1966. Own LPs: *Jack's Groove* (GNP); *Oooo-But It's Good!* (Cap.); *Jazz Profile of Ray Charles* (Reprise). Also with Shelly Manne (Cont.).

Addr: c/o Ashley Famous, 9255 Sunset Blvd., Los Angeles 69, Calif.

SHEPARD, ERNEST JR. (ERNIE), *bass;* b. Beaumont, Tex., 7/19/16; d. Hamburg, Germany, 11/23/65. Piano first, then choral work at school. First gig as singer w. Ivory Joe Hunter. Active from early 1930s in Texas, later in Calif. Worked for Eli Rice, Buddy Banks, Gerald Wilson, Phil Moore, Eddie Heywood, Billy Eckstine, Gene Ammons, Lem Davis, Dizzy Gillespie-Ch. Parker combo (briefly in Calif., 1945), Slim Gaillard, and own combo. Best known as member of Duke Ellington band Nov. 1962-Feb. '64. Left band while in Germany and spent the remainder of his life doing radio, TV and record work in Berlin, Stuttgart, Hamburg etc. Named J. Blanton as his chief influence.

LPs w. Gene Ammons (Pres.), Ch. Parker on *South of the Border* (Verve), others w. Ellington (Reprise), Johnny Hodges, Paul Gonsalves et al.

SHEPP, ARCHIE, *tenor sax, composer;* b. Ft. Lauderdale, Fla., 5/24/37. Raised in Philadelphia, Shepp studied piano, clarinet and alto as a child before switching to tenor. First job was with a rhythm & blues band that included Lee Morgan. After graduating from Goddard College with a degree in dramatic literature Shepp settled in NYC. His most important early work there was with Cecil Taylor in 1960, both in concerts and as musicians in the play *The Connection.* He later co-led group with Bill Dixon and co-led the New York Contemporary Five with John Tchicai and Don Cherry. In '64 toured the U.S.S.R. and Czechoslovakia and appeared at the Helsinki World Youth Festival with the New York Contemporary Five. Intermittently associated with John Coltrane in '65, appearing with him at various clubs and on records. Led own group with Bobby Hutcherson at Newport JF '65. Shepp is also a practicing playwright; his work *The Communist* was performed in NYC in '65.

Influenced by Webster, Hawkins, Parker, Coltrane, Rollins and Coleman, Shepp became one of the most original tenor players of the '60s. Mort Maizlish characterizes his work: "He often plays with a rough, brutal attack, reflecting both jazz origins and the sounds of the street, of rhythm & blues and of Negro folk tunes and chants. Although seemingly constructed of diverse fragments, his solos project a great deal of emotion and generally build to exciting climaxes."

Articles by Shepp have appeared in *Down Beat* and *Jazz.* As a writer and poet he has often asserted that jazz is a Negro music and that it ought to reflect and aid the Negro social revolution in America. By 1966 he had become one of the centers of the controversy over the origins and purposes of jazz.

LeRoi Jones, one of Shepp's earliest and most ardent supporters, said of him, "Archie is so much his own self that it is finally impossible to name one influence . . . his range of expression is so broad that he seems to take in or to have digested most of the ways of playing tenor saxophone." John Sinclair said that "his music posits a great power and strength, a certainty, to say, Be strong." Shepp's own position is that "Art cannot be thought of as interchangeable with life on all levels . . . IT IS LIFE. . . . Then music must at times terrify! . . . It must bring social as well as aesthetic order to our lives." (*Jazz*, September 1965)

Own LPs: *The Bill Dixon-Archie Shepp Quartet, Archie Shepp and the New York Contemporary Five* (Savoy); *Four for Trane, Fire Music, New Thing at Newport* (Impulse). Others: *The World of Cecil Taylor* (Candid); on Impulse: John Coltrane *Ascension*, three tracks with Taylor on Gil Evans *Into the Hot*, one track on *The New Wave in Jazz*.

SHEROCK, SHORTY (Clarence Francis Cherock),* trumpet; b. Minneapolis, Minn., 11/17/15. A former name-band soloist, Sherock led his own band 1945-7. Since the early 1950s he has free-lanced in Hollywood, playing mainly studio jobs with infrequent opportunities to display his jazz ability. He was heard in an album of remakes on Capitol of famous trumpet solos. Also featured on *BBB and Co.* with Benny Carter (Status).

Addr: 435 S. Peck Dr., Beverly Hills, Calif.

SHERRILL, JOYA,* singer, songwriter; b. Bayonne, N.J., 8/20/27. The former Duke Ellington vocalist appeared in 1960 in a short-lived Broadway show, *The Long Dream*. In 1962 she was a featured vocalist with Benny Goodman's orchestra on its State Dept.-sponsored tour of the Soviet Union, and in many of her appearances, singing in Russian as well as English, was the surprise hit of the show.

Own LPs: *Sugar and Spice*, (Col.); *Joya Sherrill Sings Duke* (20th Cent. Fox).

Addr: 18 Spinney Hill Dr., Great Neck, New York.

SHIHAB, SAHIB (Edmund Gregory),* alto and baritone sax, flute, composer; b. Savannah, Ga., 6/23/25. Pl. in '40s w. Roy Eldridge, T. Monk et al; in '50s with D. Gillespie, I. Jacquet and various bands in NYC. After touring in 1959-60 with the big Quincy Jones band feat. in the musical show *Free and Easy*, Shihab took up residence in Scandinavia. He was heard with the Clarke-Boland sextet and big band, scored music for a movie in Denmark, and appeared on TV in several Continental countries. In Oct. 1965 he wrote original music for a jazz ballet based on Hans Christian Andersen's *Red Shoes*. Lived in Copenhagen 1966. LPs w. Clarke-Boland (Atl., Col.), Brew Moore (Fant.); also several under his own name, not released in U.S.

Addr: c/o Gregory Sr., 323 Macon St., Brooklyn, N.Y.

SHORTER, WAYNE,* tenor sax; b. Newark, N.J., 8/25/ 33. Played w. Horace Silver, Maynard Ferguson briefly during '50s before joining Art Blakey, his first im-

portant job, in 1959. With Blakey thru '63, including tours of Japan and Europe. Joined Miles Davis in summer of '64, incl. tour of Europe and Algeria. Numerous comps. inc. *Marie Antoinette, Night Dreamer, Iris, This is for Albert, Children of the Night, Ju Ju, Armageddon, Virgo.*

Shorter attracted attention with Blakey as a hard-driving, soulful tenorman, but the increased freedom of Miles Davis' mid-'60s rhythm section allowed him to expand his vocabulary, influenced heavily by Coltrane, Rollins and Ornette Coleman. By 1965 he had already formulated much of his own style and had gained the respect of contemporary musicians. Harvey Pekar called him "an inventive solo voice," adding that "he has made a synthesis of the styles of several tenor players, and his playing is at once forceful and relaxed." John Tynan said that Shorter "is reaching out into new avenues. His playing is frequently staccato, laconic and tough-sounding." Own LPs on Blue Note, Vee Jay; others w. Davis (Col.), Hubbard (BN), Blakey (River., Epic, UA, BN, Impulse).

Addr: 2186 Fifth Ave. Apt. 14-C, New York, N.Y.

SHU, EDDIE (Edward Shulman),* tenor sax, alto, clarinet; also trumpet, harmonica, composer, singer; b. Brooklyn, N.Y., 8/18/18. Shu, who has also worked as a ventriloquist, pl. w. a variety of bands in the late '40s and early '50s incl. George Shearing, Buddy Rich and Lionel Hampton. With Gene Krupa trio '54-8; also had own group before and after in '50s. Toured w. Louis Armstrong on clar. '64-5. Rejoined Hampton in spring '66.

Addr: 16 Largo Lane, Livingston, N.J.

SILVER, HORACE WARD MARTIN TAVARES,* piano, composer, leader; b. Norwalk, Conn., 9/2/28. Prominent in the early 1950s with Stan Getz, Art Blakey and others, Silver formed his own group in 1956 and scored a series of successes as composer of *Señor Blues, The Preacher* and other popular instrumentals.

In the 1960s his career continued along similar lines as he toured the U.S. with his quintet. The group made its first tour of Japan in 1961, and visited Europe in '62 under the sponsorship of Norman Granz. Played at Antibes JF '64. Silver's compositions (in recent years) included *Horace-Scope, Blowin' The Blues Away, Finger Poppin,' Doin' The Thing, The Tokyo Blues, Silver's Serenade* and *Song For My Father.* This last, the title number of an album released in 1965, brought unprecedented popular success to the group. In August '65 the quintet was on the soundtrack for a TV soft drink commercial for which Silver wrote the arrangement.

Silver's piano style, often associated with the birth of the "funky" school in the middle and late 1950s, is constructed along Bud Powell-derived but inventive lines, with an occasional tendency to use humorous quotations. As a composer, he has made extremely effective use of the limited instrumentation at his disposal and has written many lines that represent a synthesis of post-bop jazz and various Latin influences. (Silver's father is a Portuguese from the Cape Verde Islands.)

Addr: 400 Central Park West, New York City 25, N.Y.

SIMMONS, SARNEY (NORMAN), *piano, composer;* b. Chicago, Ill., 10/6/29. Stud. Chicago Sch. of Music 1945-9. Prof. debut '46 w. Clifford Jordan. During long engagement as house pianist with the resident trio at the Bee-Hive in Chicago, he played for such visiting soloists as Charlie Parker, Lester Young, Dexter Gordon, J. J. Johnson, Kai Winding. Led nine-piece band with Frank Strozier, '57. Accompanied Dakota Staton '58, Ernestine Anderson '59. Clubs w. Johnny Griffin-Eddie Davis Quintet 1960.

In 1961 Simmons joined Carmen McRae as accompanist and musical director, touring with her throughout the U.S. and internationally, playing all leading jazz festivals etc. incl. World JF in Japan 1964.

Original infl: Duke Ellington. Other favs: Gil Evans, Hank Jones, Oscar Peterson, Ahmad Jamal. A superior accompanist and capable arranger, he made his record debut leading a trio on Argo in 1956. He feels his best work to date can be heard on *The Big Soul Band* feat. Johnny Griffin, for which he was arranger (River.) and on *Lover Man* with Carmen McRae (Col.). Other LPs with Miss McRae on Col. and Mainstream.

Addr: 2200 Cedar Ave., New York City, N.Y.

SIMMONS, RICHARD, *bass;* b. St. Louis, Mo., 8/14/27. Brothers played piano, sang. First gig w. Dick Gregory touring revue '63. Joined Quartette Tres Bien as regular bassist, playing in St. Louis and the West Coast, incl. very well-received performance at Lighthouse in LA. Favs. and infl: Ray Brown, Ron Carter, Paul Chambers. LPs: w. QTB (Decca) incl. own fav. *Steppin' Out;* w. Jean Trevor (Mains.).

Addr: 4752A St. Louis Ave., St. Louis, Mo.

SIMMONS, SONNY, *alto saxophone, composer;* b. Sicily Island, La., 8/4/33. Family moved to Oakland, Calif. when he was eight years old. Though his parents encouraged his early interest in music, they could not afford to provide him with a musical education. In 1950 Simmons bought a saxophone and began studying and working. He met Prince Lasha and during the next decade they formed several groups together, worked on a series of compositions, and appeared on a TV show in Sacramento in 1960. Two years later he made his recording debut as a member of Lasha's quintet.

Simmons, first inspired by Charlie Parker, later came under the influence of Ornette Coleman, whom he quoted as saying, "You don't use any chord changes. The only thing you have for direction is the way the melody is formed, and from that particular form and pitch, you create other vistas of music." Simmon adds: "So I tried it and found that it worked out."

LPs: *The Cry* w. Lasha (Contemp.); Eric Dolphy

Memorial Album (VJ); *Illumination* w. Elvin Jones (Impulse).

Addr: 1226 East 15th St., Oakland, Calif.

SIMONE, NINA (Eunice Waymon),* *singer, piano, arranger;* b. Tryon, No. Carolina, 2/21/33. She was the sixth of eight children. Her mother, a housekeeper by day, was also an ordained Methodist minister. Miss Simone started an playing piano by ear in 1939, and organ three years later. She took classical piano lessons privately. High school in Asheville, N.C., graduated valedictorian, then studied piano and theory for 1½ years at Juilliard School, NYC.

Supported for some time by a "Eunice Waymon Fund" established by the contributions of audiences at her childhood performances, Miss Simone later worked as an accompanist for vocal studios at a Philadelphia studio, gave piano lessons, and studied at Curtis Institute of Music.

The first job on which she sang in addition to playing was an Atlantic City night club booking in 1954. Within the next couple of years she had started recording, rose swiftly to the best seller lists, and gained national prominence. She was married Dec. 1961 to Andy Stroud, then a detective sergeant on NYC police force, now her personal manager.

A gifted musician and songwriter, Nina Simone has a voice with an unusually deep, rich timbre. As John S. Wilson has written, "She evokes and stirs her listeners' emotions more skillfully and in more varied fashion than any other popular singer." Repertoire includes folk, gospel, jazz and popular material.

LPs: Colpix, Philips.

Addr: c/o Stroud Productions Inc., 507 Fifth Ave., New York 17, N.Y.

SIMS, RAY C.,* *trombone, singer;* b. Wichita, Kansas, 1/18/21. Brother of Zoot Sims. Best known for his work w. Les Brown '49-'58, Harry James from '58. LPs: James (MGM, Dot).

Addr: 2108 Ernest Ave., N. Redondo Beach, Calif.

SIMPKINS, ANDREW,* *bass;* b. Richmond, Ind., 4/29/32. After playing clarinet and piano, started playing bass while in Army in '53. Later met Gene Harris (q.v.) and Bill Dowdy; from 1957 they were known as The Three Sounds and in the '60s their records enjoyed substantial popular acceptance. For further details see Harris, Gene.

SIMS, JOHN HALEY (ZOOT),* *tenor sax, alto sax, clarinet;* b. Inglewood, Calif., 10/29/25. Played with many big bands from 1941 including Benny Goodman, with whom he has worked on numerous occasions since '44; also Stan Kenton '53. Since '57 has frequently teamed with Al Cohn to front combo; they have toured South America and appeared several times in London as well as working off and on since 1960 at the Half Note in NYC.

In the fall of 1960 Sims toured Europe with Gerry Mulligan's concert band. In '62 he was a member of the Benny Goodman band that toured the USSR. He has appeared at numerous jazz festivals in So. Car., Virginia, Boston, etc. and took part in the Titans of the Tenor Sax concert in NYC in '66 with J. Coltrane, C. Hawkins and S. Rollins.

LPs: *New Beat Bossa Nova*, Volumes I and II (Colpix); *Jazz Mission to Moscow* (Colpix); Al Cohn-Zoot Sims Quintet (Merc.).

Addr: 354 W. Eleventh St., New York, N.Y. 10014.

SINATRA, FRANCIS ALBERT (FRANK),* *singer;* b. Hoboken, N.J., 12/12/15. Winner of innumerable jazz polls, starting with the DB Readers' Poll in 1942, Sinatra strengthened his jazz associations in the '60s through frequent night club and festival appearances backed by the Count Basie band. They recorded together for Reprise Records, the successful label founded by Sinatra in Jan. 1961. The Sinatra-Basie appearance at Newport in July 1965, despite minority reports from a few dissident critics who questioned the validity of Sinatra's participation in a jazz festival, was a popular triumph. In Nov. 1965 an extensive survey of Sinatra's career, edited and partly written by George T. Simon, and containing a detailed discography, was published by *Billboard* magazine under the title "The Sinatra Report."

LPs of jazz interest include *Sinatra and Swinging Brass; Sinatra-Basie*, both with arrs. by Neal Hefti; *Swing Along With Me*, arrs. Billy May; *It Might as Well Be Swing* with Basie band arr. Quincy Jones (all Reprise).

Addr: Reprise Records, 3701 Warner Blvd., Burbank, Calif.

SINGLETON, ARTHUR JAMES (ZUTTY),* *drums;* b. Bunkie, La., 5/14/1898. Raised in New Orleans, where he played with many pioneer bands. Went to Chicago in '25, working there and in New York with Louis Armstrong. With small combos at Nick's in Greenwich Village, NYC, late '30s. Lived in Calif. in '40s; Europe '51-3, then back to New York, where he took part in many Dixieland sessions. Worked mainly at the Metropole 1959-61; sessions at Central Plaza '62-3; Jimmy Ryan's '63-5. Seen briefly in the role of a clarinetist in film *Andy*, 1964. TV: *Chicago and All That Jazz; Salute to Eddie Condon*. Singleton's most typical work can be heard in the early L. Armstrong albums on Col.

Addr: 223 West 52nd St., New York 19, N.Y.

SLACK, FREDDIE,* *piano, composer, leader;* b. La Crosse, Wis., 8/7/10. Played in the 1930s with Ben Pollack, Jimmy Dorsey, Will Bradley-Ray McKinley. In the '40s his record of *Cow Cow Boogie* was a popular quasi-jazz hit. In later years Slack was intermittently active at clubs in and around the San Fernando Valley. He was found dead, apparently of natural causes, 8/10/65, at his apartment in Hollywood, Calif.

SLOANE, CAROL, *singer;* b. Providence, R.I., 1937. Prof. debut at 14 w. Ed Drew's band. At 18 she went to Germany with a touring musical comedy. Back in Providence '57, worked as secretary and gigged w.

Drew. Joined Les and Larry Elgart Orch. '58. After leaving the band in '60, settled in NYC. Appeared in 1960 at Pittsburgh JF, where she was heard by Jon Hendricks; a few months later he sent for her to sub for Annie Ross in his trio. Miss Sloane's big break arrived when she appeared in the 1961 Newport JF and made a strong impression on critics. She has since worked in night clubs and has been frequently heard on Arthur Godfrey's CBS radio show. Unlike most modern singers, she has researched and admires the work of such artists as Mildred Bailey and Lee Wiley. Some years ago her sound seemed to resemble Ella Fitzgerald's, but she has developed impressively since then and is one of the better jazz-influenced pop singers. Own LPs: Col.

SMITH, WILLIAM OVERTON (BILL), *composer, clarinet;* b. Sacramento, Calif., 1926. Clar. at 10; theory, harmony at 16. To NYC; stud. at Juilliard; later for several years w. Darius Milhaud at Mills Coll. in Oakland, Calif. While at Mills, met fellow-student Dave Brubeck and formed octet with him. M.A. in music 1952; became teacher at colleges while continuing to play and write all kinds of music incl. jazz. Won Prix de Rome, later settled in Rome, working on Guggenheim grant.

While in Italy, Smith represented the U.S. at the Intl. Congress of Electronic Music in Venice, giving premiere of a work for jazz combo and prerecorded tape. He became increasingly interested in electronic music. With pianist Bill Eaton he formed the American Jazz Ensemble, which toured U.S. annually playing community concerts. The group introduced the synket, a novel machine for production and transformation of sounds.

Smith is a man of prodigious talent both as composer and clarinetist. His early works incl. *Concerto for Clarinet & Combo*, rec. w. Shelly Manne, and *Divertimento*, w. Red Norvo, both on Contemp. He appeared with Brubeck on *The Riddle* (Col.), *Dave Brubeck Octet, Near Myth, Brubeck a la Mode* (Fant.). LPs by American Jazz Ensemble: Epic, RCA.

Addr: c/o American Academy, Via Angela, Mesina #5, Rome, Italy.

SMITH, CARSON RAYMOND,* *bass;* b. San Francisco, Calif., 1/9/31. Prominent in the '50s with Gerry Mulligan, Chico Hamilton and Stan Kenton, Smith later settled in Las Vegas, where he worked with the Charlie Teagarden group. He was reunited with Mulligan in a concert at the Hollywood Bowl in Sept. 1964. Toured Japan with Georgie Auld Sept. '64.

Addr: 486 Fenn St., Los Angeles, Calif.

SMITH, CHARLES (CHARLIE),* *drums;* b. New York City, 4/15/27. Heard in the Billy Taylor trio from 1952-4 and with many other leading combos and bands in the '40s and '50s, Smith moved in the '60s to New Haven, Connecticut, where he became a member of the Dwike Mitchell-Willie Ruff Trio. Smith also earned a reputation as a teacher and composer. He collaborated with Thomas Vaughan on a jazz liturgy, *A Musical Offering to God*.

After an intermittent illness Smith was hospitalized with a liver ailment and died January 15, 1966.

LP w. Mitchell-Ruff (Atl.).

SMITH, CLADYS (JABBO), * trumpet, trombone, singer, leader; b. Claxton, Ga., 1908. Rec. w. Duke Ellington in 1920s, pl. w. Cecil Scott, Ch. Johnson et al. Well known in early days as trumpeter, he later switched to trombone, which he played in 1966 at Tina's Lounge in Milwaukee. Early work heard in *The Ellington Era* (Col.), in which he has solo on *Black & Tan Fantasy.*

Addr: 2138 N. 18th St., Milwaukee, Wis.

SMITH, JAMES OSCAR (JIMMY), * organ; b. Norristown, Pa., 12/8/25. Played around Philadelphia on piano and organ. Formed own group '55 and by the following year, through his recordings, established both himself and the organ as new stars in jazz. In the '60s he continued to appear at clubs, concerts and major festivals both here and abroad, increasing his popularity into the hit record category. Won a Grammy award from NARAS for his '64 Verve album *The Cat.* For details of his numerous awards see poll tabulation pages.

Smith, more than any of his contemporaries, is responsible for the spawning of countless organ-guitar-drums trios—sometimes with saxophone added—that made themselves omnipresent in lounges and on record. In '66 he made his vocal debut on his recording of *Got My Mojo Working.*

LPs: Verve, Blue Note.

Addr: c/o Clarence Avant, 850 7th Ave., New York, N.Y.

SMITH, JOHNNY "HAMMOND" (John Robert Smith), * organ, piano; b. Louisville, Ky., 12/16/33. Private teacher. Professional pianist from 1949. Inspired by Wild Bill Davis, took up organ and formed his own combo in Cleveland in 1957. Worked w. Nancy Wilson in '58; also sideman w. Chris Columbus combo. Later led combo in NYC at Count Basie's, Minton's, Shalimar and other clubs.

LPs: River., Pres.

Addr: 34 Ford St., New Haven, Conn.

SMITH, JOHN HENRY JR. (JOHNNY), * guitar; b. Birmingham, Ala., 6/25/22. Staff musician at NBC 1947-53. Worked professionally as trumpeter, violinist, violist before concentrating on guitar. His record of *Moonlight in Vermont* was a hit of 1952. In the '60s Smith lived in Colorado Springs, running his own music store and occasionally returning to active playing by working concerts and serving on the faculty of summer jazz clinics. LP: *Reminiscing* (Roost).

Addr: 514 Salano Dr., Colorado Springs, Colo.

SMITH, HEZEKIAH LEROY GORDON (STUFF), * violin, singer, songwriter, leader; b. Portsmouth, Ohio, 8/14/09. The veteran jazz violinist spent a year at the Royal Tahitian Room in Ontario, California 1963-4. Early in '64 he went to New York to appear at the Embers

club with Joe Bushkin. After a series of free-lance engagements in California, including TV work with Steve Allen, he left in 1965 for a long series of engagements in the Scandinavian countries, and for TV and club work in England, France, Switzerland, Germany and Belgium.

Smith in his late fifties remained what he had been when he first invaded the New York scene in 1935, a totally individual artist with a fantastic capacity for swing. He has never enjoyed a reputation commensurate with his unique gifts.

Own LPs on Emarcy, Verve, 20th Century Fox; LP co-starred w. Herb Ellis (Epic); also duo-violin albums for European labels with Svend Asmussen in Copenhagen and Stephane Grappelly in Paris.

Addr: 2039 Claudina Ave., Los Angeles 90016, Calif.

SMITH, THEODORE (TEDDY), bass; b. Washington, D.C., 1/22/32. Studied trombone in high school. W. Betty Carter '60, C. Jordan and K. Dorham '61-'62, J. McLean and S. Hampton '62-'63. With Horace Silver from '63. In Paris, Antibes JF, Monterey JF '64 w. Silver. Fav: P. Chambers. Infl: John Malachi. LPs: W. Jordan (River.), Silver (BN); best work w. Dorham-McLean *El Matador* (UA).

Addr: 314 W. 103rd St., New York, N.Y.

SMITH, WILLIAM McLEISH (WILLIE), * alto sax, clarinet, singer; b. Charleston, S.C., 11/25/10. While a freshman at Fisk Univ. he met Jimmie Lunceford and played in his band for a decade, leaving in 1941. From 1944-64 he was with Harry James' band, except for a two-year absence, 1951-3, during which he worked with Duke Ellington, Billy May. After leaving James in '64 Smith was ill and largely inactive for a year. In the fall of '65 he worked with Johnny Rivers in Las Vegas, then returned to Los Angeles to play local gigs.

Smith's other activities in recent years have included record dates with Billy May and Nancy Wilson; Nelson Riddle and Ella Fitzgerald; also sound track work for the films *Pepe* and *Ocean's 11.* In late '65 he recorded his own combo album with accordionist Tommy Gumina.

LPs with James (MGM, Col., Cap.).

Addr: 3485 3rd Ave., Los Angeles 18, Calif.

SMITH, WILLIAM HENRY JOSEPH BERTHOL BONAPARTE BERTHOLOFF (WILLIE THE LION), * piano, composer; b. Goshen, N.Y., 11/25/1897. Prominent in Harlem in the 1920s, Smith was an early friend of Duke Ellington and a strong pianistic influence on him. He made a series of records for Decca from 1935-40 and was prominent in NYC traditionalist clubs in the 1940s and '50s. An entertaining, informative and well-written biography, written by Smith in collaboration with George Hoefer, was published in 1964. Entitled *Music On My Mind: The Memoirs of an American Pianist,* it included reminiscences of the early jazz scene in New York and New Jersey, incorporating data never previously available in any book on jazz. App. Newport JF '64, Hunter College concert '65.

LP: Mainstream.

SMYTHE, PAT, *piano, arranger;* b. Edinburgh, Scotland, 1927. R.A.F. pilot, practiced law in Edinburgh, before joining Dizzy Reece in London '58. '61-5 w. Joe Harriott. Led own trio and made many apps. on TV. '61 wrote score of musical *The Cure for Love.* '64 was mus. dir. for *Second City* company in West End of London. Also participated in Brit. golf championships. LPs w. Harriott (Capitol, Jazzland, Brit. Col.), Paul Gonsalves (Brit. Vocalion).

Addr: 54 Duncan Terrace, London, W.1., England.

SNOWDEN, ELMER CHESTER (POPS), *banjo, guitar;* b. Baltimore, Md., 10/9/00. Closely associated with Duke Ellington in Washington, D.C. and NYC in early '20s. Later led several bands whose sidemen included Count Basie, Jimmie Lunceford, Benny Carter.

In the early '60s Snowden, working as a parking lot attendant, was rediscovered and recorded for Prestige and Riverside. Played clubs in East '60-'61 and in No. Calif. '62-3; Monterey JF in '63. Patrick Scott and other traditional jazz enthusiasts consider him one of the foremost exponents of jazz banjo. A versatile musician, Snowden once taught guitar, banjo, mandolin and saxophone at a music institute in Berkeley, Calif.

LPs: *Ballads* w. Lonnie Johnson (Pres.); *Harlem Banjo* (River.); Beryl Booker Quartet (Riff).

Addr: 876 No. 41st St., Philadelphia, Pa.

SOLAL, MARTIAL, *piano, composer;* b. Algiers, N. Africa, 8/23/27. Moved to Paris in 1940s, working with Kenny Clarke and other U.S. expatriates. In recent years he has written the background scores for more than 20 motion pictures incl. three for Jean Paul Belmondo. He has appeared at jazz festivals in San Remo, Antibes, Berlin, Frankfurt. On visits to the U.S. he played at Newport JF, and in such clubs as The Hickory House in New York and El Matador in SF. A technically remarkable pianist with a highly personal manner of swinging.

LPs: RCA, Cap., Liberty.

Addr: 8 rue d'Héliopolis, Paris 17, France.

SOUCHON, EDMOND II, M.D. (DOC), *guitar, banjo, singer;* b. New Orleans, 10/25/1897. Has practiced medicine for more than 40 years but took up jazz as avocation in mid-1940s. Was subject of *This is Your Life* show 1961; many other TV and radio shows as performer, lecturer and interviewer. Pl. w. Sharkey Bonano and Paul Barbarin bands on syndicated TV series.

Doc Souchon is the most active and versatile figure on the New Orleans scene. He has written countless articles for various magazines, is editor of the local jazz paper *Second Line,* and has recorded an estimated 600 numbers, with his own band (on Southland) or with Doc Evans, Johnny Wiggs, Merle Koch and innumerable other combos. His most ambitious non-playing musical venture is a book, *New Orleans Jazz:*

A Pageant in Pictures (La. State U. Press), in collaboration with Al Rose. By 1966 he had delivered more than 10,000 babies, performed over 7,000 operations, had succeeded his father as medical consultant on the board of the Pan Amer. Life Ins. Co., and was working on his autobiography.

Addr: 523 Betz Place, Metairie, La., 70005.

SOUTH, EDDIE, *violin;* b. Louisiana, Mo., 11/27/04. Well known in Europe, where he toured with his own combo in the '20s and '30s, South was a vastly underrated jazz violinist whose career never brought him the success his talent warranted. In 1960 he suffered a heart attack and was forced to give up playing professionally. He died in Chicago, 4/25/62, of heart failure.

Because of the obstacles facing Negro musicians when he came to prominence, as well as the almost total lack of jazz concerts and the fact that the jazz violin was considered an anomaly, Eddie South's work was appreciated only by a relatively small in-group of admirers who were aware of his virtuosity and inspiration. He was heard on a few records with Django Reinhardt in the late 1930s. His last album was *The Distinguished Violin of Eddie South* (Merc.).

SOUTHALL, HENRY BRANCH, *trombone;* b. Richmond, Va., 8/25/31. Studied at elementary school 1943; did not study privately until he entered college. Worked jobs in Richmond while still in school. Played with Dean Hudson band 1950 and again in '55 and '60; also with Larry Elliott '56, Stan Kenton '58.

In 1962 Southall joined Woody Herman. During the next four years his peppery, humorous style and occasionally more orthodox improvisations became an increasingly important asset of the orchestra. He toured in Europe with the band in '64, '65, and '66. Appeared at Monterey and DB JF etc.

Southall says, "The style I play on *Watermelon Man* was influenced by a pianist named Eddie Powell. He was the first 'funky' pianist I'd ever heard. I feel that I play best on a ballad or a very slow blues." He names Carl Fontana, Frank Rosolino and Kai Winding as main influences.

LPs with Herman (Philips, Col.). He feels his best solos are heard on *Encores* (Philips) and *My Kind of Broadway* (Col.).

Addr: 481 Chamberlayne Ave., Richmond, Va.

SOUTHERN, JERI, *singer, piano;* b. Royal Neb., 8/5/26. Best known for her hit record, *You Better Go Now,* in early 1950s. Living in Hollywood, she appeared at the Sands and other local clubs in early '60s, then gave up public performances to become a voice teacher. LPs: Dec., Roul., Cap.

SPANIER, FRANCIS JOSEPH (MUGGSY), *cornet, leader;* b. Chicago, Ill., 11/9/06. A central figure in Dixieland jazz from the early '20s, Spanier settled on the West Coast during the late '50s, then toured Europe in 1960. At Newport JF '64. Inactive in music due to heart ailment from July '64. Own LPs: *Colum-*

bia the Gem of the Ocean (Ava), *Great 16* (RCA), *Dixieland Band* (Merc.).

Addr: 303 South St., Sausalito, Calif.

SPANN, OTIS, *piano, singer;* b. Jackson, Miss., 3/21/30. Mother pl. blues guitar; father blues piano. Learned piano by ear at age seven. Never studied formally but received instruction from an early infl., pianist Cose Davis.

When he was eight, Spann won first prize at local blues contest. Worked w. blues band for three years from age 14. After his mother's death went to Chicago, '47. With Muddy Waters band from that time. He has also rec. w. Howling Wolf, Sonny Boy Williamson, Chuck Berry and Little Walter, among others. Pete Welding has written: "I have long been of the conviction that Otis Spann currently is the most wholly stimulating blues pianist currently operative, an impressive and markedly individual soloist of great rhythmic strength, and by far the most responsive and sensitive of accompanying musicians in the whole modern blues idiom . . . easily the most forceful contemporary representative of the sturdy southern piano style exemplified in the playing of such masters as Roosevelt Sykes and Big Maceo Merriweather . . ."

Spann is equally effective as a blues singer, a powerful and individual stylist. Own LPs: Pres., Candid; LP w. Waters on Chess.

SPAULDING, JAMES RALPH JR., *alto sax, flute;* b. Indianapolis, Ind., 7/30/37. Father a professional guitarist. Studied alto, flute and clarinet in grade school, attended Chicago Cosmopolitan Sch. of Music '57 after service in armed forces. First professional gig w. Jazz Contemporaries in Indianapolis '56, then w. Sun Ra '58 and Sonny Thompson '59 in Chicago. 1960 led own quartet. To NYC, joined Freddie Hubbard '63; w. Max Roach '65, Randy Weston '65. At Newport JF '64. By 1965 Spaulding, with a clear tone and tremendous drive, was one of the most promising new saxophonists on the NY scene. Favs: Parker, Rollins, Coltrane. LPs: w. Ra (Saturn); Larry Wrice (Pac. Jazz); Hubbard, Grant Green, Wayne Shorter, Duke Pearson, Bobby Hutcherson (all on BN), Art Blakey (Colpix), Duke Pearson (Atl.). Best work on Hubbard's *Breaking Point* (BN).

Addr: 789 St. Marks Ave., Brooklyn 13, N.Y.

SPITELARA, JOSEPH T. (PEE WEE), *clarinet, saxophone;* b. New Orleans, La. 12/21/37. Studied clarinet at Nichols High School 1951. Prof. musical debut when a Ted Mack Amateur Hour appearance led to a job with Tony Almerico's band. Played with Roy Liberto 1956-8; Lawrence Welk Show, '58-'59; Santo Pecora, '59-'60. Joined Al Hirt in 1960; at that time, was a gas station attendant and played only on weekends. During the next six years, as Hirt's popularity rose, Spitelara became the most popular and valuable of Hirt's sidemen. John S. Wilson, one of many critics who singled out his work as the most valuable component of the Hirt group, has called him "a capable and well-

oriented clarinetist who also can turn in a strong, hard-driving tenor saxophone solo." Despite the New Orleans influences around him Spitelara names Buddy De Franco as his favorite.

Own LP, and many w. Hirt, on RCA.

Addr: 1409 Lake Shore Ave., New Orleans, La.

STALLINGS, MARY (Mary Lorraine Stallings Evans), *singer;* b. San Francisco, Calif., 8/16/39. No formal lessons. Sang in church choirs, later in school musicals and glee clubs. Dizzy Gillespie inspired and encouraged her interest in jazz. Supper club and concert work in Australia, 1959. LP debut '61. Toured with Billy Eckstine in Nevada, 1964-5. Monterey JF Sept. '65. Favs: Dinah Washington, Billie Holiday. LP: *Cal Tjader Plays—Mary Stallings Sings* (Fant.).

Addr: 2672 Bush St., San Francisco, Calif.

STAMM, MARVIN LOUIS, *trumpet;* b. Memphis, Tenn., 5/23/39. Studied music from age of 12. Attended North Texas State College. First important gig was with Buddy Morrow in '60. With Charlie Spivak '60, Stan Kenton '60-'62, Woody Herman '65-6. Played lead for Nancy Wilson on several dates. Has played w. Memphis and Dallas Symphonies, also in Dixieland and rock & roll groups. Taught at National Stage Band Camps from '60. A capable musician, both in solo and section-leading work. Favs: Davis, Gillespie, Edison, Terry, Hubbard et al. LPs: w. Charlie Mariano (Regina), Kenton (Cap.), North Texas Lab Band (90th Floor), George Peters (Verann).

Addr: 60 Pinehurst St., Memphis 17, Tenn.

STAPLE SINGERS. Vocal group founded by Roebuck Staple in 1948 including his daughters Mavis and Cleotha and his son Purvis. The elder Staple was born in Winona, Miss., 12/28/14. As a young man he heard and/or pl. w. Blind Lemon Jefferson, Robert Johnson, Ma Rainey and Bessie Smith, but perhaps his greatest infl. was Charlie Patton, who lived on an adjacent farm. After his first two children were born, he went to Chicago in '35, working in meat-packing plant until '41. After the family group began singing together, they became well known in Chicago churches and were soon devoting themselves completely to gospel singing. From that time they have toured, app. in clubs and concerts as well as festivals. They have not altered their approach to include R&B or R&R but have adapted folk blues to their style. Lawrence Cohn has written of them: "The Staple Singers are a tightly-integrated unit, devoid of meaningless machinations" and described their singing as "punctuated by the father's electric guitar and their magnificent antiphonal clapping. This form of clapping, a veritable art in itself, contributes to the emotional feeling emitted, and the distinctive overall sound achieved by this quite remarkable family."

Won DB critics' poll as new star vocal group '62. LPs: Epic, Riverside.

STEWARD, HERBERT (HERB),* *tenor, alto sax, flute;* b. Los Angeles, Calif., 5/7/26. Steward was one of the original "Four Brothers" in Woody Herman's 1947 band; later played with Artie Shaw, Tommy Dorsey, Harry James before settling in Las Vegas. Recorded sound track for Fred Astaire TV show. Recorded LP for Ava Records, 1961, entitled *Herb Steward Plays So Pretty.* Played lead alto in house band at Thunderbird, Las Vegas '66.

Addr: 122½ Thornton Pl., Venice, Calif.

STEWART, REX WILLIAM, * *cornet;* b. Philadelphia, Pa., 2/22/07. Celebrated for the widely imitated "half-valve" tonal effect, which he introduced to jazz on *Boy Meets Horn* while a member of Duke Ellington's band in 1939, Stewart left NYC to take up residence in Los Angeles in May 1960. During the next few years he became simultaneously engaged in three careers.

As musician, he was featured with Benny Carter at the Hollywood Bowl in 1960 and at the Monterey JF in '62. He appeared again at Monterey in '65, w. Gil Fuller band. Regular gig 1963-4 at Royal Tahitian Room, Ontario, Calif.

As a disc jockey, Stewart resumed this phase of his career in 1963, when he launched a daily radio show on KNOB, Los Angeles.

As a writer, he was widely praised for a series of reminiscences that appeared in *Down Beat* from 1964. Also wrote for *Playboy* and other publications.

Avocationally, Stewart, who attended classes at the Cordon Bleu in Paris in 1949, has catered for private parties.

Addr: 1424 Meadowbrook Ave., Los Angeles, Calif.

STEWART, LEROY (SLAM), * *bass;* b. Englewood, N.J., 9/21/14. The veteran swing and bop bassist, noted for his technique of simultaneously bowing his bass and humming in unison, and for his appearances with Art Tatum, Charlie Parker and Benny Goodman during the '40s, appeared with Rose Murphy in a duo and trios from 1956. Their tours included most of the U.S., Canada and Puerto Rico; England and U.S. Army bases in Germany and Italy '60, and appearances on BBC-TV; and an extensive tour of Australian cities in '65. At Newport JF '64 with the house band. TV shows incl. Mike Wallace, Mike Douglas, *Today, Memory Lane,* Merv Griffin. Own LPs: Savoy, UA.

Addr: 114-28 180th St., St. Albans 12, N.Y.

STIDHAM, ARBEE, *guitar, singer;* b. De Valls Bluff, Ark., 10/9/17. Father, Luddie Stidham, led Memphis Jug Bang. Arbee pl. alto saxophone in Little Rock and Memphis and eventually migrated to Chicago. Gave up saxophone due to ill health '54. After several years took up guitar and was encouraged by Big Bill Broonzy and Memphis Slim to play professionally again. Own LP: Folkways; LPs w. Memphis Slim (Candid).

STINSON, ALBERT FORREST JR., *bass;* b. Cleveland, Ohio, 8/2/44. Mother an operatic and church singer. Stud. piano, sax, trombone, tuba; bass from age 14. Worked w. many small groups incl. Terry Gibbs, 1961; Frank Rosolino, Jan. '62; then with Chico Hamilton

on tour for 3½ years. Also w. Marian McPartland in '63. In Oct. 1965 he joined the quartet led by Hamilton's ex-saxophonist Charles Lloyd.

Favs: Ch. Mingus, Ch. Haden, Israel Crosby, Slam Stewart and many others.

Stinson, who is as familiar with the work of Bartok, Ravel, Satie and Debussy as with that of Miles, Lee Konitz, John Coltrane and Thelonious Monk, is an exceptionally well-rounded musician capable of extraordinarily facile and original solos and of ensemble work compatible with the "free jazz" movement of the mid-'60s. Though he studied bass briefly with Bob West in '61, most of his present phenomenal technique and ideas are due to extensive listening and practice.

LPs with Hamilton (Col., Impulse, Reprise); Clare Fischer, Joe Pass (Pac. Jazz). Fav. own LP: *A Different Journey* (Reprise).

Addr: 996 Shelly St., Altadena, Calif.

STITT, EDWARD (SONNY), * *tenor, alto, baritone saxes;* b. Boston, Mass., 2/2/24. First prominent in D. Gillespie band 1945-6; later with Gene Ammons, JATP and own groups.

After rejoining Gillespie briefly in '58, Stitt most of the next few years worked as a single, using various rhythm sections. He was also with the Miles Davis combo for almost a year, toured Japan in a sextet with Clark Terry and J. J. Johnson in '64 and appeared at Newport and many other festivals. He visited Britain and the Continent in '64 and played at Golden Circle in Stockholm in '66. He was briefly teamed with Zoot Sims in a quintet, heard in Chicago and recorded for Cadet.

Stitt, though an early admirer of Ch. Parker, states that he was playing in a virtually identical style before he ever met or heard Parker. His technique and style matured during the '60s and he has become one of the most consistently swinging performers in contemporary jazz, both on alto and tenor sax. He was also one of the most ubiquitous recording artists, having made LPs for Argo, Roost, Jazzland, Pac. Jazz, Pres., Impulse, Atl. Perhaps his best album in recent years is *Stitt Plays Bird* (Atl.).

Addr: 7835 16th St. NW, Washington, D.C.

STOBART, KATHLEEN (KATHY), *tenor sax;* b. South Shields, Lancashire, England, 4/1/25. Pl. and rec. w. Vic Lewis, Humphrey Lyttelton, and concerts and festivals w. many gps. Married to Bert Courtley. Impressive Lester Young-based style.

Addr: 26 Norbury Court Rd., London S.W. 16., England.

STRAYHORN, WILLIAM (BILLY or SWEE'PEA), * *composer, piano;* b. Dayton, Ohio, 11/29/15. Met Duke Ellington in 1938 and joined the band '39 as associate arranger, occasional second pianist and lyricist.

Strayhorn continued to play a vital part in most phases of Ellington's activities during the '60s. An orchestra under his personal supervision played for Ellington's musical production, *My People,* presented at the Century of Negro Progress exhibit in Chicago in Aug. '63. He was heard as pianist on the Ellington-Johnny Hodges album *Side By Side* (Verve) and played briefly in *Afro-Bossa* (Reprise).

Without detracting one iota from the credit due Duke Ellington for his individual role in the music performed by the orchestra, it is impossible to under-estimate the value of Strayhorn's contribution. Until he was sidelined by serious illness in 1965-6, Ellington assigned him to write most of the arrangements of popular and standard tunes played by the band for such albums as *Ellington '65, Ellington '66* and *Will Big Bands Ever Come Back?* (Reprise). Ellington himself, however, frequently added to or changed these arrangements so that no firm dividing line can be established in the apportionment of the credit. It can certainly be stated, however, that Strayhorn's role is second only to Ellington's in the development of big band jazz on a supremely imaginative level during the 1940s, '50s and early '60s. Strayhorn's best-known compositions include *Lush Life*, for which he wrote lyrics and music; *Take The A Train*, the band's theme; *Chelsea Bridge*, and an estimated 200 others written either alone or in collaboration with Ellington.

LPs: *Billy Strayhorn—the Peaceful Side* (UA); *Johnny Hodges-Billy Strayhorn Orchestra* (Verve); others: see Ellington, Duke, and Ellington, Mercer.

Addr: 310 Riverside Dr., New York 25, N.Y.

STRAZZERI, FRANK JOHN, *piano;* b. Rochester, N.Y., 4/24/30. Played piano since age of 15, educated at Eastman School of Music. Since 1958 has worked numerous gigs with Sharkey Bonano, Charlie Ventura, Terry Gibbs, Red Mitchell, Herb Ellis, Curtis Amy, Joe Williams, Kenny Dorham, Bud Shank, Carmell Jones, Art Pepper, Benny Goodman, Buddy De Franco, Johnny Hartman. Appeared on two West Coast TV shows. Favs: Hank Jones, Wynton Kelly, Tommy Flanagan, Erroll Garner, Teddy Wilson; strongest in-fluence Hank Jones. LPs w. Amy (Pac. Jazz), Gibbs (Verve), Mitchell (Pac. Jazz & Atlantic), Ellis (Verve); own fav: *Remarkable Carmell Jones* (Pac. Jazz).

Addr: 18000 Martha St., Encino, Calif.

STREISAND, BARBRA, *singer, actress;* b. Brooklyn, N.Y., 4/24/42. Despite her victories in jazz polls con-ducted by *Playboy* Magazine and her high ratings in several DB polls, Miss Streisand is not a jazz singer and does not claim to be one. She is an exceptional dramatic personality in a vocal style associated more with the Broadway stage and popular television music than with any form of jazz.

STROZIER, FRANK R., *alto sax, flute, clarinet, piano, composer;* b. Memphis, Tenn., 6/13/37. Mother is Mildred Strozier, pl. piano. Studied piano, saxophone. Was one of a group of youngsters in Memphis who later became prominent in jazz, among them George Coleman, Hank Crawford, Harold Mabern and Booker Little; all attended the same high school.

After graduating from high school Strozier left in 1954 for Chicago, where he studied clarinet at the Chicago Cons. of Music. In 1957 he became a member of the group organized by Walter Perkins known as the MJT + 3. He remained with the group until it broke up, then moved to New York in 1959, where the combo was re-established. He made his first album as a leader in 1961 for the Jazzland label.

For three years off and on (1961-4) Strozier was a member of the Roy Haynes quartet. He also joined Miles Davis for a tour of the West Coast in '63. Early in 1965 he settled in Hollywood and became a member of the Shelly Manne quintet, playing at the Manne-Hole.

Strozier is one of the most promising young alto saxophonists in jazz, a gifted flutist, and an able com-poser. His compositions include *The Need of Love, The Crystal Ball, Long Night, She, Frank's Tune.* Fav: Charlie Parker, but says, "I appreciate most of the older musicians and a few of the younger musicians; that applies to both playing and writing."

Own LPs: *Long Night, March of the Siamese Chil-dren* (Jazzland). LPs w. McCoy Tyner (Impulse); Roy Haynes, Booker Ervin (Pres.); MJT + 3 (VJ); Shelly Manne (Cap.).

Addr: 1316 N. Fuller Ave., Hollywood, Calif.

STUART, KIRK (Charles Kincheloe), *piano, composer;* b. Charleston, W. Va., 4/13/34. Mother pl. piano, organ; brother sax, clarinet. Stud. pno. 1939 at W. Va. State Military Acad. Graduated cum laude 1952 from American Cons. An excellent accompanist, he worked w. Billie Holiday in '56; Della Reese as ar-ranger, conductor and pianist '57-9 and in a similar capacity for Sarah Vaughan '61-3. 1964-6 he was music director and led his own combo at the Inter-national Hotel in Los Angeles.

LPs: *Sassy Swings the Tivoli* (Merc.); *Shades of Gray* w. Al Gray (Tangerine); *A Date with Della Reese at Mr. Kelly's* (Jubilee). Favs: Oscar Peterson, Art Tatum, piano; Frank Foster, Thad Jones, ar-rangers.

Addr: 7822 S. Eberhart Ave., Chicago, Ill. 60619.

SULIEMAN, IDREES DAWUD,* *trumpet, alto saxo-phone;* b. St. Petersburg, Fla., 8/7/23. Worked as trumpeter w. Basie, Hampton, Gillespie, many other bands. Toured Europe (incl. Eastern Europe) and Middle East in quartet with pianist Oscar Dennard. The group disbanded after Dennard's death in Cairo in Oct. '60. In March 1961 Sulieman and his wife, singer Jamila Sulieman, settled in Stockholm. In 1962 he began doubling as saxophonist. Pl. w. Gugge Hedrenius band, later led own quintet. Made own LP for Swedish EMI label, '64. Sulieman, whom Mary Lou Williams once called "the first modern trumpet player," is also a capable alto soloist in the Parker-Stitt tradition.

Heard in *Americans in Europe* (Impulse).

SULLIVAN, IRA BREVARD JR.,* *trumpet, saxophones;* b. Washington, D.C., 5/1/31. An important part of

the modern scene in Chicago from '49, he pl. w. Art Blakey briefly in '56 but for the most part worked in Chi. until he moved to southern Florida in early '60s, app. w. groups in Miami and Ft. Lauderdale. Own LPs: Delmark, Vee Jay; LP w. Roland Kirk (Cadet).

SULLIVAN, JOE (Dennis Patrick Terence Joseph O'Sullivan),* *piano;* b. Chicago, Ill., 11/5/06. A member of the original Chicago "Austin High Gang," Sullivan enjoyed immense popularity during the '30s and '40s as a blues and swing pianist. Largely inactive during the '50s, he enjoyed a mild comeback in San Francisco, beginning with his appearance at the '63 Monterey JF and the recording of his *Little Rock Getaway* by Gerry Mulligan. Pl. at Newport JF '64. Basically a traditional musician, he has performed w. Mulligan and Bob Brookmeyer, composed and played for *Who's Enchanted?,* a documentary about blind children, and performed solo at the Trident in Sausalito, Calif. Richard Hadlock said of him in *Down Beat,* "Sullivan has retained his youthful desire to seek new avenues of expression through jazz." LPs: Verve, River.
Addr: 643 Mason St., San Francisco, Calif.

SUMMERLIN, EDGAR E. (ED),* *composer, tenor sax, clarinet;* b. Marrianna, Fla., 9/1/28. Extensive studies at colleges and music schools. Composed first liturgical jazz work in 1959, pioneering in this field. In '60 and '62 wrote and conducted music for religious TV show *Look Up and Live,* on CBS. Commissioned to write jazz liturgy for festival in Washington, D.C. In '63 he played with Don Ellis' experimental group; arranged and conducted two-piano LP for Steve Kuhn and Toshiko Akiyoshi on Dauntless label. Formed ensemble with Don Heckman for avant garde concert at Judson Hall, NYC, '65. In '66 composed, conducted and played on Canadian TV programs; lectured and played at universities.
Addr: School House Rd., Staatsburg, N.Y.

SUN RA (Le Sony'r Ra), *piano, organ, clavioline, percussion, sun harp, composer.* Sun Ra's personality has been surrounded for some years in mysticism. Naming no birthdate or birthplace, he states: "My Zodiac sign is Gemini; month of May; arrival zone, U.S.A. I studied music under the guidance of Nature's God, and this study is yet in being; at college I studied under a private tutor, Mrs. Lula Randolph of Washington, D.C." He entered music through high school classmates; John T. Whatley, he says, was a "notable sponsor."
Sun Ra played piano in Fletcher Henderson's band at the Club de Lisa in Chicago, 1946-7. For many years he was active in Chicago as the central figure in a group of experimentalists. He provided the music for a documentary film *The Cry of Jazz.* Moved to NYC in 1960s. Associated w. Jazz Composers' Guild: concerts, 1964-5, at the Cellar, Judson Hall and the Contemporary Center. Cultural tour of NY universities, colleges sponsored by Esperanto Foundation, NY

State Council on Arts. His group has been known in recent years as the Solar Arkestra.
Composer Bill Mathieu has written that "the otherworldly motif threading through Sun Ra's thought is quite whole in its poetic consistency. . . . Sun Ra plays from a place beyond everyday consciousness. He senses other planes of existence known to musicians, poets, and sorcerers for as long as there has been man. Sun Ra is unique in the way he has tied up this age-old transcendentalism with current jazz and current life."
Comps: *Friendly Galaxy, Advice to Medics, Nebulae, Dancing Shadows.*
Own LPs: Saturn, ESP, Savoy, Transition. LP w. Walt Dickerson: *A Patch of Blue* (MGM).
Addr: 48 East 3rd St., New York City, N.Y. 10003.

SWALLOW, STEPHEN W. (STEVE), *bass;* b. New York City, 10/4/40. Private teachers; piano, trumpet first; bass at 18. Joined Paul Bley Trio 1960. Later worked with George Russell, Jimmy Giuffre, Art Farmer. Joined Stan Getz Quartet June '65. One of the foremost young bassists in the new, free school of playing, he names Ch. Mingus, Ch. Haden and Wilbur Ware as favs. Won DB critics' poll as new star '64.
LPs with George Russell (River.); Steve Kuhn (Contemp.); Paul Bley (Savoy, ESP); also *Free Fall* with Giuffre (Col.).
Addr: 362 W. 19th St., New York 11, N.Y.

SWINGLE, WARD LAMAR, *singer, arranger;* b. Mobile, Ala., 9/21/27. Stud. piano from 1933. Played local gigs with brother and sister, both musicians. Alto sax and singer with Ted Fio Rito Orch. 1943-5. Masters degree in music from Cincinnati Conservatory 1951. Later in '51 Swingle went to Paris on a Fulbright Scholarship and studied piano for two years with Walter Gieseking. Back in U.S., he taught at a college in Sioux City, Iowa, but in 1956 he took up permanent residence in Paris. From 1957-61 he served as pianist for the Roland Petit Ballets and accompanist for Zizi Jeanmaire. During this period he also worked with the Blue Stars, a modern jazz vocal group, and from 1959-62 with another combo, The Double Six of Paris, which stemmed from the Blue Stars. In 1962, to improve sightreading and musicianship, he and seven colleagues began singing Bach fugues. Later they added jazz bass and drums for accompaniment. Out of this wordless vocal concept came the Swingle Singers, whose first album, *Bach's Greatest Hits,* was an immediate international success and led to tours throughout the continent and the U.S.
The Swingle Singers are all academically trained musicians, some with classical and operatic backgrounds. An associate of Swingle in the venture, heard previously as a fellow member of the Blue Stars and Double Six, is Christiane Legrand (q.v.).
The Swingle Singers have played concerts at the Albert Hall in London; Carnegie Hall; and at the White House in May 1964. Their albums have been

consistently big sellers, even more so in the U.S. and England than in France. Whether the Swingles are a jazz group has been debated, since most of their performances leave the original works of Bach, Mozart and other classical composers intact. Almost the only essential jazz touches are the rhythm section and an occasional solo moment by Miss Legrand in which a jazz improvisational influence can be sensed.

Swingle, who has done considerable writing for films, cites Gil Evans and Michel Legrand as his favorite composer-arrangers, Oscar Peterson as piano favorite and Ella Fitzgerald for vocal.

LPs: Double Six of Paris (Cap., Pathe-Marconi, Merc.); Swingle Singers (Philips).

Addr: 45, rue du Général Leclerc, Montfermeil (S et O), France.

SYKES, ROOSEVELT (Roosevelt Sykes Bey), *singer, piano;* b. Helena, Ark., 1/31/06. Studied informally with a friend, Lee Green, in 1921. Sykes' family moved to St. Louis when he was a child and it was there that he made his professional debut. He recorded for Okeh in 1929 and later, in the early '30s, was heard on RCA, Paramount, Brunswick and Champion, often under such pseudonyms as Dobby Bragg, Willie Kelly, Easy Papa Johnson. On some recordings he accompanied other singers. From 1935-40 he was on Decca and earned great popularity under the nickname "The Honeydripper." In later years his popularity persisted on RCA Victor and he toured with his own band.

Sykes later settled in New Orleans, but returned to St. Louis in 1958 and formed a blues combo. In the '60s he played local clubs, concerts in Europe, and occasionally worked in Chicago and New York.

Bob Koester has called Sykes "one of the most important urban blues-men of all time . . . a strong singer, a powerful pianist, a magnificent personality, and a profound influence on other blues men of his own and several succeeding generations."

LPs: Folkways, Delmark.

SZABO, GABOR,* *guitar, composer;* b. Budapest, Hungary, 3/8/36. The former Hungarian Freedom Fighter, a U.S. resident since 1956, joined Chico Hamilton's quintet in December 1961 and remained with Hamilton's various groups until 1965. After playing with the Gary McFarland combo, May-Aug. '65, he joined the new quartet of Charles Lloyd, his former colleague in the Hamilton groups.

Critics voting in a DB poll in 1964 elected Szabo and another Hungarian, Attila Zoller, as the best new jazz guitarists of the year. Both men had given ample evidence that the award was merited. As Dan Morgenstern of DB observed, Szabo has "a beautiful sound, great flexibility and a fine ear." He has shown himself capable of achieving considerable tonal freedom, especially in such settings as the challenging Lloyd group. His intervals and chord usages are unusual; he is a master of what Whitney Balliett has called "the sound of surprise."

First LP as leader was released on Impulse early in 1966. LPs w. Hamilton (Impulse); McFarland (Verve); Lloyd (Col.). As writer, comp. score for Roman Polanski's *Repulsion.*

TANNER, PAUL, *educator, trombone;* b. Skunk Hollow, Kentucky, 10/15/17. From a musical family; studied piano as a child, then trombone at 13. Charter member of Glenn Miller band. On staff of ABC in Los Angeles from 1950. Also pl. w. Les Brown, Charlie Spivak, Tex Beneke bands. Gave jazz courses as member of music faculty at UCLA from 1958. Active in studio work, as concert soloist, clinician for Bach-Selmer Co. Performed regularly w. numerous LA conductors, incl. H. Mancini, N. Riddle, N. Hefti, P. Rugolo, P. Weston. Appeared in three films involving Glenn Miller. Has published numerous arrangements and conducted several jazz-oriented record dates. Wrote and published three textbooks, articles in music magazines.

Addr: 12426 La Maida St., North Hollywood. Calif.

TATE, GEORGE HOLMES (BUDDY),* *tenor sax, leader;* b. Sherman, Tex., 2/22/15. Tenorman for Count Basie for over ten years, Tate has led his own big band since the '50s. Performed throughout Europe and at Newport '62, and regularly at the NYC Celebrity Club; gigs Biltmore and Waldorf-Astoria Hotels. Own LPs: Pres.

Addr: 12 Stone Blvd., Amityville, N.Y.

TATE, GRADY, *drums, singer;* b. Durham, N.C., 1/14/32. Studied at grammar school. Pl. w. Wild Bill Davis from late 1959 to early '62; Jerome Richardson combo and Quincy Jones band during the balance of '62. On the strength of his big band training with Jones, he began free-lance studio work and soon was in frequent demand for recording sessions. Worked with Cy Coleman trio for three months on Les Crane TV show in '65. Newport JF annually from '63. Concerts with Oliver Nelson at Lincoln Center and Bill Evans at Town Hall. Clubs with Billy Taylor Trio 1966. LPs with Jimmy Smith, Wes Montgomery, Stanley Turrentine, Donald Byrd, Kenny Burrell, Bill Evans (all Verve); Oliver Nelson (Impulse), Billy Taylor (Cap.); J. J. Johnson (RCA).

Addr: 2200 Madison Ave., New York City 37, N.Y.

TAYLOR, ARTHUR S. JR. (ART),* *drums;* b. New York City, 4/6/29. An ubiquitous figure on the NYC club and rec. scene in the '50s w. Bud Powell, Gigi Gryce, Art Farmer, Miles Davis, Donald Byrd and T. Monk. Pl. w. Red Garland trio and did important series of recs. w. Garland and John Coltrane. In Sept. '63 left for Europe. Living and pl. on the Continent, most often w. Johnny Griffin, except for short visit to U.S. in spring and summer of '65. Own LP: BN. LPs w.

John Coltrane (Atl.), Dexter Gordon (BN). A double-pocket set on Prestige entitled *Hard Cookin'* contains reissues of two LPs by Taylor-led groups formerly called *Taylor's Wailers* and *Taylor's Tenors.*

Addr: 67 Rue St. Jacques, Paris 5, France.

TAYLOR, WILLIAM JR. (BILLY), * *piano, composer;* b. Greenville, N.C., 7/24/21. Worked with Ben Webster, Dizzy Gillespie, Stuff Smith, Cozy Cole in '40s. Toured Europe w. Don Redman '46. House pianist at Birdland '51 with a variety of groups incl. Gillespie, Eldridge, Gaillard, Konitz, Mulligan, Pettiford, etc. Own trios from '52. In the '60s his longest engagements were at the Hickory House, NYC. Taylor also has been active in jazz other than as a player. In '59 he became a dj on WLIB, remaining there until '62 when he switched to WNEW. In '64 he returned to WLIB and in '66 became program director of the station's FM operation which includes 12 hours of jazz daily, three and a half of which are conducted by him. Produced and hosted his own jazz TV show on channel 47 '66. Initiated workshop series for George Wein at NJF and Hunter Coll. and has participated as organizer, narrator and player from '64. Concerts in schools from '62. One of the originators of the Jazzmobile in Harlem, summer '65. Lecturer at Yale Conf. on Mus. Ed. '64; Music Educator National Conf. '66. Member of advisory board on jazz for Lincoln Center; officer of NARAS.

With all his extra-curricular activities Taylor has managed to remain a pianist of warmth, grace and urbanity. Own LPs: Capitol, Mercury, Atlantic.

Addr: 555 Kappock St., Riverdale, N.Y.

TAYLOR, CECIL PERCIVAL, * *piano, composer;* b. New York, N.Y., 3/15/33. Taylor, whose conceptions and styles had identified him as one of the founders and leaders of the new music by the late 1950s, remained in New York City during most of the early '60s and continued to develop and to refine his playing. In '61 he led a quartet with Archie Shepp, Buell Neidlinger and Dennis Charles at the Five Spot and in Jack Gelber's play *The Connection.* From '62 he appeared around Greenwich Village in coffee houses and in loft concerts with groups that at times included Albert Ayler, Shepp, Jimmy Lyons, Sunny Murray and Roswell Rudd. Also gave concerts at NYC Town Hall and Philharmonic Hall. In '62 toured Europe with Lyons and Murray and was recorded at the Copenhagen Cafe Montmartre. Was one of the organizers of the Jazz Composers' Guild in '64-'65. In '65 appeared at Newport, *Down Beat* JFs.

The freedom, complexity, harmonic innovation and emotional brilliance of Taylor's playing have established him as one of the truly original minds in American music. Although he was at times influenced by Thelonious Monk, especially in his attack, Taylor's fast and intricately structured lines, almost percussive in their intensity, have had a stirring effect on the new horn techniques of the '60s. An admirer of the ballet,

Taylor has said, "I try to imitate on the piano the leaps in space a dancer makes."

A lack of acceptance by some musicians and critics and pitifully infrequent opportunities to record have kept Taylor's reputation and following limited to a small but devoted group of admirers. As did Monk during the '40s and early '50s, Taylor is said to spend most of his time practicing in his apartment and perfecting his personal form of music. By 1965 numerous avant-garde musicians looked upon him as one of their most important teachers and influences, while other pianists had begun to emulate Taylor's style of playing.

Own LPs: *The World of Cecil Taylor* (Candid), half of Gil Evans' *Into the Hot* (Impulse), *At the Cafe Montmartre* (Fant.), *Looking Ahead* (Contemp.). Others: John Coltrane *Coltrane Time* (UA).

Addr: 344 E. 4th St., New York, N.Y.

TAYLOR, CALVIN EUGENE (GENE), * *bass;* b. Toledo, Ohio, 3/19/29. Raised in Detroit. W. Horace Silver 1958-64, Blue Mitchell Quintet from '64. Toured Europe w. Silver '62, Japan w. Mitchell '65. At Newport JF '65 w. Dollar Brand, Johnny Coles. A strong, dependable bassist, Taylor has also appeared with Thelonious Monk, Howard McGhee and Lou Donaldson. Own fav. LPs: Mitchell's *Cupbearers* (River.), Roland Alexander's *Pleasure Bent* (Status). Others w. Silver (BN), Mitchell (BN).

TCHICAI, JOHN MARTIN, *alto sax;* b. Copenhagen, Denmark, 4/28/36. Father a Congolese diplomat, mother Danish. Raised in Aarhus, Denmark. Studied violin at age of 10, then alto and clarinet at 16. Attended conservatories in Aarhus and Copenhagen, where he met and played with American musicians. First appearance outside Denmark was at the 1962 Warsaw, Poland, Jazz Festival. Also in '62 led group at the Helsinki, Finland, festival. There he met Archie Shepp and Bill Dixon, who encouraged him to come to the United States.

In New York Tchicai and Shepp organized the New York Contemporary Five, which also included Don Cherry, Ronnie Boykins or Don Moore, and Sunny Murray or J. C. Moses. Tchicai took the group on an extended tour of Germany and Scandinavia in '63. In Sweden they recorded and did the music for the film *Future One.* Back in NYC, Tchicai co-led the New York Art Quartet with Roswell Rudd, Lewis Worrell and Milford Graves. Active in the Jazz Composers' Guild, they performed several concerts there and participated in the Composers' Guild orchestra's appearance at Newport '65. In concert at the Museum of Modern Art July '65.

Mort Maizlish writes of him: "Tchicai plays in a dry, metallic manner that at first makes other styles appear florid. He is, however, an extremely inventive and emotional player, whose tonal innovations do not follow even the conventions of 'originality.' " In describing his music, LeRoi Jones said, "Tchicai's tone is lean and angular. . . . He has a knack of going inside any melodic line, and shearing away any lushness and superfluity, to get at the muscular fiber of a music that at times is so pure and deeply felt that its very rhythmic impetus seems melodic and endlessly variable." Favs: Parker, Konitz, Rollins, Coltrane, Shepp, Ayler, Dolphy, Ornette Coleman. Lists most important influence on his playing as "myself."

Own LPs: w. New York Art Quartet (ESP, Phil.). Others: w. Shepp *Four for Trane* (Impulse) and *The New York Contemporary Five* (Savoy); w. John Coltrane (Impulse); two tracks on *Jazz Jamboree '63, Vol. 4* (Polish Muza).

Addr: 150 E. 46th St., New York 17, N.Y.

TEAGARDEN, CHARLES (CHARLIE),* *trumpet;* b. Vernon, Tex., 7/19/13. Played in bands of brother Jack, Paul Whiteman, Ben Pollack, Red Nichols, Bob Crosby, own groups from late '20s, then settled in Las Vegas in '59. Led own group at the Silver Slipper '61-'64 w. Bill Harris, Kay Brown. At Monterey JF '63, Aspen JF '65. Own LPs: Coral. Others: w. Jack Teagarden (Camay), Pete Fountain (Coral), Crosby (Cap.).

Addr: 1823 Pinto Lane, Las Vegas 6, Nev.

TEAGARDEN, WELDON JOHN (JACK),* *trombone, singer, leader;* b. Vernon, Texas, 8/20/05. After working with bands in Texas and around the midwest, Teagarden came to NYC in 1927. His best-known associations were with Ben Pollack 1928-33, Paul Whiteman '34-8 and as leader of his own band '39-'47. He then toured as a sideman with Louis Armstrong ('47-'51), later formed a group of his own and continued to tour as a combo leader through the '50s and early '60s. At the Monterey JF in Sept. 1963 Teagarden took part in a memorable family reunion in which the participants included both his sister and his mother at the piano, and his brother Charlie on trumpet, along with such old friends and associates as Pee Wee Russell and Joe Sullivan.

Teagarden's health by this time was not good, but he continued to tour. Negotiations were in progress for him to rejoin Armstrong's group after filling whatever bookings remained for his own sextet. The plan never materialized; after cutting short an engagement in New Orleans and visiting a hospital briefly, Teagarden returned to his hotel room and his body was found there 1/15/64; he died of bronchial pneumonia.

Jazz owes an immeasurable debt to Jack Teagarden. In the words of J. J. Johnson, "He was one of the giants." As Earl Hines commented, "Jack's only interest was music. He was always wrapped up in getting the best intonation out of his horn." Pee Wee Russell said, "He was a complete master. He owned it—that thing did his bidding. He took his time about things, his playing reflected that—it was no effort for him to play. His whole makeup was that way—easygoing." Ironically, in the next DB Readers' Poll following his death, Teagarden was not elected to the Hall of Fame,

an honor he unquestionably deserved. Always years ahead of his time, the possessor of a wholly individual sound both as instrumentalist and vocalist, he ranks with Armstrong, Beiderbecke, Coleman Hawkins and a handful of others as one of the unquestioned titans in the history of jazz. Own LPs: *At Roundtable, Dixie Sound, Jazz Maverick, Portrait of Mr. T, World* (all Roul.); *Golden Horn* (Decca); *Jack Teagarden, Mis'ry & Blues* (Verve); *King of the Blues Trombone* (Epic); *Tribute* (Cap.). Other LPs with Armstrong (Decca).

TERRY, CLARK,* *fluegelhorn, trumpet, singer;* b. St. Louis, Mo., 12/14/20. Though his nine years with Duke Ellington had established him firmly in jazz circles, and a year with Quincy Jones' band further consolidated his international reputation, it was after leaving Jones and joining NBC as a staff musician in March 1960 that Terry gradually built a following commensurate with his exceptional talents. As a member of the Skitch Henderson Orchestra on the NBC-TV *Tonight* show, he was featured with increasing frequency, and by 1965 was one of the band's leading personalities both as instrumentalist and occasional singer.

Speaking of his multiple activities, Terry once said: "I feel proud about being the first Negro to work on NBC for a long time . . . studio work is new and challenging; but at the same time I do everything from jazz dates to so-called classical, light classical and even rock 'n' roll. You have to keep your mind active and avoid stagnating."

Far from stagnating, Terry's style continued to broaden on a base that originally seemed to have been founded in the horizontal lines of Gillespie, the half-valve effects of Rex Stewart, and a general manner of phrasing that has long been entirely his own. This style has been demonstrated not only in the Henderson band, but in his frequent night club appearances with Bob Brookmeyer (q.v.), at many civil rights benefits, and on overseas tours.

In 1964 Terry toured Japan with J. J. Johnson's Sextet. Later that year he scored a surprise hit in a recording with Oscar Peterson's trio in which he sang *Mumbles*, a blues performed in a unique wordless manner that seemed to bridge the gap between traditional scat vocal and normal verbalized singing. As a result, Terry toured Europe in 1965 with Peterson and Ella Fitzgerald, also guesting on TV show w. John Dankworth in London.

Own LPs: Cameo, Mainstream, Impulse. Innumerable LPs as sideman with, among others, Lionel Hampton (Imp.); Skitch Henderson (Col.); Coleman Hawkins (Col.) et al.

Addr: 218-14 36th Ave., Bayside 61, N.Y.

TERRY, SONNY (Saunders Teddell),* *harmonica, singer;* b. Durham, N.C., 10/24/11. Blind from the age of 13, Terry worked w. Blind Boy Fuller, rec. w. him in '37. App. at *Spirituals to Swing* concert NYC

'38. Soon thereafter he teamed w. Brownie McGhee (q.v.) and their careers have run parallel ever since. LPs: see McGhee.

THIELEMANS, JEAN (TOOTS),* *guitar, harmonica, whistler;* b. Brussels, Belgium, 4/29/22. In 1959, ending his six-year membership in the George Shearing Quintet, Thielemans began to free-lance in New York and to make frequent visits to Europe. He became especially popular in Scandivania, where he recorded his own composition *Bluesette,* demonstrating a style he had developed of whistling and playing guitar in unison. *Bluesette* became a hit instrumental tune and was the subject of many recordings by jazz and pop artists. From 1963 Thielemans was a staff musician at ABC-TV, NYC, working chiefly on the Jimmy Dean show.

LP: *Too Much! Toots!* (Philips).

Addr: 279 N. Broadway, Yonkers, N.Y.

THIGPEN, EDMUND LEONARD (ED),* *drums;* b. Chicago, Ill., 12/28/30. With several modern groups during '50s, incl. Bud Powell, Billy Taylor, before becoming Oscar Peterson's drummer in Jan. '59. For work w. Peterson see Peterson, Oscar. Left Peterson June '65, free-lanced around Toronto. Published drum instruction book '65, conducted drum clinics in England and Germany '64 and '65. LPs: w. Peterson (Verve).

Addr: 26 Underhill Dr. #1020, Don Mills, Ontario, Canada.

THOMAS, JOSEPH LEWIS (JOE),* *trumpet;* b. Webster Groves, Mo., 7/24/09. One of the finest and least recognized swing era trumpeters, Thomas appeared and recorded with Fletcher Henderson, Benny Carter, Coleman Hawkins, Art Tatum and Fats Waller during the '30s and '40s. During the early '60s he free-lanced around NYC and Conn., appearing at Newport '64 w. Hawkins and at the Museum of Modern Art '65. Own LP: Atl. Others: w. Claude Hopkins (Pres.), one track on *Coleman Hawkins and the Trumpet Kings* (EmArcy); *Great Moments in Jazz Recreated at the Newport Jazz Festival* (RCA).

Addr: 473 West 158th St., New York City, N.Y. 10032.

THOMAS, KID (Thomas Valentine), *trumpet;* b. Reserve, La., 1896. Father was trumpeter and instrument custodian for the Picquit Brass Band; by sneaking into the band room, young Thomas taught himself to play valve trombone before his father bought him a trumpet. From the end of World War I he led his own band in the NO area. Until '60 pl. at places like Fireman's Hall, Tip Top and Moulin Rouge. Since then jobs have been sparse but have incl. pl. at a French Quarter art gallery; concerts at Tulane Univ.; law school picnic; and the opening of a softball league. Has held day jobs as house painter and handyman. Herb Friedwald wrote of him. "One of the few good trumpet men left in traditional jazz who has not to some degree been influenced by Louis Armstrong, he

is the closest we can hope to get to Freddie Keppard and the other pre-Louis players."

App. w. George Lewis in '60s. Own LPs: GHB, Jazz Crusade, River.

THOMAS, PATRICIA A. (PAT), *singer;* b. Chicago, Ill., 7/31/38. Self-taught, she made her debut on an amateur TV show in Chicago, then worked for some time at a local club called Budland. She gained early encouragement from pianist-arranger Norman Simmons, singing with his experimental jazz group.

With the emergence of bossa nova she was one of the first English-language singers to devote herself extensively to the idiom, appearing at a concert of Brazilian rhythms at the Academy of Music in Philadelphia Sept. '63. Later she toured England and the Continent and in 1965 played 26 cities in Japan. She was also among the first American artists to be featured in Cine-boxes (visual juke boxes).

She names Miles Davis and Sammy Davis as influences. Whether singing bossa nova, blues or ballads she displays a musicianly feeling and warmth of sound. LPs: *Desafinado, Moody's Mood* (MGM).

Addr: 40 W. 95th St., #4C, New York City, N.Y.

THOMPSON, DONALD WINSTON (DON), *bass;* also *piano, vibes;* b. Powell River, B.C., Canada. Worked in Vancouver w. Dave Robbins, Chris Gage, Conte Candoli, Barney Kessel. First U.S. job on piano, then bass, w. John Handy. Monterey JF '65 w. Handy. LP: w. Handy (Col.).

Addr: c/o 7050 Belcarra Drive, North Burnaby, B.C., Canada.

THOMPSON, JETER J. B., *piano;* b. St. Louis, Mo., 3/16/30. Family all play piano or bass. First jobs w. Chuck Berry, playing rock & roll and boogie woogie. With Quartette Tres Bien from formation 1959 in St. Louis. QTB played concert w. Count Basie, Nancy Wilson St. Louis '64; toured Midwest and West Coast, and was well received in LA '65. Thompson has composed several pieces for the QTB, incl. *Kilimanjaro, Boss Tres Bien* and *Stay My Love.* Also a cartographer for U.S. govt., real estate salesman in St. Louis. Favs: Tatum, Powell, Peterson, Jamal, Tyner. Ambition to appeal to audience with basic swing and emotion. LPs: w. QTB (Decca), incl. own fav. *Steppin' Out.*

Addr: 3944 Lexington, St. Louis, Mo.

THOMPSON, ELI (LUCKY),* *tenor, soprano saxes, composer;* b. Detroit, Mich., 6/16/24. Worked w. a variety of bands in the '40s incl. Lionel Hampton, Sid Catlett, Don Redman and Billy Eckstine. In mid-'40s became more involved in modern movement through recordings with Ch. Parker, Dodo Marmarosa and Boyd Raeburn while in LA. Own band at Savoy Ballroom, NYC in early '50s. After pl. w. Stan Kenton in mid-'50s he went to France in '57. remaining until he ret. to NYC in Dec. '62. In Europe he comp. music for and app. on TV; pl. clubs and concerts in North Africa as well as on the Continent. Since taking up residence in the U.S. again, he has worked sporadically, incl. clubs such as Half Note and a concert app. at the Little Theater, NYC, winter '64. He has, however, shown a continuing mastery of the tenor sax and perhaps the best-controlled, most mellifluous handling of the soprano sax in jazz. Own LPs on Prestige, Rivoli; one re-issue track in *The Be-Bop Era* (RCA).

Addr: Schuyler Hotel, 57 W. 45th St., New York, N.Y.

THORNHILL, CLAUDE,* *leader, composer, piano;* b. Terre Haute, Ind., 8/10/09. Leader of an excellent dance orchestra in the 1940s, several of whose sidemen formed the nucleus of the celebrated Miles Davis band that recorded for Cap. in 1949-50. Thornhill was the first to give prominence to the arrangements of Gil Evans and to make use of French horns in a modern dance band. He remained intermittently active as a leader until shortly before his death in NYC, 7/1/65.

THORNTON, TERI, *singer;* b. Detroit, Mich., 9/1/36. Raised in a musical environment and mainly self-taught, she made her professional debut in 1956 at The Ebony Club in Cleveland and spent four years working around Chicago and the midwest. Through saxophonist Johnny Griffin she was brought to the attention of Riverside Records and made her first sessions there in 1960-61. She scored a popular success in 1962 singing *Somewhere In The Night,* the theme of a television series. This was the title number of an album on the Dauntless label. Reviewing it, John A. Tynan wrote: "There's a full-bodied contralto depth in Miss Thornton's voice and a sound . . . reminiscent of Sarah Vaughan and Carmen McRae . . . Miss Thornton is unafraid to use the power of her voice—to use it but also to control it." Later LPs by Miss Thornton are on Col.

TIMMONS, ROBERT HENRY (BOBBY),* *piano, vibes, composer;* b. Philadelphia, Pa., 12/19/35. Reached prominence as a comp. through *Moanin',* written while he was w. Art Blakey '58-9, *This Here* and *Dat Dere,* rec. while a member of Connonball Adderley's group '59-'60. Rejoined Blakey for short time, also pl. briefly w. J. J. Johnson, but from early '60s has led own trio, app. in Wash., D.C. quite regularly in mid-'60s. Pl. at Village Gate, NYC spring '66.

During the "soul" fad of the early '60s, Timmons was in danger of becoming type-cast. Actually he is a versatile performer capable of many moods. In '66 he began pl. vibes as well as piano. Own LPs: Pres., River.

Addr: 339 E. 6th St. New York 10, N.Y.

TJADER, CALLEN RADCLIFFE, JR. (CAL),* *vibes, drums, piano, composer, leader;* b. St. Louis, Mo., 7/16/25. A former Brubeck and Shearing sideman, Tjader led his own combo from 1954. After several years spent mainly in San Francisco, he broadened his scope and appeared frequently during the 1960s at such night clubs as The Village Gate in NYC, Showboat in Phila., etc.; also Apollo Theatre and many

Latin dances in NYC, and various clubs along the West Coast. His group came into increasing demand for colleges; in the spring of '64 Tjader was part of a Ford-sponsored caravan that played colleges in western states. In 1965 he achieved best-selling-record stature with such albums as *Soul Sauce.*

Tjader's group is not deeply committed to conventional jazz but has achieved an effective synthesis of various Latin and Afro-Cuban moods with a jazz flavor. Though some critics have found the group's work shallow and merely pleasant, its popularity is growing steadily. Tjader's sidemen included, for a while, Clare Fischer as pianist. Fischer was also responsible for the arrangements of an excellent album featuring an enlarged group with woodwinds, *Cal Tjader Plays the Contemporary Music of Mexico and Brazil* (Verve). Tjader's pre-1962 albums are on Fantasy; later recordings are on Verve.

Addr: 349 Castenada Dr., Millbrae, Calif.

TOLLIVER, CHARLES, *trumpet, composer;* b. Jacksonville, Fla., 3/6/42. Entirely self-taught except for a brief period of tuition at Hartnett Studio, NYC. Stud. pharmacy for three years at Howard U. but then returned to New York and worked with Jackie McLean at the Coronet in Brooklyn.

Tolliver was strongly influenced by Clifford Brown during his formative years and later was given valuable guidance in New York by Freddie Hubbard. In addition to gigs with McLean he has worked with Joe Henderson, Edgar Bateman, and for a while in 1965 with Art Blakey's Jazz Messengers.

His compositions include *Cancellation, Revillot, Truth,* all heard in an LP that also shows his trumpet work to advantage, *It's Time* w. J. McLean.

TORME, MELVIN HOWARD (MEL),* *singer, composer, piano, drums;* b. Chicago, Ill., 9/13/25. Torme continued to entertain audiences in clubs with a selection of standards and current pop material delivered with a definite jazz-oriented attitude. Heard singing the title number at the beginning of film, *Sunday in New York.* One of the best and most musicianly of all pop-jazz singers. Revived his *California Suite* w. LA Neophonic Orch. '65. Own LPs: Col., Atl., Verve.

TOTAH, NABIL MARSHALL (KNOBBY),* *bass;* b. Ramallah, Jordan, 4/5/30. A dependable bassist well known for his work in the '50s with Al Cohn-Zoot Sims, Woody Herman and others, Totah played with Herbie Mann from 1958 until May 1961. Later in '61 he was heard with Bobby Hackett and Sol Yaged. From Sept. '62 to Feb. '64 he was a member of the Gene Krupa Quartet. Joined Teddy Wilson's trio July '64. In addition to these jobs he was featured with Slide Hampton and other groups during these years. LPs with Mann, Hackett, Krupa, Wilson, Roy Burns.

Addr: 64 Bruce Avenue, Yonkers, N.Y.

TRACEY, STAN, *piano, composer;* b. London, England 12/30/26. St. on accordion. Self-taught pianist; pl. w.

Jack Parnell, Ted Heath, Ronnie Scott. House pianist at Scott's club since its opening '60, pl. there and on TV w. Scott, Zoot Sims-Al Cohn, Sonny Rollins, Dexter Gordon, Roland Kirk, Ben Webster, Stan Getz, Freddie Hubbard, J. J. Johnson and many other mus. and singers.

His comp. *Baby Blue* rec. by Harry Carney, Paul Gonsalves. His suites, *Under Milk Wood* and *Alice in Jazzland* performed on British TV '66. Pl. w. New Departures (winner of *Melody Maker* polls in mid-'60s) from '61. Heard w. Rollins in film *Alfie*. Powerful, distinctive yet adaptable "composer's style" piano, chordal and percussive; prolific composer of highly personal themes. Own LPs: Brit. Col., Brit. H.M.V.; LPs w. Gonsalves (Brit. Col.), New Departures (Brit. Transatlantic).

Addr: 29a Bonham Rd., London S.W. 2., England.

TRAVIS, NICK (Nicholas Anthony Travascio),* *trumpet;* b. Philadelphia, Pa., 11/16/25. Heard during the 1940s with Woody Herman, Ray McKinley, Benny Goodman, Tommy Dorsey, Sauter-Finegan, and many other name bands, Travis became a staff musician at NBC in New York in 1957. He also worked with Gerry Mulligan's concert jazz orchestra in the early '60s and played with Thelonious Monk's ten-piece band at Lincoln Center and Carnegie Hall. After being hospitalized briefly with ulcers he died in NYC, 10/7/64. He was condsidered a superb all-around trumpeter, best known as a section man but also a capable soloist.

TRENNER, DONALD R. (DONN),* *piano, leader, composer;* b. New Haven, Conn., 3/10/27. Played with Ch. Barnet, Stan Getz, Ch. Parker in early '50s. Worked with Les Brown band off and on for several years from '53. Attained national prominence as musical director, pianist and arranger for the nightly Steve Allen TV show 1962-4. This band included such jazzmen as Conte Candoli, Bob Enevoldsen, Frank Rosolino and Herb Ellis. Trenner also acted as producer and conductor of a series of albums recorded by Allen on Dot. During 1965 he was musical director for the *Nightlife Show* on ABC-TV.

Addr: 21418 Salamanca Ave., Woodland Hills, Calif.

TRISTANO, LEONARD JOSEPH (LENNIE),* *piano, composer;* b. Chicago, Ill., 3/19/19. First important in NYC during late '40s as leader of experimental groups, he became more involved with teaching in the '50s through his own school which he opened in '51. After a long period of refusing to play in public, he began to appear at the Half Note, NYC, in '58-9. He has chosen to remain in seclusion for the most part in the '60s, teaching privately, and pl. intermittently at the Half Note. Reunited at one point in '64 with both of his principal sidemen of the late '40s, Warne Marsh and Lee Konitz, Tristano also pl. in Toronto at Le Coq D'or, and app. on CBS-TV in a *Look Up and Live* program. Pl. at Berlin JF and attendant European tour as a single, fall '65.

In '62 he rec. his first LP since 1955. An album of piano solos entitled The New Tristano (Atlantic), it was called by Harvey Pekar "a milestone in jazz piano history." Tristano uses his left hand to set up a walking bass line that fulfills the function of the absent rhythm section. Without the aid of multi-taping he utilizes a variety of time signatures. Pekar wrote of these in a DB review: ". . . not only a clever novelty, but they also are a means to an end, the end being the creation of great alternating waves of tension and relaxation."

Addr: 8667 Palo Alto St., Hollis, N.Y.

TROUP, ROBERT WILLIAM (BOBBY),* *singer, piano, composer;* b. Harrisburg, Pa., 10/18/18. Composer of hits *Daddy, Route 66;* active in club and movie work in LA during '50s. Wrote tunes for numerous films, incl. *Harlow, Will Success Spoil Rock Hunter?, The Girl Can't Help It, Man of the West, The Great Man, Voice in the Mirror, Rock Pretty Baby.* Accompanied wife Julie London on tours of Brazil '60, Japan '64. Also acted in several TV shows and films.

TUCKER, BENJAMIN MAYER (BEN),* *bass, composer;* b. Nashville, Tenn., 12/13/30. To NYC '59. Pl. w. Herbie Mann, Billy Taylor in '60s. Comp. *Comin' Home Baby,* which he rec. w. Mann. Own LP for Ava; LPs w. Taylor (Cap.), Mann (Atl.).

Addr: 408 E. 70th St., New York 21, N.Y.

TUCKER, ROBERT N. JR. (BOBBY),* *piano, composer;* b. Morristown, N.J., 1/8/23. Acc. for Mildred Bailey, Billie Holiday in '40s. Since 1949 has worked continuously for Billy Eckstine, incl. Australian tours in '60, '62, '64; Japan '63; Europe '64. Conducted N.Y. Phil. Orch. for Eckstine at Lincoln Center. Shared arranging w. Q. Jones et al on several Eckstine albums (Merc., Roul., Motown). Arr. for Mills Bros. (Dot).

Addr: 28 Cleveland Ave., Morristown, N.J.

TUCKER, GEORGE ANDREW,* *bass;* b. Palatka, Fla., 12/10/27. After working at Minton's Play House in 1957-8 Tucker pl. w. Junior Mance, then worked as a member of the group accompanying Lambert, Hendricks & Bavan; also w. Jaki Byard, Kenny Burrell, Earl Hines. He died of a cerebral hemorrhage in NYC, 10/10/65. LPs with Lambert, Hendricks & Bavan (RCA); Charles McPherson, Jaki Byard, Carmell Jones (Pres.); Earl Hines (Limelight); Stanley Turrentine, Horace Parlan (BN).

TURNER, BRUCE,* *clarinet, alto sax;* b. Saltburn, Yorkshire, Eng., 7/5/22. Toured Eng. w. Ben Webster '65, Henry Red Allen '66; won *Melody Maker* poll '66, then broke up his Jump Band to join Acker Bilk. First jazz band to play north of the Arctic Circle, Lapland '63. Own LPs on Brit. 77, Brit. Philips.

Addr: 108 Thurlow Park Rd., London S.E. 21., England.

TURNER, JEAN, *singer;* b. San Francisco, Cal., 1936. At 19, toured Europe w. USO show. After working nightclubs, she was discovered by pianist-vocal coach Eddie Beal, who introduced her to Stan Kenton. She joined the Kenton orchestra on tour from early 1962. After leaving Kenton the following year she resumed her career as a single. Own LP: Cap.

TURNER, JOSEPH (BIG JOE), * *singer;* b. Kansas City, Mo., 5/8/11. Important blues singer in KC w. Pete Johnson in '30s, he enjoyed a renaissance in the '50s with hits in the R&B field like *Shake, Rattle and Roll* and *Chains of Love.* Worked as a single ever since incl. Monterey JF '64, tours of England and Yugoslavia '65. Still one of the great blues shouters. Own LPs: Atlantic, Arhoolie.

TURRENTINE, STANLEY WILLIAM, * *tenor sax;* b. Pittsburgh, Pa., 4/5/34. After working w. Max Roach in '59-'60, formed own group which worked in various eastern clubs incl. Minton's NYC. Married organist Shirley Scott in early '60s after she had been a member of his group for a while. Own LPs for Blue Note, mostly w. small groups, but one, *Joy Ride,* w. big band.
Addr: 183 Stuyvesant Rd., Teaneck, N.J.

TURRENTINE, THOMAS WALTER JR. (TOMMY), * *trumpet;* b. Pittsburgh, Pa., 4/22/28. Pl. w. Mingus, Max Roach in '50s. W. Lou Donaldson in '60s but mostly free-lance in NYC. LPs w. Jackie McLean, Sonny Clark, Horace Parlan (BN).

TYNER, ALFRED McCOY (Sulaimon Saud), *piano, composer;* b. Philadelphia, Pa., 12/11/38. His mother played piano and encouraged his early interest in music ("Although I didn't study the classics extensively, I think I had a pretty good foundation"). Around 1953 Tyner had his own jazz combo of teenagers. He was mainly influenced by the brothers Bud and Richie Powell, who were neighbors ("I was impressed by the harmonies Richard Powell used to play and by his use of the sustaining pedal on chords").

Tyner worked with local groups including Calvin Massey's band around Phila. He was first introduced to John Coltrane when he and Massey worked a week with the saxophonist at the Red Rooster.

In 1959, after playing concerts with Benny Golson in Phila. and San Francisco, Tyner became part of the Jazztet, organized by Golson and Art Farmer. He remained with the group six months, then joined John Coltrane and stayed with him until Dec. 1965. In '66 he free-lanced mainly with his own trio in NYC.

During the years with Coltrane, Tyner developed into one of the most important young pianists of the 1960s. In Coltrane's own words, "First there is McCoy's melodic inventiveness . . . the clarity of his ideas . . . he also gets a very personal *sound* from his instrument; and because of the clusters he uses and the way he voices them, that sound is brighter than what would normally be expected from most of the chord patterns he plays. In addition, McCoy has an exceptionally well developed sense of form, both as a soloist and an accompanist. Invariably in our group, he will take a tune and build his own structure for it. He is always, in short, looking for the most personal way of expressing himself. He doesn't fall into conventional grooves. And finally, McCoy has taste. He can take anything, no matter how weird, and make it sound beautiful."

Tyner's experiments with modes, strongly influenced by Coltrane, were in turn influential on many other pianists. He won the DB Critics' Poll in the New Star category, 1963. He is represented in numerous LPs on Impulse, both with Coltrane and various groups of his own. Those under Tyner's name include *Inception,* (AS-18); *Reaching Fourth* (AS-33); *Live At Newport* (A-48); *Today and Tomorrow* (A-63); *McCoy Tyner Plays Ellington* (A-79).

His earliest LP is *Meet the Jazztet* (Cadet 664). In addition to the Powell brothers, Tyner acknowledges as influences Thelonious Monk ("Truly an honorable contributor") and Art Tatum ("an inspiration to music"). He also feels that his religious activity has been of utmost importance to him. He belongs to the Ahmadiyya Movement in Islam.
Addr: 140-14 183rd St., Jamaica, 13, N.Y.

URTREGER, RENE, * *piano, composer;* b. Paris, France, 7/16/34. Worked with many U.S. musicians on Continent incl. Miles Davis, Lester Young. Won the Prix Django Reinhardt in 1961. Except for a period in '64 when he toured with a pop singer, Urtreger has remained active in jazz, playing concerts in Germany, Switzerland, Italy, etc. Working on music for films and TV in recent years, he has also accompanied the Double Six vocal group and played on an LP with Stéphane Grappelly and Stuff Smith. Worked in trio with Daniel Humair and Pierre Michelot at Club St. Germain in Paris. LP w. Lester Young (Verve).
Addr: 7 bis, Rue Des Eaux, Paris 16, France.

VALDEZ, CARLOS (POTATO), * *conga drum;* b. Havana, Cuba, 11/4/26. Featured w. Herbie Mann's various combos since June '59, he has app. w. him on Columbia, Atlantic and UA LPs.

VAN EPS, GEORGE, * *guitar;* b. Plainfield, N.J., 8/7/13. A graduate of many name bands of the 1930s including Freddy Martin, Benny Goodman, Ray Noble, Van Eps is a pioneer guitarist of the pre-electric era. His guitar method was published by Plymouth Music in 1961. A folio of solos was issued by the same publishers in '64. Van Eps has occasionally appeared in concerts in recent years including the annual jazz festivals in Aspen, Colo. since '64.

Addr: 436 So. Fairview St., Burbank, Calif.

VAN LAKE, TURK (Vanig Hovsepian),* *guitar, composer;* b. Boston, Mass, 6/15/18. During the early 1960s Van Lake spent much of his time as accompanist for singers, among them Miriam Makeba, Brock Peters, Edie Adams and Nancy Wilson. His intermittent association with Benny Goodman, begun in the 1940s, was renewed in April 1962, when he joined a band that left soon afterward on a tour of the Soviet Union. Van Lake wrote a 50,000-word diary of the trip but was unable to find a publisher who would accept it.

LPs w. Goodman (RCA); Terry Gibbs (Time); Herbie Mann (Atl).

Addr: 30 Daniel Low Terrace, New York, N.Y. 10301.

VAUGHAN, SARAH LOIS,* *singer;* b. Newark, N.J., 3/27/24. First heard with Earl Hines and Billy Eckstine bands in '40s, she later went on her own usually acc. by a piano-bass-drums combo. The most important singer to emerge from the bop era, she reflected her association w. Parker and Gillespie through her great harmonic awareness.

Although she has remained a jazz-influenced singer, since the '50s she has worked more in the pop field, gaining international recognition and acclaim. In '63 she rec. an LP on location at the Tivoli Gardens in Copenhagen, Denmark, *Sassy Swings the Tivoli;* on Mercury, and many other LPs on Mercury (incl. *Vaughan Sings the Mancini Songbook;* and *Vaughan With Voices* arr. by Robert Farnon) and Roulette (incl. *Sarah Vaughan & Count Basie*).

In early '65 she performed at the White House for President Johnson and his guests after a state dinner.

VENTURA, CAROL, *singer;* b. 3/3/37. Father and mother were in show business. Prof. debut at 17 with small jazz and show groups, also big bands. Repl. Keely Smith in Louis Prima show in Nevada lounges 1961. Has since worked as single and has been praised by critics as a strongly jazz-oriented singer with an attractive timbre. Favs: F. Sinatra, E. Fitzgerald, T. Bennett, J. Garland.

Own LPs: Pres.

Addr: 133 W. 12th St., New York City, N.Y.

VENTURA, CHARLIE,* *saxophones;* b. Philadelphia, Pa., 12/2/16. Became well-known as tenor man w. Gene Krupa in '40s, then led own big band and combos into early '60s, when he rejoined Krupa. Illness curtailed his activities in '65-6. He can be heard w. the *Metronome All Stars* and w. his own group in tracks on the RCA reissue, *The Be-Bop Era;* also w. Dizzy Gillespie in *New Wave* (Philips).

Addr: 1609 Porter St., Phila., 45, Pa.

VENUTI, GIUSEPPE (JOE),* *violin;* b. 9/1/04. Internationally known since the 1920s as the first great jazz violinist, heard on innumerable records with his own

Blue Four and other groups led by Red Nichols, Paul Whiteman et al. In recent years has been working in lounges in Las Vegas and Seattle. His definitive early performances have been made available again in a two-volume LP, with booklet and photographs, recalling his partnership with guitarist Eddie Lang, in *Stringin' The Blues* (Col. C2L 24).

VIALE, JEAN-LOUIS, *drums;* b. Paris, France, 1/22/ 33. Self-taught on drums. Led own band at age of 18. By 1951 was one of the founders of cool jazz in Paris, playing with B. Jaspar, H. Renaud, M. Solal, B. Wilen. During '50s and '60s led own groups and accompanied visiting U.S. musicians including C. Brown, S. Getz, D. Gordon, Lester Young, S. Stitt, Z. Sims. Toured Canada, Brazil w. Sacha Distel; made TV appearance '62 in Italy w. D. Byrd and J. Griffin. In concert w. the Double Six '65, André Hodeir '65. Favs: Blakey, Roach, Clarke. LPs: all on French Vogue: w. Renaud, Solal, Brown-Art Farmer, Jaspar, R. Thomas, F. Foster, G. Wallington, Sims, Cy Touff-Bill Perkins.

Addr: Le Jal Des Pres, Route du Moulin, Orgeval, France.

VICK, HAROLD EDWARD, *tenor sax, clarinet, flute, composer;* b. Rocky Mount, N.C., 4/3/36. Piano at nine. Played w. cousin, Thomas Cofield, in high school combo composed of music teachers. Later, w. Cofield, pl. local dances. Stud. psychology, sociology, Howard U.; grad. 1958, worked briefly for Welfare Dept. NYC. Worked w. rhythm and blues groups, then big bands and some show orchs. A period of working with organists was followed by jobs mainly with piano and rhythm. Infl. by Stitt, Rollins, Coltrane.

Own LP: *Steppin' Out* (Blue Note). Fav. own solos on *Oh Baby* w. John Patton BN). Others w. Lloyd Price (ABC-Par.), Jack McDuff (Pres.), Gene Ammons' *Soul Summit Vol. II* (Pres.), Ray Charles' *Country & Western Vol. II* (ABC-Par.), Grant Green's *His Majesty King Funk* (Verve).

Addr: 1171 Fulton Ave., Bronx 56, N.Y.

VIG, TOMMY, *vibes, drums;* b. Budapest, Hungary, 7/ 14/38. Father a prominent Hungarian jazz altoist and clarinetist. Vig toured Europe as drum prodigy at age of seven. Graduated Bartok Conservatory, Budapest; later studied at Juilliard. Comps. incl. *I Miss You Today, Depression in a New Town, Short Story.* He fled from Hungary during the revolt of 1956, eventually reaching U.S., where he studied at Juilliard. Took jobs w. Meyer Davis, Martin Denny, Esquivel, but also played w. Bill Evans, Duke Jordan, Peter Ind, Mat Mathews. Appeared in Steve Perlow concert at Las Vegas Flamingo '65. His work *Four Pieces for Neophonic Orch.* was played by LA Neophonic Apr. 1966. Fav: Emil Richards. Infl: Bartok, Monk, Miles Davis, Ellington, Goodman, Gillespie, Parker et al. Own LP: *The Tommy Vig Orchestra* (Take V).

Addr: 1746 Monroe Ave., Bronx 57, N.Y.

VINNEGAR, LEROY,* *bass, composer;* b. Indianapolis, Ind., 7/13/28. In LA from 1954; with Shelly Manne

'55-6; pl. on best-selling *My Fair Lady* LP with Manne, Andre Previn. In 1959-61 worked mainly wih Joe Castro in Cal. and Europe.

One of the busiest free-lance bassists in the West Coast, Vinnegar is known more for his "walking" beat than for complex melodic solos, though he is an imaginative pizzicato and arco improviser. He has gigged and recorded with Les McCann, Teddy Edwards, Phineas Newborn, Jack Wilson, Gerald Wilson's band, The Jazz Crusaders. TV and/or concerts with Theo. Bikel, Odetta, G. Mulligan, Josh White et al. Hollywood Bowl with Stan Getz; Monterey JF. Tour of Japan with all-star group '64. He has written several popular instrumental works, among them *For Carl* (used as theme in film *An Affair of the Skin*), *Subway Grate, Hard to Find*.

Own LPs: Contemp., VJ. LPs with T. Edwards, S. Rollins, H. McGhee (Cont.); L. McCann, K. Dorham, G. Wilson (Pac. Jazz); J. Castro (Clover).

Addr: 6235 Primrose Ave., Los Angeles, Calif. 90028.

VISOR, CARRINGTON LIVINGSTON JR., *tenor sax, flute, clarinet, composer;* b. Washingon, D.C., 5/14/34. Father pl. tpt. in symph. bands. Started pl. sax in high school; while still there, pl. w. Howard U. Swingmasters. Worked in Howard Theater house band and many local groups; to LA '58, working w. Curtis Counce, Lighthouse All Stars, nine months w. Chico Hamilton Quintet '60-'61. Later spent year and a half with Louis Bellson band in Pearl Bailey show. Several months in Terry Gibbs combo on nightly Regis Philbin TV show '64-5. LPs w. Bellson (Roul.).

Addr: 1509 S. Hauser Blvd., Los Angeles 19, Calif.

WAITS, FREDERICK DOUGLAS (FRED), *drums;* also *flute;* b. Jackson, Miss., 4/27/43. Studied flute in high school both in Jackson and Detroit. Majored in flute at Jackson St. Coll. but became more interested in drums during percussion class. Pl. rock and roll jobs while in college. Ret. to Detroit '62 and pl. w. Jimmy Wilkins big band into '63; Terry Pollard, Dorothy Ashby, and rock gigs '63. Joined Paul Winter '63, remaining until Dec. '65, incl. two So. American tours. While w. Winter also worked w. Kenny Dorham, Curtis Fuller, Cedar Walton in NYC. Member of big band assembled for Gerald Wilson at Basin St. East, March '66. Backed Damita Jo, Betty Carter '66. W. Sonny Rollins trio June '66. Orig. infl.: Roach, Blakey, Philly Joe Jones. LPs w. Winter, Denny Zeitlin (Col.), Ray Bryant (Cadet), Groove Holmes (Pres.), Wild Bill Davis (RCA).

Addr: 343 W. 84th St., New York 24, N.Y.

WALDRON, MALCOLM EARL (MAL),* *piano, composer;* b. New York, N.Y., 8/16/26. Most noted for his excellent work with Charles Mingus and Billie Holiday during the middle and late '50s, Waldron expanded his scope both as composer and musician during the '60s. In 1961 and '62 he appeared at the NYC Five Spot in a remarkable group headed by Eric Dolphy and Booker Little, which also included Richard Davis and Ed Blackwell. Wrote film scores for *The Cool World* '63 and *Three Bedrooms in Manhattan* and *Sweet Love Bitter* '65; and music for LeRoi Jones' plays *The Slave* and *The Dutchman*. In Europe '65 appeared at Bologna, Italy, Jazz Festival and in concert throughout Italy and in Paris. Made several appearances in NYC and the Midwest. At Newport JF '62.

A melodically and rhythmically exciting soloist, Waldron, like Monk, often builds his solos on deceptively simple single-note lines. More controlled than Monk's, they are usually symmetrically designed and, aided by Waldron's sparse but punctuating left hand, convey an emotional message even when understated. As a composer Waldron uses the simplicity of his playing to effective advantage. Nat Hentoff called him "one of the most probing and unpredictable forces in modern jazz," while Joe Goldberg says that "there are few more committed to the music than Waldron, few who play it with more skill and dedication, and few as overdue in their acceptance." Own LPs: several with trios, and *The Quest* w. Dolphy and Booker Ervin (Pres.). Others: w. Mingus (Atl., Fant., Savoy), Dolphy (Pres.), Ron Carter (Status), numerous others as sideman on Pres.

Addr: 107-39 166th St., Jamaica, N.Y.

WALKER, AARON (T-BONE),* *singer, guitar;* b. Linden, Tex., 1913. Acc. Ida Cox, Ma Rainey, Blind Lemon Jefferson; pl. w. Les Hite band '39-'40. From that time has worked as a single all over the country. In mid-'60s app. at Apollo Theater and Half Note, NYC. Still a powerful exponent of blues singing and playing, and occasional acrobatics. LP: reissue of material from 1945-50 on *The Great Blues Vocals and Guitar of T-Bone Walker* (Cap.)

WALTON, CEDAR ANTHONY JR.,* *piano, composer;* b. Dallas, Texas, 1/17/34. Played in late 1950s with Lou Donaldson, J. J. Johnson. After leaving Johnson, worked with Benny Golson-Art Farmer Jazztet July '60-Aug. '61. Then toured as pianist-arranger with Art Blakey's Jazz Messengers Aug. '61-June '64, including two European tours and one tour of Japan. In Oct. '64 he visited Japan again with a group composed of former Blakey sidemen. In '65-6 his trio accompanied singer Abbey Lincoln, for whom he served as musical director at Wells' Supper Club, NYC.

LPs with Blakey: *Free For All, Mosaic* (Blue Note); *Three Blind Mice* (UA); *Ugetsu* (River.). Other LPs: *Body and Soul* with Freddie Hubbard (Imp.), Eddie Harris (Atl.)

WARD, CLARA,* *singer;* b. Philadelphia, 4/21/24. A gospel singer from childhood, she studied under her mother, who led a choral group.

The Ward Singers first came to prominence at a

Baptist Convention in '43 and during the next two decades traveled over a million miles, enjoying a success unique among gospel groups. Among their greatest successes were: Frequent appearances at the New Frontier in Las Vegas from Oct. '62 through July '65; theatre engagements in the *Jack Benny Show* in NYC and Toronto '63; TV shows such as *Dial M for Music, Hootenany,* a triumphant engagement at the Olympia Theatre in Paris Nov.-Dec. '65, and engagements at the Village Gate in NYC. Miss Ward and the five other singers in her group have a dynamic and exciting quality that is related to the roots of jazz, though their repertoire has usually been that of the gospel idiom. In 1965 the group began to broaden its range of material, recording such popular songs as *Smile* and the Beatles' hit *Help.*

As a side enterprise, Miss Ward runs the unique Ward Record Shop in Philadelphia, which sells only gospel music. LPs: Col., Vanguard, Verve.

Addr: c/o Monte Kay, 200 West 57th St., New York 19, N.Y.

WARREN, EARLE RONALD,* *alto sax, composer;* b. Springfield, Ohio, 7/1/14. The veteran ex-Basie alto player, also active during the '50s as a free-lance mus. dir. and manager, toured Europe w. Buck Clayton and the Basie All-Stars in 1961. Also w. Lena Horne '61. W. Clayton on U.S. tours '62-'63. Conducted several rock & roll shows, played in studio orchs. '65 teamed w. Emmett Berry, appearing in night clubs, etc. Newport JF '61. Has own furniture store. LPs w. Basie (Bruns., Col. etc.).

Addr: 58 Hilltop Rd., Newfoundland, N.J.

WARREN, EDWARD (BUTCH), *bass, composer;* b. Washington, D.C., 8/9/39. His father, Edward Warren Sr., plays piano and once led a band in which the younger Warren played. Worked around Washington w. Stuff Smith and many local groups before coming to NYC in '58 to play w. Kenny Dorham at Five Spot. In the '60s free-lanced w. many combos before joining Thelonious Monk '63. Left in '64 to return to Wash. where he worked w. small groups such as Eddie Phyfe '66. Comp. *Lost, The Backbone, Eric Walks.* Favs.: Jimmy Blanton, Paul Chambers, Ray Brown. Warren, one of the most talented young bassists to emerge in the '60s, in his duets with Monk often echoed the style of Blanton. LPs: Monk (Col.), Dorham, Joe Henderson, Dexter Gordon, Sonny Clark, Herbie Hancock (BN).

WARWICK, DIONNE, *singer;* b. Orange, New Jersey, 12/12/40. Mother is Lee Warwick, formerly with Drinkard Singers, a gospel group. Attended Hart Coll. of Mus., Hartford, Conn.; stud. piano 1959-61. First prof. work as background vocal group singer. Became a top-selling record artist in early '60s, heard on a series of singles. Her appearances have incl. the Cannes Film Fest. in '64; Olympia Theatre, Paris '64, '65 and '66; Savoy Hotel, London, Apr. '65; Carnegie Hall,

NYC, and Symphony Hall, Boston, Dec. '65; Basin Street East, NYC, Apr. '66.

Though she has had a wide appeal to teen-aged audiences, Miss Warwick is not a rock 'n' roll performer. Most jazz experts consider her a first-class performer in a style that indicates the influences of her favorite singers, Billie Holiday and Frank Sinatra. Her best-known records include *Anyone Who Had A Heart,* which she considers her outstanding work, *Walk On By, Don't Make Me Over, Who Can I Turn To* and *Message To Michael* (Scepter).

Addr: 254 W. 54th St., New York, 19, N.Y.

WASHINGTON, DINAH (Ruth Jones),* *singer;* b. Tuscaloosa, Ala., 8/29/24; A vocalist with Lionel Hampton's band 1943-6, Miss Washington became a recording star after her first session, featuring blues compositions by this writer (incl. *Evil Gal Blues, Salty Papa Blues*), was released on Keynote. During the late '40s and the '50s she concentrated more frequently on popular songs, but her background of religious singing and her deep feeling for the blues could be discerned even in her most commercial work. She died suddenly 12/14/63 at her home in Detroit.

Miss Washington, billed in her early years as "Queen of the Blues," had in her voice a terse, sardonic quality that gave a personal meaning to every lyric she touched. Her timbre had a gutty, vinegarlike character; her phrasing was exceptionally free of orthodox restrictions. Her career was synthesized in a two-volume album, *The Dinah Washington Story,* recorded not long before her death, in which she sang new versions of many of her biggest hits (Merc.). Some of the original versions, cut in the 1940s, can be heard on *Dinah Sings The Best in Blues* (Merc.). Other LPs on Roul., Merc. and a few tracks in one album on Grand Award; one tune with Lionel Hampton on *All American Award Contest* (Decca).

WASHINGTON, RONALD JACK,* *baritone sax;* b. Kansas City, Mo., 1912. Well known as the anchor man of the Count Basie reed section from 1935-50, Washington later gigged in Oklahoma City, where he died in 1964.

WATERS, ETHEL,* *singer;* b. Chester, Pa., 10/31/00. Popular recording star in 1920s, best known for her first big hit, *Dinah,* 1924. In '30s and '40s established herself as a fine dramatic actress (*Mamba's Daughters, Member of the Wedding*). Many motion pictures incl. *Cabin in the Sky, Pinky.* Autobiography: *His Eye is On The Sparrow* (Doubleday). In the 1960s Miss Waters, seriously ill, lived in Pasadena, Calif. and limited her singing to occasional appearances at religious events. She also appeared in revivals of her early stage hits. An album of her early hits was due for reissue on Col. in 1967.

WATERS, MUDDY (McKinley Morganfield),* *singer, guitar;* b. Rolling Fork, Miss., 4/4/15. To Chicago 1943. Worked in local clubs and achieved prominence through recordings in '50s, making first overseas tour in '58. During the '60s he was one of the more prominent figures in the revival of traditional blues. He appeared at the Newport JF 1960. In addition to working in Britain and on the Continent he enjoyed great popularity in Canada, where he appeared on many television shows. His voice has a rough, harsh urgency and a great emotional intensity rarely found among contemporary blues artists.

LPs: *Muddy Waters at Newport* & others (Chess); as "Dirty Rivers" w. Otis Spann (Pres.).

Addr: 4339 Lake Park, Chicago, Ill.

WATKINS, DOUGLAS (DOUG),* *bass;* b. Detroit, Mich., 3/2/34. One of the wave of youthful jazzmen from Detroit who reached New York in the mid-'50s, Watkins pl. w. Art Blakey in 1955, later w. Horace Silver, then free-lanced with Hank Mobley and various others around NYC. While driving to San Francisco to join Philly Joe Jones' group, Watkins fell asleep at the wheel and was killed instantly in a collision near Holbrook, Arizona, 2/5/62. The loss of this unusually capable musician was widely mourned in jazz circles.

WATKINS, JULIUS,* *French horn;* b. Detroit, Mich., 10/10/21. Pl. w. Oscar Pettiford in '50s; also co-led Les Jazz Modes w. Charlie Rouse. In '60s has pl. w. pit bands for Broadway shows; w. Charlie Mingus' brass ensemble '65. LPs w. Curtis Fuller (Status), Milt Jackson (River.).

WAYNE, CHUCK (Charles Jagelka),* *guitar, banjo;* b. New York, N.Y., 2/27/23. One of the early bop guitarists; free-lanced around NYC with a variety of bands during '40s and '50s. On staff of CBS from '59. Appeared w. own trio at The Most during '60s. Taught privately and studied classical guitar. On several record dates. Own LPs: *Tapestry* (Focus), which included a modern banjo solo; *Morning Mist* (Pres.).

Addr: 90 Bayview Ave., Princess Bay, N.Y.

WEBSTER, BENJAMIN FRANCIS (BEN),* *tenor sax;* b. Kansas City, Mo., 2/27/09. Played with many swing bands including Benny Carter, Fletcher Henderson, Cab Calloway. Came to prominence with Duke Ellington 1939-43. Rejoined Ellington briefly in '48 and has often been associated with ventures involving present and past Ellington sidemen.

In the early 1960s Webster, living in Los Angeles and NYC, was in relative obscurity, working too irregularly for a man of his incomparable talent. Despite the many changes in tenor playing and the influences that could have modified his style, Webster's great intensity and implacable swing on up tempos, and his control, lyricism and beauty in interpretations of ballads remained unaffected by the passage of time. In 1965-6 he found a greater measure of acceptance by moving to England and working clubs and concerts there and on the Continent.

Best LPs as leader incl. *Webster-Oscar Peterson, Webster & Associates* w. Coleman Hawkins; *Soul of Ben Webster* w. Art Farmer (Verve); *Warm Moods* w. string quartet, arr. J. Richards (Reprise); *See You*

At the Fair (Impulse); *Webster-Sweets Edison* (Col.). Others see Clark Terry (Impulse); Johnny Hodges (Verve). See also Ellington, Duke, and Ellington, Mercer.

WEBSTER, PAUL FRANK,* *trumpet;* b. Kansas City, Mo., 8/24/09; d. New York City, 5/5/66. After pl. w. Geo. E. Lee, Bennie Moten, Andy Kirk, earned reputation as outstanding lead trumpeter w. Jimmie Lunceford band 1935-42. Later w. Cab Calloway, Ch. Barnet. From 1954 worked in Immigration Office job, but continued to play gigs around NYC, and worked in pit band of Langston Hughes' play *Simply Heavenly* on Broadway. One of the first high-note jazz specialists, he was best known for his solo on Lunceford's *For Dancers Only.* LPs w. Lunceford (Dec., Col.), Sy Oliver (Dec.).

WEIN, GEORGE THEODORE,* *piano, singer, leader;* b. Boston, Mass., 10/3/25. Played with Dixieland combos in Boston from mid-1940s but is best known as producer of the annual Newport JF, which he started in 1954. After a riot erupted outside the festival grounds in 1960 Wein was not associated with the event for one year, but he came back to build it into an even greater success than in the pre-riot years. In addition, he has produced the annual Ohio Valley JF in Cincinnati since 1962; the Pittsburgh Catholic Youth Organization Festival since '64 (the first such official sponsorship of jazz by the Catholic Church); the Down Beat JF in Chicago, in collaboration with the magazine, '65; and the first Southern presentation of this kind, The Longhorn JF in Austin, Texas, April '66.

Wein created the Newport Folk Festival and Foundation, active from 1963. In '66 he expanded to produce the first opera festival with the Metropolitan Opera at Newport. His overseas ventures have included numerous tours with Thelonious Monk, with an all-star show featuring four drummers, a general festival seen in Berlin and other capitals from 1964, and the World JF, with U.S. and Japanese musicians, in five Japanese cities in '64.

Wein has continued to play piano at most of the events he has presented. His LPs include *That Newport Jazz* (Col.); *Great Moments in Jazz—Re-created at the Newport JF* (RCA).

Addr: 50 Central Park West, New York 23, N.Y.

WELLINS, BOBBY, *tenor sax, soprano sax, composer;* b. Glasgow, Scotland, 1936. Pl. w. Buddy. Featherstonhaugh, Tony Crombie, toured France w. own group; U.S. w. Vic Lewis. W. New Departures jazz and jazz-poetry gps. from '61, incorporating free improvising. His extended comp. *The Battle of Culloden Moor,* for himself, Stan Tracey, Laurie Morgan and orchestral acc., was performed in London '61 (he has rec. a quartet version w. New Departures). Feat. in Stan Tracey's *Under Milk Wood* suite, pl. it w. Tracey's quartet on TV in Eng. and Germany '66. Considered by many Eng. mus. and critics to be the most original and creative jazzman yet produced in Europe, Wellins has a style of great subtlety and inventiveness, and a distinctive fragile sound with strong Scottish folk roots. LPs on Brit. labels w. Stan Tracey (Col., H.M.V.), New Departures (Transatlantic), Tony Crombie (Tempo).

WELLS, WILLIAM (DICKIE),* trombone; b. Centerville, Tenn., 6/10/09. Soloist in many of the big swing bands, most notably that of Count Basie, with whom he worked 1938-45 and '47-'50. Wells toured Europe in late 1959. After working for a while with Ray Charles' band he again free-lanced in NYC and continued to consolidate his reputation in Europe. He made a highly successful tour in the fall of 1965 with the British traditionalist band of Alex Welsh.

Wells was discussed at length in a chapter entitled *The Romantic Imagination of Dickie Wells* in the book *Jazz: Its Evolution and Essence* by André Hodeir, Grove Press. In it, Hodeir analyzed at length the symmetry and contrasts of Wells' style, his ability to use subtle inflections and vibratos to optimum effect, and the skillful technique discernible in his early records. Some of Wells' solos can be heard in the first Basie albums on Decca and Brunswick. He is also featured in *Classic Tenors* with Lester Young (Contact) and in *At His Very Best* w. Young (Emarcy).

Addr: 153 W. 139th St., New York City, N.Y.

WELLS, AMOS JR. (JUNIOR), singer; b. Memphis, Tenn., 12/9/34. Raised in an environment that produced B. B. King and other authentic blues artists, Wells was indoctrinated with the blues feeling from an early age. He moved to Chicago in 1946, bought his first harmonica two years later and soon began sitting in at local taverns. He became acquainted with Muddy Waters and worked as an added attraction on some of Waters' engagements. After Army service 1953-5 he again played in groups around Chicago and enhanced his reputation through such appearances as a concert at the Swarthmore College Folk Festival.

Wells' style is based on the knowledge he picked up listening to Sonny Boy Williamson and other contemporaries. First heard on such independent labels as States, Chief, and Profile, he is heard leading his own Chicago blues band in *Hoodoo Man Blues* (Delmark).

WELLSTOOD, RICHARD MacQUEEN (DICK),* piano; b. Greenwich, Conn., 11/25/27. Pianist w. Jimmy Archey, Roy Eldridge, Conrad Janis during late '40s and '50s. House pianist at Metropole '59-'61, Nick's '61-'63. Free-lanced NYC '63-'64. W. Gene Krupa quartet from '64. Toured S. America '65, Israel '66 w. Krupa. Columnist for *Sounds & Fury* magazine. Own LP: Pres. Others: w. Bob Wilber, Clark Terry (Clas. Jazz), w. John Letman (Beth.), w. Odetta (RCA, River.).

Addr: 268 E. Virginia Ave., Manasquan, N.J. 08736.

WELSH, ALEX, trumpet; b. Edinburgh, Scotland, 7/9/29. Led own band at Brit. concerts, festivals and clubs from '55. Since '63 it has toured Brit. acc. Bud Freeman, Henry "Red" Allen, Pee Wee Russell, Earl Hines, Ruby Braff, Dickie Wells, Rex Stewart. Musicianly

and tasteful Dixieland band. Own LPs on British labels (Col., Pye).

Addr: 10 Pennant Mews, London W.8., England.

WESS, FRANK WELLINGTON,* alto and tenor saxes, flute, composer; b. Kansas City, Mo., 1/4/22. Worked for some years in Wash., D.C.; toured w. Blanche Calloway, Billy Eckstine et al. Acquired major jazz reputation as one of the first modern jazz flutists and as tenor (later alto) soloist w. Count Basie, June 1953-Aug. '64. In pit band of B'way show *Golden Boy* Sept. '64-March '66. TV work with Sammy Davis, Edie Adams, Judy Garland; LPs with Basie (q.v.), Sinatra, Fitzgerald, Sammy Davis.

Addr: 185-40 Ilion Ave., St. Albans 12, N.Y.

WEST, BOB, bass; b. Milledgeville, Georgia, 3/1/37. Brother an organist, mother a music teacher. Studied with Jimmy Bond, Stanley Keath, then joined Charles Lloyd quartet in LA. Did some TV background writing '60. Joined Sarah Vaughan, incl. tour of Europe, '61. With LA Neophonic Orch. '66. Also a full-time racing driver. Favs: Red Mitchell, Ray Brown, Scott La Faro. LPs: w. Clare Fischer (Pac. Jazz), Andrew Hill (Contemp.), Billy Eckstine (Motown).

WESTBROOK, MICHAEL (MIKE), composer, piano, valve trombone; b. High Wycombe, Buckinghamshire, England, 3/21/36. '58 began writing and formed own band in Plymouth. '62 moved to London and reformed, '63 expanded to eleven pieces, '65-6 cut down to six. Members have inc. Henry Lowther, John Surman, Keith Rowe, Lawrence Sheaff, Lou Gare. Pl. many concerts and arts festivals from '64. Westbrook and Surman are responsible for all comps., inc. several extended works, which leave most of the detail to improvisation. Band's aggressive style has attracted much critical attention. Westbrook is also a qualified art teacher. Favs: Ellington, Mingus.

Addr: 2 Crescent Mansions, Elgin Crescent, London W.11., England.

WESTON, RANDOLPH E. (RANDY),* piano, composer; b. Brooklyn, N.Y., 4/6/26. Sideman with rhythm-and-blues and jazz combos from '49 to '54. Began to achieve a reputation as composer and pianist in late '50s. Toured colleges with his quartet and a team of jazz dancers annually from '59 to '64; organized series of concerts for high schools and libraries in NYC at which he outlined the history of jazz. Collaborated with Rev. John G. Gensel in presenting jazz worship services in several churches 1963-6. Has also given a number of lectures on the Negro in the U.S.

From 1952-66 Weston frequently played summers at Berkshire resorts in Lenox, Mass. He has been heard intermittently at numerous NYC clubs, incl. the Half Note, whose jazz policy he inaugurated. His concert appearances have included several for the United Nations Jazz Society and many benefits for a variety of causes. To Nigeria for a Performing Arts Festival '61; visited Nigeria again '63.

His most successful compositions have been *Hi-Fly*

and *Little Niles.* Others incl. *Berkshire Blues, African Cookbook, Uhuru Afrika Suite, Blues Suite, In Memory Of, Where?, Pam's Waltz.* In 1966 Weston launched his own Bakton record label. He continued to show a strength and individuality, both as composer and instrumentalist, that has yet to achieve adequate public recognition. Whether his inspiration stems from Africa or the Berkshires, he writes and plays in an outstandingly melodic and attractive style that invariably creates the mood he set out to achieve.

LPs: Bakton, UA, Roul., Colpix.

Addr: 330A Lafayette Ave., Brooklyn, N.Y.

WETTLING, GEORGE GODFREY,* *drums;* b. Topeka, Kans., 11/28/07. In Chicago and Dixieland jazz from the early days, Wettling appeared occasionally with Eddie Condon from the mid-'50s, incl. Condon's Carnegie Hall concert July '64. At NY Gaslight Club regularly from '64. Newport JF '64, Chicago Down Beat JF '65. TV appearance on *Salute to Eddie Condon* '64. Continued activity as painter. Columns and features published regularly in DB, other jazz magazines.

Addr: 406 W. 57th St., New York, N.Y.

WETZEL, BONNIE,* *bass;* b. Vancouver, Wash., 5/15/26. Widow of trumpeter Ray Wetzel, with whom she worked in Tommy Dorsey band. Later prominent as member of Beryl Booker's all-girl trio, which toured Europe in 1954. Died of cancer in Vancouver 1965.

WHIGHAM, HAYDN (JIGGS), *trombone;* b. Cleveland, Ohio, 8/20/43. '61-2 and '64 w. Glenn Miller Orch. dir. by Ray McKinley as lead and soloist, '63 w. Stan Kenton. '65 freelanced in NYC, then left to join Kurt Edelhagen in Cologne. Toured Japan w. McKinley, Britain w. Kenton '63, Africa w. Edelhagen '66. LPs w. Kenton (Capitol), McKinley (RCA), Johnny Richards (Roulette).

Addr: 5 Cologne-Zollstock, Kendenicher Str. 18, Germany.

WHITE, CHRISTOPHER WESTLEY (CHRIS), *bass;* also *guitar, trombone;* b. New York City, 7/6/36. Stud. pno. privately in Brooklyn. Bass w. Cecil Taylor off and on 1955-9; Bernard Peiffer '60, Nina Simone '60-'61. From 1962-6 he toured w. the D. Gillespie Quintet, visiting Europe in '62 and '65. His excellent sound, imaginative playing and informal humor were invaluable factors in the group's popularity. White left Gillespie in Jan. '66 to study and play in NYC. Joined Billy Taylor trio, Apr. '66.

LPs w. Gillespie: Philips, Limelight.

Addr: 308 E. 8th St., New York City, N.Y. 10009.

WHITE, JOSHUA DONALD JR. (JOSH), *singer, guitar;* b. New York City, 11/30/40. Son of the distinguished singer and guitarist of the same name. A professional singer since the age of four, when he appeared with his father at Cafe Society in NYC. Attended New York Professional Children's School; never studied music. Continued to work off and on with his father until 1961, when he started out on his own. Has played dra-

matic roles in five Broadway shows, including *Only In America, The Long Dream;* TV appearances on *Armstrong Circle Theatre* and many variety shows. Clubs and concerts throughout U.S., Canada and Europe, including Carnegie Hall and Town Hall NYC. Joint concerts with Henry Mancini and Glenn Miller band. White, much of whose style is clearly derived from his father, became increasingly popular with college concert audiences in the mid-'60s. Own LP: *I'm On My Own Way* (Merc.).

Addr: 156 E. 52nd St., New York City, New York.

WHITE, MICHAEL WALTER, *violin;* b. Houston, Tex., 5/24/33. Raised in Oakland, Calif.; began study of violin at age 9. Played in Vancouver, B.C. 1965. At the 1965 Monterey Jazz Festival White caught the public attention in a surprising performance with the John Handy quintet. He is one of the first violinists to adapt avant-garde techniques and ideas to that instrument. Favs: Stuff Smith, Joe Kennedy, Stephane Grappelly. Lists O. Pettiford, Sun Ra, B. Powell, T. Monk, D. Ellington, C. Brown as influences. LP w. Handy (Col.)

Addr: 1076 59th St., Oakland, Calif.

WHITLOCK, BOB,* *bass;* b. Roosevelt, Utah, 1/21/31. Worked w. Mulligan, De Franco, many others on West Coast in '50s. Toured w. Geo. Shearing Quintet 1965-1966.

LPs w. Shearing (Cap.), Vi Redd (UA), Mulligan (Wor. Pac.).

Addr: P.O. Box 692, Malibu, Calif.

WHITSELL, RICHARD GUILES (DICK), *trumpet, piano;* b. Chicago, Ill., 7/18/36. Played local jobs while in college, where he met Paul Winter and formed a band that later became professional. Played with Tex Beneke and other dance bands, but most of his work has been as a member of Winter's Sextet, including six-month tour of Latin America for State Department during first half of '62 and concert at White House Nov. '62.

In 1963 Whitsell left music to become a doctor, but ran into difficulties and was rejected by American medical schools. He later went to Europe and Mexico. In 1966, still inactive in music, he planned to enter law school.

LPs with Paul Winter (Col.).

Addr: 10534 S. Seeley, Chicago, Ill., 60643.

WHITTLE, TOMMY, *tenor sax;* b. Grangemouth, Scotland, 10/13/26. From '43 pl. w. Johnny Claes, Lew Stone, Carl Barriteau, Harry Hayes. '47-'52 w. Ted Heath, left to join Tony Kinsey. '52-5 was feat. weekly on Eng. radio w. Cyril Stapleton. Left to lead own band after winning polls '55. Freelance since '57, but toured U.S. and France w. own gps. Fluent and inventive soloist in Lester Young-based style. Own LPs on Brit. labels.

Addr: 203 Merry Hill Rd., Bushey, Hertfordshire, England.

WIGGINS, GERALD FOSTER,* *piano;* b. New York City, 5/12/22. Best known as acc. for Lena Horne,

Kay Starr and many other singers in '50s. In recent years has free-lanced as Hollywood studio musician, played regularly at Memory Lane Club and played on LPs with Nat Cole, Lou Rawls, Ernie Andrews (Cap.); Sweets Edison, Sam Fletcher (VJ). Acc. for Maria Cole '65-6.

Addr: 1404 So. Hobart Blvd., Los Angeles 6, Calif.

WILBER, ROBERT SAGE (BOB), * *clarinet, soprano sax;* b. New York City, 3/15/28. Prominent in many traditionalist groups in the 1940s and '50s, Wilber worked in 1960-61 with Tony Bennett and Bobby Hackett. He also free-lanced at Eddie Condon's and other clubs. In 1962-4 he played with Max Kaminsky's group for Jackie Gleason. Various dates at Metropole and Condon's, '64-6, also free-lanced composing and arranging. Studied piano with Sanford Gold '66. Own LPs: *New Clarinet In Town, Blowing the Blues Away* (Classic Jazz).

LPs with B. Hackett (Cap.), Jack Teagarden (UA), M. Kaminsky (Seeburg).

Addr: 302 No. Main St., New City, New York 10956.

WILDER, JOSEPH BENJAMIN (JOE), * *trumpet;* b. Colwyn, Pa., 2/22/22. Many pit bands for Broadway shows in '50s except for Jan.-June '54 when he was w. Count Basie. Joined staff at ABC-TV '57. Time off to tour USSR w. Benny Goodman '62. LP w. Goodman (RCA).

Addr: 640 Riverside Drive, New York 31, N.Y.

WILKERSON, DON, *tenor sax, composer;* b. Moreauville, La., 1932. After informal musical education at home, he began playing alto while at high school in Houston, Texas. Professional debut in Dayton, Texas. Joined Amos Milburn 1948; also worked in Los Angeles '48-9 with Charles Brown. Returned to Houston and remained there until 1954, when he joined the early Ray Charles band, playing tenor solos on such early records as *Come Back Baby, I Got A Woman* and *This Little Girl of Mine.* Through the encouragement of Ike Quebec, he was brought to the attention of Blue Note Records and made his debut as a leader on *Preach Brother!* His style shows a combination of bop and blues influences.

WILKINS, DAVE, *trumpet;* b. Barbados, B.W.I., 9/25/14. Came to London '37, pl. w. Ken "Snakehips" Johnson until the latter was killed when a bomb fell on the band '41 during the Blitz. Then pl. w. Ambrose, Harry Parry, Eric Winstone, Ted Heath, and many other bands up to '49. Toured Europe '50, and since then pl. mostly w. Wally Fawkes and Bruce Turner. Retired due to illness '62-6. Rec. w. Fats Waller, Una Mae Carlisle, Ambrose, Ted Heath. Fav. own solo *Body and Soul* w. Parry.

Addr: 62 Westbere Rd., London N.W.2., England.

WILKINS, ERNEST (ERNIE), * *composer, alto, tenor saxophones;* b. St. Louis, Mo., 7/20/22. Played w. George Hudson, Earl Hines bands in '40s; Count Basie '51-5. Settled in NYC, writing scores for Basie, Tommy Dor-

sey, Harry James in '50s. Toured overseas w. Dizzy Gillespie '56. In '60s has divided his time between NYC and Detroit, writing for his brother Jimmy's band in the latter city. More arrs. for James. LPs: *Bursting Out* w. Oscar Peterson (Verve), James (MGM).

WILLETTE, "BABY FACE," *organ, composer;* b. New Orleans, La., 9/11/33. Studied piano from 1938 with his uncle Fred Freeman, a local musician. His mother was a missionary and pianist; his father was minister of a church in Little Rock, Ark. Willette made his professional debut playing piano with rhythm and blues and gospel groups in the early '50s, touring the U.S., and visiting Cuba and Canada. At one time he had his own trio playing in Milwaukee and Chicago. As a sideman he worked with Guitar Slim, Joe Houston, King Kolax, The Caravan Gospel Singers and Roy Brown. Inspired by Charlie Parker records and by the work of two church organists, he gradually changed over from rhythm and blues to jazz and from piano to organ. Favs: Powell, Monk, Garner, Peterson; Jimmy Smith, Shirley Scott. Own LPs: Blue Note, Argo.

WILLIAMS, CLARENCE, * *composer, pianist, leader;* b. Plaquemine, La., 10/8/93. In the 1920s Williams was well known as the producer and director (sometimes pianist) on a series of important recordings featuring Louis Armstrong and other early jazz artists. He also accompanied Bessie Smith on some of her classic blues recordings and wrote many of the compositions for these sessions. During the '30s and '40s he concerned himself mainly with the operation of a music publishing company. Inactive in later years, he died in NYC 11/6/65. Williams was best known as the composer of *Sugar Blues, Gulf Coast Blues, I Ain't Gonna Give Nobody None of My Jelly Roll,* and (in collaboration w. Spencer Williams) *Royal Garden Blues.*

WILLIAMS, CHARLES MELVIN (COOTIE), * *trumpet;* b. Mobile, Ala. 7/24/08. A member of Duke Ellington's orchestra from the spring of 1929 until Nov. 1940, Williams played with Benny Goodman for a year before forming his own big band. He later worked with a combo and by the early 1960s was active mainly as a nightclub act accompanied by a rhythm section. In the fall of 1962, after an absence of 22 years, he rejoined Ellington. During the next four years his clear, engaging open sound and inimitable plunger-mute solos were frequently featured with the band, sometimes in Ellington originals but also in some of the band's best performances of pop songs such as *Fly Me To The Moon.* Numerous LPs with Ellington, the most recent being on Col. and Reprise.

Addr: 119-64 New York Blvd., Jamaica 34, N.Y.

WILLIAMS, JOE (JOSEPH GOREED), * *singer;* b. *Cordele,* Georgia 12/12/18. After six very successful years as featured vocalist with Count Basie Orch., Williams left in January, 1961 to go out as a single artist. For the first year he was accompanied on his tours by the Harry

"Sweets" Edison Quintet, and later by the Junior Mance Trio. He appeared at the NJF annually from 1962; at Monterey in '64. In the fall of '62 he played two weeks of concerts in England; returned to London September, '65 for engagement at Annie Ross's Room.

During the years that followed his departure from the Basie band Williams expanded his scope conspicuously. Though still an extraordinarily convincing blues performer in a relatively sophisticated (urban) blues style, he also developed into one of the most outstanding pop singers of the 1960s, thus achieving a duality of talents attained by no other male singer.

LPs: Prior to September 1962 Williams was heard first on Verve, then on Roulette, with Count Basie band and on his own. After that date he recorded a series of albums for RCA, most of them devoted to pop songs rather than blues. Among the best are *Jump For Joy, Me And The Blues, The Song Is You,* and *The Exciting Joe Williams.*

Addr: c/o John Levy Enterprises, 119 W. 57th St., New York 19, N.Y.

WILLIAMS, JOHN TOWNER,* *piano, composer;* b. Flushing, N.Y. 2/8/32. Pianist-arranger for movies, TV, pop singers from '55. Mus. Dir. *Alcoa Theater, Ben Casey, Chrysler Theater, Kraft Theater,* etc.; several films incl: *John Goldfarb Please Come Home, Diamond Head, None But the Brave.* Wrote *Essay for Strings,* performed by many symphonic orchestras. Comp. *Prelude and Fugue for Jazz Orchestra* performed by L.A. Neophonic Orch., '65. LPs: w. Shelly Manne (Cap.), Andre Previn.

Addr: 4161 High Valley Rd., Encino, Calif.

WILLIAMS, MARION, *singer;* b. Miami, Fla., 8/29/27. Both parents sang in Holiness churches. Her father died when she was nine; Miss Williams left school after the ninth grade to support her family, working as maid, nurse, and laundress, and singing in storefront churches and street-corner revivals on weekends. She joined the Clara Ward Singers in 1947 and remained with the group as lead voice for eleven years.

In 1958 Miss Williams and four other members of the Ward Singers formed their own group, the Stars of Faith. In 1961 Langston Hughes wrote a gospel musical play, *Black Nativity,* in which Miss Williams was featured in the U.S. and overseas 1961-5. She also sang the lead in *Prodigal Son* in Europe '55-6. Concerts: President Kennedy's International JF, Washington, D.C., May, '62; Spoleto, June '62; Coventry Cathedral, Sept. '62; Philharmonic Hall, Dec. '62; Antibes JF, July '65; Town Hall, '66. Kenneth Tynan called Miss Williams "Unforgettable . . . her voice zooming from coloratura exaltation to cavernous contralto reproach, she is a mobile magnificat." LPs: Epic, Savoy, VJ; also guest with Ray Brown-Milt Jackson *Much in Common* (Verve).

Addr: 1020 W. Columbia Ave., Philadelphia, Pa.

WILLIAMS, MARY LOU (Mary Elfrieda Winn),* *piano, composer;* b. Pittsburgh, Pa., 5/8/10. The first feminine

pianist brought to prominence by the swing era, Miss Williams played in Andy Kirk's orch. 1931-42. She has also arranged for Benny Goodman, led numerous combos of her own, and worked in England and France in 1953-4.

A deeply religious woman, she was responsible for the launching of a foundation through which she gave help to many musicians afflicted with personal problems. Though the foundation occupied much of her time in the early 1960s, after a period of relative inactivity she played at such New York clubs as The Prelude in '60, The Embers in '61 and Joe Wells' in '62. In 1964-5 she spent a year and a half at the Hickory House on 52nd St. Other appearances: Manhattanville Catholic School of Music, '64; Pittsburgh JF '64-5; Monterey Festival '65. At Monterey she introduced a liturgical work, *St. Martin de Porres,* arranged for trio and voices. She recorded it for her own label, Mary Records. Billy Taylor, speaking of Miss Williams in an interview with Marian McPartland, said, "She has the most consistent way of swinging; even with a rhythm section that isn't quite hanging together, she can make it swing. She does not overpower the rhythm section; on the contrary, she plays so subtly that she seems to be able to isolate herself and swing, though the others may not be . . . she'll take something pianissimo and swing just as hard as if it were double forte. She's one of the very few people I know that can do this—consistently swing in any context."

Addr: 63 Hamilton Terr., New York 31, N.Y.

WILLIAMS, RICHARD GENE, *trumpet, composer;* b. Galveston, Texas, 5/4/31. Played tenor saxophone in high school; worked with local bands, Air Force 1952-6, then joined Lionel Hampton, Sept. 1956, on trumpet, touring Europe with him. Also worked intermittently with Gigi Gryce 1959-62, Charles Mingus '59-'64, Lou Donaldson '60, Quincy Jones '61, Slide Hampton '61-3, including trip to Paris in '62; Orchestra USA '64; briefly with Duke Ellington '65. Thad Jones-Mel Lewis '66.

A schooled musician who has played with the Radio City Symphony, Williams has a Master's degree in music from Manhattan School. Infl: Fats Navarro (playing), Charlie Parker (writing), Gil Fuller. Own LP: Candid. LPs w. Gigi Gryce, Oliver Nelson (Pres.); John Handy (Roul.); Max Roach, Yusef Lateef (Impulse); Charles Mingus (Col.); Yusef Lateef (River.).

Addr: 91 Schenectady Ave., Brooklyn 13, N.Y.

WILLIAMS, SPENCER,* *songwriter;* b. New Orleans, La., 10/14/1889. Most of Williams' life from the 1930s was spent in England and Sweden; before this time, however, he had established himself as the composer of many songs that became jazz standards, notably *Squeeze Me* (written with Fats Waller in 1918), *Royal Garden Blues, I Found A New Baby* and *Basin St. Blues.* Williams died in NYC, 7/14/65.

WILLIAMS, ANTHONY (TONY), *drums, composer;* b. Chicago, Ill., 12/12/45. Began studying music in 1955 in Boston. Drum teacher was Alan Dawson. Gained early advice and guidance from tenor saxophonist Sam Rivers, with whom he collaborated on a series of experimental concerts with the Boston Improvisational Ensemble. Moved to NYC in December 1962 and played gigs and concerts with Jackie McLean's combo. Miles Davis heard him with McLean and hired him for the Davis quintet. During the next two years, working mainly with Davis but also with other groups in New York and Boston when Davis was inactive, Williams made a profound impression on both musicians and critics as the youngest and most imaginative representative of the new and freer style of drumming of the 1960s. He won the DB critics' poll as New Star on drums in 1964.

Williams' natural musical inclinations are toward the avant garde, as is discernible in the company he kept, and in the compositions he wrote, for his first LP as a leader, a remarkable set entitled *Life Time*, released in 1965 on Blue Note. Other LPs with Davis (Col.), Herbie Hancock, Jackie McLean, Grachan Moncur (BN).

WILLIAMSON, SONNY BOY (Rice Miller), *singer, harmonica;* b. Glendora, Miss., ca. 1893; d. West Helena, Ark., 5/24/65. Not to be confused with John Lee (Sonny Boy) Williamson, who died in '48. Active in the '30s, he did not begin to receive wide recognition until his records made in the period following World War II. A performer in the same genre as Muddy Waters, Memphis Slim and Willie Dixon, Williamson app. at the American Folk and Blues Festival, London '63. LPs: *Sonny Boy Williamson and the Yardbirds* (Mercury); *The Real Folk Blues* (Chess).

WILSON, GERALD STANLEY,* *composer, leader, trumpet;* b. Shelby, Miss., 9/4/18. Early experience in Detroit. Toured with Jimmie Lunceford band 1939-42. Since then, based in LA, has led bands off and on; also pl. w. D. Gillespie and C. Basie bands 1948-9.

In 1957 Wilson started a rehearsal workshop band, making occasional personal appearances. The orchestra's first major appearance took place at the Flamingo in Las Vegas, in a show with Earl Grant, in 1961. During the next few years Wilson appeared in numerous locations in and around LA including Basin Street West, '63; The Lighthouse, Hermosa Beach, '64. He scored a notable success when the orchestra appeared at the Monterey JF in '63.

Movies: Under Geo. Stoll, Wilson scored five scenes and played trumpet in *Where The Boys Are*, 1960, and wrote some sequences for the Ken Murray TV special in '62. Under David Raksin he scored scenes for *Love Has Many Faces*, '64. Wilson has accomplished much of his best-known work in recent years as arranger and conductor for singers in a series of albums, including five for Al Hibbler, Bobby Darin, Johnny Hartman, Julie London. He has also had an intermittent association with Duke Ellington, occa-

sionally writing arrangements for the Ellington band or subbing in its trumpet section. His tune *Imagine My Frustration* was sung by Ella Fitzgerald with the Ellington band in the album *Ella At Duke's Place* (Verve).

Wilson won NARAS nominations in '63 and '64 and was a DB Critics' Poll winner in the big-band division in '63 and the composer category in '64.

Gerald Wilson's orchestra was the most successful organized jazz band to come to prominence in the early 1960s. Its strength has rested almost entirely on the individuality of Wilson's writing. (Though he is an excellent trumpet player, he rarely plays solos.) There is a consistent quality to his original compositions that carries through in his orchestrations of the works of others. Several of his best-known originals, such as *The Moment of Truth*, have been inspired by a love of Mexico and his interest in bullfighting.

Wilson appeared in New York in two concerts with Al Hirt at Carnegie Hall in 1965; the following year his band played an engagement at Basin Street East in NYC. For all these appearances, however, because of the economics of the music business in this decade, he was obliged to assemble a new band composed of New York musicians.

Wilson's compositions include his band's theme, *Blues for Yna Yna, Viva Tirado, Teri, Latino, Josefina, Paco, Ravi, Eric, Los Moros de Espana, Musette* and *El Viti*.

The band's albums, all on Pacific Jazz, include *You Better Believe It!* (feat. Richard "Groove" Holmes' organ); *Moment of Truth; Portraits; On Stage* and *Feelin' Kinda Blue*. Soloists on most of these albums include Joe Pass, guitar; Teddy Edwards, Harold Land tenor saxes; Carmell Jones, trumpet; Jack Wilson, piano or organ. *Al Hirt Live At Carnegie Hall*, arr. and cond. by Wilson, is on RCA. Wilson tpt. solos on *Leroy Walks* (Contemp.).

Addr: 4625 Brynhurst Ave., Los Angeles 43, Calif.

WILSON, JACK JR., *piano;* also *harpsichord, organ, vibes, drums;* b. Chicago, Ill., 8/3/36. Studied music in Ft. Wayne, Ind., then joined a local band at age of 14. Played w. James Moody in '53. While attending Indiana U. gigged w. Dave Baker, Slide Hampton; to Columbus, Ohio, playing w. Roland Kirk and own trio. With Dinah Washington '56-'57, then free-lanced in Chicago w. S. Stitt, J. Griffin, G. Ammons. To Los Angeles in '62; worked with G. Wilson, S. Vaughan, N. Wilson, L. Donaldson, J. McLean, B. Collette, J. Rushing, J. Witherspoon, H. Land, J. Hartman, C. Amy, E. Kitt, S. Davis Jr., D. Dandridge, B. Jennings, A. Hibbler, H. Rumsey, S. Manne, G. Fuller, C. Terry-B. Brookmeyer, L. Alexandria. In Monterey JF house band '63. Formed own quartet '65 w. Roy Ayers. Soloist in film *Bus Riley's Back in Town;* pl. in *Alfred Hitchcock, Peyton Place, Bob Hope Presents* TV shows.

Harvey Pekar wrote that Wilson "displays excellent

technique, a firm touch and a fruitful imagination." Ira Gitler called him a pianist of "warmth and facility." Wilson's experience and diversity have made him one of the most important pianists on the West Coast. Favs: Tatum, Powell, Monk, Peterson, Shearing, Byard et al. Own LPs: Atl., Vault. Others: w. Gerald Wilson, Amy, E. Anderza (Pac. Jazz); R. Evans (Cadet); Ayers (UA); D. Washington (Merc.); N. Wilson (Cap.); S. Vaughan (Roul.); J. London (Lib.).

Addr: 2525 Dearborn Dr., Los Angeles, Calif.

WILSON, NANCY,* *singer;* b. Chillicothe, O., 2/20/37. Discovered in August 1959 by Cannonball Adderley, she was signed by Capitol Records and beginning in 1960 made a steady climb to national popularity. Her first hit record was *Guess Who I Saw Today.*

Miss Wilson, unlike most singers with a jazz background, did not play in clubs catering to jazz audiences. She succeeded in bypassing them and was soon playing major rooms and hotels. In 1963 she worked at the Waldorf-Astoria, NYC. In 1965 she played to a capacity audience at the Shrine Auditorium in Los Angeles. She has worked as a main attraction in Las Vegas casinos, toured successfully in Europe, and has formed a corporation, Wil-Den Enterprises, in partnership with her husband, drummer Kenny Dennis, to manage other artists, publish music, produce TV shows, etc.

Miss Wilson is an extremely capable and self-possessed performer whose style, at one time reminiscent of Dinah Washington, soon evolved into something completely personal and established her as one of the major new singers. Analyzing her own performance, she has said, "Some things I sing are jazz-oriented and others are not. I am neither a jazz singer exclusively nor a pop singer exclusively. I loved making records with people like Cannonball. But on a lot of things I do, there just isn't any invention, any spontaneity in the jazz sense." From the jazz standpoint, Miss Wilson's best albums are *The Swingin's Mutual* with George Shearing Quintet; *Nancy Wilson/ Cannonball Adderley; The Nancy Wilson Show* (Live at the Cocoanut Grove); *Yesterday's Love Songs, Today's Blues,* arranged by Gerald Wilson (all Cap.). Many other LPs of a more pop-oriented nature are also on Cap.

Addr: c/o Wil-Den Enterprises, 9465 Wilshire Blvd., Beverly Hills, Calif.

WILSON, PHILLIPS ELDER JR. (PHIL), *trombone, composer;* b. Belmont, Mass., 1/19/37. Stud. piano privately; trombone at New England Conserv. and Navy School of Music. Played with Jimmy Dorsey orch. on either trombone or piano, off and on from 1956-8. Led own band and quartet '59; Al Belletto sextet '59; NORAD Command Band 1960-62 as trombone, pianist, arranger. Joined Woody Herman orch. 1962, remaining until '65.

Teacher of trombone, theory and arranging at Berklee School, Boston, 1966.

Favs: J. Teagarden, B. Harris, D. Wells, T. Dorsey. Comps: *Two Moods of Summer, Basically Blues.*

Wilson is a remarkable technician and inspired soloist whose talent was first noticed in his solo with Herman on *It's A Lonesome Old Town* in the album *Woody Herman—1963* (Philips). He is on all other Herman LPs on Philips, also *My Kind of Broadway* (Col.); *Woody Herman and the 4th Herd* (Surrey); *Music From NORAD* (Norad).

Addr: 7 Marston St., Exeter, N.H.

WILSON, THEODORE (TEDDY),* *piano, composer;* b. Austin, Texas, 11/24/12. Featured with Benny Goodman from 1935-9 in a trio that broke down segregation in jazz, Wilson was one of the most influential instrumentalists of the swing era, succeeding Earl Hines as the most imitated jazz pianist. He led his own excellent big band in 1939-40. During the '40s and '50s he divided his time between staff jobs at NYC radio and television stations, led sextets and trios in clubs, and was occasionally reunited with Goodman. Since 1960 Wilson has appeared several times on such national TV shows as *The Telephone Hour, Tonight, Today,* and the Mike Douglas show. Night club engagements have taken him from New York to Washing, Cleveland, Boston, etc. He has also made annual appearances at the JF in Aspen, Colo.

His foreign tours have included as JF in Australia in 1960; a tour of the USSR with Benny Goodman in '62; and a European JF tour in '65.

Wilson has retained the firm, neatly swinging and orderly style of his formative years. He has recorded several albums in the '60s, most of them on Columbia and a more recent set on Cameo. He is also heard on *Benny Goodman In Moscow* (RCA) and *Together Again!,* a reunion of the original Goodman quartet (RCA).

Addr: 213 Knickerbocker Ave., Hillsdale, New Jersey.

WINCHESTER, LEMUEL DAVIS (LEM),* *vibes;* b. Philadelphia, Pa., 3/19/28. This promising vibraphonist, a member of the Wilmington, Delaware police force, was brought to Newport JF 1958 as a protege of L. Feather and soon achieved prominence in jazz, resigning from the police force in 1960 to devote all his time to music. His career was tragically cut short when he was demonstrating a trick with a revolver and accidentally killed himself, 1/13/61, in Indianapolis, Ind. LPs: Prestige.

WINDING, KAI CHRESTEN,* *trombone, composer, leader;* b. Aarhus, Denmark, 5/18/22. To U.S. 1934. With dance and jazz bands from 1940, incl. Kenton '46-7. Co-led quintet w. J. J. Johnson, '54-6. Led own septet and free-lanced as NYC studio musician.

In 1962 Winding was appointed musical director at the NYC Playboy Club. The following year, his experiments with unusual instrumentations, such as the use of electronic instrumentation behind a 12-piece brass ensemble, led to his recording of such albums as *More* (1963) and *Mondo Cane #2* (1964), both of which were non-jazz items aimed at the mass commercial market and enjoyed resounding commercial success. These and other Verve LPs have greatly broadened his popularity; meanwhile he has continued to play jazz from time to time, leading a quartet at the Playboy Club in 1966.

LPs: Verve; Impulse; *The Great Kai and J.J.* (Impulse); *Trombone Panorama* (Col.).

Addr: 120 Bellair Drive, Dobbs Ferry, N.Y.

WINTER, PAUL THEODORE JR., *alto sax, leader, composer;* b. Altoona, Pa., 8/31/39. Studied piano from age of 6, then organized own band while attending Northwestern Univ. in Chicago. Won first place at Intercollegiate, Georgetown JFs '61. In '62 suggested an extended tour of Asia or Latin America to the State Dept. and took sextet to 23 Latin American countries, playing 160 concerts in 61 cities.

Following that success, Winter's sextet, made up entirely of college students, was the first jazz group to perform at the White House. The concert, in late 1962 and organized under the direction of Mrs. Kennedy, was well received by the press and by officials.

Winter's group then appeared at several JFs in '63 and '64 and at a UNICEF concert in June '63. On *Today, Tonight, Jazz Casual* TV shows '63-'65. Own LPs: Col.

Addr: 973 Lexington Ave., New York, N.Y.

WISKIRCHEN, REV. GEORGE, *teacher, leader;* also *trumpet;* b. Quincy, Ill., 10/14/28. A graduate of Notre Dame U.; holds an M.A. in music education from Northwestern U. A Catholic priest and member of the Congregation of the Holy Cross, Wiskirchen began teaching music at Notre Dame High School in Niles, Ill., a suburb of Chicago, in 1956. There he pioneered the high school stage band movement in the Chicago area and organized the Jazz Lab at Notre Dame H.S. His bands, composed of high school students, appeared at the Chicago Downbeat JF, Chicago's McCormick Place, and at the Notre Dame U. Collegiate JF '60-'65. Author of several books on stage band teaching techniques. Taught course in stage band methods at Eastman Sch. of Music Summer '65. Active as teacher and judge in numerous music clinics throughout Midwest. Directed Northwestern U. Jazz Workshop '63-'65. His two excellent columns, "Jazz on the Campus," concerning college band developments, and "From the Top," a review of stage band materials, appear in *Down Beat* regularly.

Addr: c/o Notre Dame High School, Niles 48, Ill.

WITHERSPOON, JAMES (JIMMY),* *singer;* b. Gurdon, Ark., 8/8/23. W. Jay McShann in '40s; popular in R&B field in '50s. Scored big success at Monterey JF '59. In '60s toured U.S. and Europe. Won DB critics' poll as new star '61. App. at Monterey in Jon Hendricks' *Evolution of the Blues Song* and on Columbia recording of same. Own LPs: Pres., Reprise.

WOOD, WILLIAM CLIFFORD (BILL), *bass;* b. North Wilkesboro, N.C., 11/7/37. Father played reeds. After grammar school moved to Detroit. Played trumpet in high school, then switched to bass. Studied theory and harmony at Detroit Inst. of Mus. Arts. First prof. job w. Dorothy Ashby '57; later worked w. Yusef Lateef, Joe Henderson. To NYC '62. Free-lancing w. groups such as Kenny Dorham, Carmen McRae, Terry Gibbs, Leo Wright, Gloria Lynne, Roy Haynes and Archie Shepp, but from '63 associated mainly w. Randy Weston. Also toured w. Robert de Cormier folk singers in first half of '66. Orig. inf.: Paul Chambers; favs.: Richard Davis, Ron Carter. LPs w. Weston (Bakton), Gibbs (Time).

Addr: 80 Jefferson St., New York 2, N.Y.

WOODE, JAMES BRYANT (JIMMY),* *bass, composer, piano;* b. Philadelphia, Pa., 9/23/29. Free-lanced during early '50s, then w. Ellington for five years from '55. After leaving Ellington emigrated to Stockholm, Sweden. Worked for Swedish radio and gigged w. top Swedish musicians, own groups, in France w. Kenny Clarke and Francy Boland. Became well known as TV vocalist, sideman on numerous Swedish recordings. Wrote dance sequence for film *Cycodromen* w. Harriet Anderson. Moved to Cologne, Germany '64 to manage own publishing company. Appeared yearly at Prague, Lugano, Berlin, San Remo, Vienna, Frankfurt JFs. Contributed several articles to trade journals, Swedish newspapers. In many other concerts, films, TV shows, recording dates throughout Europe. Own LP: Col. Others: w. C. Hawkins, Clarke-Boland, B. Powell, J. Griffin, S. Shihab, E. Fitzgerald, T. Thielmans, F. Gulda, Q. Jones, Rune Ofuerman, Knud Jorgenson, R. Fol, Jan Johansson.

Addr: Molen Oord, Horndijk 7, Oud Loosdrecht, Holland.

WOODMAN, BRITT,* *trombone;* b. 6/4/20, Los Angeles, Calif. In 1960 Woodman left Duke Ellington after almost ten years with him. He appeared with Quincy Jones at Newport, '61; recorded with Ch. Mingus for Candid, Jimmy Hamilton for Prestige. Later went into commercial work, w. B'way show bands incl. *Little Me*, '62, *Half a Sixpence*, '65. Also w. Leon Leonidoff at NY World's Fair, '64.

Addr: 239 West 16th St., Apt B-2, NYC, 10011.

WOODS, JAMES H. (JIMMY), *alto sax;* also *tenor sax, flute;* b. St. Louis, Mo., 10/29/34. Parents moved to Seattle, Wash., where Woods studied clarinet at age of 13. First recording date was w. Joe Gordon 1961 for Contemporary; also did two LPs w. own groups for same label. Intermittently w. Gerald Wilson band as alto soloist from '63. W. Chico Hamilton from Jan. '64 to Apr. '65, incl. Johnny Carson and Steve Allen TV shows, 8 weeks in London, tour of Japan. Monterey JF '63 w. Wilson. Favs: Parker, Rollins, Coltrane.

Woods plays strong alto with an exceptionally full, rich tone. Nat Hentoff said of him, "The qualities most evident in Woods' playing are his passionate, penetrating sound and speech-like phrasing; fiercely secure sense of swing; and an empirical commitment to freedom that leads him into new ways of expanding the jazz language." Own LPs: *Awakening* and own fav. *Conflict* (Contemp.). Others: w. Gordon (Contemp.).

Addr: 4349 El Prieto Rd., Los Angeles, Calif.

WOODS, PHILIP WELLS (PHIL),* *alto sax, clarinet, composer;* b. Springfield, Mass., 11/2/31. Came to prominence in mid-'50s; U.S., overseas w. Dizzy Gillespie band in 1956. From late '59 until '61 Woods worked mainly with Quincy Jones' band, touring Europe extensively. In the spring of '62 he was a member of the Benny Goodman band that toured the Soviet Union. He was in the band that played *The Lost Continent* with Gillespie at Monterey JF '62.

Though still best known for his fluent and passionate Parker-inspired alto work, Woods won the DB Critics' Poll in 1963 as "Deserving of Wider Recognition" on clarinet. In the past few years he has generally busied himself with recording and TV work in New York, private teaching, and a summer job as music director at Ramblerny, a creative arts camp with an extensive jazz department in New Hope, Pa.

As a composer he wrote an extended work, *Rights of Swing,* recorded in 1960 on Candid. His *Piece for Alto and Piano* and *Three Improvisations* for saxophone quartet were both performed at Town Hall.

LPs: *Quintessence* w. Q. Jones (Imp.). With Oliver Nelson: *Fantabulous* (Cadet); *Full Nelson* (Verve); *More Blues and the Abstract Truth* (Imp.). W. Th. Monk: *Orchestra at Town Hall* (River.); *Big Band and Quartet* (Col.). With Joe Morello: *It's About Time* (RCA).

Addr: RD1, Box 266, New Hope, Pa.

WOODYARD, SAMUEL (SAM),* *drums;* b. Elizabeth, N.J., 1/7/25. Joined Duke Ellington's orchestra 1955. Left in the summer of '59 but rejoined after a few months' absence. He was out of the band again in July '65 but once more returned to the orchestra during its European tour in Jan. '66.

LPs: see Ellington, Duke.

WORKMAN, REGINALD (REGGIE), *bass;* b. Philadelphia, Pa., 6/26/37. Father played trombone. Studied piano at age of eight, tuba and euphonium in high school. Began playing in r & b bands in 1955. First jazz gig w. G. Gryce '58. W. Red Garland '59, R. Haynes '59, J. Coltrane '60, J. Moody '62, A. Blakey's Jazz Messengers '63-'64, A. Heath '64, Y. Lateef '65. Toured Europe '63, Japan '64 w. Blakey. Fav. work was w. Coltrane group, which at the time included Eric Dolphy. Workman, a strong, rhythmic and versatile bassist, by the mid-'60s was coming into increasing demand for recording in NYC with both hard-bop and avant-garde groups. Toured with Herbie Mann, 1966. LPs: W. Gryce (Pres.), Duke Jordan (BN), Grant Green (BN), Coltrane (Atl., Impulse), F. Hubbard (Impulse, BN), Blakey (River., Colpix),

W. Shorter (BN), A. Shepp (Impulse), Lateef (Impulse).

Addr: 525 W. 146th St., New York, N.Y.

WRAY, KEN, *valve trombone, trombone;* b. Manchester, England, 2/2/27. Pl. in Eng. w. Jack Parnell, Tony Crombie, Ronnie Scott, Jimmie Deuchar, Johnny Dankworth, Tubby Hayes and Harry South big bands, Woody Herman, Benny Golson, and Germany '57-9 w. Kurt Edelhagen. Individual, economical trombone style, heavily vocalized. LPs w. Jimmie Deuchar (Brit. Tempo), Tubby Hayes (Brit. Fontana).

Addr: 21 Lowndes St., London S.W. 1., England.

WRIGHT, EUGENE JOSEPH (GENE),* *bass;* b. Chicago, Ill., 5/29/23. Worked with Ammons, Basie, Cobb, De Franco, Norvo before joining Dave Brubeck in Feb. '58. Many U.S. and overseas concerts and festivals with the quartet (see Brubeck, Dave). LPs w. Brubeck (Col.), Paul Desmond (RCA).

Addr: 9902 S. Forest Ave., Chicago 28, Ill.

WRIGHT, LEO NASH,* *alto sax, flute, clarinet, piccolo;* b. Wichita Falls, Tex., 12/14/33. Worked with bands in San Francisco and New York before joining Dizzy Gillespie August 1959. During his three years with Gillespie appeared at Newport and Monterey Festivals. Also recorded first album as leader, *Blues Shout* (Atl.) in '61.

After leaving Gillespie, worked in NYC with Kenny Burrell, Gloria Coleman and briefly with his own quintet; during the next year made numerous record dates with Jimmy Witherspoon, Lalo Schifrin, A. C. Jobim, Bob Brookmeyer, Johnny Coles, Gloria Coleman, Brother Jack McDuff. Late in 1963 he was offered a tour of Europe. He worked mainly in Scandinavia, but later played the Blue Note club in Berlin, liked the city, and has remained there since. In 1966 he played in the house band at Dug's Night Club.

LPs w. Gillespie (Verve, Philips), *Jazz At The Philharmonic* (Verve) and other artists as listed above; also European LPs with George Gruntz and the Recklinghausen '65 Jazz Workshop Band.

Addr: Hauptstr. 15, 1 Berlin 62, Germany.

WRIGHT, CHARLES (SPECS),* *drums;* b. Philadelphia, Pa., 9/8/27. Played with Dizzy Gillespie, Cannonball Adderley, Carmen McRae, Benny Golson in 1950s; Lambert, Hendricks & Ross 1960-61. Died of a heart attack in Philadelphia, Pa., 2/6/63.

WROBLEWSKI, PTASZYN (JAN),* *tenor sax, composer;* b. Kalisz, Poland, 3/27/36. Played in festivals in Poland and USSR from '57; visited Newport with International Band '58; led own groups 1960-61; pl. w. Kurylewicz Quintet '62-3; since then has led his own Polish Jazz Quartet. Since '63 has been composer-arranger for Polish radio bands. Toured for six months in West Germany 1963-4 and has made many other appearances throughout Europe. Wroblewski is vice president of the Polish Jazz Federation. Fav. arr: Ellington, Strayhorn, G. Evans, O. Nelson. LP: *New-*

port *International Band* (Col.); others on Polish labels Metronome and Muza.

Addr: Pulaskiego 1, Kalisz, Poland.

YAGED, SOLOMON (SOL),* *clarinet;* b. Brooklyn, N.Y., 12/8/22. Featured with innumerable Dixieland bands, Yaged led the last group of this type to play at Nick's in Greenwich Village before it closed. Worked for several years at The Metropole, NYC. Led quintet for two seasons at Bistro Cafe in N.Y. World's Fair 1964-5. Own LP: *Jazz At The Metropole* (Philips), *Keith Brasselle Sings Dixieland* (Mardi Gras).

Addr: 2832 W. 28th St., Brooklyn, 24, N.Y.

YANCEY, WILLIAM EARL (BILL), *bass, tuba;* b. Kansas City, Mo., 7/30/33. Raised in Chicago. Began playing at Du Sable High School in 1950; later studied at American Conserv. for three years and with various private teachers. Worked w. Sol Hicks '52-3, Jack McDuff '54-6; Army service '56-8; Ike Cole '58; John Young Trio '59-'61; Eddie Harris, late '61. After touring w. Lambert, Hendricks & Bavan he joined the George Shearing Quintet in '63. In '64 he was a member of Ella Fitzgerald's rhythm section, touring England and the Continent with her. Worked at Playboy Club in Chicago '65. Feat. w. George "Stardust" Green Trio '66. A well-schooled, superior bassist, inspired by Israel Crosby, Richard Davis and Ray Brown.

LPs with Eddie Harris, John Young (Cadet); Shearing (Cap.); Ella Fitzgerald (Verve).

Addr: 400 East 33rd St., Chicago 16, Ill.

YOUNG, EL DEE,* *bass;* also *cello;* b. Chicago, Ill., 1/7/36. Worked with r&b groups in early '50s, then joined Ramsey Lewis Trio. The group rose to national popularity in 1965. Left Lewis summer '66.

LPs: Cadet, Merc.

YOUNG, JOHN MERRITT, *piano;* b. Little Rock, Ark., 3/16/22. Studied piano in Chicago from age of nine. With Andy Kirk 1942-45 and '46-'47, Dick Davis '47-'50, Eddie Chamblee '51-'55. From '55 led own trio in Chicago; also accompanied many major visiting artists. Fav: Phineas Newborn Jr. Infl. on playing: Hines, Tatum; on writing: Ellington. Own LPs: Delmark, Cadet. Own fav. *Themes and Things* (Cadet).

Addr: 5320 Drexel Blvd., Chicago 15, Ill.

YOUNG, LARRY (Khalid Yasin), *organ, composer;* b. Newark, N.J., 10/7/40. Father, an organist, was major influence on him. Stud. piano with Mrs. Olga von Till; did not study organ formally. After several years of relative inactivity in music he began playing the blues around 1957 in Elizabeth, N.J. Worked with rhythm and blues groups, later with many jazzmen incl. Lou Donaldson, Donald Byrd, Kenny Dorham, Grant Green, Tommy Turrentine, Hank Mobley.

Young says his musical evolution began with a 1960 recording, *Groove Street* (Prestige). Made a strong impression in 1965 with *Into Something* (Blue Note), which presented him as a fluent, vital organist with an unusual flexibility and genuine knowledge of the instrument. Comps: *Testifying, Tyrone, Paris Eyes, Backup, Ritha.* Young visited Europe, in 1964-5, spending two months in France and a month in Germany, where he recorded on piano with Nathan Davis for the Saba label. Other LP w. Grant Green (BN).

Addr: 26 Clinton Place, Newark 8, N.J.

YOUNG, LEONIDAS RAYMOND (LEE),* *drums;* b. New Orleans, La., 3/7/17. Brother was Lester Young. Swing drummer from mid-'30s; w. Nat King Cole '53-'62. Formed own record company in LA. A&R man for Vee Jay Records '64-'65; produced 15 albums, incl. Russ Morgan, Red Norvo, Damita Jo, Harry Edison.

Addr: 7501 Denker Ave., Los Angeles 47, Calif.

YOUNG, EUGENE (SNOOKY),* *trumpet;* b. Dayton, Ohio, 2/3/19. Prominent w. Lunceford and Basie in '40s. Own group in Dayton '47-'57, then rejoined Basie. In '60s on staff at NBC-TV; frequently seen on Johnny Carson *Tonight* show. Organized band for Gerald Wilson's app. at Basin Street East '66; lead man w. Thad Jones-Mel Lewis orch. '66. LPs with Jones-Lewis (Solid State), Basie (Roul.), Hawkins (Imp.).

Addr: 35-18 215th Pl., Bayside 61, N.Y.

YOUNG, JAMES OSBORNE (TRUMMY),* *trombone, singer;* b. Savannah, Ga., 1/12/12. One of the best-known soloists in the great Jimmie Lunceford band 1937-43. Lived in Hawaii 1947-52, then joined Louis Armstrong combo and remained with him for 11 years. After a few months in LA he returned to Hawaii. LPs w. Armstrong (Col. etc.), Lunceford (Decca).

Addr: 3030 Lakimau St., Honolulu, Hawaii.

ZAWINUL, JOSEF (JOE),* *piano, composer;* b. Vienna, Austria, 7/7/32. Worked with French, German and Austrian groups before emigrating to U.S. in 1959. After playing with Maynard Ferguson and Slide Hampton, accompanied Dinah Washington from fall of '59 until Mar. '61. Worked briefly with Harry Edison and Joe Williams, then joined Cannonball Adderley and became a key member of his group during the next five years, touring the U.S. and Japan and visiting Europe several times. He displayed a sparkling, exuberant up-tempo style and a harmonically beautiful ballad feeling.

In addition to recording more than a dozen albums with Adderley, he was featured on sessions with Yusef Lateef, Coleman Hawkins, Clark Terry, Ben Webster,

Charlie Rouse, Jimmy Forest, Ernie Wilkins, Oliver Nelson, Victor Feldman, Roy Haynes, Philly Joe Jones, Thad Jones, J. J. Johnson, Curtis Fuller.

Co-leader on *Soul Mates* with Ben Webster (River.). Own LP: Atl. As writer, he arranged *Fiddler On The Roof* for C. Adderley (Cap.), arr. and cond. the Nat Adderley *Autobiography* album (Atl.) and wrote arrangements for the Nancy Wilson-Cannonball Adderley LP (Cap.). Comps: *Scotch & Water, Midnight Mood;* also *Riverbed* (recorded by Friedrich Gulda).

Addr: 382 Central Park West, New York 25, N.Y.

ZEITLIN, DENNIS JAY (DENNY), *piano, composer;* also *bass, drums;* b. Chicago, Ill., 4/10/38. Parents both pl. piano. Stud. privately 1944-52. Heard jazz while at high school; never studied it formally. Harmony, comp. w. several teachers incl. Geo. Russell.

After a brief Dixieland period, he gigged around Chicago with modern groups, then in Champaign, Ill., and in Baltimore, where he was resident at Johns Hopkins studying medicine. By now he had decided on two careers, one in music and the other in psychiatry.

Before beginning medical school he traveled through Europe in the summer of 1960, sitting in with Oscar Pettiford in Copenhagen and with various groups in Paris. First LP w. Jeremy Steig Quartet Nov. '63 (Col.). Obtained M.D. from Johns Hopkins June '64. Interned at SF Gen. Hosp. July '64-'65. Resident in psychiatry at Langley Porter Neuropsychiatric Clinic from July '65.

Under the sponsorship of John Hammond, Zeitlin recorded as leader of his own trio, starting in the spring of '64, and was soon one of the most talked-about new pianists. He was enthusiastically received at the Newport and Monterey JF in '65. Despite the time demanded by his medical career, he worked one night a week at the Trident in Sausalito, Calif., '65-6, made several appearances on the *Tonight* TV show, etc.

Zeitlin is a perfectionist on many levels, in music and medicine, the study of literature, Epicureanism, as a connoisseur of wines, and as an avocational photographer. In music this quality is manifested in a broad spectrum of performances and original compositions, ranging from simple riff tunes to long, lyrical, complex works of great melodic and harmonic charm. He was the most versatile young pianist to come to prominence in the early 1960s.

Comps: *The Carnival, Mirage, Carole's Waltz, Carole's Garden, After The War.* LPs: Col.

Addr: 189 Commonwealth, San Francisco, Calif.

ZENTNER, SIMON H. (SI),* *trombone, leader;* b. Brooklyn, N.Y., 6/13/17. A former sideman in the Les Brown, Harry James and Jimmy Dorsey bands and a Hollywood studio musician for almost a decade, Zentner started his own dance band in 1957. He achieved great popularity in 1960 with a hit record, *Lazy River,* arranged by Bob Florence. As a consequence, his was the only new jazz-oriented dance band to achieve a measure of economic stability in the early 1960s; he

toured the U.S. regularly, playing concerts with Johnny Mathis in 1964 and with Nancy Wilson in '65. In '64 he switched from Liberty to RCA Records. He inaugurated the big-band policy at the Hotel Tropicana in Las Vegas in '65. LPs: Liberty, RCA.

Addr: 14155 Magnolia Blvd., Van Nuys, Calif.

ZITANO, JAMES HAROLD (JIMMY), *drums;* b. Boston, Mass., 1/14/28. Began studying trombone in '49, then switched to drums. Gigged around Boston w. H. Pomeroy, J. Byard, C. Mariano, S. Chaloff, R. Twardzik. Intends to pursue career as composer and arranger. Favs: Roy Haynes, Max Roach, Kenny Clarke. LPs: w. Donald Byrd (Trans.), Al Hirt (RCA).

Addr: 2226 Gen. Pershing St., New Orleans, La.

ZITO, RONALD (RONNIE), *drums;* b. Utica, N.Y., 2/17/39. Father, three brothers (incl. composer Torrie) all musicians. Started pl. w. family. In Utica w. J. R. Monterose, 1958; Bobby Darin's personal drummer for four years; Frank Rosolino combo in LA, '61; acc. Peggy Lee, '62; toured w. Woody Herman '65-6. Infl. by Elvin and Philly Joe Jones, Rich, Roach, Blakey, Bobby Higgins. LPs w. Herb Ellis (Verve), Herman (Col.).

Addr: 629 Kappock St., Brooklyn, N.Y.

ZOLLER, ATTILA CORNELIUS,* *guitar;* also *bass, trumpet;* b. Visegrad, Hungary, 6/13/27. With Jutta Hipp, Hans Koller in Europe during '50s, then to U.S. in '59. Joined Herbie Mann '62 and remained with him until Jan. '65, then organized own quartet with Don Friedman and played in several spots around NYC. From '60 made yearly tours of Europe for concerts, radio, TV and recording work. W. own group at Newport JF '65. Taught at several summer jazz clinics. Won German film prize '62 for music for *The Bread of Our Early Years.* Won DB Critics' Poll for guitar '64, numerous European polls. Own LPs: *Lyrics and Jazz, The Horizon Beyond* (Phil.). Others: w. Mann (Atl.), Friedman (River.).

Addr: 69-01 35th Ave., Woodside 77, N.Y.

ZWERIN, MICHAEL, *bass trumpet;* also *trombone, piano;* b. New York City, 5/18/30. Studied violin 1936. Later attended High School of Music and Art. In 1948, while on summer vacation from college, he played trombone with Miles Davis' band at Royal Roost. Later gave up trombone and spent several years in Paris. Returning to U.S. in '58, gigged with Billy May, Sonny Dunham; toured with Claude Thornhill '58-9, Maynard Ferguson '59-'60, Bill Russo '60. From 1962-5 he played trombone and bass trumpet with Orchestra USA and was musical director and arranger for a sextet drawn from this orchestra. Gigged at Five Spot, NYC, 1962-4, as member of Upper Bohemia Six. Toured USSR w. Earl Hines '66.

Though still active in jazz, Zwerin since 1960 has been president of a manufacturing company, Capitol Steel Corp. He has also devoted some time to journalism and has written a number of witty and sensitive columns for the *Village Voice, Down Beat* and *Sounds and Fury*. Favs: J. J. Johnson; Gil Evans, Duke Ellington. Other infls: L. Young, Ch. Parker, J. Coltrane.

Own LP with sextet of Orchestra USA playing Kurt Weill themes (RCA). Also with Orchestra USA (Colpix, Col.); John Lewis-Gary McFarland (Atl.); Maynard Ferguson (Roul.).

Addr: 43 Morton St., New York City, N.Y.

The blues and folk scene by Pete Welding

Though they have been root and center of jazz and most American popular music for many decades, the blues are brewing in the 1960s to a degree and in a manner as never before. It has been only in the last five or six years that the blues has begun to receive its share of serious investigation and critical attention. In a sense, the situation of blues scholarship and research is akin to that of jazz in the mid- and late-1930s, when the first dedicated and knowledgeable jazz enthusiasts began to publish their critical and discographical findings about a music that had been born and come to maturity some decades earlier.

In the case of blues scholarship, however, the problems have been rendered far more complex by the fact that work which should have been begun perhaps thirty or more years ago is only now being undertaken. The first commercial recordings of blues singers were made at much the same time as the earliest jazz recordings, and many of the important early blues artists—who might possibly have provided significant information about the evolution and dissemination of the blues in the rural South—have either died or disappeared with the same curious ease with which they appear to have entered the recording studios more than four decades ago. When one considers the often haphazard and indiscriminate manner in which blues artists were recorded in the early days of "race" recording (i.e., recordings made solely for the then huge and untapped Negro record market), the complexity of the problems facing the blues historian begins to emerge.

A surprisingly wide stylistic range of blues performers found their way into the mobile recording studios that plied the South in the '20s, and in their ignorance of what would appeal to the burgeoning Negro record audience, the large recording firms recorded a fantastic number of country bluesmen, in styles ranging from the most primitive and archaic to the most sophisticated and complex, as well as the majestic and often moving female singers who originally had initiated the blues boom of the 1920s.

Though the blues might rightly be viewed as a central experience of the American Negro, the music itself—in obedience to the laws of cultural determinism—has undergone a number of stylistic transformations, generally as a result of its perhaps necessary alliance with the world of commercial music. The blues progressed from a rough, personalized country form to a trim, glossy and often formulized urban music that was in turn supplanted by a harsh, clamorous return to country sources in the work of the electrically amplified blues bands of the post-World War II years. And in the years since, this has given way to more sophisticated, less individualized offshoots, rock and roll, "soul" music, and related forms.

For contemporary Negro audiences the blues of the 1960s has become less a music of introspection and personal commentary than a musical symbol of cultural identity, less a music of direct, individual human contact than a sort of communal ritual to which slightly more than lip service need be rendered. The contemporary urban bluesmen—B. B. King, Bobby Blue Bland, Junior Parker, even Ray Charles—may be viewed more properly as representatives or embodiments of a peculiarly modern Negro life "style," a stance or posture, than as practitioners of a music of total engagement or commitment to the Negro life experience. To remark this is not either to demean the work of the younger bluesmen or to imply that their music has no meaning or relevance for their listeners. Quite the opposite is true.

The transformation of the music accurately mirrors the vast changes that have taken place in the fabric of American Negro culture over the last five decades or so; the evolution of the blues, in fact, might properly be interpreted as an index of acculturation. And it is surely no mere accident that much of the current popular music favored by the young Negro closely resembles—or is identical with—that of his white counterpart.

At much the same time, however, as the modern urban blues forms were supplanting the older styles among Negro audiences, there was developing an interest—largely intellectual, to be sure—in the archaic folk-styled blues among young white listeners. As part of the great revival of interest in America's traditional folk musics in the late 1950s an appreciable and sympathetic audience for the traditional country blues was created. Triggered by the pioneering book-length studies *The Country Blues* (currently being updated in light of subsequent findings) by Samuel Charters in 1959 and *Blues Fell This Morning* by British blues writer Paul Oliver in 1960, serious attention was begun to be paid the archaic blues styles and artists, many of whom were sought out, re-discovered, re-recorded (often with a frequency far beyond their ability to sustain), and introduced to the new, adulatory folk music audience. A circuit of folk music clubs, coffee houses, and university and festival stages rapidly developed, and many an aged blues veteran suddenly found himself in the midst of a renewed career in the twilight of his life.

But the re-discovery of the old country blues on rare shellac 78-rpm discs, coupled with the corollary re-discovery of a number of the performers behind them, has resulted in a virtual re-writing of blues history. Most important has been the belated recognition of the on-going, fecundating role of Mississippi in the mainstream of the blues. Chief agent in this awakening was Origin Records, a small New York independent record label whose re-issue on LP of many rare and often obscure examples of the work of the important Mississippi Delta bluesmen was vastly instrumental in focusing attention on the powerful, influential music of the region. It was largely as a result of Origin's two re-issue albums of his work that the great Charley Patton (born in the Mississippi Delta, ca. 1885) became to be recognized as one of the wellsprings of the harsh, introspective Mississippi blues style, and his musical offspring have been virtually legion.

Many of the veteran Mississippi bluesmen who have followed in his wake have been re-discovered in recent years, a number of them embarking on careers of varying success. Among them are singer-guitarists Eddie "Son" House (born Lyon, Miss., March 12, 1902); Nehemiah "Skip" James (Bentonia, Miss., June 9, 1902)—also a pianist; Mississippi John Hurt (Teoc, Miss., March, 1894); Robert Wilkins (Hernando, Miss., Jan. 16, 1896); Big Joe Williams (Crawford, Miss., Oct. 16, 1899); and Booker Washington "Bukka" White (Houston, Miss., Nov. 12, 1909), while a recent discovery, Fred McDowell (Rossville, Tenn., Jan. 10, 1904?), performs the old blues as though time has stood still for him.

At the head of the Mississippi Delta basin, the border blues traditions of Memphis, Tennessee, are perpetuated today in the still exciting and viable singing and playing of Walter "Furry" Lewis (born Greenwood, Miss., March 6, 1900); Will Shade (Memphis, Tenn., Feb. 5, 1898); Gus Cannon (Red Banks, Miss., Sept. 12, 1883); and Memphis Willie Borum (Memphis, Tenn., Nov. 4, 1911), among others. Cannon, virtually inactive for many years, and Shade (also known as "Son Brimmer") were moving forces in the two colorful and exub-

erant jug bands with which Memphis has been identified over the years, Cannon's Jug Stompers and the Memphis Jug Band.

A bit farther east, in Brownsville, Tenn., lives one of the greatest poets in the blues—frail, blind John Adam "Sleepy John" Estes (Lauderdale county, Tenn., Jan. 25, 1904), along with his longtime harmonica player Hammie Nixon (Brownsville, Tenn., 1913). Another representative of the region's music, singer-mandolinist-guitarist James "Yank" Rachel (born near Brownsville, Tenn., March 16, 1908), currently resides in Indianapolis, though he has worked and recorded with Estes in the years since his re-emergence in the folk-blues revival.

The strongly musical traditions of the East Coast are perhaps most manifestly continued in the work of the popular team of singer-guitarist Brownie McGhee (Knoxville, Tenn., Nov. 30, 1915) and singer-harmonica player Sonny Terry (real name Saunders Teddell, Durham, N.C., Oct. 24, 1911), though much of their recent recorded work bears the strain of their having recorded too prolifically and indiscriminately. Other workers in these traditions are Pink Anderson (Lawrence, S.C., Feb. 12, 1900), whose work bears considerable influence from his days with the touring patent-medicine shows that plied the rural South, and Elizabeth Cotten (Chapel Hill, N.C., ca. 1900), a particular favorite of the folk audience as a result of her charming, melodious and intricate guitar style (as is Mississippi John Hurt for much the same reason). Harlem religious street singer-guitarist Rev. Gary Davis (Lawrence County, S.C., ca. 1896) might likewise be included in this category.

Sam "Lightnin'" Hopkins (Centreville, Texas, March 15, 1912) has recorded so extensively—though rarely at the expense of genuine emotional depth—that he, for all practical purposes, represents the blues style of his native state for many of today's listeners. An extraordinarily gifted singer and guitarist whose work is thoroughly rooted in tradition, Hopkins has been successful in bridging the demands of popular recording and the folk music audience to a degree unmatched by perhaps any other bluesman. Other contemporary Texas bluesmen include singer-guitarist Lowell Fulson (Tulsa, Okla., 1921), who most often works as a latter-day urban rhythm-and-blues stylist, and singer-guitarist Melvin "Lil' Son" Jackson (Tyler, Texas, Aug. 17, 1916), and singer-pianist Robert Shaw (Stafford, Texas, Aug. 9, 1908); though the latter two have recorded recently, they are inactive musically, preferring to pursue non-musical careers. The Texas blues traditions still remain the least-investigated of all regional blues styles, though Paul Oliver and Houston playwright-folklorist Mack McCormick are currently engaged in the arduous work of formulating an approach to the state's music.

A significant discovery has been Mance Lipscomb (Navasota, Texas, April 9, 1895), a singer-guitarist who brings to life in his strong, vigorous music the broad range of Negro folk music traditions that flourished in the early years of this country—of which the blues is only one part—and which have largely gone by the board as a result of a one-sided emphasis on the blues after recordings created a vogue for this form. Elizabeth Cotten also represents an aspect of this broad "songster" tradition, as do Maryland singer-guitarist Bill Jackson (Granite, Md., Feb. 22, 1906) and one-man-band Jesse Fuller (Jonesboro, Ga., March 12, 1896).

The development of the modern blues style—primarily a heavy, unsubtle ensemble approach utilizing electrically amplified guitar, bass and harmonica—owes much to the pioneering work of Muddy Waters (born McKinley Morganfield in Rolling Fork, Miss., 1915), whose recordings for the Chicago independent label, Chess Records, beginning in 1948 signaled a return to the powerful, individualized blues of his native state (albeit updated and simplified by amplification). Following in his path were such performers as singer-harmonica players Little Walter Jacobs (Alexandria, La., ca. 1931), Big Walter Horton (Memphis, Tenn., April 6, 1918), and Amos "Junior" Wells (Memphis, Tenn., Dec. 9, 1934)—all three of whom were members of the Waters band at various times—and Sonny Boy Williamson, No. 2 (born Willie "Rice" Miller, Glendora, Miss., ca. 1896, died Helena, Ark., May 24, 1965), an exemplary singer-harmonica player who assumed the name of "Sonny Boy Williamson" upon the death of John Lee Williamson (the "original" Sonny Boy) in 1948. Other influential Chicago bluesmen in the postwar years were singer-guitarists Howling Wolf (born Chester Burnett, Aberdeen, Miss., June 10, 1910) and Jimmy Reed (Leland, Miss., 1926).

The most recent extensions of the Waters approach are seen in the more sophisticated work of such younger Chicago bluesmen as George "Buddy" Guy (Lettsworth, La., July 30, 1930) and Otis Rush (Philadelphia, Miss., April 29, 1934), both exciting singer-guitarists whose work is still solidly within the blues mainstream. Both have drawn inspiration from the hugely influential modern bluesman B. B. King (real name Riley B. King), a Mississippi-born, Memphis-reared performer whose magnificent jazz-based playing and emotive singing owe not a little to the earlier work of Aaron "T-Bone" Walker (Linden, Texas, 1913), a pioneer in the fleet, multi-noted blues guitar approach. Two other influential blues stylists have been Chuck Berry (St. Louis, Mo., 1931) and Bo Diddley (real name Ellis McDaniel, McComb, Miss., Dec. 30, 1928), Chicago-based singer-

guitarists who were largely instrumental in forging the prototypes of rock-and-roll in the mid-'50s and whose work since that time has progressively moved in that direction—i.e., away from the hard-core blues and into the area of teen-directed big beat popular music, though the blues feeling remains strongly central to their music.

Both the popular blues and the folk music-directed approach to blues appreciation have tended to stress the role of the guitar in the music. There are at present, however, a number of expressive and individual blues pianists at work in the blues (primarily as accompanists, it must be admitted). Among the most successful in having attracted the folk-blues audience have been Memphis Slim (born Peter Chatman, Memphis, Tenn., Sept. 3, 1915); Champion Jack Dupree (New Orleans, La., July 4, 1910); Curtis Jones (Cass City, Texas, Aug. 18, 1906)—all three of whom are currently resident in the more congenial locale of Europe; Sunnyland Slim (born Albert Luandrew, Lambert, Miss., Sept. 5, 1907); Eurreal "Little Brother" Montgomery (Kentwood, La., April 8, 1906); Roosevelt Sykes (St. Louis, Mo., 1913); Robert Shaw; Robert McCoy (Aliceville, Ala., 1908); and Otis Spann (Vicksburg, Miss., ca. 1931), who is currently pianist in the Muddy Waters Band.

Admittedly, any mere "highlight" approach to the blues, such as this far too brief survey of current activity, cannot touch upon everything or everyone. Or even upon very many, for that matter. In assessing the blues today one must necessarily omit, in so short a review, mention of the countless, often anonymous bluesmen who keep the music alive at the most fruitful and meaningful level—that of home, family circle, or neighborhood—that is, at the very roots of the music. There is a huge, bewilderingly complex, widespread and continuing blues activity teeming beneath the surface of American Negro life even today, whether in the rural South or in the urban North. The range of the music is broad—from primitive to polished, from archaic to contemporary, from highly personal songs created out of the life experience of the singer and sung for self or a small circle of friends to the sleek, meticulously contrived creations manufactured in the cold, unreal atmosphere of a recording studio.

However, the blues prevail, a living reminder of where the Negro has been, an emblem of where he is, and perhaps an augury of where he will be. Always, though, they are a touchstone.

Introduction to poll tabulations

The following tabulations of poll winners are intended to serve as a yardstick of the respective opinions of jazz fans, critics and leading musicians. Their inclusion should not be construed to imply that the musicians listed are necessarily the most important or most successful. They are simply the most popular with these groups of voters.

The *Down Beat* readers' poll is the oldest and best known of all, having been conducted annually for the past 30 years. The same publication has conducted a poll of jazz experts since 1953. In recent years the critics' poll has included votes from an increasingly large number of jazz writers overseas.

Voters in this poll elect two winners in each instrumental division. The first is designated as "Established Talent"; the second, originally known as the "New Star" category, was modified from 1963 to include "Talent Deserving of Wider Recognition."

The *Playboy* poll is included because this magazine has a circulation of over 3,000,000 and therefore repre-sents a substantial segment of the public that has expressed an interest in jazz. However, the victories in these polls of Peter, Paul & Mary and of other singers (and a few instrumentalists) who could hardly by any standards be called jazz performers would appear to indicate that mass popularity, rather than an essential link with jazz, has governed the selection of winners.

Far more valuable is the *Playboy* "All Stars' All Stars" poll, in which the winners of *Playboy* readers' polls are themselves asked to participate as voters. It should be borne in mind that by virtue of having won a readers' poll, such performers as Peter, Paul & Mary earn the right to cast their votes as jazz experts in this poll; nevertheless, the results by and large reflect the views of the important jazz musicians of the 1960s.

An initial annual readers' poll was inaugurated in 1966 by *Jazz* magazine. The results are included here. For comparative purposes a typical foreign poll, conducted by the long-established London publication *The Melody Maker,* is also listed.

	Down Beat Critics' Poll **1960**	*Down Beat Readers' Poll* **1960**	*Down Beat Critics' Poll* **1961**
Hall of Fame		Dizzy Gillespie	Coleman Hawkins
Trumpet	Dizzy Gillespie *Nat Adderley	Miles Davis	Dizzy Gillespie *Freddie Hubbard
Trombone	J. J. Johnson *Al Grey	J. J. Johnson	J. J. Johnson *Julian Priester
Alto	Cannonball Adderley *Ornette Coleman	Cannonball Adderley	Cannonball Adderley *Eric Dolphy
Tenor	Coleman Hawkins *Johnny Griffin	John Coltrane	John Coltrane *Charlie Rouse
Baritone	Gerry Mulligan *No Contest	Gerry Mulligan	Gerry Mulligan *Sahib Shihab
Clarinet	Buddy De Franco *Pete Fountain	Buddy De Franco	Buddy De Franco *Rolf Kuhn
Piano	Thelonious Monk *Ray Bryant	Oscar Peterson	Thelonious Monk *Junior Mance
Guitar	Kenny Burrell *Wes Montgomery	Barney Kessel	Wes Montgomery *Les Spann
Bass	Ray Brown *Sam Jones	Ray Brown	Ray Brown *Charlie Haden
Drums	Max Roach *Billy Higgins	Shelly Manne	Max Roach *Louis Hayes
Flute	Frank Wess *Les Spann	Herbie Mann	Frank Wess *Leo Wright
Vibes	Milt Jackson *Lem Winchester	Milt Jackson	Milt Jackson *Mike Mainieri

* Artist deserving of wider recognition.

Down Beat Readers' Poll **1961**	*Down Beat Critics' Poll* **1962**	*Down Beat Readers' Poll* **1962**	*Down Beat Critics' Poll* **1963**
Billie Holiday	Bix Beiderbecke	Miles Davis	Jelly Roll Morton
Miles Davis	Dizzy Gillespie *Don Ellis	Miles Davis	Dizzy Gillespie *Don Cherry
J. J. Johnson	J. J. Johnson *Dave Baker	J. J. Johnson	J. J. Johnson *Roswell Rudd
Cannonball Adderley	Johnny Hodges *Leo Wright	Paul Desmond	Johnny Hodges *Jackie McLean
John Coltrane	Sonny Rollins *Wayne Shorter	Stan Getz	Sonny Rollins *Dexter Gordon
Gerry Mulligan	Gerry Mulligan *Cecil Payne	Gerry Mulligan	Gerry Mulligan *Jay Cameron
Buddy De Franco	Pee Wee Russell *Jimmy Hamilton	Buddy De Franco	Pee Wee Russell *Phil Woods
Oscar Peterson	Bill Evans *Cecil Taylor	Oscar Peterson	Bill Evans *McCoy Tyner
Wes Montgomery	Wes Montgomery *Grant Green	Wes Montgomery	Jim Hall *Joe Pass
Ray Brown	Ray Brown *Art Davis	Ray Brown	Charles Mingus *Gary Peacock
Max Roach	Philly Joe Jones *Roy Haynes	Joe Morello	Elvin Jones *Pete La Roca
Herbie Mann	Frank Wess *Eric Dolphy	Herbie Mann	Frank Wess *Roland Kirk
Milt Jackson	Milt Jackson *Walt Dickerson	Milt Jackson	Milt Jackson *Dave Pike

	Down Beat *Readers' Poll* **1963**	*Down Beat* *Critics' Poll* **1964**	*Down Beat* *Readers' Poll* **1964**
Hall of Fame	Thelonious Monk	Art Tatum	Eric Dolphy
Trumpet	Miles Davis	Miles Davis *Carmell Jones	Miles Davis
Trombone	J. J. Johnson	J. J. Johnson *Grachan Moncur III	J. J. Johnson
Alto	Paul Desmond	Johnny Hodges *Jimmy Woods	Paul Desmond
Tenor	Stan Getz	John Coltrane *Booker Ervin	John Coltrane
Baritone	Gerry Mulligan	Gerry Mulligan *Charles Davis	Gerry Mulligan
Clarinet	Buddy De Franco	Pee Wee Russell *Bill Smith	Jimmy Giuffre
Piano	Oscar Peterson	Bill Evans *Don Friedman	Bill Evans
Guitar	Charlie Byrd	Jim Hall *Gabor Szabo	Jim Hall
Bass	Ray Brown	Charles Mingus *Steve Swallow	Charles Mingus
Drums	Joe Morello	Elvin Jones *Tony Williams	Joe Morello
Flute	Herbie Mann	Frank Wess *Yusef Lateef	Herbie Mann
Vibes	Milt Jackson	Milt Jackson *Bobby Hutcherson	Milt Jackson

* Artist deserving of wider recognition.

Down Beat Critics' Poll 1965	*Down Beat* Readers' Poll 1965	*Jazz Magazine* Readers' Poll 1966	*Melody Maker* (England) Readers' Poll 1966
Earl Hines	John Coltrane		
Miles Davis *Johnny Coles	Miles Davis	Miles Davis	Miles Davis
J. J. Johnson *Albert Mangelsdorff	J. J. Johnson	J. J. Johnson	J. J. Johnson
Johnny Hodges *Charlie Mariano	Paul Desmond	Johnny Hodges	Johnny Hodges
John Coltrane *Archie Shepp	John Coltrane	John Coltrane	John Coltrane
Harry Carney *Jerome Richardson	Gerry Mulligan	Gerry Mulligan	Gerry Mulligan
Pee Wee Russell *Paul Horn	Buddy De Franco	Buddy De Franco	Pee Wee Russell
Bill Evans *Andrew Hill	Oscar Peterson	Oscar Peterson	Oscar Peterson
Jim Hall *Bola Sete	Jim Hall	Jim Hall	Wes Montgomery
Charles Mingus *Ron Carter	Charles Mingus	Richard Davis	Ray Brown
Elvin Jones *Alan Dawson *Dannie Richmond }	Elvin Jones	Joe Morello	Art Blakey Elvin Jones }
Roland Kirk *James Moody	Herbie Mann	Yusef Lateef	Roland Kirk
Milt Jackson *Gary Burton	Milt Jackson	Bobby Hutcherson	Milt Jackson

	Down Beat Critics' Poll 1960	Down Beat Readers' Poll 1960	Down Beat Critics' Poll 1961
Accordion		Art Van Damme	
Misc.	Julius Watkins *Steve Lacy	Don Elliott	Julius Watkins *John Coltrane
Comp.-Arr.	Duke Ellington *Quincy Jones	Gil Evans	Duke Ellington *George Russell
Big Band, Jazz	Duke Ellington *Quincy Jones	Count Basie	Duke Ellington *Gerry Mulligan
Big Band, Dance		Les Brown	
Combo	Modern Jazz Quartet *Farmer-Golson Jazztet	Modern Jazz Quartet	Modern Jazz Quartet *John Coltrane
Vocal Group	Lambert, Hendricks & Ross *No Contest	Lambert, Hendricks & Ross	Lambert, Hendricks & Ross *Double Six of Paris
Male Singer	Jimmy Rushing *Bill Henderson	Frank Sinatra	Ray Charles *Jimmy Witherspoon
Female Singer	Ella Fitzgerald *No Contest	Ella Fitzgerald	Ella Fitzgerald *Aretha Franklin
Organ			
Jazzman of the Year			
Record of the Year			

* Artist deserving of wider recognition.

Down Beat Readers' Poll 1961	Down Beat Critics' Poll 1962	Down Beat Readers' Poll 1962	Down Beat Critics' Poll 1963
John Coltrane	John Coltrane *Roland Kirk	Jimmy Smith	John Coltrane *Eric Dolphy
Gil Evans	Duke Ellington *Oliver Nelson	Gil Evans	Duke Ellington *Gary McFarland
Count Basie	Duke Ellington *Terry Gibbs	Duke Ellington	Duke Ellington *Gerald Wilson
Count Basie		Count Basie	
Modern Jazz Quartet	Miles Davis *Al Grey-Billy Mitchell	Dave Brubeck	Miles Davis *Clark Terry-Bob Brookmeyer
Lambert, Hendricks & Ross	Lambert, Hendricks & Ross *Staple Singers	Lambert, Hendricks & Ross	Lambert, Hendricks & Ross *Stars of Faith
Frank Sinatra	Ray Charles *Lightnin' Hopkins	Frank Sinatra	Ray Charles *Mark Murphy
Ella Fitzgerald	Ella Fitzgerald *Abbey Lincoln	Ella Fitzgerald	Ella Fitzgerald *Sheila Jordan

	Down Beat Readers' Poll 1963	Down Beat Critics' Poll 1964	Down Beat Readers' Poll 1964
Accordion			
Misc.	Roland Kirk	Roland Kirk *Yusef Lateef	Roland Kirk
Comp.-Arr.	Duke Ellington	Duke Ellington *Gerald Wilson	Duke Ellington
Big Band, Jazz	Duke Ellington	Duke Ellington *Harry James	Duke Ellington
Big Band, Dance	Count Basie		Count Basie
Combo	Dave Brubeck	Thelonious Monk *Art Farmer	Dave Brubeck
Vocal Group	Lambert Hendricks & Bavan	Double Six of Paris *Swingle Singers	Double Six of Paris
Male Singer	Ray Charles	Ray Charles *Muddy Waters	Ray Charles
Female Singer	Ella Fitzgerald	Ella Fitzgerald *Jeanne Lee	Ella Fitzgerald
Organ		Jimmy Smith *Freddie Roach	Jimmy Smith
Jazzman of the Year			
Record of the Year			

* Artist deserving of wider recognition.

Down Beat *Critics' Poll* **1965**	*Down Beat* *Readers' Poll* **1965**	*Jazz Magazine* *Readers' Poll* **1966**	*Melody Maker* *(England)* *Readers' Poll* **1966**
Roland Kirk *Stuff Smith	Roland Kirk	John Coltrane	Roland Kirk
Comp.—Duke Ellington Arr.—Gil Evans *Comp.—Ornette Coleman *Arr.—Clare Fischer	Comp.—Duke Ellington Arr.—Gil Evans	Duke Ellington	Duke Ellington
Duke Ellington *Johnny Dankworth	Duke Ellington	Duke Ellington	Duke Ellington
	Count Basie		
Miles Davis *Al Cohn-Zoot Sims	Dave Brubeck	Miles Davis	Modern Jazz Quartet
Double Six of Paris *No Contest	Double Six of Paris		Swingle Singers
Louis Armstrong *Johnny Hartman	Frank Sinatra	Louis Armstrong	Frank Sinatra
Ella Fitzgerald *Cleo Laine	Ella Fitzgerald	Ella Fitzgerald	Ella Fitzgerald
Jimmy Smith *John Patton	Jimmy Smith	Jimmy Smith	Jimmy Smith
	John Coltrane	John Coltrane	Duke Ellington
John Coltrane: "A Love Supreme" (Impulse)	John Coltrane: "A Love Supreme" (Impulse)	John Coltrane: "A Love Supreme" (Impulse)	Blues Artist of the Year: Jimmy Witherspoon

**ALL-STAR
JAZZ BAND**
(Voters are readers of Playboy magazine)

	1960	1961	1962
Leader	Stan Kenton	Stan Kenton	Stan Kenton
Trumpet	Miles Davis	Miles Davis	Miles Davis
	Louis Armstrong	Louis Armstrong	Dizzy Gillespie
	Dizzy Gillespie	Dizzy Gillespie	Louis Armstrong
	Chet Baker	Jonah Jones	Maynard Ferguson
Trombone	J. J. Johnson	J. J. Johnson	J. J. Johnson
	Kai Winding	Kai Winding	Kai Winding
	Bob Brookmeyer	Bob Brookmeyer	Bob Brookmeyer
	Jack Teagarden	Jack Teagarden	Jack Teagarden
Alto Sax	Paul Desmond	Paul Desmond	Cannonball Adderley
	Earl Bostic	Cannonball Adderley	Paul Desmond
Tenor Sax	Stan Getz	Stan Getz	Stan Getz
	Coleman Hawkins	Coleman Hawkins	John Coltrane
Baritone Sax	Gerry Mulligan	Gerry Mulligan	Gerry Mulligan
Clarinet	Benny Goodman	Benny Goodman	Pete Fountain
Piano	Erroll Garner	Dave Brubeck	Dave Brubeck
Guitar	Barney Kessel	Barney Kessel	Barney Kessel
Bass	Ray Brown	Ray Brown	Ray Brown
Drums	Shelly Manne	Shelly Manne	Shelly Manne
Misc. Instrument	Lionel Hampton, vibes	Lionel Hampton, vibes	Lionel Hampton, vibes
Male Vocalist	Frank Sinatra	Frank Sinatra	Frank Sinatra
Female Vocalist	Ella Fitzgerald	Ella Fitzgerald	Ella Fitzgerald
Instrumental Combo	Dave Brubeck Quartet	Dave Brubeck Quartet	Dave Brubeck Quartet
Vocal Group	Four Freshmen	Lambert, Hendricks & Ross	Lambert, Hendricks & Ross

ALL-STARS' ALL-STARS (Voters are musicians who won previous year's Playboy readers' poll)

Leader	Duke Ellington	Duke Ellington	Duke Ellington
Trumpet	Dizzy Gillespie	Dizzy Gillespie	Dizzy Gillespie
Trombone	J. J. Johnson	J. J. Johnson	J. J. Johnson
Alto Sax	Paul Desmond	Cannonball Adderley	Cannonball Adderley
Tenor Sax	Stan Getz	Stan Getz	John Coltrane
Baritone Sax	Gerry Mulligan	Gerry Mulligan	Gerry Mulligan
Clarinet	Buddy De Franco	Buddy De Franco	Buddy De Franco
Piano	Erroll Garner	Oscar Peterson	Oscar Peterson
Guitar	Barney Kessel	Barney Kessel	Wes Montgomery
Bass	Ray Brown	Ray Brown	Ray Brown
Drums	Shelly Manne	Philly Joe Jones	Philly Joe Jones
Misc. Instrument	Milt Jackson, vibes	Milt Jackson, vibes	Milt Jackson, vibes
Male Vocalist	Frank Sinatra	Frank Sinatra	Frank Sinatra
Female Vocalist	Ella Fitzgerald	Ella Fitzgerald	Ella Fitzgerald
Instrumental Combo	Modern Jazz Quartet	Miles Davis Quintet	Miles Davis Quintet
Vocal Group	Lambert, Hendricks & Ross	Lambert, Hendricks & Ross	Lambert, Hendricks & Ross

1963	1964	1965	1966
Stan Kenton	Henry Mancini	Henry Mancini	Henry Mancini
Miles Davis	Miles Davis	Miles Davis	Miles Davis
Dizzy Gillespie	Al Hirt	Al Hirt	Al Hirt
Louis Armstrong	Dizzy Gillespie	Louis Armstrong	Dizzy Gillespie
Al Hirt	Louis Armstrong	Dizzy Gillespie	Louis Armstrong
J. J. Johnson	J. J. Johnson	J. J. Johnson	J. J. Johnson
Kai Winding	Kai Winding	Kai Winding	Kai Winding
Bob Brookmeyer	Si Zentner	Si Zentner	Si Zentner
Jack Teagarden	Bob Brookmeyer	Bob Brookmeyer	Bob Brookmeyer
Cannonball Adderley	Cannonball Adderley	Cannonball Adderley	Cannonball Adderley
Paul Desmond	Paul Desmond	Paul Desmond	Paul Desmond
Stan Getz	Stan Getz	Stan Getz	Stan Getz
John Coltrane	John Coltrane	John Coltrane	John Coltrane
Gerry Mulligan	Gerry Mulligan	Gerry Mulligan	Gerry Mulligan
Pete Fountain	Pete Fountain	Pete Fountain	Pete Fountain
Dave Brubeck	Dave Brubeck	Dave Brubeck	Dave Brubeck
Chet Atkins	Charlie Byrd	Charlie Byrd	Charlie Byrd
Ray Brown	Ray Brown	Charles Mingus	Charles Mingus
Joe Morello	Joe Morello	Joe Morello	Joe Morello
Lionel Hampton, vibes	Lionel Hampton, vibes	Lionel Hampton, vibes	Lionel Hampton, vibes
Frank Sinatra	Frank Sinatra	Frank Sinatra	Frank Sinatra
Ella Fitzgerald	Ella Fitzgerald	Barbra Streisand	Barbra Streisand
Dave Brubeck Quartet	Dave Brubeck Quartet	Dave Brubeck Quartet	Dave Brubeck Quartet
Lambert, Hendricks & Bavan	Peter, Paul & Mary	Peter, Paul & Mary	Peter, Paul & Mary

Duke Ellington	Duke Ellington	Duke Ellington	Duke Ellington
Dizzy Gillespie	Dizzy Gillespie	Dizzy Gillespie	Dizzy Gillespie
J. J. Johnson	J. J. Johnson	J. J. Johnson	J. J. Johnson
Cannonball Adderley	Paul Desmond	Cannonball Adderley	Paul Desmond
Sonny Rollins	Stan Getz	Stan Getz	Stan Getz
Gerry Mulligan	Gerry Mulligan	Gerry Mulligan	Gerry Mulligan
Buddy De Franco	Buddy De Franco	Buddy De Franco	Buddy De Franco
Oscar Peterson	Oscar Peterson	Oscar Peterson	Oscar Peterson
Wes Montgomery	Wes Montgomery	Wes Montgomery	Wes Montgomery
Ray Brown	Ray Brown	Ray Brown	Ray Brown
Philly Joe Jones	Philly Joe Jones	Elvin Jones	Elvin Jones
Milt Jackson, vibes	Milt Jackson, vibes	Milt Jackson, vibes	Milt Jackson, vibes
Frank Sinatra	Frank Sinatra	Frank Sinatra	Frank Sinatra
Ella Fitzgerald	Ella Fitzgerald	Ella Fitzgerald	Ella Fitzgerald
Oscar Peterson Trio	Dave Brubeck Quartet	Dave Brubeck Quartet	Modern Jazz Quartet
Lambert, Hendricks & Bavan	Four Freshmen	Double Six of Paris	Swingle Singers

ABC-PARAMOUNT, 1330 6th Ave., New York 19, N.Y.

A & M, 8255 Sunset Blvd., Suite 201, Hollywood 46, Calif.

ANGEL, 1750 N. Vine St., Hollywood 28, Calif.

ARGO (see CADET)

ARHOOLIE, Box 5073, Berkeley 5, Calif.

ATCO, 1841 Broadway, New York 23, N.Y.

ATLANTIC, 1841 Broadway, New York 23, N.Y.

AUDIO FIDELITY, 770 11th Ave., New York 19, N.Y.

BAKTON, P.O. Box 249, Cooper Station, New York 3, N.Y.

BETHLEHEM (see KING)

BLUE NOTE, 43 West 61st St., New York 23, N.Y.

BRUNSWICK, 445 Park Ave., New York 22, N.Y.

CADET, 2120 S. Michigan, Chicago 16, Ill.

CAEDMON, 461 8th Ave., New York 1, N.Y.

CAMAY, 1721 Broadway, New York 19, N.Y.

CAMBRIDGE, 473 Washington St., Wellesley, Mass.

CAMEO-PARKWAY, 1405 Locust St., Philadelphia 2, Pa.

CAPITOL, 1750 N. Vine St., Hollywood 28, Calif.

CHECKER, 2120 S. Michigan Ave., Chicago 16, Ill.

CHESS, 2120 S. Michigan Ave., Chicago 16, Ill.

COLPIX, 711 5th Ave., New York 22, N.Y.

COLUMBIA, 51 W. 52nd St., New York, N.Y. 10019.

COMMAND (see GRAND AWARD)

CONTACT (see JAZZ PRESS)

CONTEMPO (see UNITED ARTISTS)

CONTEMPORARY, 8481 Melrose Pl., Los Angeles 69, Calif.

CONTINENTAL, 500 5th Ave., New York 17, N.Y.

COOK LABORATORIES, 101 2d St., Stamford, Conn.

CORAL, 445 Park Ave., New York 22, N.Y.

CRESCENDO, 3720 27th St., Long Island City 1, N.Y.

CROWN, 1435 S. La Cienega Blvd., Los Angeles 35, Calif.

DAUNTLESS (see AUDIO FIDELITY)

DECCA, 445 Park Ave., New York 22, N.Y.

DEL-FI, 6277 Selma Ave., Hollywood 28, Calif.

DELMARK, 7 W. Grand, Chicago 10, Ill.

DEUTSCHE GRAMMOPHON, 350 5th Ave., New York 1, N.Y.

DIXIELAND JUBILEE, 9165 Sunset Blvd., Hollywood, Calif.

DOT, 1507 N. Vine St., Hollywood 28, Calif.

ELEKTRA, 51 W. 51st St., New York 19, N.Y.

EMERALD, c/o Philles Records, 9130 Sunset Blvd., Los Angeles 69, Calif.

EPIC, 51 W. 52nd St., New York, N.Y.

ESOTERIC (see EVEREST)

EVEREST, 1313 N. Vine St., Hollywood 28, Calif.

FANTASY, 855 Treat Ave., San Francisco 3, Calif.

FOCUS (see ATLANTIC)

FONTANA (see SMASH)

FOLKWAYS, 165 W. 46th St., New York 36, N.Y.

GNP CRESCENDO, 9165 Sunset Blvd., Los Angeles 69, Calif.

GLAD-HAMP, 165 W. 46th St., New York, N.Y.

GOLDEN CREST, 220 Broadway, Huntington Sta., N.Y.

GOOD TIME JAZZ (see CONTEMPORARY)

GRAND AWARD, 1501 Broadway, New York 36, N.Y.

GROOVE (see RCA VICTOR)

HOME OF THE BLUES, 107 Beale St., Memphis 3, Tenn.

IMPERIAL, 1586 N. La Brea, Hollywood 28, Calif.

IMPULSE, 1330 6th Ave., New York 19, N.Y.

JAZZLAND (see RIVERSIDE)

JAZZOLOGY, P.O. Box 748, Columbia 2, S.C.

JAZZ PRESS, 1841 Broadway, New York 23, N.Y.
JUBILEE, 318 W. 38th St., New York 18, N.Y.

KAPP, 136 E. 57th St., New York 22, N.Y.
KING, 1540 Brewster, Cincinnati 7, Ohio.

LIBERTY, 6920 Sunset Blvd., Hollywood 28, Calif.
LIMELIGHT, 35 E. Wacker Dr., Chicago 1, Ill.
LONDON, 539 W. 25th St., New York 1, N.Y.

MAINSTREAM, 1290 6th Ave., New York 19, N.Y.
MERCURY, 35 E. Wacker, Chicago 1, Ill.
MGM, 1540 Broadway, New York 36, N.Y.
METRONOME, 117 E. 43rd St., New York, N.Y.
MINGUS, CHARLES, RECORD CLUB, Box 2637,
    Grand Central Station, New York 17, N.Y.
MIRA, 9145 Sunset Blvd., Hollywood 69, Calif.
MODERN, 5810 S. Normandie Ave., Los Angeles,
    Calif.
MONOGRAM, 1650 Broadway, New York 19, N.Y.
MOTOWN, 2648 W. Grand Blvd., Detroit 8, Mich.

NOBILITY, 516 Bourbon St., New Orleans, La.

OFFBEAT (see RIVERSIDE)
ONWARD, 2313 Lakeshore Blvd. W., Toronto 14, Ont.

PACIFIC JAZZ, 8715 W. 3rd St., Los Angeles 48, Calif.
PHILIPS, 35 E. Wacker, Chicago 1, Ill.
PLAYBOY, 232 E. Ohio, Chicago 11, Ill.

PRESTIGE, 203 S. Washington Ave., Bergenfield, N.J.

RCA CAMDEN (see RCA VICTOR)
RCA VICTOR, 155 E. 24th St., New York 10, N.Y.
REGINA, 2742 E. Tremont Ave., New York 61, N.Y.
REPRISE, 4000 Warner Blvd., Burbank 5, Calif.
RIVERSIDE, 235 W. 46th St., New York 36, N.Y.
ROULETTE, 1631 Broadway, New York 19, N.Y.

SATURN, P.O. 7124, Chicago, 7, Ill.
SAVOY, 56 Ferry St., Newark, N.J.
SEECO, 39 W. 60th St., New York 23, N.Y.
SMASH (see MERCURY)
SUE, 265 W. 54th St., New York 19, N.Y.

TAMLA (see MOTOWN)
TANGERINE, c/o RPM Enterprises, 2107 W. Wash-
    ington Blvd., Los Angeles 18, Calif.
TIME (see MAINSTREAM)
20th CENTURY FOX, 444 W. 56th St., New York 19,
    N.Y.

UNITED ARTISTS, 729 Seventh Ave., New York 19,
    N.Y.

VEE JAY, 1449 S. Michigan, Chicago, Ill.
VERVE, 1540 Broadway, New York 36, N.Y.
VOCALION (see DECCA)

WORLD PACIFIC (see PACIFIC JAZZ)

A specially assembled album under the above title, comprising outstanding performances by leading jazz artists of the 1960s, and including a number of works recorded specifically for inclusion in this package, will be found on the Verve label. For full details of *Encyclopedia '67,* see Verve release lists.

The quantity of jazz LP records released since 1960 has been conspicuously in excess of the quality. Because the output has been so vast, there has nevertheless been a substantial number of releases that should be in every collector's library.

Some records have been highly praised by the critics; some have gained popular success and made a vital impact on the trends in contemporary jazz despite a poor reception on the part of the critics. The list below includes items from both these categories, along with others that impressed the author as representative of the artist featured. Some are simply typical of the artist rather than the greatest or best or winners of the highest ratings. A few important reissues of pre-1960s recordings have been included and are indicated by (R) after the artist's name. The recommendations have been limited to records still listed and generally available.

Cannonball Adderley. Nippon Soul (Riverside 477).

Laurindo Almeida-Bud Shank (R). Brazilliance (World-Pac. 142).

Laurindo Almeida-Modern Jazz Quartet. Collaboration (Atl. 1429).

Louis Armstrong. Hello Dolly! (Kapp 1364).

Louis Armstrong, Dave Brubeck, Carmen McRae, Lambert, Hendricks & Ross. The Real Ambassadors (Col. 5850).

Albert Ayler. My Name is Albert Ayler (Fant. 6016).

Mildred Bailey (R). Her Greatest Performances (Col. C3L 22).

Clifford Brown (R). The Immortal Clifford Brown (Limelight LS2-8601).

Kenny Burrell (arrs. by Gil Evans). Guitar Forms (Verve 6812).

Benny Carter. BBB & Co. (Prest.-Swingville 2032).

Ray Charles (R). The Ray Charles Story (Atl. 2-900).

Ray Charles. Genius Plus Soul Equals Jazz (Imp. 2).

Nat King Cole (R). The Vintage Years (Cap. 2529).

Ornette Coleman. Ornette! (Atl. 1378).

Ornette Coleman at the Golden Circle, Stockholm (Blue Note 84224-5).

John Coltrane. Giant Steps (Atl. 1311).

John Coltrane. A Love Supreme (Imp. 77). Won *Jazz Magazine* Album of Year award, 1965; *Down Beat* Record of Year, 1965.

Miles Davis-Gil Evans. Sketches of Spain (Col. 1480).

Miles Davis in Europe (Col. 8983). Won *Jazz* Magazine Album of Year award, 1964.

Eric Dolphy. Out to Lunch (Blue Note 4163).

Duke Ellington. Afro-Bossa (Reprise 6069). Won *Jazz* Magazine Album of Year award, 1963.

Duke Ellington. The Nutcracker Suite (Col. 8341).

Duke Ellington's Concert of Sacred Music (RCA 3582).

The Indispensable Duke Ellington (R) (RCA 6009).

The Symphonic Ellington (Reprise 6097).

The Ellington Era (R), Vols. I & II. (Col. C3L37, C3L39).

Duke Ellington-Ella Fitzgerald. Ella at Duke's Place (Verve 4070).

Booker Ervin. Freedom Book (Prest. 7295).

Bill Evans. Conversations with Myself (Verve 8526).

Bill Evans-Jim Hall. Undercurrent (United Artists 14003).

Gil Evans. Out of the Cool (Imp. 4).

Gil Evans. Into the Hot (Imp. 9).

Clare Fischer. First Time Out (Pac. Jazz 52).

Ella Fitzgerald. These Are the Blues (Verve 4062).

Stan Getz. Focus (Verve 8412).

Stan Getz-Charlie Byrd. Jazz Samba (Verve 8432).

Dizzy Gillespie. Gillespiana (Verve 8394).

Dizzy Gillespie. Perceptions (Verve 8411).

Dizzy Gillespie. The New Continent (Limelight 86022).

Dizzy Gillespie & The Double Six of Paris (Philips 600-106).

The Greatest of Dizzy Gillespie (R) (RCA 2398).

John Handy. The John Handy Quintet (Col. 9262).

Jon Hendricks. Evolution of the Blues Song (Col. 8383).

Woody Herman '63 (Philips 200-065).

Woody Herman '64 (Philips 200-118).

Andrew Hill. Black Fire (Blue Note 4151).

Earl Hines. Grand Reunion, Vols. I & II (Limelight 82020, 82028).

Billie Holiday (R). The Golden Years, Vols. I & II (Col. C3L21, C3L40).

Billie Holiday (R). Lady Love (United Artists 14014).

Lightin' Hopkins. Down Home Blues (Prest.-Bluesville 1086).

Paul Horn (arrs. by Lalo Schifrin). Jazz Suite on the Mass Texts (RCA 3414).

Stan Kenton. Adventures in Time (Cap. 1844).

B. B. King. Live at the Regal (ABC-Par. 509).

Roland Kirk, Rip, Rig & Panic (Limelight 86027).

Eddie Lang-Joe Venuti (R). Stringin' The Blues (Col. C2L24).

Yusef Lateef. 1984 (Imp. 84).

John Lewis. Music for Brass: The Golden Striker (Atl. 1334).

John Lewis. Essence: Comps. of Gary McFarland (Atl. 1425).

Ramsey Lewis. The In Crowd (Argo 757).

Carmen McRae. Live at Sugar Hill (Time 52104).

Herbie Mann at the Village Gate (Atl. 1380).

Charles Mingus. Black Saint and the Sinner Lady (Imp. A-35).

Charles Mingus Revisited (Limelight 86015).

Modern Jazz Ensemble (R). Little David's Fugue (Verve VSP 18).

Modern Jazz Quartet. Pyramid (Atl. 1325).

Modern Jazz Quartet, Jimmy Giuffre Three and Beaux Arts String Quartet. Third Stream Music (Atl. 1345).

Grachan Moncur III. Evolution (Blue Note 4153).

Thelonious Monk. Monk's Greatest Hits (River. 421).

Wes Montgomery. Goin' Out of my Head (Verve 8642).

Lee Morgan. The Sidewinder (Blue Note 84157).

Gerry Mulligan. Night Lights (Philips 600-108).

New Wave In Jazz (Imp. 90).

Phineas Newborn, Jr. A World of Piano (Contemp. 3600).

Orchestra U.S.A. Sonorities (Col. 2395).

Outstanding Jazz Compositions of the 20th Century (R) (Col. C2L31).

The Essential Charlie Parker (R) (Verve 8409).

Joe Pass. For Django (Pac. Jazz 85).

Oscar Peterson with Swinging Brass (Verve 8364).

Oscar Peterson. Canadiana Suite (Limelight 86010).

Don Redman (R). Master of the Big Band (RCA 520).

Sonny Rollins. The Bridge (RCA 2527).

George Russell. The Stratus Seekers (River. 412).

Pee Wee Russell. New Groove (Col. 1985).

Gunther Schuller-Jim Hall. Jazz Abstractions (Atl. 1365).

Archie Shepp. Four for Trane (Imp. 71).

Horace Silver. Song for My Father (Blue Note 84185).

Bill Smith-Johnny Eaton. American Jazz Ensemble in Rome (RCA 2557).

Jimmy Smith. The Cat (Verve 8587).

Billy Strayhorn. The Peaceful Side (United Artists 15010).

Swingle Singers. Bach's Greatest Hits (Philips 600-097).

Cecil Taylor at the Cafe Montmartre (Fant. 86014).

Jack Teagarden (R) (RCA 528).

Dinah Washington. This is My Story (Merc. SRP-2-603).

Randy Weston. Randy! (Bakton 1001).

Gerald Wilson. You Better Believe It (Pac. Jazz 34).

Lester Young. Pres at His Very Best (Merc. MRC 26010).

Denny Zeitlin. Carnival (Col. 2340).

Following is a list of books concerned with jazz published in the U.S. during the 1960s and still generally available.

ASCH, MOSES, & ALAN LOMAX (editors). *The Leadbelly Songbook* (Oak). 97 pp. 1963.

BALLIETT, WHITNEY. *Dinosaurs In The Morning* (J. B. Lippincott). 224 pp. 1962.

BECHET, SIDNEY. *Treat It Gentle* (Hill & Wang). 245 pp. 1960.

BERENDT, JOACHIM (translated by Dan Morgenstern). *The New Jazz Book* (Hill & Wang). 314 pp. 1962.

BRADFORD, PERRY. *Born With the Blues* (Oak). 175 pp. 1965.

BRUNN, H. O. *The Story of the Original Dixieland Jazz Band* (Louisiana Press). 268 pp. 1960.

CARMICHAEL, HOAGY, with STEPHEN LONGSTREET. *Sometimes I Wonder* (Farrar, Straus & Giroux). 313 pp. 1965.

CERULLI, DOM, with BURT KORALL & MORT NASATIR (editors). *The Jazz Word* (Ballantine). 249 pp. 1960.

CHARTERS, SAMUEL B. *The Poetry of the Blues*. (Oak). 111 pp. 1963.

CHARTERS, SAMUEL B., & LEONARD KUNSTADT. *Jazz: A History of The New York Scene* (Doubleday). 382 pp. 1962.

COKER, JERRY. *Improvising Jazz* (Prentice-Hall). 115 pp. 1964.

COURLANDER, HAROLD. *Negro Folk Music USA* (Columbia Univ. Press). 324 pp. 1963.

DAVIS, SAMMY JR., with JANE & BURT BOYAR. *Yes I Can* (Farrar, Straus & Giroux). 612 pp. 1965.

DEXTER, DAVE JR. *The Jazz Story: From the 90s to the 60s* (Prentice-Hall). 192 pp.

ERLICH, LILLIAN. *What Jazz Is All About* (Julian Messner). 181 pp. 1963.

FEATHER, LEONARD, with JACK TRACY. *Laughter from the Hip* (Horizon). 175 pp. 1963.

FEATHER, LEONARD. *The Book of Jazz from Then Till Now* (Horizon). 280 pp. 1965.

FRANCIS, ANDRÉ. *Jazz* (Grove Press, Evergreen paperback). 189 pp. 1960.

GILLENSON, LEWIS (editor). *Esquire's World of Jazz* (Esquire, Inc.). 224 pp. 1963.

GITLER, IRA. *Jazz Masters of the Forties* (Macmillan). 285 pp. 1966.

GOLD, ROBERT S. *A Jazz Lexicon* (Alfred A. Knopf). 363 pp. 1964.

GOLDBERG, JOE. *Jazz Masters of the Fifties* (Macmillan). 246 pp. 1965.

GREEN, BENNY. *The Reluctant Art* (Horizon). 191 pp. 1963.

HADLOCK, RICHARD. *Jazz Masters of the Twenties* (Macmillan). 255 pp. 1965.

HENTOFF, NAT. *Jazz Country* (Harper & Row). 146 pp. 1965.

HENTOFF, NAT. *The Jazz Life* (Dial). 255 pp. 1961.

HODEIR, ANDRÉ. *Toward Jazz* (Grove). 224 pp. 1962.

HORNE, LENA, with RICHARD SCHICKEL. *Lena* (Doubleday). 300 pp. 1962.

JONES, LEROI. *Blues People* (Wm. Morrow). 244 pp. 1963.

KAMINSKY, MAX, with V. E. HUGHES. *My Life In Jazz* (Harper & Row). 242 pp. 1963.

KELLEY, WILLIAM MELVIN. *A Drop Of Patience* (Doubleday). 237 pp. 1965.

LEONARD, NEIL. *Jazz and the White Americans* (Univ. of Chicago Press). 215 pp. 1962.

MAURERER, HANS J. (editor). *The Pete Johnson Story* (U.S. & Europe Fund Raising Project for Pete Johnson). 102 pp. 1965.

MEHEGAN, JOHN. *Jazz Improvisation, Books I, II, III, IV* (Watson-Guptill).

MELLERS, WILFRED. *Music in a New Found Land* (Knopf). 543 pp. 1965.

MILLER, WILLIAM ROBERT. *The Christian Encounters the World of Pop Music and Jazz* (Concordia). 1965.

MYRUS, DONALD. *I Like Jazz* (Macmillan). 118 pp. 1965.

OLIVER, PAUL. *Blues Fell This Morning* (Horizon). 355 pp. 1961.

OLIVER, PAUL. *Conversation with the Blues* (Horizon). 217 pp. 1965.

OSTRANSKY, LEROY. *The Anatomy of Jazz* (University of Washington Press). 362 pp. 1960.

RAMSEY, FREDERIC JR. *Been Here and Gone* (Rutgers Univ. Press). 177 pp. 1960.

REISNER, ROBERT G. *Bird: The Legend of Charlie Parker* (Citadel). 256 pp. 1962.

RUSSELL, ROSS. *The Sound* (E. P. Dutton). 287 pp. 1961.

SCARBOROUGH, DOROTHY. *On The Trail of Negro Folklore* (Folklore Associates). 295 pp. 1963.

SHIRLEY, KAY (editor). *The Book of The Blues,* annotated by Frank Driggs (Leeds Music & Crown Publishing). 301 pp. 1963.

SIMON, GEORGE T. *The Feeling of Jazz* (Simon & Schuster). Illustrations by Tracy Sugarman. 1961.

SMITH, WILLIE THE LION, with GEORGE HOEFER. *Music On My Mind* (Doubleday). 318 pp. 1964.

TANNER, PAUL A., & MAURICE GEROW. *A Study of Jazz* (Wm. C. Brown).

WALKER, LEO. *The Wonderful Era of the Great Dance Bands* (Howell-North). 315 pp. 1965.

WILLIAMS, JOHN A. *Night Song* (Farrar, Straus & Giroux). 219 pp. 1961.

WILLIAMS, MARTIN (editor). *Jazz Panorama* (Crowell-Collier). 318 pp. 1962.

WILLIAMS, MARTIN. *Where's the Melody?* (Pantheon). 195 pp. 1966.

LEADING AMERICAN PERIODICALS

Coda, P.O. Box 87, Station "J", Toronto 6, Ontario, Canada.

Down Beat, 222 West Adams Street, Chicago, Ill. 60606

Jazz: 1841 Broadway, New York, N.Y. 10023

Sounds & Fury, Castell Publishing Co., Inc., 240 Genesee St., Utica, N.Y. 13502

The Second Line, New Orleans Jazz Club, 2417 Octavia St., New Orleans, La. 70115